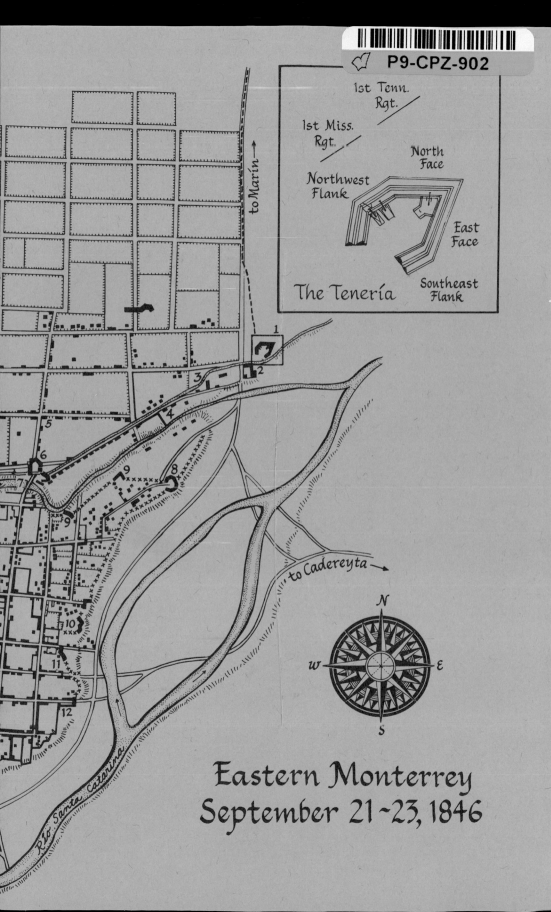

to Marín →

The Tenería

1st Tenn.
Rgt.

1st Miss.
Rgt.

North
Face

Northwest
Flank

East
Face

Southeast
Flank

to Cadereyta →

N

W   E

S

Río Santa Catarina

Eastern Monterrey
September 21-23, 1846

THE PAPERS OF
Jefferson Davis

SUPPORTED BY
The National Historical Publications and Records Commission
The Moody Foundation
The William Stamps Farish Fund
The Wortham Foundation
Mississippi Department of Archives and History
Damon Wells, Jr.
Harris Masterson III
Mississippi Historical Society
Mississippi American Revolution Bicentennial Commission
The United Daughters of the Confederacy
Albert Sidney Johnston Camp No. 67, Sons of Confederate Veterans
Varina M. W. Stewart

SPONSORED BY
William Marsh Rice University
The Jefferson Davis Association

Defeat of Mexican Lancers by the Mississippi Rifles

THE PAPERS OF
Jefferson Davis

VOLUME 3
July 1846–December 1848

James T. McIntosh, EDITOR
Lynda L. Crist, ASSOCIATE EDITOR
Mary S. Dix, ASSISTANT EDITOR

LOUISIANA STATE UNIVERSITY PRESS
BATON ROUGE AND LONDON
1981

LIBRARY OF CONGRESS CATALOGING IN PUBLICATION DATA (Revised)
Davis, Jefferson, 1808–1889.
  The papers of Jefferson Davis.
  Vol. 2–   edited by J. T. McIntosh.
  Includes bibliographies.
  CONTENTS: v. 1. 1808–1840.—v. 2. June 1841–
July 1846.—v. 3. July 1846–December 1848.
  1. Davis, Jefferson, 1808–1889. 2. United
States—Politics and government—1815–1861—Sources.
3. United States—History—Civil War, 1861–1865—
Sources. 4. Confederate States of America—History
—Sources. 5. Statesmen—United States—Correspond-
ence. 6. Confederate States of America—Presidents
—Correspondence. I. Monroe, Haskell M., ed.
II. McIntosh, James T., ed.
LIBRARY OF CONGRESS CATALOGING IN PUBLICATION DATA
E467.1.D2596   973.5   76–152704
ISBN 0–8071–0943–6 (v. 1)   AACR1
ISBN 0–8071–0028-x (v. 2)
ISBN 0–8071–0786-7 (v. 3)

INTRODUCTION

by K. Jack Bauer

THE MEXICAN WAR offered Jefferson Davis a chance for military glory and public notice, which he exploited to the fullest. During the two and a half years covered by this volume Davis rose from a little-known congressman and former soldier to a genuine war hero and nationally recognized politician.

If Davis' acceptance of command of the 1st Mississippi Regiment struck some of his contemporaries as too hasty and too carefully orchestrated not to be contrived, his performance as colonel was stellar. Once in command, Davis successfully argued for the equipping of the unit with Eli Whitney's percussion rifles. As a result, it was the only rifle regiment to serve with Zachary Taylor's army. Davis drafted a special drill manual for his men and trained them intensively until they became a steady, disciplined combat unit. Few, if any, volunteer regiments in Mexico surpassed its performance on the battlefield.

Part of the regiment's reputation stemmed from the partiality that Taylor showed to his former son-in-law. As soon as Davis reached the war zone, Taylor penned a warm, welcoming letter saying, "I am more than anxious to take you by the hand, & to have you & your command with or near me." Taylor directed the regiment to join the main army for the Monterrey campaign. At Monterrey the Mississippians fought well in the mishandled assault on the city's eastern defenses.

It is in the aftermath of the Monterrey battle that Davis' less-attractive side appears. Among his regiment's actions was a joint assault on Fort Tenería with the 1st Tennessee. It was a confused attack and, like most battlefield actions, the actual events were as obscured by the smoke of battle as the reconstruction of them has been hampered by the selective recall of the participants. Davis' brigade commander, Brigadier General John A. Quitman, intended

v

for the Tennesseans to make the assault, but without his approval the Mississippians joined the attack. Whether they did so by order of Davis or at the urging of his second-in-command is uncertain, but the resulting dispute over credit continued long after the war. That controversy, however, paled before one initiated by Davis with the Tennesseans over which regiment first entered the fort. The extreme lengths to which he went to establish his unit's claim to primacy are evident in the reports collected from his subordinates. Reflected are both Davis' concern over developing the esprit of his men and a preoccupation with establishing his own image as a valiant warrior. Many observers, unable to determine who indeed was first into the Tenería, have come to suspect with Balie Peyton that Davis "only wished to make a little Locofoco capital at home for Miss. consumption." Yet in all these discussions there is no question that the Mississippians and their colonel had proved themselves on the field of battle.

Less controversial were the contributions of the regiment to the victory at Buena Vista. The details of its participation in that fight appear in the mass of reports collected by Davis. Even without Davis' considerable public relations campaign, the role of the Mississippians received full coverage in contemporary accounts of the battle. An interesting aspect of Davis' presentation of the battle was his stress on the innovative V formation adopted by his men and the 3d Indiana to break up a Mexican cavalry attack. Several participants insisted that the American line was at best only slightly bowed, although none questioned the effectiveness of the fire of the two regiments. Nor was Davis' personal image harmed by the painful and laming wound received during the battle.

The publicity given the Mississippi Regiment and its commander forced President James K. Polk to offer Davis a commission as brigadier general. Davis refused on grounds that illuminate his growing ability to argue issues on narrow and precarious constitutional bases. Insisting that the volunteers were actually militiamen, a towering leap of logic accepted by few others, Davis claimed for them "a constitutional right to be under the immediate command of officers appointed by State authority." Therefore, organization into brigades commanded by federally appointed generals would cause them to "lose their distinctive character of State troops." The argument appears so contrived as to lead some observers, who noted that Davis while in the U.S. House of Representatives had apparently not opposed the legislation creating the generals, to suspect that the more likely reason was Davis' recognition that the opportunity for more military glory had departed.

The war showed other, more positive, traits. Davis quickly developed a close personal relationship with Zachary Taylor. Their surviving correspondence attests the regard that the older man held for the younger. He chose Davis to serve with Brigadier General William J. Worth and Governor J. Pinckney Henderson of Texas as American negotiators for the armistice following the Monterrey assault. Taylor's later reliance on Davis as one of his political spokesmen is a particular mark of confidence considering their differences in party affiliation. That role illuminates Davis' moral character. He honestly responded to queries about Taylor's strengths but never became a partisan. Equally, Davis, whose well-recognized personal involvement with "Old Rough and Ready" would have excused him from taking sides in the 1848 presidential election, made no attempt to hide his intention to vote for Lewis Cass. Nor did that disturb his relations with Taylor.

Just as Davis' war record won him the offer of the stars of a general, it prevented Governor Albert G. Brown from offering an interim senatorial appointment to any other politician. The return of Davis to Washington in December 1847 opened a new era in his life. He played upon his Mexican experiences and military reputation to support the administration's vain effort to secure authorization for ten additional regular regiments to prosecute the seemingly unending war with Mexico. Although he believed the treaty negotiated by Nicholas P. Trist to end the conflict did not bring the United States enough territory, he supported ratification. His desire for additional Mexican land, like his later support of the annexation of Yucatan and Cuba, reflected Davis' continuing efforts to secure additional slaveholding territory. That and his belief, strongly stated during the debate on the Oregon territorial government bill, that Congress lacked the constitutional authority to forbid slavery in a territory were the start of a drumfire of similar arguments that would become familiar to his listeners during the next decade.

Few readers of these letters will find Jefferson Davis an attractive personality. He appears humorless, stuffy, and highly demanding.

INTRODUCTION

"I have remembered your request on the subject of profanity and have improved," he pompously assured his wife before demanding of her: "Have you remembered mine on the subject of prayer." He also instructed her to "be pious, be calm, be useful, and charitable and temperate in all things." Nor can one glimpse compassion in his long April 1848 letter complaining of "how far your treatment of me was injurious" in the midst of a litany of half-spoken self-pity over her failure to follow "a line of conduct suited to the character of your husband, and demanded by your duties as a wife."

The Jefferson Davis of later years who rose to prominence by strength of personality, sharpness of mind, utter self-confidence, and a constant watch on the objective ahead is clearly visible during the Mexican War years. Whether those years exercised much influence on his later actions or thoughts is less evident beyond their oft-noted enhancement of his own view of his military prowess.

ACKNOWLEDGMENTS

A LEGION of friends, scholars, and professionals in many fields have contributed to the preparation of Volume 3. Most have offered assistance far beyond that requested, and we are deeply grateful to all.

For continuing support and thoughtful direction by the board of directors and the board of advisory editors we are most appreciative. Likewise, we are indebted to the board of governors, Rice University, for continuing sponsorship, shelter for the editorial offices, and staff participation in university services.

Vital financial aid has been provided by the National Historical Publications and Records Commission; the Moody Foundation; the William Stamps Farish Fund; the Wortham Foundation; the Mississippi Department of Archives and History; Damon Wells, Jr.; Harris Masterson III; the Mississippi Historical Society; the Mississippi American Revolution Bicentennial Commission; the United Daughters of the Confederacy; Albert Sidney Johnston Camp No. 67, Sons of Confederate Veterans (Houston); and Varina M. W. Stewart. In addition, we have received gifts from many others, including several members of the Davis Family Association: Peggy M. Allen; Reva N. Carpenter; Timothy B. Cole; Ruth D. Deiss; Charles L. Graves; Howard E. Haller; Suzanne H. Herrick; Gen. and Mrs. Maurice Hirsch; Davis Marret; Frank W. Michaux; Ruth H. Mullis; National Historical Society through the late Bell I. Wiley; Mrs. H. W. Nugent in memory of her husband; Charlotte W. Padon; Eugenia Porter Rayzor; Lt. Col. Alvin L. Small; Albert Stedman; F. G. Strachan; Rutledge S. Thomas; Gen. James H. Lane Chapter (Charlotte, N.C.), Robert E. Lee Chapter (Lake Charles, La.), and the Texas Division, United Daughters of the Confederacy; Clarence Parker Post, Veterans of Foreign Wars (Beaumont, Miss.); Phyllis

ix

ACKNOWLEDGMENTS

Whinrey; Mrs. Will A. Whitaker; and Mrs. Richard H. Wills, Jr. For all these donations we express our sincere thanks.

The members of the National Historical Publications and Records Commission, the executive director Frank G. Burke, and the members of the commission staff have proved unfailingly helpful. We particularly wish to cite the valuable research performed by Sara Dunlap Jackson and the assistance of Roger A. Bruns, Diane M. Buncombe, Joyce Eberly, H. B. Fant, Mary A. Giunta, Anne H. Henry, Richard N. Sheldon, Fred A. Shelley, George L. Vogt, Richard E. Wood, and former director E. Berkeley Tompkins. The cooperation of the National Archives has also been generous, thanks to the good offices of James B. Rhoads, former archivist of the United States. Karl L. Trever and the late Mildred Hobbs, two retired members of the Archives staff, undertook the preliminary, time-consuming search for Davis materials, and they are specially commended for their diligent, creative efforts in our behalf.

Without the never-ending flow of data, aid in the transcription of manuscripts, and answers to numerous queries provided by the following archivists, librarians, editors, scholars, and researchers, Volume 3 would be less complete and useful: Diane Campbell and Helen L. Cripe, American Antiquarian Society; Whitfield J. Bell, Jr., American Philosophical Society; John L. Ferguson, Arkansas History Commission; Ann L. Wadsworth, Boston Athenaeum; Marion B. Bragg; Natalie Cowan, M. K. Swingle, and Jay Williar, California Historical Society; Madeleine A. Darcy, Thomas M. Fante, and Miriam T. Pike, California State Library; Betty Fox, Carnegie-Stout Public Library (Dubuque); Gail E. Balman, Central State College (Edmond, Okla.); Archie Motley, Chicago Historical Society; Frances Forman and Anne B. Shepherd, Cincinnati Historical Society; Margaret Cook, College of William and Mary; Rolf Klep, Columbia River Maritime Museum (Astoria, Ore.); Kenneth A. Lohf, Columbia University; Rachel Shute, Columbus and Lowndes County (Miss.) Historical Society; John A. Baule, Dubuque County Historical Society; Kenneth W. Berger, David W. Brown, Sharon E. Knapp, and Mattie U. Russell, Duke University; David E. Estes, Emory University; James R. Bentley, The Filson Club (Louisville, Ky.); Frances L. Hopkins, Franklin and Marshall College (Lancaster, Pa.); David K. King, Free Library of Philadelphia; Connie L. Stephenson, Georgia Historical Society;

ACKNOWLEDGMENTS

Rodney G. Dennis, Harvard University; Bruce Henry, Huntington Library; Roger D. Bridges and Paul Spence, Illinois State Historical Library; Tom Rumer, Indiana Historical Society; Edith Walden, Indiana State Library; Lida Lisle Greene, Iowa Department of History and Archives; Hambleton Tapp, Kentucky Historical Society; John C. Broderick, C. F. W. Coker, and John McDonough, Library of Congress; Ingeborg R. Baum, Library of the Supreme Council, 33° (Washington); Robert Klein, Loras College (Dubuque); Rose Lambert and Aline H. Morris, Louisiana State Museum; Margaret Fisher Dalrymple, Louisiana State University Archives; Mary Eleanor K. Wyatt, Marshall County (Miss.) Historical Society; Clinton I. Bagley, Patti Carr Black, Charlotte Capers, the late Harriet Heidelberg, Elbert R. Hilliard, Michelle Hudson, Caroline Allen Killens, Lisa Reynolds, and particularly Ronald E. Tomlin, Mississippi Department of Archives and History; Frances H. Stadler, Missouri Historical Society; Eleanor S. Brockenbrough and Edward D. C. Campbell, Jr., Museum of the Confederacy; Michael P. Musick, National Archives; Gen. Francis S. Greenlief, National Guard Association of the United States; Betty C. Menges, New Albany–Floyd County (Ind.) Public Library; James B. Bell, New England Historic Genealogical Society (Boston); Collin B. Hamer, Jr., New Orleans Public Library; William Asadorian, New-York Historical Society; Jean R. McNiece, New York Public Library; James L. Murphy, Ohio Historical Society; Gordon A. Cotton and Blanche Terry, Old Court House Museum (Vicksburg); Douglas M. Preston, Oneida Historical Society (Utica, N.Y.); fellow editors Mary-Jo Kline and Joanne W. Ryan (The Papers of Aaron Burr), Clyde N. Wilson and Walter K. Wood (John C. Calhoun), Richard A. Bland (Henry Clay), William B. Willcox (Benjamin Franklin), John Y. Simon (Ulysses S. Grant), Nathan Reingold (Joseph Henry), Patricia P. Clark, Marion O. Smith, and C. James Taylor (Andrew Johnson), Robert A. Rutland (James Madison, and Charles M. Wiltse (Daniel Webster); Barbara W. Finney, James K. Polk Memorial Auxiliary (Columbia, Tenn.); Earle E. Coleman and Mardel Pacheco, Princeton University; Hal H. Will, Puget Sound Maritime Historical Society (Seattle); Robert E. May, Purdue University; Kathleen E. Kuczynski, Rensselaer County (N.Y.) Historical Society; Dorothy W. Knepper and Barbara Rawlings, San Jacinto Museum of History Association (Deer Park, Texas); James A. Steed, Smithsonian In-

ACKNOWLEDGMENTS

stitution Archives; Louis B. Rauco, State Library of Pennsylvania; Fran Eads and John H. Thweatt, Tennessee State Library and Archives; Jean Carefoot, Texas State Library; Wilbur E. Meneray and Sue Woodward, Tulane University; Richard J. Sommers, United States Army Military History Institute (Carlisle Barracks, Pa.); Marie T. Capps, Herbert Leventhal, and Michael E. Moss, United States Military Academy; William W. Jeffries, United States Naval Academy; Frances P. Barton and Joyce H. Lamont, University of Alabama; William M. Roberts, University of California (Berkeley); Phyllis Moore Sanders, University of California (Los Angeles); Jacqueline Bull, the late Holman Hamilton, and Richard Lowitt, University of Kentucky; Robert A. Linder, University of Mississippi; Brenda M. Eagles, Pattie B. McIntyre, Ellen Neal, Richard A. Shrader, and Carolyn A. Wallace, University of North Carolina; Richard E. Beringer, University of North Dakota; Nettie Lee Benson, Jane Garner, Goldia Hester, Chester V. Kielman, and Victoria Reed, University of Texas Archives; Carolyn M. Beckham, University of Virginia; Charles D. Spurlin, Victoria (Texas) College; Howson W. Cole, Virginia Historical Society; Delbert J. McBride, Washington State Capitol Museum; Patricia L. Bodak and Judith A. Schiff, Yale University.

A number of persons, among them Davis descendants, have shared their private collections of documents and family records; several have even undertaken additional research. We are especially indebted to Leisa West Bates, Percival T. Beacroft, Jr., Florence N. Bruce, Myrtie C. Byrne, Ernesto Caldeira, Julia Courtenay Campbell, Robert E. Canon, Barbara Clarke, Richard W. Davis, Lucinda Goldsborough Dietz, Ralph W. Donnelly, Emily Driscoll, George H. Edwards, Frank E. Everett, Harold C. Fisher, the late Albert F. Ganier, Bertram Hayes-Davis, the late Jefferson Hayes-Davis, Karen B. Henderson, Thomas W. Henderson, Janet Hermann, Mrs. Joe H. Howie, Kathryn Compton Kimble, Elizabeth Kerrigan Kuebel, Mary Ella B. Logan, Natalie S. Lowry, Marie W. McLaurin, William J. Miller, Douglas M. More, Margaret Moss, Ben S. Nelms, Thomas V. Noland, Gerard O'Brien, Kathleen O'Fallon, Esselyn G. Perkins, William L. Richter, Elizabeth Smith Ricks, Joseph Rubinfine, Charles W. Sachs, Adele Davis Sinton, Rosa Cole Spencer, Mrs. Fred Swaney, Lt. Col. David L. Traxler, Elizabeth Garth Vestal, Col. Charles F. Ward, Newton Wilds, and Clarence L.

ACKNOWLEDGMENTS

Yancey. Although not specifically intended for use in Volume 3, the valuable Davis items recently given to the project by George M. Britton, James L. Britton, and Richard C. Hulbert are greatly appreciated.

Of the many State Department officials who assisted us in gaining access to the Defense Archives in Mexico City, we would like to thank Richard B. Phillips, then cultural affairs officer of the United States Embassy, and his assistant Javier Corona for the inordinate amount of time they donated to our research concerns. Professor Luis G. Ceballos also generously provided assistance.

We have been fortunate in our association with the Rice University community, many of whom have been unstinting in their cooperation and warm support. In particular, we thank Joan R. Boorman, Nathan Broch, Walter L. Buenger, Samuel M. Carrington, Gilbert M. Cuthbertson, Robert H. Dix, Katherine F. Drew, Kay A. Flowers, the Friends of Fondren Library, Leonard J. Fullenkamp, Charles M. Gibson, Fannie M. Haynes, S. W. Higginbotham, Ferne B. Hyman, Harold M. Hyman, John S. Hughes, Marian M. Jordan, Barbara A. Kile, Holly L. Leitz, John V. Leskowitz, Fredericka Meiners, Nicolo Messana, Ola Z. Moore, Jeanette E. Monroe, James W. Mooney, Richard O'Keeffe, Nancy B. Parker, Richard H. Perrine, William L. Pinkston, Susan G. Pridmore, Linda M. Quaidy, Richard R. Seim, Ann-Marie Vermillion, Kristine Wallace, Joseph F. White, and Elizabeth S. Wray.

Ably assisting in the preparation of Volume 3 were several students and part-time employees: John R. Anderson, Mary S. Butler, Ruth McCotter, Mrs. William A. McGinnis, Jr., and Diana L. Walzel. A special note of appreciation is due to George W. New for long hours of painstaking research, volunteered enthusiastically. As was our good fortune for Volumes 1 and 2, Barbara Long has again prepared splendid maps, this time to complement the Mexican War documents.

Finally, our colleagues at the Louisiana State University Press—director Leslie A. Phillabaum, executive editor Beverly Jarrett, managing editor Martha Lacy Hall, designer Albert Crochet, and especially Marie G. Carmichael, our talented editor—deserve praise for their collective skills in the production of Volume 3.

EDITORIAL STAFF

xv

EDITORIAL METHOD

DURING THE preparation of Volume 3, the prospectus for the complete letterpress edition was carefully reviewed. Rising production costs dictated a reduction in the total number of volumes as well as substantial changes in the methodology of document selection and annotation. In this and subsequent volumes, items composed by Davis are given preference for publication in full, especially those documents that illuminate his character, opinions, philosophy, and personal relationships. Special consideration is given to letters, speeches, and documents not previously printed. An appended calendar lists all Davis material known to exist from the period, allowing an overview of incoming correspondence, routine letters, and congressional activities.

Documents

The printed version closely resembles the original manuscript. Spelling, grammar, punctuation, abbreviations, contractions, and repeated letters, words, and phrases are reproduced as written. Interlined words are enclosed in virgules: "/added/." Material marked for deletion is preceded and followed by short dashes and enclosed in angle brackets: "<–out–>." Superscript is lowered, standard paragraph indention is used, and page numbers are omitted. Always footnoted, marginalia are incorporated at the place intended or, if the place cannot be determined, appear at the end of the item. In documents taken from newspapers and other printed sources, heads and subheads are deleted and obvious printers' errors, such as inverted letters, corrected without comment. Square brackets, unless otherwise noted, indicate editorial insertions, most often added because the manuscript is damaged. Indecipherable words appear in the printed version as "[illegible]."

When the background or context of an item is unclear, an editorial note is inserted below the title (see the speech of June 10, 1847).

Although frequently written on two or three lines and occasionally located at the end of the manuscript, the place and date are always positioned at top right and whenever possible treated in one line. If the place and date are derived from internal evidence or other sources, they are enclosed in brackets and footnoted (see Davis' letter of February 8, 1847). Unless bearing a specific date, monthly military returns have been assigned the first day of the following month (see the calendar for examples). In some cases, an exact date cannot be determined even though the month is known; such documents appear in what seems a logical sequence (see the letter from James H. R. Taylor, [March 1847]). Undated items known to be of the period are printed in an appendix following the dated documents.

Salutations are capitalized for consistency and are placed at top left; inside addresses are omitted. The complimentary close immediately follows the last sentence of the letter. Whether written on the last page, in the margin, or on verso, postscripts follow the signature (see the letter from William H. Sparke, November 17, 1848).

Enclosures either are printed in full at the date written or are listed in the calendar. If not Davis items, they are described in footnotes (see Davis to John Jenkins, August 4, 1847).

Annotation

The descriptive note records the following information: the character of the manuscript, whether an ALS, AL, LS, LbC, D, or L, copy (see the list of symbols); the locations of known contemporary copies, the one listed first being that which is transcribed (in a few instances, an item is transcribed from two versions; see July 1, 1848); the postmark and outside address, if useful; relevant endorsements, especially those of Davis and Varina Davis; if the document is an enclosure, a notation of the letter of transmittal (see the letter from Daniel R. Russell, November 24, 1847); the physical condition of the original, if damaged or incomplete; unusual provenance.

Numbered footnotes identify and explicate. A brief biographical sketch emphasizing any special relationship with Davis accompanies the first mention of an individual. If no biographical sketch appears, the person has been identified previously or insufficient information was found. The location of each person's sketch, whether in the current or a previous volume, is provided in the index. For places, events, and things, numbered notes are used to clarify, correct, and give pertinent comments by Davis and others. All Mexican War place-names appear on the maps. Textual irregularities—manuscript damage, marginalia, Davis' emendations—are detailed in numbered notes.

All citations are by short titles; see the list of sources for full bibliographical data. Most abbreviations used in the notes are self-explanatory. Repository designations are adopted from *Symbols of American Libraries* (11th ed.). For some less common abbreviations and all repository symbols, see the lists following in the front matter. *Webster's New International Dictionary* (3d ed.) and the Chicago *Manual of Style* (12th ed.) are standard references. Most of the city directories used may be found in the microfilm collection produced by Research Publications, Inc. All citations of federal census schedules refer to population unless otherwise specified. In certain cases, a National Archives microfilm series is given instead of the record group designation, since the film is generally more accessible (for example, see the calendar entry for November 21, 1848; see also the National Archives section in the list of sources). In citations of government documents, the congress and session numbers appear as arabic numerals separated by a colon; e.g., *Cong. Globe*, 30:1, 798, refers to the *Congressional Globe*, 30th Congress, 1st Session, page 798. Likewise, volume and page numbers of other printed sources are in arabic, including references to previous volumes of *The Papers of Jefferson Davis*. For example, *Davis Papers*, 2:17, refers to Volume 2, page 17, not item 17. Documents cited only by writer and recipient (or title) and date are printed or calendared in this volume (see the letter from Francis G. Baldwin, November 19, 1848, n3).

Calendar

Appendix II, the calendar, summarizes all extant Davis documents from the period covered by the volume. When several of Davis' actions are known on a certain issue, particularly a legislative matter, the calendar entry is the date of his first involvement (see, for examples, April 13 and May 21, 1848). Routine letters of transmittal are simply noted (see the entry for March 3, 1848). All citations are by short titles, and abbreviations are used when appropriate. Senate proceedings as reported in the *Senate Journal* are preferred over those in the *Congressional Globe*.

Addenda

Recently discovered items that fall in the time period covered by previous volumes are calendared in Appendix III.

Volume 3

There are 533 calendar entries covering almost 600 items. Of the 152 documents printed in full, 68 are letters by Davis, 10 are his Mexican War reports and statements, and 19 are speeches. The Davis items represent the holdings of 50 repositories and 11 private collections, as well as the contents of 17 newspapers and various other printed sources.

SYMBOLS AND ABBREVIATIONS

A	Autographed
D	Document: unaddressed items, such as proclamations, speeches, oaths, deeds, commissions, etc.
E	Endorsement
Encl	Enclosure
L	Letter
LbC	Letterbook copy
MS(S)	Manuscript(s): a general category used when other descriptions are inapplicable
S	Signed
AGO	Adjutant General's Office
AHA	American Historical Association
ann.	annotator; annual
app.	appendix
applic.	application
appt.	appointment
a.q.m.	assistant quartermaster
art.	artillery; article
aud.	auditor
BDAC	Biographical Directory of the American Congress
btn.	battalion
bty.	battery
cat.	catalog
cav.	cavalry
chron.	chronicle
coll.	collection
comnd.	commissioned
comns.	commissions

SYMBOLS AND ABBREVIATIONS

comp.	compiler
compt.	comptroller
comr.	commissioner
consol.	consolidated
Cont.	Continental
corres.	correspondence
DAB	*Dictionary of American Biography*
dir.	directory
dismtd.	dismounted
doc.	document
ex.	executive
f/w	filed with
inf.	infantry
Intell.	*Intelligencer*
JSH	*Journal of Southern History*
lt.	light; lieutenant
mtd.	mounted
mvmts.	movements
NCAB	*National Cyclopaedia of American Biography*
n.d.	no date
n.p.	no place; no publisher
OED	*Oxford English Dictionary*
OR	*Official Records of the Union and Confederate Armies*
pubs.	publications
rec.	record
recoms.	recommendations
ref.	referred
reg.	regulation; register
RG	record group
rgt.	regiment
rgtl.	regimental
ser.	series
SWHQ	*Southwest Historical Quarterly*
USMA	United States Military Academy
vol.	volunteer
WPA	Works Progress Administration

REPOSITORY SYMBOLS

AU	University of Alabama
CSmH	Henry E. Huntington Library
CtY	Yale University
DLC	Library of Congress
DNA	National Archives
DSI	Smithsonian Institution
GEU	Emory University
ICHi	Chicago Historical Society
IHi	Illinois State Historical Library
In	Indiana State Library
InHi	Indiana Historical Society
InNea.	New Albany–Floyd County Public Library
KyLoF	Filson Club
KyLx	Lexington Public Library
KyLxT	Transylvania University
LNT	Tulane University
LU-Ar	Louisiana State University, Department of Archives and Manuscripts
MB	Boston Public Library and Eastern Massachusetts Regional Public Library System
MH-H	Harvard University, Houghton Library
MiU-C	University of Michigan, William L. Clements Library
MnHi	Minnesota Historical Society
MWA	American Antiquarian Society
Ms-Ar	Mississippi Department of Archives and History
MsU	University of Mississippi
MsVO	Old Court House Museum Library

REPOSITORY SYMBOLS

N	New York State Library
NBuHi	Buffalo and Erie County Historical Society
NcD	Duke University
NcU	University of North Carolina
NHi	New-York Historical Society
NIC	Cornell University
NjP	Princeton University
NN	New York Public Library
NNC	Columbia University
NNPM	Pierpont Morgan Library
NWM	United States Military Academy
OOxM	Miami University
PHi	Historical Society of Pennsylvania
ScCleU	Clemson University
T	Tennessee State Library and Archives
Tx	Texas State Library and Historical Commission
TxHR	Rice University
TxU	University of Texas, Austin
ViHi	Virginia Historical Society
ViRC	Museum of the Confederacy
ViU	University of Virginia
ViW	College of William and Mary

CONTENTS

ILLUSTRATIONS

CHRONOLOGY
July 1846–December 1848

Brackets indicate those dates that follow logically from information in primary sources but are not explicitly stated.

1846

July 3	Ordered to report with his regiment to Gen. Zachary Taylor in Mexico Votes in favor of the Walker tariff bill
July 4	Leaves Washington for Vicksburg to assume command of the 1st Miss. Rgt.
July 13	Arrives at Vicksburg; leaves for Davis Bend
July [14]	Leaves Davis Bend
July 17	Arrives at New Orleans
July 18	Assumes command of the 1st Miss. Rgt.
July 26	Sails from New Orleans
July [29 or 30]	Arrives at Brazos Island
August 3	Moves to the mouth of the Rio Grande
August 24	Leaves the mouth of the Rio Grande
August 31	Arrives at Camargo
September 7	Leaves Camargo for Monterrey
September 7–8	Camps at Guardado Abajo
September 9	Camps at the hacienda of Bartelo Andreas
September 10	Camps at Mier

CHRONOLOGY

September 11   Camps at Chicharrones

September 12   Camps at Puntiagudo

September 13–14   Camps at Cerralvo

September 15   Leaves Cerralvo

September 16   Camps at Papagayos

September 17   Camps at Marín

September 18   Camps at San Francisco

September 19   Leaves San Francisco for Monterrey; camps at Walnut Springs

September 21–23   Commands the 1st Miss. Rgt. in the Battle of Monterrey

September 21   Captures the Tenería and a nearby fortified stone building; withdraws from the attack on El Diablo; reconnoiters the *tête-de-pont*; repulses a lancer attack; retires to Walnut Springs

September 22   Garrisons the fortified stone building and redan at the Tenería

September 23   Occupies El Diablo; advances toward the central plaza; retires to Walnut Springs

September 24   Appointed a commissioner to negotiate the capitulation of Monterrey

September 25   Sent to the Mexican headquarters to obtain signed copies of the capitulation

October 17   Letter of resignation from Congress is forwarded to the governor of Mississippi by Joseph E. Davis

October 18   Granted a sixty-day furlough

October [19 or 20] Leaves for the United States

October 29   Sails from Brazos Island

CHRONOLOGY

October 30	Stops at Galveston
November 1	Arrives at New Orleans
November 2	Leaves for Davis Bend
November 4	Arrives at Davis Bend
November 10	Addresses a banquet honoring the 1st Miss. Rgt. at Vicksburg
November [19]	Leaves Davis Bend
November 21	Arrives at New Orleans
December 1	Sails from New Orleans
December 4	Arrives at Brazos Island
December [7 or 8]	Leaves for the camp at the mouth of the Rio Grande
December [10]	Embarks for the trip upriver
December 14	Reaches Camargo
December 16	Leaves Camargo for Monterrey
December [25]	Meets Gen. Zachary Taylor near Montemorelos; proceeds with him to Victoria

1847

January 4	Arrives at Victoria; rejoins the 1st Miss. Rgt.
January 16	Leaves Victoria
January 25	Arrives at Monterrey
January 30	Leaves Monterrey
January 31	Camps at Rinconada Pass
February 2	Arrives at Saltillo
February 5	Leaves with Taylor's headquarters for Agua Nueva
February 21	Returns to Saltillo

CHRONOLOGY

February 22	Leads the 1st Miss. Rgt. to Buena Vista; returns to Saltillo at nightfall
February 23	Commands the 1st Miss. Rgt. in the Battle of Buena Vista; wounded in the regiment's first engagement; returns to Saltillo after dark
March [25 or 26]	Leaves Saltillo by ambulance
March 27	Arrives at Monterrey
May 17	Appointed brigadier general
May [17]	Leaves Monterrey with part of his regiment
May [19 or 20]	Joins the rest of his regiment at Cerralvo; leaves for Camargo
May 22	Camps several miles beyond Camargo
May 24	Arrives at Reynosa
May [25]	Leaves Reynosa
May 27	Arrives at the mouth of the Rio Grande
May 28	Moves to Brazos Island
May 30	Sails from Brazos Island
June 6	Arrives at New Orleans
June 10	Speaks at a reception for the 1st Miss. Rgt.
June 12	Leaves New Orleans
June 14	Stops at Natchez; speaks at a reception for the 1st Miss. Rgt.
June 15	Arrives at Vicksburg; speaks at a reception for the 1st Miss. Rgt.
June [16]	Returns to Brierfield
June 20	Declines the appointment as brigadier general
August 10	Appointed United States senator

CHRONOLOGY

August 15	Accepts the appointment as senator
November 11	Leaves Davis Bend for Washington
November 17	Arrives at Louisville, Kentucky
November 18	Arrives at Cincinnati; visits with former President Tyler
November 25	Arrives at Washington
November 27	Calls on President Polk
December 6	Takes his seat in the Senate
December 9	Attends a dinner at the White House with cabinet officers and other members of Congress
December 14	Appointed to the Military Affairs, Pension, and Library committees
December 25	Engages in a fight with Henry S. Foote
December 30	Appointed to the Board of Regents, Smithsonian Institution

1848

January 11	Elected United States senator by the Mississippi legislature
February 15	Sworn in as a duly elected senator from Mississippi
March 10	Votes to ratify the peace treaty with Mexico
March 17	Votes in favor of the bill to raise ten regiments
June 13	Speaks at a dinner honoring John J. Crittenden
June 20–21	Consults with President Polk concerning the reduction of the army after the war
June 23	Reports to President Polk on recent events in Cuba

xxxv

CHRONOLOGY

July 12	Delivers a major speech protesting formal prohibition of slavery from the Oregon Territory
July 27	Votes for the Senate's compromise bill on Oregon
[late August]	Visits Blue Lick Spring, Kentucky
September 3	Stops at Lexington, Kentucky, en route to Mississippi
September 22	Visits Vicksburg; speaks at Raymond
September 23	Speaks at Jackson
September 26	Speaks at Vicksburg
October 19	Speaks at Port Gibson
[October 31]	Speaks in Yazoo County
November 20	Arrives in New Orleans en route to Washington
December [1]	Arrives in Washington
December 4	Attends opening of second session
December 12	Appointed to the Military Affairs and Library committees
December 13, 18, 20	Attends meetings of the Smithsonian Board of Regents
December 22	Assumes chairmanship of the Military Affairs Committee
December 23	Attends convention of southern members of Congress
December 27	Attends meeting of the Smithsonian Board of Regents

THE PAPERS OF JEFFERSON DAVIS

Volume 3

1846–1848

To the People of Mississippi

Steamer Star Spangled Banner,
Mississippi River, July 13, 1846.

FELLOW CITIZENS: I address you to explain the cause of my present absence from the seat of the federal government.

Those of our fellow-citizens who, in answer to a call of the President, had volunteered to serve the U. S. in the existing war with Mexico, have elected me for their Colonel,[1] and the Governor has furnished to me a commission[2] in accordance with that election. Having received a military education and served a number of years in the line of the army, I felt that my services were due to the country, and believed my experience might be available in promoting the comfort, the safety and efficiency of the Mississippi Regiment in the campaign on which they were about to enter—Such considerations, united to the desire common to our people to engage in the military service of the country, decided me unhesitatingly to accept the command which was offered. The regiment was organized and waiting to be mustered into service preparatory to a departure for the army of operation.[3] Under such circumstances, I could not delay until the close of the Congressional session, though then so proximate that it must occur before a successor could be chosen and reach the city of Washington

It was my good fortune to see in none of the measures likely to be acted on at this session such hazard as would render a single vote important, except the bill to regulate anew the duties upon imports. The vote on this was to occur very soon (in two days) after the receipt of my commission as Colonel, and I have the satisfaction to announce to you that it passed the House the evening before I left Washington; and I entertain no doubt of its passing through the Senate and becoming the law of the land.[4] An analysis of the votes upon this bill will show that its main support was derived from the agricultural and exporting States. To these in a pecuniary view it was the measure of highest importance. But whilst I rejoice in it for such considerations, because tending to advance the great staple interest of our State, and thus to promote the prosperity of all indus-

3

try among us, I am not less gratified at it as a measure of political reform. In adopting the ad valorem rule and restricting its operation to the revenue limit, the great principle of taxing in proportion to the benefits conferred is more nearly approximated, and the power to lay duties is directed to the purpose of raising money, for which alone it was conferred in the constitution of our confederacy. Thus it was exercised by the fathers of our Republic in the first tariff enacted under the federal constitution; when for the benefit it would confer upon American producers and manufacturers they chose to raise revenue by imposts rather than direct taxation. Since then, as in the bill of 1842, (to be substituted by that lately passed through the House of Representatives,) the collection of revenue has been the subordinate; the benefit to particular classes, the main object of duties. And the extent to which this was pursued was concealed by specific duties and minima valuations—rendering the law unintelligible on its face, and in many cases wholly prohibitory in its operation—destroying revenue but leaving taxation. A tariff "for pretection" must discriminate against the necessaries of life to favor manufactures in a rude or "infant" state; a tariff for revenue may, and generally would, impose its highest duties upon luxuries, for reasons so just and equalizing in their practical effects, that one could have no inducement to conceal the policy or shrink from its avowal.

Commercial changes and the wants or superfluities of the treasury must require occasional modifications in the rates of duties upon imports; but a salutary check is held by the people so long as all modifications are made by changing the rate per cent. on enumerated articles, by which it is seen at once what tax is imposed upon consumption, and whether or not the limit of revenue is passed.

I trust we shall never again witness the spectacle, so revolting to every idea of self government, of a law in which, by specific duties and minima valuations, the purpose and effect is as absolutely concealed as in the edicts of the ancient tyrant, which were written in a hand so small and hung so high as to be illegible to those upon whom they were to operate.[5]

During this session, as your Representative, I have acted upon all measures as seemed to me best to accord with the principles upon which I was elected, and most likely to correspond with the wishes and interests of the people of Mississippi. Thus my support was given to the law for the separation of the fiscal affairs of the general government from all connection with banks. The bill passed by the House of Representatives will, it is confidently expected, pass the Senate of the United States probably with an amendment extending the time at which it is to go into full effect.[6] This is supposed to be necessary to prevent an injurious revulsion in the trade of the country, consequent upon the sudden contraction of the discounts of those banks, which have extended their accommodations upon the government deposites Evils however positive, cannot always be immediately abated; and in this extension of the time it is only designed to make a temporary concession of policy, that by an easy, gradual change the prosperity of trade may be secured and monetary derangement be avoided. These two, the "tariff" and "Independent Treasury," are the measures which seem to me most deeply to involve the interests of Mississippi. Without mountain slopes, and mountain streams to furnish water power; without coal mines permanently to supply large amounts of cheap fuel at any locality, we cannot expect, in competition with those who enjoy either or both of these advantages, ever to become a manufacturing people. We must continue to rely, as at present, almost entirely upon our exports; and it requires no argument, under such circumstances, to maintain the position that the interest of our State will be most advanced by freeing commerce from all unnecessary burthens, and by measuring the value of our purchases by the standard used in our sales—the currency of the world.

By the active exertion of our Senator Speight, a bill was passed through the Senate, granting to the State of Mississippi alternate sections of land to aid in the construction of the proposed Mississippi and Alabama rail road. It is scarcely to be hoped that the House will act upon this measure at the present session, but placed upon the calendar of unfinished business, I think it will become a law at the next session of this Congress.[7] I have also hoped that at the same session, a law would be passed to enable the Postmaster General to make contracts for a long term of years with rail roads under construction, by which the government would be secured from the exorbitant charges monopolies have it in their power to impose, and such certainty conferred upon the value of rail road stock as would greatly aid in the completion of an entire chain of rail ways from the Mississippi at Vicksburg to the Atlantic, and to the metropolis of our Union—a chain like a system of nerves to couple our remote members of the body politic to the centre of the Union, and rapidly to transmit sensation from one to the other; or like great sinews uniting into concentrated action the power of the right hand and the left—the valley of the Mississippi and the coast of the Atlantic—whenever the necessities of one or the other shall require the action of both.

Much has been done during the past winter to adjust suspended and conflicting claims to land purchased from the U. S., and it is to be hoped that the action of this Congress will relieve our people from the uncertainty and harassing delays under which so many of them have labored for years past.[8]

The bill to graduate and reduce the price of the public lands, will no doubt become a law;[9] and we may expect from it an important increase to our population and State wealth; such as has been the result in the northern portion of our State, where under the Chickasaw treaty,[10] a graduation system has been in operation, it is to be supposed, will be the result of a similar graduation in those districts where the public land has remained long unsold. The coast survey, now in progress along the Gulf of Mexico, cannot fail to have an important influence upon that portion of our State which borders on the Gulf, by giving correct charts of the channels and points of entrance safe for coasting vessel. Beyond this, I anticipate that the survey will establish as a fact that the best point west of Cape Florida for a navy yard to repair or construct vessels of the largest class, is the Harbor of Ship Island; and further, that it will lead to the speedy establishment of the necessary lights along the Coast and upon its adjacent Islands. The difficulty of obtaining appropriations for these has heretofore been greatly increased by the want of official information. The Legislature of our State memorialized Congress upon the propriety of re-opening the Pass Manchac. I was fully impressed with the propriety of the claim. Under more favorable circumstances, an appropriation for the purpose might have been obtained; and I yet hope that we shall get a survey and report upon the contemplated work, in time for action at the next session of this Congress.

Since I took a seat as your Representative in Congress, the country has been disturbed; its political elements agitated and thrown into confusion; its peace with England seriously endangered by a question of boundary in what is known as the Oregon Territory. We have now satisfactory reasons to believe that this question is amicably adjusted. The exact terms of the agreement have not transpired; but in general language it may be stated as settled on the basis of the 49th parallel of north latitude, with a temporary permission to the Hudson's Bay Company to navigate the Columbia River. That there should have been a desire among our people generally to hold the whole Territory was but natural, and this not merely from a wish to extend our territory, but also from a more creditable desire to reserve as far as we might, the North American Continent for republican institutions. As few will contend that this desire would have justified our Government in waging a war for territorial acquisition, the question was narrowed down to this: how far are our rights clearly defined, and how shall we best secure what is clearly our own, and upon what terms shall we compromise for what is disputable? There were some who claimed for the parallel of 54° 40′ N. L a talismanic merit—that it was the line to which patriotism required us to go, and short of which it was treasonable to stop. This opinion could only rest on the supposition that by purchase from Spain we acquired a perfect title. But this was to assume too much. The assumption carried with it the element of its own destruction. The Spanish claim extended as far as the 61st degree. If the boundary had been well defined, and the title perfect, then there was no power in our Government to surrender any part of it, and the Convention with Russia is void. But if, as must be generally admitted, the line of 54° 40′ was a compromise with Russia growing out of the fact that our title was imperfect and the boundary unsettled, then was 54° 40′ merely a line of expediency, as any other parallel would have been—good only as against Russia, and subject on the same principle to further adjustment with the other claimant in that territory.

The history of our past negotiations with Great Britain in relation to that territory gave little foundation for the expectation that we could get amicably, the whole country we have now secured south of the 49th parallel of latitude; and if the information I have derived from the officers who have explored different portions of that country be correct, a few years will satisfy our people that we have obtained nearly all which would have been valuable to us—a territory extending further north than the most northern point ever occupied by any portion of our people, and if the term "Oregon Territory" was properly applicable to the valley of the Columbia, or Oregon River, a territory far more valuable than could be claimed in the valley drained by that stream and all its tributaries

In the south we had another question of boundary unsettled; and though all proper efforts were made to adjust it amicably, they proved abortive. The minister sent to Mexico under a previous understanding that diplomatic relations should be renewed, and invested with full powers to treat of all questions in dispute, was rejected, without even being allowed to present his credentials.[11] It could not be permitted to our rival claimant thus to decide the question, and though the insult would have justified an immediate declaration of war, in a spirit of forbearance, the administration refrained from recommending this measure, and merely moved forward our troops to take possession of the entire territory claimed as our own, when there was no longer a prospect of adjustment by negotiation. This led to such hostilities as rendered it necessary to recognize the existence of war. Our government made the declaration in the mode provided by the constitution; and proceeded steadily to supply the means for a vigorous prosecution of the war into which we have been so unexpectedly drawn. In this connection it is worthy of remark that before a declaration was made on our part, the President of Mexico had made a similar declaration, and the appointments of the Mexican army which crossed the Rio Grande to attack the forces of General Taylor, clearly show that it had advanced on that frontier for the purpose of invading the State of Texas.

The zeal shown in every quarter of the Union to engage in the service of our common country—the masses who have voluntarily come forward in numbers far exceeding the necessities of the occasion—attest the military strength of our Republic, and furnish just cause for patriotic pride and gratulation. I regret the disappointment felt by so many of my fellow-citizens of Mississippi at not being called into service; and I have not failed to present the case fully to the Executive of [th]¹²e U S. Your patriotic anxiety is well appreciated; nor is the propriety of your conduct in waiting until regularly called for, forgotten; and if the war should continue, as further supplies of troops be required, there is no doubt but that our State will be among the first looked to for new levies.

There are several subjects connected with the local interests of Mississippi upon which it would have been agreeable to me to have said something; but the great length to which this letter is already extended, induces me with a few remarks bearing more particularly upon myself, to terminate it.

Unless the government of Mexico shall very soon take such steps as to give full assurance of a speedy peace, so that I may resume my duties as your Representative at the beginning of the next session of Congress, my resignation will be offered at an early day, that full time may be allowed to select a successor.[13]

Grateful to the people for their confidence and honor bestowed upon me, I have labored as their representative industriously. Elected on avowed and established principles, the cardinal points to guide my course were always before me. How well that course has accorded with your wishes; how far it is approved by your judgment, it is not for me to anticipate; but I confidently rely on your generous allowance to give credit to my motives; and for the rest, as becomes a representative, I will cheerfully submit to your decision.

JEFF'N: DAVIS.

Vicksburg *Sentinel and Expositor,* July 21, 1846.

[1] The other members of the 1st Miss. Rgt. staff were Lt. Col. Alexander K. McClung; Maj. Alexander B. Bradford; Richard Griffith, adj.; Seymour Halsey, surgeon; James D. Caulfield, contract asst. surgeon (employed Sept. 15, 1846); John Thompson, asst. surgeon (appointed Dec. 1, 1846); Thomas P. Slade, acting a.q.m.; Kemp S. Holland, asst. commissary of subsistence (died Dec. 4, 1846); Christopher H. Mott, asst. commissary (appointed Oct. 24, 1846); Humphrey Marshall, sgt. maj. (resigned Aug. 23, 1846); Charles T. Harlan, sgt. maj. (Aug. 23–Oct. 24, 1846); Horace H. Miller, sgt. maj. (appointed Jan. 8, 1847). The following served as company officers:

Co. A—Capt. John M. Sharp, 1st Lt. Philip J. Burrus (resigned July 21, 1846), 1st Lt. Ferdinand Bostick (Sept. 6–17, 1846), 2d Lt. Amos B. Corwine (elected 1st lt. Feb. 15, 1847), 2d Lt. Seaborne M. Phillips (elected Mar. 6, 1847), 2d Lt. Thomas P. Slade.

Co. B—Capt. Douglas H. Cooper, 1st Lt. Carnot Posey, 2d Lt. James Colhoun, 2d Lt. Samuel R. Harrison.

Co. C—Capt. John Willis, 1st Lt. Henry F. Cook, 2d Lt. Richard Griffith, 2d Lt. Rufus K. Arthur.

Co. D—Capt. Bainbridge D. Howard, 1st Lt. Daniel R. Russell, 2d Lt. Lewis T. Howard (resigned Dec. 30, 1846), 2d Lt. Leon Trousdale (elected Jan. 5, 1847), 2d Lt. Benjamin L. Hodge (resigned Aug. 19, 1846), 2d Lt. Thomas J. Kyle (Sept. 6–Dec. 31, 1846), 2d Lt. E. W. Hollingsworth (elected Jan. 5, 1847).

Co. E—Capt. John L. McManus, 1st Lt. Crawford Fletcher, 2d Lt. James H. Hughes, 2d Lt. Charles M. Bradford.

Co. F—Capt. William Delay, 1st

Lt. William N. Brown, 2d Lt. Frederick J. Malone (resigned Oct. 31, 1846), 2d Lt. Josephus J. Tatum (Nov. 16, 1846–Jan. 20, 1847), 2d Lt. John P. Stockard (elected Jan. 29, 1847), 2d Lt. William W. Redding.

Co. G—Capt. Reuben Downing, 1st Lt. Stephen A. D. Greaves, 2d Lt. William H. Hampton, 2d Lt. Francis McNulty (killed Feb. 23, 1847), 2d Lt. Samuel Thomas (promoted Mar. 6, 1847).

Co. H—Capt. George Crump (furloughed Oct., resigned Nov. 1846), Capt. John S. Clendenin (2d lt., elected capt. Jan. 29, 1847), 1st Lt. Robert L. Moore (killed Feb. 23, 1847), 1st Lt. James E. Stewart (elected Mar. 6, 1847), 2d Lt. John Bobb (resigned Sept. 24, 1846), 2d Lt. Hugh M. Markham (resigned Oct. 19, 1846), 2d Lt. John J. Poindexter (elected Jan. 26, 1847), 2d Lt. Richard Hopkins (elected Mar. 6, 1847).

Co. I—Capt. James H. R. Taylor, 1st Lt. Christopher H. Mott, 2d Lt. Samuel H. Dill, 2d Lt. William Epps.

Co. K—Capt. William P. Rogers, 1st Lt. William H. H. Patterson, 2d Lt. William P. Townsend, 2d Lt. William B. Wade.

2 Albert G. Brown was governor of Mississippi; his signed commission to Davis has not been found. In the 1880s Davis received a letter from T. M. Thorpe of New York City, reporting that the commission could be acquired for $150. Obviously Davis did not avail himself of the offer, for in January 1888 Samuel W. Smith of Kansas City, Missouri, informed the Virginia State Library that he was willing to sell a collection of historical records that included Davis' commission (Thorpe to Davis, May 12, ViRC; Smith to Davis, La. Hist. Assn.—Davis Coll., LNT). The present location of Smith's collection is unknown.

3 Probably a reference to Zachary Taylor's command, first called the "corps of observation" but later re-named the Army of Occupation (Roger Jones to Taylor, Apr. 27, 1844, DNA, RG94, Letters Sent, 20: 257; DNA, M-29, roll 1, Gen. Orders No. 1, Aug. 6, 1845).

4 The Walker tariff, passed by the House on July 3, was approved July 30, 1846 (U.S. Statutes at Large, 9:42–49).

5 Davis refers to the Roman emperor Caligula, who concealed a severe tax law in the manner described (Suetonius, Lives, 280).

6 The independent treasury bill passed the House on April 2, 1846. As Davis expected, the Senate amended the measure before passage on August 1. Five days later it was signed into law (Cong. Globe, 29:1, 595–96, 1164, 1176, 1196–97; U.S. Statutes at Large, 9:59–66).

7 Jesse Speight's railroad bill was passed by the Senate on May 4, but not acted upon by the House. Not until 1848 was aid forthcoming for a railroad from Jackson to the Alabama line (Cong. Globe, 29:1, 751, 753, 1197; U.S. Statutes at Large, 9:237). As senator, Davis submitted his own railroad bill on December 26, 1848.

8 On May 19 the Senate passed a bill to adjust all suspended preemption claims. After Davis' departure from Washington, the House acted, and on August 3 the bill became law (Cong. Globe, 29:1, 839, 1145; U.S. Statutes at Large, 9:51–52). See Davis Papers, 2:488, 537, for Davis' concern with preemption.

9 House and Senate action on the pricing of public lands was inconclusive during the Twenty-ninth Congress (Cong. Globe, 29:1, 1073, 1093–94, 1179–80, 1196; see also Davis Papers, 2:335).

10 See Davis Papers, 2:260, for a discussion of the treaties of 1832 and 1834.

11 John Slidell had traveled to Mexico in December 1845.

12 Letters missing from the original newsprint.

[13] Editorial comment on Davis' decision not to resign at this time was mixed. For conflicting views, see the Jackson *Southron*, July 22, 1846, and the Vicksburg *Sentinel and Expositor*, July 28, 1846.

To Varina Howell Davis and Joseph E. Davis

Editorial Note: Davis reached Hurricane, his brother's plantation, on July 13. He intended to board the *Paul Jones* for the trip downriver the next evening, a plan he probably carried out, since the steamer docked in New Orleans on July 17, the day he is known to have arrived. Even before assuming command of his regiment the following day, Davis arranged for the Mississippians to leave their campground, where they were exposed to the inclement weather, and move to some large, empty sheds on the outskirts of the city (DNA, RG94, Vol. Muster Rolls, Mexican War, 1st Miss. Rgtl. Return, Aug. 1846; Vicksburg *Tri-Weekly Whig*, July 14, 25, 1846; New Orleans *Picayune*, July 18, 1846; New Orleans *Jeffersonian*, July 20, 1846; Yazoo City *Whig*, Aug. 7, 1846).

18th July 1846

MY DEAR WIFE

I am so late that I have only time to say I am well very busy making arrangements to start and with a heart full of love to my own Winnie[1]

It will be two or three days before we leave here though a part of the Regt. will be off in a day or at most two— I will write again

YOUR HUBBIE

BROTHER,

I will write to you very soon

JEFF

ALS (Barbara Clarke). Addressed: "J. E. Davis Hurricane [via] Paul Jones."

[1] Davis' nickname for his wife.

To Robert J. Walker

Confidential

Camp at New orleans 22d July 1846

DEAR FRIEND,

The first detachment of three companies from the Mississippi

11

Rgt. have just sailed.[1] The rifles have not arrived and from a letter sent me by Col. J. Roach[2] it appears that they were not turned over to him but sent in the ordinary way—may I ask of you to make some inquiry concerning this matter.[3]

This evening and to morrow I hope to get the balance of the Rgt. under way[4]—I have put my ow[n][5] affairs first and in this I have followed certainly a natural order; but the great question upon which I wish to address you concerns others. From all I can discover, the two men of our party who stand first here and hereabouts are Govr. Cass, and Sectry. Walker, the latter would have nothing to fear from the former in a democratic rivalry were it not for the influence exerted by the Custom house officers—they appear odious to the american population and the Surveyor[6] to have influence no where and I will add from all I can learn he don't deserve it— These men hang a dead weight upon you— The Jeffersonian[7] has been touching the Surveyor quite closely about his connexion with a contract he is recommending the government to make with a Capt. Fullerton[8] to run steam b[oats] to Brazos Santiago—you will recollect that I called your attention to his hostility to the "Jeffersonian" it is believed to continue as I am informed by the same authority I gave you at the time I handed a letter to you from the publisher of that paper.[9]

The only democratic paper here could do much good if unembarassed—more harm if rendered hostile to us. You will understand much more from this short letter than I have time in the midst of embarking preperations to write— I am <–of–> decidedly of the opinion that a friend of mine would be benefitted and the party advanced by the removal of surveyor Hayden   Very sincerely your friend

JEFF'N: DAVIS

ALS (Z735, Davis Papers, Ms-Ar).

[1] Cos. F, G, and I, commanded by Lt. Col. Alexander K. McClung, left New Orleans for Brazos Island on the *New York* July 22 and arrived on either July 26 or 27 (New Orleans *Jeffersonian*, July 25 [23], 1846; Holly Springs *Gazette*, Aug. 7, 14, 1846; Z355f, Browning Diary, Aug. 5, 1846, Ms-Ar).

[2] James Roach's letter has not been found.

[3] Since the rifles were shipped from New Orleans on cutters of the revenue service, which was under the control of the secretary of the treasury, it is possible that Walker used his influence to expedite their shipment (Jackson *Mississippian*, Aug. 12, 1846).

[4] Cos. A, D, F, and K, under Maj.

12

Alexander B. Bradford, sailed on the *Massachusetts* July 23 and arrived off Brazos Island on July 27. The three remaining companies, B, C, and H, led by Davis, did not leave New Orleans until July 26, when they sailed on the *Alabama* (Vicksburg *Tri-Weekly Whig*, July 30, 1846; Jackson *Mississippian*, Aug. 12, 1846).

[5] Square brackets throughout indicate material supplied where original is damaged.

[6] David Hayden, a native of New England, was deputy collector of customs at Natchitoches, Louisiana, before being named surveyor for the district and inspector of revenue for the port of New Orleans in 1844. Replaced in 1850, he moved to San Francisco, where in 1854–55 he was employed at the customhouse as deputy naval officer (*U.S. Reg. of Officers and Agents, 1845*, 185, *1855*, 74; 1842 New Orleans dir., 2:114; *Senate Ex. Jour.*, 6:367, 374, 8:24, 29, 236). Although Davis later revised his estimate of Hayden (see Davis to Walker, Aug. 24, 1846), a mutual acquaintance described Hayden as an "adventurer" and sycophant (Claiborne, *Quitman*, 2:19–20; see also Hayden's correspondence with Walker during this period in Walker Papers, DLC).

[7] The New Orleans *Jeffersonian*, a Democratic weekly.

[8] Undoubtedly a reference to either Hugh or Samuel Wiley Fullerton, both engineers and natives of Pennsylvania, who resided in New Orleans. In the summer of 1846 Hugh Fullerton received a federal contract to transport men and supplies on the steamer *Fashion*. Samuel Fullerton, a former employee of the Mobile & New Orleans Mail Line and for several years captain of the *Fashion*, became owner of the ship, which he sold to the government in 1846 (DNA, RG92, Reg. of Contracts, 1846–47, 89, 125–26, 132, 136, 361, 455; 1842 New Orleans dir., 1:159; 1850 Census, La., Orleans, 2d munic., 4th ward, family 563; *State v. Fullerton*, 7 Rob. 210, 211, 214 [La. 1844]).

[9] Watson Van Benthuysen, related by marriage to Davis' brother Joseph.

To Varina Howell Davis

off Brazos Santiago 29th July 1846

MY DEAR WIFE,

after an extraordinarily quiet voyage we are at anchor, waiting for a Lighter to get ashore on the Brazos Island – Several times I have thought may it not be[1] the calm sea over which we are running is type of my fortune where agitation is to me of far greater moment than in the waters of the gulf – may god have preserved you as calm – your affectionate letter[2] reached just before starting from New orleans. I was much gratified to see that you been engaged in useful and domestic things. However unimportant in themselves each may be, it is the mass which constitutes the business of life, and as it is pursued so will it generally be found that a woman is happy and contented. To one of exacting and devoted temper the cultivation of shrubs furnishes an appropriate and inexhaustible field of employment. I say appropriate because no suspicion of in-gratitude or faithfulness can exist towards them.

Joe.[3] is well except the injury to his ancle of which you have been informed — I asked him to write to his Mother he said he had done so.

Present me affectionately to all and receive a Husbands love for sweet Winnie—[4]

Again farewell and again I <–ask–> that the season of our absence may be a season of reflection bearing fruits of soberness, and utility, and certainty of thought and of action. My love for you placed my happiness in your keeping, our vows have placed my hono[r][5] and respectability in the same hands. K[i][5]ss Ma and the Children.[6]

Hubbin would kiss the paper he sends to wife, but is in the midst of the men, who though talking & whistling and wondering when the Lighter will come have time enough to observe any thing the Col. does — I send a kiss upon the wires of love and feel earth, air & sea cannot break the connection

AL (Davis Papers, KyLxT). Ad-dressed to Varina Davis in Natchez. Manuscript repaired with tape; por-tions of the second page excised.

[1] Manuscript torn.
[2] Not found.
[3] Varina's elder brother Joseph Davis Howell was a pvt., Co. C, 1st Miss. Rgt.

[4] The lower part of page one and top of page two have been removed; approximately twelve lines missing.
[5] Manuscript folded.
[6] A reference to Davis' mother-in-law Margaret Kempe Howell and Varina's several younger siblings. After this sentence approximately five lines of text have been cut away.

From Zachary Taylor

Head Qrs, Ary, of Occupation or Invasion
Matamoros Mexico Augt, 3d, 1846

MY DEAR COL,

I lean with much pleasure of your safe arrival at Brazos Island,[1] with your excellent Regt, of Mississippi Volunteers, & very much regret I cannot at once order you with your Comd, <–at once–> to Camargo, where the greater portion of the army will be concen-trated, <–but–> which is impracticable at the present time, but will do so as soon as possible with our limited means of transportation, the want of a more ample suplly has embarrassed us not a little, & I fear will /continue to/ do so to some extent— I propose bringing up the Regts, from their encampments on the banks of the Rio Grande, where I flatter myself they will be pleasantly situated, as regard pure air, heath, wood & water, pretty much in the order in which they arrived in the country, & must say it is a source of mortification that yours was not among the first which reached Brazos Island,[2] as I can assure you I am more than anxious to take you by the hand, & to have you & your command with or near me,[3] & flatter myself if we are not disappointed in the arrival of several Boats which are daily expected from N. Orleans & else where in addition to those now here, we will very soon be able to bring you up—

I expect /to/ leave <–here–> by the first boat which reaches here from below on her way to Camargo,[4] & should have been highly gratified could I have seen you before <–leaving–> /my departure/ for that place, but trust it will not be long before I shall have that pleasure— Wishing you continuued health & prosperity I remain Truly & Sincerely Your Friend

Z. TAYLOR

ALS (MS Coll., MB). Addressed: "Col. Jefferson Davis Comdg Missi, Volunteers Bra[zo]s Island Texas." Endorsed: "Capt. Ogden will forward this H. W."

[1] Davis and Cos. B, C, and H joined the rest of the regiment at Brazos Island on either July 28 or 29 (Giddings, *Campaign*, 25–26; New Orleans *Delta*, Aug. 8, 1846; Woodville *Repub.*, Aug. 15, 22, 1846; Carrollton *Miss. Dem.*, Aug. 19, 1846).

[2] Contrary to his statement, Taylor already had issued orders giving the 1st Miss. Rgt. precedence over several regiments that had reached Brazos Island before the Mississippians (DNA, M-29, roll 1, Gen. Orders No. 93, July 30, 1846; Sioussat, ed.,

"Mexican War Letters," *Tenn. Hist. Mag.*, 1:138; Smith, *Campaign*, 7).

[3] Taylor's eagerness to see Davis belies the assertion that the two men, so long estranged, were reconciled on the battlefield of Buena Vista (N. Y. *World*, Jan. 12, 1890; Anderson notes, Wood Papers, box 12, folder 8, S. Hist. Coll., NcU; Thomas C. Reynolds to Davis, Jan. 4, 1883, ViRC). Both Davis and his wife later wrote that the reconciliation took place when Davis and Taylor happened to meet on a Mississippi steamboat before the Mexican War (Davis to George W. Jones, Dec. 27, 1882, Dubuque *Herald*, Jan. 14, 1883; V. Davis, *Memoir*, 1:199).

[4] Taylor left Matamoros the next day, August 4 (Taylor, *Letters*, 39).

South Central United States and the Rio Grande, ca. 1846

T E X A S

Pecos River

Brazos River

Austin

Colorado River

San Antonio

Nueces River

M E X I C O

Laredo

Corpus Christi

Mustang Isla

Monclova

Padre Island

Camargo

Rio Grande

Reynosa

Matamoros

Brazos Island

Monterrey

Saltillo

N

W E

S

Victoria

0   50   100   200

Miles

Tampico

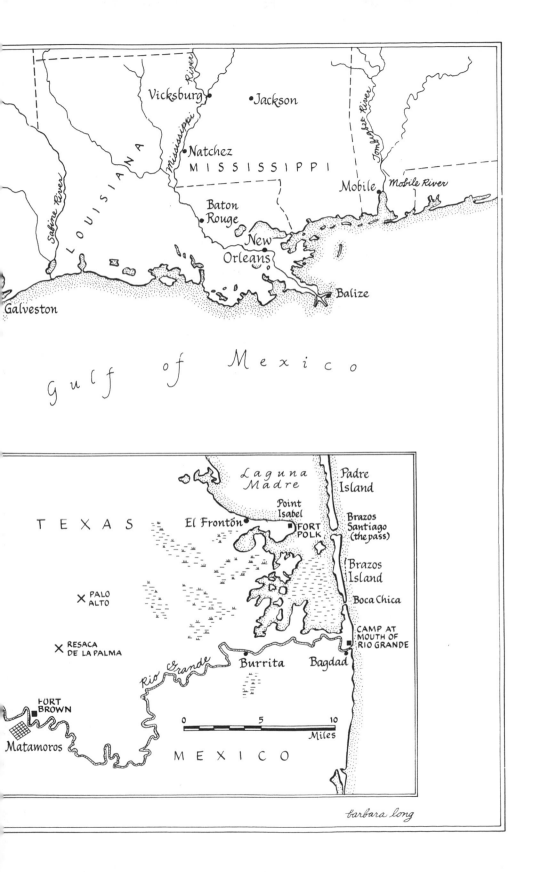

Vicksburg • • Jackson

Mississippi River

Natchez •

M I S S I S S I P P I

Mobile • | Mobile River

L O U I S I A N A

Tombigbee River

Sabine River

Baton
Rouge

New
Orleans

Balize

Galveston

G u l f   o f   M e x i c o

Laguna
Madre

Padre
Island

T E X A S

Point
Isabel

El Frontón •

■ FORT
POLK

Brazos
Santiago
(the pass)

Brazos
Island

✕ PALO
ALTO

Boca Chica

CAMP AT
MOUTH OF
RIO GRANDE

✕ RESACA
DE LA PALMA

Rio Grande

Burrita •

Bagdad

FORT
BROWN

0   5   10
                  Miles

Matamoros

M E X I C O

barbara long

To Varina Howell Davis

Mouth of Rio Grande[1] 16th Aug 1846

DEAR WIFE,

I am here daily expecting boats to ascend the River, much chafed by delay but in good health, Your Brother is in good health though from change of diet and water we have had very many on our sick report. The future has an aspect as peaceful as you desire, and sorely to the disappointment of the Missi patriots we can hear nothing of warlike preperations by the mexicans.

I have remembered your request on the subject of profanity and have improved— Have you remembered mine on the subject of prayer, and a steady reliance on the justice of one who sees through the veil of conduct to the motives of the heart. Be pious, be calm, be useful, and charitable and temperate in all things

My love to our family and believe me to think the balance of two sheets at least which I would like to write to my sweet Winnie— Farewell wife

YOUR HUSBAND

AL (ViRC). AL, retained copy (Davis Papers, GEU). Endorsed: "Letters from my own dearest Jeff Varina H. Davis."

[1] On August 3 the 1st Miss. Rgt. moved from Brazos Island to the army's makeshift encampment at the mouth of the Rio Grande, a distance of nine or ten miles (Vicksburg *Tri-Weekly Whig*, Aug. 25, 1846).

To John McNutt[1]

Mouth of R[io Grande][2]
20th A[ugust 1846]

SIR,

Maj. Bradford of the 1st Mi. Vol. will hand you this, I have sent to your post to request you if possible to send me some rifle ammunition and percussion caps, we may get on without the ammunition having a small allowance of that furnished to the two rifle companies as originally armed but now that the percussion Rifles have arrived the caps are indispensable and we have *none*.[3] By some means then I hope you can send us some caps and if it shall not greatly promote the public service, it will at least greatly oblige me, and inspir[e] some additional confidence in the men.

Capt. Whitely[4] sent on the 3d of Aug. a small supply of Sabres and pistols for the officers of this Regt. to Col. Hunt.[5] a. q. m. at New orleans; have you heard of them?

The arms sent over to be <–condemned–> repaired for this Regt. will not be required and I suppose may be included in the invoices [whi]ch will accompany the arms returned to y[ou] [Consul?]t Maj. Bradford on this point   yrs. truly

JEFFN. DAVIS

ALS (W. Americana MSS, S-527, D294, CtY).

[1] John McNutt (c1819–81), an 1840 West Point graduate, was commander of the ordnance depot at Point Isabel (1846–47) and Monterrey (1847–48). Chief of ordnance for the Department of Kansas during the Civil War, he retired from the army in 1878 (Cullum, *Biog. Reg.*, 2:26; Heitman, *Hist. Reg.*, 1:680).

[2] Square brackets enclose material supplied where the edges of the original are frayed.

[3] The rifles that President Polk had promised to the 1st Miss. Regt. reached Davis on August 19 and 21 (Z618, Smith Diary, Aug. 18, 20, 1846, Ms-Ar). Prior to their arrival only Cos. A and I had been issued rifles, in accord with a regulation that permitted the two flank companies of a volunteer regiment to choose rifles rather than muskets (Yazoo City *Whig*, Aug. 7, 1846; Jackson *Southron*, Sept. 2, 1846; Mahon and Danysh, *Infantry*, 19). The rifle, which as Davis had predicted came to be known as the "Mississippi rifle," was the first such army weapon to have a percussion ignition system (Wilcox, *Mexican War*, 75–76; V. Davis, *Memoir*, 1: 247; Sawyer, *Our Rifles*, 141–42). Since infantry regiments did not carry rifles at this time, there was no applicable manual of arms. Consequently Davis was compelled to prepare a manual himself and give his officers daily instructions (New Orleans *Times-Dem.*, Dec. 6, 1889, 1).

[4] Robert Henry Kirkwood Whitely, commander of the Baton Rouge arsenal, 1841–51, graduated from West Point in 1830. Retiring from the army in 1875, he died in 1896 (Cullum, *Biog. Reg.*, 1:454–55; Heitman, *Hist. Reg.*, 1:1029).

[5] Thomas F. Hunt (1793–1856), a North Carolina native and a veteran of the War of 1812, was deputy quartermaster gen. at New Orleans during the Mexican War (Heitman, *Hist. Reg.*, 1:557; Risch, *Quartermaster Support*, 240–41).

To Robert J. Walker

Mouth of Rio Grande 24th Aug. 1846

DEAR SIR,

A part of our Regt. has started to Comargo, I embark in a few

hours with another detachment making a total of five Companies[1]—
We have met delay and detention at every turn, the quar[ter][2]
masters at New orleans have behaved eith[er] most incompetently
or maliciously, and I am now but two days in possession of the
Rifle[s] ordered forward before I left Washington.

But don't give the quarter master's Dept. credit for that, my acknowledgements for having them *now* are due to your Naval Militia— Maj. Roach despairing of the q.M. Dept. applied to Capt
Webster[3] of the revenue service who placed the arms on the cutters
"Ewing" and "Legare" and brought them to the Brazos Santiago.
The ammunition and accountrements sent from Baton Rouge to be
forwarded by the quarter Master have not arrived and the ordnance
stores /on the frontier/ above, have a very insufficient supply of
Rifle ammunition. <–and–> All this arises from having a bundle
of papers and prejudices against Volunteers charged with the duties
of quarter Master at New Orleans—Viz. Lt. Col. & Asst. Qr. Master
Hunt of the U. S. Army.

I must acknowledge the debt due from the Missi. volunteers for
service timely and and courteously rendered by Capts. Webster and
Moore[4] Codg. the Cutter "Ewing" and the Captain comdg. the
"Legare."[5] If you can notice their conduct, I hope we may so use
the rifles as to show the service was not to us alone.

Maj. Roach informs me that the surveyor of the port of New
orleans Mr. Hayden gave him kind assistance and feeling that it
was done as a favor to your friends causes me to regret that I
heard the statements in new orleans which were communicated to
you.[6]

The mouth of this River has but little to invite one seeking the
Land of promise to to enter it the banks are low and without trees,
but the current meets the sea with such force as to keep the entrance generally smooth, and it has been to me a matter of supprise
that goods bound up the river were not brought ashore here,
<–here–> instead of being carried over the breakers at the Brozos
in lighters & then brought in other lighters here— The anchorage
is said to be equally good and the entran[ce] habitually more quiet,
though somewhat more shallow. I have not received the letter you
intended to send me but hope always abides and cheering us onward leads to the expect a letter from at Army Head Qrs.

"Claiborne"[7] went off on the Louisiana Volunteers, (as I understand it a mere pretext) for the fact is they were sick of the job, and but very of all I have seen wished to remain longer in this country.[8] Our Regt. have suffered much from disease, had transportation been furnished promptly we would gone with a full Regt. and what is more important with /men/ full of zeal, and vigor; into the Campaign[9]—

Though we pick the mill ston[e] we can't see through it, if ever I find a hole it will give me pleasure to communicate to you the wonders found within.[10]

Present me to Mrs. Walker in the kindest terms and give my remembrances to my young friends your Children— With great regard I am yrs. &c

Jeffn. Davis

ALS (Misc. MSS-Walker, NHi).

[1] Co. G and a portion of Co. C had left on the *Exchange* August 20; Davis, with Cos. A, E, H, and parts of B and C, boarded the *Virginian* on August 24. The balance of the regiment embarked two days later on the *Col. Cross* (DNA, RG94, Vol. Muster Rolls, Mexican War, 1st Miss. Rgtl. Return, Aug. 1846; Z618, Smith Diary, Aug. 24, 1846, Ms-Ar; Jackson *Southron*, Sept. 23, 1846; Vicksburg *Tri-Weekly Whig*, Sept. 24, 1846).

[2] Square brackets indicate material supplied where the edges of the original are frayed.

[3] John A. Webster (1787–1877), an officer in the U.S. Revenue Service, 1819–59, was appointed commander of the revenue cutters operating off the Texas and Mexican coasts in 1846 (N.Y. *Times*, July 5, 1877, 5, July 12, 1877, 2; Smith, *Revenue Marine*, 35, 77; DNA, RG26, Rec. of Revenue Marine Officers, 1797–1920, 49–51).

[4] Gay Moore was commander of the schooner *Ewing*, 1845–47 (DNA, RG26, Rec. of Revenue Marine Officers, 1797–1920, 106–108).

[5] Napoleon L. Coste (DNA, RG26, Rec. of Mvmts., Coast Guard Vessels, 1790–1933, 1:109–10).

[6] See Davis to Walker, July 22, 1846.

[7] John F. H. Claiborne was co-proprietor of the New Orleans *Jeffersonian*.

[8] Since the Louisianians had volunteered in April 1846, they were enrolled under a law limiting their service to three months. Thus in July Gen. Taylor, following the directions of the War Department, gave the Louisiana volunteers the option of reenlisting for twelve months or returning to New Orleans for mustering out. Most chose to leave Mexico, "greatly dissatisfied" (Vicksburg *Tri-Weekly Whig*, Aug. 20, 1846; DNA, M-29, roll 1, Gen. Orders No. 91, July 21, 1846; *House Doc. 196*, 29:1, 72–73, 120, *Ex. Doc. 60*, 30:1, 281–82, 309–10; *U.S. Statutes at Large*, 1:424–25, 9:9–10; New Orleans *Picayune*, Aug. 2, 1846).

[9] By the end of August 108 members of Davis' regiment had been discharged, most for medical reasons; 70 others were listed as "present sick" (DNA, RG94, Vol. Muster Rolls, Mexican War, 1st Miss. Rgtl. Return, Aug. 1846).

[10] Davis is probably thinking of the phrase "to see far in (into, through) a millstone," conveying an "ironic commendation of pretended extraordinary acuteness" (*OED*).

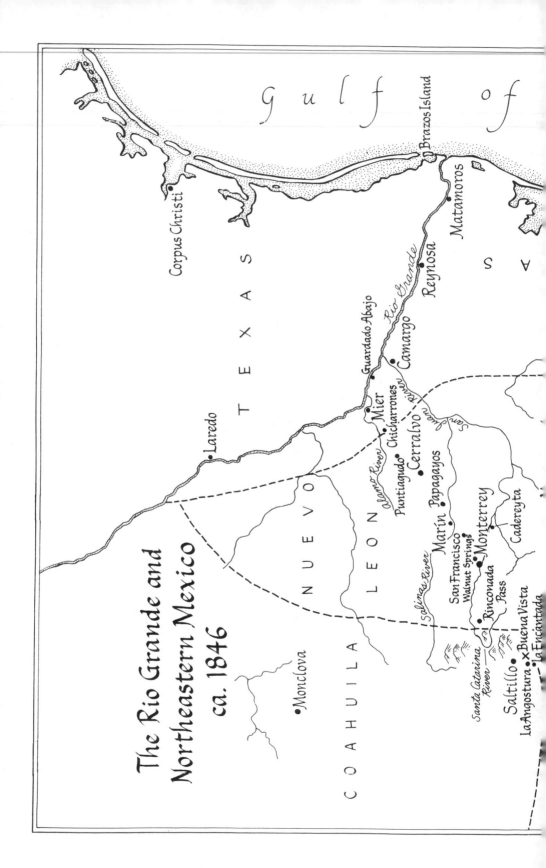

The Rio Grande and
Northeastern Mexico
ca. 1846

Gulf of

Corpus Christi

Brazos Island

Matamoros

Reynosa

Rio Grande

Guardado Abajo

Camargo

Laredo

Mier

Chicharrones

Puntiagudo

Cerralvo River

Cerralvo

Papagayos

San Juan River

TEXAS

NUEVO

LEON

Alamo River

Marín

San Francisco

Walnut Springs

Monterrey

Cadereyta

Salinas River

Rinconada

Pass

Monclova

COAHUILA

Santa Catarina River

Saltillo

La Angostura

Buena Vista

La Encantada

A S

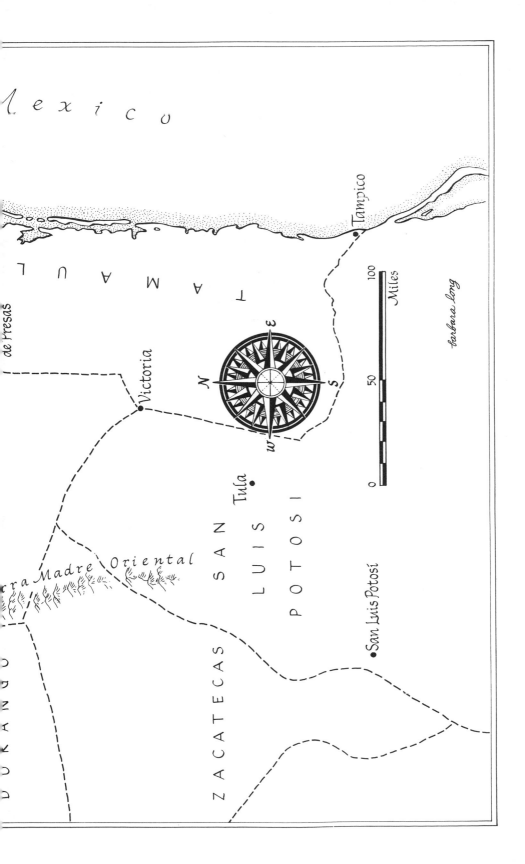

From Albert G. Brown

Executive Chamber
Jackson Miss. 29th aug. 1846

SIR

The Secr of War[1] has forwarded to Me the letter of resignation of Lt. Burrus[2] of the Yazoo Volunteers under your command, with an intimation from the Adgt. Genl U. S Army[3] endorsed thereon that the resignation should have been tendered to the Governor of Missi. The Secr forbears to decide as to the correctness of the Adjt. Genl intimation but says the consent of the Prest. & the Dept is given to the withdrawal of Lt Burrus from the service.

I enclose several blank commissions to be used by you as occasion may require not doubting that they will be safe in your hands— This is done to facilitate the operations of your command to releive you from any embarrassment growing out of deaths and resignations among your officers— In every case when a resignation is tendered and accepted by you, my approval is hereby given, and you have my consent to issue a commission to a successor from the inclosed blanks— I shall expect you of course to make a return to the adjt. Genl of this State[4] or to myself and also the Dept at Washington of the name of the officer succeeding together with the date of his commission— I have communicated the contents of this letter to the Secr of War[5] Very Respfl Your obt Sevt

A G BROWN

LbC (RG27, Vol. 42, Ex. Jour., 94, Ms-Ar).

[1] William L. Marcy.
[2] 1st Lt. Philip J. Burrus of Co. A, a Benton resident, had resigned in July (DNA, M-863, roll 1; RG33, Vol. 19, Rec. of Comnd. Officers, 13, Ms-Ar).
[3] Roger Jones.
[4] Wiley P. Harris (RG33, Vol. 21, Rec. of Comnd. Officers, 1, Ms-Ar).
[5] In response Marcy advised Brown that Gen. Taylor had been authorized to grant officers' discharges and to fill vacancies, thus would "doubtless avail himself" of the blank commissions sent to Davis (Sept. 21, 1846, DNA, RG94, Entry 12, Letters Recd., 1805–89, 580-B-1846; see also Brown to Davis, Jan. 4, 1847).

To George H. Crosman[1]

Near Camargo[2] 3d Sept. 1846

DEAR CROSSMAN, I met a "musician" going over to fill the wind instruments and sent him on without any other credentials than his Mississippi face to appear in court—

The bearer a drummer being a man of resources and anxious to make a noise in the world,[3] has suggested that if he had time and sheepskins he could make heads, without which you will agree no man should make a noise.

What says the Don about the mule— Let the old soldier come this evening— Very truly I am as ever yrs.

JEFF'N. DAVIS

ALS (DNA, RG92, Consol. Corres. File: Col. J. Davis). LbC (ibid., Letters Recd. by Crosman, 1:758–59). Addressed: "Capt. Geo. H. Crossman Camargo [via] orderly."

[1] George Hampton Crosman (1798–1882) graduated from West Point in 1823 and served in the army until 1866, most of the time in the Quartermaster's Department. He and Davis probably first met sometime between 1832 and 1834 at Jefferson Barracks, Missouri (Cullum, *Biog. Reg.*, 1:315–16).

[2] Davis, traveling on the *Virginian* with Cos. A, E, H, and parts of B and C, reached Camargo on August 31, two days before Co. G and the rest of Co. C. The remainder of the 1st Miss. Rgt. left the camp at the mouth of the Rio Grande August 26 on the *Col. Cross* and arrived at Camargo September 4 (Jackson *Southron*, Sept. 23, 1846; Vicksburg *Tri-Weekly Whig*, Sept. 24, 1846; Vicksburg *Weekly Sentinel*, Sept. 29, 1846; Z355f, Browning Diary, Sept. 4, 1846, Ms-Ar; Pace, ed., "Rogers Diary," *SWHQ*, 32:261–62).

[3] "I have made noise enough in the world already, perhaps too much"— Napoleon, speaking in October 1816 to his British surgeon (O'Meara, *Napoleon in Exile*, 1:78–79).

Terms of Capitulation

Editorial Note: Soon after reaching Camargo Davis learned that the 1st Miss. and 1st Tenn. rgts. would form the 2d Brig., Field Div. of Vols., under the command of John A. Quitman. On September 7 the brigade began the march to Monterrey; six days later, after stops at Guardado Abajo, Mier, Chicharrones, and Puntiagudo, it reached Cerralvo. Awaiting it there were the 1st Ky. and 1st Ohio rgts., commanded by Thomas L. Hamer and composing the 1st Brig. of the volunteer division. Thus united, the Field Div. led by William O. Butler left Cerralvo September 15 and proceeded via Papagayos to Marín, where on September 17 it joined David E. Twiggs's and William J. Worth's 1st and 2d divs. of army regulars. By the following day, when Taylor moved on to the hacienda of San Francisco, J. Pinckney Henderson and his Texas Div. had arrived, and Taylor's army was complete. On September 19 the Americans finally approached the strongly fortified city of Monterrey. After three days of fighting (September 21–23), the enemy proposed a conditional surrender. Davis was appointed a commissioner to negotiate the terms of capitulation (Vicksburg *Tri-Weekly Whig*, Sept. 22, Oct. 15, 1846; Woodville *Repub.*, Oct. 16, 1846; Robertson, *Reminiscences*, 122–24; Henry, *Campaign Sketches*, 178, 188; DNA, M-29, roll 1, Gen. Orders Nos. 112, 119, 120, Sept. 2, 17, 18, 1846; *House Ex. Doc. 60*, 30:1, 417–18; DNA, RG94, Vol. Muster Rolls, Mexican War, 1st Miss. Rgtl. Return, Sept. 1846).

Done at Monterey
sept. 24th 1846

Terms of Capitulation of the City of Monterey, the Capital of Nueva Leon, agreed upon by the undersigned Commissioners, to wit, Genl. Worth of the United States Army, Genl. Henderson[1] of the Texan Volunteers, and Colonel Davis of the Mississippi Riflemen, on the part of Major general Taylor commanding in[2] Chief the United States forces; and General Requena[3] and General Ortego[4] of the army of Mexico and Señor Manuel M. Llano[5] governor of Nuevo Leon on the part of Senor General Don Pedro Ampudia[6] Commanding in Chief of the army of the North of Mexico.

Art. I As the legitimate result of the operations before this place and the present position of the contending armies, it is agreed that the City, the fortifications, Cannon, the Munitions of War and all other public property, with the undermentioned exceptions be surrendered to the Commanding General of the United states forces now at Monterey.

Art. II. That the Mexican forces be allowed to retain the following arms, to wit, the commissioned officers their side arms, the Infantry their arms and accoutrements, the Cavalry their arms and accoutrements, the Artillery one field battery not to exceed six pieces with twenty one rounds of ammunition

Art. III. That the Mexican armed forces retire within seven days from this date, beyond /the line formed by the/ Pass of the Riconada, the City of Linares and San Fernando de presas

Art. IV. That the Citadel[7] of Monterey be evacuated by the Mexican, and occupied by the American forces to morrow morning at ten O.Clock.

Art. V. To avoid collisions and for mutual convenience: That the Troops of the United States will not occupy the City until the Mexican forces have withdrawn, except for hospital and storage purposes.

Art. VI. That the forces of the United States will not advance beyond the line specified in the 3d Article before the expiration of eight weeks or until the orders or instructions of the respective governments can be received

Art VII. That the public property to be delivered shall be turned over and received by officers appointed by the Commanding generals of the two Armies—

Art. VIII. That all doubts as to the meaning of any of the preceding articles shall be solved by an equitable construction and on principles of liberality to the retiring Army

Art. IX. That the Mexican flag when struck at the Citadel may be saluted by its own battery.

PEDRO DE AMPUDIA

W. J WORTH Brg Gnl U.S.A
J PINCKNEY HENDERSON
Major Genl Commanding
The Texian Volunteers
JEFF N. DAVIS
Col. Missi. Riflemen
MANL. M. LLANO

T. REQUENA
[J?] MA [DE?] ORTEGA
Approved,[8]
Z. TAYLOR,
Majr Genl U.S.A. Comdg—

ADS (Mexican War Papers, NWM). DS (Archivo Militar, Secretaría de la Defensa Nacional, Fracción 1/a, Legajo 18, Operaciones Militares, 1846, 22). D, copy (DNA, RG94, Letters Recd., 390-T-1846, Report 91 and Encls.).

[1] James Pinckney Henderson (1808–58), governor of Texas, 1846–47, commanded two mounted regiments during the Mexican War (*Handbook of Texas*; *House Ex. Doc. 60*, 30:1, 418).

[2] The word *in* is written over the word *it*.

[3] Tomás Requena (1804–50), second-in-command of the forces in the north, was said by some observers to be the ablest of the Mexican generals (*Diccionario Porrúa, Suplemento*; Balbontín, *Invasión Americana*, 46).

[4] José María Ortega (1793–1871)

served under Antonio López de Santa Anna at the Battle of San Jacinto, where he was captured, and again at Buena Vista, where he commanded the reserve division (*Diccionario Porrúa*; Jenkins, ed., *Papers of the Texas Revolution*, 8:404).

[5] Manuel María Llano (1799–1863), Mexican politician and a former governor of Nuevo León (*Diccionario Porrúa*).

[6] Pedro Ampudia (1805–68) served as Mariano Arista's lieutenant at Palo Alto and Resaca de la Palma, before being appointed commander for northern Mexico by Santa Anna in July 1846. Despite widespread criticism of his surrender of Monterrey, Ampudia held another important command at Buena Vista (*Diccionario Porrúa*; Bancroft, *Works*, 13:346–402,

passim; Smith, *War with Mexico*, 1: 502).

[7] The one important fortification still in Mexican hands, the Citadel, which had been erected around an un-finished church, dominated the northern approaches to the city (Giddings, *Campaign*, 153).

[8] In the left margin.

To Joseph E. Davis

MONTEREY, Sept. 25th, 1846.

MY DEAR BROTHER:— The town is ours after a severe conflict. The Mississippians were brought into action on the 21st and performed some brilliant service. On the 22nd preparations were made, and we held an advance post. On the morning of the 23rd we (the Mississippians) opened the action early, and continued firing and advancing into the town until near sunset, when we were ordered to withdraw. On the 24th propositions having been received to capitulate, Gen. Worth, and Gen. Henderson of Texas, and myself, were appointed commissioners to arrange the terms of capitulation. We agreed, and the papers have been exchanged. *It was reported to us, by the Mexican General, that Mexico had received commissioners from the United States.*[1]— They were whipped, and we could afford to be generous. We hope soon to return as the war is probably over.[2]

With love to all—I am your brother.

Vicksburg *Weekly Sentinel*, Oct. 27, 1846.

[1] Gen. Ampudia's assertion proved incorrect. However, it is true that on July 27, 1846, Secretary of State James Buchanan had written the Mexican minister of foreign relations offering to send an envoy with full powers to draw up a peace treaty. The Mexican government replied that no action could be taken until a new congress convened in December. Although Gen. Taylor may have been aware of his government's proposal, he was not advised of the Mexican response until October 11 (Buchanan, *Works*, 7:40; Polk, *Diary*, 2:144–45; Taylor, *Letters*, 61, 64). Thus Joseph Davis was to characterize as wholly "g r a t u i t o u s" the Vicksburg *Tri-Weekly Whig*'s observation (Oct. 24, 1846) that Davis was "easily humbugged" if he had been convinced that commissioners had been received by Mexico (Vicksburg *Weekly Sentinel*, Nov. 3, 1846). See also Davis' memorandum of October 7, 1846.

[2] Omitted from the printed version, according to Joseph Davis, was a final sentence in which Davis stated that two relatives serving in Co. C, 1st Miss. Rgt.—Robert H. Davis and Joseph D. Howell—"'were unhurt.'" Shown a copy of the complete letter, the editor of the Vicksburg *Tri-Weekly Whig* (Oct. 24, 1846) took Davis to task for failing to report on

the casualties suffered by his regiment at Monterrey, saying that "the part he took in the battle, and the safety of himself and his relations, were all that burthened his mind." In a published response dated October 30, Joseph Davis explained that his brother's private letter had been made available for publication only because of the "anxiety of the public for the smallest scrap of news" (Vicksburg *Weekly Sentinel*, Nov. 3, 1846).

To John A. Quitman

Monterey, Mexico 26th Sept. 1846.

SIR,

In conformity with your instructions I have the honor to report such facts in relation to the conduct of the Regiment of Miss. Riflemen on the 21st and 23d. Insts:[1] as came under my immediate observation, and will add such explanations as may seem necessary. When on the morning of the 21st. the 1st. Division[2] was drawn up in order of battle before the City of Monterey, you will remember that the position of the Regt. under my command was thought to be too much exposed, and that it was detached to the left. Seperated from the division, I did not hear the orders by which it was put in motion, but seeing the other Regiment of your Brigade (Col. Campbell's)[3] <–in motion–> /moving/ towards the enemy, I ordered the Miss. Riflemen to advance by the left of the Battalion[4] and follow it.

<–By this means–> /Thus/ when the Regiments of your Brigade were united their natural order was inverted.[5] In this order /under a cross fire of artillery/[6] we advanced <–to the–> /in/ front of the Fort[7] upon our left, to a point within the range of the enemy's musketry, but beyond the effective fire of our Rifles.[8] Under your orders to fill an interval which had been created upon my left, I ordered the <–companies of my command–> /Mississippi Riflemen/ to advance obliquely by the left of companies to a line which I estimated as effectively near /to the enemy/, and then ordered the Battalion into line[9]—the companies being directed, <–as soon as–> /when/ formed, to commence firing as in open order. In a few minutes the fire of the enemy had so far diminished as to indicate the propriety of a charge, and /being without instructions/ it was accordingly ordered.[10]

Lieut. Col. McClung[11] sprung before his old company and called

25

on them to follow him.[12] The call was promptly answered. In an instant the whole Regiment rushed forward, the flanks converging to the sally-port[13] which lay nearly before our centre, and it became a contest of speed who first should reach the Fort. The enemy fled from the rear sally-porte[14] as we entered the front, leaving behind his Artillery, a considerable number of Muskets, his dead and wounded. Passing immediately through the Fort, we found the Enemy flying in disorder—some to a fortified stone building immediately in rear, others across the stream to the Fort[15] which stands beyond it. Our pursuit was so close that we reached the gate of the stone building before it was secured, and upon forcing it open the men inside fled behind the pilasters of the Portico and held up their hands in token of submission. An Officer offered me his sword and announced the surrender. I received it and retired to select an officer to take charge of the prisoners, and receive their arms. Lieut. Townsend[16] of Co. "K" was directed to discharge this duty, and the pursuit of the enemy /was/ immediately resumed. Leading those who had come up across the ford, we advanced within Rifle range of the Fort beyond <-it-> /the stream/, and opened a fire upon such of the enemy as showed themselves above the wall. The intention being to storm the Fort as soon as a sufficient number of our Regiment came up. In this position we received no fire <-of-> /from/ the enemy's Artillery, and his Musketry had not proved destructive, up to the time when I was ordered to retire.

Until after we withdrew I knew nothing of the position or co-operation of the forces <-up->on our right. In accordance with my instructions, and expecting to find the main body of my Regiment, I passed up the street to our then right with the force just withdrawn across the stream. We soon became mingled with other troops which we found along the wall, and <-upon-> /again/ rallying my command for a forward movement, I found it <-decidedly-> /much/ reduced. Capt. Cooper[17] had kept, say twenty of his company together; with these and about ten others of our Regiment, I advanced until we met with Capt. Field[18] of the U. S. Army, who led us to a point where he had discovered a considerable body, probably one hundred of the enemy; on our approach they fled beyond a street[19] which was enfiladed by the fire of a strong party sheltered behind the Tete du Pont of the principal bridge. Capt. Cooper with the party accompanying <-him-> us was posted in an interior building[20] to act as sharp shooters against the men of the Tete du pont, until we should be sufficiently reinforced for more offensive operations. After a brief period we were joined by Major Mansfield[21] of the U. S. Engineers with a small party of the 1st Infantry under his command. Whilst the men were resting we reconnoitered the position, and decided on a plan of attack.[22] At this instant we were joined by Genl. Hamer[23] with a portion of his Brigade,[24] and from him we received orders to retire; as I was afterwards informed to give protection to a Battery of Artillery[25] threatened by Lancers[26] in the rear.

In the mean time a few individuals, but no organized portion of my Regiment, had joined me, and we followed in rear of Genl. Hamer's column. After having proceeded the half of a mile or more, the enemy's cavalry <–approached–> /appeared/ on our left, and the troops in front began to close and form on a Chapparel fence in advance of us. The men under my command had undergone such severe fatigue that their movements were necessarily slow, and some of them fell behind, when a party of Lancers dashed forward to attack the rear. I ordered the Riflemen to face about and returned to the relief of our comrades. The movement was readily executed, and though the files were in loose order, their effective fire soon drove the enemy back, leaving several dead behind him.[27] Soon after this I was joined by Major Bradford with the portion of our Regiment which had served under his orders a great portion of the day; and for whose conduct during that period, I refer to Major Bradford's report accompanying this statement. We were now on the ground where for the third time during the day we had been under the cross fire of the enemy's Batteries, and where I learned from you the position of another portion of my Regiment, and received your orders to join <–it–>, and consolidate <–my Regiment–> /it/.[28] Were I to mention all the instances of gallantry and soldierly firmness which came under my observation, this statement would extend beyond a convenient limit. I saw no exhibition of fear, no want of confidence, but on every side the men who stood around me were prompt and willing to execute my orders. I cannot omit to mention the gallant bearing of Lieut. Col. McClung. At the storming of the Fort, he first mounted the parapet, and turning to the Regiment waved his Sword over his head in token of the triumph of our Arms. Leaving him in that position to cheer the

men on to further danger, it was my misfortune soon after to lose
his services. At the fortified stone building he was dangerously
wounded. <-Nor can-> I <-omit to->/must also/ mention Lieut.
Patterson[29] who sprung into the Sally-porte[30] as Col. McClung
mounted the parapet, and fired the first American piece within
the <-lines-> /work/ of the enemy. Capt. Downing[31] in whom
<-was-> /is/ happily combined the qualities of a leader and com-
mander, was <-also-> severely wounded (whilst among the foremost) cheering his company to the charge, and I /have/ felt severely the loss of his <-future-> services. <-When advancing->

Corporal Grisham of Capt. Taylor's Company "I", fell near me
after we had crossed the stream, and were advancing upon the Fort
beyond it. He had fired his Rifle several times, and was advancing
firing with exemplary intrepidity, when he fell pierced by two
wounds and died as he had fought—calmly, silently, and with his
eye upon the foe. Lieut. Calhoun[32] attracted /my/ notice by the
gallantry with which he exposed himself, and the efforts he made
to shelter others. Pleased with the enthusiasm and dashing spirit of
all, I was yet more struck with many instances of coolness which
verged upon indifference to danger, but which the limits of this
communication will not allow me specially to notice. Subjoined is
a list of the killed and wounded, in the action of the 21st. of September, 1846.

Killed Seven, viz:

Corpl. Wm. H. Grisham,	Co. "I"
Private L. M. Turner,	" "C"
" Silas Meecham,	" "E"
" Samuel Potts	" "G"
" Jos. P. Tennille	" "H"
" Joseph Heatron	" "I"
" Joseph Downing	" "I."

Wounded in the same action forty seven, viz:
Four commissioned officers, five non-com'd & thirty eight privates,
as follows,

Lieut. Col. A. K. McClung — dangerously
Captain R. N. Downing — severely
Lieuts. H. F. Cook & R. K. Arthur[33] — slightly.
Sergt. E. W. Hollingsworth, Co. "D", & Sergt. J. H. Langford, Co.
"E", slightly; Sergt. F. A. Wolf,[34] Co. "I", and Sergt. W. H. Bell,[35]

Co. "K", dangerously Corpl. John B. Markham, Co. "C", severely.

Five privates of Company "B", viz: W. H. Miller[30] & J. H. Jackson dangerously; A. Lanehart,[37] severely; J. L. Anderson & G. H. Jones, slightly.

One private of Company "C", viz: H. B. Thompson,[38] slightly.

Seven privates of Company "D", viz: G. W. Ramsey, mortally and since died; Alpheus Cobb, dangerously; Geo. Wills,[39] O. W. Jones, and W. Huffman[40] severely; Wm. Orr and D. Love, slightly.

Nine privates of Company "E", viz: A. P. Burnham, mortally and since died; H. W. Pierce[41] and Wm. Shadt, dangerously; Wm. H. Fleming severely; Jacob Fredericks,[42] John Coleman, W. P. Spencer, M. M. Smith,[43] and James Kilvey, slightly.

Four privates of Company "G", viz: J. Williamson[44] and A. W. Teague,[45] dangerously; Warren White[46] & Robt. Bowen, severely.

Three privates of Company "H", viz: Fredk. Mathers [Mathews], mortally; B. F. Roberts and Avery Noland,[47] slightly.

Three privates of Company "I", viz: C. F. Cotton[48] and G. Williams,[49] severely; Nat. Massie, slightly.

Six privates of Company "K", viz: E. B. Lewis, <–and–> D. B. Lewis[50] and Charles Martin,[51] dangerously; John Stewart, James L. Thompson[52] and John McNorris, slightly. Very respectfully

<–JEFF'N DAVIS–> /JEFF'N DAVIS/[53]

Col. Miss. Riflemen

(<–Copy–>)

<–R. GRIFFITH ADJUT.

Regt. Miss. Riflemen–>[54]

LS, copy by Richard Griffith (DNA, RG94, Letters Recd., 423-T-1846, f/w 38-T-1847). L/ALS, partial copy by Davis and V. Davis (RG27, Vol. 26, Corres., Mexican War Docs., Ms-Ar). Significant textual differences between the two versions are pointed out in footnotes.

[1] This report covers only the events of September 21. Davis' official report for September 23 is printed as the following item. For other Davis accounts of the Battle of Monterrey, see his speech of November 10, 1846, his letter to John Jenkins of November 16, his memorandum dated [December 31], his letter to Albert G. Brown, September 20, 1847, and his two undated statements.

[2] Davis probably intended the Field Div., of which his regiment was a part; the Field Div. was placed in line of battle to the right of the 1st Div., about a mile from the city.

[3] William Bowen Campbell (1808–67) commanded the 1st Tenn. Rgt., which with Davis' unit formed the 2d Brig. of the Vol. Div. A former Whig congressman, Campbell became governor of Tennessee and served briefly as a Union general (*DAB*).

Principally because of the controversy over the storming of the Tenería at Monterrey, the relationship between Davis and Campbell was hostile (see, for example, Sioussat, ed., "Mexican War Letters," *Tenn. Hist. Mag.*, 1: 154–56).

[4] Davis perhaps refers to his regiment as a battalion because it did not have its full complement of companies, A and F having been left in garrison at Cerralvo (DNA, RG94, Vol. Muster Rolls, Mexican War, 1st Miss. Rgtl. Return, Oct. 1846).

[5] Since the 1st Miss. was on the left of the brigade line, in a movement by the left flank it would ordinarily have preceded the 1st Tenn.

[6] Quitman's command was under cannon fire from the Citadel, the Tenería, and El Diablo (*House Ex. Doc. 17*, 30:1, 24).

[7] The Tenería, an earthen lunette on the eastern edge of Monterrey. Named for the tannery (fortified stone building) that it covered, the fort was commanded by Col. José María Carrasco and was manned by a garrison of 350 infantrymen, divided between it and the tannery to its rear. Its artillery consisted of two 8-pounders, a 4-pounder, and a mountain howitzer (Balbontín, *Invasión Americana*, 26–30).

[8] The 1st Miss. fronted at about three hundred yards from the Tenería (Davis' memorandum dated [Dec. 31], 1846).

[9] Other accounts of the movement to the interval on the left and the formation in line of battle are given in John Willis' and Douglas H. Cooper's reports (Nov. 1, 1846; n.d.; see also Davis' description in his memorandum of [Dec. 31], 1846).

[10] Quitman apparently did not intend for the 1st Miss. to charge the Tenería. As he wrote in his battle report, the 1st Tenn. was to charge "so soon as the enemy should have received the full fire of the rifle regiment," but both Campbell and Davis anticipated his order, the 1st Miss. moving to a new position to which Quitman had directed them and "some of the companies never stopping, but advancing in a charge upon the works" (*House Ex. Doc. 17*, 30:1, 15–16). See also n12 below.

[11] Alexander Keith McClung (1811–55), a nephew of Chief Justice John Marshall, was born in Kentucky. After a brief, turbulent navy career (1828–29) McClung settled in Jackson to practice law and edit a Whig newspaper (1840). Named federal marshal for northern Mississippi in 1841, McClung was living in Columbus when he organized the Tombigbee Vols. (Co. K, 1st Miss. Rgt.) for service in Mexico; he was elected lt. col. in July 1846. Badly wounded at Monterrey, McClung saw no further action. In 1847 he ran for Congress, in 1848 was a presidential elector, and in 1850–51 served as chargé d'affaires to Bolivia. After losing a second congressional race in 1853 and failing to secure an army commission the next year, McClung committed suicide in a Jackson hotel. Reportedly there was "some personal trouble" between Davis and McClung in Mexico; however, Davis twice endorsed McClung's applications for military appointments. McClung evidently was unreconciled, confiding to a friend that he wanted to fight a duel with Davis " 'because I think the United States will be better off without him. . . . He is a dangerous and wily politician, loaded down with vanity and self conceit, wishing only for his own aggrandizement' " (Eaton, Ohio, *Weekly Reg.*, June 13, 1861; Paxton, *Marshall Family*, 175–77; DNA, RG45, Acceptances of Comns., 1827–28, No. 211, Resignations of Officers, 1812–33, Nos. 171–73; Vicksburg *Tri-Weekly Sentinel*, Sept. 28, 1840; *Senate Ex. Jour.*, 5:387, 419, 8:110, 151, 351; McClung to Robert J. Walker, Feb. 17, 1847, DNA, RG107, Applics. for Appt.; Jackson *Southron*, Nov. 26, 1847;

Jackson *Mississippian*, Jan. 24, 1834, Aug. 18, 1848; Vicksburg *Tri-Weekly Whig*, Nov. 12, 1853; Rowland, *Courts, Judges, and Lawyers*, 307–308; McClung subject file, Ms-Ar).

[12] Although in a public speech (Nov. 10, 1846) Davis stated that he and McClung simultaneously gave the order to charge, here and in other accounts (Davis to Jenkins, Nov. 16, 1846, and Davis' memorandum dated [Dec. 31], 1846) the sequence in which Davis relates the events leading to the charge suggests that McClung was responding to a Davis order when he led the rush on the Tenería. Apparently neither version satisfied McClung, who heatedly claimed to have taken the initiative, stating that he did so "as I explained to Col. Davis from no disrespect to him, but because I really thought it very likely he was shot (I had not seen him for about a quarter of an hour) and because I thought that he himself was withheld from giving it in consequence of the strictness of his military education and habits, which would induce him to wait for orders from *his* superior; and I was the more induced to this opinion by the last remark I heard him make about fifteen or twenty minutes before, when I saw him walking up the line, which was an angry and vehement complaint that he had no orders. . . . I have certainly no purpose of either expressing a denial or doubt that Col. Davis also gave the order, but I think it perfectly apparent . . . that I gave it first." As proof, McClung cited corroborating statements from several Mississippi officers (Vicksburg *Tri-Weekly Whig*, July 13, 1847).

[13] The embrasure on the northwest flank of the Tenería. On the copy made by Davis and his wife, the phrase "the sally porte" is crossed out and "an open embrasure" interlined.

[14] The gorge of the Tenería.

[15] El Rincón del Diablo (The Devil's Corner), an earthen fort commonly known as El Diablo, was defended by two pieces of artillery (Smith, *War with Mexico*, 1:249; Balbontín, *Invasión Americana*, 34).

[16] William Purnell Townsend (1822–82) returned to Lowndes County after his Mexican War service. About 1852 he moved to Texas, serving during the Civil War as capt. and later maj., 4th Texas Inf., before a wound forced him to resign. He died in Calvert (Lipscomb, *Hist. of Columbus*, 34; *Vedette*, Dec. 1882, 9; Parker, *Robertson County*, 202–203).

[17] Douglas Hancock Cooper (1815–79), capt., Co. B, was a Wilkinson County planter and lawyer. With Davis' assistance he was appointed federal agent to the Choctaw Indians in 1853; he later served as the Confederate superintendent of Indian affairs and was commissioned a brig. gen. in 1863. After the war he lived at Fort Washita (Davis to Franklin Pierce, Feb. 3, 1853, DNA, RG48, Appt. Div., Applics. and Papers re Indian Comr.; Wright, "Gen. Cooper," *Chron. of Okla.*, 32: 142–84; "Notes and Docs.," ibid., 44:221; Morris, "Choctaw and Chickasaw Agents," ibid., 50, 428–32).

[18] George P. Field of the 3d Inf. An 1834 West Point graduate, Field took part in the military occupation of Texas and saw action at Palo Alto and Resaca de la Palma. He was killed during the withdrawal from Monterrey on September 21 (Cullum, *Biog. Reg.*, 1:577).

[19] The street running north from the Purísima bridge.

[20] See no. 5 on the map of Monterrey.

[21] Joseph King Fenno Mansfield (1803–62), chief engineer of Taylor's army, conducted the reconnaissances before the battles of both Monterrey and Buena Vista. In 1853, upon Davis' recommendation, he was appointed col. and inspector gen. He was killed at Sharpsburg while commanding XII Corps (*DAB*).

22 Davis later gave a slightly variant account of the events leading to the proposed attack on the Purísima bridge: "I moved off across a small stream [an irrigation ditch], and through a field to the front of the *tête-de-pont*, which covered the front of the Purissima Bridge, where I met Captain Field, of the United States Infantry, with his company, and Colonel Mansfield, of the United States Engineers. Under their advice, a plan was formed for immediate attack" (Davis to William P. Johnston, n.d., Johnston, *A. S. Johnston*, 139).

23 Thomas L. Hamer (1800–46), an Ohio politician, was commissioned a brig. gen. of vols. in July 1846. He fell ill at Monterrey in November and died soon after. Davis observed that, although Hamer was undoubtedly "a man [of] talent and promise in civil career," there was nothing in him "to show a genius for war. He was said to have frankly confessed his inaptitude soon after the battle of Monterey" (Davis, notes on Monterrey, Apr. 18, [1875], Barret Coll. of Johnston Papers, LNT; *BDAC*).

24 The 1st Ohio; the 1st Ky. had been assigned to guard the mortar and howitzer battery north of the city (*Senate Doc. 1*, 29:2, 84).

25 Hamer had been ordered to support Braxton Bragg's battery (*House Ex. Doc. 17*, 30:1, 10).

26 Although American soldiers frequently referred to all Mexican cavalry as lancers (see, for instance, the Buena Vista battle reports), a contemporary Mexican account notes that, though the "greater number" of the cavalry carried lances, many were armed only with saber and musket (Balbontín, *Invasión Americana*, 78).

27 For another Davis account of the withdrawal and attack by the Mexican cavalry, see Davis to William P. Johnston, n.d., Johnston, *A. S. Johns-*

ton, 139; see also Estes, "Monterey," Fort Worth *Gazette*, Jan. 5, 1885.

28 The 1st Miss. was dispersed after the attack on the Tenería, some troops remaining in the captured forts to the end of the day, others advancing into the lane, still others taking shelter in the area around the Tenería in order to fire on El Diablo. A number were eventually reorganized under Maj. Bradford and rejoined Davis after the withdrawal from the city; the remainder apparently came up in "small detachments" before the regiment returned to its encampment (see the reports of the various company commanders, Sept. 26–Oct. 18, 1846, and n.d.; *House Ex. Doc. 17*, 30:1, 25; Joseph D. Howell to Margaret K. Howell, Sept. 25, 1846, Z790f, Howell Papers, Ms-Ar).

29 William Henry Harrison Patterson, 1st lt., Co. K. A native Virginian, Patterson was accidentally shot in a fight at Monterrey on April 20, 1847, and lost a leg as a consequence. He returned to his home in Lowndes County, where he was later (1853) elected sheriff, dying in 1856 during his second term (DNA, M-863, roll 3; Pace, ed., "Rogers Diary," *SWHQ*, 32:284; Vicksburg *Daily Whig*, Nov. 4, Dec. 11, 1846; Columbus *S. Standard*, Nov. 12, 1853; RG28, Vol. 284, Reg. of Comns., 445, Ms-Ar; Jackson *Mississippian*, Mar. 7, 1856).

30 On the Davises' copy the phrase "sally porte" has been struck and "open embrasure" interlined.

31 Reuben N. Downing, capt., Co. G, was wounded in the arm and returned to Mississippi on leave before rejoining his company on the eve of the Battle of Buena Vista (DNA, M-863, roll 1; Natchez *Courier and Jour.*, Dec. 2, 1846).

32 2d Lt. James Colhoun (c1815–49) of Co. B. An Irishman and a saddler by trade, he lived in Woodville before moving in 1849 to Waterproof, Louisiana (DNA, M-863, roll 1;

Woodville *Repub.*, Aug. 13, 1850).

[33] Rufus K. Arthur (c1816-55), born in Maryland, was a Vicksburg attorney. During the war he served in Co. C and acted as correspondent for the Vicksburg *Whig*, edited by his brother Alexander. Elected district attorney for Mississippi's third district in 1848, Arthur also served a term in the legislature (1850), then edited the *Whig* from 1851 until his death (DNA, M-863, roll 1; Arthur to Samuel Stamps, Aug. 28, 1848, RG 28, Vol. 7, Corres., Ms-Ar; *Miss. Official Reg., 1908*, 65; 1850 Census, Miss., Warren, family 539; Everett, "Vicksburg Lawyers," 86–87; Vicksburg *Weekly Whig*, July 9, 1851; Fisher Funeral Home recs., MsVO).

[34] Francis A. Wolff, the son of a German saddler, was born in one of the Carolinas about 1824. In the decades after the Mexican War he was a Tippah County legislator (1854, 1865–67, 1880) and during the Civil War was capt., 3d Miss. Inf. A longtime admirer and correspondent of Davis', Wolff was living as late as 1887 (Wolff to William T. Walthall, May 15, 1879, La. Hist. Assn. Davis Coll., LNT; 1860 Census, Miss., S. Tippah, family 1183; *Miss. Official Reg., 1908*, 63, 123; DNA, RG109, Comp. Service Recs.; Davis to Wolff, May 27, 1848, Aug. 24, 1887, Ben S. Nelms).

[35] William Henry Bell (c1825–78), a native of Alabama, lost his left arm at Monterrey. In 1848, on Davis' recommendation, he was appointed an Indian subagent and in the 1850s migrated to California. There he became a justice of the peace (1866) and later sergeant-at-arms in the state senate (DNA, RG15, Mexican War Pension Applics., WC 2776; Davis to Robert J. Walker, Dec. 6, 1848; *American Almanac, 1850*, 109; San Francisco *Alta Calif.*, Aug. 3, 4, 1878; *Index to San Francisco Great Reg., 1872*).

[36] William H. Miller (c1826–76), a Natchez resident, was discharged in January 1847. After the Mexican War he moved to Mason County, Kentucky (DNA, RG15, Mexican War Pension Applics., WC 6451; DNA, M-863, roll 2; Henry, *Masons*, 198).

[37] Adam Lanehart, a native Mississippian born about 1822, returned home to Woodville in December 1846; he was a planter by occupation (1850 Census, Miss., Wilkinson, family 505; Woodville *Repub.*, Dec. 26, 1846).

[38] Henry B. Thompson, born in Maine in 1824, was a druggist before the Mexican War. Discharged at Monterrey in October 1846, he moved to California in 1849 and was residing in San Francisco as late as 1887 (DNA, RG15, Mexican War Pension Applics., SC 10375; DNA, RG217, Paymaster Accts., Van Buren, Sept.–Oct. 1846, Acct. 5141, Voucher 88).

[39] Born in Germany about 1822, George Wills was a tailor and later (1850) a grocer in Carroll County (DNA, RG217, Paymaster Accts., Van Buren, Sept.–Oct. 1846, Acct. 5141, Voucher 103; 1850 Census, Miss., S. Carroll, family 547).

[40] Warren Huffman (c1823–64) was discharged on October 22 and lived in Carroll County before returning to his native Warren County in the 1850s. In August 1861 he enlisted in the Miss. Lt. Art.; he was promoted sgt. shortly before his death in action in June 1864 (DNA, RG217, Paymaster Accts., Van Buren, Sept.–Oct. 1846, Acct. 5141, Voucher 94; 1850 Census, Miss., S. Carroll, family 181; DNA, RG15, Mexican War Pension Applics., OWIR 15266; DNA, RG109, Comp. Service Recs.).

[41] Hugh W. Pierce (c1823–71), a native Mississippian, was discharged in October 1846. A printer by trade, Pierce edited and published the Brandon *Republican*, a Whig journal, in 1848–49. Several years later (1854)

he taught at Madison College in Sharon and from 1866 until his death headed the Jackson public school system (1850 Census, Miss., Rankin, family 265; DNA, M-863, roll 3; Jackson *Mississippian*, Aug. 24, 1849; *Mississippian and State Gazette*, Sept. 13, 1854; Natchez *Courier and Jour.*, July 5, 1848; DNA, RG15, Mexican War Pension Applics., WC 5327; McCain, *Jackson*, 1:209, 215).

[42] Jacob Fredericks (Friedrichs) was born in Germany about 1820 and had lived in Raymond since 1843. Discharged from the Mississippi regiment in October, he returned to his trade as a carpenter in Hinds County. He died during the 1853 yellow fever epidemic (DNA, RG217, Paymaster Accts., Van Buren, Sept.–Oct. 1846, Acct. 5141, Voucher 54; 1850 Census, Miss., Hinds, family 272; Jackson *Mississippian and State Gazette*, Nov. 4, 1853).

[43] Born in Tennessee about 1826, Marshall M. Smith was a resident of Canton before the Mexican War. After President Polk and Davis unsuccessfully recommended him for a customs inspectorship in 1848, Smith turned to law, opening an office in Jackson in 1852. He also served as state librarian, 1852–54 (DNA, RG 217, Paymaster Accts., Van Buren, Nov. 1846, Acct. 5141, Voucher 15; Davis to Robert J. Walker, Mar. 30, 1848; Smith to Polk, June 1, 1848, Polk Papers, DLC; Jackson *Mississippian and State Gazette*, July 22, 1853; *Miss. Official Reg., 1908*, 33).

[44] James Williamson (c1824–89) was a Virginia-born blacksmith. After losing an arm at Monterrey, he worked as a laborer, living in Tennessee for about forty years before his death in the Davidson County asylum (DNA, RG217, Paymaster Accts., Van Buren, Sept.–Oct. 1846, Acct. 5141, Voucher 92; 1850 Census, Tenn., Franklin, family 1536; DNA, RG15, Mexican War Pension Applics., WO 8535).

[45] Abner Washington Teague (1821–1900), born in South Carolina, was a farmer who had lived at Benton before the war. Discharged in December 1846, he returned to South Carolina (DNA, RG15, Mexican War Pension Applics., WC 12469; DNA, RG217, Paymaster Accts., Van Buren, Dec. 1–11, 1846, Acct. 5141, Voucher 51).

[46] Samuel Warren White, born in 1825, was the son of a Charleston, South Carolina, attorney who settled in Yazoo County in the 1830s. White left Yale at the end of his sophomore year to enlist in Davis' regiment; he was appointed quartermaster sgt. in February 1847. After the war he returned to Yazoo, residing there as late as 1849. According to university records, he was still alive in 1910 (Webber, ann., "Recs. from Blake and White Bibles," *S.C. Hist. and Geneal. Mag.*, 36:50, 113, 37:42; DNA, M-863, roll 3; New Orleans *Delta*, June 10, 1847; Henry, *Masons*, 173; CtY to Davis Assn., Aug. 7, 1979).

[47] Avery Noland (1828–83), a native Mississippian and a graduate of Oakland College in Lorman, recovered from his wounds and saw action at Buena Vista. He settled at Milliken's Bend, Louisiana, in the 1850s and reportedly served as an officer in the Civil War (family recs. of Florence N. Bruce and Thomas V. Noland).

[48] Charles F. Cotton, born in Tennessee about 1821, was discharged from the Mississippi regiment in November. A farmer, he lived in Ripley after the war. He died sometime before February 1856 (1850 Census, Miss., Tippah, 3d dist., family 434; DNA, RG15, Mexican War Pension Applics., OWIF 9231).

[49] Gideon Williams (c1825–82), a Tennessean, had lived in Marshall County before the war. In the 1850s he moved to Texas, becoming a farmer in Hill County (DNA, RG217, Paymaster Accts., Van Buren, Nov. 1846, Acct. 5141, Voucher 76; DNA,

RG15, Mexican War Pension Applics., WC 2080; 1880 Census, Texas, Hill, enumeration dist. 76, 4).

50 Daniel B. Lewis, born in South Carolina about 1817, was a farmer who migrated to Cherokee County, Texas, in the early 1850s. He lived there with his family until at least 1860 (DNA, RG217, Paymaster Accts., Van Buren, Nov. 1846, Acct. 5141, Voucher 27; DNA, RG15, Mexican War Pension Applics., OWI 4578; 1860 Census, Texas, Cherokee, family 160).

51 Charles Martin (1821–76) was born in South Carolina but was a resident of Lowndes County when he enlisted in the 1st Miss. Rgt. He died in Union County (DNA, RG217, Paymaster Accts., Van Buren, Nov. 1846, Acct. 5141, Voucher 84; DNA, RG 15, Mexican War Pension Applics., WC 2274).

52 Easily confused with John L. Thompson of the same company, James Thompson had no middle initial (DNA, M-863, roll 3).

53 Here Davis strikes the copied signature on Griffith's copy and interlines his own.

54 Undoubtedly struck by Davis.

To John A. Quitman

[Monterrey, September 26, 1846][1]
Additional Report

SIR, Omitting to notice those occurrences which transpired whilst with you holding the Fort on the 22nd.,[2] I resume my statement at the point when ordered out to reconnoiter the movements and position of the enemy on the morning of the 23d. My command consisted of Company "H," commanded by 1st Lieut. Moore;[3] company "G," commanded by 1st Lieut. Greaves;[4] and two companies of Col. Campbell's Regiment,[5] under the command of Lieut. Col. Anderson.[6] Having been deprived of the very valuable services of Adjutant Griffith[7] of the Riflemen by an injury received in his Shoulder, which compelled him to remain in Camp, Lieut. Cook, at a time when the duty we had to perform was both difficult & perilous,[8] offered me his services and rendered great assistance. As we advanced into the Town, armed bodies of men fled through the streets at our approach. Having turned the flank of the Fort,[9] we found it evacuated—the Artillery removed, as I suppose, under cover of the night, and we took possession of it; but as it was commanded by the Forts in rear of it, and the *terre pleine* exposed to their fire, it was necessary to take shelter upon the outer side.[10] At this time I was accompanied by, and received valuable assistance and advice from Lieut. Scarrett[11] of the Engineers. After a reconnoissance still further to the left,[12] I received your orders to advance

35

to what my examination induced me to believe a better position; and my command was changed in relieving Company "G," by Capt. Cooper's company "B" of our Regiment, and by substituting for one of the Companies of Col. Campbell's Regiment, Company "D," of the Mississippi Riflemen, commanded by 1st Lieut. Russell.[13] Finding no enemy within our range at the next position,[14] we advanced to a breast-work thrown across the termination of a street to our left.[15] Whilst examining <–the–> it, I was twice fired at by sharp-shooters. The files of my command nearest to me stepped forward to punish the assailants, and in a few moments we were in action. Our fire was effective upon the right, but the enemy posted upon the top of a large building on our left,[16] continued to fire from his place of security, and killed one of our men, whose gallant conduct had, I remember, attracted your attention—private Tyree of Co. "K" whose /his/ company being in rear, had voluntarily come up & joined us.[17] We had (I think) done all which we could effect from that position when you directed us to a place of greater safety, to which you had ordered the remaining companies of my Regt. to advance.[18] <–I regret that–> Capt. Taylor[19] /and his company/ was not relieved from the duty with which I had charged him; <–though the–> /that of holding a/ post[9] /in the rear/ which <–he held–> was very important in the event of our being compelled to retire, I had found him so efficient on the previous occasion, and his company so prompt and gallant, that I regretted his absence. After we were joined by the Texan Volunteers[20] under Genl. Henderson, I derived great support from them as well from their gallantry as their better knowledge of the construction of Mexican houses.[21]

We continued to advance and drive the enemy by passing through courts, gardens, and houses, taking every favorable position to fire from the house tops, which from their style of architecture furnishes a good defence against Musketry, Until near the Plaza where we found all the streets barricaded, and swept by so severe a fire, that to advance from our last position,[22] it became necessary to construct a defence across the street. For this purpose we used the baggage and pack saddles found in the houses; and though under a fire of Artillery as well as Musketry, had more than half finished the work, when we received orders to retire. This was done in good order, though I regret to say that the Enemy, emboldened by the first retrograde movement, followed our retreat by a cross street and wounded several of our party; among others Lieut. Howard[23] of the Miss. Riflemen, who was bringing up the rear. As on the former occasion, to name those whose conduct equalled my highest expectations and hopes, would be to furnish a list of the officers and men engaged in the action.

I wish to mention for your notice two gentlemen who joined my Regiment and served in the ranks as Volunteers on the 23rd.— Major E. R. Price[24] of Natchez, and Capt. J. R. Smith[25] late of the Louisiana volunteers: they were both conspicuous for their gallantry and energy[26] on every trying occasion—always with the advanced detachment, and as prompt in the observance of orders, as in the encounter of danger.

Whilst I cannot mention all who deserve commendation, and feel that you will bear me out in claiming the highest credit for each, I cannot forbear from naming Capt. Cooper, Lieuts. Moore, Russell[27] and Cook, and Sergeant Major Harlan,[28] who being especially under my observation and generally out of your view, might otherwise pass without that notice which their most soldierly conduct so well merits.

The conduct of Regimental Surgeon, Seymour Halsey, is worthy of the highest credit, and claims especial notice. On the 21st. he was on the field of battle, and exposed several times to much personal danger whilst giving early relief to the wounded, and has effected much by his attentions since. To his vigilance and skill it is fair to assign the fact that but one case of amputation has occurred in our Regiment up to this date.[29]

List of the killed and wounded in the action of the 23d.

Private John M. Tyree, of Com. "K".

Wounded, four viz:

Private R. W. Chance,	of Com. "B".	mortally
do P. W. Johnson,	″ "C",	severely
do Platt Snedicor,	″ "K",	mortally
2d Lieut. Howard,	″ "D",	severely

Killed on the 22d., viz:

Private, Danl. D. Dubois, of Com. "H"

Wounded on the 22d. viz:
Private Robert Grigg,   of Com. "H", slightly.

JEFFN. DAVIS
Col. Mi. Riflemen

LS, copy by Richard Griffith (DNA, RG94, Letters Recd., 423-T-1846, f/w 38-T-1847). L/ALS, partial copy by Davis and V. Davis (RG27, Vol. 26, Corres., Mexican War Docs., Ms-Ar). AL, fragment (ViRC). Significant textual differences between Griffith's and the Davises' copies are pointed out in footnotes.

[1] Davis evidently intended this report as a continuation of the preceding one.
[2] On September 22 the 1st Miss. was posted in the fortified stone building and a redan connecting the building with the Tenería.
[3] Robert L. Moore (c1815–47) of Vicksburg, a Virginia-born attorney. Because Capt. George P. Crump had fallen ill, Moore assumed command of Co. H on September 23. He was killed at Buena Vista (Z133, Crutcher Notes, 195, Ms-Ar; DNA, M-863, roll 2; Vicksburg Daily Whig, Dec. 11, 1846).
[4] Stephen Arne Decatur Greaves (1817–80) commanded Co. G from September 22, 1846, to February 22, 1847, in the absence of Capt. Downing. A lawyer and state legislator from Hinds County, Greaves was active in Mississippi Democratic politics into the 1850s. After the Civil War he lived at Livingston (DNA, M-863, roll 1; Jackson S. Reformer, Feb. 23, 1846; Jackson Mississippian, June 15, 1849; Jackson Mississippian and State Gazette, Dec. 12, 1851; Vicksburg Weekly Sentinel, Jan. 12, 1848; Vicksburg Sunday Post, Mar. 11, 1973, 32).
[5] Cos. A and B of the 1st Tenn. (House Ex. Doc. 17, 30:1, 27–28; DNA, RG94, Vol. Muster Rolls, Mexican War, 1st Tenn. Rgtl. Return, Sept. 1846).

[6] Samuel Read Anderson (1804–83) commanded because Col. William B. Campbell was ill on September 23. Later cashier of the Bank of Tennessee and for eight years postmaster of Nashville, Anderson saw action during the Civil War as commander of the Tenn. Brig., CSA, and as director of the Tennessee conscription bureau. After the war he was a merchant in Nashville (House Ex. Doc. 17, 30:1, 27–28; DNA, RG94, Vol. Muster Rolls, Mexican War, 1st Tenn. Rgtl. Return, Sept. 1846; Warner, Gens. in Gray).
[7] Richard Griffith (1814–62) of Co. C was appointed adj. in July 1846. A Vicksburg merchant, he later moved to Jackson, became a successful banker, and was elected to two terms as state treasurer (1847–51). He also served as marshal for the southern district of Mississippi (1853–61). Commissioned a Confederate brigadier in 1861, Griffith was mortally wounded at Savage Station, Virginia, and was mourned by the Davises as a valued friend (DNA, M-863, roll 1; Biog. and Hist. Memoirs of Miss., 1:826–27; Senate Ex. Jour., 9:131, 142, 10:402, 415; Warner, Gens. in Gray; Vicksburg Tri-Weekly Whig, Sept. 26, 1846; Griffith subject file, Ms-Ar; Davis, Rise and Fall, 2:141; V. Davis to Davis, July 6, 1862, Adele D. Sinton).
[8] The Davises' copy reads "was considered both difficult, and perilous."
[9] El Diablo.
[10] The Mexicans manning improvised fortifications between El Diablo and the cathedral plaza could fire into the rear of the fort.
[11] Jeremiah M. Scarritt (c1817–54), an 1838 West Point graduate, served as chief engineer during the Second

Seminole War and was brevetted capt. for his conduct at Monterrey. After the Mexican War he continued his engineering duties, chiefly as superintendent of repairs at Fort Morgan, Alabama (Cullum, *Biog. Reg.*, 1:699).

[12] Davis made two reconnaissances from El Diablo: the first, with Scarritt, to the redoubt on the right of El Diablo; the second, with Lt. Moore of the 1st Miss., to the left of the fort, along the eastern edge of Monterrey.

[13] Daniel R. Russell, born about 1820 in Washington, D.C., commanded Co. D at both Monterrey and Buena Vista in the absence of Bainbridge D. Howard. A prominent Whig, Russell was elected clerk of the district chancery court (1847), a victory won with some assistance from Davis; he also served as state auditor (1851–55). In 1863 he resigned his commission as col., 20th Miss. Inf., because of poor health and returned to his home in Carrollton, dying there sometime after 1870 (DNA, M-863, rolls 2–3; Russell to Davis, Nov. 24, 1847; Russell to Samuel Stamps, June 26, 1848, RG28, Vol. 7, Corres., Ms-Ar; Hamilton, *Carroll County*, 17–18; *Miss. Official Reg.*, 1908, 31, 621; 1870 Census, Miss., Carroll, Carrollton, family 51).

[14] Probably the tenaille mentioned by Davis in his letter to Brown, September 20, 1847.

[15] See no. 11 on the map of Monterrey.

[16] The hospital at the southeastern corner of the city; see no. 12 on the map.

[17] John M. Tyree, killed while serving temporarily with Co. H (DNA, M-863, roll 3).

[18] Cos. C, E, G, and K, under Maj. Alexander B. Bradford.

[19] James H. R. Taylor (c1820–67), capt., Co. I, was born in North Carolina. A lawyer from Holly Springs, he was recommended by Davis for a place on the Mexican claims commission after the war, served as a state legislator (1852), and sought a Democratic congressional nomination in 1853. He was active in the Know-Nothing party during the mid-1850s. After brief service in 1861 as lt. col., 15th Tenn. Inf., Taylor returned to Mississippi and was elected as a Democrat to the state senate (DNA, M-863, roll 3; *Miss. Official Reg.*, 1908, 61, 117; Davis et al. to James K. Polk, July 31, 1848, Taylor to Davis, Mar. 29, 1853, Davis Papers, KyLxT; Overdyke, *Know-Nothing Party*, 121–22, 277; Rawson, "Party Politics," 167, 284; DNA, RG109, Comp. Service Recs.; 1860 Census, Miss., Marshall, Holly Springs, family 186; Natchez *Weekly Dem.*, Nov. 18, 1867).

[20] The 2d Texas Mtd. Vols., under the command of Col. George T. Wood (*Senate Doc. 1*, 29:2, 88).

[21] During their war for independence the Texans had discovered the utility of advancing through fortified city buildings by boring through the walls, a method they and the Mississippians used to advantage during the third day's fighting at Monterrey. The same procedure had been suggested earlier to Davis by Lt. Scarritt, who left to obtain the necessary tools but failed to return (*Senate Doc. 1*, 97; Kendall, "Hist. of the War," ch. 5, 46n, Kendall Papers, TxU; Walthall, *Davis*, 20; Davis to Brown, Sept. 20, 1847).

[22] A two-story house at the corner of the plaza (see no. 13 on the map of Monterrey). In an account written shortly before his death Davis stated that the Texans joined the Mississippians only at this point (*Davis Papers*, 1:lv).

[23] Lewis T. Howard of Co. D was born in Mississippi about 1821. Hospitalized for the wound he received at Monterrey, he resigned his commission in December 1846 and returned to Carroll County (DNA, M-863, roll 2; 1850 Census, Miss., N. Carroll, family 414).

[24] Ezra R. Price (c1816–48), a Natchez attorney, had served as 1st lt.

and adj. of the disbanded 4th La. Inf. Determined to take part in the war, Price and John R. Smith walked from Camargo to Monterrey, where they fought alongside the 3d and 4th Inf. as well as the 1st Miss. In January 1847 Price was elected maj., 2d Miss. Rgt., but chronic poor health forced him to take a leave of absence in October. He died in Lexington, Kentucky (Heitman, *Hist. Reg.*, 2:65; New Orleans *Picayune*, Oct. 22, 1846; Natchez *Courier and Jour.*, July 26, 1848; DNA, M-863, roll 6).

[25] John Rodes Smith, formerly of the 4th La. Inf. After the Battle of Monterrey, he returned to New Orleans, where he was in business as a commission merchant as late as 1860 (Heitman, *Hist. Reg.*, 2:68; New Orleans *Picayune*, Oct. 30, 1846; 1846–60 New Orleans dirs.).

[26] The Davises' copy reads "for their good conduct."

[27] On the Davises' copy an asterisk following the name Russell refers to a marginal note: "The names of *Posey, Greaves*, and *Hampton* should have been here inserted."

[28] Charles Theodore Harlan, reportedly born in Virginia about 1817, was mustered into Co. H as a sgt. but in August 1846 was promoted sgt. maj. Discharged in October, he returned to his home in Vicksburg and lived there until 1849, when he went to California. After several unsuccessful years as a prospector he settled in Sacramento; he apparently was living as late as 1856 (Vicksburg *Daily Whig*, Dec. 11, 1846; DNA, M-863, roll 2; Harlan Letters, passim, TxU). Davis recommended him for an army commission in 1847, and in 1850, when Harlan again sought his former commander's assistance, Davis responded with letters that, according to Harlan, were "very flattering in their tenor" (Davis to Polk, Nov. 30, 1847; Harlan to Julia E. LeGrand, Feb. 24, 1850, Harlan Letters, 243, TxU).

[29] The Davises' copy reads "not a case of amputation has yet occurred in our Regiment."

From Alexander B. Bradford

Camp Near Montery Mexico September 26' 1846

Sir I was called upon by you last evening to make such Report of the Conduct of the Mississippi Riflemen as came within my immediate observation during the Battle of Montery, and in conformity thereto I herein send you a statement which I vouch to be correct as far as it proposes to detail. On the morning of the 21d. Instant our Brigade under the Command of General Quitman moved out on the direction of Monterey; the Tennessee Regiment on the Right, when we arrived opposite the city we halted a short time, and then were ordered to move South by the Left flank, the Tennesseeans Still being in front;[1] a brisk cannonade was kept up upon us until we had Moved our Regiment with its whole front Nearly opposite the lower fort or redout[2] of the town, the Tennesseeans Still being on the Left; at this moment a most distructive fire opened

40

from the fort of grape Canister and muskety raking our whole Line from Right to Left, we instantly received orders to charge; and they were as promptly executed, & the Fort Carried by Storm. As far as my attention was directed to the first occupation of the Fort by our troops I can say that Lieut Col McClung of our Regiment was the first on the wall followed immediately afterwards by others of the Regiment:[3] at this moment I /heard/ Adjutant Griffith proclaim we had taken the Fort. As to the Conduct of the Officers & soldiers of the Regiment on this day, I say with pleasure they done their duty nobly. on the 22nd Genl. Worth on the part of the American Army had the field,[4] and we had but little to do except To receive Such Shots at the lower Fort[5] which was in Our possession as the enemy thought proper to send at us.

On the Morning of the 23rd. you were ordered out by General Quitman with two Companies of our Regiment & two Companies of the Tennesseeans to take the Fort No 3.[6] opposite to our then position which you promptly done. In about an hour there after I was ordered by General Quitman to Move out quickly with the balance of the Regement except Captain Taylors Company which was ordered by you to remain & guard The Fort to sustain him in an attack made with the Detachment under your Command on the lower part of the town;[7] we instantly Moved out, and immediately after passing the creek a heavy fire of grape & muskety opened by which we were annoyed & exposed to for several hundred Yards; yet it was met with admirable firmness by the Riflemen until their arrival in town when a warmer Salute awanted them, which was received with equal spirit by the whole Regiment. We remained Some time under cover of the Houses, during which time a portion of the Regiment joined your Command and a portion remained with me. We were afterwards ordered by Gen Quitman to charge on the town, and the Command was executed with almost unparralleled firmness. We Carried the Street west for Several hundred yards under a Continued Shower of grape & Cenister Shot accompanied with Musketry; and took a position in the heart of the town and maintained it, firmly for several hours under a most galling fire the whole time, and until we were ordered by the Commanding General[8] to draw o[f]f, and then retired in good order. The officers with me of the Mississippi Riflemen as far as now recollected, were Captains Willis & McManis[9] & Lieuts /Patterson

Townsend Wade[10]/ Arthur Bradford[11] & Markum[12] who all behaved with great presence of mind & courage as did evry Soldier who accompanied us. Indeed their gallanty was Conspicuous through out, & met my entire approbation. I cannot close without making mention of Captain Bennett[13] of the 1s Ten. Regiment under Col Campbell and Captain Truitt[14] of the 2d Regiment of Texas Mounted Men under Col Woods[15] who voluntarily served with my Command, and under my Orders: They both together with their companies behaved with great galantry, & from them I received <-the-> most efficient Aid— <-I hope their respective Cols.-> Dr. Veech[16] Quarter Master of Col. Woods Regiment was also with me the whole time & with his great coolness & courage rendered me essential Service.

All reflected on themselves the highest honour. I have the honour to be Your Most Obt Sert

A B BRADFORD Major
Miss Riflemen

ALS (DNA, RG94, Letters Recd., 423-T-1846, f/w 38-T-1847). L, copy by Richard Griffith (RG27, Vol. 26, Corres., Mexican War Docs., Ms-Ar).

[1] While in line before the city the 1st Tenn. filed past the Mississippians and thus preceded them on the march to the Tenería.

[2] The Tenería.

[3] Bradford refers to the controversy that arose between the 1st Tenn. and the 1st Miss. rgts. over the taking of the Tenería. When William B. Campbell claimed the honor for the Tennesseans, Davis took exception, defending his unit on several occasions. In addition, presumably seeking support for his argument, Davis asked his company commanders and Maj. Bradford to submit battle reports, a departure from prescribed military procedure (U.S. War Dept., *Army Regs.,* [1821], 128, 1847, 119). All the officers noted that McClung was first to mount the walls of the Tenería, several stated directly that no Tennessee soldier preceded the Mississippians, and some gave reasons why the Tennessee charge was delayed. Indeed, the relative positions of the two regiments and the manner in which they charged were central to the dispute. To Campbell's assertion that the 1st Tenn., lined up before the fort's north face, had been more directly in front of the Tenería and closer than the 1st Miss. at the time of the charge, Davis countered with evidence that his men had been nearer the fort, had formed directly in front of the northwest flank, and had charged "by the front at full speed," while the 1st Tenn. "was marched up by a flank" (see his undated fragment on the battle and his letter to John Jenkins, Nov. 16, 1846). Campbell himself admitted privately to some confusion in his ranks and conceded that "individuals of another regiment may have entered with the first of my regiment" (*House Ex. Doc. 17,* 30:1, 25; Sioussat, ed., "Mexican War Letters," *Tenn. Hist. Mag.,* 1:143–45, 154–55). Alexander McClung, a central figure in the charge,

stated that at both the Tenería and the tannery "we took all the prisoners," adding later that the Tennesseans "were not in the fort . . . when I mounted the breastwork, I naturally looked across at them and saw them coming" (Vicksburg *Weekly Whig*, Apr. 21, *Tri-Weekly Whig*, July 13, 1847). Gen. Quitman, whose battle report is ambiguous about the charge, consistently declined to take sides in the controversy. However, he wrote to a friend in November that, although the two regiments charged simultaneously, the 1st Tenn. "was impeded by a deep ditch" and he believed that "M'Clung was first on the rampart" (Claiborne, *Quitman*, 2:304; *House Ex. Doc.* 17, 30:1, 15). Davis' effort to obtain a clear statement from Quitman was unavailing, and despite his attempts to resolve the dispute it was revived as late as 1862, when Andrew Johnson recalled that Davis once had "scurrillously impugned the courage" of the 1st Tenn. Rgt. (Davis to Quitman and to Joseph E. Davis, Jan. 13, 26, 1847; N.Y. *Times*, Apr. 1, 1862, 2).

⁴ On September 22 Gen. William J. Worth's 2d Div., operating on the western side of Monterrey, captured the summit of Independence Hill and the Bishop's Palace (Smith, *War with Mexico*, 1:246–48).

⁵ The 1st Miss. was posted in the fortified stone building and in a redan between the building and the Tenería.

⁶ Cos. G and H, 1st Miss. Rgt., along with Cos. A and B, 1st Tenn. Rgt., were ordered to capture El Diablo.

⁷ In the interim Cos. B and D had joined Davis, Co. G returning to the Tenería. Thus Bradford brought Cos. C, E, G, and K to Davis' support. Capt. James H. R. Taylor commanded Co. I.

⁸ Zachary Taylor.

⁹ John L. McManus (1816–95) of Co. E. A resident of Jackson, he was elected clerk of the circuit court in 1847; he subsequently was reelected (1858) and served through the war. Late in life McManus moved to Louisiana; he was residing in Grangeville at his death (DNA, RG15, Mexican War Pension Applics., WC 10080; *Jour. Confed. Cong.*, 3:404, 408; Vicksburg *Weekly Sentinel*, Nov. 10, 1847; Jackson *Mississippian*, Sept. 14, Nov. 9, 1849, Oct. 20, 1858; RG28, Vol. 285, Reg. of Comns., 315, Ms-Ar).

¹⁰ William B. Wade of Co. K was born in Virginia about 1824. A Whig, he represented Lowndes County in the state legislature (1854) and during the Civil War commanded a company of the 10th Miss. Inf. He was killed shortly after the war by federal troops (DNA, M-863, roll 3; *Miss. Official Reg., 1908*, 120, 595–96; Columbus *S. Standard*, Dec. 3, 1853; 1850 Census, Miss., Lowndes, Columbus, 4th ward, family 38; McFarland, "Forgotten Expedition," *Miss. Hist. Pubs.*, 9:23).

¹¹ Charles MacPherson Bradford (1825–67), 2d lt., Co. E. After the Mexican War he moved from Jackson to New Orleans, where, as a leader in the Whig and Know-Nothing parties, he was elected justice of the peace and district attorney. He saw brief service during the Civil War as lt. col., 15th La. Inf. (RG33, Vol. 19, Rec. of Comnd. Officers, 125, Ms-Ar; DNA, M-863, roll 1; Booth, comp., *La. Confed. Soldiers*; New Orleans *Crescent*, Sept. 27, 1867; DNA, RG15, Mexican War Pension Applics., WC 1460).

¹² Hugh Mercer Markham (c1815–64), born in Virginia, was a clerk by occupation. Resigning as 2d lt. of Co. H in October 1846, he returned to service briefly in 1847 as acting quartermaster of the 2d Miss. Rgt. After a trip to California in 1850, he resided in Vicksburg and near Raymond (DNA, M-863, roll 2; Vicksburg *Daily Whig*, Jan. 5, 1847; Vicks-

burg *Weekly Whig*, Apr. 3, 1850; 1860 Census, Miss., Warren, family 127; DNA, RG15, Mexican War Pension Applics., WC 5988; family recs. of Kathryn C. Kimble).

[13] Robert A. Bennett (1822–75), a native Virginian, was later a Democratic state legislator (1859–61) from Gallatin and served as capt., 9th Tenn. Cav., CSA, during the Civil War (McBride and Robison, *Biog. Dir.*; *Tennesseans in the Civil War*, 1:74).

[14] Alfred M. Truit (c1817–64) was later maj., 1st Texas Mtd. Vols. Born in North Carolina, he figured in the Shelby County, Texas, "Regulator-Moderator War" of the early 1840s. A state legislator after the Mexican War, he served during the Civil War as capt. and a.q.m., 28th Texas Dismtd. Cav. (DNA, RG94, Comp. Service

Recs., Mexican War, 1st and 2d Texas Mtd. Vols.; DNA, RG109, Comp. Service Recs.; 1860 Census, Texas, Shelby, family 58; Terrell, *Truitt Family*, 22–23; *Texas Legis.*, 10).

[15] George Tyler Wood (1795–1858) was a state legislator in his native Georgia (1837–38) and in Texas (1846) before organizing the 2d Texas Mtd. Vols. He was subsequently governor (*Handbook of Texas*).

[16] John Allen Veatch (1808–70), born in Kentucky, was a physician and schoolteacher before the Mexican War. He served with three different Texas units (1846–48) and afterward pursued a scientific career in California, Nevada, and Oregon (*Handbook of Texas*; DNA, RG94, Comp. Service Recs., Mexican War, 2d Texas Mtd. Vols., Co. B).

From Reuben N. Downing

Camp near Monterey, Sept. 26th 1846

SIR: At your request I send you a brief statement of the storming of the Mexican Battery[1] on the morning of the 21st so far as the same came under my observation.

When the attack on the Mexican Battery commenced, the Company under my command was on the extreme left of the Mississippi Regiment, and next to the Tenessee Regiment. It appears that the Tenessee Regiment, under the command of Col. Campbell moved forward to the attack by the right flank, which, when they halted and faced the enemy, owing to the position in which they were placed, threw their (then right) left in front.[2]

The Mississippi Regiment moved by the left flank, and consequently when they halted, and fronted the enemy's battery, the left was in front. The fire of the enemy was tremendous and most destructive; and I suppose continued for thirty minutes before the charge began. When the charge was ordered, I ordered my company to cease firing, load and charge. At this time Col. Campbell rode up to the left of his Regiment, next to me, and ordered them to charge. The Company on the extreme left, rose from the Chaparral and grass where they had been firing, and commenced advancing on the Battery at shouldered arms, in a walk. The Mississippi Regiment now commenced the charge in double quick time, and in advance of the Tenessee Regiment who were moving to the charge by a flank; and when the Battery was stormed and the whole force of the enemy driven from it, and the Mississippi Regiment in complete possession of it, the Company on the left of the Tenessee Regiment, which was in advance of that Regiment had not yet reached the Battery, and were firing to the left, on the retreating Mexicans as they were attempting to reach the second Battery,[3] beyond the Fort. I, with several other officers of the Mississippi Regiment were calling on the Tenesseeans to cease firing as they would shoot our men, who were then passing the fort in pursuit of the retiring enemy. Col. Campbell was riding by the side of his Regiment, and also called to his Command to cease firing. At this time the Tenessee flag was unfurled by their standard bearer on the Battery. Before, however, the Tenesseeans got into the Battery, the Mississippians were in possession of the Fort,[4] where Col. McClung was shot.

I am very certain that Col. McClung was the first man on the Breast works, and that the Mississippians had taken the Battery and Fort before the Tennesseeians arrived   Yours respectfully

(signed) R. N. Downing

Comdg. Compy. "G."

1st R. M. Vols.

In addition to the above facts; when you ordered the charge sounded, which was simultaneous to the order of Genl. Quitman, the whole regiment moved promptly & together to the execution of the order

R. N. Downing

L, copy by Davis (RG27, Vol. 26, Corres., Mexican War Docs., Ms-Ar). Endorsed by Davis: "No. 9 Compy 'G.' Statement of Capt. Downing and Lieut. Greaves." Enclosed. Davis to Albert G. Brown, Oct. 3, 1847.

[1] The Tenería.

[2] Observing an inversion of the usual order of the 1st Tenn. companies in line of battle, Downing offers the logical explanation that the regiment had marched to the Tenería

by the right flank. In fact, however, the Tennesseans marched by the left flank: the inversion came about when the leading company halted, forcing each succeeding company to file around it to the left (*House Ex. Doc.* 17, 30:1, 25).

[3] El Diablo.

[4] The fortified stone building.

From William P. Rogers

Camp near Monterey, Sept. 26, 1846

SIR: I was in twenty paces of the fort[1] on the 21st Sept. when it was mounted by Lieut. Col. McClung the Col. was followed instantly by crowds of the Mississippians.

My means of judging whether the Riflemen were followed by the Tennesseeans or not was limited, for I stopped but a moment in the fort to gather my men and then passed on. I remember however to have seen a few say four or five Tennesseeans in the fort— and I think these men were with the Mississippians during the remainder of the fight. By far the greatest portion of those who crossed the creek in advance upon the second fort[2] were Mississippians — Respectfully

(signed) W. P. ROGERS[3]

L, copy by Davis (RG27, Vol. 26, Corres., Mexican War Docs., Ms-Ar). Endorsed by Davis: "no. 11 Compy 'K.' statement of Capt. Rogers and Lieut. Patterson." Enclosed: Davis to Albert G. Brown, Oct. 3, 1847.

[1] The Tenería.
[2] El Diablo.
[3] William P. Rogers (1819–62), capt., Co. K, was an Aberdeen lawyer and Whig newspaper editor. Defeated in a campaign for the chancery court clerkship in 1848, he next sought the marshalcy of Mississippi's northern district and was a candidate for state auditor in 1849, when he was appointed consul to Veracruz. He resigned in September 1851 after an investigation of an alleged embezzlement by one of his agents. Shortly afterward Rogers moved to Texas, where he resumed his law practice and was active in state politics. As col., 2d Texas Inf., he was killed at Corinth while attempting to place his regimental flag within enemy lines (DNA, M-863, roll 3; *Mississippiana*, 2:2; Jackson *Mississippian*, Dec. 1, 1848, Oct. 12, 1849; Rogers to Davis, Feb. 23, 1849, DNA, M-873, roll 75; *Senate Ex. Jour.*, 8: 355; Corres., Dec. 9, 1849–Sept. 15, 1851, passim, DNA, M-183, rolls 5–6; *Handbook of Texas*). For the journal Rogers kept during the Mexican War, see Pace, ed., "Rogers Diary," *SWHQ*, 32:259–85.

46

From Daniel R. Russell

Camp Near Monterey 26th. Septr '46

DEAR SIR—

At your request I, send you, a hurried account, of such occurrences of the battle of the 21st inst, as came within my own observation—

About ten Oclock on the morning of the 21st. whilst your regiment was lying down under cover, upon the right /(left)/[1] of the Tenneesee Regt, both regts. being in front <–& to the right–>[2] of the Town, & nearly a mile to the right of the fort[3] which was first taken that morning, A very sharp firing of small arms was heard[4] <–in–> /proceeding from/ the direction of the last mentioned fort, You exclaimed "they are getting the start of us," & in a few moments your Battalion was ordered up, & marching by the left flank moved <–upon–> towards the fort. The rear of the column, near which was my company, being the third company from the right, marching in double quick time, the Tennesee Regiment being upon your left was now the head of the column. <–While on our march to the fort–> Meantime the fort towards which we were moving kept up a heavy fire <–of round shot, whose calibre I do not know–>[2] & /<–grape as I supposed–>/[2] while a large fort[5] upon the right of the Town & in front of which we had just been posted <–under lying–>[6] (under cover,) threw a number of heavy shot upon the column — The head of the column was moving diagonally upon the fort when filing to the left the Brigade was thrown into line right in front upon a line paralell with the front face[7] of the fort & about 140 yards distant from it,[8] <–The firs–> Your Battalion was placed immediately opposite to the fort, The Tennesee Battalion, Col Campbell being in a straight line further to the left.[9] <–The–> Col Campbell's battalion suffered a heavy loss from Killed & wounded <–by shots from the fort we were moving upon–>[2] <–as I–> while advancing, as I judged from the numbers of his command whom I observed lying upon the road side. The first firing from the Brigade /upon the fort/ which I observed, proceeded from your left companies who <–I–> began to fire as they formed upon the line of battle[10] — By the time my command arrived within 50 or 60 yards of that line order had disappeared & the movement of the companies in front of me was a rush upon the line. Mr Griffith the adjutant directed me to my place in the line, My attention was then confined for a time to the movements of My men under the direction partially of the adjutant & yourself <–and all–>, The attempt was made to make the firing regular, but <–it–> was futile for every man, loaded & fired with the utmost rapidity—I observed & was cheered by the presence & coolness of Mr Griffith, & by your casual[11] presence as your duty brought you near my position, You at length in 5 minutes from the time we halted (say 10, but it was quick work) demanded <–Damn it–>[2] why do not the men get nearer to the fort? why waste amunition at such distance I then moved my men some 30 or 40 yards nearer those <–in advance–> /of my then most advanced/ being some 20 yards still nearer, Twas but a moment before, I was aroused from the side of a wounded man over whom I had bent for a moment, by your voice above the din of the battle shouting loudly for a charge, I arose & saw you 50[12] yards before the general line (/2/[13] for the men were now in <–an–> a position <–in–> which they had never been /before/[13] taught to occupy in line the most advanced /being [were?]]/[14] Some 50 yards a head of the more laggard) /1/[13] with your sword upraised waiving over your head Cheering on the Battalion to charge upon the fort,.[15] Not wishing to be left I <–leapt–> rushed to the head of my <–fort–> company & found myself in the midst of your command en route, with the fury peculiar to an american charge in battle, for the <–fort,–> Mexican fort, Lieut Col McClung of your command was the first man I saw upon the walls of the fort, he leaped upon it & waved his sword in triumph. You were immediately <–be[hind?]–> /afterwards/ within the fort, I think you passed Col McClung before he left the wall, I am sure when I arrived at the fort that I was in the midst of the men of your battalion, I am sure, with a certainty that cannot err, that none but men of your Battalion preceeded me into the fort, & I am sure, that I had spent some moments after getting within the fort in silencing the guns of our own men, <–before my eyes–> by the command of some Superior whose /name/ I now forget, & had partially succeeded, almost entirely, when <–the–> I observed the /front/ wall<–s–> of the fort to be covered by Col Campbell's men who reopened the fire upon such of the enemy as presented themselves to view. <–when–> I appealed to an officer of that command to silence his men & left the fort for the city— while we were before the fort & firing from the line, the Shot /as I supposed grape and from small arms/[13] fell thick, <–plentifully–>[2] upon us. <–from the fort, & as I supposed cannon, round shot, grape as I supposed, & from small arms.–>[16] I forgot to mention that a large house[17] strongly fortified in rear of the fort was manned & fired small arms upon us. /Previous to the charge/[13] There, was firing from the chapperel between the <–righ–> right of your Battalion & the fort. <–before the charge,–>[2] I was at one time directed by a field officer of your command to fire upon those men thus placed supposing them to be the enemy, but I /did not do so &/ never knew <–whether–> who they were,

I have thus hurriedly related such facts as I now remember connected with the attack upon the fort— Yours respectfully

DANL R. RUSSELL 1st Lt
commdg company "D–" 1st
Regt Miss Vols,

ALS (Davis Papers, DLC). L, copy by V. Davis (RG27, Vol. 26, Corres., Mexican War Docs., Ms-Ar). Significant textual differences between the two copies are pointed out in footnotes.

In July 1863 Davis' personal papers and library, hidden near Jackson, Mississippi, were discovered and pillaged by Union troops. Despite the vandalism a number of manuscripts, among them this report, Russell's second report dated October 18, 1846, Douglas H. Cooper's undated report, and an undated page concerning the capture of the Tenería, were taken to Gen. Hugh B. Ewing, who turned them over to William T. Sherman. Sherman in turn sent them to Ulysses S. Grant's headquarters in Vicksburg. Duly forwarded to the Adjutant General's Office in Washington, the documents were deposited in the State Department in September 1863, remaining there until 1906, when they were transferred by presidential order to the Library of Congress (Lise Mitchell memoirs, 9–10, Elizabeth K. Kuebel; Hopkins, *Seventh Rgt.*, 110; Ewing to Philemon Ewing, Aug. 4, 1863, Richards, "Autographs," cat. 84 [1978], item 9; Sherman to John A. Rawlins, Aug. 5, 1863, DNA, RG94, Letters Recd., 288-T-1863; U.S. Lib. of Cong., *Rep., 1906*, 26–27, 132). See also Davis to Brown, October 3, 1847.

[1] Interlined in another hand, possibly Davis'; on Varina Davis' copy *left* is written over *right*. The 1st Tenn. was initially on the right, but when the advance on the Tenería was ordered it filed to the Mississippians' left and thus headed the column of march.

[2] Marked for deletion in another hand, possibly Davis'; omitted on Varina Davis' copy.

[3] The Tenería.

[4] Gen. Taylor had ordered a force composed of the 1st and 3d inf. and the Btn. of Baltimore and District of Columbia Vols. (Baltimore Btn.), commanded by Lt. Col. John Gar-

land, to make a demonstration on the eastern side of Monterrey. Meeting strong resistance at the Tenería, Garland's command was diverted into the suburbs west of the fort. There a small body of regulars under Electus Backus was able to seize a building to the rear of the Tenería (no. 3 on the map of Monterrey) and fire into the fort, an action that in Taylor's opinion "contributed largely" to the Tenería's fall (*Senate Doc. 1*, 29:2, 84–85; Backus, "Brief Sketch" and "Controversy," *Hist. Mag.*, 10:207–13, 255–57).

5 The Citadel.

6 The word *lying* marked for deletion by Davis or Varina Davis.

7 The northwest flank of the Tenería.

8 Davis estimated that the 1st Miss. formed its final line of battle at 180 yards; see his memorandum dated [December 31], 1846.

9 Campbell described his position as "about 95 yards from the North west corner of the fort and the line extending thence to the east slightly obliking from the fort so that the extreme left was about 130 [yards] from the fort," that is, from the north

face of the fort (Sioussat, ed., "Mexican War Letters," *Tenn. Hist. Mag.*, 1:155).

10 The Mississippi companies formed from left to right in the following order: G, E, C, K, I, D, H, B (Vicksburg *Tri-Weekly Whig*, July 13, 1847).

11 Varina Davis' copy reads *usual*.

12 Russell first wrote *20*.

13 Interlined in another hand, probably Davis'.

14 Second word interlined by Davis or Varina Davis.

15 Varina Davis' copy reads, "I arose and saw you fifty yards before the general line with your sword upraised <–above–> /over/ your head cheering on the Battalion to charge upon the fort, for the men were now in a position which they had never been before brought to occupy in line, the most advanced were some fifty yards ahead of the more laggard."

16 The phrase "& as I supposed cannon" struck by Russell; "from the fort" through "from small arms" struck by Davis.

17 The fortified stone building.

From James H. R. Taylor

Camp before Monterey. Sept 27th. 1846.

DEAR SIR,

Allow me to make known to you through this report all things that fell under my immediate observation during the battle of the 21st. at Monterey. Early in the morning Genl Butlers[1] division moved from the camp, and were posted behind the mortar planted about a mile and a half from the city. While the division were thus stationed an engagement was brought on to the left of the City by the third, and fourth Infantry,[2] and Baltimore Battalion. Genl Butler's division was ordered into /action/ to their support. The Tennessee Regiment commanded by Col Campbell filed by us. In consequence of the other Regiments (Genl Hamer's Brigade) not being loaded, the Mississippians closed up upon the Tennesseeans[3] A Brisk cannonading was kept up upon us from the Fort to the right of the City, and also from the Fort[4] attacked by the troops first mentioned. For before we had arrived within musket shot of the Fort the firing had ceased or nearly so The Tennesseeans passed in column to the left of the Fort while the Mississippians were brought up in line immediately opposite, and in direct line with the main embrasure— The third and fourth Infantry as well as the Baltimore Battalion retiring on the right as far as I could judge— Here the action was brought on in earnest, and continued with encreasing heat for some time. One or two of the companies were a few paces in advance of the Regiment and Genl. Quitman rode down the line, <–and ordered–> and ordered an advance alignment upon them.[5] About the time the column reached that point, I heard the command to charge. The person who gave the command, must have been very near me, or else amidst the roar of <–the–> cannon, and small arms I should not have been able to have heard it. At the time the command was given you yourself was the nighest officer to me being amongst my company encouraging them on.[6] Left: Col: McClung was the first person upon the battlement of the Fort followed closely by the main body of the Mississippians. I remained in the fort <–for–> a few seconds for the purpose of collecting my company, during which time I saw no bayonet<–s–> within the Fort, and I stand convinced that none passed in before me.[7] From there we were led on past the second Fort[8] which surrendered about the same time of the first. There Left: Col: McClung who had acted with so much gallantry was seriously wounded.

Passing the second Fort— we were led on by your self across the creek to make a charge upon the third Fort.[9] Here a heavy fire was gallantly sustained by those who had crossed the creek. The numbers across the creek were minutely increasing while you were arranging a charge upon the <–fort–> third Fort when you were ordered back by Gen Quitman. After we recrossed the creek I encountered many of the Tennesseeans filing up the lane leading to the right of the Fort. In this lane all the troops acted with great firmness, and courage being exposed to ball, grape, cannister, and musket shot from the <–street–> Fort, and a heavy fire enfilading the street.[10] I[11] would further state that from an examination of the ground across the creek,[12] had your command advanced forty yards further the Fort would have been at their mercy. For even in the position that we occupied the enemy could not depress their cannon so as to bear upon us, and a few yards further we would have been sheltered by an embankment that led intirely up to the fortification

The remainder of the Mississippi Riflemen were upon the bank of the Creek and crossing when they were ordered back. Allow me to recommend to your notice the conduct of both the officers and men under my command; who acted with great courage and daring. I cannot conclude this report without mentioning the Conduct of Joseph Heatron who fell advancing upon the first fort, and dying, encouraged his comrades to the charge. I would further bring to your recollection the conduct of Corporal Grisham of my Company who fell, under your own eye, across the Creek. He fell in advance of all and every one, advancing on the third fort. Respectfully

(signed) JAMES H. R. TAYLOR
Comdg. Com. "I." 1st Regt.
Missi. Volunteers
Marshall guards

L, copy by V. Davis and Davis (RG 27, Vol. 26, Corres., Mexican War Docs., Ms-Ar). Endorsed by Davis: "No. 10 Compy. 'I.' Statement of Capt. Taylor." Enclosed: Davis to Albert G. Brown, Oct. 3, 1847.

[1] William Orlando Butler (1791–1880), a Kentucky native, served in the War of 1812, the legislature (1817–18), and the House of Representatives (1839–43). Appointed maj. gen. of vols. in June 1846, he was wounded at Monterrey, participated in the Mexico City campaign, and superseded Winfield Scott as commander-in-chief in January 1848. Later that year he was the Democratic candidate for vice-president (*DAB*).

[2] The 1st Inf., not the 4th, participated with the 3d Inf. in the engagement under John Garland's command; however, three companies of the 4th Inf. preceded Quitman's brigade to the Tenería and attacked before retiring into the suburbs (*Senate Doc. 1*, 29:2, 84–85).

[3] Davis stated that his regiment followed the 1st Tenn. and preceded the 1st Ohio because the 1st Tenn. and 1st Miss. "were of the same brigade" (see his memorandum dated [Dec. 31], 1846).

[4] The Citadel and the Tenería.

[5] Quitman wrote in his battle report that, when he ordered Cos. B and H on the regiment's right flank to advance sixty yards, "this movement was promptly effected . . . in good order, the whole regiment moving briskly up to the new alignments under a heavy fire from the fort—some of the companies never stopping, but advancing in a charge upon the works" (*House Ex. Doc. 17*, 30:1, 15). Lt. Col. McClung noted that at one point the right flank was "drawn in like the arc of a circle" (Vicksburg *Tri-Weekly Whig*, July 13, 1847).

[6] Taylor is perhaps alluding to the

dispute between Davis and McClung, both of whom claimed to have ordered the charge. Reaffirming his statement, Taylor later wrote Mc-Clung that "when I came to make out my official report, I stated that I did hear the order to charge but knew not personally from whom it proceeded. I would state here, as in my official report, that Col. Davis was the highest field officer to me. You asked me what induced me to lead my company to the charge and where the charge began. I heard the order and saw you in or about the centre of the regiment, waving your sword and making every demonstration towards a charge. I then saw you dash off towards the fort. The charge commenced about the centre of the regiment" (Vicksburg *Tri-Weekly Whig*, July 13, 1847).

[7] A reference to the controversy that arose between the 1st Tenn. and 1st Miss. rgts. over the storming of the Teneria. The Tennesseans, unlike the Mississippians, carried bayonets (*House Ex. Doc. 17*, 30:1, 16).

[8] The fortified stone building.

[9] El Diablo.

[10] The enfilading fire came from the *tête-de-pont* at the end of the street.

[11] At this point the hand is that of Davis.

[12] The letter *c* is written over the letters *st*.

From Varina Howell Davis

[September 1846][1]

MY DARLING BANNY,

I was so hurried by the reliable gentle man who was to take the letter, and warrant to you that I fear my letter was unsatisfactory[2]— And now I have nothing to say, only to pray for you, and to beg you to let me know if anything happens to you or to Joe[3] in the battle, I don't fear defect except from treachery, and panic—

Last night I dreamed we were taking leave before a multitude, and every time I left you, you rushed back and kissed me again, and I actually waked with your kisses so warm upon my lips that I could not believe you were not in my arms. Dearest, best beloved, may God bring you these arms once more, and then at least for the time I clasp you I shall be happy.

As God is your shield, and buckler may he shelter you, and bear you up, and give his angels charge over you[4] is the prayer of your devoted Wife.

WINNIE—

I sent the warrant by Dr W. R. Holt[5] of Lexington. N. C.

ALS (Adele D. Sinton).

[1] As early as August 28 the New Orleans *Picayune* reported the likelihood of a battle in northern Mexico. First word of Monterrey was printed in New Orleans papers on October 4.

[2] No previous letter from Varina Davis has been found.

[3] Varina's brother Joseph D. Howell.

[4] Ps. 91:4, 11.

[5] William Rainey Holt (1798–1868), a graduate of the University of North Carolina and Jefferson Medical College, was a physician and planter known for the scientific development of his crops and livestock (Ashe, *Biog. Hist.*, 7:172–81). Any contact between him and Davis during the Mexican War is unknown.

To ———

Monterey, October 5, 1846.

"Before this reaches, you will have heard of the success of our arms at this place. From the bearer (Major Price) you can learn all accurately and in detail; he can say, as did the pious AEneas, *cuncta quorum vide*,[1] and I will add that which his modesty might prevent him from doing, that he played a conspicuous part in all he saw. After forced marches, a hard press being made on the morning of the action, he joined the Mississippi Regiment, in the hour of engagement and remained with the advance. I had abundant opportunity to observe him and can say to you that a more gallant fellow never stood under fire. He was prompt to enter every scene of useful danger, and was cool as brave in the discharge of his duties."[2]

Miss. Free Trader and Natchez Gazette, Dec. 1, 1846.

[1] Perhaps a printer's error, since Davis doubtlessly intended *cuncta quorum vidi* ("all things of which I have seen"), a phrase he used again many years later in the conclusion of his *Rise and Fall of the Confederate Government*. He may have been thinking of the phrase from Virgil's *Aeneid* (2.5–6)—"what most wretched events I myself saw and of which I was a great part"—with which Aeneas introduces the story of the fall of Troy.

[2] Davis' commendation was one of four that the editor of the *Free Trader* published to promote Price's election as maj., 2d Miss. Rgt.

To Varina Howell Davis

Monterey 5th Oct. 1846

My Dear Wife,

I wrote to you soon after the capitulation of this city, since then the most important event to you and to me which has transpired is the arrival of your letter of Spt. 5th.[1]

My health is very good and my ignorance of our future movements as entire as your own— The Mexican General assured us before the terms of Capitulation were agreed on that commissioners from the United States had been received at Mexico,[2] if this was half true a portion of the forces here must be soon disbanded— yr. Brother is well— My love to your parents and the young folks. affectionately your husband

JEFFN. DAVIS

ALS (ViRC). Endorsed: "copied Mexican War?"

[1] Neither Davis' letter to his wife nor hers of September 5 has been

found. After this sentence approximately twelve lines of text have been excised.

[2] See also Davis to his brother, September 25, 1846.

From Joseph E. Davis

Hurricane [October][1] 7th, 1846

MY DEAR BROTHER

Yesterday we read accounts of the Battle of Monterrey. You may easily imagine the feeling of intense anxiety with which the news was read & listened to by all parties. I came to the list of killed & wounded, here my eyes failed me, my voice grew tremulous. But Heaven be praised you were not in the list. When the family[2] assembled at breakfast I read it again, and never had so attentive an audience. Yet much as I rejoice at this victory I am constrained to think it barren of the fruits that such an expenditure of blood should have produced. All accounts are imperfect and all the circumstances should be known to form a just opinion, but scant as the means of judging are, the enquiry forces itself why after forcing them into the narrow streets under circumstances that compelled a surrender unconditionally, were such terms accepted. Such an opportunity will surely never occur again and then the *Armistice of eight weeks*, this is worse than all the rest. I feel that I am dealing with a subject that I do not understand. I hope to hear your opinion & such other matters as may shed more light upon the matter.

I have looked for some speedy termination of the war, and have therefore withheld your resignation from Congress. I have talked with some of your friends who seem very much opposed to your resignation.

Of domestic affairs, no new features since I wrote to you. James[3] informed me the night before last that he had one hundred & seventy thousand pounds picked. He still holds the opinion that he will make three hundred bales—this will be near as much as the Hurricane crop. The health of the people pretty good. The health of the family not so well. Poor Mary[4] was visited by the priest, who administered to the Sacrament & extreme unction.

I feel inclined to wait for your answer to this before sending in your resignation, and in the mean time some new facts may be developed.[5]

Some complaints have been uttered against you for severity of training,[6] but the battle I suppose will silence all murmurings, and the grumblers will hide their heads. We are anxious to hear more, to see the list of the killed,[7] etc. I told Lise[8] you had the Mexicans penned and let them go again, she wanted to know why you let them go, this I could not give a satisfactory reason for but promised you would tell her when you come home, for which she is not alone in expressing & feeling a strong desire.

YR BROTHER

Davis, *Private Letters*, 42–43. Although the present location of the original is not known, it was once owned by Mary Hamer O'Kelley, Joseph E. Davis' great-granddaughter (Hudson Strode to Davis Assn., Nov. 1970).

[1] From internal evidence it is clear that Joseph Davis' letter was written in October, not September as dated in the printed version.

[2] Joseph E. Davis' household comprised his wife Eliza, his ward Joseph D. Nicholson, and probably his daughter, his son-in-law, and their three children, in addition to Davis' widowed sister Amanda Bradford and several of her offspring.

[3] James Pemberton, manager of Brierfield during Davis' absence.

[4] Mary Lucinda Davis Mitchell, Joseph Davis' second daughter, died November 22, 1846.

[5] On October 17 Joseph Davis sent Governor Brown the letter of resignation that his brother had entrusted

to him. When the Jackson *Mississippian* (Oct. 28) printed the writ of election for Davis' successor, it noted that Davis' letter was "dated at Monterey September 29th," which suggests that Davis postdated his letter or that Joseph Davis received a second between October 7 and 17. Neither Davis' resignation nor Joseph Davis' letter of transmittal has been found (Albert G. Brown to Joseph E. Davis, Oct. 22, 1846, RG27, Vol. 42, Ex. Jour., 107, Ms-Ar).

[6] Comments on Davis' strict discipline had appeared in Mississippi newspapers beginning in August (Vicksburg *Tri-Weekly Whig*, Aug. 18, 1846; Jackson *Southron*, Sept. 23, 1846; Woodville *Repub.*, Oct. 2, 1846; see also Estes, "Miss. Rifles," Mexican War subject file, Ms-Ar).

[7] The list of killed and wounded in the New Orleans *Picayune* of October 4 was of officers only; a complete list of names did not appear until a month later.

[8] Mary Elizabeth (Lise) Mitchell

(Feb. 22, 1842–May 11, 1927), daughter of Mary Lucinda Davis and Dr. Charles J. Mitchell, was reared and educated by her grandparents Joseph and Eliza Davis. She accompanied them when they were forced to flee from Hurricane in 1862 and in a journal still extant chronicled their wanderings during the remainder of the war. On June 12, 1873, Lise married William David Hamer (1840–80), a Florence, Alabama, attorney. They later settled at Hurricane, which Lise had inherited from Joseph E. Davis. She remained there despite widowhood, debt, and floods until 1899, when she moved to Rosswood plantation in Jefferson County. She died in New Orleans, survived by her children Mary Lucie (1876–1960) and William David, Jr. (1878–1933); another son and daughter had died in infancy (tombstone, Vicksburg city cemetery; *Biog. and Hist. Memoirs of*

Miss., 1:845–49; Lucinda B. Mitchell to Hamer, Apr. 15, 1898, Mary Rose L. Mitchell to Ann Matilda B. Miles, Feb. 9, 1899, Jefferson County tax receipt, Dec. 27, 1912, Lise Mitchell Papers, and Lise Mitchell Jour., LNT; Lise Mitchell memoirs, Elizabeth K. Kuebel; Fisher Funeral Home recs., MsVO; Marriage Book II, 412, Warren County Courthouse; Z774, *Davis v. Bowmar* [1874], 14, Ms-Ar; Davis genealogy files, Ernesto Caldeira). The close relationship between Davis and Lise was ended in the mid-1870s, when a lawsuit placed them on opposite sides of a bitter family dispute (Davis, *Private Letters*, 231, 244, 332, 346; *Davis v. Bowmar*, 55 Miss. 671 [1879]; "Story of Brierfield," St. Louis *Globe-Dem.*, Oct. 24, 1886, 8; Davis to Hamer, Jan. 6, 1887, Adele D. Sinton; Davis to Hamer, Mar. 6, 1887, Davis Coll., AU).

Memorandum on the Capitulation of Monterrey

CAMP NEAR MONTEREY, October 7th, 1846.
Memoranda of the transactions in connexion with the capitulation of Monterey, capital of Nueva Leon, Mexico.

By invitation of General Ampudia, commanding the Mexican army, General Taylor accompanied by a number of his officers, proceeded on the 24th September, 1846, to a house designated as the place at which General Ampudia requested an interview. The parties being convened, General Ampudia announced, as official information, that commissioners from the United States had been received by the government of Mexico; and that the orders under which he had prepared to defend the city of Monterey, had lost their force by the subsequent change of his own government, therefore he asked the conference. A brief conversation between the commanding generals, showed their views to be so opposite, as to leave little reason to expect an amicable arrangement between them.

General Taylor said he would not delay to receive such propositions as General Ampudia indicated. One of General Ampudia's party, I think, the governor of the city, suggested the appointment of a mixed commission; this was acceded to, and General W. G. Worth of the United States army, General J. Pinckney Henderson, of the Texan volunteers, and Colonel Jefferson Davis, of the Mississippi riflemen on the part of General Taylor; and General J. Ma. Ortega, General P. Requena, and Señor the Governor M. Ma. Llano on the part of Gen. Ampudia, were appointed.

General Taylor gave instructions to his commissioners which, as understood, for they were brief and verbal, will be best shown by the copy of the demand which the United States commissioners prepared in the conference room here incorporated:

Copy of demand by United States Commissioners.

"I. As the legitimate result of the operations before this place, and the present position of the contending armies, we demand the surrender of the town, the arms and munitions of war, and all other public property within the place.

"II. That the Mexican armed force retire beyond the Rinconada, Linares, and San Fernando, on the coast.

"III. The commanding general of the army of the United States agrees that the Mexican officers reserve their side arms and private baggage; and the troops be allowed to retire under their officers without parole, a reasonable time being allowed to withdraw the forces.

"IV. The immediate delivery of the main work,[1] now occupied, to the army of the United States.

"V. To avoid collisions, and for mutual convenience, that the troops of the United States shall not occupy the town until the Mexican forces have been withdrawn, except for hospital purposes, storehouses, &c.

"VI. The commanding general of the United States agrees not to advance beyond the line specified in the second section before the expiration of eight weeks, or until the respective governments can be heard from."

The terms of the demand were refused by the Mexican commissioners, who drew up a counter proposition, of which I only recollect that it contained a permission to the Mexican forces to retire with their arms. This was urged as a matter of soldierly pride, and as an ordinary courtesy. We had reached the limit of our instructions, and the commission rose to report the disagreement.

Upon returning to the reception room, after the fact had been announced that the commissioners could not agree upon terms, General Ampudia entered at length upon the question, treating the point of disagreement as one which involved the honor of his country, spoke of his desire for a settlement without further bloodshed, and said he did not care about the pieces of artillery which he had at the place. General Taylor responded to the wish to avoid unnecessary bloodshed. It was agreed the commission should reassemble, and we were instructed to concede the small arms; and I supposed there would be no question about the artillery. The Mexican commissioners now urged that, as all other arms had been recognised, it would be discreditable to the artillery if required to march out without anything to represent their arm, and stated, in answer to an inquiry, that they had a battery of light artillery, manœuvred and equipped as such. The commission again rose, and reported the disagreement on the point of artillery.

Gen. Taylor hearing that more was demanded than the middle ground, upon which, in a spirit of generosity, he had agreed to place the capitulation, announced the conference at an end; and rose in a manner which showed his determination to talk no more. As he crossed the room to leave it, one of the Mexican commissioners addressed him, and some conversation, which I did not hear, ensued. Gen. Worth asked permission of Gen. Taylor, and addressed some remarks to Gen. Ampudia, the spirit of which was that which he manifested throughout the negotiation, viz: generosity and leniency, and a desire to spare the further effusion of blood. The commission reassembled, and the points of capitulation were agreed upon. After a short recess we again repaired to the room in which we had parted from the Mexican commissioners; they were tardy in joining us, and slow in executing the instrument of capitulation. The 7th, 8th, and 9th articles were added during this session. At a late hour the English original was handed to Gen. Taylor for his examination; the Spanish original having been sent to General Ampudia. Gen. Taylor signed and delivered to me the instrument as it was submitted to him, and I returned to receive the Spanish copy with the signature of General Ampudia, and send that having Gen. Taylor's signature, that each general might countersign the original to be retained by the other. Gen. Ampudia did not sign the instrument as was expected, but came himself to meet the commissioners. He raised many points which had been settled, and evinced a disposition to make the Spanish differ in essential points from the English instrument. Gen. Worth was absent. Finally he was required to sign the instrument prepared for his own commissioners, and the English original was left with him that he might have it translated, (which he promised to do that night,) and be ready the next morning with a Spanish duplicate of the English instrument left with him.[2] By this means the two instruments would be made to correspond, and he be compelled to admit his knowledge of the contents of the English original before he signed it.

The next morning the commission again met; again the attempt was made, as had been often done before by solicitation, to gain some grant in addition to the compact. Thus we had, at their request, adopted the word *capitulation* in lieu of *surrender*; they now wished to substitute *stipulation* for *capitulation*. It finally became necessary to make a peremptory demand for the immediate signing of the English instrument by General Ampudia, and the literal translation (now perfected) by the commissioners and their general. The Spanish instrument first signed by Gen. Ampudia was destroyed in presence of his commissioners; the translation of our own instrument was countersigned by Gen. Taylor, and delivered.[3] The agreement was complete, and it only remained to execute the terms.

Much has been said about the construction of article 2 of the capitulation, a copy of which is hereto appended.[4] Whatever ambiguity there may be in the language used, there was a perfect understanding by the commissioners upon both sides, as to the intent of the parties. The distinction we made between light artillery equipped and manoeuvred as such, designed for and used in the field, and pieces being the armament of a fort, was clearly stated on our side; and that it was comprehended on their's, appeared in the fact, that repeatedly they asserted their possession of light artillery, and said they had one battery of light pieces. Such conformity of opinion existed among our commissioners upon every measure which was finally adopted, that I consider them, in their sphere, jointly and severally responsible for each and every article of the capitulation. If, as originally viewed by Gen. Worth, our conduct has been in accordance with the peaceful policy of our government, and shall in any degree tend to consummate that policy, we may congratulate ourselves upon the part we have taken. If otherwise, it will remain to me as a deliberate opinion, that the terms of the capitulation gave all which could have followed, of desirable result, from a further assault. It was in the power of the enemy to retreat, and to bear with him his small arms, and such a battery as was contemplated in the capitulation. The other grants were such as it was honorable in a conquering army to bestow, and which it cost magnanimity nothing to give.

The above recollections are submitted to Generals Henderson and Worth for correction and addition that the misrepresentation of this transaction may be presented by a statement made whilst the events are recent and the memory fresh.[5]

JEFFERSON DAVIS,
Colonel Mississippi Riflemen.

Washington *Union*, Feb. 10, 1847. Enclosed: Davis to Thomas Ritchie, Jan. 6, 1847.

[1] The Citadel.

[2] Davis was sent to Ampudia's headquarters on the morning of September 25 to receive the signed document (Johnston, *A. S. Johnston*, 142–44).

[3] Davis apparently served as secretary for the American commission members, at least in the final stages of their work, for the English copy is in his hand. The final Spanish version, with Davis' signature, is preserved in the Archivo Militar in Mexico City.

[4] The Washington *Union* of Feb-

ruary 10, 1847, printed the text of the capitulation agreement with Davis' memorandum, the two endorsements discussed in n5 below, and Davis' letter of January 6.

[5] The annexed endorsements by J. Pinckney Henderson and William J. Worth are dated October 12. Both verified Davis' account and agreed that Taylor had concluded the best possible agreement. Henderson admitted some hesitation in accepting the Mexican counterproposals about armaments but was convinced to accede by Taylor's response that he "wished to avoid the further shedding of blood" and by Taylor's belief that the Polk administration would approve the terms.

To Robert J. Walker

Monterrey, October 12, 1846
"If any moral effect could be produced by military achievement enough has been done at this place to produce it. Here we found an Army about double the size of our own; yet we were allowed to approach through a country offering every opportunity that an enterprising officer would ask to check an advancing army; without

a battering gun, or a trenching tool, we invested the Town, so strong in its defences, so strong in its natural advantages, as to have been considered impregnable before the recent additions to its works. Indeed it is said that a superstitious confidence existed among the people that Monterey could not be taken. Three days sufficed to make them ask for terms, and the commanding officer even told us at the beginning of the conference that his government had received commissioners from ours, resorting to falsehood as it now appears, to obtain a capitulation."[1]

Autograph dealer's cat. entry (Dodd, Mead, & Co., "Autographs & MSS," cat. 75 [Apr. 1905], item 36).

[1] Another sentence from this letter is quoted in a biography of Robert J. Walker: "our Mississippians have been in a situation which tried both the men and the new rifles, and the experiment has proved them equal to my highest expectations" (Shenton, *Walker*, 102, 240).

From William P. Rogers

Camp Near Monterey[1] Oct- 12th 1846

SIR

Haveing been prevented by sickness from making a full report[2] of the conduct of the company (which I have the honor to command) before Montery on the 21st of Sept– I now ask to report as follows. I marched from Camp on that morning with 38 non,commissioned officers and privates.

The position of my company when the fireing commenced was directly in front of the centre of the fort[3] which we were attacking, which position we maintained except that we advanced upon the fort until /I heard/ the order to charge* <–was given–> from Lieut- Col- Mc.Clung (he being the only field officer near me at the time,

The order to charge was promptly obeyed by my company, and I entered the fort followed by a majority of my company 15 or 20[5] paces behind Col. Mc.Clung. Lieuts- Patterson & Townsend fol-

* Which order was given, as am credibly informed, by Col Davis in several different forms on the right. & extended up the line[4]

lowed by 8 or 10 others entered the fort, immediately behind Liut-Col. Mc.Clung. <–Lieut Wade–> Lieutenant- Wade during this entire time occupied his proper position with the Company and gallantly urged it to the Charge. During the charge and previous thereto four of my company were wounded Two but slightly and two <–severely–> very badly. We halted but a moment in fort and passed out in persuit of the flying enemy. In this chase we passed the sugar House or Distillery,[6] which the enemy had converted into a fortification (in rear of the fort- crossed the creek a short distance beyond it and reached a position 50 or 75 yds. beyond the creek Here we were /temporarily/ halted*[7] by your command You immediatly returning to the Creek, as I supposed to urge the remainder of the Regiment to follow, we being then in charge upon the 2sd fort[8] into which the enemy <–were–> had taken shelter and from which they were now pouring upon us a galling fire, This position we maintained some 10 or 15 minutes when we received the order to fall back to the right and rear and advance up a lane or street. This we did, when I recrossed the creek and advanced a short distance up the street, I fell under the command of Major Bradford, you having passed on.[9] We advanced slowly up the lane all the time exposed to a gallig fire from the enemy, which was returned with equal warmth, We advanced up this lane one or two hundred yds.. Occupying /it/ for several hours when we returned to the fort,[8] from which place we were marched out in order across the plain for a mile or possibly farther where we rejoined the portion of our regiment with you.

I would be doing injustice were I to individualize, any single one of the officers or men under my command. All acted bravely and all done their duty.

On the morning of 22sd, I marched from Camp with 28 non-commissioned officers and privates— we were marched to the breastworks in front of the sugar House, where we remained—At night I returned to Camp by the permission of yourself and Gen-Quitman. I was not in the engagement of the 23rd. Respectfully Yours &c

W. P. ROGERS
Comdg. co. K
1st Reg- Missi- Vol.

ALS (Z777f, Davis Papers, Ms-Ar).
L, copy by Davis (RG27, Vol. 26,
Corres., Mexican War Docs., Ms-Ar).
Rogers' original report was donated
to the Mississippi Archives by Davis'
grandson, Jefferson Hayes-Davis.

[1] Probably Camp Allen, where
Quitman's brigade was encamped
from September 29 to December 14,
1846. The site, near Taylor's headquarters at Walnut Springs, was
selected by Davis and several other
officers (DNA, M-29, roll 2, Special
Orders No. 146, Sept. 28, 1846; Henry
C. Long to Davis, Feb. 12, 1861,
DNA, RG109, Citizens File; DNA,
RG94, Muster Rolls, Mexican War,
1st Miss. Rgtl. Return, Jan. 1847).
[2] Rogers had written a brief report
of the battle on September 26.

[3] The Tenería.
[4] A reference to the dispute between Davis and Lt. Col. McClung,
both of whom claimed to have ordered
the charge.
[5] Rogers first wrote "25 or 30."
[6] The fortified stone building,
which housed both a tannery and a
distillery (Roa Bárcena, *Recuerdos*,
1:109–10; Electus Backus' rep., Sept.
24, 1846, encl. map, DNA, RG393,
W. Dept. and Div., Reps. of Div.
Comdrs. Engaged with the Enemy in
Mexico).
[7] Rogers provided no explanation
of this asterisk.
[8] El Diablo.
[9] Davis with a small party of Mississippians had moved on to attack
the *tête-de-pont*.

From Stephen A. D. Greaves

Camp Allen, Near Montery
October 18th. 1846.

SIR: At your request, I herewith furnish you, with a short statement, of what occured, under my observation, on Wednesdey the
23d. of September, in Montery.

[Soo][1]n after you had taken possession. of the Field-work,—in
the rear of the old Fort[2]—which commanded the entrance to the
city of Montery, Genrl. Quitman ordered me to take the Raymond
Fencibles,– Company G.— and advance upon the city, to see what
effect it would have upon the enemy, I did so immediately; and
approached within a few paces of the fortifications which had been
thrown up by the Mexicans, around that end of the City. I soon
discovered that the enemy had abandoned them; & by approaching
the breast-works, and looking along the streets, I could see them
moving on towards the Grand Plaza, where, I was informed by
some Mexican prisoners[3] taken by Lieut. Hampton[4]— they had
assembled to make the last resistance, From this place, I discovered,
to my left, some Mexicans standing upon the top of a large stone
building,[5] watching our movements, through a *spy glass*, I moved

up, with the Company, within rifle [sh]ot of the building, when
Genrl. Quitman, ordered me to halt. I did so, and remained within
the range of the fire of that building for fifteen or twenty minutes,
A Company of Tennesseans had been ordered up by Genrl Quitman
to support me, & had halted some two hundred yards in our rear.
The enemy, to my astonishment,, did not fire upon us; although, I believe, they could have done so with effect. I was then ordered back
to the Field work occupied by our troops; & did so, slowly and in
order. During our halt in front of the enemy, I discovered, a few
paces to my right, where they had mounted a Cannon, but which
had been taken away, as I supposed, the night previous, and planted
on the Plaza. Very soon after, the attack was made on the city of
Montery; and my command[6] had the honor & gratification of shar-
ing the Danger and glory. of that day,[7] As we approached the city,
the fire of the eneny was exceeding warm[&?]. I noticed, a well
directed fire was kept up from the large stone building, which I had
approached so near, an hour before, In advancing upon the city,
we were all entirely exposed to the fire of the eneny who were
concealed in Stone houses, & protected from our fire. As soon,
however, as we had passed over their strong fortifications, and
entered the city of Monterey, we entered their houses where the
doors were open, and broke those down <–they–> were closed,
We continued to fire upon them, from house to house, & from
square to square, until ordered to retire from the city by Genrl
Taylor, late in the evening, We advanced,—following *your* lead,—
within a square or two, of the grand Plaza, near the Cathedral;
where the enemy made a most desperate and obstinate resistance.
The men, under my immediate command, fought gallantly throughout the day, as did others, whom I had an opportunity of seeing.
The scene was exceedingly inspiring, when Lieut. Bragg[8] entered
the city, late in the evening, with his train of Flying Artillery, &
commenced firing along the streets, & driving the eneny back upon
the Plaza, That end of the City was then in the possession of the
Americans, who were in allmost every house firing upon the eneny,
As soon as our troops saw him enter the streets of Monterey, gallop-
ing, fearlessly, at the head of his Artillery, they commenced cheering, & seemed to enter into the fight with more spir[it] & enthusiasm. Just after him, Came Ex. President Lamar of Texas, on horse
back. /at full speed,/ with his sword drawn, <–at full speed–>—

cheering on the men, & urging them <–most–> to battle nobly for Texas & the U. States.[9]

Fortunately, I did not lose a man that day. I did not even have one wounded. I think, we entered the city of Montery, about 9: o,clock in the morning, & retired from it, about 5.o,clock in the evening. The fire, during those eight hours, was uninterrupted, Your's respectfully.

S. A. D. GREAVES, 1st. Lieut.–
Commanding Company .G.

ALS (Davis Papers, KyLxT). L, copy by Davis (RG27, Vol. 26, Corres., Mexican War Docs., Ms-Ar). Addressed: "Col. Jefferson Davis Present." Greaves's report was donated to Transylvania University by Davis' grandson Jefferson Hayes-Davis.

[1] Square brackets enclose letters supplied where the original is water stained.

[2] El Diablo and the Tenería.

[3] A group of about fifteen Mexicans had been captured by Davis and Lt. Hampton during a reconnaissance to the right of El Diablo.

[4] William Henry Hampton (c1822–55), born in Virginia, was a resident of Raymond, Mississippi. A Whig, Hampton served as Hinds County probate court clerk (1848–52). He was living in Vicksburg at the time of his death (DNA, M-863, roll 2; Jackson Mississippian, Oct. 1, 1847, Nov. 16, 1849; Jackson Mississippian and State Gazette, Nov. 4, 1853; Henry, Masons, 77; 1850 Census, Miss., Hinds, family 386; Vicksburg Daily Whig, Nov. 24, 1855).

[5] The hospital.

[6] Co. G returned to the Tenería when Co. B was ordered up and subsequently went into action as part of Maj. Alexander B. Bradford's command.

[7] The word day is written over the word attack.

[8] Braxton Bragg (1817–76), later Davis' commander of the armies, was a brevet capt. in September 1846. He led Co. E, 3d Art., at Monterrey and succeeded to the command of Co. C before the Battle of Buena Vista (DAB; McWhiney, Bragg; Bragg's reps., Sept. 24, 26, 1846, DNA, RG 393, W. Dept. and Div., Reps. of Div. Comdrs. Engaged with the Enemy in Mexico; Senate Ex. Doc. 1, 30:1, 203).

[9] Mirabeau Bonaparte Lamar (1798–1859), president of Texas from 1838 to 1841 (DAB). As inspector and acting adj. for J. Pinckney Henderson's Texas Div., Lamar played a conspicuous part at Monterrey: it was his suggestion that the 2d Texas Mtd. Vols., then fighting on the western side of the city, be transferred to the east to support Quitman's brigade on September 23. In a speech three decades later Davis recalled the dramatic entry that Lt. Greaves observed: " 'At Monterey, with a bright red vest, heedless of danger, [Lamar] rushed into the thickest of the fray, and, with the cry of "Brave boys, Americans are never afraid!" at the head of the gallant Second regiment, charged home to victory. He was an ideal Texan—a man of rare genius and tender affection' " (Lubbock, Memoirs, 609; Senate Doc. 1, 29:2. 98–99).

From John L. McManus

Camp Allen near Monterey,
18th Oct. 1846.

SIR.

Owing to my indisposition ever since the battle I have not been able to comply with your request sooner.

I will endeaver to give you a plain and succinct account of everything that occurred, or come under my immediate attention during the engagements, as nearly as I can now remember.

On the morning of the 21st. Sept. we took up the line of march <–leading–> on the road leading into Monterey, when we arrived in about one mile and a half of the city, we were ordered to halt, and remain under cover of a small hillock, to protect us from the batteries,[1] that were occasionally playing upon us, we had not remained in this position long before we heard a quick firing of small arms,[2] about one mile upon our left, very soon thereafter you ordered us down in the direction of the firing. Gen Quitman's Brig. moved off there. the Tennessee Regt. in front, your Regt. marching by the left flank; (whether the Tennesseeans were marching by the left flank, I know not,)[3] we proceeded in that direction in double quick time, running over some armed troops,[4] who they were I have never learned, nor have enquired since. We marched on under a heavy fire of artillery all the way when in about two hundred yards of the fort we commenced our fire, we advanced slowly, and fired. About this time I discovered the Tennessee Regt. was in some confusion, which caused us to get the start of them. I turned my attention to my own company, and did not see what became of them afterwards. When we arrived within fifty or sixty yards, I heard you order the charge, and exclaim about the same time "now is the time, Great God, if I had thirty men with knives I could take that fort."[5] this seemed to encourage the men, and they rushed forward immediately upon the fort. Lieut. Col. McClung ran in front of Capt. Rogers company, and called upon them by name to follow him, there was then a general foot race to the fort.— Col McClung arrived first upon the fort, soon followed by Lt. Patterson, and some others I do not now recollect.—we passed through the Fort where I discovered you. Lt. Col McClung, and Lt. Patterson some short distance ahead of me. I lost sight of you as you passed round the west end of the second fort,[6] when I arrived there I was met by some five, or six men, bearing Col McClung out of the fort severely wounded. I stopped, and pulled off my coat to bear him away, which threw me some distance in your rear, when I saw you again you were upon the opposite side of the <–stream–> stream, that is in about sixty yards of the Fort,[7] I turned up the stream, and took shelter with several others behind some Ranches, we remained there some time firing at the Fort, until we were ordered to retire by Maj. Bradford, during all this time we were under a continual fire of artillery, and small arms. We returned to camp that night.

On the 22nd., wearied, and worn down we <–had already–> started to the Forts we had already taken, we arrived at the fort[8] with but little loss, and remained there all day, and <–all–> night.

On the 23d. you took a detachment of two companies one commanded by 1st. Lt. Greaves, the other by 1st. Lt. Moore,[9] and took the third fort,[7] meeting with no resistance You, proceeded on towards town where you did meet with resistance, the remaining companies under Maj. Bradford were <–then–> ordered to your support,[10] we succeeded in getting into town, under a heavy fire of musketry—we extended our line along the street until we advanced some two or three hundred yards, where I first met with you, we were seperated again., Major Bradford ordered me to form my company, and follow him up the street. Lt Bradford, and myself with some fifty, or sixty men, followed him, nothing of much importance occurred on that day, the fire was kept up about five hours. Yours respectfully.

(signed) J. L. McManus.
Capt. Company "E." 1st Regt Missi
Riflemen.

L, copy by V. Davis (RG27, Vol. 26, Corres., Mexican War Docs., Ms-Ar). Endorsed by Davis: "No. 8 Co. 'E.' Statement of Capt. McManus." Enclosed: Davis to Albert G. Brown, Oct. 3, 1847.

[1] The guns of the Citadel.
[2] A reference to John Garland's attack on the Tenería.
[3] The 1st Tenn. marched to the Tenería by the left flank.
[4] Several units, including Garland's command and part of the 4th Inf., had preceded the Mississippians to the Tenería; the 1st Miss. also passed a group of Tennesseans cut down by a cannonball during the march (*House Ex. Doc. 17*, 30:1, 24; Claiborne, *Quitman*, 2:277).
[5] Lt. Col. McClung, seeking proof of his contention that he, not Davis,

had ordered the charge, solicited an additional statement about the order from McManus. In response Mc-Manus wrote: "I presumed Col. Davis had ordered the charge, because I heard an order; the charge was made, and I took it for granted that the order I heard was from the Col. Commanding, having seen him a short time before. At or about the time the order to charge was given, I saw you in front of the Tombigby company calling upon the men, waiving your sword and walking rapidly backwards towards the field work. . . . I am now inclined to think that I may have been mistaken in supposing the charge to have been first ordered by Col. Davis, because the charge commenced in the companies on the left, which were under your command, and you were first on the wall of the fort" (Vicksburg *Tri-Weekly Whig*, July 13, 1847).

[6] The fortified stone building.

[7] El Diablo.

[8] One of the buildings in the Tenería complex.

[9] Cos. G and H. Later Co. G returned to Bradford's command, and Cos. B and D joined Davis.

[10] Cos. C, E, G, and K came up with Bradford.

From William H. H. Patterson

Camp Allen, Oct. 18th 1846

Sir, at your request, I proceed to inform you of the action of Compy. "K." of Missi. Riflemen in Battle in the Town of Monterey on the 23d Sept. 1846[1]— On Wednesday morning about a half hour after sun rise, you left us in the fort at the Distillery[2] with two companies under your command and took possession of the *small fort*[3] that had been evacuated the night previous. about 10 o.Clock we received orders from Genl. Quitman's aid de Camp[4] to march immediately to your support. you having commenced an attack upon the Town with the small force under your command.[5]— Company "K." being the first formed and ready to move we marched off, Compy. "C". I think followed next to us. We crossed the Creek in this order and entered the Town opposite the small fort under a very heavy fire from the small arms of the Enemy. At this point we got into action in connection with Compy "B."

Shortly afterwards the Texan Rangers[6] joined us, <-&-> a very warm fire was kept up on the enemy during the day. We had only their heads to aim at as they would show them over the stone walls to fire at us. I cannot therefore state the amount of damage sustained by the Enemy from our Rifles. We forced them however from one square to another, until we got very near the *church*.[7] at which time we had orders to retire to the fort, we obeyed this order with much reluctance.

The loss sustained by Comp. "K" on this day was Private Snedicor who was mortally wounded while crossing a street, and Private Tyree who had strayed off from his Company early in the morning, & at the time the action commenced joined the Vicksburg Vols. He was shot dead, I believe in the presence of yourself and Genl. Quitman.

I have the honor to inform you that the Officers, non Com. officers and Privates all showed great coolness and bravery on this day. Very Respectfully your's &c

(signed) WM. H. H. PATTERSON
1st Lieut. Comdg. Co. "K."
Missipi. Riflemen

L, copy by Davis (RG27, Vol. 26, Corres., Mexican War Docs., Ms-Ar). Endorsed by Davis: "no. 11 Compy 'K.' statement of Capt. Rogers and Lieut. Patterson." Enclosed: Davis to Albert G. Brown, Oct. 3, 1847.

[1] Patterson commanded Co. K on September 23 because Capt. William P. Rogers was ill (Pace, ed., "Rogers Diary," *SWHQ*, 32:263).

[2] The fortified stone building.
[3] El Diablo.
[4] William A. Nichols.
[5] At this point in the battle Davis had with him Cos. B, D, and H of the 1st Miss.; Co. K, along with Cos. C, E, and G, came to his support under the command of Maj. Alexander B. Bradford.
[6] The 2d Texas Mtd. Vols.
[7] The cathedral.

From Daniel R. Russell

18h October 1846 Camp Allen

DEAR SIR—

In my statement made in my communication to you under date of 26 ult— I say nothing of the occurrences of the 21st. after relating the capture of the fort,[1] by your Battalion — Being at leisure, I will now further add such facts as I observed afterwards—

I cannot say how many men remained in the fort or the "large house"[2] (a distillery I believe) in the rear of the fort, /after the surrender/ I saw you pass out from the fort towards the city a very few moments after I entered the fort, men of your command were <–now–> constantly leaving it—in your footsteps, As I left the fort Genl Twiggs[3] I think it was, appeared, mounted, shouting, go on! go on! secure your victory &c.—There were /a/ goodly number of Americans now in the fort, but the movement was gen-

eral for the city, While under the walls of the Distillery my attention was called by one of my company, to two Mexicans Officers
standing upon the roof of the building behind the parapet, holding
up their swords, the hilts upward One of the Officers held a small
white flag in one hand, I stopped & attracted their attention & by
signs sought to obtain a sword, one of the Officers was shot, /at this
moment/ & the other darted down from his dangerous position—
passing on <–I–> a few paces, I discovered Lt Col McClung evidently wounded, Lt Kyle[4] of my company was in the act of raising
him from the ground. This was immediately opposite & near to the
only entrance, upon that side, to the distillery, The entrance was a
double gate—The route which you had taken <–& which was
rapidly being filled by your men &–> led by the above mentioned
double gate down a small hill, & crossing a creek, which was about
knee deep at the ford, led onto <–a–> another fort.[5] We crossed
the creek, which I suppose <–was–> is an hundred & fifty yards
from the 2nd fort, & proceeded some 50 or 60 steps, when the men
who were with me took cover behind a small hillock immediately
upon the road side & to the left. They were 20 or 25 in number,
perhaps, some company officers were amongs[t]? them but I do not
remember, <–There–> 10 or 12 of them were of my company, I
now saw you for the first time since I saw you go out of the first
fort, At this time to my right & rear behind a chapparel fence were
some twenty more riflemen, Many were scattered over the open
plain to the left pursuing the retreating Mexicans & some were to
the right in an old field shooting at the retreating enemy, Some of
those who had left the fort went <–into–> to the right in to a
street which is now known as the lane, There were I think when
I first saw you beyond the creek fifty men in view & about you.
You told me on my asking for orders, that we could take that
fort. pointing to the 2nd fort, in five minutes, & ordered me to form
my men. I asked you, where? you said where we stood.— while I
was engaged executing your command, <–you–> I again <–saw–>
met you (you had disappeared for a few moments,) you were
cursing bitterly you ordered me to retire from my position to
recross the creek & form in the lane, you said you had been ordered
to withdraw your men, & repeated, you would have taken the fort
in five minutes if you had <–gone–> been allowed to proceed,
The firing upon us while in the position last spoken of, that is, be-

tween the creek & the fort, was extremely hot, but from small arms alone, as the guns from the fort did not bear on us, I saw several men shot around me, We retreated to the other side of the creek, wading it where it was <-very-> /waist <-d->/[7] deep. <-"It took me", about the hips others were in, waist deep.->[8] I again saw you in the lane & <-side-> my men following me, went with you to <-behind-> a small house which protected us from <-the-> firing, There being exhausted we sat down & rested for the first moment, since we<-r-> arose from our position & moved upon the first fort—While sitting down Genl Quitman rode up, & dismounted I went to him & telling him I had been ordered "to withdraw", desired to know what was the order? to whatplace we were to retire? He told me, to stand where I was & stop every riflemen & bring up the rear of the Brigade as it left the Town— Capt Cooper with Lts: Posey[9] & Colhoun were there, & some 12 or 15 of their men, a good many regulars, some 12 or 14 of my company /with Lt Kyle/ & stragglers from several others companies of your Regt.[10]— From behind a small house in the lane which we had passed some 15 or 20 riflemen & a few musketeers were firing upon the fort.—While behind the house where I saw. Genl Quitman my attention was attracted by a sharp firing in the lane, of musketry; upon my right as I faced the fort, /I saw/ Genl Hamers Brigade[11] were in line behind a low stone wall, & firing.—They fired several vollies, & <-aros-> in a few moments, formed a column & moved off from the Town. Before their rear passed us. you rejoined us, & taking command of the riflemen, brought up the rear of the column. Here I insert an extract from My official record of the occurrences in my company book, noted down a day or two after the battle—to wit—"At length <-the-> Genl Hamer's Brigade withdrew from the Town & some 50 riflemen a part of Capt Cooper's company, with Capt Cooper Lt Posey & Lt Calhoun, & a part of my own company with Lt Kyle & myself, under col Davis brought up the rear, by order of Genl Quitman

We left the Town passing to the westward of the fort we had taken, & crossing the first battle field directed our march to some fields of corn surrounded by chapparel fences, Our men were tired down, some of them wounded, & unable to keep well up, were straggling behind the column, some of them 50 yards from the rear of the close column, <-Now-> upon our left as we were retiring, was a chapparel fence, beyond was an open plain, extending to the "black fort," or the "citadel" It was discovered that a regt <-as was supposed->, /2/ of lancers, (/1/ of the enemy's)[12] had sallied out from the citadel, & were evidently intending to attack us— As many riflemen as we had /up with us/ were immediately thrown into line, & ordered to reserve their fire, x x x x x[13] & The Ohio Brigad[e][6] had been faced to the front & posted behind & along the fence, x x x x x —The left of their line was fifty yards or more to our right, we <-ab-> abandened the muskets & prepared our little band to recieve the lancers, They came up gallantly, their fiery little chargers prancing & rearing, handsomely, We now saw about fifty of them had passed around our left flank & were approaching through the corn upon our rear, a volley from a few of the rifles upon those in front seemed to check their headway, our men faced about, & moved down towards those who had passed to our rear, Two of the enemy rode up to within about 60 or 70 yds, of us[14] <-squad->, just to the edge of the corn, They were both brought from their saddles by shots from our rifles. x x x x x x x x x— We were then marched for a reason most probably known to Genl Hamer x x x x x x — backwards & forwards (within the compass of an half mile in range of heavy cross fire <-from-> of cannon from three forts[15]—five times[16] —At length most of our regt. coming up in small detachments we abandoned Genl Hamer, & under our own Colonel were <-en route for camp-> /withdrawn It was/[17] now within an hour & a half of night, /when/[17] We were again brought out to be fired at by said cannon, by Genl Quitman & halted, He said Genl Taylor had sent for the Brigade that had done the service during the day, & we must go back to Town, We again turned our faces Montereyward & after marching a few hundred yards, were again halted & finding our amunition was exhausted, were marched to camp"—

I have written this very carelessly, & hastily, only seeking to be correct & explicit Yous &c

DANL R. RUSSELL

ALS (Davis Papers, DLC). L., copy by V. Davis (RG27, Vol. 26, Corres., Mexican War Docs., Ms Ar). Significant textual differences between the two versions are pointed out in footnotes.

[1] The Tenería.

[2] The fortified stone building.

[3] Brig. Gen. David E. Twiggs, nominally in command of the 1st Div., was ill on the morning of September 21 and did not appear on

the battlefield until sometime after Lt. Col. Garland had led the division's attack on the Tenería (*Senate Doc. 1*, 29:2, 85, 88; see also Davis to James K. Polk, Apr. 13, 1848).

[4] Thomas J. Kyle (c1820–73), 2d cpl. and later 2d lt., Co. D, resigned his commission in December 1846. Born in Alabama, he lived in Holmes County, Mississippi, and during the Civil War commanded Co. G, 3d Miss. Inf., State Troops. After being captured at Hudsonville and released, he reenlisted as capt., Co. C, 3d Miss. Cav., State Troops (DNA, M-863, roll 2; 1850 Census, Miss., Holmes, family 547; ibid., 1860, family 568; DNA, RG109, Comp. Service Recs.; DNA, RG15, Mexican War Pension Applics., WC 425).

[5] El Diablo.

[6] Manuscript torn.

[7] The word *very* marked for deletion and the word *waist* <–d–> interlined in another hand, probably Davis'.

[8] Probably marked for deletion by Davis; does not appear in Varina Davis' copy.

[9] Carnot Posey (1818–63), a Woodville attorney, had submitted his resignation as 1st lt., Co. B, in October 1846 but apparently changed his mind and remained with his regiment. Federal attorney for southern Mississippi before the Civil War, Posey organized the Wilkinson Rifles in 1861, was soon elected col., 16th Miss. Inf., and on November 1, 1862, was pro-

moted brig. gen. He was fatally wounded at Bristoe Station, Virginia (DNA, M-863, roll 3; Warner, *Gens. in Gray*; *Senate Ex. Jour.*, 11:127, 134; *Miss. Free Trader and Natchez Gazette*, Dec. 10, 1860). During the Mexican War Posey publicly praised Davis' conduct but privately was critical of his "repulsive and abrupt manner." Later relations between the two were cordial (Posey to George H. Gordon, Feb. 19, 1847, Harold C. Fisher; Woodville *Repub.*, Oct. 31, 1846; Day, "Posey," Woodville *Repub.*, 1975 Pilgrimage Ed., 11).

[10] According to Davis, Cooper and some thirty other Mississippians had accompanied him in the movement toward the *tête-de-pont* (see Davis' report to Quitman, Sept. 26, 1846, and his memorandum dated [Dec. 31], 1846).

[11] Thomas L. Hamer's 1st Brig. of the Field Div., at this point comprising only the 1st Ohio Rgt.

[12] Numbers *2* and *1* interlined, perhaps by Davis. The passage was rearranged on Varina Davis' copy to read "of the Enemy's Lancers."

[13] Russell uses *x*'s to indicate ellipses.

[14] The word *us* is written over *our*.

[15] The Citadel, El Diablo, and the *tête-de-pont*.

[16] Another account mentions only four countermarches (Douglas H. Cooper to Davis, n.d.).

[17] Interlined in another hand, probably by Davis.

From John Willis

Editorial Note: Granted a sixty-day furlough to return home, Davis left Monterrey on October 19 or 20 for Camargo, where he boarded the steamer *Hatchee Eagle*. On October 29 he and John Willis sailed from Brazos Santiago on the *Galveston*. The following day their ship called at Galveston, Texas, and on November 1 they reached New Orleans (DNA, M-29, roll 2, Special Orders No. 159, Oct. 18, 1846;

1 NOVEMBER 1846

Z618, Smith Diary, Oct. 22, 1846, Ms-Ar; New Orleans *Jeffersonian*, Nov. 2, 1846; Nashville *Whig*, Nov. 12, 1846).

Steamer Galveston, Novr. 1st 1846

DEAR SIR,

I herewith hand you a report of such occurrences of the battles of the 21st & 23d of September as I witnessed.

On the morning of the 21st the Missi. Riflemen under your command and a Regiment of Tenn. Volunteers commanded by Col. Campbell marched out of Camp under Genl. Quitman towards the city of Monterey. When within about a mile of the "Citadel" the Brigade was halted in a hollow, where we found Capt. Ramsey[1] with a heavy mortar firing shells at the City. We remained a short time and took up our line of march in the direction of the eastern part of the City, where we had heard the report of small arms.[2] Our Regt. marching by the left flank and following the Tennesseeians who marched by the right flank.[3]

We continued to advance in this order under a heavy cannonade <–cannonade–> (which cut down a number of Tennesseans and a few of our men) until within about three hundred yards of the Mexican Forts, when our Regiment was by your order thrown into column of Companies /and the whole moved by left of companies/ for a short time, and then formed in order of battle, bringing the centre of our Regt. directly opposite the fort.[4]

Then it was the action commenced—our men by your orders advancing & firing with great coolness. The Regiment still continued to advance on the Fort, and when within some eighty yards of it, I heard Lieut. Col. McClung who was near to me call to the men to follow him and he moved rapidly towards the embrasure of the Fort, mounted the parapet & waved his sword several times.[5] A number of our Regiment passed into the Fort immediately & followed the Enemy who were retreating to their forts beyond the creek. The remainder of the Regt. followed in a run, took possession of the Fort and a large & very strong stone distillery immediately in rear of it and strongly manned by the Enemy.

So far as the capturing of these works are concerned I am satisfied that it was all accomplished by our Regiment without the assistance of the Tennesseeans who were too far removed from them, to assist in the assault. On the morning of the 23d you marched out of the fort with three companies[6] and took possession of a strong fort,[7] evacuated the night previous by the Mexicans. You then advanced into the Town & commenced an attack on the Enemy strongly posted on the hospital & other strong buildings. After you commenced the attack Maj. Bradford was ordered to your assistance with four companies,[8] my own among the number. After we had reached the town we were joined by the eastern Regiment of Texan Rangers,[9] and in company with them moved down into the city several squares, exposed to a severe fire from the Barricades thrown across the streets. From our position in town we were ordered to retire, which was done, and we returned to the Fort which you took possession of in the morning— remained there a short time and then retired to the fort & distillery taken by us on the 21st.—

I neglected to mention in it's proper place that after our attack upon the Fort & distillery on the 21st, many of our Regiment passed down to the creek & several across it in pursuit of the enemy and were ordered to retire, by whom I do not know.[10] I am very respectfully your obt. Servt.

(signed) JNO. WILLIS
Comdg Com. "C."
1st Missi. Riflemen

L, copy by Davis (RG27, Vol. 26, Corres., Mexican War Docs., Ms-Ar). Endorsed by Davis: "No. 6 Compy 'C.' Statement of Capt. Willis." Enclosed: Davis to Albert G. Brown, Oct. 3, 1847.

[1] George D. Ramsay (1802–82), capt. and later chief of ordnance for Taylor's army. Commander of a number of arsenals during a lengthy military career, he rose to the position of brig. gen. and chief of ordnance for the Union army in the Civil War (DAB).

[2] A reference to Garland's attack on the Tenería.

[3] Both regiments marched by the left flank.

[4] Ordered by Davis to fill an interval on the regimental left, the Mississippians moved to within 180 yards of the Tenería, opposite the fort's northwest flank (see Davis' memorandum dated [Dec. 31], 1846).

[5] Both Davis and McClung claimed to have ordered the charge on the Tenería. McClung later sought an additional statement from Willis, who reaffirmed his original description: "I did not hear any one but yourself give any thing like an order to charge. . . . the whole line moved in an instant to the charge as soon as you began it" (Vicksburg Tri-Weekly Whig, July 13, 1847).

[6] Davis left the Tenería complex on September 23 with Cos. G and H of the 1st Miss. and Cos. A and B of the 1st Tenn.; later Co. G was sent

back to Bradford's command; Cos. B and D joined Davis.

[7] El Diablo.

[8] Cos. C, E, G, and K.

[9] The 2d Texas Mtd. Vols.

[10] The order was Quitman's.

To Balie Peyton[1]

New Orleans 1st Novr 1846

SIR

In the daily Picayune of this city bearing date 23d Oct 1846 I have seen a letter published as yours[2] containing an account of what occured at the west end of the town during the attack and capture of the city of Monterey,[3] Mexico.

In the letter refered to there is a statement of an occurrence in the East end of the town, to wit, the capture of a fort on the 21st Sept.[4] which is so inaccurate and does so much injustice to the Miss: Regt: as to require me to ask of you in such manner as you may elect to remove the impression created by this statement, bearing as it now does the sanction of your name. Very Respectfully yr: Obt: Svt:

(signed) JEFFER DAVIS

L., copy by William B. Campbell (Campbell Family Papers, Perkins Lib., NcD). Enclosed: Peyton to Campbell, Nov. 5, 1846 (ibid.).

[1] Balie Peyton (1803–78) served as Gen. Worth's aide-de-camp at Monterrey. A native of Tennessee and former Whig congressman (1833–37), Peyton was practicing law in New Orleans when the Mexican War began (BDAC; Caldwell, Bench and Bar, 241–45).

[2] Balie Peyton's letter of September 25 to John A. Rozier, a New Orleans lawyer (1846 New Orleans dir.; Capers, Occupied City, 22).

[3] The letters onte have been written over exico.

[4] Concerning the capture of the Tenería, Peyton had written that "the 1st Regiment of Tennessee volunteers, commanded by Col. Campbell . . . charged under the lead of its gallant colonel and other officers, and was the first regiment which stormed the fort, mounted the breast-works, and unfurled the stars and stripes upon its walls, amidst a perfect hail-storm of balls, which was pouring upon it."

From Balie Peyton

New Orleans 3d Novr 1846

SIR

I have the honor to acknowledge the receipt of your favour of the 1st inst: which came to hand yesterday & regret that my engagements prevented an earlier reply. You say that in a letter of mine published in the Picayune of the 23d Oct: in reference to the storming of Monterey, "There is a statement of an occurrence in the east end of the town, to wit, the capture of a fort on the 21st Sept which is so inacurate & does so much injustice to the Mississippi Regt as to require me to ask of you, in such manner as you may elect to remove the impression created by this statement."

I regret that you did not more particularly point out the inacuracy & injustice to which you allude & thereby enable me to amend the one & rectify the other. Nothing surely could be further from my wish or intention than to do injustice to the Miss: Regt or to detract in the slighest degree from the fame so gallantly won by them & indeed on reverting to my letter I can find nothing which will warrent any such conclusion.[1]

It is true that in refering to the storming of a fort on the east end of the town I alluded in terms of Commendation to the conduct of the Tennessee Regt, but I could not suppose for an instant that such commendation could be construed into injustice to any other Regt. The Miss: Regt I doubt not bore itself as gallantly as the Tennessee Regt & it seems to me that there were too many laurels won by each to render it necessary to cavil about their distributive share.

As you are aware I know nothing personally of the operations on the East end of the town. I was at the time on the West end with general worth's division. The facts stated by me were derived from Col Campbell of the Ten. Rgt soon after the battle & I <–can–> am well assured that he is not capable of intentional misrepresentation & if there is any inacuracy in my statement I must leave it to you in the absence of Col Campbell "in such manner as you may elect" to correct the same in as much as you have not pointed it out & I am not aware that any exist Very Respectfully Your Obt: svt:

(Signed) BALIE PEYTON

L, copy by William B. Campbell (Campbell Family Papers, Perkins Lib., NcD). Enclosed: Peyton to Campbell, Nov. 5, 1846 (ibid.).

[1] Peyton sent William B. Campbell copies of his correspondence with Davis on November 5, commenting: "You will perceive that I have been hauled up by Col. Davis for the statement which I made in relation to your Regt. being the first Regt, which scaled the breastwork, & stormed the fort on the 21.st, at Mon-

terey. I consulted [Seargent S.] Prentiss who knows the Col. well, & we come to the conclusion that he only wished to make a little Locofoco capital at home for Miss. consumption. I have indeavoured to so answer his communication that he should not play the heroe at my expense. . . . He is very far from wishing to provoke a dificulty with you or I, for I am sure that he heard before he left Montery that you claimed for your Regt, at least as much as I stated in their favour, & why did he not correct /it/ then, & there? . . . The Col. went to Miss before he recieved my answer" (Campbell Family Papers, Perkins Lib., NcD).

Speech at Vicksburg

[November 10, 1846][1]

FRIENDS AND COUNTRYMEN: Whatever may be considered the value of the services I have been enable to render, I feel they are now more—far more than rewarded by the approbation extended so generously by my fellow-citizens. I feel, too, that not so much to my own services, as to those of the gallant men it has been my pride and good fortune to lead to battle, this warm gushing of approval is tendered. It shall be my grateful duty to convey to these glorious spirits the approval you have expressed—to convey to them the only reward for which the Mississippi Volunteers took arms—the thanks and smiles of their State and countrymen.

It has been the high fortune of the Mississippi Regiment to add by their valor and conduct at Monterey, another chaplet to the honor of the chivalry of our State. It has not been done without sacrifices, labors, privations, and dangers. A few months ago you saw a band of patriots leave your shores—exulting in hope and youth and looking forward to laurels and victory. Few in that band of enthusiastic volunteers knew what were the stern realities of military life; and at the very threshhold of the service upon which they entered, detention, disappointment, and hardships attended them.

When they landed on the inhospitable shores of their future field of operations they did so but to encounter yet severer trials. Young men reared to ease and the refinement of life had suddenly to enter upon the forbidding and homely duties of the Soldier. Added to this, sickness in its most relaxing form did its dreadful work; and often—often did I see the high hopes almost ready to yield—the proud spirit almost discouraged by the delays and idleness and disease that unnerved them. How painful was my situation at that time! I saw the men who had trusted themselves to my care in the generous confidence that I could serve them, fretted by delays—wasted by sickness—galled by seeing regiment after regiment pass before them to that front to which *they* aspired; and I was forbid by the very confidence given me to tell them that notwithstanding all, when the time of trial came, theirs *should* be the foremost post of honor.[2] I could not tell them this, and was forced to see their growing disgust and despair. But not for a single moment in all these trials did I fail to see the evidences—did I lose the firm conviction—that when danger arose and the time for action came, the ardor and valor, dimmed but not quenched, would flame up anew—and the chivalry and bravery of the Mississippians be gloriously vindicated!

We spent the time of our delays in the discipline that was to fit us for the front position we intended to claim. And without arrogating undue credit, let me say that this time was not fruitlessly wasted, as the result soon showed. We became known as the best drilled Regiment in the volunteer army. And, when at Camargo the line of march was formed, and our regiment was at last put in the proud leading position to which we intended to assert our right, it was asked how we came to be put in this advanced position in preference to others who had moved before us, I answered, irritatingly, but yet truthfully—"*Their merits place the Mississippi Regiment in front.*"[3]

It is not my purpose to weary you with the details of the actions in which our regiment bore so distinguished a part at Monterey, nor would have time to notice all that should be noticed were I to undertake it. I can only in brief allude to some of the conduct that marked our corps, and have won them the admiration of the army and country.

It has been said that volunteers were adequate indeed to one impulsive charge, but after the noise and confusion of actual battle, would forget their discipline and could no longer be controlled by their officers. In front of the first fort taken at Monterey,[4] I disproved this fallacy; and I must be excused for mentioning it with the pride I feel. When our forces were advancing under the deadly fire of the Forts—when the havoc of battle raged hottest and fiercest—when the dying and the dead lay around us, and balls were hissing through our ranks at every step, I saw an opening allowed

by a movement of the regiments in our neighborhood, and determined to seize the opportunity to place the Mississippians at once
in the post of most efficient action. By a manœuvre and a flank
movement by companies which I shall not attempt to explain, we
could take the place desired.[5] The words of command were given
and reechoed. The trial movement had come. With anxiety, yet
with confidence, I watched the result. Coolly, silently, firmly and
bravely that regiment of volunteer Mississippians went through the
complicated evolution, in the midst of the roar of cannon and the
crashing of death-shots around them, with the self command of
veterans and as quietly and perfectly as if on a peaceful parade
field!

Others, who have been more successful in writing their valor on
paper with a pen, than on the bodies of our enemies with lead and
steel, may have beaten the Mississippians in blazoning their deeds
to the country.[6] But of one thing we can boast; none of them beat
the Mississippians in storming the enemy's ramparts; and we shall be
content that deliberate, and sometimes slowmoving truth, shall travel
behind these impetuous rumors, and finally set all things right.

It is true, we have not so many reported killed and wounded as
others. The reason is that *we were so far in advance that the enemy's shot, aimed at the body of the army, passed over our heads.*[7]
A true reckless soldier in our regiment whom we all know remarked
in the midst of the fight, that with plenty of powder he could never
get out of ammunition—he could hold up his cap, and catch it full
of bullets in a minute.[8]

After we had taken this front position covering the fort, the
sharp crack of our rifles within point blank distance, soon made it
no holiday work for the Mexicans to stand to their guns. Their
fire grew slack, and a panic and dread of our deadly aim were
evidently coming over them. The favorable moment was seen; and
tho' without bayonets—without any expectation of so doing when
we entered on the attack—I determined on a charge. I looked on
the right and left to see who of our boys were ready to follow, and
gave the word. At the very moment, our brave Lieut. Colonel, the
glorious McClung—with the quick decision and military judgment
that mark him made by heaven for the soldier—also came to the
same conclusion. Without hearing, as I have been assured, the word
given by me at the other end of the line, he gave the same order to

those around him, and taking advantage of the authority he held over the Tombigbee Volunteers on account of having once commanded them as Captain, he called particularly upon them, and dashed forward in the impetuous race for victory. The advance was now a mere question of speed. The Mexicans—poor fellows— did not stay to look—did not remain to raise the question whether we had bayonets or not—but rushed pell mell out of the fort; and the game form of our Lieut. Colonel, standing upon the ramparts, and waving his sword in triumph, proclaimed the victory.

The first fort being taken, the second[9] was stormed in much the same way; though here the brave McClung received the wound we so long feared would prove mortal. The third fort[10] was now before us, and the object of our aim. From house to house, in the intervening space, our gallant riflemen fought their way. The sharp, angry crack of their arms made no idle report, and many a Mexicans fell from his station when our Mississippi aim was taken. We were in the full tide of success, sanguine of victory and the conquest of the fort, when to our chagrin and mortification the order to retire reached us, and we were forced to abandon our pursuit.

I will not undertake to recount the trying hardships of the following night, when our men were left to guard the forts already taken.—We had every reason to anticipate an attack.—Signals were fired by the enemy in the city.—Rockets were sent up at intervals, evidently concerting for some movement at a certain hour; and in this state of expectation we were forced to keep awake and under arms the whole night. Such fatigues were enough to weary the hardiest veterans, but our boys bore all without a murmur, and only seemed eager for a renewal of the conflict; and in the morning, when, from some experience in field works, I observed that the enemy were evacuating the fort we had before approached, and the order was given for its attack; they rushed forward with the same impetuosity as before, and were mortified to find that no enemy staid to receive them, and that it was a bloodless conquest.

Nor will I undertake to detail all the incidents of the conflicts in the streets, and the heroic advance made into the very heart of danger. Through the whole of the fighting, and in all their movements, our men conducted themselves with the skill and courage of veterans, and have wholly silenced all doubts as to the efficiency of volunteers. In the scattering demonstrations of the last day's fighting, it was necessary for each man to act as his own leader, and in every moment did our volunteers evince a skill and coolness that showed nearly each himself fitted for command. In the fighting through the streets our men distinguished themselves scarcely less than in the first day's charge upon the forts; and be it remembered, that before the capitulation the Mississippi soldiers were the only ones who had looked into the Grand Plaza.[11]

The result of the campaign, this far, of the Mississippi Volunteers, is to me the more gratifying that it verifies an opinion I have always entertained, that for incurring hardships with an unflinching will—meeting danger with a spirit that holds death in contempt—and even for enduring the drudgery of bodily fatigue and exposure—the best soldiers are *gentlemen.* They it is who have a high spirit of honor—a noble emulation for approval to sustain them; and with that spirit the immortal mind asserts its power, bides the toil and suffers without fatigue, mocks the danger and death, and relinquishes exertion and advance, only with life itself. To such a band of spirits in our Mississippi Volunteers I shall bear from you, my friends, the meed for which they have bled and endured; and the hour when I shall lay before them the testimony of the approval their country awards them will be the proudest and happiest of my life.

Holly Springs *Gazette* (Whig), Dec. 12, 1846.

[1] Davis spoke at Southrons' Hall in Vicksburg to some 300–400 persons gathered for a dinner meeting in honor of himself, Capts. George P. Crump and John Willis, "and all the returned Volunteers" (Vicksburg *Daily Whig*, Nov. 12, 1846).

[2] Davis refers to the selection of the 1st Miss. for the advance on Monterrey as part of the 2d Brig., Field Div., later the subject of protest by a regiment left behind on the Rio Grande. Gen. Taylor explained that the selection was made because the Mississippians were armed with rifles and because Davis had orders from the War Department to report directly to headquarters (Smith, *Campaign,* 93–94; Huntsville, Ala., *Dem*, Mar. 31, 1847; *Davis Papers,* 2:693).

[3] Publication of Davis' speech, this statement in particular, and the subsequent letter to John Jenkins provoked a vehement response from several Tennessee writers, who interpreted Davis' comments to mean that the 1st Miss. had led its brigade's march from Camargo. Col. William B. Campbell took issue as well with Davis' assertion that the Mississippi was the "best drilled" of the volunteer units. Most offensive to the Tennesseans, however, and the subject of lengthy rebuttals, were Davis' description of the first charge and his claim to have captured the Tenería (*Tri-Weekly Nashville Union,* Dec. 3, 1846; Nashville *Whig,* Dec. 5, 10, 1846; Sioussat, ed., "Mexican War

Letters," *Tenn. Hist. Mag.*, 1:154–56; Robertson, *Reminiscences*, 167–74).

4 The Tenería.

5 The maneuver that Davis ordered brought the regiment within rifle range of the fort.

6 Doubtless a reference to the published letters of Balie Peyton and William B. Campbell, crediting the 1st Tenn. Rgt. with having taken the Tenería (Davis to Peyton, Nov. 1, 1846; Nashville *Whig*, Oct. 24, 1846).

7 At Monterrey the 1st Miss. suffered sixty-two casualties, including eight killed; the 1st Tenn. had seventy-six wounded and twenty-nine killed (Return, Sept. 25, 1846, RG27, Vol. 26, Corres., Mexican War Docs., Ms-Ar; DNA, RG94, Vol. Muster Rolls, Mexican War, 1st Tenn. Rgtl. Return, Sept. 1846). Although Davis' Tennessee critics assumed from its context that his statement referred to the charge on the Tenería, it seems more apposite to the attack on El Diablo. Compare Davis' observation that the latter's guns could not be brought to bear on the attacking volunteers (memorandum dated [Dec. 31], 1846). For other comments on the greater number of Tennessee casualties, see John A. Quitman's battle report (*House Ex. Doc. 17*, 30:1, 16; see also Vicksburg *Tri-Weekly Whig*, Oct. 27, 1846, Huntsville, Ala., *Dem.*, Nov. 4, 1846, and —— to "My dear Mother," Sept. 25, 1846, Mexican War Coll., T).

8 For variant versions of Pvt. Edward M. Cohea's declaration, see Holly Springs *Gazette*, Oct. 31, 1846, Jackson *Southron*, Jan. 1, 1847, and Estes, "Monterey," Fort Worth *Gazette*, Jan. 5, 1885.

9 The fortified stone building.

10 El Diablo.

11 Davis submitted several corrections to the reported version of his speech, including a request that this sentence read "the Mississippians *and Col. Wood's Texan Riflemen* were the only ones" who had seen the main plaza. In a postscript he noted that "'Wood's Regiment, as gallant and as serviceable as any, has fared badly in the unofficial accounts, and I am the more reluctant to omit notice of them'" (Vicksburg *Weekly Sentinel*, Dec. 2, 1846).

To Balie Peyton

Warren County Miss 14 Novr. 1846

SIR

Your letter of the third inst, in answer to mine of the first was received through the Post office three days since. You regret that I did not more distinctly point out the inaccuracy and injustice to which I alluded as contained in your published letter—

Capt Willis who bore my [Attentre?]¹ was competent & authorized to have given any additional information which you required; or had you stated to me your difficulty at our interview it would have been done by myself—

As you say I was aware that you "knew nothing personally" of what<–of–> occurred occurred at the "east end of the town".

But your published letter contains a paragraph in reference to an event which occurred in that locality & in which the Tenn & Missi: Regt: were the sole actors. The relative position of these regts: in that event (the storming of a fort)[2] was a controverted point, your statement covered the whole ground of controversy. It was stated as upon your own authority and as no exception was made of this from the body of your letter, no commander named no place designated one less informed than ourselves would necessarily include this among those events to which in the latter part of your letter you say your narration was confined.

I could not expect less or desire more than that you would correct such impression, so far as produced by your published statement by an equally public disclaimer of all knowledge of this transaction— For this purpose it was unnecessary that I should specifically present the points in dispute, they could only be settled by others—

The Mississippians claim, first to have reached the parapet, first to have entered the fort. This claim will be substantiated.[3] In the mean time it was only for you to withdraw from the position of a voucher in a controversy about the merits of which you were not informed, & to relieve the question from the weight of your authority[4]— Commendation of the Tennesseeans, our comrads in battle, could only give pleasure to me, & surely neither their gallantry, nor the character of their Colonel[5] are issues which I have made

I have not brought this question before the public & was willing that our commanders should assign to each that "distributive share" of the "laurels won" which might be due.

Should I not be disappointed I will be in New Orleans by 20th inst[6] & will be glad to hear from you at the St Charles Hotel— Vy: respectfully yr obt: svt:

Signed   JEFFER: DAVIS

L, copy by William B. Campbell (Campbell Family Papers, Perkins Lib., NcD).

[1] Since Campbell overwrote this word, it cannot be read clearly. Davis may have written the French word *attente*, meaning that his letter to Peyton called for reply.

[2] The Tenería.

[3] To support his claim Davis seems to have asked the Mississippi captains to provide details on the taking of the Tenería. He also requested statements from several other officers (Davis to John A. Quitman, Jan. 13, 1847, and to Joseph F. Davis, Jan. 26. 1847).

[4] Peyton evidently published no disclaimer of his account.

[5] William B. Campbell.

[6] Davis arrived in New Orleans on November 21. By then Peyton had gone to Tennessee and apparently did not return before Davis left for Mexi- co on December 1 (Jackson *South- ron*, Nov. 26, 1846; Natchez *Courier and Jour.*, Dec. 23, 1846; New Orleans *Picayune*, Nov. 22, Dec. 2, 15, 1846).

To John Jenkins

BRIERFIELD, NOV. 16, 1846

SIR—My ideas of military propriety prevented me from publishing any statement of the conduct of the Mississippi Regiment in the seige at Monrerey.

Secure in the consciousness of its gallant and valuable services, even without such restraint, I should probably have remained silent and allowed the official reports of commanders to reach an unbiased public.

But by the publications of others a question has been prematurely raised as to the capture of the first Fort at the east end of the city on the 21st Sept.[1] Deferring to some subsequent period a full account, I will now only present some of the main facts bearing upon this event.

In the forenoon of the 21st Sept., a part of Gen. Twiggs division[2] made a demonstration upon the advanced work at the east end of Monterey—Gen Butler's division from the positson occupied heard the firing of small arms, but were not in sight of the combattants, when three Regiments, to-wit, the Tennessee, the Mississippi and the Ohio, were put en route in the direction of the firing, which was obliquely to our left and front.

After we had proceeded a short distance, the Ohio Regiment was diverged to the front, and the Tennessee and Mississippi Regiments continued their line of march in the order named, and moving by a flank.

During the whole march we were exposed to a cross fire of artillery. A round shot raking the Tennessee Regiment made great havoc, but did not check the advance.

The firing of small arms which had attracted us, ceased, and when we halted before the Fort and fronted to it, a small body of troops in the undress of our "regulars"[3] was standing in such a position as to mask the right companies of the Mississippi Regiment. I pointed out the fact to Brig. Gen. Quitman commanding in person, and the closing or other movement of the Tennessee Regiment having created an interval on our left, it was agreed that I should occupy it. We were within the effective range of the enemy's fire but beyond that of our Rifles. I therefore executed a movement which gained ground to the front and left and when the Regiment was again formed into line, the troops who had stood upon my right were gone.

The attacking force now consisted of the Tennessee and Mississippi Regiments. The latter on the right, was directly in front of the Fort.[4]

A deep, wide embrasure (which seems to have been used as a sally port) was immediately before our fifth company,[5] numbering from the right; the piece of artillery which belonged to this embrasure was run behind the parapet. We commenced firing, advancing; the men were directed to select their objects and aim as sharp shooters. Their fine rifles told upon the enemy so that in a short time, say ten minutes, his fire was so reduced as to indicate the propriety of a charge. I had no instructions, no information as to the plan, no knowledge of any sustaining troops except the Tennesseans on our left, and seeing nothing to justify delay, gave the order to charge.[6]

Lieutenant Col. McClung led the company before the embrasure at full speed upon it, the flanks ran, converging to this line of approach, which was over a smooth piece of ground from which the corn had been lately cut. When the movement commenced, I saw Col. Campbell directing his Regiment in some flank manoeure; thereafter I do not recollect to have looked back, and did not see him; but I have been informed that he led his Regiment by a flank.[7]

When I crossed the ditch our Lieutenant Col. was the only man upon the parapet. I sprang into the embrasure beside Lieutenant Patterson of our Regiment. The defence of the place was abandoned; the last of its garrison were crowding out of the sally port at the other extremity; we pursued them, firing upon them as they fled to a fortified stone building in rear of the Fort and across a stream to a fort still further to the rear.[8]

When I saw Col. Campbell's letter (recently published) claiming for his Regiment the credit of storming this fort, carrying it at the point of the bayonet, and giving to the Mississippi Regiment the merit of only having sustained him, my supprise at such an arrangement of the Regiments, was only equalled by that which I felt at learning that the bayonet had been put in requisition. No one could go upon the ground, examine the position of the Regiments and the condition of the parapet and ditch of the fort, and the surface over which it was necessary to approach, without coming at once to the conclusion, that our Regiment must have entered the fort first, or faltered in the charge. Why this claim has been put forth it is not for me to determine. It is improbable, unjust, injurious to us, and unnecessary to our comrades in that attack, when the conduct of the whole was the property of each. As a duty to my Regiment, I will follow this question, raised by others, until a mass of concurrent testimony from a variety of witnesses shall incontestably established our claim to whatever credit attaches to the storming party on that occasion.[9] Your friend, &c.,

JEFFERSON DAVIS.

Vicksburg *Weekly Sentinel*, Nov. 24, 1846.

[1] Both Balie Peyton and William B. Campbell had published letters asserting that the 1st Tenn. Rgt. had captured the Tenería.

[2] The 1st and 3d Inf. rgts. and the Baltimore Btn., under the command of John Garland.

[3] Probably members of the 4th Inf.

[4] The 1st Miss. line faced the Tenería's northwest flank, while Campbell's line obliqued away from the fort's north face.

[5] Co. K.

[6] In his November 10 speech Davis stated that he and Lt. Col. McClung simultaneously gave the order to charge.

[7] Campbell, "finding some difficulty in getting the men to form in line of battle," ordered his captains to lead their companies to the charge by a flank (*House Ex. Doc. 17*, 30:1, 25; Sioussat, ed., "Mexican War Letters," *Tenn. Hist. Mag.*, 1:144).

[8] El Diablo.

[9] See Davis to John A. Quitman, January 13, 1847, and to Joseph E. Davis, January 26, 1847.

From J. Pinckney Henderson

Austin Nov. 25, 1846

MY DR COLN

I give you above a copy of a letter which I felt it my duty to address Genl Taylor after arriving here and finding what some malicious prints were saying in regard to my course and opinions as one of the Commissioners who signed the Armistice. If they had abused us all including Genl Taylor I should only have[1] defended the Armistice and explained nothing but seeing /in/ the Genls. despatch the above quoted paragraph I was surprized & provoked tho' I shall not believe until I hear it from himself that he ever intended to say or intimate that we made the terms without his previous knowledge & instructions yet the language he uses will bear that construction & is so understood by most persons whom I have heard speak on the subject.[2] I am perfectly willing to bear all the blame which those who are opposed to the Capitulation can jusly place upon me. I shall still defend it upon the ground that Genl Taylor honestly believed it would meet the views of the Govt   I remain with great respect your friend & obdt Sevt

HENDERSON

ALS, retained copy (Governor's Papers, Tx). Endorsed: "Gov. Henderson to Col's Davis & Worth Enclosing copies of his letter of Nov. 23d. to Maj. Genl. Taylor."

[1] The word *have* is in the margin.
[2] In his dispatch Zachary Taylor had informed the government that, although the terms of capitulation were "less rigorous" than first proposed, "the gallant defence of the town, and the fact of a recent change of government in Mexico, believed to be favorable to the interests of peace, induced me to concur with the commission in these terms." On his return to Austin, Henderson found Texas newspaper editors blaming the commissioners, and himself in particular, for the unpopular agreement. In fact, as Henderson reminded Taylor, "we received our instructions from you on both occasions of our retiring with the Mexican commissioners to draft the articles of capitulation" (*House Ex. Doc. 60*, 30:1, 346; Henderson to Taylor, Nov. 23, 1846, Governor's Papers, Tx; Houston *Dem. Telegraph and Texas Reg.*, Nov. 30, 1846).

To Robert J. Walker

New Orleans 30th Novr. 1846

DR. SIR, I wrote to you some time since[1] in relation to the position of our government towards Mexico, and also to ask of you such information as you might be pleased to communicate on that subject— You will in view of the anxiety I feel, upon every account, excuse me for again approaching you on this subject. Though others may be more clamorous probably none are so truly anxious to obtain an early and cheap peace, as the *free trade Democrats*. If our state Dept. were filled with the trophies of war, and we left free to extend our boundary wherever we chose, I should think the acquisitions dearly purchased if it cost us what we have gained in <-the-> progress to free trade.

To the Mexicans there can be but two motives to continue the war, viz. to arouse the resentment of the people and by hostility to invaders to create a national feeling—the other, to raise and maintain an Army sufficiently large to secure the political objects of those who command it – Invasion or the prospect of invasion is necessary to excite such resentment or to maintain such an Army. The people of Southern Mexico care little for the country we have conquered, if relieved from the apprehension of our further advance into the interior, they would become quiet and all efforts to increase and provide their Army would probably fail; whilst those who looked to war to <-re->generate a national feeling, deprived of their compensation for the evils of invasion must become recruits to the peace party of their country. And as heretofore I believe that the establishment of a line of posts along the Sierra Madre, resting on the Gulf of Mexico at Tampico, and the Pacific at any favorable point, with operations to seize and occupy the entrepots of their commerce, would immediately bring us offers of negociation. If it did not, As a military movement, I would still believe it the best which the nature of the country and the character of the government of Mexico present.[2] I have been waiting here eight days for transportation to the Brazos Santiago, expect to leave this evening or in the morning for Army head quarters.[3] Our Mississippians at the seige of Monterey did much more than they have received credit for, had we been under the immediate command of an experienced Soldier our services would have been noticed not as part of a Brigade but as the fact was, a Regiment often acting independently, and seizing advantages which the Genl. of Brigade saw after they had been taken.[4]

We have too many new generals, seeking a reputation for other /(political)/ spheres,[5] as you must have seen by the puffs direct which have filled the news papers in the form of correspondence, & which bear on every feature the impress of a Mexican atmosphere.

There have been rumors here which have been reported to me to the effect that the custom house officers at this place were about to start a new paper to be edited by W. M. Smyth,[6] and that the enterprise was sanctioned by yourself. I regretted to hear these things not the less because I knew the designs of the proprietor of the "Jeffersonian"[7] were so friendly towards you, that even the writer of this, cautioned him to wait awhile and let us see. To be plain he wished to commence the presentation of your name for the next presidency, and whilst I thought it advisable to defer action, I did not wish to see him cooled in his ardor, or weakened by the defection of any part of the Democracy – I know him to be so far superior to the venal class who control the great body of /news/ papers, to be so reliable in any case requiring confidential correspondence, that I gave him a letter of introduction[8] to you and hoped he would have made your personal acquaintance.

Present my kindest remembrances to Mrs. Walker— and accept assuranc[es][9] of the regard of your friend

JEFFN. DAVIS

ALS (Z659f, Walker Papers, Ms-Ar).

[1] Davis' letter to Walker has not been found.

[2] For an elaboration of the defensive line Davis proposed, see his remarks in the Senate on February 3, 1848.

[3] Davis sailed December 1 on the *Alabama* (New Orleans *Picayune*, Dec. 2, 1846). On his return he found that headquarters, moving with Zachary Taylor, had left Monterrey for Victoria (DNA, M-29, roll 1, Gen. Orders Nos. 156, 160, Dec. 10, 22, 1846).

[4] Davis is doubtlessly thinking of the Mississippians' attacks on El Diablo and the *tête-de-pont* on September 21 and their approach to within one block of the central plaza on September 23, initiatives unrecognized in Brig. Gen. John A. Quitman's report. Angered by what he viewed as Davis' insubordination and envy, Quitman commented privately that at Monterrey Davis "neither did nor was authorised to make any dispositions but under my orders, /yet/ he claims the merit of having done every thing" (Quitman to Eliza T. Quitman, Feb. 20, 1847, Quitman Family Papers, S. Hist. Coll., NcU).

[5] Upon receiving congressional authorization (June 1846) to appoint "such number of major-generals and brigadier-generals as the organization of such volunteer forces . . . may render necessary," Polk selected William O. Butler and Robert Patterson as maj. gens. and Thomas L. Hamer, Joseph Lane, Thomas Marshall, Gideon J. Pillow, John A. Quitman, and James Shields as brig. gens. All were Democrats, owing their appointments more to political influence than to military experience. Opinions varied concerning the competence of all except Pillow, the president's former law partner, who was generally seen as lacking military ability (*U.S. Statutes at Large*, 9:20; Sellers, *Polk: Continentalist*, 434–37; Smith, *War with Mexico*, 1:546).

[6] Early in December William M. Smyth announced that the *Daily Atlas* would make its debut in New Orleans on January 4, 1847. By the following May the new journal was defunct (New Orleans *Delta*, Dec. 8, 1847; Vidalia, La., *Concordia Intell.*, May 8, 1847).

[7] Watson Van Benthuysen was

editor and proprietor of the New Orleans *Jeffersonian*.

[8] On August 21, 1846, Van Benthuysen had addressed Walker concerning the privilege of printing postal lists in the *Jeffersonian* (Walker Papers, DLC). Davis' enclosed letter of introduction has not been found.

[9] Right margin cropped.

To Elizabeth Maury Holland[1]

Mouth of Rio Grande 8th Dec. 1846

MY DEAR MADAM,

It is my painful duty to announce to you an event of deepest affliction to you and of most lasting regret to myself.

Your gallant and honorable husband is no more. He died on the 4th of this month and was buried the next day at this place. Immediately on my arrival[2] I inquired for and found his grave. It is in an elevated position and the head board distinctly marked with his name.

I stood beside the grave of my late friend, and the memory of his lofty and noble spirit, whilst it inreased the regret I felt at his loss, gave me the consolation that all who knew him as I did would like myself pay the tribute of friendship and esteem to a name which was adorned by all that enobles man, and unstained by any thing which could detract from the loftiest reputation.

Capt. Holland had been attacked by measles when on the march to Monterey he continued with the army and though that particular disease passed away his constitution was undermined, and his health so bad that I applied to have him relieved and sent to new orleans soon after the battle of "Monterey." Since I left the Regt. he started on his way home and died on a steam boat descending the Rio Grande, the body was brought on and as I have before stated interred at this place.[3] A physician[4] who was on board gave him all the medical assistance which could be rendered. Though he died in a strange land he was with friends who did all that could be done to supply the tender cares of which devotion to his country had deprived him. Dr. Wilson took charge of his personal effects and received his instructions as to their disposal, from him you will learn more minutely the immediate cause of dissolution.

Under such calamity I feel that words of consolation would be idle and will leave it to him who tempers the wind to the shorn lamb[5] to sustain you under this irreperable loss. In after times it will be for you and for his children to remember with pride, that he died in the cause of his country, honored as a patriot, and soldier, and lamented as a friend by those to whom severest trials had made him known.

Accept my dear Madam my profoundest sympathy and if it shall be in my power to serve you, do not hesitate to command me. Very Respectfly your friend &c.

JEFF'N: DAVIS

ALS (DNA, RG15, Mexican War Pension Applics., OWWF 8943). Addressed: "Mrs. K. S. Holland Holly Springs Mississippi." In 1849 Davis' letter of condolence was sent to the Pension Office in support of Elizabeth Holland's claim, with the request that it be returned to her since she valued it highly; her request apparently was overlooked.

[1] Elizabeth M., older sister of oceanographer Matthew Fontaine Maury, was born in Virginia about 1802. She married Kemp S. Holland in Tennessee in 1823, moved with him to Marshall County, Mississippi, in the 1830s, and was a resident of Holly Springs as late as 1871 (Corbin, *Maury*, 7; Williams, *Maury*, 120, 468; 1850 Census, Miss., N. Marshall, family 417; DNA, RG15, Mexican War Pension Applics., OWWF 8943).

[2] Davis reached Brazos Island December 4 and subsequently proceeded to the mouth of the Rio Grande (Matamoros *American Flag*, Dec. 12, 1846).

[3] Holland's body was later reinterred at Holly Springs (Holly Springs *Gazette*, Feb. 26, 1847).

[4] John T. Wilson, 2d Texas Mtd. Vols. (Albert G. Turney to James K. Polk, Jan. 28, 1847, DNA, RG107, Applics., 1846–47, Mil.).

[5] Davis' paraphrase of a sixteenth-century French proverb, "Dieu mesure le froid à la brebis tonduc," is similar to that found in Laurence Sterne's *A Sentimental Journey* (Stevenson, ed., *Home Book of Quotations*, 789).

To Varina Howell Davis

Mouth of Rio Grande 10th Dec. 1846

DEAR WINNIE,

I have lost much time as the date of this letter will show you which could I have foreseen the events which have fallen out might have been passed with you. But let us believe that all is ordered for the general good & tutor our minds to act as becomes contributors, to feel as becomes creaturis bound by many obligations to receive with gratitude whatever may be offered, and wait with patience and confidence the coming result.

93

Thus speak I sweetest wife whilst the winds lash the waves and the waves tumble Jim[1] and the greater part of my baggage on the board the ship, leaving me expectant on the shore and anxious to ascend the River. For reasoning as above under such circumstances please give me credit. It is reported that Genl. Taylor is preparing to move towards Tampico and that the Mississippians are to go with him— Santa Anna is said to be making some demonstration of an attack upon what however is not indicated.[2]

Letters of Marke are said to have been issued by Mexico and that thirty or forty privateers are fitting out at Havanna to attack some one of our depots.[3] How true this is you know as well as I do, but the probability is increased by the palpable advantage which our defenceless depots offer.

At some time I hope to have an opportunity to introduce you to a Lady friend of mine now staying in New orleans, she is the wife Maj. McCree[4] of the Army. During the absence of her husband she remains with their children at New Orleans, and through our long acquaintance commenced at Prairie du Chien,[5] I have never known her to do an improper act. She gave me a letter to her husband and when he read it he seemed to be happy for two days that we were together, he said it had put him in a good humor with all the world. That letter was written when she was surrounded by annoyances especially disturbing because affecting her children, and was addressed to a husband whom she knew to be chafed by and disatisfied with his situation.[6] One of these days God willing I will give you the history of several of my female acquaintance, of whom I lost trace when I left the army and refound in New Orleans— When in a speculative mood they will furnish food for contemplation. I have seen several volunteers from Monterey they report your brother[7] well— Don't let the whigs find out that I communicated this to you and said nothing about other members of the Regt.[8] I could not find the Bradford letter[9] if you see it in the Room we occupied please send it to me.

My dear wife you have taken upon yourself in many respects the decision of your own course, and remember to be responsible for ones conduct is not the happy state which those who think they have been governed too much sometimes suppose it.

To rise superior to petty annoyances to pity and forgive the weakness in others which galls and incommodes us is a noble exhibition of moral philosophy and the surest indication of an elevated nature. To be able to look over the conventionalisms of society yet to have the good sense which skillfully avoids a collision with is the power and the practice I desire in my wife— With the practice and without the power a woman may be respectable. With the power and without the practice she will often be exposed to remarks, the fear of which would render me as a *husband* unhappy. This among other weaknesses which belong to a morbid sensibility I early confessed to you,[10] had I not done so you must after our marriage have discovered it. Please consult Brother Joe. and have such a house built as with his advice you desire, & endeavor to make your home happy to yourself and those who share it with[11]— Before this reaches you I hope your Mother will be with you.[12]

To all our family give my love. Tell Brother Joe. I will write to him soon.

There was no cause sufficient to justify your anxiety about the Tennesseans.[13] Farewell, ever with deepest love and fondest hope,

YOUR HUSBAND

AL (Davis Letters, Woodson Research Center, TxHR). According to the autograph dealer who previously owned them, this letter and another Davis item were acquired from an Arizona stamp merchant, who had obtained them from a local woman. She had found the two documents among the effects left behind by one of her tenants (The Scriptorium to Woodson Research Center, June 23, 1977).

[1] Jim Green, also known as "Big Jim," was Davis' body servant during the Mexican War. Although his particular assignment at Brierfield was the care of Davis' horses, Green was a house servant when he accompanied the Davises to Washington in the late 1850s. He returned to Warren County soon after the 1860 election, but when Davis Bend was evacuated in April 1862 he fled eastward with members of the Davis family, returning with them to Vicksburg in 1865. He died at Hurricane plantation in 1867 (V. Davis, *Memoir*, 1:285; Shepperd, "Montgomery Saga," 10, 15–16, 21, 25, 32, 38, Montgomery Papers, DLC; Joseph Davis to Davis, Aug. 24, 1863, Davis Papers, KyLxT, Joseph Davis to Samuel Thomas, Oct. 21, 1865, DNA, RG105, Office of Comr., Letters Recd., D-6, 1865, Vol. 2; Ben Montgomery to Joseph E. Davis, Nov. 14, 1867, Z1028, Joseph Davis Papers, Ms-Ar).

[2] On December 6 a reporter who had arrived in Mexico with Davis reported in like vein on Zachary Taylor's future movements and added that Santa Anna was said to have 10,000 "choice troops" near Victoria to resist the American advance (New Orleans *Picayune*, Dec. 15, 1846).

[3] To overcome a shortage of ships and mariners, the Mexican government in July 1846 authorized the issuance of letters of marque, and several months later enacted legislation to confer citizenship on foreigners entering its naval service. Reports that naturalization papers and privateer

commissions were readily available in the West Indies and Europe alarmed American shipping interests along the Gulf Coast (Smith, *War with Mexico*, 1:191–93; Bauer, *Mexican War*, 112).

⁴ Mary H. Wheaton (c1809–89) had married Samuel MacRee in 1829 and was widowed twenty years later. A lifetime friend of Davis', she died in St. Louis (DNA, RG15, Mexican War Bounty Land Applics.; New Orleans *Delta*, July 31, 1849; N.Y. *World*, Jan. 12, 1890).

⁵ The site of Fort Crawford, where Davis was stationed, 1831–33, and where MacRee was posted, 1832–33 (*Davis Papers*, 1:212–66 passim).

⁶ A major in the Quartermaster's Department, MacRee was stationed at Point Isabel but undoubtedly hoped to participate in battle, an opportunity denied him in the eighteen months he served in Mexico (New Orleans *Delta*, July 31, 1849; Cullum, *Biog. Reg.*, 1:257–58).

⁷ Joseph D. Howell.

⁸ The Vicksburg *Whig* and its ally the Jackson *Southron* had taken Davis to task for his letter of October 8.

⁹ Perhaps a reference to correspondence with Maj. Alexander B. Bradford.

¹⁰ Davis made a similar admission when he was courting Varina Howell in 1844 (*Davis Papers*, 2:208).

¹¹ Although Davis' stated reason for requesting a furlough was his wife's health, he may have been impelled to return home because of the strained relations that had developed in his family (John A. Quitman to Eliza T. Quitman, Oct. 19, 1846, Quitman Family Papers, S. Hist. Coll, NcU; V. Davis, *Memoir*, 1:310; Z774,

Davis v. *Bowmar* [1874], 364–66, Ms-Ar). One biographer believed that the source of discord was a will Davis drew up before leaving for Mexico; Varina Davis stated, however, that her husband made his will while home on leave. The provisions of the 1846 document were not detailed but very likely resembled those of a will composed the following year with the assistance of Joseph E. Davis. It provided that Davis' estate be divided among his wife, three widowed sisters, and two orphaned nieces (Strode, *Jefferson Davis*, 1:173–74; V. Davis, *Memoir*, 1:311; *Davis* v. *Bowmar*, 55 Miss. 671, 770, 772 [1879]; Z774, *Davis* v. *Bowmar* [1874], 349–51, 357–58, Ms-Ar). Whether or not the will was a factor, a clear cause of contention in the mid-1840s was Davis' plan to build a house at Brierfield to accommodate his sister Amanda and her children as well as his own family, an arrangement Varina Davis adamantly opposed (*Davis Papers*, 2:247). The most serious family disagreements—those between Joseph and Varina Davis—were undoubtedly rooted less in specific issues than in the character of those two people, each extraordinarily strong willed and jealous of the other's influence with Davis (Goldsborough, notes on V. Davis, Lucinda G. Dietz).

¹² Margaret K. Howell and her two youngest children visited at Brierfield for three weeks in January and February 1847.

¹³ Varina Davis may have feared that her husband's dispute with members and partisans of the 1st Tenn. Rgt. after the Battle of Monterrey would lead to a duel.

From Joseph E. Davis

Hurricane Decr. 16th '46

MY DEAR BROTHER

It gratifies me to be enable to give you the most favorable account of Varina both mentally & bodily, she has been occupied, with some little improvments such as planting trees shrubs & flowers and some additions to her Cotage, fencing the yard &c and has still on hand some work which she seems anxious to finish it seems, she is expected to Visit her mother at Christmas, and I believe would prefer to remain than to suspend her improvments but for the feeling that her mother would regard it as wanting in affection I have just finished a letter to Mr. H expressing my opinion of the evil of interupting her labours in their progress and desiring him to write to her the concurance of her mother in the propriety of her staying &c upon this answer will depend her movment, and I feel no doubt of the view he will take of it.[1] Luther Anna Bradford &c are going to Feliciana[2] on friday to spend the Christmas and we shall have none here but Mary Jane[3] & Varina, Dr. Mitchell & Jo[4] are in Madison & Amanda is going over, to arrange to bringg her things over, the river is rising and the bayou is probably navagable[5]

I have seen some of the Genl officers reports of the battle of monterey & as John Randolp[6] one said of Dallas's report[7] the most remarkable thing in it was the entire absenc of truth, some of them in which the public feels most interest have not been published Genl Quitmans to Genl. Butler of the 21st[8]

We are looking for the Message, and the opening of Congress but contrary to the opinion of the press generally I expect a Session of less importance than usual, so far as war measures are concerned they may raise some additional regts. of regular troops[9] for by this time the most unobserving must see the error in a mixture of volunteer force and regulars, mutual Jealesy & dislike will exist requiring more generosity than is found among men as they are to avoid colisions of a serious Kind. Genl Scott /it/ Seems is to take the field but for /what/ purpose does not appear I expect for the forces destined for Vera Crus[10] but you will be in possession of correct information before this letter reaches you.

Varina will wrote you and more fully of the affairs of Brierfield, the Health of the is good and things are going on slowly, more slowly than if you were there but [no very?] great omissions are known. I hope the war may soon be closed and once more see my Brother & talk over the events it has brought forth

YR BROTHER

as I never ask for that which I have no hope of receiving— I will not ask you to write to me; I well know how much of your time is consumed & when you have leisure for a thought of home, there are others that claim it— I have some little trials occasionally but as I feel conscious that I deserve to have such, I will not complain— as for instance giving up that miniature— may it be the last & may you never feel the neglect of one that has been to [you][11] as a sister Yours

ELIZA[12]

The clothing will be ready for shipment about the 26th inst— when I will forward them as soon as possible[13]

W. V. B.[14]

AL (ViRC). Addressed: "Cal Jefferson Davis Miss. Volunteers Army of Occupation Monterey Mexico."

[1] Varina Davis' parents, William B. and Margaret K. Howell, were longtime friends of Joseph E. Davis'. Varina seems to have visited them at Christmas but returned to Brierfield before the new year (V. Davis to her parents, [Jan. 4–5, 1847], Davis Coll., AU).

[2] Davis' nephew Luther L. Smith, Jr., his niece Anne Bradford, and probably other members of his sister Amanda Bradford's family were planning a visit to Davis' eldest sister, Ann Eliza Smith, who lived at Locust Grove plantation in West Feliciana Parish, Louisiana.

[3] Mary Jane Bradford, a close friend of Varina Davis' and the Davises' niece.

[4] Joseph Davis' eldest grandchild, Joseph Davis Mitchell (Oct. 9, 1839–Dec. 19, 1911). Born in Paris and adopted by his grandfather after his mother's death in 1846, Mitchell was educated privately and in Switzerland. During the Civil War he served in Co. E, 21st Miss. Inf., on John C. Breckinridge's staff, and as an aide to his uncle, the Confederate president. He lived briefly with his father in Texas after the war. From Joseph Davis he inherited Diamond Place plantation, his residence during the last decade of his life (tombstone,

Vicksburg city cemetery; family recs. of Albert F. Ganier; *Biog. and Hist. Memoirs of Miss.*, 1:845–48; Lise Mitchell Jour., 30, 38–39, 58, 104, LNT; DNA, RG109, Comp. Service Recs.).

[5] Amanda Bradford, Davis' sister, and Charles J. Mitchell owned adjacent plantations on the southern bank of Brushy Bayou (also Bayou Vidal) in Madison Parish, Louisiana. Brushy Bayou flowed into the Mississippi directly opposite Davis Bend (Lockett, *La. as It Is*, 105; Z774, *Davis* v. *Bowmar* [1874], 480, 557–59, Ms-Ar; DNA, RG77, map 519-#8).

[6] John Randolph of Roanoke (1773–1833) represented Virginia in the House and Senate during the first three decades of the nineteenth century (*BDAC*).

[7] Alexander James Dallas (1759–1817), a Pennsylvania attorney who was secretary of the treasury, 1814–16 (*DAB*). Randolph's comments have not been found.

[8] The report of John A. Quitman, Davis' brigade commander, on the events of the first day's fighting at Monterrey was conspicuously absent from the public prints. As one of Davis' officers confirmed, its not having been circulated "excite[d] surprise—and has elicited some remark" (Douglas H. Cooper to Quitman, Jan. 23, 1847, Z239, Claiborne Coll., Ms-Ar). Undoubtedly in response to his constituents' queries, Mississippi

representative Jacob Thompson called upon the president to provide the report, which was duly sent to the adjutant general by Zachary Taylor on April 10, 1847 (*Cong. Globe*, 29:2, 296, 303; *House Ex. Doc. 17*, 30:1, 1–2, 14–17). Taylor offered no explanation for the delay but may have withheld Quitman's account because of the controversy over capture of the Tenería.

9 The president's annual message was delivered on December 8; it appeared in the Vicksburg *Daily Whig* on December 18. Although New Orleans and Vicksburg papers had commented that the session would be eventful, Joseph Davis' forecast proved more accurate. A bill to raise ten additional regular regiments was signed into law on February 11 but no major legislation was enacted during the remainder of the Twenty-ninth Congress (Vicksburg *Daily Whig*, Dec. 8, 1846; New Orleans *Jeffersonian*, Dec. 12, 1846; *U.S. Statutes at Large*, 9:ix-xi, 123–26).

10 On November 19 Winfield Scott was informed that he would command an expedition against Veracruz, a plan the administration did not publicize but which was rumored widely in the press. Assuming that Scott had revealed his mission, President Polk fumed that "no doubt the Mexican Government . . . [is] as well apprised of the secret instructions which were given to Gen'l Scott . . . as he is himself" (Elliott, *Winfield Scott*, 439–45; Polk, *Diary*, 2:393–94).

11 Manuscript damaged.

12 Eliza Van Benthuysen Davis, Joseph Davis' wife.

13 Thomas P. Van Benthuysen, clothing agent for the 1st Miss. Rgt., left New Orleans for Mexico on January 4, 1847 (New Orleans *Jeffersonian*, Jan. 5, 1847; Saltillo *Picket Guard*, Apr. 19, 1847). Since no regulations governed volunteers' uniforms, considerable variety existed even within a regiment. By the Battle of Buena Vista the Mississippians seem to have adopted a common uniform consisting of "a red shirt worn outside of . . . white duck pants," with "black slouch hats" (see the frontispiece), and one volunteer recalled that on their trip home they wore blue suits supplied by the state of Mississippi (Chamberlain, *My Confession*, 122–23; Bloom, "With the American Army into Mexico," 17–19; Estes, "Miss. Rifles," Mexican War subject file, Ms-Ar). The government provided each volunteer private and noncommissioned officer with a clothing allowance of $42.00, which in Mississippi was supplemented by state funds and local public subscriptions. Moreover, in 1850 the Mississippi legislature voted to reimburse Davis for the $2,950.26 that he had expended from his personal funds to purchase uniforms for his regiment (*U.S. Statutes at Large*, 9:18; Woodville *Repub.*, May 16, 1846; Vicksburg *Sentinel and Expositor*, June 2, 9, 1846; *Miss. Laws, 1850*, 489–90).

14 Joseph Davis' brother-in-law Watson Van Benthuysen.

From Joseph E. Davis

Hurricane Decr. 30th 1846

MY DEAR BROTHER

I have but little to add <–since I wrote–> since I wrote you last week aur affairs remain much as the were at that time

Varina returned yesterday in good health and went to the Brierfield with Mary Jane and Came up this evening I have not been down since sunday.

I have removed Sister Amandas peopple and effects from the bayou with some difficulty, from obstructions in the Bayou

We have also removed the remains of poor David[1] and reintered in the bur[y]ing ground here, yesterday evening, poor David I could but think of his many good qualities his truth his freedom /from/ envy, or petty malice, his generosity, his chivalry, with all his want of worldly wisdom he was man

The Senate have passed a resolution of inquiry, & the house reported a bill for the increase of the pay &c of the army[2] it seems a scramble who shall be foremost in this clap trap. Varina will write a post script[3] to this and I will close here with the wish for your substantial happiness and safty and the hope that your duties will soon close & you may be with us

YR BROTHER

AL (Adele D. Sinton).

[1] The Davises' brother-in-law David Bradford was killed in 1844 and evidently first buried at his plantation in Madison Parish.

[2] On December 14 a Senate resolution instructed the Committee on Military Affairs "to inquire into the expediency of increasing, during the continuance of the present war with Mexico, the pay of the non-commissioned officers, musicians, and privates of the army . . . including the volunteers." A bill with such provisions was soon reported in the House but was not enacted. Only a year later, however, Congress voted three months' additional pay to all who had served in the war (*Cong. Globe*, 29:2, 30, 53; *U.S. Statutes at Large*, 9:248).

[3] There is no postscript.

Memorandum on the Battle of Monterrey

[December 31],[1] 1846

Memoranda of events connected with the Mississippi Riflemen during the siege of Monterey, New Leon, Mexico.

On the 19th of Sept. we were encamped with Genl. Taylors main Army in the wood of San Domingo about a league to the north of the City.

On the 20th Genl. Worth was detached with a division to take position on the west end of the city and occupy the main Saltillo road

On the 21st the remaining force except a camp guard was marched out to make a demonstration upon the East end of the city, which would serve to attract attention from the movements of Genl. Worth and which it was also hoped might lead to more substantial results. This force was composed of two divisions the 1st commanded by Genl. Twiggs[2] and the 3d commanded by Maj. Genl. Butler. The Mississippi Regt. formed part of Genl. Butlers Division, and with the Tennessee Regt. under Col. Campbell constituted the left Brigade commanded by Brig. Genl. Quitman

Genl. Butler halted his division in a ravine about a mile from the City and then occuppied by our shell battery. The Kentucky, Ohio, and Tenessee Regts were formed in line on the right of Capt. Ramsey's Mortar. The Mississippi Regt. was detached to the left[3] — Here the whole division lay under cover of a ridge which protected it from the Enemy's shells— In the mean time Genl. Twiggs division was ordered to the left and in a short time we heard a rapid fire of small arms in the direction of a Fort[4] at the East end of the City, and which I had discovered whilst examining the ground to the front and left of the position of the Missi. Regt. Soon after the commencement of this firing I saw a movement in Genl. Butlers division from which we had been detached so far, that I did not hear the order which produced it. The Tenessee and Ohio Regts. moved by a flank towards the left inclining to the front. The Kentucky Regt was left in position. Being a portion of the command to which these Regts. belonged and seeing that their march was in the direction of the firing, I moved the Missi. Regt. by advancing from the left and filed in at the head of the Ohio Regt. and in rear of the Tenessee Regt. claiming that position from Col. Mitchell[5] of the Ohio Regt. because the Mississippians and Tenesseeans were of the same brigade. The Ohio Regt. was subsequently filed off to the front. The firing ceased. Our Brigade[6] continued to march obliquely to the left and front exposed to a cross fire of Artillery until we halted in front of the advanced work of the Enemy on the East of the City

When the Mississippi Regt. fronted (about three hundred yards from the Fort) I observed a small body of Troops[7] before the right companies of my Regt. and asked Genl. Quitman if I should not take some space on our left which had become vacant since we halted– and as we were exposed to the enemys fire but not yet within the range of our rifles– I determined in taking the ground to the left, also to advance in a mode which would expose the men less than a movement in line.

The companies were ordered to advance by left, then to incline to the left, and then Battalion was formed into line when about one hundred and eighty yards from the fort– The companies to commence firing, the movement brought the left company[8] first into line and the firing extended to the right. Two Companies having been left as a Garrison at Seralvo we had eight on the field.[9] The fort before us was a round work[10] with a low, wide embrazure which formed the easiest entrance to the fort. This embrasure (which I think was used as a sally porte) was immediately in front of <–the–> our fifth company numbering from the right.[11] The men were cautioned to fire only when a distinct object was presented and steadily to advance firing– Their accuracy of aim seemed to intimidate the enemy, <–and their fire was slackened–> their artillery was silenced, the fire of their small arms was so diminished as to indicate the propriety of a charge. I had no orders, no information as to what was designed– The Troops who had been on my right were gone, and except the Tenesseeans on the left, I had no knowledge of any supporting force. A charge could have benn made on the right or on the left of the fort, whilst the enemy were occupied with our fire, but seeing nothing, hearing nothing, to warrant the expectation of such a movement, and believing the moment was passing which should not be lost I gave the order to charge.

I expected but little resistance, I announced to the men my conviction of the ease with which we could storm the place, by saying that twenty men with butcher knives could take it.

The Regt. was advancing firing, the formation had thus become loose, I was passing from the centre towards the right <–urging–> directing and bringing forward the men, when Lt. Col. McClung, who had <–[illegible]–> been on the left sprung before the fifth company, of which he was the former Captain, and I heard him call on the men to follow him, and at their head he dashed rapidly off towards the Fort, so rapidly that who should reach it first was a question to be decided by speed and position at the start.[12] I have said that the fifth, Capt. Rogers Company "K." was in front of the entrance, the left Co. which was next to the Tenessee Rgt. though the Capt. R. N. Downing made his utmost efforts, could not be first because they had further to go. As to the position of the men and of the Companies at the fort, I consider it the result of their position in line of battle, and as all equally struggled for the first place full credit is due to all.

I crossed the ditch with the advance of the Mississippi Regt. Lt. Col. McClung first mounted the parapet, Lieut Patterson sprang into the embrasure and shot down a Mexican in the fort, I stepped by Lieut Patterson's side, the garrison had abondoned the defence of the place, and the last of their men were crowding out of the sally porte in rear of the work, upon the parapet the only person visible was our Lt. Col. who stood looking to the rear and waving his sword in token of the triumph of our arms. Intent on the pursuit I <–scarcely–> /only/ paused to glance around the fort, and then led through it. When the Missi. Regt. commenced its charge I saw Col. Campbell near the flank of his Regt. directing some movement, the nature of which I have since learned I did not understand. and I did not see his Regiment afterwards.[13]

Having passed through the fort we found the Mexicans flying /some/ to a stone building which was fortified by a breast work of earth in front and one of sand bags upon its top, others fled across a stream in rear of this building to a Fort[14] which stood beyond it.

Between the fort which we had captured, and the fortified building in its rear I saw Genl. Twiggs, he was alone and after I passed him, heard him call to our men and in his striking, peculiar manner point out the advantage of a close pursuit. The enemy made no attempt to enter the stone building by its front, but passed on to an entrance on the right side of the building. I was so close behind the last who entered that as they closed the heavy door, I ran with all my force against it, before it could be barred and threw it open.

The enemy some twenty odd in number ran under a portico on the left side of the inner court and held up their hands in token of submission, an officer <–called out–> announced their surrender, and approached me and delivered his sword. I then passed out closing the door to prevent any one from firing through ignorance of the surrender and looked among the bystanders for an officer to whom I would entrust the duty of receiving the arms and taking charge of the prisoners. This duty was assigned to Lieut Townsend of Co. "K." and I immediately renewed the pursuit of the enemy.[15]

With some twenty or thirty men crossed the stream[16] and from such cover as the ground afforded opened a fire on the fort to which the enemy had fled. Our position was favorable, the enemy having no artillery posted to bear upon it, and our advance upon the fort in the direction of its gorge would have been sheltered for a great part of the way by the natural declivity of the ground, so as to compel the enemy in firing upon us in the then condition of his wall to expose a great part of his person[17]

I was standing in the road near the ford calling and making signals to the men in rear to follow me when I received an order from Genl. Quitman through his aid de Camp Lieut Nichols,[18] directing me to retire, and soon afterwards Genl. Quitman came in person and rode into the stream whence he called to me to renew the order

I believed then as now that the enemy were panic stricken, and that the men who were coming to me with those already across the stream would have taken the fort with very little loss, I obeyed the order reluctantly, as did the men who were with me; but cannot censure an order which could spring alone from a desire to save our men and a belief, though never realised, that the same end could be more easily attained.[19] After recrossing the stream, as directed we moved through a street to the right, where we again joined the ohio Regt. posted under a deadly fire and so far as I could see without any commensurate advantage in the position. Here Col. Mitchell fell severely wounded a<–n–> moment after having given me his congratulation on my safety, here <–Genl. B–> and very nearly at the same time, Genl. Butler was wounded, and

<–From this position with all of as many of my Regt. as I could collect I moved to the right–> here we lost a number of men especially from the ohio Regt. Though the works of the enemy[20] were detached, their relation to each other gave to this position the dis advantages which would belong to attacking the curtain of a bastion front. After a hasty examination I indicated to Genl. Butler a route by which the salient on our right[21] could be attacked, <–he seemed–> he seemed preoccupied, and after speaking to the other Genls. on the ground I called the attention of Inspector Genl. /A. S./ Johnston to the movement I proposed, he suggested to me to commence it, with as many of my Regt. as I could collect,[22] we

proceeded to the right a short distance, when we met Capt. Field (accompanied by but one man) he <-told-> had discovered a party of the enemy moving on our rear, and led us to their position, though at least three times our number we attacked them and drove them back until they crossed a street[23] enfiladed by the Tete du pont which was the salient of the system of works we were attacking. Here we were joined by Maj. Mansfield of the Engrs. with a party of the 1st U. S. Infy. <-and determined-> Capt. Cooper the senior officer <-of our Regt.-> with me was placed with the men of our Regt. in a stone house /on the left side of the street/[24] to pick off the enemy whenever he appeared above his parapet. Maj. Mansfield selected the opposite side of the street and commenced cautiously crossing his men over to advance on the right whilst we advanced on the left side of the street. At this time Genl. Hamer /division commander Genl. Butler having left the field/ came up /with a large body of volunteers/ and directed us to retire. Against the advice of Maj. Mansfield and my own opinion distinctly expressed, but as I have understood by the consent of his Comdg. Genl.[25] he withdrew the Troops from this position. We were now conducted a half mile or more to the rear. When passing out of a corn field the line was threatened by the Enemy's cavalry. The Mississippians were in rear, the exertions of the day had been so severe that when the Troops in front of us began to move rapidly to form under cover of a brush fence, our men could /not/ keep up with them. A detachment of the enemy's cavalry say fifty men dashed over the broken fence in our rear and attacked two persons who were in the corn behind us— I called on the men of my Regt. to return and make a counter attack <-upon-> they did so with their usual spirit and drove the enemy back, killing four of his men. After various countermarches we were joined by Genl. Quitman, the Brigades were reorganized as well as might be and we took a position to which ammunition was directed, but before the arrival of the Rifle cartridges, were marched back to our Encampment.

On the 22d with the Tenessee Regt. <-the-> we marched to the fort captured the day previous, and relieved Col. Garlands Brigade[26] which had held the place from the evening of the 21st.

The Tenessee Regt. commanded by its Lt. Col. Anderson took post in the Round Fort — The Mississippi Regt. held the work in rear[27] and the stone building to which it was attached. We had gone

out without preperation, and remained, without food or other than
the very light clothing we wore, <–watching–> through the night
<–which because–> exposed to a severe north<–er–> wind and
penetrating rain. It was too dark to see any thing except the signal
Rockets and fires of the enemy,– but we could from time to time
hear cavalry moving, and [ow]ing[28] the great superiority in numbers w[hic]h the enemy possessed over us, and his [in]timate knowledge of all the approaches <–around us–> were kept constantly
on the alert. At day break I saw enough to convince me that the
enemy were withdrawing from the works near us, but couldnt[29]
perceive that he had removed his artillery this was communicated
to Brig. Genl. Quitman Comdg. and I was sent out with two Missi.
and two Tenn. companies[30] to reconnoitre and gain any advantage
which should be offered. We passed to the right and crossing a
deep irrigating canal entered the gorge of the Fort known as "del
Diablo" and found it evacuated.

With Lieut Scarrett of the Engineers /and a small party of Rifle-
men/ I examined the proximate flanking works, & agreed with /him/
that they were untenable in their then condition, but with slight
labor and some pieces of artillery could be made very available in
future operations— /<–We took some thirty prisoners, who
claimed to be peasants–>/ This report I made to Genl Quitman
whom I found on my return to the "Fuerte del diablo", and Lt.
Scarrett went to report to Genl. Taylor. /During this reconnoissance we took some thirty prisoners[31] who said they were peasants/

My reconnoissance was extended to the left[32]– the command was
changed to three Missi.[33] and one Tenn. Companies. Lt. Col. Anderson remained in charge of the Fort del Diablo,[34] and I advanced
upon the flanking works to the left, until fired on by the enemy
who seemed to be advancing to dispute the possession of a barricade
on which I was standing[35] [My] command formed on the reverse
[side] of the barricade and drove the contendin[g pa]rty back
with a reported loss of fo[urtee]n— We lost one Mississippian
than whom /there was/ none more gallant.[36] We were still exposed to a fire from a building[37] which was beyond the range of
our rifles and known to be occupied by a large force— I therefore
withdrew the men placed them under cover and awaited the arrival
of reinforcements. The remainder of the Mississippi Regt. (except
one company on duty in the rear) came up,[38] a part of Col. Woods

Regt. of Texan Rangers having dismounted joined us as Riflemen, we now advanced into the Town, from house to house passing generally through the court yards and driving the enemy steadily back from house tops, eack of which formed a place for attack and furnished a very secure defence— The advance was composed in about equal numbers of Mississippians and Texans and we were abreast of the Main plaza[39] <-when-> on the evening of the 23d when we received orders to retire — I /had/ sent the sergt. Major[40] of the Missi. Regt. back to find Genl. Quitman, and that portion of the Regt. which I had left with Maj. Bradford, to inquire also what had become of the peice of artillery which had been sent to cooperate with me[41]— He returned and informed me that orders had been sent some time before to Genl. Henderson and myself to withdraw and that all the Troops in our rear had retired.[42] [Abou]t this time we were engaged in fo[rmi]ng a barricade to cross a street which wa[s li]tterally swept by fire of both artillery and [s]mall arms, this we had nearly complete[d u]sing such material as was found in the neighboring houses, and it had been agreed between Genl. Henderson comdg. the ad[v]ance of Col. Woods Texan Regt. and myself, with the advance of the Mississippi Riflemen, that we would take possession of a stone house in our front, which from its <-great-> height would enable us to fire down into the main plaza, in which the great body of the /enemy's/ Troops had been collected, <-and where-> /In that building/ we had determined to pass the night. It is to be attributed to the fact that we were so far in advance that but little was known of the advantages we had gained that the order to withdraw was sent to us.

    <-The enemy had when driven back from his advanced positions uniformly removed his artillery->

    To this may be added the influence which reports of sorties against us, and false rumors of the loss we were sustaining /must have produced./ The enemy did not again take possession of the advanced positions from which he had been driven, probably because, they had withdrawn their artillery and feared again to risk it, or to go out without it, therefore our withdrawal<-l-> had no evil consequences

    On the morning of the 24th a flag [of t]ruce was sent in by the Mexican [com]mander,[43] to ask for terms of capitula[tion] A conference was granted and [the w]ell known capitulation was the [resul]t. <–[illegible]–> As to the wisdom of the [course a]dopted in this capitulation men [did an]d probably will differ, for myself, [I approve]d it when it /was/ done, and now [reviewing it a]fter the fact, I can see much [to con]firm me in the view I originally [took]. We gained possession of a fort large [an]d well constructed,[44] we had neither [a ba]ttering train nor trenching tools, to re-[d]uce it, to carry the work by storm must have cost us many men when we had not one to spare. We gained a large amount of powder and fixed ammunition, much of this was stored in the main cathedral, and the fire of our mortars[45] must have produced an explosion of the magazine directed against that building must have produced an explosion, which would have destroyed the ammunition, a great number of houses which have been useful to us, and with the enemys troops in the plaza, must have destroyed many of the advance of our own forces.

JEFFN. DAVIS

ADS (Ricks Coll., IHi). DS (Z777f, Davis Papers, Ms-Ar). The Mississippi Archives version, copied in part by Davis' wife and daughter, bears an endorsement signed by Davis and dated April 6, 1885: "The forgoing . . . is a copy of a memorandum, made by me in 1846. . . . It was, with other papers lost when my library was pillaged from the place where it /was/ deposited in Hinds Co Missi for safety during the war between the States. . . . In the month of Jan last, the Revd F[rank] M. Bristol, of Chicago. Illinois, informed me that he had possession of a paper which he described purporting to have been written by me and which he desired to have verified. . . . I asked Mr Bristol to send the paper to me for verification or condemnation, also requesting, if it was a true paper, that I might be permitted to copy it. With his assent, the foregoing copy has been made and the original returned to him as an innocent holder." Within months after it was purloined in 1863, the manuscript was displayed at the Great Western Sanitary Fair in Cincinnati, one of four Davis items donated by Thomas M. Hunter, a former officer of the 1st Ohio Vol. Inf. On March 15, 1864, the memorandum was purchased at auction by Joseph P. Leavitt of Cincinnati for $5.25. When the document was acquired by Bristol is not known; it was accessioned by the Illinois State Historical Library as part of the Jesse J. Ricks autograph collection in 1937 (Boynton, comp., *Sanitary Fair*, 426–27, 439, 546; *Ohio Roster*, 1:3; Bristol to Davis, Jan. 17, Feb. 14, 1885, ViRC; *NCAB*, 25:406–407; IHi to Davis Assn., June 2, 1978).

[1] The manuscript is dated only "1846."
[2] Twiggs's division was commanded by John Garland on the morning of September 21.
[3] Ramsay had advised Davis to move the 1st Miss. from its position behind the mortar in order to avoid enemy fire (Carrollton *Miss. Dem.*, Jan. 6, 1847).
[4] The Tenería.
[5] Alexander Mebane Mitchell

(c1813–61), an 1835 West Point graduate and veteran of the Seminole wars, left the army in 1837 and after several years as an engineer opened a law practice in Cincinnati. Severely wounded at Monterrey, he recovered to serve as military governor of the city in 1847. In 1850–51 he was marshal of the Minnesota Territory (Cullum, *Biog. Reg.*, 1:615; *Senate Ex. Jour.*, 8:134, 170, 293; DNA, RG15, Mexican War Pension Applics., OWWF 27796).

6 The letters *Bri* are written over *Mis.*

7 Probably members of the 4th Inf.

8 Co. G.

9 Cos. A and F remained in garrison at Cerralvo until October 31.

10 Although others besides Davis mentioned that the Tenería was round, a plan published in an account by one of the Mexican defenders shows it was polygonal (reports of Douglas H. Cooper and Carnot Posey, n.d.; Balbontín, *Invasión Americana*, 29).

11 Co. K.

12 For McClung's rebuttal of Davis' statement that speed and position determined who entered the Tenería first, see Vicksburg *Tri-Weekly Whig*, July 13, 1847.

13 A reference to the controversy between the 1st Miss. and 1st Tenn. over capture of the Tenería.

14 El Diablo.

15 McClung, noting "some difference of opinion between Col. Davis and myself, as to the occurrences at the distillery," published statements to the effect that he had preceded Davis into the building (Vicksburg *Tri-Weekly Whig*, July 13, 1847).

16 Davis was reportedly "mortified that more of the men" had not followed him across the stream (Vicksburg *Weekly Sentinel*, Nov. 3, 1846).

17 Two of Davis' captains echoed his conviction that the position before El Diablo was an advantageous one; see the reports of James H. R. Taylor

and Daniel R. Russell, September 27 and October 18, 1846.

18 William Augustus Nichols (c1818–69), Quitman's aide from August to early October 1846, subsequently served with Winfield Scott. A West Point graduate and career army officer, he was assigned to the Adjutant General's Office during the 1850s and 1860s; he was William T. Sherman's chief of staff, 1866–69 (Cullum, *Biog. Reg.*, 1:707–709; Heitman, *Hist. Reg.*, 1:747).

19 Less charitably, Davis wrote in 1875 that Quitman had "wholly misconceived the case" in ordering the withdrawal from El Diablo (notes on Monterrey, Apr. 18, [1875], Barret Coll. of Johnston Papers, LNT). For other evidence of Davis' disappointment at being called back, see Z618, Smith Diary, October 22, 1846, Ms-Ar, and Walthall, *Davis*, 18.

20 El Diablo and the *tête-de-pont*.

21 The *tête-de-pont*.

22 In another account Davis wrote that he "approached General Johnston, and told him I had been recalled when about to take the salient on our left, that we were uselessly exposed where we were, and said, 'If not the left, then let the right salient be attacked.' He answered, with his usual calm manner and quick perception, 'We cannot get any orders, but if you will move your regiment to the right place the rest may follow you.'" That Butler, Hamer, and Quitman insisted on remaining in the lane Davis found inexplicable: "Genl Butler and Col. Mitchell were both wounded in that position to which I offered objections in the remarks made to [Johnston]. Why they huddled men together where they could'nt inflict any injury on the Enemy and where the Enemy's artillery bore on them, must be answered by those who can justify the selection of politicians rather than tried soldiers for the command of troops" (Johnston, *A. S. Johnston*, 138–39;

Davis, notes on Monterrey, Apr. 18, [1875], Barret Coll. of Johnston Papers, LNT).

[23] The street running north from the Purísima bridge.

[24] See no. 5 on the map of Monterrey.

[25] Zachary Taylor.

[26] The infantry units of the 1st Div., along with Randolph Ridgely's battery and the 1st Ky., held the Tenería complex under Garland's command (*Senate Doc. 1*, 29:2, 86).

[27] A redan resting on the fortified stone building.

[28] Square brackets indicate letters or words written in at a later date where the original manuscript is damaged. Most of the missing material appears to have been added by Davis himself, perhaps when he examined the manuscript in 1885. In this case only the added letters *ow* are visible; in her copy Varina Davis transcribed the word *owing*.

[29] The letters *nt* are in the margin, added in an unknown hand.

[30] Cos. G and H of the 1st Miss. and A and B of the 1st Tenn.

[31] Since Davis states in another account that he took fifteen prisoners while reconnoitering to the right, this statement perhaps includes the Mexicans occupying El Diablo when it was captured (Davis to Albert G. Brown, Sept. 20, 1847).

[32] Accompanied by Lt. William H.

Hampton, Davis examined the works along the eastern edge of the city.

[33] Cos. B, D, and H; Co. G was sent back to Bradford's command.

[34] Anderson was later ordered to return to the Tenería (*House Ex. Doc. 17*, 30:1, 28).

[35] See no. 11 on the map of Monterrey.

[36] Pvt. John M. Tyree.

[37] Probably the hospital.

[38] Maj. Bradford brought up Cos. C, E, G, and K. When the regiment was reunited, a portion joined Davis and the rest remained with Bradford. Co. I was left to guard El Diablo.

[39] See no. 13 on the map of Monterrey.

[40] Charles T. Harlan.

[41] Two of Braxton Bragg's guns had been withdrawn about three o'clock (Bragg's report, Sept. 26, 1846, DNA, RG393, W. Dept. and Div., Reports of Div. Comdrs. Engaged with the Enemy in Mexico).

[42] Davis later commented that, although he and Henderson considered it more dangerous to retire than to remain, they obeyed the order (Sexton, "Henderson," *Texas Hist. Quar.* [*SWHQ*], 1:196).

[43] Pedro Ampudia.

[44] The Citadel.

[45] The mortar, transferred to Worth's command on September 23, had begun to fire on the main plaza by sunset (*Senate Doc. 1*, 29:2, 106).

To Thomas Ritchie

VICTORIA,[1] TAMAULIPAS, MEXICO,
January 6, 1847.

DEAR SIR: After much speculation and no little misrepresentation about the capitulation of Monterey, I perceive by our recent newspapers, that a discussion has arisen as to who is responsible for that transaction.[2] As one of the commissioners who were entrusted by General Taylor with the arrangement of the terms upon which the city of Monterey and its fortifications should be delivered to our forces, I have had frequent occasion to recur to the course then adopted, and the considerations which led to it. My judgment after the fact has fully sustained my decisions at the date of the occurrence; and feeling myself responsible for the instrument as we prepared and presented it to our commanding general, I have the satisfaction, after all subsequent events, to believe that the terms we offered were expedient, and honorable, and wise. A distinguished gentleman with whom I acted on that commission, Governor Henderson, says, in a recently published letter,[3] "I did not at the time, nor do I still like the terms, but acted as one of the commissioners, together with General Worth and Colonel Davis, to carry out General Taylor's instructions. We ought and could have made them surrender at discretion," &c., &c.

From each position taken in the above paragraph I dissent. The instructions given by General Taylor only presented his object, and fixed a limit to the powers of his commissioners; hence, when points were raised which exceeded our discretion, they were referred to the commander; but minor points were acted on, and finally submitted as a part of our negotiation. We fixed the time within which the Mexican forces should retire from Monterey. We agreed upon the time we would wait for the decision of the respective governments, which I recollect was less by thirty-four days than the Mexican commissioners asked—the period adopted being that which, according to our estimate, was required to bring up the rear of our army with the ordnance and supplies necessary for further operations.

I did not then, nor do I now, believe we could have made the enemy surrender at discretion. Had I entertained the opinion it would have been given to the commission, and to the commanding general, and would have precluded me from signing an agreement which permitted the garrison to retire with the honors of war. It is demonstrable, from the position and known prowess of the two armies, that we could drive the enemy from the town; but the town was untenable whilst the main fort (called the new citadel) remained in the hands of the enemy. Being without siege artillery or entrenching tools, we could only hope to carry this fort by storm, after a heavy loss from our army; which, isolated in a hostile country, now numbered less than half the forces of the enemy. When all this had been achieved, what more would we have gained than by the capitulation?

General Taylor's force was too small to invest the town. It was, therefore, always in the power of the enemy to retreat, bearing his light arms. Our army—poorly provided, and with very insufficient transportation—could not have overtaken, if they had pursued the flying enemy. Hence the conclusion that, as it was not in our power to capture the main body of the Mexican army, it is unreasonable to suppose their general would have surrendered at discretion. The moral effect of retiring under the capitulation was certainly greater than if the enemy had retreated without our consent. By this course we secured the large supply of ammunition he had collected in Monterey—which, had the assault been continued, must have been exploded by our shells, as it was principally stored in "the Cathedral," which, being supposed to be filled with troops, was the especial aim of our pieces. The destruction which this explosion would have produced must have involved the advance of both divisions of our troops; and I commend this to the contemplation of those whose arguments have been drawn from facts learned since the commissioners closed their negotiations.[4] With these introductory remarks, I send a copy of a manuscript in my possession, which was prepared to meet such necessity as now exists for an explanation of the views which governed the commissioners in arranging the terms of capitulation, to justify the commanding general, should misrepresentation and calumny attempt to tarnish his well-earned reputation, and, for all time to come, to fix the truth of the transaction.[5] Please publish this in your paper, and believe me your friend, &c.,

JEFFERSON DAVIS.

Washington *Union*, Feb. 10, 1847.

[1] Davis rejoined his regiment at Victoria on January 4. Leaving the mouth of the Rio Grande on the *J. E. Roberts*, he arrived at Camargo on December 14, the same day the Mississippians marched from Monterrey. On December 16 Davis left Camargo on horseback with a small party; they overtook Gen. Taylor on December 25 near Montemorelos and traveled to Victoria with him (Z618,

Smith Diary, Dec. 14–16, 1846, Ms-Ar; *House Ex. Doc. 60*, 30:1, 385–86; Coleman, ed., *Life of Crittenden*, 1: 270; Henry, *Campaign Sketches*, 278–79; McCall,. *Letters from the Frontiers*, 471; New Orleans *Picayune*, Dec. 2, 1846; New Orleans *Delta*, Mar. 13, 1853).

[2] Although some believed that responsibility for the unpopular capitulation agreement rested entirely with Zachary Taylor, others criticized the commissioners, either as a group or

individually, for granting overly generous terms. The Washington *Union* (Oct. 28, 1846), for example, singled out Worth, and Texas newspapers blamed Henderson for conceding too much (New Orleans *Delta*, Oct. 6, 21, Dec. 1, 1846; *Miss. Free Trader and Natchez Gazette*, Oct. 6, 27, 31, 1846; Houston *Dem. Telegraph and Texas Reg.*, Nov. 30, 1846; *Civilian and Galveston Gazette*, Dec. 5, 1846).

[3] Undoubtedly the letter J. Pinck-

ney Henderson wrote the editor of the Austin *Democrat* on October 4, 1846, an extract of which was printed in the New Orleans *Delta* on December 1.

[4] In a speech before a meeting of Mexican War veterans in 1876, Davis reiterated the same defense of the capitulation agreement (*Address*, 9–10).

[5] Davis' memorandum of October 7, 1846.

To John A. Quitman

Camp near Victoria 13th Jany. 1847

SIR,

The accompanying publications will sufficiently explain to you the controversy which has arisen upon a point of Regimental history, and I hope be considered a sufficient justification for my calling upon you, our immediate commander on the occasion when the event occurred, for a full statement of such particulars as came within your observation, and bear upon the question involved.[1] Very Respectfully I am yrs. &c.

JEFFN. DAVIS.
Col. Missi. Rifln.

note

These are the only copies I have of the enclosed publications please preserve them for me   yr. friend

JEFFN. DAVIS

ALS (Quitman Papers, MH-H). Addressed: "Genl. J A. Quitman U.S. Army Victoria." Endorsed: "Col. Davis asks Genl. Quitman to decide between the merits of the Miss & Tenn. Regts. at the battle of Monterey."

[1] Davis refers to the controversy with the 1st Tenn. Rgt. over capture of the Tenería. Although the enclosures are missing, perhaps returned as

Davis requested, one of them must have been Davis' letter of November 16. Other items that may have been included are: Balie Peyton's letter from the New Orleans *Picayune* (Oct. 23); William B. Campbell's from the Nashville *Whig* (Oct. 24); and the newspaper account of a speech Davis delivered in Vicksburg on November 10 (see the following letter from Davis to his brother).

To Joseph E. Davis

Monterey 26th Jany 1847

MY DEAR BROTHER,

After a march to Victoria and back (near 400 miles)[1] I arrived here yesterday and am [enca][2]mped near to the position we occupied on our first arrival at this place in Sept. last. All this has come to pass in this wise. At Victoria Genl. Taylor was informed by dispatches from Genl. Scott that he had come out to conduct an attack against Vera cruz and thence the city of Mexico, that he would require a large part of Genl. T.s Army indicating parts which he would take, and said he would leave Genl. T. 2000 Regulars and 5000 volunteers; to hold the line of our conquests until reinforced he could advance by the interior line to make a junction of the two columns at the city of Mexico.[3] Genl. T. sent on the force he had with him except Col. May's squadron of Dragoons; two batteries of light artillery;[4] and the Missi. Riflemen with which force as small as was deemed competent he made his way back to this place with his supply train. On our arrival we find that instead of leaving 2000 Regulars from Genl. T.s army Scott has even stripped Genl. Wool of the Regulars who were with his command,[5] taken off. the Engineer officers[6] who were construct/ing/ defences at Saltillo and made Genl. T. "safe" as his rival in this race.[7]

During my visit to the United States Genl. T. found that by directing his march on the route to Zacatecas instead of San Louis de Potosi he could find sufficient water and soon reach a country so closely cultivated that he could subsist his army upon it.[8] Had he not been ordered to limit his advance to Saltillo[9] he would have taken that route a month since, had Genl. Scott left the force he spoke of and created a diversion at Vera Cruz, Genl. T. would have advanced without delay and this opened to my hopes visions of constant confli[ct], the campaign of an isolated army, the thing of which american Soldiers have never been able to speak as eye witnesses, an invading force pressed by the enemy on every side and bristling to repel approach. But why dwell on a hope which has almost left me. I believe I'll take the other side and reason like old Tarpoley. Such I take for the orthography of the name of the old Choctaw at Greenville.[10]

When I reached Victoria I sent my published letter to Col.

Campbell with a note that it was for his perusal and offered to receive a proposition from for a joint investigation of the question. He asked time, and after three days Maj. Bradford /who bore my note/ reported that Col. Campbell was sore [u]nder my letter that he had not yet made up his mind and I might not expect him to do anything[11]

I then put inquiries to Genl. Twiggs and his aid Lieut McDonald[12] and to Maj. J. J. Abercrombie[13] and to Genl. Quitman. The first answered well, the second not much to the purpose but well as far as it went the third did not answer (we were suddenly and unexpectedly seperated)[14] the last declined to answer and made paltry excuses and petty complaints, such as his fear the inquiry might lead to a breach of the peace, and that officers were prohibited from writing about the operations of a campaign and that he had been treated with injustice, how? the members of the Regt. writing accounts of the battle had not mentioned *him*.[15] I avoided any inquiry as to Col. Campbells condemnation of his regiment, which many persons say was loud and violent.[16] To me it seemed unecessary to notice this and I did not wish unless it became necessary to injure any one.

I can say little of the future Genl. T. will go in a few days to Saltillo if he can get a force even a small one he will advance at the first opportunity on the enemy,[17] for our Regt. I expect any honorable service which he can give us. He is deeply chafed by the course of the war department, not only has he been stripped of his command but to this date is without advice from the Secty. of War even of the intent to send Genl. Scott out here.[18] In selecting our Regiment as an escort he paid us a high compliment. I think unfair means have been used to supplant him. I have no confidence in Genl. Scott, none in the line from Vera cruz as an approach.[19]

The desire to be in every battle fought during my term of service is strong, but I could not in the present condition of Genl. Taylor ask to leave him and in other considerations especially the belief that Vera cruz will not be defended must seek content if I remain upon this line.

Before we left Victoria it was reported among the Mexicans that Vera Cruz had been abandoned by the Mexican forces & it is supposed that the Navy, good at taking evacuated Towns, has made a descent upon it.[20] Give my love to all the family which is so far as

I can judge from my latest letters, now small. God grant that all your hopes in relation to Varina[21] may be realized. If she shall be excited by /my/ absence to such action and self command as to restore her health and spirits it will be a boon cheaply purchased by all the sacrifices and inconveniences it costs me. This letter already long will grow sad if I speak of home and we have Byron's Johnson against mingling those ingredients together[22]– Now that my thoughts have gone home I should do ill to write of other things not thinking of them. Farewell my dear Brother— yours

JEFFN. DAVIS

ALS (Davis Coll., ICHi).

[1] Davis left Victoria on January 16 (DNA, RG94, Vol. Muster Rolls, Mexican War, 1st Miss. Rgtl. Return, Jan. 1847).

[2] Square brackets enclose letters supplied where the original is damaged.

[3] On January 3 Winfield Scott had addressed letters of instruction to both Zachary Taylor and William O. Butler, detailing his plans for an expedition to Veracruz, Tampico, and ultimately Mexico City. Taylor was to hold Monterrey, the Rio Grande, and possibly Victoria and Saltillo until later in the spring when his army and Scott's might be reinforced, allowing a two-pronged advance to the capital (*House Ex. Doc. 60*, 30:1, 1151–54).

[4] Bvt. Lt. Col. Charles A. May led a ·squadron of the 2d Dragoons; Capts. Braxton Bragg and Thomas W. Sherman commanded Cos. C and E, 3d Art. (Smith, *War with Mexico*, 1:555; Heitman, *Hist. Reg.*, 1:698).

[5] John E. Wool's command had arrived at Agua Nueva on December 21 after a two-month march from San Antonio. Numbering about 3,000 regulars and volunteers, Wool's force was diminished by the loss of three infantry companies, an independent unit of Kentuckians, and a detachment of the 2d Dragoons. After January 1847 only a squadron of 1st Dragoons and Co. B, 4th Art., represented the regulars in Wool's division (Hinton, "Career of Wool," 193–206; Smith, *War with Mexico*, 1:509; Baylies, *Wool's Campaign*, 22–23; Brooks, *Mexican War*, 199).

[6] Scott's instructions to Taylor ordered Capt. Robert E. Lee, then an engineer officer at Saltillo, to join the Veracruz expedition (*House Ex. Doc. 60*, 30:1, 1156).

[7] In two private letters written in late January Taylor expressed the belief that Scott's appointment as commander-in-chief was part of an administration intrigue and that "one of the principal objects in getting up the [Veracruz] expedition . . . was to break me down." He was also convinced that his having become a potential presidential candidate had "disconcerted and annoyed General Scott and other aspirants, who deemed it no doubt necessary to have me at once killed off" (Taylor, *Letters*, 84; Coleman, ed., *Crittenden*, 1:275–76). See also Taylor's letter to Davis of July 27, 1847. For Davis' later estimate of Scott's conduct, see a speech delivered at Memphis in the summer of 1852 (Davis, *Papers*, ed. Rowland, 2:174–76).

[8] Early in November Taylor had informed the government that the arid terrain between Saltillo and San Luis Potosí would not sustain his army. The alternate route via Zacatecas, though portrayed as a rich

mining district offering abundant provisions and forage, in fact was also dry and desolate, presenting monumental difficulties for an invading force (*House Ex. Doc. 60*, 30:1, 361; Bakewell, *Silver Mining*, 2–3).

[9] On October 22 the secretary of war instructed Taylor not to advance beyond Monterrey unless it was necessary to occupy the mountain passes on the route to Saltillo. Taylor replied on November 12 that he considered it imperative to occupy Saltillo itself; he did not attempt any further forward movement at that time (*House Ex. Doc. 60*, 30:1, 364, 375).

[10] Davis refers to the now-extinct hamlet of Greenville in Jefferson County, where his brother Joseph lived in the 1810s and where Davis himself reportedly attended a plantation school (Lynch, *Bench and Bar*, 73; RG60, Vol. 18, Source Material on Jefferson County, 19, 106–107, Ms-Ar). The area formerly was inhabited by Choctaw Indians, some of whom remained after the cession of 1802 (U.S. Cong., *American State Papers*, Class II, Indian Affairs, 1:658–59; De-Rosier, *Removal of the Choctaw Indians*, 29–30).

[11] Undoubtedly Davis sent his letter of November 16, 1846, to the Tennessee colonel, with whom he disagreed on whether Davis' or Campbell's regiment had first entered the Tenería; Davis' covering note has not been found. Although he apparently never replied directly to the inquiry, Campbell wrote privately that Davis' claim was "presumptuous" and that he intended to expose its falsity as soon as he had "time to devote to that subject" (Sioussat, ed., "Mexican War Letters," *Tenn. Hist. Mag.*, 1:154).

[12] Philip W. McDonald (c1818–51), a Pennsylvanian, graduated from West Point in 1841. Assigned to the 2d Dragoons, he had served in several frontier posts before his assignment to David E. Twiggs's staff in July 1846 (Cullum, *Biog. Reg.*, 2:73).

[13] John J. Abercrombie, an officer in the 1st Inf., whom Davis had known in his previous military service.

[14] The replies of Twiggs and McDonald have not been found. Abercrombie had left Monterrey in November 1846 to join Gen. Robert Patterson's command in Camargo (DNA, M-29, roll 2, Special Orders No. 171, Nov. 5, 1846).

[15] Quitman wrote to a friend that, as commander of both the Tennessee and Mississippi regiments, he felt he should not participate in any controversy between them. In addition, the personal relationship between Quitman and Davis was strained in the months after Monterrey. Quitman resented the fact that Davis had not called on his family while on leave in Mississippi and also believed Davis was "jealous of my reputation." It is not literally true that Quitman was unmentioned in the Mississippi battle accounts, but notices of him did not confirm his own estimate of his performance. He later complained specifically of neglect by Davis, who had failed to name the general in his Vicksburg speech (Claiborne, *Quitman*, 1:303–304; Quitman to Frederick H. Quitman, Jan. 11, 1847, Z156f, Quitman Papers, Ms-Ar; Quitman to Eliza T. Quitman, Jan. 27, Feb. 20, 1847, Quitman Family Papers, S. Hist. Coll., NcU).

[16] Campbell's "condemnation" of his men occurred when the Tennesseans recoiled from the destructive fire of Mexican forces in the Tenería. As he wrote after the battle, "I hastened to ride to them and get in rear and by all artifice of language—by threats and by commands, I halted them and ordered them to form in line and charge the fort" (Sioussat, ed., "Mexican War Letters," *Tenn. Hist. Mag.*, 1:143–44; see also Robertson, *Reminiscences*, 139–40).

[17] Taylor left Monterrey on January 31, the day after the Mississippians broke camp. Reports that enemy

cavalry was near Saltillo and that two American reconnaissance parties had been captured prompted Taylor to move without waiting for reinforcement. "Should [the enemy] offer us battle," he vowed, "I shall indulge them" (Taylor, *Letters*, 84, 86; *House Ex. Doc. 60*, 30:1, 1106).

[18] Taylor complained in both official and private letters that he was "personally mortified and outraged" by the administration's failure to advise him in advance of its plans (*House Ex. Doc. 60*, 30:1, 863; Coleman, ed., *Crittenden*, 1:274).

[19] For Davis' opinion of a superior strategy, see his letter to Robert J. Walker of November 30, 1846.

[20] The navy had occupied Tampico on November 14, two weeks after the town was abandoned. Veracruz did not surrender until March 29, after a three-week investment (Dufour, *Mexican War*, 163–64, 197–210).

[21] Davis may have just received his brother's December 16 letter.

[22] A character in Byron's *Don Juan*, Johnson was an Englishman captured by the Turks. Meeting Don Juan in a Constantinople slave market, Johnson advised him that "a sad tale saddens doubly when 'tis long" (canto V, stanza 16, line 8).

To Varina Howell Davis

[Agua Nueva, February 8, 1847][1]

We are here on the table-lands of Mexico, at the foot of the Sierra Madre. We came expecting a host and battle, have found solitude and externally peace.[2] The daily alarms of this frontier have ceased, the enemy I believe has retired to San Luis de Potosi,[3] and we are waiting reinforcements,[4] while General Scott is taking all who can be seized and incorporates them in his division of the army. We have a beautiful and healthy position, and are waiting only action or such excitement as reconciles man to repose.

V. Davis, *Memoir*, 1:314–15.

[1] Place and date supplied by Varina Davis.

[2] The 1st Miss. Rgt., in company with Zachary Taylor, left Monterrey on January 30, camped the following night at Rinconada Pass, and reached Saltillo February 2. Three days later, "to restore confidence among the volunteer troops . . . [and] cause the return of the inhabitants of Saltillo," Taylor moved his headquarters eighteen miles south to Agua Nueva, where it remained until February 21 (*House Ex. Doc. 60*, 30:1, 1109; DNA, RG94, Vol. Muster Rolls, Mexican War, 1st Miss. Rgtl. Returns, Jan.–Feb. 1847).

[3] Evidently Davis believed, as did Taylor, that most of Santa Anna's army had turned south to meet the Americans at Veracruz. In fact the Mexicans had already begun to march northward toward Agua Nueva (Smith, *War with Mexico*, 1:373, 379–80).

[4] Not until March 20, a month after the Battle of Buena Vista, did the first of the expected reinforcements arrive (*House Ex. Doc. 60*, 30:1, 1120).

From Joseph E. Davis

Hurricane Feby 13th 1847

MY DEAR BROTHER

We have just heard though Mr. Van Benthuysen of your return to Monterey,[1] & he intimates your dissatisfaction at the arrangment, I feel on the Contrary that it may exempt you from an exposure that I dread More than the enemy the Yellow fever which plevails So early as to render it unsafe for you even to embark there at the experation of your term of Service.[2]

The letter of Genl. Taylor Said to have been writen to Genl. Gaines is attracting a good deal of notice, the Censure Cast on it by Some of the Supporters of the Administration is beyound what is due and yet I regret Some parts of it, Such as ascribing <-t-> his exertions to a desire to Sustain the Adm. And the propriety of other parts of the letter is[3] Condemned, in a military point of View, Still it is the publication more than the writing of the letter that is blamable and that impropriety it might well have been Supposed, could Scarcely have been committed by Genl. Gains.[4] The Sceme of a Lieut. Genl. will Scarcely be revived, and little as I know of millitary matters think it could only have been productive of mischief, it now Seems Benton was offered this appointment, and appears sorely disappointed and has had the indiscretion to exhibit that feeling in the Senate.[5]

Ficklin[6] & Our Jake Thompson has had the folly to expose themselves by a speech upon military affairs I send you Thompsons which I received under his Frank last night[7] Some portions of the Speech must have been writen by somebody else but you will See it, &c

Mrs. Howell[8] with the little folks Maggy[9] Jenny[10] & Jeff[11] have been up Some weeks & are are now waiting for a boat Varina goes down with her for a few weeks,[12] her health much as at the date of my last[13]

The family here are also about as usual, the weather has been cold Since the first Jany a part of time severely so Our plantation labour is not forward but but if favoured by good weathe will be in time James[14] estimates 125 bales of cotton still to gin, the teams being now required for ploughing[15] I will stop them after this week and haul the balance to the Steam Gin,[16] The price has improved

119

Since you left here & according to my usual way of hoping I still look for a further improvment, it may be quoted 10. & 11. I expect <-s-> -12 cp[er?] and 15. by april[17] but this you will attach as much importance to as the guess of any body else that knows nothing about it. The Legislature of this state at the last session passed a levee[18] law, and under it they assessed a tax of $1160. upon me $636 upon you this I felt as a flagrant injustice and determed to resist it, I have therefore injoined them from Collecting the tax and more over injoined them from making it all,[19] as by the Slopage of the water at the Conger field it increase the rise in the river upon us[20]

The Boat is in hearing

YR BR.OTHER

AL (ViRC).

[1] Joseph Davis' brother-in-law Watson Van Benthuysen, who lived in New Orleans, may have received news of Davis from recently arrived military personnel.

[2] The 1st Miss. Rgt., due to leave Mexico in late May or early June, sailed from Brazos Santiago, where the yellow fever season began earlier than in Mississippi.

[3] The word *are* is overwritten.

[4] Smarting under official criticism of his Monterrey capitulation agreement, Zachary Taylor had written a long letter on November 9, 1846, to his cousin Edmund P. Gaines. In it he defended the terms, complained of inadequate support, and outlined his views on past and future strategy. On January 22 most of the letter appeared in the New York *Morning Express* and soon afterward in papers across the country. Gaines assumed responsibility for the letter's publication, but the administration was not placated. Polk and the cabinet agreed that Taylor should be censured and further decided to revive paragraph 650 of the 1825 army regulations, which provided that an officer writing for publication or allowing his writings to reach the press might be cashiered (Silver, *Gaines*, 5; Polk, *Diary*, 2:355–57; Dyer, *Zachary Taylor*, 242–43; *House Doc. 119*, 29: 2, 109–10).

[5] A frequent visitor to the White House during November 1846, Senator Thomas Hart Benton not only counseled a vigorous campaign into the heart of Mexico but also suggested creation of the office of lt. gen., a position he was willing to accept. On January 4 Polk proposed to Congress the "appointment of a general officer to take command of all our military forces in the field." The plan was speedily rejected, partly because it was known that Benton would receive the office. On January 25 the Missourian indignantly denied that Polk had contrived to choose the next president by appointing a Democrat to the new command (Polk, *Diary*, 2:227, 346–47; *Cong. Globe*, 29:2, 104–105, 246–47).

[6] Orlando Bell Ficklin (1808–86) was the nephew of the Lexington postmaster with whom Davis had boarded while a student at Transylvania University. An attorney, Ficklin served in the Illinois state legislature and in the House of Representatives (1843–49, 1851–53). He was married to Elizabeth Colquitt, a friend of Varina Davis' (*BDAC*; Ficklin,

Genealogy, 2–3; Washington *Union*, Aug. 27, 1846; *Davis Papers*, 1·9, 2: 421, 535).

⁷ On January 9 and 21 both Ficklin and Mississippi Representative Jacob Thompson had criticized Zachary Taylor's "victories without advantages" in Mexico. On January 30 Thompson attempted to amend a resolution commending Taylor's capture of Monterrey with a statement disapproving the capitulation terms (*Cong. Globe*, 29:2, 153–61, 226–28, 295–99). Thompson's January 9 address was issued as a pamphlet, undoubtedly the one Davis' brother had just received.

⁸ Davis' mother-in-law Margaret Kempe Howell.

⁹ Varina's sister Margaret G. Howell, aged about four.

¹⁰ Jane Kempe Howell, Varina Davis' youngest sister, was probably born in Natchez about 1844; she was educated in New Orleans and Washington. On November 12, 1863, she married William G. Waller, John Tyler's grandson. Two of the Wallers' three children survived their mother, who died sometime in the 1870s (1850 Census, La., Orleans, right bank, family 450; Margaret K. Howell to William B. Howell, Oct. 29, 1854, Z790f, Howell Papers, Ms-Ar; Joseph D. Howell to V. Davis, June 29, 1859, Davis Papers, DLC; *Burke's Presidential Families*, 230; Richmond *Dispatch*, July 25, 1894, 3; ViHi to Davis Assn., Feb. 24, 1977).

¹¹ Jefferson Davis Howell (1846–Nov. 7, 1875), Varina Davis' youngest sibling, was born in Natchez. Since the Davises volunteered to oversee his education, "Jeffy D" was frequently a member of their household during the 1850s. As Davis wrote in early 1876, he "bore to us . . . the relation of a son" (Davis to George O. Kelly, and V. Davis to Margaret K. Howell, Nov. 21, 1858, Davis Coll., AU). During the Civil War Howell first joined a New Orleans militia unit and in 1863 was appointed to the

Confederate navy as a midshipman, seeing action with the Charleston squadron and in Raphael Semmes's brigade. Captured with the Davises in May 1865, Howell was imprisoned at Fort McHenry and Savannah. Afterward he traveled to Canada and to Europe, worked briefly for the New York *News*, and was a transient seaman before settling in San Francisco in 1870. Eventually the commander of several ships, he was lost at sea in the wreck of the *Pacific* (V. Davis, *Memoir*, 1:576, 2:796, 819–22; V. Davis to Margaret K. Howell, [1857], Davis Coll., AU; Scharf, *Hist. Confed. Navy*, 779n–81n; Wright, ed., *Lewis & Dryden's Marine Hist.*, 224n).

¹² Margaret Howell had arrived at Brierfield on January 22. Rather than visiting in Natchez "for a few weeks," Varina apparently stayed with her parents until Davis' return from Mexico in June (Margaret K. Howell to [William B. Howell], Jan. 22, 1847, Davis Coll., AU; Davis to V. Davis, May 27, 1847; V. Davis, *Memoir*, 1:358).

¹³ Joseph Davis' last extant letter is dated December 30; he certainly had written others in the interim (see Joseph Davis to Davis, Apr. 23, 1847).

¹⁴ James Pemberton, Davis' plantation manager.

¹⁵ The letters *ugh* have been written over *wing*.

¹⁶ The steam gin to which Joseph Davis refers was probably his own. In the mid-1840s Brierfield had "a fine gin on the place," but it was horse powered (Z774, *Davis* v. *Bowmar* [1874], 241, and memorandum of arguments, 4–5, *Joseph E. Davis* v. *Rice C. Ballard et al.*, RG8, Superior Court of Chancery case no. 3973, Ms-Ar; *Davis Papers*, 1:438).

¹⁷ When Davis left home in late November 1846, short-staple cotton was selling in New Orleans for an average 9.2 cents per pound. By January the price had climbed to 10.1 but thereafter failed to meet Joseph

Davis' expectations, reaching only a median 10.7 cents per pound by April (Bruchey, ed., *Cotton*, table 3P).

18 The letters *a le* are written over *asse*.

19 Signed into law on February 23, 1846, the Warren County levee law was the first to provide for protection of the entire riverfront and the first state levee statute to include building specifications. The cost was to be borne by the riparian proprietors and by those owners of inland tracts that would be safeguarded (*Miss. Laws, 1846*, 172–78; Harrison, *Levee Districts*, 3–5). Although the levees constructed on Hurricane and Brierfield were deemed adequate by the local inspectors, on December 5 the Davis brothers were assessed one dollar per acre for protection of their 1,796 acres of backland. On January 13 Joseph Davis was officially notified of the assessment. Three weeks later, on February 3, he filed a bill of complaint against the county sheriff (who was also the tax collector) and the three levee commissioners. His case hinged on the contentions that his land was improperly inspected, that he was allowed no appeal of the commissioners' decision, that the proposed levee above his property would cause flooding on Davis Bend, and that the law was a perversion of the taxing power. After several years of litigation, the superior court of chancery ruled in his favor, a decision upheld by the state supreme court in 1856. As Varina Davis recalled, the suit was brought in behalf of both brothers, whose plantations shared common levees. While Davis was in Mexico, she said, Joseph Davis "spoke to me of it several times as a matter of pecuniary interest to both of us" (Z774, *Davis* v. *Bowmar* [1874], 373–75, 588–96, and *Joseph E. Davis* v. *Rice C. Ballard et al.*, RG8, Superior Court of Chancery case no. 3973, Ms-Ar; *R. C. Ballard et al.* v. *Joseph E. Davis*, 31 Miss. 525, 535–37 [1856]).

20 Once owned by Jonathan Conger, the tract referred to was located on the Mississippi River above the Davis plantations and below Diamond Place (see *Davis Papers*, 2:endpaper map). Joseph Davis believed that new levees upstream would block the river's natural outlet across the lowlands above him and thus cause flooding on Davis Bend, a contention supported by several of his neighbors and a number of hydrographers (*Joseph E. Davis* v. *Rice C. Ballard et al.*, RG8, Superior Court of Chancery case no. 3973, passim, Ms-Ar; Ellet, *Miss. and Ohio Rivers*, 60; Humphreys and Abbot, *Report*, 411–12, 416; U.S. Miss. River Comn., *Improvement of the Lower Miss. River*, 37, 173).

To Varina Howell Davis

Satillo   25th Feby 1847

MY DEAR WIFE,

I wrote to you a few days since anticipating a battle[1]—we have had it— The Mississippians did well— I fear you may feel some anxiety about me and write to say that I was wounded in the right foot and remained on the field so long afterwards that the wound has been painful but is by no means dangerous[2]— I hope soon to be up again— My friend Mr. Crittenden[3] will write on this sheet to Brother Joe and give him more particulars[4]— God bless you affectionately

YOUR HUSBAND

ALS (ViRC).

[1] Davis' last known letter to his wife was dated February 8.

[2] A musket ball pierced Davis' right foot near the ankle during the Mississippi regiment's first charge at Buena Vista. When he refused to retire from the field, a preliminary dressing was applied while he remained in the saddle. After the action he was tended in a field hospital and later in the American hospital at Saltillo. According to Varina Davis, he was on crutches for many months and "suffered intensely from his wound . . . for five years." As late as October 1887 Davis complained of discomfort "in the foot that was broken in Mexico" (N.Y. *Tribune*, Dec. 8, 1889, 16; V. Davis, *Memoir*, 1:332, 359; Davis to James L. Power, Oct. 6, [1887], Z1401m, Power Papers, Ms-Ar).

[3] Thomas Leonidas Crittenden (1819–93), son of Senator John J. Crittenden, and Davis became good friends when they traveled to Mexico together in December 1846. Crittenden served on Taylor's staff as a volunteer aide at Buena Vista and saw additional service with the 3d Ky. Inf. He was a Union general during the Civil War (*DAB*; Warner, *Gens. in Blue*; Davis to John J. Crittenden, Jan. 30, 1849, Crittenden Papers, DLC; Washington *Nat. Intell.*, Apr. 2, 1847; see also Davis to Crittenden, Jan. 23, 1848).

[4] Crittenden's letter to Joseph E. Davis gave a summary of the battle, praised the contributions of Davis and his men, and assured the family that Davis' wound was "not at all dangerous." A long endorsement indicates that Joseph Davis' wife copied the Crittenden letter as well as part of an undated communication from Davis' nephew Joseph D. Smith for transmittal to Varina Davis, then visiting her parents in Natchez. Smith's information, derived from an army officer, confirmed that Davis' wound was slight, that "he was able to get about . . . & his health [was] good other wise."

From Crawford Fletcher

Camp Near Soltillo Mexico
Feby 28th 1847

D SIR

In compliance with your request I Report,

That on the 22d Feby my command with that of Capt Coopers were left to Guard Camp,[1] that during the whole day we were under arms, fearful that the enemy <–would–> a Body of some two or three thousand Lancers,[2] who were in the neighbourhood

123

would attack our camp, and that my men behaved remarkably well obeying all orders with the greatest alacrity being desirous of meeting the enemy

That on the 23th Feby 1847 my Company with others of the Mississippi Regt[3] under your immediate command took up the line of march for Buena Vista, that about nine oclock we arrived on that field, when the day to all appearances was lost, the Enemy having turned our left flank and defeated one of the Indiana Regt driving the greater portion of them off the Field.[4] The Lancers in hot persuit of our cavalry who were retreating before them and coming down up on our Camp[5] supported by their infantry a body of six or seven thousand <–in Number–> Men,[6] Just at this particular crisis, joined by a fiew Indianaians under the Command of Col. Boules[7] who rallied and came to our support[8] we Commenced the attack upon the Enemy and succeeded in stopping there onward course for a short time:[9] Being attacked by the Lancers /on the right/ and the Infantry <–driving–> moving down upon us in front supported by a verry large body of Lancers.[10] I <–had–> Recieved your orders to retire and in doing so lost six of the best men in my company all of them were wounded in the first charge and left on the field and afterwards murderd in cold blood by the Mexicans and six wounded who were carried off the Field[11]

That after retreating a short distance I rallied my men aided by Lut J. H. Hughs[12] and joyned the Regt by the side of a deep ravine,[13] One Regt of Indianians under Comdg of Col Lane[14] and a piece of artilery under comd of Let. Kilburn[15] coming to our support we resisted the charge of a verry large body of Lancers, who were repulsed with a considerable loss,[16] that my commd in company with others of the Regemt under your Commd made several other attacks upon the enemy at different points and places, and always succeeded in carrying our points. About three oclock we recieved orders to support the Kentucky Regt under comd of Col. McGee[17] & Col Hardings[18] Regt of Illinois troops who were retreating before the Enemy,[19] we did so, and repulsed them considerable loss[20] recapturing two pieces of Artelery, they had taken,[21] they inded this day work,

That the men of my company indivedually and as a body behaved with the greatest coolness and courage I noticed many instances of daring courage & gallant conduct on there part Let. Hughes the only commissioned /officer/ of the company who was in the action besides myself always assisted me in rallying the men and came to my aid on all occasions behaving nobly and Ganantry,

I regret exceedingly that captain McManus[22] whose long debility & severe illness prevented him from particitakng in the actions of the day as also Let Bradford who is absent on Furlougs

CRAWFORD FLETCHE[23] 1st Let
Comdg Comp "E" Miss Rflmen

ALS (RG27, Vol. 26, Corres., Mexican War Docs., Ms-Ar). Endorsed by Davis: "No. 6 Com. 'E.'" Enclosed: Davis to Albert G. Brown, Oct. 3, 1847.

[1] Crawford Fletcher was commanding Co. E because Capt. John L. McManus was ill; Capt. Douglas H. Cooper's Co. B shared guard duty with Fletcher's men on February 22. See the inset on the map of Buena Vista for location of the campsite.

[2] Gen. José Vicente Miñón, commanding approximately 1,200–1,500 cavalrymen, was charged with attacking the American forces at Saltillo (*Niles' Reg.*, Apr. 24, 1847, 118; Balbontín, *Invasión Americana*, 71, 79; Matamoros *American Flag*, June 23, 1847).

[3] Cos. A, B, C, E, F, G, H, and I participated in the action at Buena Vista on February 23.

[4] Enemy infantry led by Gens. Francisco Pacheco and Manuel María Lombardini turned the American left early on February 23, sweeping before them an outnumbered force that included the 2d Ind. Rgt. Posted on the extreme left flank, the Indianans held their ground for about half an hour before the regimental commander misunderstood an order to advance and called instead for a retreat. Because of the confusion, the uneven terrain, and the colonel's failure to designate a rallying point, the retreat became a disorderly rout (Carleton, *Buena Vista*, 53–63; Smith,

War with Mexico, 1:557; *Ind. in the Mexican War*, 300–11). See letter D on the Buena Vista map.

[5] At approximately the same time that the Americans on the main plateau were dispersed, Gen. Pedro Ampudia's force drove back a small group of riflemen—Ky. and Ark. Cav., Ind. and Ill. Rifle Btns.—stationed on and near the eastern mountains (letters E and F on the map). Once the volunteers reached more level ground, some 1,000–2,000 Mexican cavalrymen pursued them toward Gen. John E. Wool's camp at Buena Vista, near which was parked "a conspicuous prize" of some 200 supply and baggage wagons (Carleton, *Buena Vista*, 70–71, 79, 89–93; Roa Bárcena, *Recuerdos*, 1:172–73; New Orleans *Jeffersonian*, Apr. 3, 1847; Gregg, *Diary and Letters*, 2:48–49; *Senate Ex. Doc. 1*, 30:1, 147–48, 166–67, 171–73, 190–91).

[6] Approximations of Mexican strength on the American left varied from 6,000 to 12,000. Given the number in Santa Anna's army on the eve of battle, the troops assigned to the reserve or operating elsewhere, and the dispersal of some of Pacheco's forces, Fletcher's estimate is plausible (Smith, *Campaign*, 49–50; Vicksburg *Daily Whig*, Mar. 31, Apr. 2, 1847; Santa Anna, *Apelación*, Pt. 2, 67).

[7] William A. Bowles (c1795–1873), a native of Maryland, was a physician, resort developer, and Indiana state legislator (1838–41, 1843–44). In 1846 he was chosen col., 2d Ind. Rgt.,

a position for which he displayed little aptitude. Because of the disorderly retreat of his men at Buena Vista, he was arrested and his actions were officially investigated. Bowles later became active in the Know-Nothing party in Indiana. His identification with several secret prosouthern groups during the Civil War led to his arrest and imprisonment for treason, 1864–66 (1870 Census, Ind., Orange, French Lick, family 164; "Bowles," English Coll., InHi; Buley, "Ind. in the Mexican War," *Ind. Mag. Hist.*, 15:299–301, 16:51–53; Fesler, "Secret Political Societies," ibid., 14:200, 266–68; Brand, "Know Nothing Party," ibid., 18:203).

[8] The number of soldiers from the 2d Ind. Rgt. who fought with Davis' command was a question that recurred for years after the battle. From the evidence in Mississippi battle reports and other accounts, it seems that Bowles and about twenty to forty Indianans served with the 1st Miss. from the time of the latter's first engagement until the close of the action (Jackson *Southron*, Apr. 16, 1847; *Cong. Globe*, 31:2, App., 291; Carleton, *Buena Vista*, 75; DNA, RG 153, Court Martial Case Files, FF123, 49–50; see also the reports of Amos B. Corwine and Davis, Mar. 1, 2, 1847, and Davis' testimony in the Bowles court of inquiry, Apr. 20, 1847).

[9] Davis' regiment engaged Ampudia's command, a force of perhaps 4,000 infantrymen and cavalrymen (Carleton, *Buena Vista*, 76–77; Jackson *Southron*, Apr. 16, 1847; *Senate Ex. Doc. 1*, 30:1, 148). See no. 2 on the map of Buena Vista.

[10] The attack by the lancers occurred at or near the site numbered 4 on the map of Buena Vista.

[11] During the first charge the Mississippi regiment sustained most of its casualties. From Co. E the six killed were: Sgts. Joseph H. Langford and William W. Phillips, Cpls. Joseph C. Reville and Francis M. Robinson, and

Pvts. Robert A. Joyce and William Sellers. The wounded, all of whom recovered, were Pvts. Richard Clariday (Clardy), Robert J. Fox, John Kennedy, Isham C. Laird, Anthony B. Puckett, and James Waugh (DNA, RG94, Vol. Muster Rolls, Mexican War, 1st Miss. Misc. Rgtl. Papers).

[12] James H. Hughes (1823–90), 2d lt., Co. E, was the son of a Jackson circuit judge and a native Tennessean. By 1850 he had become a farmer in Texas; he eventually settled in Harrisburg, where he worked for the Houston Direct Navigation Co. and the Southern Pacific Railroad (Jackson *Southron*, Apr. 16, 1847; Rowland, *Courts, Judges, and Lawyers*, 257; DNA, RG15, Mexican War Pension Applics., WC 7074; 1850 Census, Texas, Goliad, family 38; ibid., 1870, Harris, family 37; ibid., 1880, enumeration dist. 77, 8).

[13] The Mississippians retired through the northern ravine to the point marked no. 5 on the map of Buena Vista. Although the site was described as both "a piece of vantage ground" and "a small bottom," one of the Mississippi officers stated in 1851 that Davis himself, on horseback and readily visible, became the rallying point (Greenville, S.C., *Mountaineer*, June 4, 1847; William R. Haddon to Davis, July 4, 1853, Haddon Coll., In; Woodville *Repub.*, Oct. 28, 1851).

[14] James Henry Lane (1814–66) was col., 3d Ind. Rgt., and later led the 5th Ind., which also served in Mexico. After the war he was lieutenant governor and congressman before moving to Kansas, where he led the drive for statehood and became one of the first senators (*DAB*; *BDAC*).

[15] Charles Lawrence Kilburn (1819–99), a Pennsylvania native, graduated from West Point in 1842 and during the Mexican War served in Co. C, 3d Art. In 1853 he transferred to the Commissary Department, was brevetted brig. gen. in 1865, and after the Civil War was successively chief com-

missary in four different army divisions (Cullum, *Biog. Reg.*, 2:129–30; Heitman, *Hist. Reg.*, 1:597).

[16] Fletcher refers to the famous stand of the Mississippi and Indiana regiments in the V formation; see no. 7 on the map.

[17] William Robertson McKee (1808–47), an 1829 West Point graduate, had known Davis at the Academy. After serving in the army for seven years, McKee settled in Louisville, where he was one of the operators of the Lexington & Louisville Transportation Line, a railroad engineer (1844–46), and an attorney. Like Davis, McKee returned to the army in 1846 as commander of a volunteer regiment, the 2d Ky. He died "while gallantly leading a charge" at Buena Vista (*Biog. Ency. Ky.*, 275–76; Cullum, *Biog. Reg.*, 1:427; Heitman, *Hist. Reg.*, 1:671; Coleman, "Ky. River Steamboats," *Ky. Hist. Reg.*, 63:309; Clark, *Hist. Ky.*, 185).

[18] John J. Hardin (1810–47), an attorney, Whig legislator (1836–42), and congressman (1843–45), was also a militia general who had fought in the Black Hawk War and led troops against the Mormons before his election as col., 1st Ill. Rgt., in 1846. He was killed at Buena Vista (*DAB*).

[19] At midafternoon the 1st Ill., 2d Ill., and 2d Ky. rgts. were overwhelmed on the main plateau by a Mexican force of several thousand under Gen. Francisco Pérez. Unable to hold their position, the volunteers fled into a deep ravine where scores were killed, among them Cols. Hardin and McKee and Lt. Col. Henry Clay, Jr. (Carleton, *Buena Vista*, 107–11).

[20] The site of the Mississippians' last engagement is shown on the Buena Vista map as nos. 9 and 10.

[21] Only Fletcher's fellow officer in Co. E confirmed that the Mississippi regiment "retook a piece of cannon." The 4th Art. lost two 6-pounders on the main plateau, but those guns were not recaptured until the Battle of Contreras (Jackson *Southron*, Apr. 16, 1847; Smith, *War with Mexico*, 2: 109–10).

[22] John L. McManus assisted in the defense of the headquarters camp; see William P. Rogers' report of March 6.

[23] Crawford Fletcher (c1824–76) was born in Tennessee but when elected 1st lt. of the State Fencibles was a Jackson resident. After the war he moved to Red Fork, Arkansas. In 1855 he asked Davis' aid in obtaining an army commission and until 1861 served as capt., 9th Inf. Resigning because he was "not willing to bear arms against [his] country," Fletcher subsequently became a planter in central Arkansas (1870 Census, Ark., Jefferson, family 123; DNA, RG15, Mexican War Pension Applics., WC 2687; DNA, M-863, roll 1; Heitman, *Hist. Reg.*, 1:425; Fletcher to Davis, Feb. 13, 1855, DNA, RG107, Applics. for Appt., 1820–61; Fletcher to Davis, Mar. 22, 1861, DNA, RG109, Citizens File: Washington Fletcher; *Senate Ex. Jour.*, 10:84, 87).

To Waddy Thompson

SALTILLO, MEXICO, March 1, 1847.

DEAR SIR:—After having received your esteemed favor of Nov. 10, 1846,[1] I offered my personal services to your friend, Mr. JOYCE,[2] of my Regiment, and it gives me pleasure to have secured in a small degree one of your friends. It is now my melancholy duty to inform you that he is no more. At the same time, I offer the stern consolation, that he died gallantly, as became a soldier and patriot. He was killed in the battle of Buena Vista, on the 23d ult., in our first and most desperate charge upon the enemy. He was buried, with many of his comrades, near the spot he fell upon.

Gen. SANTA ANNA in person commanded the Mexican forces, amounting to 20,000 or more veteran troops, according to his own statement to Gen. TAYLOR,[3] whilst our own did not exceed 5,000 in the action.

The battle commenced on the 22d and ended on the following day—the enemy leaving the field with great loss, the precise number not ascertained. Our loss, in killed and wounded, is very severe, amounting to more than 700.

From a painful wound, I have used the hand of a friend[4] to write this note. With great regard, I am your friend, &c.

JEFFERSON DAVIS.

Greenville, S.C., *Mountaineer*, Apr. 9, 1847.

[1] Thompson's letter has not been found.
[2] Robert A. Joyce, a native of Greenville, South Carolina, was thirty-six years old when he fell at Buena Vista (Greenville *Mountaineer*, Apr. 9, May 7, 1847).

[3] Davis refers to Santa Anna's surrender demand of February 22, in which he declared to Taylor: "You are surrounded by twenty thousand men, and cannot in any human probability avoid suffering a rout" (*Senate Ex. Doc. 1*, 30:1, 98).
[4] Probably Thomas L. Crittenden (see Davis to V. Davis, Feb. 25, 1847).

Douglas H. Cooper to Richard Griffith[1]

Saltillo March 1st 1847

SIR: In compliance with your request, I have the honor to report, for the information of the Colonel commanding, such facts as came under my own observation during the recent operations against the enemy at this place & Buena Vista & which may not be known to him <–Col.–> Having been left in command of the camp guard, consisting of my company. (B) & (E) company, Lt. Fletcher commmdg on the 22nd Febry, the operations of that day, of course, are not within my personal knowledge. Nothing of any moment occured at camp, except the appearance of some two thousand of the Enemy's cavalry, who came through a mountain pass on the east side of Saltillo, & marched down to the Factory near the Monterey road;[2] where they remained during that day & night.

Apprehending an attack their appearance was at once communicated to Gen Taylor & toward night, dispositions of the wagons & artillery (one piece under Lt Shover[3]) were made with a view to the defence of the camp & baggage. The wagons were parked under the direction of Capt Sibley[4] Qt. Master assisted by Lt Slade[5] Regimental Quartermaster. Lt Slade also rendered <–my–> great assistance in visiting the videttes & communicating with other points near the camp. Mr Wetmore sutler was also very active as a vidette. Capt McManus 'tho' unable to undergo any fatiegue, was constantly present and ready to render whatever aid in his power. The men remained under arms all day & exhibited great coolness & determination, when momentarily in <–danger–> /expectation/ of /an/ attack – on the 23rd my company was ordered out to the field; & being directly under the eye of the Col, it is unnecessary for me to say any thing as to our movements on that day. I cannot refrain however from bearing testimony to the gallantry of Lts. Posey Calhoun & Harrison[6] during that trying time. My admiration was also excited by the very brave & gallant bearing of Lt Greaves of Capt Downings Company—in the first charge upon the enemy. Sgt. Maj. Miller's[7] conduct /also/ fell under my observation, which was cool & every way worthy of praise.

I cannot make any distinction among the men of my company, (with one exception prvate Schneider who left the ranks & fell in the hands of enemy on the road to town)[8] where all behaved with great coolness & bravery. Privates Thos Titley, Lewis Turberville, William Wilkinson. & Seaborne Jones were found dead, having fallen in the front of the fight. I have reason to believe some of them were only wounded, at first, but were afterwards murdered by the Mexicans. It is gratifying to notice the difference, between our soldiery in the treatment of wounded. One case as an example happened with private Gayden[9] of my company. A Mexican Lancer' horse had been shot & fallen upon the leg or foot of the man He was observed struggling, but Gayden would not fire upon him for *fear he might be a wounded* man. Soon however he extricated himself & ran. When Gayden & another man fired & the mexican fell. This illustrates the feeling of our men, even when excited almost to madness by a knowledge of the inhuman barbariety of the Mexican soldiery. I should have mentioned in the proper place that I observed & was struck with perfect coolness under fire, which was exhibited by Capt Downing, Capt Delay[10] & Lt. Corwin who was in command after Capt Sharp's wounds forced him to retire from the field. I refer to the short time while we occupied our lost position on the hill side near Capt Shermans battery & were fired upon from the enemy's battery near the foot of the mountain.[11] The conduct of the artillery officers /Capt. Sherman[12] & Lt. Killburn/ while with us came directly under the eye of Col Davis & no doubt excited his admiration as it did that of every officer & man present – Respectfully—

D. H. Cooper
Capt. Miss. Riflemen

ALS (RG27, Vol. 26, Corres., Mexican War Docs., Ms-Ar). Endorsed by Davis: "No. 4 Com. 'B.'" Enclosed: Davis to Albert G. Brown, Oct. 3, 1847.

[1] Although the outer address is to Davis, the inside addressee was Griffith. As adj., Griffith received four battle reports for Davis, who was in Saltillo recovering from his wound.

[2] See the inset on the Buena Vista map for the pass of Palomas Adentro and the location of the cotton factory. The pass had been fortified by American volunteers in mid-February but abandoned on February 21 when Santa Anna's approach was discovered (Little Rock Ark. State Gazette, Mar. 27, Apr. 24, 1847).

[3] William H. Harrison Shover, an 1838 West Point graduate, commanded a 6-pounder from Co. C, 3d Art. Brevetted for gallantry at Monterrey and Buena Vista, Shover taught at the Military Academy from 1848 until his death in 1850 at the age of thirty-six (Cullum, Biog. Reg., 1:703; Carleton, Buena Vista, 45).

[4] Ebenezer Sproat Sibley (1805–84) graduated from West Point in 1827 and served in the 1st Art. and in the Quartermaster's Department. He was

brevetted maj. after Buena Vista, served as deputy quartermaster gen. during the Civil War, and retired in 1864 (Cullum, Biog. Reg., 1:386–87; N.Y. Times, Aug. 15, 1884, 4).

[5] Thomas Pugh Slade, 2d lt., Co. A, was born in North Carolina about 1810. A resident of Benton, he became district court clerk (1838–46) and a state legislator (1847–48). After trying his luck in the California goldfields, he remained in the West, living at Del Mar as late as 1887 (Benton Yazoo Banner, Oct. 13, 1838, Nov. 8, 1839, Dec. 10, 1842; Jackson Mississippian, Nov. 5, 1847; DNA, RG15, Mexican War Pension Applics., SC 10586; Miss. Official Reg., 1908, 113).

[6] Samuel R. Harrison (c1819–67), a native Mississippian, was elected additional 2d lt., Co. B, on July 1, 1846. After the Mexican War he tried twice, once with Davis' assistance, to obtain a regular army commission. In 1861 Harrison was chosen 1st lt., Co. I, 1st (Nelligan's) La. Inf.; promoted col. in April 1862, he resigned in June and in November was appointed maj. and commissary for the brigade commanded by Davis' nephew Joseph R. Davis (1850 Census, Miss., Wilkinson, family 130; DNA, M-863, roll 2;

Davis to Polk, Nov. 30, 1847; Douglas H. Cooper to Davis, Mar. 15, 1853, DNA, RG107, Applics. for Appt., 1820–61; DNA, RG109, Comp. Service Recs.; *Jour. Confed. Cong.*, 3: 394; Woodville *Repub.*, Apr. 27, 1867).

7 Horace H. Miller (c1826–77), an attorney born in Kentucky, was appointed sgt. maj. in January 1847. After the war he copublished the Vicksburg *True Issue* (1851), a Union party journal, and was chargé d'affaires to Bolivia (1851–53). Later, claiming to have been first to fire on a United States flag (in January 1861), Miller was an officer in the state troops before receiving a commission as lt. col., 20th Miss. Inf., in 1862. Captured at Fort Donelson, Miller subsequently (1865) was col., 9th Miss. Cav. He served as Warren County circuit judge in 1866 and in 1874 led a mounted force during a Vicksburg race riot (1850 Census, Miss., Warren, family 29; Patridge, "Miss. Press," *De Bow's Rev.*, 20:506; *Senate Ex. Jour.*, 8:367, 9:223; Hopkins, *Seventh Rgt.*, 92; Miller to Davis, Mar. 30, 1861, DNA, RG109, Citizens File: Laurence F. O'Brian; *Jour. Confed. Cong.*, 1:841, 4:451; *Miss. Official Reg., 1908*, 36; Gibson, *Memoirs*, 78–80; DNA, M-863, roll 2; Fisher Funeral Home recs., MsVO; Stone, *Brokenburn*, 143).

8 Frederick M. Schneider was returned in a prisoner exchange early in March (DNA, M-863, roll 3). See also Davis' report of March 2.

9 Iveson Greene Gayden (1825–96), born in Amite County, attended Oakland College and later prospered as a planter in East Feliciana Parish (Clar-

ence L. Yancey to Davis Assn., Apr. 5, 1976; *Biog. and Hist. Memoirs of La.*, 1:441–42).

10 William Delay (1814–71), capt., Co. F, was born in Kentucky and settled as a young man in Oxford, Mississippi, where he published and edited several Democratic newspapers (1843–55). He was also postmaster in the mid-1840s and late 1850s. During the Civil War he organized and commanded Co. C, 9th Miss. Inf. (1861–62), and was county probate clerk (1862–67). Davis and Delay maintained a lifelong friendship, strengthened by their Mexican War service and their mutual devotion to the Democratic party (Rainwater, ed., "Thompson Letters," *JSH*, 6: 104n; *Mississippiana*, 2:56–57; Kendel, "Reconstruction," *Miss. Hist. Pubs.*, 13:227, 230; RG28, Vol. 285, Reg. of Comns., 419, Vol. 286, 327, Ms-Ar; DNA, RG109, Comp. Service Recs.; Oxford *Falcon*, Oct. 12, 1867; Davis to Robert McClelland, Nov. 9, 1854, Lincoln Shrine; Davis to Delay, Dec. 6, 1869, Miss. Coll., MsU).

11 For the site of the last position held by the Mississippians, see no. 11 on the map of Buena Vista. The "enemy's battery" may have been the 18- and 24-pounders on the main plateau, reportedly manned in part by the San Patricio Btn. of American deserters (Carleton, *Buena Vista*, 83, 87).

12 Thomas West Sherman (1813–79), a Rhode Island native, graduated from the Military Academy in 1836, served in the 3d Art., and during the Civil War was a brig. gen. of vols. (*DAB*).

From Amos B. Corwine

Camp near Saltillo, Mexico, March 1st,/47.

In obedience to the request of Col. Jeff. Davis, I submit the following report:

On the morning of the 22d ultimo, information having been received by the commanding Genl. that the enemy was advancing, the 1st Regt. Miss. Riflemen, together with the other troops attached to Head Quarters, was ordered under arms, and, after the necessary prperation, took up the line of march from its encampment near Saltillo, to *Buena Vista.*

The incidents of that day were trivial and unimportant, & our Regiment not getting into action, it was ordered back to camp late in the evening. The next morning, however, at an early hour, it again repaired to *Buena Vista*—

Arriving upon the field, a scene of the greatest consternation presented itself to our view—Some of the troops belonging to Genl. Wool's <–command–> division[1] were seen retreating before the enemy in great confusion, the enemy having succeeded in making his way around the left wing of our line and secured a position at the base of the mountain which gave him greatly the advantage over us, and rendered the fortunes of the day somewhat problomatical.[2] At this critical crisis, our regiment was ordered up to a point where the enemy, in great numbers, had drawn up in line ready to give us battle.

We were marched up by the right flank, and when within suitable distance of the enemy were halted, brought into line and then advanced in the same position, by the front—Col. Davis giving the order to fire advancing. A deadly fire was poured upon the enemy which greatly thined his ranks and caused him to retire in great confusion.[3]

In this charge Capt. Sharp was wounded in both legs, and from the serious nature of his wounds, the command of the company necessarilly devolved upon me, although he remained on the field the greater part of the day, encouraging his men by his presence and appeals, to "stand to their arms."

After making this successful charge, which, I regret to say, was <–not un–> attended with heavy loss on our side—many of our most gallant and skillful officers and bravest men having fell—Col. Davis, perceiving a large body <–approaching–> of Cavalry approaching our left, gave the order for us to retire, that we might gain a more advantagious position and receive support.[4]

In a short time the 3d Indiana Regt. commanded by Col. Lane and one piece of Light Artillery from /Capt./ Bragg's Battery,

commanded by Lieut. Kilbourn, came to our assistance. Cal. Davis
then gave the order to again advance which was promptly obeyed;
and at the approach of the Cavalry halted his command and cautioned it to stand fast and reserve its fire until the nearer approach
of the eneny. Cal. Lane did the sam to his command, which was
on our right and front—the two regiments forming a half-square.
As the Cavalry came near us, a <–deadly–> heavy and deadly fire
was directed at their ranks which caused them quickly to disperse,
with great loss.[5] The brilliant achievements of the day were at
length crowned with success by another charge of our regt. supported by the 3d Indiana, upon the heights of the revine on our
right, upon a column of infantry who were completely driven from
their position, which they had just before gained.[6]

The conduct of my command generally, was so meritorious that
I forbear mentioning individual instances of gallantry, lest I do injustice to others.

It may not be improper here to mention that a fragment of Col.
Bowls' 2d Indiana Regt. who had been rallied by the exertions of
Major Bradfor and Ajutant Griffith, after the route in the early
part of the action, put themselves under my immediate command,
and their conduct throughout the day was commendible in the
higest degree. There were from 16 to 18 of them. I regret that I
cannot procure their names, as such an exhibition of bravery is
rarely <–to be–> met with—their comrads having been driven
from the field in dismay, <–and–> whilst they, but a handful, were
left to bear the brunt of battle with /comparative/ *strangers*!

AMOS B. CORWIN,[7] Lieut.

Com'd'g. company "A." 1st Regt.

Miss. Riflemen

ADS (RG27, Vol. 26, Corres., Mexican War Docs., Ms-Ar). Endorsed
by Davis: "No. 3 Com 'A.' Lieut.
Corwine's *Statement*." Enclosed: Davis
to Albert G. Brown, Oct. 3, 1847.

[1] John E. Wool was left in command of the American troops at
Buena Vista when Taylor, the Mississippi regiment, and other units of the
headquarters command returned to
camp near Saltillo on February 22.

[2] Corwine refers to the flight of
several volunteer units from the
American left, particularly the 2d
Ind., Ky., and Ark. Cav. rgts. Letters
D, E, and F on the map indicate their
assigned posts.

[3] Davis' men marched from the hacienda along the road and through
the northernmost ravine, turning by
the right flank to gain the plateau
(Woodville *Repub.*, Apr. 17, 1847;
Alexander B. Bradford's report to

Davis, Mar. 2, 1847). Nos. 2 and 3 mark the places of their encounter with the enemy.

[4] No. 5 on the map of Buena Vista shows the approximate place where the Mississippians regrouped.

[5] A reference to the V formation, no. 7 on the map.

[6] See nos. 9 and 10 on the map for the location of the Mississippi regiment's final engagement.

[7] Amos Breckinridge Corwine (1815–80), a native Kentuckian, was associated with newspapers in Mississippi and Cincinnati before serving as United States consul in what is now Panama, from 1850 until 1861. Thereafter he practiced law in New Rochelle, New York. He and Davis, whom Corwine described as his "best Earthly friend and benefactor," maintained throughout their lives the friendship forged in Mexico (Corwine to Davis, Feb. 2, 1860, Davis Papers, KyLxT, Mar. 10, 1853, Davis, *Papers*, ed. Rowland, 2:187–88, Oct. 21, 1878, ViRC; N.Y. *Times*, June 24, 1880, 2; *Vedette*, Aug. 15, 1880, 11; DNA, RG15, Mexican War Pension Applics., WC 3221).

Reuben N. Downing to Richard Griffith[1]

Camp 1st Regt Mississippi Riflemen
Saltillo 1st March 1847

SIR

I herewith submit, a statement of the operations <–of the operations–> of the first Regement of Mississippi Riflemen commanded by Col Jeff Davis, and G. company, same regement, in the battles of Buena Vista fought near this place on the 22nd & 23rd Ultimo. I assumed the command of G company on the evening of the 22nd,[2] when the troops were being arranged in order of battle, near the ranch of Buena Vista, at the pass of En Cantada,[3] for a conflict with the enemy who was advancing with a large and superior force Whilst engaged in arranging the order of Battle, skirmishers became engaged with the enemy in the mountains, on the left of the line, and continued a brisk fire until night fall, without any material result on either side[4] when our regement which was in reserve,[5] was ordered to return to Camp at this place, a distance of near eight miles, Early in the morning of the 23rd we returned to the battle field. As we approached the roar of Cannon & the heavy discharges of musketry, were distinctly heard, giving assurance that the battle had earnestly commenced, As we approached nearer rumors of every character reached our ears, the most alarming, that the day was going against us—that our left wing had been turned & that the enemy were pouring into the plain to attack us in rear, Our regement moved forward & not a man did I hear expressing any fear or alarm as to the result. When we arrived in sight, we discovered < our > /the/ left wing had broken & were flying in every direction, & were being pursued by a large & overwhelming force of the enemy. We met many of our friends flying in haste from the field, We endeavrd to rally them but in vain—but few could be rallied, who joined us & fought gallantly through the day.[6] The enemy were following the fugitives cutting them down at every step, Our arrival in the field arrested their attention, I counted six heavy armed regements of Infantry & four detachments of cavalry of the enemy, in echelon at the base of the mountains and on the plain, Our regement <–in column–> /in column/ commenced moving rapidly, <–up–> in the direction of the enemy having a ravine on our right,[7] I looked behind to see what assistance we would receive. I could see none. When we arrived in proper distance we deployed into line,[8] gave three hearty cheers & rushed impetuously on the enemys lines, Such was the impetuousity of the onset, one regement of the enemy retired rapidly to a heavy reserve in their rear, at this time my attention was directed to a large body of Lancers, approaching us on our right, evidently with the intention of attacking us in rear, I called all the riflemen I could around me, crossed the ravine in the direction of the enemy placed them in a safe position & commenced a fire on the head of their column,[9] when I received orders to retire, which was done, the enemy firing down the ravine at us, retiring & we returning the fire. Two riflemen were killed <–by–> /near/ me in retiring, On emerging from the ravine I discoverd the Lancers had retired, as also their Infantry & took a position near their reserve During this time we had received no assistance from any arm in the service, at the moment we commenced the rapid movement on the enemy, he was evidently making his disposition to advance on the <–op–> open plain, (which was altogether open to him)[10] & attack our army in rear, he was waiting for the arrival of the heavy body of Lancers who made the demenstration on our right to make the movement The charge in our part checked therer /movement/ effectually & compelled them to fall back on their heavy reserve, Our regement retired about two hundred yards to the rear,[11] & rapidly formed <–our–> /a/ line, when an Indiania Regement came to our support, together with Leut Kilborn with one piece of light artillery, We commenced moving slowly upon the enemy with the artillery in the centre,[12]

This piece was admirably served & with such effect, that Col Davis perceived a demonstration in the part of the enemy to charge us, This we prepared for by changing the line, forming in right angle, the Indianna Regement on our right, their flank protected by a deep ravine & our left by artillery, as we had finished making this disposition the enemys Lancers came down upon us in gallant style, to within <–60–> sixty or one hundred yards, when they received a fire from the whole line which was so destructive, it caused them to wheel & retreat rapidly from us,[13] Being reenforced at this juncture by Capt Sherman & three pieces, light artillery & Col May[14] with the dragoons, we continued to advance upon them, with the artillery, Col May with the dragoons moving up on our left, making a demonstration to charge, the Infantry & artillery moving directly upon them, had the effect of dispersing them in the mountains or driving them entirely from the field.[15] After resting from the fatigues of the <–day–> /charge/[16] we were ordered to the front near the centre of our line, to assist our friends who were gallantly struggling against terrible odds, When advancing to their relief we discovered a large body of Mexicans, charging in fine style down the hill on the artillery,[17] We opened a fire upon them at the distance of two hundred yards, which arrested their progress, We gave many hearty cheers & charged them[18]—the enemy broke & fled over the point of the hill, we pursuing—we perceived a Mexican Battery to our left next the mountains which commanded this hill;[19] I <–directed–> /ordered/ my company & those of the Riflemen, who followed, to pass with me rapidly over the point of the hill, to the next ravine where I supposed the enemy were[20]— This was performed by a portion of the regiment & the enemy commenced retreating from the ravine, we received a raking fire from their Battery, & were ordered to retire, which was done, not however until we had succeeded in killing & despersing this force of the enemy. Nothing farther occured worthy of mention during the remainder of the evening, We had been engaged with the enemy near eight hours, The conflict for the day was over the enemy had been driven from all our line, & we remained victors of the day, Tewards night our regement was ordered to return to Camp[21] & after the nights repose, we again prepared ourselves for the field; when we received intelligence that Genl Santa Anna with all his forces had retreated in the direction from which he came, in great haste & apparently in great confusion, <–1 ta–>

I take pleasure in mentioning the good conduct of Leuts Greaves & Hampton who were very efficient & rendered good service throughout the day, Also the good conduct of the non commissioned officers of G, Company & Sergeant McNair[22] of E. Company who acted with me a portion of the day, [&?] *all* the men of my company, Of the four corporals one was killed & three were wounded, Corperal<–s–> Atkinson,[23] Prvates Thompson.[24] Neely,[25] Gibbs,[26] Saunders,[27] who were wounded, continued the fight during the day, Leut McNulty[28] fell while leading a portion of the Company against the enemy in the morning, Private James H Graves Bond Felts. Parr. Seay L a Cooper & /Cerpl/ Alexander, also fell in the first conflict with the enemy in the morning Very Respty yr obt Sevt

R N Downing
Capt Comdg G. 1st Rgt M R

ALS (RG27, Vol. 26, Corres., Mexican War Docs., Ms-Ar). Endorsed by Davis: "No. 8 Com. 'G.'" Enclosed: Davis to Albert G. Brown, Oct. 3, 1847.

1 Regimental adj. Griffith received this and three other reports on Davis' behalf.

2 Wounded at Monterrey, Downing had been in Mississippi on furlough. Already on his way back to the war, he had hastened from Monterrey when he heard of the Mexican advance. He joined the Mississippi regiment early in the afternoon of February 22 (DNA, M-863, roll 1; New Orleans *Picayune*, Jan. 3, 1847; Vicksburg *Daily Whig*, Apr. 2, 1847).

3 Downing confused two geographical entities, the pass of La Angostura and the nearby ranch of La Encantada. Taylor's forces were deployed at the pass on the afternoon of February 22 (Smith, *War with Mexico*, 1:384).

4 About 3:00 in the afternoon eight rifle companies and the Ky. Cav. under Col. Humphrey Marshall engaged the troops of Gen. Ampudia on the extreme left of the field. Because of some initial confusion the enemy succeeded in gaining an advantageous position but, according to Marshall, "overshot their mark . . . killed no one, and wounded only seven." Mexican losses were said to be "considerable" (*Senate Ex. Doc. 1*, 30:1, 146, 164–65, 171). See letters E and F on the Buena Vista map.

5 The Mississippi regiment's position on February 22 is marked as no. 1 on the map.

6 Downing refers to the retreat of several volunteer regiments from the American left; some members of the 2d Ind. Rgt. fell in with Davis' command.

7 The northern ravine.

8 No. 2 on the map marks the place at which the Mississippians first met the enemy.

9 While falling back from the first charge the Mississippi regiment re-

pulsed a lancer attack at about no. 4 on the map.

[10] The northern plateau. Because the American left had collapsed, Davis' men were the only fresh troops standing between the Mexican advance and Buena Vista.

[11] The point where the Mississippians regrouped is no. 5 on the map of Buena Vista.

[12] In addition to the 3d Ind. Rgt. and a piece of light artillery under Charles L. Kilburn, a substantial portion of the 2d Ind. Rgt., rallied under Lt. Col. William R. Haddon, reinforced the Mississippians after the first charge (Haddon to Davis, July 4, 1853, Haddon Coll., In). From the rallying point the combined force moved toward Gen. Ampudia's troops, forcing them back to the base of the mountains (no. 6 on the Buena Vista map; Carleton, *Buena Vista*, 79–81).

[13] As Downing indicated, the 3d Ind. and the rallied 2d Ind. formed on the Mississippi right, the 3d Ind. anchored on the northern ravine (Gibson, *Buena Vista*, 5). The Mississippi left was flanked by Capt. Thomas W. Sherman's 12-pound howitzer since Lt. Kilburn by then had returned to his command. See Davis' report of March 2 for details of the V formation; see also no. 7 on the map and Davis' sketch of the V.

[14] Charles Augustus May (1818–64), capt., 2d Dragoons, was an early hero of the Mexican War. Brevetted col. after Buena Vista, he was promoted maj., 1st Dragoons, in 1855. After the fall of Fort Sumter, May resigned his commission and settled in New York City (Heitman, *Hist. Reg.*, 1:698; N.Y. *Tribune*, Dec. 28, 1864, 8; *NCAB*, 4:321).

[15] Downing has counted Sherman's 12-pounder as well as another 12-pounder and a 6-pounder under the command of Lt. John F. Reynolds as the Mississippians' artillery support. In conjunction with his own squadron of 2d Dragoons, May had

organized a sizable contingent of other cavalry, infantry, and artillery at the Buena Vista hacienda. The combined advance—May's command and the troops that included the Mississippi regiment—was successful. As one observer noted, "the dismayed Mexicans retired before us in disorder" and were effectively trapped near the foot of the eastern mountains (Carleton, *Buena Vista*, 89–93, 101–105; *Senate Ex. Doc. 1*, 30:1, 198–99, 203–205; Grayson M. Prevost to John E. Wool, Aug. 3, 1847, Wool Papers, N). See no. 8 on the map.

[16] A lull in the fighting occurred early in the afternoon as the two sides exchanged white flags. Taylor sent his aide Thomas L. Crittenden to propose that the imperiled enemy force surrender (see the note above). At about the same time one or more Mexican officers approached the main plateau to ask Taylor what he wanted. Taylor then ordered a ceasefire and sent Gen. Wool to confer with Santa Anna. Both Crittenden and Wool failed in their missions, however, and the Mexicans took advantage of the quiet to elude their erstwhile pursuers and rejoin the main army (Washington *Union*, Apr. 2, 1847; *Senate Ex. Doc. 1*, 30:1, 136, 148–49, 202; Alcarez et al., *Other Side*, 126–27).

[17] Combining all his forces under the command of Francisco Pérez, Santa Anna launched a massive assault on the main plateau. The units under attack were the 1st Ill., 2d Ill., and 2d Ky. rgts., a section of the 2d Art., and two guns of the 4th Art. As the Americans yielded, Capt. Braxton Bragg arrived with his Co. C, 3d Art., "advanc[ing] several hundred yards" on the plateau. Capt. Thomas W. Sherman's guns and the Mississippi and Indiana regiments joined the action shortly after Bragg (*Senate Ex. Doc. 1*, 30:1, 202, 204–205; *Niles' Reg.*, Apr. 24, 1847, 119; Carleton, *Buena Vista*, 107–14).

[18] See no. 9 on the Buena Vista map

for the site of the Mississippians' last charge.

[19] See letter 1 on the map of Buena Vista.

[20] No. 11 on the map.

[21] Other than the wounded and the Mississippi regiment, which was ordered to protect the camp near Saltillo during the night, all the American troops remained on the field, expecting an attack the following morning (Vicksburg *Daily Whig*, Apr. 2, 1847; Carleton, *Buena Vista*, 126–29).

[22] Evander McNair (1820–1902), born in North Carolina and reared in southern Mississippi, operated a store in Brandon after the Mexican War. He settled in Washington, Arkansas, about 1856; early in 1861 he raised a battalion to form part of the 4th Ark. Inf., which he was elected to command. Promoted brig. gen. after the battle at Richmond, Kentucky, McNair was wounded at Chickamauga and later saw action in the Trans-Mississippi Department. He later was a merchant in New Orleans (Warner, *Gens. in Gray*; Rowland, *Heart of the South*, 3:519–22).

[23] Asa B. Atkinson, born in North Carolina about 1816, was a mechanic and sawmill operator in Hinds County in the 1850s (1850 Census, Miss., Hinds, family 1180; ibid., 1860, family 796; DNA, M-863, roll 1).

[24] Joseph H. Thompson, born in 1821, was a native Tennessean who lived in Natchez and in Hinds County, where he was a farmer. As late as 1887 he was residing in Scott County (DNA, RG15, Mexican War Pension Applics., SC 1780; 1860 Census, Miss., Hinds, family 828).

[25] Andrew J. Neely, a resident of Brownsville, died en route to California in the spring of 1849; he was about thirty-four years old (DNA, M-863, roll 2; Vicksburg *Tri-Weekly Whig*, May 17, 1849).

[26] Charles H. Gibbs, a merchant born in Virginia early in the 1820s, died of yellow fever at Raymond in October 1855 (1850 Census, Miss., Hinds, family 354; Vicksburg *Tri-Weekly Whig*, Oct. 16, 1855).

[27] Romulus M. Saunders was born about 1825 in Alabama. In 1847 he returned to Hinds County but apparently was living in Seguin, Texas, by 1862, when he requested Davis' assistance in securing a Confederate army position (1850 Census, Miss., Hinds, family 1311; Jackson *Southron*, May 28, Nov. 5, 1847; DNA, M-863, roll 3; Saunders to Davis, Feb. 28, 1862, DNA, RG109, Citizens File).

[28] Francis J. McNulty, aged approximately twenty-six, was an 1846 graduate of the Louisville Medical Institute and a resident of Raymond (DNA, M-863, roll 2; Anderson, ed., *La. Swamp Doctor*, 266; Henry, *Masons*, 79).

To William W. S. Bliss[1]

Satillo, Mexico 2d March 1847

SIR:

In compliance with your note of yesterday,[2] I have the honor to present the following report of the service of the Mississippi riflemen on the 23d ultimo.

Eearly in the morning of that day the Regiment was drawn out from the Head-quarters encampment, which stood in advance of, and overlooked, the town of Saltillo. Conformably to instructions, two companies were detached for the protection of that encampment, and to defend the adjacent entrance to the town. The remaining eight companies were put in march to return to the position of the preceding day,[3] now known as the battle-field of Buena Vista. We had approached to within about two miles of that position, when the report of artillery-firing, which reached us, gave assurance that a battle had commenced. Excited by the sound, the regiment pressed rapidly forward, manifesting upon this, as upon other occasions, their more than willingness to meet the enemy.

At the first convenient place the column was halted for the purpose of filling the canteens with water;[4] and, the march being resumed, was directed towards the position which had been indicated to me, on the previous evening, as the post of our Regiment. As we approached the scene of action, horsemen recognised to be of our troops, were seen running, dispersed and confusedly, from the field; and our first view of the line of battle, presented the mortifying spectacle of a regiment of infantry flying disorganized from before the enemy.[5] These sights, so well calculated to destroy confidence, and dispirit troops just coming into action, it is my pride and pleasure to believe, only nerved the resolution of the Regiment I have the honor to command.

Our order of march was in column of Companies advancing by their centres. The point which had just been abandoned by the regiment alluded to,[6] was now taken as our direction. I rode forward to examine the ground upon which we were going to operate, and in passing <–[illegible]–> through the fugitives, appealed to them to return with us, and renew the fight; pointing to our Regiment as a mass of men behind which they might securely form. With a few honarable exceptions, the appeal was as unheeded as were the offers which, I am informed, were made by our men, to give their canteens of water to those who complained of thirst, on condition that they would go back.

General Wool was upon the ground making great efforts to rally the men who had given way. I approached him, and asked if he would send another regiment to sustain me in an attack upon the enemy before us. He was alone; and after promising the support, went in person to send it.[7]

Upon further examination, I found that the slope we were ascending[8] was intersected by a deep ravine, which, uniting obliquely with a still larger one upon our right,[9] formed between them a point of land difficult of access by us; but which, spreading into a plain towards the base of the mountain, had easy communication with the main body of the enemy. This position important from it's natural strength, derived a far greater value from the relation it bore to our order of battle, and line of communication with the rear.[10] The enemy in number many times greater than ourselves, supported by strong reserves, flanked by cavalry, and elated by recent success, was advancing upon it. The moment seemed to me critical, and the occasion to require whatever sacrifice it might cost to check the enemy.

My Regiment having continued to advance was near at hand. I met and formed it rapidly into order of battle; the line then advanced in double quick time, until within the estimated range of our rifles, when it was halted, and ordered to "fire advancing."[11]

The progress of the enemy was arrested. We crossed the difficult chasm before us under a galling fire, and in good order renewed the attack. <–upon the other side.–> The contest was severe,— the destruction great upon both sides. We steadily advanced,[12] and as the distance was diminished, the ratio of loss increased rapidly against the enemy; he yielded, and was driven back on his reserves.

A plain now lay behind us—the enemy's cavalry had passed around our right flank, which rested on the main ravine,[13] and gone to our rear. The support I had expected to join us was nowhere to be seen. I therefore ordered the regiment to retire, and went in person to find the cavalry, which after passing round our right, had been concealed by the inequality of the ground.

I found them at the first point where the bank was practicable for horsemen, in the act of descending into the ravine— no doubt for the purpose of charging upon rear. The nearest of our men ran quickly to my call, attacked this body, and dispersed it with some loss.[14] I think their commander was among the killed.

The Regiment was formed again in line of battle behind the first ravine we had crossed;[15] soon after which, we were joined upon our left by Lieut. Kilbourne with a piece of light artillery; and Col. Lane's, the 3d Regiment of Indiana volunteers.[16]

Lieut. Kilbourn opened a brisk and very effective fire: the enemy immediately receded; we advanced,[17] and he retired to the mountain. No senior officer of Lieut. Kilbourn's corps being present upon this occasion, it gives me pleasure to bear testimony to the valuable services he rendered, and to express my admiration of the professional skill and soldierly qualities he manifested.

We now occupied the ground where the Mississippi regiment first met the enemy. A heavy fire was opened upon us by a battery which the enemy had established near the centre of his line. The Indiana regiment was most exposed and passed from the left into the ravine upon our right.[18]

The artillery was retired to the battery from which it had been drawn. I had sent forward some parties, to examine the ground on which we had fought in the morning, for the purpose of bringing in the wounded: when these parties had returned, our Regiment retired by it's left flank, and marched along the bank of the ravine, heretofore noticed, as being on our right. The Indiana regiment, moving down the hollow, was concealed from the view of the enemy, who was probably thereby encouraged to make an attack.

We had proceeded but a short distance, when I saw a large body of cavalry[19] debouche from his cover on the left of the position from which we had retired, and advance rapidly upon us.[20] The Mississippi Regiment was filed to the right and fronted, in line across the plain; the Indiana Regiment was formed on the bank of the ravine, in advance of our right flank, by which a reentering angle was presented to the enemy.[21] Whilst this preperation was being made, Serjeant Major Miller, of our regiment, was sent to Captain Sherman for one or more pieces of artillery from his battery.

The enemy who was now seen to be a body of richly caparisoned lancers, came forward rapidly and in beautiful order—the files and ranks so closed, as to look like a /solid/ mass of men and horses. Perfect silence, and the greatest steadiness prevailed in both lines of our troops, as they stood at shouldered arms waiting an attack. Confident of success, and anxious to obtain the full advantage of a cross fire at short distance, I repeatedly called to the men not to shoot.[22]

As the enemy approached, his speed regularly diminished, until, when within 80 or 100 yards, he had drawn up to a walk, and seemed about to halt. A few files fired without orders, and both lines then instantly poured in a volley so destructive, that the mass yieded to the blow, and the survivors fled.[23] Captain Sherman having come up with a field piece from his battery, followed their retreat with a very effective fire, until they had fled beyond the range of his gun.

Soon after this event, a detachment of our artillery and cavalry moved up on our left, and I was directed to cooperate with it, in an attack upon the enemy at the base of the mountain.[24]

We advanced parallel to this detachment, until it was halted. I then placed our men under such protection, as the ground afforded,[25] from the constant fire of the enemy's artillery, to which we were exposed, to wait the further movement of the force with which we were to act. At this time, the enemy made his last attack upon the right, and I received the Generals order, to march to that portion of the field.[26]

The broken character of the intervening ground concealed the scene of action from our view; but the heavy firing of musketry formed a sufficient guide for our course. After marching two or three hundred yards, we saw the enemy's infantry advancing in three lines upon Capt. Bragg's battery; which, though entirely unsupported, resolutely held it's position,[27] and met the attack, with a fire worthy of the former acheivements of that battery,[28] and of the reputation of it's present meritorious commander. We pressed on, climbed the rocky slope of the plain on which this combat occurred, reached it's brow so as to take the enemy in flank and reverse,[29] when he was about one hundred yards from the battery. Our first fire—raking each of his lines, and opened close upon his flank—was eminently destructive. His right gave way, and he fled in confusion.[30]

In this the last conflict of the day, my regiment equalled—it was impossible to exceed—my expectations. Though worn down by many hours of fatigue and thirst, the ranks thinned by our heavy loss in the morning, they yet advanced upon the enemy with the alacrity and eagerness of men fresh to the combat. In every approbatory sense of these remarks, I wish to be included a party of Col. Bowles' Indiana regiment, which served with us during a greater part of the day, under the immediate command of an officer from that regiment, whose gallantry attracted my particular attention, but whose name I regret is unknown to me.[31]

When hostile demonstrations had ceased, I retired to a tent upon the field for surgical aid, having been wounded by a musket ball, when we first went into action. Our Regiment remained inactive until evening, and was then ordered to the encampment of the previous night, under the command of Major Bradford.

We had seen the enemy retire; but his numerical superiority over

us would scarcely admit the supposition that he had finally retreated. After my arrival at our encampment, which was some time after
dark,[32] I directed Capt. Rogers, with his Company "K." and Lieut.
Russell, commanding Company "D." to proceed with their commands to the field of battle, and report to the commanding General
for orders. These were the two companies which had been left as a
guard at Head-quarters encampment, as stated in the beginning of
this report. They had been threatened during the day by a strong
detachment of the enemy's cavalry; and had performed all the duties
which belonged to their position, as will be seen by the accompanying statement of Capt. Rogers,[33] in a manner creditable to themselves and their Regiment; but they were disappointed, because they
had not been with us in the battle of the day, and were gratified at
the order to march upon night service, and probably to a dangerous
post.

Every part of the battle having been fought under the eye of the
commanding General, the importance and manner of any service it
was our fortune to render, will be best estimated by him:[34] but in
view of my own responsibility, it may be permitted me to say in
relation to our first attack upon the enemy, that I considered the
necessity absolute and immediate. No one could have failed to perceive the hazard. The enemy, in greatly disproportionate numbers,
was rapidly advancing. We say no friendly troops coming to our
support, and probably none except myself expected reinforcement.
Under such circumstances, the men cheerfully, ardently entered into
the conflict; and though we lost in that single engagement, more than
thirty killed, and forty wounded,[35] the Regiment never faltered,[36]
nor moved except as it was ordered. Had the expected reinforcement arrived, we could have prevented the enemy's cavalry from
passing to our rear, results more decisive might have been obtained,
and a part of our loss have been avoided.

To enumerate the instances of gallantry, and good conduct, which
I witnessed, would exceed the limits proper to this communication,
and yet could not fail to omit very many which occurred. I will
therefore attempt no other discrimination than to make an exception
of the two <–privates–> privates who were reported as "missing,"
and who have since been returned by the enemy, taken prisoners
without a wound.[37] <–and–> Upon all others both officers and
men, I have the pleasure to confer my unqualified commendation.

To Major Bradford, I offer my thanks for the prompt and creditable manner in which he executed all the orders I gave him; and would especially refer to the delicate duty assigned him, of restoring order among the files of another regiment, when rendered unsteady by the fire of the enemy's artillery.[38]

Adjutant Griffith rendered me important aid, as well in his appropriate duties, as by the intelligence and courage with which he reconnoitred the enemy, and gave valuable information.

I must also notice the good conduct of Sergeant Major Miller, and Quarter master Sergeant White, of the Regimental staff.

First Lieut. Mott[39] acting assistant Commissary of subsistence, joined his Company, (capt. Taylor's) and performed good service throughout the day.

Second Lieut Slade acting assistant Quarter master, was left, in charge of his train, at our encampment. It has been reported to me, that when the enemy's cavalry threatened our encampment, he formed his teamsters and others into a party, mounted them on waggon horses, and joined Lieutenant Shrover of the artillery, in his brilliant sortie, by which the enemy was driven from his position on our line of communication.[40]

Captain Sharp's Company "A." and Captn. Delay's company "F." having been on "detached service" when the battle of Monterey was fought, seemed anxious on this occasion to bring up any arrears in which they might be supposed to stand to the Regiment. They formed the first division,[41] and did their duty nobly.

Three of the Companies were by unavoidable causes, deprived of the presence of their Captains on this occasion,[42] viz.

Company "C," commanded by Lieut. Cook, whose gallantry at the storming of Monterey received my notice, and whose good conduct on this occasion is worthy of the highest commendation.

Company "E." commanded by Lieut. Fletcher, who showed himself equal to all the emergencies of that eventful day.

Company "H," commanded by Lieut Moore, who so gallantly led it on the 23d of September, in the storming of Monterey. Cool, brave, and well informed, he possessed my highest respect and entire confidence. He fell in our first engagement, and on our most advanced position. The command of the Company then devolved upon 2d Lieut. Clendennin[43] (Captain elect) who continued to lead it during the battle.

145

Captain Taylor of Company "I," was present with his command throughout the day, and, as on former occasions, proved himself worthy to be the leader of that gallant Company.

Captain Cooper, with his company "B," upon the left flank of the Regiment, seized every opportunity which his position gave him, and rendered distinguished service.

Captain Downing joined his company "G," on the 22d at Buena Vista. He had heard at the Rinconada that we were about to be attacked, and though the road was beset by "Rancheros," he hastened forward, and took command of his Company in the morning. In the first engagement of the 23d, this company was particularly distinguished, and fulfilled the expectations which it's high state of discipline warranted. Second Lieut. McNulty was killed when leading a portion of the company to the charge. First Lieut. Greaves, /and Second Lieut Hampton/ for their gallantry in battle and uniform good conduct, deserve the highest consideration.

There were many instances of both officers and men, who after being wounded remained upon the field, and continued to discharge their duties until active operations had ceased. Such was the case with Captain Sharp; who though shot through both thighs, evinced so great reluctance to leaving the field, that he was permitted to remain and follow his Company on horseback. Lieuts. Posey, and Corwine, and Stockard[44] were wounded, but set the valuable example of maintaining their posts.— such also, was the conduct of Sergeants Scott,[45] of Company "C," and Hollingsworth,[46] of Comp. "A;" of Private Malone[47] of Company "F;" and of others whose names have not been reported to me.

In addition to the officers already commended in this report, I would mention as deserving especial consideration for their gallantry and general good conduct, Lieuts, Calhoun, & Dill,[48] and Arthur, and Harrison, and Brown[49] and Hughes.

It may be proper for me to notice the fact, that early in the action Col. Bowles of Indiana, with a small party from his Regiment, which he stated was all of his men that he could rally,[50] joined us, and expressed a wish to serve with my command. He remained with us throughout the day, and under all circumstances, displayed much personal gallantry.

Referring for the casualties in in my Regiment to the list which has been furnished,[51] I have the honor to be very respectfully, yr. mo. obt. svt.

JEFFN: DAVIS
Col. Missi. Rifln.

ALS (RG27, Vol. 26, Corres., Mexican War Docs., Ms-Ar). LS (DNA, RG94, Letters Recd., 257-T-1847, f/w 169-T-1847). Enclosed: Davis to Albert G. Brown, Oct. 3, 1847.

[1] William Wallace Smith Bliss (1815–53), born in New York, graduated from West Point in 1833. Appointed Zachary Taylor's chief of staff in 1845, he served through the war and became Taylor's son-in-law (1848) and private secretary (1848–50). He died of yellow fever at his home on the Mississippi coast (Cullum, *Biog. Reg.*, 1:543–45; Taylor, *Letters*, xii–xiii).

[2] Bliss's note has not been found.

[3] No. 1 on the map of Buena Vista.

[4] See the map of Buena Vista for the springs near the hacienda.

[5] The retreat of the Ark. Cav., Ky. Cav., and 2d Ind. rgts. from the American left. See letters D, E, F, on the map.

[6] The 2d Ind. Rgt. had been posted on the southeastern edge of the main plateau (Carleton, *Buena Vista*, 50); see letter D on the map.

[7] Davis, "having left the road and taken a diagonal direction towards the [main] plateau," met Wool about midway between Buena Vista and the plateau (Baylies, *Wool's Campaign*, 33; Wool to Henry B. Dawson, May 21, 1860, Wool Coll., ICHi).

[8] The northern plateau.

[9] The northern ravine and its eastern branch.

[10] If the Mexicans had seized the northern plateau, they would have entrapped the American army, since the mountains provided natural barriers on the east and west and Santa Anna would have gained control of the road leading north and south. See the map of Buena Vista.

[11] For the route taken by the regiment, see the map of Buena Vista. No. 2 indicates the starting point of the Mississippians' first charge.

[12] No. 3 approximates the site of the regiment's farthest advance in the first attack.

[13] By "plain" Davis means the northern plateau, one of the few relatively level tracts on the battlefield. The "main ravine" is the northern ravine.

[14] The repulse of the lancers occurred at about no. 4 on the map of Buena Vista. Davis later recalled that his regiment "poured such a destructive fire into the [Mexican cavalry] that it was instantly put to rout" (Davis to William A. Buck, June 21, 1859, ViRC).

[15] The rallying point on the northern plateau is no. 5 on the Buena Vista map.

[16] In addition, about 200 members of the 2d Ind. Rgt. who had rallied under the command of Lt. Col. William R. Haddon, joined Davis' command (Haddon to Davis, July 4, 1853, Haddon Coll., In).

[17] No. 6 is the approximate site that the volunteers and Kilburn's artillery reached in their advance. It was at the start of the movement that Davis reportedly uttered the command "*Forward-guide centre-march,*" which was adopted by Mississippi Democrats as their party slogan in June 1847 (Vicksburg *Daily Whig*, Mar. 31, 1847; Jackson *Mississippian*, June 11, 1847).

[18] Col. James H. Lane, 3d Ind., confirmed that "enfilading fire" from the

enemy battery forced him to retire through the northern ravine (*Senate Ex. Doc. 1*, 30:1, 187). The exact location of the battery is not known.

[19] According to a knowledgeable reporter, the Mexicans sent forward "a fresh brigade of cavalry, covered by infantry," numbering perhaps 2,000 (Carleton, *Buena Vista*, 94; Jackson *Mississippian*, Apr. 16, 1847; Gibson, *Buena Vista*, 5).

[20] Although Lane evidently had noticed the cavalry when the Indiana and Mississippi regiments advanced to the mountains, Davis was surprised at their approach: "the charge of Mexican cavalry was not anticipated—indeed the presence of such a force on our left was not known until it debouched from a ravine about four hundred yards distant and commenced advancing on us" (Davis to William A. Buck, June 21, 1859, ViRC; *Senate Ex. Doc. 1*, 30:1, 187).

[21] Davis has described the V formation, no. 7 on the Buena Vista map. The Mississippi regiment was aligned perpendicular to and some distance from the bank of the northern ravine, forming the left side of an obtuse angle; the 2d and 3d Ind. rgts. formed the right side of the angle, which rested on the ravine's northern bank. Davis' own position was on the right flank of his regiment (Davis, *Papers*, ed. Rowland, 8:487–88). Among the many descriptions given of this unusual defense against cavalry, none was more often repeated than that of Lt. Charles P. Kingsbury: "Col. Davis immediately threw his command into the form of a V, the opening towards the enemy" (New Orleans *Jeffersonian*, Apr. 3, 1847). Davis later explained that the V was not devised by "previous design, but familiar from a military education and many years of military service with the advantage of a <–[illegible]–> /converging/ fire it was a natural and ready conclusion from the conviction that our fire would repel the attack, that the troops should be so disposed as to give the greatest effect to our fire" (Davis to

William A. Buck, June 21, 1859, ViRC). See also Davis' sketch of the V formation.

[22] A member of the 2d Ind. Rgt. who served in the ranks of the Mississippi regiment recalled Davis' words as they awaited the lancers' charge: "'Hold your fire, men, until they get close, and then give it to them!'" (Scribner, *Camp Life*, 65). According to Davis, in obedience to his orders his men "stood motionless as a rock, silent as death, and eager as a greyhound" (Nov. 11, 1858, Davis, *Speeches*, 46).

[23] After the battle two Indianans claimed that the 3d Ind. Rgt. deserved credit for the success of the V formation. One declared that the lancers were repelled "before the Mississippians delivered a fire," and the other stated that the head of the enemy column was stopped 170 paces from the Mississippi right flank, beyond the range of the Mississippians' rifles (Indianapolis *Ind. State Sentinel*, June 9, 1847; Brookville *Ind. American*, June 25, 1847).

[24] Referring to the advance toward the eastern mountains in conjunction with a large force commanded by Capt. Charles A. May. See no. 8 on the map.

[25] After the advance and during the exchange of white flags, Davis' men were resting in a sheltered position near the edge of the northern plateau (Jackson *Southron*, Apr. 16, 1847).

[26] Davis recalled that in midafternoon one of Zachary Taylor's aides "called from the other side of the ravine . . . that General Taylor wanted support" (McElroy, *Davis*, 1:91–92; Crawford Fletcher's report, Feb. 28, 1847).

[27] The Mississippians marched with trailed arms in double-quick time toward the position marked no. 9 on the map of Buena Vista. Braxton Bragg had placed his three pieces of artillery on the southeastern edge of the main plateau (Woodville *Repub.*, Apr. 17, 1847; Carleton, *Buena Vista*, 112).

[28] Co. C, 3d Art., was the first unit

in the American army to be designated horse artillery (1838). Commanded first by Samuel Ringgold and later (1846) by Randolph Ridgely, the "flying artillery" had "dazzled observers with its speed and precision" (McWhiney, *Bragg*, 54, 61, 74; Birkhimer, *Hist. Sketch*, 54–63).

29 The site of the Mississippians' last charge is shown as no. 9 on the map of Buena Vista.

30 Omitted from Davis' and other Mississippi accounts is any notice of seeing the retreating Illinois and Kentucky regiments, an omission that lends credence to the claims of the 3d Ind. that they were first on the plateau, firing twice before Davis and his men arrived. The 3d Ind. suffered heavy casualties on the main plateau, while Davis' command apparently had none (Washington *Union*, Aug. 25, 1847; Gibson, *Buena Vista*, 6; Indianapolis *Ind. State Sentinel*, Aug. 30, 1848; Vicksburg *Weekly Whig*, Apr. 7, 1847).

31 Davis later learned that 2d Lt. David S. Lewis of the 2d Ind. was the officer whose actions he noted.

32 Davis arrived at the camp near Saltillo "in a common wagon" about 10 P.M. He evidently spent the night there and, anticipating a renewal of the fighting the next morning, "ordered himself to be placed in a wagon, and remained at the head of his regiment" (French, *Two Wars*, 82; Pace, ed., "Rogers Diary," *SWHQ*, 32:277n; Matamoros *American Flag*, Apr. 10, 1847).

33 Rogers' report is dated March 6.

34 In his official report Taylor warmly praised Davis and his men; a member of Co. G wrote that after the victory Taylor sent a special messenger to compliment them for "having that day covered themselves with immortal honor" (*Senate Ex. Doc. 1*, 30:1, 139; Jackson *Southron*, Apr. 16, 1847). Taylor's apparent partiality for Davis' men was resented by many, especially members and friends of the Indiana regiments (Smith, *Campaign*, 74–77; Washington *Union*, Aug. 25, 1847).

35 According to Davis' figures, about 70 percent of the total Mississippi casualties was accounted for in the first charge.

36 Braxton Bragg believed that the Mississippi was the only volunteer unit that did not waver during the battle, but William R. Haddon recalled that some of Davis' men were "rendered a little unsteady" by artillery fire just before the V formation. Haddon ordered them back into position, "telling them that the lines was their safest place." Davis reportedly concurred, remarking, " 'Well said, the place of duty is the place of safety' " (Haddon to Davis, July 4, 1853, Haddon Coll., In; Bragg to William T. Sherman, Mar. 1, 1848, Sherman Papers, DLC).

37 Pvts. Frederick M. Schneider, Co. B, and James W. Vinson, Co. I, are believed to have fled the field after the Mississippians' first engagement. No stigma attached to the capture of Cpl. James E. Stewart, who was taken after being wounded. All three were returned about March 1 (DNA, M-863, roll 3; Vicksburg *Daily Whig*, Apr. 7, 1847).

38 Bradford rallied members of the 2d and 3d Ind. rgts., as well as some stragglers who had joined the Mississippians before the V formation. See his report of March 2.

39 Christopher Haynes Mott (1826–62), born in Kentucky and reared in Holly Springs, had attended Transylvania University. After the war he practiced law with L. Q. C. Lamar, was a state legislator (1850), county probate judge (1857), and special United States commissioner to California. Col., 19th Miss. Inf., in 1861–62, Mott was mortally wounded near Williamsburg, Virginia (Rowland, ed., *Ency. Miss. Hist.*; Mayes, *L. Q. C. Lamar*, 61; *Miss. Laws, 1856–57*, 93).

40 Slade's command consisted of "a promiscuous crowd of mounted and foot volunteers, teamsters, and citizens" who joined Lt. William H. H. Shover's 6-pounder, another piece of artillery, and an Illinois company in

pursuit of the Mexican cavalry that threatened both the headquarters camp and the town itself (Carleton, *Buena Vista*, 119–21). For details, see the report of William P. Rogers dated March 6.

[41] The companies on the right flank (Hardee, *Rifle and Light Inf. Tactics*, 1:5–6).

[42] Capts. John Willis, John L. McManus, and George P. Crump were absent. Willis, left ill in Monterrey, arrived with reinforcements the morning of February 24; McManus was also ill but participated in the defense of Saltillo; Crump had resigned in November 1846 (Vicksburg *Daily Whig*, Apr. 2, 1847; DNA, M-863, rolls 1–3).

[43] John S. Clendenin (1818–57), a Pennsylvanian, lived in Yazoo County before the Mexican War. In 1848–49 he was inspector of customs in New Orleans, practicing law there for several years before his appointment as federal attorney for Washington Territory (1853–57). In 1852 Davis wrote two letters for Clendenin, describing him as "a zealous, consistent Democrat," a personal friend, and "my comrade in Mexico" (Wash. State Capitol Mus. to Davis Assn., Mar. 24, 1978; Jackson *S. Reformer*, July 12, 1845; DNA, M-863, roll 1; 1849–52 New Orleans dirs.; New Orleans *Delta*, May 13, Oct. 20, 1849; *Senate Ex. Jour.*, 9:80, 90, 10:173; Davis to Franklin Pierce, Dec. 9, 1852, DNA, RG60, Appt. Papers: Wash. Terr.; Davis to Richard Brodhead, Dec. 9, 1852, Goodspeed's, "Flying Quill," May 1955).

[44] John P. Stockard (c1820–60), born in Tennessee, was elected 2d lt., Co. F, in January 1847. After the Mexican War he was probate judge of Lafayette County (1850 Census, Miss., Lafayette, family 1351; DNA, M-863, roll 3; DNA, RG15, Mexican War Pension Applics., WC 4556).

[45] William Henry Scott (c1823–61) of Virginia was in the mercantile business in Vicksburg by 1843. Leav-

ing the 1st Miss. Rgt. upon his appointment to the 11th Inf. in April 1847, he saw action at Contreras and Churubusco and was recommended by Davis for a promotion. Soon after resigning his army commission in 1853, Scott reportedly killed a Mexican War comrade in a duel; subsequently he was rumored to be involved in a Nicaraguan filibustering expedition. In 1861 he served briefly as capt. 1st (Strawbridge's) La. Inf. (Heitman, *Hist. Reg.*, 1:870; DNA, M-863, roll 3; Vicksburg *Tri-Weekly Whig*, July 6, 1843; Davis to James K. Polk, Dec. 13, 1847; Scott to Davis, Mar. 15, 1861, DNA, RG109, Unfiled Papers and Slips; Jackson *Mississippian and State Gazette*, Oct. 7, 1853; *Daily Vicksburg Whig*, Oct. 9, 1860; Booth, comp., *La. Confed. Soldiers*).

[46] David M. Hollingsworth (1824–91), a Georgian, was a cabinetmaker in Yazoo County after the Mexican War. In the 1850s he settled in New Orleans, eventually becoming proprietor of a "carriage repository" (DNA, RG15, Mexican War Pension Applics., WC 7703; 1850 Census, Miss., Yazoo, family 867; Jackson *Mississippian*, May 3, 1859; 1866, 1874, 1881 New Orleans dirs.).

[47] Frederick James Malone (1826–91), a native of Alabama, had resigned as 2d lt., Co. F, in October 1846, but reenlisted as a private in January. After the war he ventured to California before becoming a rancher in Bee County, Texas. During the Civil War he commanded a state cavalry company and at his death was serving as county commissioner (DNA, RG15, Mexican War Pension Applics., SC 4864; DNA, M-863, roll 2; Confed. Muster Roll Index, Tx; Madray, *Hist. Bee County*, 53).

[48] Samuel H. Dill, 2d lt., Co. I, was born in Tennessee about 1804. A resident of Holly Springs, he served as postmaster (1850) and participated in Democratic party activities (1850

Census, Miss., N. Marshall, family 37; DNA, M-863, roll 1; Henry, *Masons*, 143; Holly Springs *Miss. Palladium*, Aug. 8, 1851, Jan. 22, 1852).

[49] William N. Brown (c1827–87), 1st lt., Co. F, was born in Tennessee and reared near Oxford. After the Mexican War he became a prosperous landowner in Bolivar County. In 1861 he organized and led Co. A, 20th Miss. Inf. Captured at Fort Donelson, Brown later participated in the defense of Vicksburg and was wounded at Franklin, Tennessee, in 1864. By 1880 he had settled in Victoria County, Texas (Rose, *Victor Rose's Hist.*, 101–102; Victoria County Probate Recs., 7:210; Sillers, comp., *Bolivar County*, 139, 145, 147, 404–405; DNA, M-863, roll 1; *OR*, Ser. 1, 7: 379–83, 45, Pt. 1:684, and 52, Pt. 1:64–65).

[50] In 1851 Davis remembered the circumstances of Bowles's having joined the Mississippians at Buena Vista. Davis said he saw about twenty of Bowles's men assembled by a lieutenant and several others "scattered in the files of the Mississippi regiment." Bowles then approached Davis "and with very deep feeling, almost bursting into tears, said, 'my regiment has run away; there is all I have left; and I wish permission to fight with your regiment'" (*Cong. Globe*, 31:2, App., 291). See also Davis' deposition of April 20, 1847, concerning Bowles.

[51] In a separate undated return, thirty-nine Mississippians were listed as killed and fifty-six as wounded. The Mississippi regiment suffered proportionately more casualties than any other unit at Buena Vista (Smith, *War with Mexico*, 1:561).

From Alexander B. Bradford

Saltillo March 2nd 1847

SIR, late this evening I was called upon for a report of such transactions as took place at the Battel of Buena wista <–having immediate–> on the 23rd. /ult/ which have immediate connection with our Regiment. If I had been called on sooner it would have given me pleasure to have went into detail, but time will not admit, and I shall therefore confine myself to the more important occurrences of the day. Your Regiment was on the field of Buena vista on the 22nd, & remained there until near sundown when we was ordered down to this place that night as I understood to guard the City which was threatened, & to return to the feild as soon as practicable next morning. Some time before we moved off on the evening of the 22nd there was a brisk fire of small arms on General Taylors left between his troops and the enemy which lasted until some time after Dark & then ceased with but little damage to either side as I am informed.[1] On the night of the 22nd. Your Regiment encamped on the heights adjacent to this city, & as soon as the troops breakfasted in the morning of the 23rd you took up the line of march for the feild of action,—and when in about two miles of it the battle again commenced on General Taylors left, & by the time we arrived on the Ground the action had became General. Immediately before we took our position the Second Regiment of Indiana troops under the Command of Col Bowls gaveway on the hight to our Right,[2] & many of them /were/ leaving the field in Route, when I succeeded in stoping a a portion of one of the companies apposite to our line, who fell in with us, & they together with <-our-> /their/ brave Col fought with us through the battle—we formed rapidly on the Right flank,[3] and at this moment the fortunes of the day seemed against us— There was a heavy column of Infantry of about 4000 of the enemy that had completely turned General Taylors left & were moving to fall on his rear, & many think if it had not been checked by the Mississippi Riflemen, might have lost our ours the brilleont victory which followed.

You perceived the critical position in which the army at this crises was placed, and determined to move forward upon them rapaidly Keeping up a fire upon them as we advanced, and arrest their progress if possible— You gave the word and like veterens the Regiment moved off, under one of the heaviest fires I ever saw, which was returned by our Regiment with equal spirit, until we came to a deep ravine[4] which impeded our progress for a short time as its bonks were from 10 to 15 <-f->[5] high and very abrupt, yet this did not check the ardour of the men, they very soon crossed it & steadily advanced upon the enemy Keeping their fire, until the enemy began <-rapidly-> to give way; a heavy body of Lancers seeing this, bore down on our left, and we were about being over wheeled between these two colums, until <-for-> your timely direction to fall back by the right down <-the-> /a/ ravine.[6]— we retired under the circumstances in good order, & formed on the opposite /side/ of the ravine which we had crossed in our advance movement—with the utmost proptness— Never did troops behave with more unflinching courage than did the Riflemen in this dangereous, but necessary movement– I crossed the Ravine with them, and moved in their midst, & altho they were rapidly falling on all sides, each officer & soldier, seemed to present a gallent & noble bearing till the moment the order to retire was given, <-&-> At /&/ beyond the ravine towards the enemy we lost between 80 & 90 Officers & men[7]—there the brave Lieuts Moore & McNulty were Killed, & Captain Sharp wounded – I can say with pride

& pleasure <–I was [transputed?] to behold–> that I have never witnessed any entire body of troops display such unwavering Cour age as did the Riflemen on this occasion— Shortly after we took position a second time[8] the third Indiana Regiment commanded by Col Lane a portion of the 2d Indiana & some straggles from other Regiments took, position on our left for mutual protection— The enemies battery opened upon us, & at the Same time the Lancers made a demenstration on us from the Left, at which the troops above named seemed to take a panic, and a portion of them were rapaidly giving way; seeing the imminent danger we w[ere][9] in if they left their position, /I/ threw aside militay etiquet for a moment, & rode around them & ex[ho]rted them to rally and return to their ranks & sustain their Eagle; they moved back to the line, & their brave officers with my humble /exertions/ sudceeded <–ag–> in again forming them—

The Indians chengeed positition very[10] soon from our left to right flank, & we formed at a right angle on the left;[11] In the mean time the ruthless Lancers not satisfied with the Slaughter they had made amongst us thought by one desperate effort to enterminate us prepared to charge us <–& did so–> & in a few minutes advanced rapaidly in column upon us; and when they arrived in proper distance we poured in altogether such a volly upon /them/ as to Sweep off all their entire front and /they/ retired in the utmost disorder. Our Regiment flanking Col. Lanes Regiment, some time before the close of the action, made a handsome & very distructive charge upon the enery who were pressing <–the [illegible]–> /e/ a portion of our troops on our right & repulsed them with great loss on <–our–> /their/ part[12]— After this our Regiment was ordered to flank the Artilley[13] & did so until we were ordered to leave the feled which was not until the enemy had <–left th–> ceased firing & <–with drawing–> were with drawing their forces – I cannot distinguish between the gallant officers of our Regement, as to /who/ are most deserving to be named all are worthy of a place in a report;– but I respectfully suggest that as Captain Taylor of the Guerds & his subalterns were not named at the battle of Montery,[14] & Captains Sharp & Delay and their Subalterns. were on detached Service and did not participate in the honour of that day, that for their distinguished conduct on the field of Buena Vista, [that] they may be named in your report.

In conclusion I am pleased to say that I observed with pleasure the devotion you manifested towards your Regimnt & your county, by remaining for honours[15] after receiveing a severe wound on the fiuld inded that you did not retire, until the close of the battle—

All which is respectfully submitted I have the honour to be your most obt servent

A. B. BRADFORD Maj
Miss[16] Riflemen

ALS (RG27, Vol. 26, Corres., Mexican War Docs., Ms-Ar). Endorsed by Davis: "No. 2 Maj: Bradford." Enclosed: Davis to Albert G. Brown, Oct. 3, 1847.

[1] American forces under Col. Humphrey Marshall skirmished with Mexican troops in the eastern mountains from midafternoon until nightfall. See letters E and F on the map.
[2] The main plateau. The Mississippians had left the road and were marching in a southeasterly direction.
[3] The Mississippians turned to their right to meet the advancing Mexican army.
[4] The northern ravine, particularly its eastern branch.
[5] Bradford seems to have started writing the word *feet*, then marked it for deletion.
[6] The northern ravine. The Mississippi regiment was moving in a northwesterly direction. See nos. 3, 4, 5 on the map for the regiment's advance and its movement in retiring.
[7] Davis estimated the losses at upwards of seventy.
[8] The Mississippians regrouped at approximately no. 5 on the map of Buena Vista.

[9] Square brackets indicate the presence of ink blots.
[10] The word *after* appears to have been overwritten.
[11] The 3d Ind. Rgt. took a position parallel to the northern ravine, forming the right side of the V formation; see no. 7 on the map.
[12] The Mississippi regiment's last engagement, on the main plateau, is marked as no. 9 on the map of Buena Vista.
[13] According to two Mississippians, the regiment was posted in support of Lt. George H. Thomas' and Capt. Thomas W. Sherman's batteries on the main plateau (report of Douglas H. Cooper, Mar. 1, 1847; Jackson *Southron*, Apr. 16, 1847). See no. 11 on the map.
[14] James H. R. Taylor was not named in Davis' report of the first day's action at Monterrey but was commended in the report covering September 23.
[15] The word *hours* is doubtlessly intended.
[16] Bradford first seems to have written "Comdg Mi," identifying himself as commander of the regiment in Davis' absence.

John S. Clendenin to Richard Griffith[1]

Camp near Soltilo   March 2nd. 1847

DEA[2] SIR

On approaching th field of action, in th morning of the 23rd. th left wing of our army which had been engaged by an overwhelming force was, giving way, and heavy columns of the eneny, both of infantry and cavalry, were turning our flank.[3] The fot of th day seemed already to be irretievably against us, and our /reget/ without being halted, was moved with all possible speed against the the enemy who, were triumphantly advancing in immense masses from our left flank, in direction of the rear of th main body of our arny. After a few minutes rapid advance we engaged th foe in terrible conflict, but our advance and fire upon them were unfortunatily <–inter–> for us interrupted by a deep ravine,[4] which we had to cross, and which /(gave)/ to th enemy in addition to their far superior numbers, an advantage over /us/ too great <–to great–> to be resisted with immediate success; yet we gained /postion/ across th ravine and renewed <–an–> /a/ fire upon th columns of th eneny, which halted and confused them. But being unable to <–mointain–> /sustain<–ed–>/ so unequal a combat long, and being entirely <–unsuported–> without any support whatever we retired from th then contested ground, until we <–we–> were joined by a few pieces of light artillery which were wisely ordered to our assisstance,[5] This junction soon being formed we advance against a tenfold force of th enemy, and opening a most distrutive fire upon them, they soon became th retreating party.[6] After this we were joined by a portion of th Indiana troops who had been rallied and /(formed)/ <–fr–> at our side. They in connexion with our regiment (th credit of which belongs to the latter) success-fully and without loss repulsed a large body of Lancers who during th engagements of th day came down upon us in solid col-umns.[7] Our Regiment during th day, frequently engaged /(large)/ <–large–> bodies of the enemy and drove them, with great slaughter to <–them–> /(themselves)/ but with inconsiderable loss to us. Nearly th entire loss <–in killed and–> of th regiment in killed and wounded, was in th first conflict. It was then that my own company suffered its entire loss in killed and th number after-wards /(wounded)/[8] were but two. <–in number.–> It was then that 1st Lieut, R L Moore fell while nobly serving his country. In the death of Lt Moore our Regiment and the service have lossed <–one–> a brave and worthy officer. His cool courage and his capacity to command, united to a regid determination to do that which /(was)/ right rendered his services almost beyond estimate. Near him fell three privates of the company who, left behind them no better soldirs than they were themselves.

Of my own company who were with me on the field I could not

speak of one in higher terms than another All did their duty brave-ly and well. Whether in resisting a charge of cavrly or /in/ th hot fire of infantry coolness and courage characterized them. It is also due to 2nd. Lt. J J Poindexter[9] <–th–> to say in this report that the services rendered me, by <–him–> him in th command of th company[10] on that trying /(occasion)/ were most eminent and worthy of notice

Th <–behaviour of the–> officers of the regiment as far as met my observation behaved with courage & capacity.

I submit th above with due respect and am Yours &c

J. S. CLENDENIN Capt.
Commanding Company

ALS (RG27, Vol. 26, Corres., Mexican War Docs., Ms-Ar). Endorsed by Davis: "No. 9 Com. 'H.'" Enclosed: Davis to Albert G. Brown, Oct. 3, 1847.

[1] Since Davis was recuperating from his wound, Griffith received this and three other battle reports.
[2] Clendenin omitted the final letter of numerous words in his report.
[3] The 2d Ind., the Ky. and Ark. Cav., and some artillerymen had been driven from their positions (letters D, E, and F on the map) on and near the main plateau.
[4] The northern ravine. For the location of the Mississippi regiment's first charge, see nos. 2 and 3 on the Buena Vista map.
[5] The Mississippians retreated from the map site marked no. 3 to no. 5. It was there that they were joined by the 3d Ind., part of the 2d Ind., and a piece of light artillery commanded by Charles L. Kilburn.
[6] Once reinforced, the Mississippi regiment advanced toward the base of the mountains; see no. 6 on the map.
[7] Clendenin refers to the V formation in which the Mississippi regiment acted with the Indianans; see no. 7 on the map.
[8] Co. H reported a total of four killed and nine wounded (Return, RG27, Vol. 26, Corres., Mexican War Docs., Ms-Ar).
[9] John J. Poindexter (1816–81) was a merchant in Jackson for several years before the Mexican War. Afterward he settled in New Orleans and later lived in Galveston (McCain, *Jackson*, 1:76, 77; 1854, 1859, 1861, 1866–67 New Orleans dirs.; Galveston *Daily News*, Nov. 10, 1881).
[10] Clendenin, a 2d lt. in 1846, was elected capt., Co. H, after the resignation of George Crump, but 1st Lt. Robert L. Moore had refused to turn over the command until Clendenin received his official commission from the governor of Mississippi. After Moore's death Clendenin and Poindexter were the only two company officers present (New Orleans *Delta*, Oct. 20, 1849).

From Henry F. Cook

Camp at Saltillo March 3 1847

COL DAVIS

I beg leave to submit to you the following report of the Battle of Buena Vista on the 22 & 23 of Feb last so far as it refers to C Compay Miss Riflemen.

on the morning of the 22 of Feb the Regement left their Camp at Saltillo for the Pass of "Buena Vista", when it arrived there, a position was assigned to it in rear of the line of Battle then being formed.[1] We remained in this position during the day, in the course of which we were the silent but anxious spectators of a skirmish in the mountains on the left of our line of battle between a large body of Mexicans & two or three Companis of Kentucky Regement.[2]

We returned to our Camp at night, and on the next morning the 23rd again left for the approaching scene of action. Before we had reached the field however, we saw that the action had already commened and that the left wing of our army were closely engaged with a largely superor force of the enemies Infantry & Cavalry. In a short time this entire line gave way & fled from the scene of action.[3] leavig the eneny in possession of the field—

The Regiment continued to move steadily forward, marching by the <-right flank-> center of Companies until within a short distance from the enemy. Then formed into line and marched to the front. When within about two hundred yards of a large body of Infantry you gave the Command to "Advance firing"[4]

Unsupported by any other force the Regt faultered not; but continued to advance and fire upon the eneny whose numbers were five times greater than our own.

Crossing a deep ravine whose precipitous banks seemed to oppose no obstacle to their way, they continue their charge until they had gained the opposite bank of another ravine[5] still neare to their now retreating foe : When at this instant you perceived that a large body of Cavalry were apprachig the flanks of the line with the evident intention of cutting of their retreat, and gave the order to the Regement to retire. This well timed retreat was effected in good order, the men rallied and formed in line without confusion after they had passed beyond the reach of the enemis fire.[6]

157

The Regiment was then reinforced by a piece of Artillery from Command by Lt Kilbourn— And in a short time afterwds was further reinforce by a Regement of Indiana Volunters, who were formed on the right of our line.[7]

With this force we met and dispersed a large body of Cavalry who were formed for the purpose of makig a charge upon us.[8]

Still later in day we were reinforced by two additional pieces of Cannon & Col Mays Dragoons.[9]

With this force we continue to move forwar drivng the enemy before us, until we had regaind posession of the field, which appeared to have been so hopelessly lost to us in the mornig.[10]

the day being now far spent & the firing have ceased on both sides, the Regimet returned to <–the–> Camp, rejocing over the victory which their arms had so essentially contributed to secure. The casuality of the Company have already been reported to you.[11] In conclusion I <–take great pleasure in–> /I beg leave to/ say- <–ing–> that the company who were in the action durig the day under my command behaved with such uniform gallantry that I refrain from calling your attention to particular individuls, lest others might think themselvs slighted by my silence.

All of which is Respectfel submitted by [yrs?]

H F. Cook

1 Lieut Comdg C Co[12]

Miss Riflemen

ALS (RG27, Vol. 26, Corres., Mexican War Docs., Ms-Ar). Endorsed by Davis: "No. 5 Com. 'C.'" Enclosed: Davis to Albert G. Brown, Oct. 3, 1847.

[1] For the Mississippians' position, see no. 1 on the map of Buena Vista.

[2] The Ky. Cav., Ind. Rifle Btn., and part of the Ark. Cav. were first to engage the enemy at Buena Vista.

[3] The 2d Ind. Rgt. retreated from the main plateau; the volunteers skirmishing in the mountains also were forced to fall back. See letters D, E, and F.

[4] Where the Mississippi regiment first fired on the enemy is shown as no. 2 on the Buena Vista map.

[5] Traversing the eastern branch of the northern ravine, the Mississippians reached approximately the point marked no. 3.

[6] The rallying point is no. 5.

[7] The 3d Ind., part of the 2d Ind., and a piece of light artillery under Charles L. Kilburn arrived to support the Mississippi regiment. After the advance toward the mountains (no. 6 on the map), which Cook failed to mention, the Indianans moved from the Mississippi left to the right.

[8] The V formation; no. 7 on the map.

[9] John F. Reynolds commanded two pieces of light artillery, which operated with a large force of 2d Dragoons and other cavalry and in-

fantry under the leadership of Capt. Charles A. May. In the early afternoon May's command and the units that included the Mississippi regiment moved parallel with each other against the enemy near the base of the mountains. For the Mississippians' estimated position during the advance, see no. 8.

10 The Mississippi and Indiana regiments along with Capt. Thomas W. Sherman's battery aided in the final defense of the main plateau. See no. 9 on the map.

11 Four members of Co. C were killed, and eight were wounded (Return, RG27, Vol. 26, Corres., Mexican War Docs., Ms-Ar).

12 Capt. John Willis was absent because of ill health.

From William P. Rogers

Camp near Saltillo, Mxo. March 6th. 1847.

Sir,

It affords me pleasure to call your attention to companies "D" and "K" of the Mississippi Regiment, which were left in Camp at Head Quarters on the 23d Ult: for its defence and protection, under my command.[1]

Early on the morning of the 23d, a larger body of the enemy were seen on the plain two or three miles east of our camp. They were mounted men, and evidently threatened an attack upon camp, which disposition was apparent at a later hour of the day.[2] Soon after you had lead your regiment to the field of Battle, a large number of American Soldiers were seen flying from the field of battle toward my post in great disorder and confusion. With the assistance of Lieut: Russell, who was in command of Com. "D", and other officers under my command, I succeeded, after great exertion in rallying about two hundred of them.[3] Those of them who were on foot I placed under the command of Captain McManus,— to whom I am indebted for assistance on that occasion. Those on horses I placed under the command of Lieut: Slade.

Soon after these dispositions were made the enemy <–offered–> appeared in large force on the road leading from Saltillo to "Buena Vista" about one mile from camp and between my post and the main Army.[4] I now deemed an attack certain, and after striking tents, formed my command in rear of the Gun under the command of Lieut: Shover, who instantly opened a heavy fire upon the enemy. Soon after this Lieut. Shover ran his gun out half mile more and continued his fire, which soon drove the enemy from their position.

In the mean time however Lieut: Slade gallantly led his mounted men on in support of the Gun, which followed the enemy a mile or more, <–and–> from my post, and drove them from the field.[5]

I cannot fail to mention the cool and intrepid conduct of the officers and men under my command, and the ready willingness evinced by all to meet the enemy as much probably from a desire to divide the dangers of the day and withdraw a portion of the enemy from the main field[6] as from a personal disposition to share in the glories of the battle of "Buena Vista."

On the night of the 23d. in obedience to your orders I re-reported the two companies under my command to the comdg General whom I found at the advanced post of our Army, and by him was ordered to a position in rear of Captain Sherman's <–battery–> /field/ Battery,[7] where I remained until the morning of the 24th. when it was found that the enemy were gone. We then gave *three cheers* for the American flag and *Genl: Taylor*, and by orders I rejoined my regiment. Respectfully yours

Wm: P. Rogers
Captn: Com: "K"
Miss: Riflemen

L, copy by Richard Griffith (RG27, Vol. 26, Corres., Mexican War Docs., Ms-Ar). Endorsed by Davis: "No. 11 Com. 'K.'" Enclosed: Davis to Albert G. Brown, Oct. 3, 1847.

[1] In a repetition of his insubordination at Monterrey, Rogers refused to stay in Saltillo on February 22. But on the 23rd, as he recounted, Davis "came to me early and told me that I was the only captain in the Regiment who had not been on detatched service and that he hoped inasmuch as we were surrounded by Mexicans that I would not again refuse to take a separate command and defend that post of headquarters. He further said that he knew I had for him no kind feeling but that endangered as we were he hoped that might be forgotten. The post he assigned me he said was a post of honor and that he desired that I might have the glory of leading an independent command

to action. . . . I could not again refuse" (Pace, ed., "Rogers Diary," *SWHQ*, 32:276n–77n).

[2] By midmorning a force of cavalry under the command of Gen. José Vicente Minón was close enough to draw fire from the redoubt near the Mississippians' camp; it was driven back with some loss (*Senate Ex. Doc. 1*, 30:1, 206–207). See the inset on the map of Buena Vista for the relative location of the town, redoubt, camp, and road.

[3] Rogers refers to those members of the 2d Ind., 1st Ky., and Ark. Cav. rgts., as well as the Ill. and Ind. Rifle btns., who had fled the battlefield.. He later estimated their total number at 600; Zachary Taylor believed no more than about 200 reached Saltillo (Vicksburg *Weekly Sentinel*, Apr. 21, 1847; Matamoros *American Flag*, Apr. 28, 1847).

[4] About noon "two heavy squadrons of the enemy lancers" blocked

160

the road, stopping communication between Saltillo and Buena Vista and seizing a number of prisoners (*Senate Ex. Doc. 1*, 30:1, 206–207; Matamoros *American Flag*, Apr. 28, 1847).

[5] About midafternoon Lt. Shover noted that the enemy was moving "towards the mountain and obliquely towards Buena Vista." Believing the time propitious for an attack, he moved his 6-pounder forward, supported by a howitzer under the command of Lt. James L. Donaldson and by Slade's disparate force. The Americans followed Miñón's cavalry as far as Arispe's Mill, nearly three miles from the camp and redoubt (*Senate Ex. Doc. 1*, 30:1, 208–209; Carleton, *Buena Vista*, 120–23).

[6] The American volunteers and artillerymen near Saltillo, augmented by civilians and fugitives from Buena Vista, numbered only a few hundred, yet prevented Miñón's much larger force from capturing Saltillo and attacking the American rear at Buena Vista (Matamoros *American Flag*, June 23, 1847; Balbontín, *Invasión Americana*, 84; Smith, *War with Mexico*, 1:555–56).

[7] Rogers reported elsewhere that his position on the main plateau was "in 400 yards of the enemy's strongest works," in fact "nearer the enemy than any other troop" (Pace, ed., "Rogers Diary," *SWHQ*, 32:278n; Vicksburg *Weekly Sentinel*, Apr. 21, 1847).

From James H. R. Taylor

[March 1847][1]

COL: DAVIS

In pursuance to your request I will attemp to Give a report of the action of the 23d at Buena Vista so far the Regement or rather my Company as forming a part of the Mississippi participated in the engagement of the day Early in the morning of the 22nd Feb the Regement was put in motion from Saltillo to Buena Vista in quik time a distance of six miles. On reaching the hights occupied by our troops we were drawn up in line of battle during the day.[2] Towards evening a scattering fire was brought on at the base of the mountain at the extreme left flank of our Army.[3] About five oclock in the evening the fire became much Greater Clearly Shewing that the Mexican had largely increased even attempting to Gain the hight next to the Mounta[in][4] Sometime after Sun Set our Regement wer put in motion for our Cam at Saltillo Early on the following morning we were en route for scene of action Before reaching it however a heavy fire Commenced on the left flank of the Army the Enemy having succeeded in Gaining the desired heights. Our Regement Moved directly to the scene of opperations in double Quick time. on Coming near the engaged forces we discovered the Indianna routed and retreating in Great confusion.[5] It seemed to be the desire both of our officers and men as they passed us to rally them to the fight. Col Bowles joined us without a Command so also Leut: Lewis[6] with a few men and here let me add that through out the day Leut Lewis rendered his Country efficient service and Col Bowls distinguished himself for his bravery and Gallantry. In the face of the Mexican forces were we led single hand without Arttilery to back or other troops to sustain us. Flashed with their success the Mexican moved against us at a rapid stride but well dressed ranks Onward the Mississippi Regement moved until within one hundred and fifty Yards when we were Ordered by You to fire and Advance.[7] The Regement advanced stadely upon the Eneny until we Came to a deep Ravine forty or fifty feet deep and almost perpendicular. Here wer wer ordered to march on and no sooner ordered then Your Regement had decended and Scaled the opposite precepce and were advancing upon the enemy;[8] they Giving away. In this Charge the most Gallant I dare say on Record the enemy suffered Great loss as well as mamy brave and Gallant Mississippians fell. The Regement was advancing when the Order to fall back was Given for just then we were almost surrou[nd][4]ed by the enemy and a large body of lancers were endeavoing to get possion in our rear. The Regement with You at its head fell back to the Ravine and down the Ravine and Repulsed a heavy body lancers that had formed above us.[9] In Gaining a favorable position the Regement was halted and formed by Battallion front.[10] We had then been joined by the Indianna Regement Commanded by Col Lane[11] And To Maj Bradford belongs Great Creat for the rallying that Regement to sustain a charge about to be made upon us by a large body of appoaching us on the left. The Lancers churched up within about fifty yards of our line and here every officer did his duty exhorting the men to his duty. The Lancers were repulsed with Great loss.[12] From early in the morning until late in the evening even until sun set the Mississippi Regement were hotly and actively engaged and it were idle for me to undertake to enumute the many regement-[al?] feats of daring and the many untakings bold and fearless It is useless for me here to state that my Company shareds its fatigues, danges and acchivenments. I can make no distinction like a band of brothers each /did his duty/ emulating the Good example. I would recommed to Your notice my brave Leut Mott & Dill. The officers all did their duty they in particular were prominent. As for my

heroic dead their deeds are their Epitaphs. Sergt Anderson [an]⁴d
Henry Frotter¹³ /A Collingsworth¹⁴ & John Branch/ and J Peace
were distinguished in the fight and fell as [far?] that day as a Mississippian dared Go. To You Col: Davis here permit me in behalf of
my Company to express our thank for Your remaining with Your
Regement though wounded early in the action and our high esteem
for coolness and fore[sight?] during the day Obt Yours I remain

J. H. R. TAYLOR
Caept Comdg Com"I" Miss:
Riflemen

ALS (RG27, Vol. 26, Corres., Mexican War Docs., Ms-Ar). Endorsed
by Davis: "No. 10 Com. 'I.'" Enclosed: Davis to Albert G. Brown,
Oct. 3, 1847.

¹ Since Taylor does not mention
the absence of Pvt. James W. Vinson,
who was believed killed until returned in a prisoner exchange on
March 4, and because Taylor addressed Davis in Saltillo—Davis left
for Monterrey on March 25 or 26—
this report most likely was written
during that interim

² See no. 1 on the Buena Vista map
for the Mississippi regiment's position in reserve.

³ The first skirmishing at Buena
Vista was between Gen. Ampudia's
forces and a group of Americans
commanded by Col. Humphrey Marshall. See letters E and F.

⁴ Edge of manuscript clipped.

⁵ The 2d Ind. Rgt. retreated in
some disorder from their position on
the main plateau early on February
23 (letter D).

⁶ David S. Lewis, born in Kentucky
about 1799, was 2d lt., Co. B, 2d Ind.
Rgt. After the Mexican War he returned to Lawrence County, Indiana,
where he was an "R B Minister"
(1850 Census, Ind., Lawrence, family
94; DNA, RG15, Mexican War
Bounty Land Applics.).

⁷ For the route taken by the Mississippians, see the Buena Vista map.
No. 2 marks the approximate location where the regiment fired its first
volley.

⁸ The men of Davis' command
crossed the eastern branch of the
northern ravine, advancing to the
position marked no 3.

⁹ At approximately the place marked
no. 4, the Mississippians repelled a
cavalry attack while retiring.

¹⁰ The rallying point is shown as
no. 5 on the map of Buena Vista.

¹¹ James H. Lane commanded the
3d Ind. Rgt.; part of the 2d Ind. and
a piece of light artillery also arrived
as reinforcements.

¹² The V formation, no. 7 on the
map.

¹³ Henry G. Trotter, born about
1827, probably in Monroe County,
was the son of Mississippi supreme
court justice James F. Trotter (DNA,
M-863, roll 3; Vicksburg *Daily Whig*,
Apr. 2, 1847; Lynch, *Bench and Bar*,
205–206).

¹⁴ Although reported killed at Buena
Vista, Addison S. Collingsworth ap-
parently survived the war, residing in
New Albany, Indiana, for several
years before his death in 1891 (DNA,
RG15, Mexican War Pension Ap-
plics., WO 9619; InNea to Davis
Assn., Oct. 21, 1978).

To John E. Wool

Saltillo 25th March 1847[1]

MY DEAR GENL.

I have just read with great pleasure the copy of your letter to genl. gibson,[2] which you did me the honor to send me this evening.

It shall be preserved for the use permitted & be assured under circumstances requiring, that it will give me great satisfaction thus to apply it.

In these times of petty jealousy and ignoble strife for public approbation it is quite refreshing to see one so prominent in the scenes you describe forgetting himself to sustain and commend his commander.[3]

With assurances of my regard,[4] I am cordially yrs.

JEFFN. DAVIS

ALS (Ford Coll., MnHi).

[1] The day before, Wool had issued a special order that Davis and other wounded officers and soldiers leave Saltillo on March 25 in a wagon train escorted by Mirabeau B. Lamar. Davis reached Monterrey on the 27th (DNA, RG94, Wool's Orders; Vicksburg *Tri-Weekly Whig*, May 11, 1847; Indianapolis *Ind. State Sentinel*, May 12, 1847).

[2] Wool's letter to George Gibson, commissary gen. of subsistence, has not been found.

[3] Although Wool had written to Gibson and other prominent Washingtonians describing Taylor's performance at Buena Vista in "flattering terms," it was later reported that while Davis was recuperating in Saltillo he heard that Wool was critical of Taylor's leadership. Davis then "addressed a note to Gen. Wool, stating his intention to make such publication as would set the matter in its true light. Gen. Wool called upon Col. Davis, and asked him to defer such statement until he (Gen. W.) should address him a letter. This letter was sent to Col. Davis, and was a distinct disclaimer, on the part of Gen. Wool, of any more credit than he deserved, and giving to Gen. Taylor, as was his due, the highest meed of praise" (Jackson *Mississippian*, Jan. 12, 1858; Taylor to Joseph P. Taylor, May 9, 1847, Taylor Papers, DLC; Washington *Union*, Apr. 5, 1847, Mar. 18, 1849; Wool to John A. Dix, Mar. 2, 1847, Dix Papers, NNC; New Orleans *Delta*, Apr. 3, 1847; N.Y. *Tribune*, Apr. 17, 1847).

[4] Davis seems to have overwritten the word *highest*.

From Joseph E. Davis

Hurricane April 16th 47

DEAR BROTHR

I am still without any letter from you since the Battle, Mr. Crittenden and Doct. Halsey were both considerate enoug[h][1] to write some particulars of your wound.[2] st[ill?] I feel great anxety to hear from you

We have been for some time past in a state of allarm for fear of an overflo[w] the river is now somthing higher than in 1844, and still rising slowly, and from the best information, a fall may be looke[d] for in a few days Stamps[3] wrote on the 5th inst from Louisville stating that it was at a stand at Memphis on 1st and had follen 15 inches at New Madrid on the 2nd. & 15 feet at Louisvill on the 5th[4] so far we suffered no loss and hope we shall not.

You will see from the papers an increased disposition to run Genl. Taylor for Presidency, If he could be the candidate of the nation instead of a party, if Genl T. is apposed to the ultra Powers claimed by the whigs for the federal Govt. such as the protective and internal improvment policy, I could say that many of the Democrats would rejoice at an oppertun[ity] to vote for him, You may have some oppertunity of knowing from him and I should be glad to know.[5]

The news papers have signified the begining of June as the time for aur state convention if you have any view to public life it migh[t] be well to say to your friends or some of them if you desire a nomination.[6]

We are done planting and most of the first planting is up the season is quite dry— Eliza has planted your mountain seed and it is up she watches closely as a favorite of her garden.

Your people are quite well, the family here & people also & things generally as usual Some dozen colts that Jim[7] would be glad to hear of

YR BROTHR

AL (Davis Papers, NWM). Right margins, especially of first page, cropped; water stained.

[1] Letters in square brackets supplied where manuscript edge clipped.
[2] Thomas L. Crittenden addressed a letter to Joseph Davis on February 25 (see Davis to V. Davis, Feb. 25); Seymour Halsey was the surgeon for the 1st Miss. Rgt.
[3] William Stamps, Davis' brother-in-law.
[4] On April 15 the Mississippi River was reported to be three inches above the high-water mark of the 1844 flood at Vicksburg and still rising (Monette, "Miss. Floods," *Miss. Hist. Pubs.*, 7:466).
[5] As is evident in the letters Taylor wrote Davis during 1847–48, the two frequently discussed a wide range of political issues.
[6] The state Democratic convention was scheduled to meet in Jackson June 7–8 to nominate candidates for state offices, including governor. As early as February 26 the Jackson *Mis-*

sissippian reported that Davis was suggested as a gubernatorial candidate, and a week later Davis' mother-in-law marveled that a prominent Whig had become an admirer of Davis', predicting he could be governor if he chose to run. But on March 26 the editors of the *Mississippian* announced that Davis would not be a candidate for any office while serving as col., 1st Miss. Rgt. Certainly by early May Davis had informed his brother that he would not accept the nomination for governor (Margaret K. Howell to William B. Howell, Mar. 6, [1847], Z790f, Howell Papers, Ms-Ar; Jackson *Mississippian*, Mar. 12, 26, June 11, 1847; Matamoros *American Flag*, May 22, 1847; Joseph E. Davis to Davis, May 13, 1847).

[7] Jim Green, Davis' body servant.

Court of Inquiry Deposition

Editorial Note: Immediately after Buena Vista questions arose concerning the retreat of the 2d Ind. Rgt. As intimations of cowardice increased, Joseph Lane, commander of the Ind. Brig., became convinced that Col. William A. Bowles was culpable and insisted that he be court-martialed. Lane preferred two formal charges: that Bowles was incompetent and that he had "misbehaved . . . before the enemy." Doubting that the charges could be substantiated, Zachary Taylor denied a court-martial. Lane consequently demanded and received a court of injuiry into his own conduct and was acquitted of any blame. Meanwhile Bowles, who had been arrested pending Taylor's decision, also requested a court of inquiry (Indianapolis *Ind. State Sentinel*, May 12, 1847, Sept. 9, 1848; Viola, "Taylor and the Ind. Vols.," *SWHQ*, 72:339–43). On April 12 the court convened at Buena Vista to hear the testimony of more than forty witnesses, including Davis, whose deposition was taken in Monterrey. Davis' answers to a series of interrogatories by the judge advocate were recorded by the secretary of the Monterrey military commission and entered in the court proceedings on April 24.

twentieth day of April 1847
at Monterey Mex

The time at which Col Bowles joined my Regt, and the force with which he joined it, I have not the power conclusively to state. When I reached the battle field, I rode forward in advance of my Regt and met a large number of men retiring before the enemy in seeming confusion. I have since been informed this was Col. Bowles' <–evidence.–> Regt.

I passed them, and after reconnoitring the enemy, returned to the head of my Regt, promptly formed it from column into line of battle and rapidly advanced to attack–

After the first engagement, Col. Bowles reported to me, he offered his services with those of a small party of men, I think as embodied about twenty, said that his Regt had run away, that these were the only men he could rally, and that he wished to serve with my regt.

I accepted his services and gave him choice of position for his men, they served the greater part of the day on our right under the immediate command of a gallant officer who I have since <–learned–> been informed is Lt. Lewis of the 2. In. Vols–

Circumstances convince me that Col. Bowles and the men of his Regt, must have joined my command before our first engagement, but as he would necessarily fall in rear of a marching column to which he wished to unite a detachment, as I was in advance of my regt, and immediately on returning to it commenced preparations for an attack which was rapidly made, and as I had no previous acquaintance with Col. Bowles, there is nothing surprising in it, if his presence remained unobserved until he reported, and became personally known to me. In accepting the services of Col. Bowles when tendered to me, it was of course in his appropriate grade of field officer, He did not command the Miss. Regt or any part of it, nor was this possible, as the Regt was embodied throughout th-<–at–> battle, and I commanded it in person.

The conduct of Col. Bowles was marked by self possession, by quiet, genuine courage, and by entire propriety so far as it came under my observation

(signed) JEFFERSON DAVIS
Col. Miss. Riflen.[1]

D (DNA, RG153, Court Martial Case Files, FF123, 48–49).

[1] The last witness to be heard by the court was Maj. Alexander B. Bradford, who brought Davis' deposition from Monterrey. Later the same day (April 24) the court concluded that "Col. Bowles evinced no want of personal courage or bravery, but, that he did manifest a want of capacity and judgement as a commander" (DNA, RG153, Court Martial Case Files, FF123, 51).

From Joseph E. Davis

Hurricane 23rd. April '47

MY DEAR BROTHER

Your letter of the 12th from Saltillo came to hand on Tuesday, since then I have a copy of one to Mr Van Benthuysen of the 23rd.[1]

Knowing that you must feel anxious about things at home I have write[n][2] to you weekly thinking some of them at least would reach you.

We are much occupied in attention to the levees, and so far by a good deal of labour have prevented any injury except the seepage which is less than in '44. the /river/ is 5 or 6 inches higher I think although the marks <–are–> of that year have been long covered that it is not certainly kno[wn][2] I have but little information that can be relyed on but should expect a fall in a few days the rise for the last 24 hours is very slight.[3]

You will see by the papers that the whigs and natives wish to monopolize the popularity of Genl. Taylor.[4] I have thought he might be nominated without respect to party what is the same thing by all parties, the country is more tired of the political War than the Mexican War, the people have no other interest than to secure the blessing of good government, a candidate there fore who was in favor of a strict construction of the federal constitution, who would be the president of the nation and not of a party, who in his appointments to office would ask no other question than of the honesty and capacity of the purson to be appointed, would be Elected by acclamation, and do much to restore the government to its purity and proper dignity, you may have some oppertunity of conversing with him before you return, I wish to vote for him if I can do so, without a surender of principles that I deem sacred, and the mor[e][5] from a feeling that it has been the purpose of the Administration to depress him

We are all well I would write to Doct Mitchell if I thought there was much chance for a letter to reach him[6] the children are very well, Lise[7] on being told that her uncle Jeff would have to hop a long with a crutch said "I would rather die than he should be so"

AL (Adele D. Sinton).

[1] Neither Davis' letter of March 12 nor his letter to Joseph Davis' brother-in-law Watson Van Benthuysen has been found.

[2] Edge of first page cropped.

[3] Two days after Joseph Davis wrote, the water level at Vicksburg increased to four inches above the 1844 record; thereafter it began to fall and by mid-May had dropped fifteen feet (Monette, "Miss. Floods," *Miss. Hist. Pubs.*, 7:466–67). The Davises suffered no major losses as a result of the 1847 flood (Zachary Taylor to Davis, July 27, 1847).

[4] The New Orleans *Delta* (Apr. 10, 16, 20, 1847) noted that members of the American party in New York and Philadelphia were recommending Taylor for president. Meanwhile, so

many Whig editors were supporting Taylor that the *Delta* (Apr. 17) asked, "By what right do these party papers undertake to monopolize for the whig party all the glory achieved by Gen. Taylor in this war."

5 Manuscript damaged.
6 Charles J Mitchell, Joseph Davis' son-in-law, was in Mexico.
7 Joseph Davis' granddaughter Mary Elizabeth Mitchell and her two brothers lived at Hurricane.

To Joseph E. Davis

Monterey, 30th April, 1847.

DEAR BROTHER:

I am here partaking of the general quiet and inaction which surrounds us. The time is near at hand when the twelve months volunteers must be discharged. No information has been sent to the gen'l of any plan by which he is to supply the deficiency that will be created by the discharge of the troops now with him. The four regiments of volunteers sent out and three companies of mounted Texans, so far as is known, will constitute the whole force.[1]

For it is not probable that any of the new regiments will be in the field soon enough to relieve the last of the twelve months men, say the early part of June. Under the case, as it will probably exist, the majority will then arise to draw in the advance. Presto, if the enemy be active as far as the Rio Grande. Can it be possible that this is desired and thus indirectly sought, that it may be done without incurring any responsibility.[2]

Provision has been made for 20 regiments, 10 only have been raised. If the 20 were in the field they would only replace the 21 that are to go out. As Gen'l Scott will claim the largest share of these troops[3] no hope can be entertained of much service for this column. However much this may be regretted, particularly here, it is yet more to be regretted because of the very favorable opportunity now presented of going on this route to the City of Mexico.

I do not know when our regiment will start home, but it must be soon and whilst my wish to return certainly predominates over every other feeling it is with regret that I look forward to leaving this country before the war is concluded.

Capt. Chilton of the Dragoons, the brother of John M. Chilton, leaves in the morning.[4] He will stop at Vicksburg and if you find it convenient please show him some civilities on my account. His attention to me when wounded entitles him to much consideration from me. My foot is steadily improving and I hope to be able to use it. Thank Eliza for her letter and say to her that if I do not write to her by this conveyance,[5] I will do so very soon.[6]

I received a letter from Varina written at Natches on the 30th Ult. she then spoke of returning to the Brierfield and I suppose will have done so before this reached you. I wrote to her twice recently and as I sent the letter under cover to you, they have probably by your attentions reached her[7]—

Give my love to sisters Ama[8] and Eliza, to Varina if with you and all the young people.[9] It will be to me a joy which from day to day I more desire to see again the happy, truly affectionate faces

From Elizas letter I regretted to learn that you were unwell, God grant that this may find you well an[d][10] with the happiness you so well [de]ser[ve to e]njoy. affectionately Your Brother

JEFFN DAVIS

Omaha *World-Herald*, June 13, 1926, mag. sec., 3; part of the letter was reproduced in facsimile. Discovered by E. R. Smisor, an Omaha jeweler, the original was taken from one of the Davis plantations in Warren County during the Civil War by Smisor's uncle, a steamboat captain.

[1] Davis refers to the volunteer regiments from Massachusetts, Virginia, North Carolina, and Mississippi and to a battalion of Maj. Michael H. Chevallie's Texas Mtd. Vols., which had recently arrived at Monterrey. In addition, Zachary Taylor's command included several companies of artillery and portions of two dragoon regiments. His force was augmented in May 1847 by four regular army regiments, bringing his total strength to 6,350, or approximately two-thirds the number under his command in April (Smith, *War with Mexico*, 2: 417; *House Ex. Doc. 60*, 30:1, 1146–48; DNA, M-29, roll 3, Gen. Orders No. 36, Apr. 20, 1847).

[2] Davis seems to suggest, as did Taylor himself, that the administration was deliberately placing the general in a perilous position while publicly maintaining that he was receiving adequate support (Taylor, *Letters*, 95, 110–11; Washington *Union*, Mar. 29, 1847).

[3] Taylor was losing thirteen regiments; Winfield Scott, seven regiments and two companies. Ten volunteer units were called up in November and December 1846, but not until March 1847 did Congress authorize ten new regular regiments. As Davis predicts, twelve of the twenty regiments were sent to Scott (Smith, *War with Mexico*, 1:537, 2:63, 75–76, 363–65; *House Ex. Doc. 60*, 30:1, 1121).

[4] Recently appointed to the 1st Dragoons, Robert H. Chilton was on his way to Washington for orders. He arrived in New Orleans on May 10 (DNA, M-29, roll 3, Special Orders No. 38, Apr. 20, 1847; New Orleans *Picayune*, May 11, 1847).

[5] No correspondence between Davis and his sister-in-law Eliza Davis has been found.

[6] Beginning with the next paragraph, transcription is from the facsimile.

[7] Varina Davis' letter of March 30 and any letters Davis wrote her after February 25 have not been located.

Instead of returning to Brierfield, she evidently remained with her family in Natchez until June.

⁸ Davis' widowed sister Amanda Bradford was living at Hurricane with Joseph E. Davis. Davis' sister Ann Eliza Smith resided in Louisiana.

⁹ Referring to Joseph Davis' three grandchildren and several Bradford nieces and nephews, all staying at Hurricane.

¹⁰ Square brackets enclose letters supplied because the facsimile is partially obscured by a superimposed photograph.

To Jackson Citizens

MONTEREY, May 7, 1847.

GENTLEMEN¹—Your letter of the 5th ult., conveying the resolutions of a public meeting,² held in the capital of our State, on the 3d of April, 1847, has just been received.

For the approbation thus conferred on the officers and men of the 1st Mississippi Rifles, I feel most sincerely thankful. For myself, and for those whom it has been my honor and good fortune to command, I will say, that in such manifestations of regard and esteem of our brethren at home, is contained the reward for whatever we have borne of toil, privation or loss; for whatever we may have achieved of honorable service in the cause of our country.

The necessary directions will be given, to place your letter on the records, and ensure its reading at the head of each company of our Regiment.

For the very kind and highly complimentary terms in which you, as the organ of the meeting have presented its resolutions, I am truly sensible, and offer my grateful acknowledgements.

Cordially, I am your friend and fellow citizen,

JEFF'N DAVIS,
Colonel 1st Mississippi Rifles.

Vicksburg *Tri-Weekly Whig*, June 8, 1847.

¹ Members of the committee appointed to transmit the resolutions were: Collin S. Tarpley, John D. Freeman, James J. Deavenport, Henry S. Foote, Caswell R. Clifton, Charles Scott, Daniel Mayes, John I. Guion, Anderson Hutchinson, and John Mayrant. Their letter has not been found.

² Convened at the Jackson Theatre, "a numerous and brilliant assembly" passed a set of resolutions sent to Zachary Taylor as well as to Davis. Two praised Taylor, John A. Quitman, and the 1st Miss. Rgt.; two expressed sympathy for the families of the fallen Mississippians and called for erection of a memorial monument; one prayed for the safe return of the regiment (Jackson *Mississippian*, Apr. 9, 1847).

From Joseph E. Davis

Hurricane 13th May 1847

MY DEAR BROTHR

Your letter of the 5th april[1] was recd. a few days since and althoug old was still of interest. Although we have intelegenc of you as late as the time Col Rogers left Monterey,[2] Capt. Chilton I think may have something for me[3] but he did not stop I may receive it tonight by return of the Concordia[4]

The news is now that Mexico has solicited the mediation of England, and will make no resistance at the Capital.[5] I hope all this may be true, for if a peace should be of [een?] so short duration it will free the country from Mr. Polk's Political Genl.[6] and other job appointees.

I was at Vicksburg on Monday & Tuesday last, I saw many of your frinds, some were disposed to nominate you for Congress some still wished to make you Govr. [a]⁷nd others to make you Senator in *Place* of Speight lately dead[8] of which you are apprised, to this my reply was that my opinion was that you wished no public service but was un authorised to speake except as to the office of Govr. this you could not under any considerations accept.[9]

A meeting will be holden on Saturday to make arrangments for the reception of the volunteers at Vicksburg & to Elect delegates to the Jackson Convention 1st monday in June, (Dem)[10]

We are impatient for your return, if "nought should return but the *broken Car*" I hope the quet of home, and the freedom from the thousand vexations anoyances may amelerate your recovery; A feeling to render respect to the Volunteers is general I fear they may claim too much by asking offices they are not qualified to fill,[11] that ill fated 2n. Regt. Miss. Rifles[12] I learn from the papers has the small pox I feel some anxiety on that account.

I have sent down most of your cotton[13] and will send the balanc by the next trip of the Concordia except some not gined

The selishness & vanity of Genl. Scott must ever detract from his merit & as man and a general Genl. Scott <-h-> is in his eys the only pupose of this war all else subordinate, but he may win laurels but [h]⁷is political aspirations may stop for he is never to rise to distinction in civil life. I have been anxious to know somthing of Genl. Taylor, and had a mind to write to him not that I expected him to have time to reply or that it would be prudent for him to do so, but there is a tide in the affairs men[14] and must be taken &c if he is free from ultraFederal priniples, if /in/ truth he is a Southern man he may be president and president of the nation not of a party may for the first time for many years ask "is he honest is he capeable"

I have heard nothing from Dr. Mitchell since he reached Camargo, say to him I will send his letters to new Orleans if still with you[15]

I was at Brierfield yesterday all well the Negroes all seen desirous to see and hear from you I told some of them that you would be there before the crop was ready for inspection

This is disjointed letter and bad as it is I fear you may not get it.[16]

hoping to see you soon and talk over all the little things ride about with you again see the colts although like the crop not in order for inspection may still afferd you some pleasure is the most anxious wish of your Brothr

---

AL (ViRC).

[1] Davis' letter has not been found.

[2] Jason Rogers (1803–48), lt. col., 1st Ky. Rgt., was a native New Yorker and a West Point graduate (1821) who had settled in Louisville. He was related by marriage to Albert Sidney Johnston, one of Davis' closest friends. During the Mexican War Rogers saw action at Monterrey and in 1847 was named military commander of the city. Leaving Mexico in April, he arrived in New Orleans on May 4 (Dorman, "Genealogy of the Preston Family"; Johnston, *A. S. Johnston*, 134; DNA, M-29, roll 3, Gen. Orders No. 26, Apr. 2, 1847; New Orleans *Picayune*, May 5, 1847).

[3] Robert H. Chilton was charged with delivery of Davis' letter dated April 30.

[4] A packet steamer on the New Orleans–Milliken's Bend route, the *Concordia* stopped regularly at Davis Bend.

[5] Recent articles in New Orleans newspapers noted that the Mexican government had "solicited the friendly mediation" of England and that

"the impression was gaining ground in the army that there would be no more fighting. . . . it was even doubted if the Mexicans would defend their capital" (*Delta* and *Picayune*, May 11, 1847).

[6] Most likely referring to the unpopular appointment of Gideon J. Pillow as maj. gen. of vols.

[7] Manuscript torn.

[8] Jesse Speight, senator from Mississippi, died on May 1.

[9] When Davis gave this authorization to his brother is not known; he did run for governor in 1851 "as a duty" to the Democratic party (*Davis Papers*, 1:lx).

[10] Joseph Davis and his two sons-in-law David McCaleb and Thomas E. Robins were among the Warren County delegates elected at the May 15 meeting. Davis' brother and Robins attended the June 7–8 convention, which nominated a slate of state officers (Vicksburg *Weekly Sentinel*, May 19, 1847; Jackson *Mississippian*, June 11, 1847). After the convention tabled a resolution recommending Davis for senator, the state Whig newspaper commented that

Davis' friends were "much disheartened." Subsequently the *Southron* charged that by "pre-concert and arrangement" several delegates had cautioned against the claims of military heroes solely to undermine Davis, who was "a Lion in the path of every Loco aspirant in the State." Further, it was predicted that "the aspirants, their friends and retainers [would] *smuggle down* his claims in the legislature as they did in caucus" (Jackson *Southron*, July 9, 23, Aug. 13, 1847).

11 Joseph Davis seems to anticipate that a number of Mississippi veterans would run for office in the upcoming state election. Many did so, including Maj. Alexander B. Bradford, Adj. Richard Griffith, and Capts. Reuben N. Downing and John L. McManus (Jackson *Mississippian*, Nov. 19, 1847). Also he may have believed, quite rightly, that some members of his brother's command would seek military or government appointments. See, for example, Davis' recommendations of William H. H. Patterson and Samuel R. Harrison (Feb. 8, 20, 1847).

12 On November 27, 1846, Governor Brown issued a call for ten infantry companies to form the 2d Miss. Rgt., which was organized within a matter of weeks. Representing counties from every section of the state, the men of the 2d Miss. chose Reuben Davis, Joseph H. Kilpatrick, and Ezra R. Price as col., lt. col., and maj., respectively. From the time of its formation the regiment was so ravaged by pneumonia, smallpox, and measles that recruiting teams sought replacements during the summer and fall of 1847 (R. Davis, *Recollections*, 221–53; DNA, M-863, roll 5; *Miss. Official Reg., 1908*, 415–17).

13 Referring to the shipment of cotton from Davis' Brierfield plantation, undoubtedly sent to New Orleans for sale.

14 From *Julius Caesar*, act IV, scene iii.

15 Joseph Davis' son-in-law arrived at the camp near Monterrey on April 24 (Zachary Taylor to Joseph P. Taylor, Apr. 25, 1847, Taylor Papers, DLC).

16 Davis started the trip home on May 17, probably leaving Monterrey with Cos. E, H, and K and joining the rest of the 1st Miss. Rgt. at Cerralvo about May 19 (Matamoros *American Flag*, May 26, 1847; Vicksburg *Tri-Weekly Whig*, June 3, 1847).

From Albert G. Brown

Executive Chamber
Jackson Mi 17 May 1847

SIR

I have the honer to enclose a Copy of a letter written by me to the Secretary of War[1] requesting that officers & men in your Regement be allowed to retain their arms on retir<-e->ing from the service or that said arms be issued to Mississippi as a part of her *quota* from the Genl Government.[2] The Sec't. has not yet replied to the letter, but it is not doubted by me that he will at least yield

174

to the last request.[3] Expecting to be absent from home for some weeks I have instructed the Sec of State to forward Gov Marcy's answer to you when it is received.[4] Should either of My requests be complied with, you will allow the Men under your command to retain their arms when you disband them. If they are issued to the State, I cannot render a more acceptable service to the people for whom your ever glorious Reg't has wove such imperishable honer than to say in their name "there shall be no divorce between the gallant soldier & his Gun."[5] Very Respy Your obt. serv't

A. G. BROWN

LbC (RG27, Vol. 42, Ex. Jour., 170–71, Ms-Ar). Enclosed: Davis to John Jenkins, Aug. 4, 1847.

[1] Brown's letter to William L. Marcy was dated April 20 (Vicksburg *Weekly Sentinel*, Aug. 25, 1847).

[2] A statute of April 23, 1808, provided that arms be transferred by the Federal government "in proportion to the number of the effective militia in each state and territory" (*U.S. Statutes at Large*, 2:490–91).

[3] Marcy replied to Brown on May 11 that the men of the 1st Miss. Rgt. could not personally retain their arms but that the rifles would "be issued to the State as a part of her quota." He enclosed a report from the Ordnance Department stating that "one thousand Percussion Rifles" had been issued and that all would be charged to Mississippi until it was ascertained how many had been lost or destroyed in Mexico (Vicksburg *Weekly Sentinel*, Aug. 25, 1847).

[4] See Wilson Hemingway to Davis, May 21, 1847.

[5] In March 1848 the Mississippi legislature acted on Brown's declaration by resolving that each soldier of the 1st Miss. Rgt. be permitted to keep his rifle (*Miss. Laws, 1848*, 535).

From James K. Polk

Washington City   May 19th. 1847:

MY DEAR SIR:

The Secretary of War will transmit to you a Commission as Brigadeir General of the U. S. Army. The Brigade which you will command will consist of Volunteers called out to serve during the war with Mexico. It gives me sincere pleasure to confer this important command upon you.[1] Your distinguished gallantry and military skill, while leading the noble Regiment under your command and especially in the battles of *Monterey* and *Buena Vista* eminently entitle you to it. I hope that the severe wound which you received at the latter place, may soon be healed, and that your country may have the benefit of your valuable services, at the head of your new command. I am Very faithfully Your friend

JAMES K POLK

LbC (Polk Papers, DLC).

[1] Although Polk had intended to name Robert Armstrong, a personal friend, to the brigadier generalship, he explained to Armstrong that after Buena Vista public sentiment was clearly in Davis' favor. "So strong is the popular feeling in Mississippi," he continued, "that I have reason to believe—, that the political character of the State—would have been changed, at least for a time, if Col Davis had not been appointed." He added that Davis, "a scientific and most gallant officer . . . richly merits the promotion." To a Mississippi congressman Polk wrote that he would have promoted Davis "some weeks" earlier but was "embarrassed by . . . causes, which if explained to his friends, would be satisfactory to them." Whatever the president's rationale, Zachary Taylor was convinced that Davis was granted the commission "under the expectation of keeping him out of the Senate" (Polk to Armstrong, June 13, and to Stephen Adams, May 17, 1847, Polk Papers, DLC; Taylor, *Letters*, 109).

From Joseph E. Davis

Hurricane 21st May '47

MY DEAR BROTHR

As the time draws nea[r][1] for your return a feeling of increased anxiety is entertaind by your relatives and friends. On Tuesday Mr. Robins[2] came down with a document from Gov Brown he felt sure it was a commission for you as Senator in place of Speight deceased, he deliv[er]ed to me & feeling somthing more than Curiosity, I opened it turned ou[t] to be small affair as you will find regarding the Rifles &c.[3] this un[im]portant communication I closed up and enclosed to Mr. Van Benthuysen with directions to deliver it to you on your arrival at New Orleans. Brow[n] has been put upon the Boad of Visitors for the Military acadamy, and has gone to the dissatisfaction of those I have hear[d] speak of the matter. a general opinio[n] seems to be that the Academy could get on without him. Preparations to receive the Regt. at Vicksburg on a large Scale /are making/ and it is thought Brown should have remained and delered an address being the head of the military power in the State.

I perceive some troops have departed for the Brasos which it is hoped will enable Genl. Taylor to hold his posstions if not to advance and this it would seem is not intended. Scott has discharged his Volunteers before the expiration of their term of service[4]

[O][5]ur home affairs remain much as in my former letters of which I have writen you a bout two a week, since Dr. Mitchells departure for whom we feel some anxety as no word of him since he left the mouth of the Rio Grande, 10th of April has been in.

After a long drought we have a rain to day quite as much as desired the Genl. Health of the family & the people here and at the Brierfield is good and geting on [illegible], the Cotton is small for the season. and not as clean as the dry season would lead you to expect.[6]

I feel the uncertainty of a letter reaching you and if this should not the loss will be small although it may be of some interest to Know at the latest date the Condition of affairs at home—

YR BROTHER

AL (Adele D. Sinton). Addressed: "Col Jefferson Davis 1 Missi. Rifles New Aleans Care Messrs. W. Laughlin & co."

[1] Unless otherwise noted, square brackets indicate letters supplied where the right margin of the manuscript is cropped.

[2] Thomas E. Robins, Joseph Davis' son-in-law, lived in Vicksburg.

[3] Albert G. Brown to Davis, May 17.

[4] Scott was concerned for the volunteers' health during the approaching yellow fever season, hence his early dismissal of several regiments on May 6–7. In 1848 he was censured by the War Department for his actions (Scott, *Memoirs*, 2:453; Smith, *War with Mexico*, 2:64; *House Ex. Doc. 60*, 30:1, 1245).

[5] Manuscript torn.

[6] Because of the dry weather planters undoubtedly expected their fields to be relatively free of the weeds and grass destructive to young cotton plants (Lyman, *Cotton Culture*, 28–29).

To George H. Crosman

Rhenosa[1] 24th. May 1847

DEAR FRIEND,

We arrived here this evening and find the 2nd. Ky. and part of the Ky. Cavalry waiting transportation.— The "Roberts" has just come up and another Boat is in sight.—

By taking the Rough and Ready the whole of my Regt. can be placed on her, the "Troy" left as a lighter until she returns and the other boats will releive the immediate press for transportation, such considerations have induced me to require the Rough & ready to continue on to the mouth, and the "Troy" to remain until she returns.[2]

I hope the arrangement will not incommode you or be otherwise unsatisfactory— you will appreciate the reluctance with which I have given any directions which might possibly derange your plans.— As ever Yours

(Signed) JEFFER. DAVIS
Colo. Mi. Rifle—

LbC (DNA, RG92, Letters Recd. by Crosman, 2:860). Endorsed: "(Received 27th. May 1847)."

[1] The Mississippians had undoubtedly expected to board a steamer at Camargo for the trip downriver, but the Rio Grande was so low that navigation was temporarily suspended above Reynosa (New Orleans *Delta*, June 2, 1847). Davis and his men had reached Camargo on May 22, camping several miles below town before marching on to Reynosa (Z355f, Browning Diary, Ms-Ar; Barringer, ed., "Lane Jour.," *Ind. Mag. Hist.*, 53:433).

[2] Contrary to Davis' expectation, the 1st Miss. Rgt. did not travel together on the *Rough and Ready*; two companies of Mississippians passed Matamoros on May 27 aboard the steamer *Whiteville* (Matamoros *American Flag*, June 2, 1847).

To Varina Howell Davis

Mouth of Rio Grande 27th May 1847

DEAR WIFE,

I have just arrived here and have a moment to say that we are on our way to New orleans and will leave by first conveyance. Early in next month we will probably be in new orleans and soon thereafter I shall be at home— I cannot walk yet but am steadily recovering— God bless you my dearest, and preserve you in all things for the great end of our life substantial, mutual happiness— Farewell

YOUR HUSBAND.

AL (Davis Coll., AU). Addressed: "Mrs. Varina Davis care of W B Howell Eq *Natchez Miss*: pr Dallas."

To Thomas B. Eastland[1]

Mouth of R. Grande 27th May 1847

DEAR SIR, I have arrived at this place with eight companies of the Missi. Regt. and anxious to proceed to New orleans with the least delay.

Can you arrange so as to give us prompt despatch in a *steam vessel*. I would have gone over to see you if I had been able to ride on horseback, but as I suppose you have been apprised from genl. Head Qrs. of our coming and know you will be predisposed to oblige us, I have felt more than ordinarily easy about arrangements at this point— Very truly yr. friend

JEFFN. DAVIS
Col. Mi. Rifln.

ALS (DNA, RG92, Letters Recd. by Eastland, No. 252).

[1] Thomas B. Eastland, born about 1807 in Kentucky, had been a merchant in Nashville and New Orleans before his appointment in 1846 as maj. and quartermaster of vols. Discharged in 1849, he lived briefly in California before returning to Tennessee (1850 Census, Tenn., Davidson, Nashville, family 544; ibid., 1860, White, family 66; *Senate Ex. Jour.*, 8:101, 105; Heitman, *Hist. Reg.*, 1: 394; Watson and Huggins, eds., "To Calif.," *Calif. Hist. Quar.*, 18:99–100).

To Thomas B. Eastland

Mouth of Rio grande 27th May 1847—

DEAR MAJ.

Thank you for your kind letter and think with you that *one* steamer might have been left to keep up communications between new orleans and the column *above*.[1] I will come over[2] in the morning and the next day if you say so the Troops can be ready to embark, or if other things can be prepared the Rgt. will be ready to move to morrow.[3]

Until I see you in the morning Farewell—as ever very truly yours

JEFFN DAVIS

ALS (DNA, RG92, Letters Recd. by Eastland, No. 271).

[1] Davis refers to Zachary Taylor's command stationed in northern Mexico. Winfield Scott and most of the American forces were far to the south, preparing for an advance on Mexico City (Bauer, *Mexican War*, 268–74).

[2] Eastland's office was at Brazos Santiago.

[3] Despite Davis' request for transportation by steamboat, he and eight companies of the Mississippi regiment were taken to New Orleans on the schooner *P. B. Savory* and the brig *Forest*, both of which sailed on May 30, reaching New Orleans June 5 and 6 respectively. Two companies,

D and G, followed a few days later, arriving in New Orleans on June 11 (New Orleans *Delta*, June 6, 1847; New Orleans *Bee*, June 7, 1847; New Orleans *Picayune*, June 8, 12, 1847).

To John C. Calhoun

Brazos Sant Iago 28th May 1847

MY DEAR SIR,

your esteemed favor of the 30th March[1] after unusual delay has reached me, nothing could add to my willingness to serve the young gentleman[2] who was the subject of your communication. His gallantry in battle and soldeirly conduct on all occasions has attracted my notice and received my highest commendation. I had very little power to serve the deserving, my reccommendations have in no instance been noticed[3] and the Regimental appointments within the power of a Colonel are limited to the non. com. Regtl. Staff. Before the battle of Buena Vista, I appointed our your young friend Quarter Master Sergeant. On the day of the battle he shouldered his rifle and took his place in the ranks of his old company.

His conduct as at Monterey was worthy of the highest praise, and had the better fortune to escape from wound. He has entirely recovered from the effects of the wound he recived at Monterey[4] and if there be any way in which I can promote his views be assured that it will always be with the greatest pleasure my exertions will be made in his behalf.

He is now with the rear detachment of the Regt. but will join us probably in the early days of June at New Orleans, at which place our Rgt. will be mustered out of service.

Please accept my best wishes and most cordial assurances of Regard: as ever yr. friend

JEFFN. DAVIS

ALS (Calhoun Papers, ScCleU).

[1] Not found.

[2] Samuel Warren White.

[3] Davis had recommended three members of his regiment—William H. H. Patterson, Samuel R. Harrison, and Stephen D. Carson—for regular army commissions; none of them was appointed. His recommendations in behalf of Philip A. Roach and Clinton W. Lear, however, were successful.

[4] White was wounded in the leg at Monterrey; he was not wounded during the Battle of Buena Vista (DNA, M-863, roll 3).

Speech at New Orleans

Editorial Note: Citizens of New Orleans had planned for a week the reception honoring Davis and the 1st Miss. Rgt. On the afternoon of June 10 a "grand and imposing" parade marched along Camp Street to Lafayette Square for the official ceremonies. After the welcoming address, Davis rose, supporting his wounded leg on a chair, and delivered the following remarks, which "created the liveliest admiration in the vast crowd" (New Orleans *Delta*, June 3–5, 11, 1847; New Orleans *Picayune*, June 11, 1847; Tarpley, *Jeff. Davis*, 21–22).

June 10, 1847

"Citizens of New Orleans—no language can express the emotions of the returned volunteers under the reception you give them. But the heart feels, and it spontaneously thanks you. We are unconscious of having done any thing which merits a reception like this. When our country called us, we went, as dutiful children, to her defence; and if you think we have been fortunate in the discharge of our duty we thank you. Next to the approval of his own conscience, the soldier values the approbation of his country.

"Your organ to-day with his peculiar eloquence[1] has been pleased to speak of Gen. Taylor. He has not said more of him than justice demands. Our hearts are bound in sympathy to his. As soldiers we have learned to reverence him for his military judgment; as men we have learned to admire him for his simplicity of character; and we love him for the blended virtues of a good and great man. On the battle-field, calm—no emergency disturbs his composure. His features, as if of iron, show his sternness in the discharge of duty; but when the battle is over, he is the soldier's best and kindest friend. There is not a volunteer before me who will not tell you that his heart beat more proudly on the morning of Buena Vista, when he saw the old General ride upon the plateau, and with his glass survey the field already crimsoning with the blood of the wounded and the slain. The sense of danger was lost in the enthusiasm which sought death rather than retreat.

"Your orator, Mr. Prentiss, has spoken of volunteers as revealing in this war a new faculty. Their effectiveness in defensive war was tested on the plains of Chamette;[2] but under a leader as dearly-beloved, they have lately exhibited an endurance of toil, and a cheerfully sustained courage which entitled them to be termed the true strength of the Republic. Regulars of the service—men enlisted for war as profession—have won bright laurels; but I feel no hesitation in saying, what my long connection in the regular service enables me to say without invidiousness, that neither the exactest discipline nor the severest drill, without that spirit which volunteers eminently possess, will make the truly effective soldier. The same feeling that made the French soldier have a place in his knapsack for a marshal's batoon,[3] gave to him his daring. Individual courage, sustained by a sense of individual responsibility—the mind kindling beneath a consciousness of personal dignity and personal character—this is the feeling that, when truly excited, exalts the commonest man into the hero.

"But our hearts, when we would exult, are shadowed with sorrow. You ask for those who went forth with us; but are not here to-day. Where are they? The drooping heads, and half-inverted countenances of those embrowned men before me give solemn answer. Hardin, McKee, Yell,[4] Clay,[5] Watson,[6] Lincoln,[7] and others, gave themselves to their country, and their country will do them eternal honor. I speak in behalf only of a portion of the returned volunteers; but McKee and Clay were endeared to me by the holiest ties. In boyhood, when the impulses of nature are strong, and the affections intense, we mingled our sports together. At school and in the academy, our associations were the same; and now the heart sinks in the reflection that they are not.

"But there are others who are not here to-day. Honored are those who fell upon the field of battle. But who will tell the struggle of those who met death in disease? A soldier's rough hand ministered to their wants; a soldier's tear may well water the flower that grows upon their grave.

"To die is sometimes a privilege. For many of the returned volunteers there was a harder task than to die—to thirst for glory and not to realize it—to burn with desire to mingle in the strife, and not be able—to know that friends search their names in vain upon the public records. This is the volunteer's hardest fate—unwritten heroes. The courage to submit to silence, and in the discharge of duty to be inactive, where action is glory—this is moral greatness.

"In conclusion, I again thank you, citizens of New Orleans, for this welcome, and the orator whom you have selected to communicate it. My old friend, in leaving Mississippi,[1] has brought with him the enchanter's wand; and though he has told you that the age of chivalry has passed when the bard sung of the warrior's return, he has at the same time convinced us that the age of oratory has succeeded. I again thank you.'

New Orleans *Southerner* (Dem.), quoted in Jackson *Mississippian* (Dem.), June 25, 1847.

[1] Seargent S. Prentiss, formerly of Vicksburg, gave the welcoming address (for the text of his speech, see *Vedette*, Mar. 1884, 3–5).
[2] A reference to Andrew Jackson's victory at New Orleans (1815), a battle fought on Ignace de Lino de Chalmette's plantation (Carter, *Blaze of Glory*, 249–80).
[3] Napoleon Bonaparte: "Every French soldier carries in his knapsack the baton of a marshal of France" (Stevenson, ed., *Home Book of Quotations*, 1430).
[4] Democratic congressman and former governor of Arkansas, Archibald Yell (1797–1847) died at Buena Vista, where he led the 1st Ark. Rgt. (*DAB*).
[5] Henry Clay, Jr. (1811–47), attended both Transylvania University and West Point with Davis. An attorney and state legislator in the mid-1830s, Clay was lt. col., 2d Ky. Rgt., when he fell at Buena Vista (Houston *Dem. Telegraph and Texas Reg.*, May 10, 1847; *Appletons'*; Collins, *Hist. of Ky.*, 2:170). Recalling his friendship with the elder Clay, Davis remembered that "his favorite son was killed with me in Mexico, and he always associated me with that boy" (Burr, "Davis at Home," *Tyler's Quar.*, 32:171).
[6] William H. Watson (1808–46), lt. col., Washington and Baltimore Btn., was an attorney and state legislator who was killed at Monterrey (*Tercentenary Hist. of Md.*, 4:887–88).
[7] George Lincoln (1816–47), son of Massachusetts governor and congressman Levi Lincoln, was a regular army officer killed at Buena Vista while serving on Gen. John E. Wool's staff (Lincoln, *Lincoln Family*, 417–19).

Speech at Natchez

Editorial Note: Davis and four companies of the 1st Miss. boarded two steamers at New Orleans on June 12 for the trip to Natchez. Greeted at the public park by an enthusiastic crowd, the guests of honor were welcomed officially by Adam L. Bingaman. After both Davis and Alexander K. McClung spoke, the volunteers continued their journey upriver, arriving in Vicksburg on June 15. Davis was reunited with his wife at Natchez, taking her to the steamboat landing "in a barouche, nearly hidden with flowers. . . . The journey was one long ovation" (Natchez *Courier and Jour.*, June 16, 1847; Vicksburg *Tri-Weekly Whig*, June 17, 1847; V. Davis, *Memoir*, 1:358).

June 14, 1847

After thanking the people for his regiment and himself, for the very kind reception that had been extended to them, he declared that whatever hardship they had endured—whatever service they had rendered in the field—they had been more than repaid by the approbation of their country. To the brave men he had had the honor to command, he said he owed all that, under the circumstances, one man could owe to others. That when they reached the field of Buena Vista, the battle had commenced, and they met a regiment of their countrymen flying from the enemy,[1] yet with the greatest alacrity they advanced, firing, upon ten times their own numbers. When their flanks were threatened, they were manoeuvred to, and fought upon, either flank—were halted, changed their position to the rear, formed again to the front, and in the coolest manner, and without bayonets, they stood fast without firing a shot, till the Mexican Lancers, in "perfect array," and with confidence beaming on their banners, came upon them, when they poured on them a volley, such as none but American Riflemen can deliver, repulsing at once, and with great slaughter, the Mexican Cavalry.[2]

The honor of taking the first work at Monterey, he said, had been unjustly appropriated by others; but he claimed it for his own Regiment; there ought to be no question about it; there could be no doubt, for, said he, with a flashing eye, and most emphatic tone of gesture, "Lieut.-Col. McClung, whose mangled form now sits before you,[3] was the first man to enter a battery at Monterey, and I, speaking, saw it with my own eyes."[4] He denounced in no measured terms the conduct of the government in withdrawing from Gen. Taylor his troops[5]—declared that if he had known to what extent the capitulation of Monterey had been used in the United States to injure Gen. Taylor, his defence of it would have been more perfect and complete—that he had the means in his possession—that at Monterey it was noticed that "those who complained most of the capitulation were those who were not quite up to the mark in the fight." He concluded by stating, he was about to restore to their country and their friends, the remnant of his gallant regiment, "melted down from that terrible engine of power, disciplined Mississippi courage, into the mechanic, the professional man, the husbandman, and the peaceful citizen."

"Sporting Epistle from the South-West," July 10, N.Y. *Spirit of the Times* (nonpartisan), July 31, 1847, 267.

[1] The retreat of the 2d Ind. Rgt.

[2] Referring to the V formation of the Mississippi and Indiana regiments.
[3] Alexander K. McClung was severely wounded at Monterrey.
[4] A reference to the Mississippians' capture of the Tenería, a claim dis-

puted by members of the 1st Tenn. Rgt.

[5] Privately Davis had denounced the strategy of leaving Zachary Taylor with a small force in northern Mexico (Davis to Joseph E. Davis, Jan. 26, Apr. 30, 1847). His public criticism was noticed immediately, reprinted in other newspapers, and quickly denied by the New Orleans *Southerner*, whose reporter declared: "We were within three feet of Col. Davis during the whole of his speech and know that he DID NOT use any remarks reflecting upon the administration for their conduct towards Gen. Taylor" (Richmond *Enquirer*, Oct. 1, 1847). Nearly a year later, however, the Vicksburg *Tri-Weekly Whig* (June 29, 1848) noted that Davis had never retracted the comments.

To James K. Polk

WARREN COUNTY, MISS., June 20, '47.

MY DEAR SIR:—Your very kind and complimentary letter of the 19th May last, was received in New Orleans, together with the commission to which you therein referred.

To be esteemed by you as one whose services entitled him to promotion, is to me a source of the highest gratification; which will remain to me undiminished, though my opinions compel me to decline the proffered honor.

I will this day address to the Adj't. Gen'l. U.S. Army, an official note informing him that the commission has been received, and is declined. To you I wish to give an explanation, being too sensibly affected by your expressions of honorable estimation and friendly regard, willingly to run any hazard of a misapprehension of the motives which have decided my course.

You inform me that my command will consist of volunteers. I still entertain the opinion expressed by me, as a member of Congress, in May and June 1846,[1] that the "volunteers" are militia. As such, they have a constitutional right to be under the immediate command of officers appointed by State authority: and this I think is violated by any permanent organization made after they have passed into the service of the United States; by which they lose their distinctive character of State troops, become part of a new formation, disciplined by, corresponding and only recognised through the head, which the federal government has set over them.

Such I consider the organization of Volunteer regiments into Brigades, under Brigadiers appointed by the President, as provided for in the law of June 1846;[2] and entertaining this opinion, my decision, as stated to you was the necessary result.

For the gratifying notice you have taken of myself and the regiment I had the honor to command; for the distinction you have been pleased to confer upon me by this unsolicited appointment; and for the kind solicitude you express for my welfare, receive, Sir, my sincerest thanks. Very truly your friend,

JEFFERSON DAVIS.

Vicksburg *Weekly Sentinel*, Oct. 6, 1847. Enclosed: Charles J. Searles to John Jenkins, n.d. (ibid.). While writing his *Rise and Fall of the Confederate Government*, Davis asked friends in Washington to search for the original of this letter. It was recovered by his research assistant early in 1878, but its present whereabouts is unknown (J. L. Jones to William T. Walthall, Nov. 12, 1877, W. J. Tenney to Walthall, Feb. 5, 1878, Z37, Walthall Papers, Ms-Ar).

[1] On June 26, 1846, there was extended debate about presidential appointment of general officers for volunteer units. Any remarks Davis may have made and his vote on an amendment concerning the naming of such officers by states are not recorded in the *Congressional Globe*. For a later reiteration of his feelings about volunteer officers, see *Davis Papers*, 2: 699–700.

[2] The act to organize the volunteer forces and provide general officers for them was approved June 26, 1846 (*U.S. Statutes at Large*, 9:20).

To Robert J. Walker

Warren County 20th June 1847

DR. SIR, First permit me to thank you and your most esteemed Lady for your kind remembrance of myself and family, and [th][1]en to say that I hope you will not be d[is]appointed when you hear that I have th[is] day written to the Adjt. Genl. and to the Presdt. declining the appointment of Brigadier Genl.

I have always held that "volunteers were Militia as such could be temporarily commanded as the exigencies of service required by federal officers, but could be permanently organized only under state autho[r]ity. The President (in a very kind letter) informed me that I had been appointed to command a Brigade of Volunteers with this knowledge I could not accept, without violation to a constitutional opinion. If the War continues I hope to [be?] again in the field and to see the end of it—With my kindest remembrances to all your family and best wishes for yourself I am as ever yr. friend &c

JEFFN. DAVIS

ALS (Z659f, Walker Papers, Ms-Ar).

[1] Square brackets enclose material supplied because the manuscript has been damaged, probably by tape.

To George E. Metcalf[1]

Brierfield, Mi. 23d June 1847

MY DEAR SIR,

Seldom have I more regretted the want of power than on the receipt of your letter, which gives such indication of good judgement, and well directed military enthusiasm, that I feel most deeply my inability to put you at once into the position most favorable for it's cultivation. Very few at your age returning from a successful campaign, would instead of seeking a commission to continue the practice of war, have asked an opportunity to learn the elements of it's science; and this it is which even beyond my personal regard for you, renders me so anxious that you[r][2] wish should be gratified.

Cadet's warrants are granted on the nomination of the Representatives of Congressional d[is]tricts, except ten which are by presentation of the President of the United States. Mr. Gildart[3] of Wilkinson Co. has the appointment for the district in which you reside, and until a vacancy occurs no other can be made therefrom. The Executive nominations are sought by so many applicants that there would be little hope of obtaining an appointment through that channel for some time to come. Should you be willing to wait for a vacancy the application had best be made to both sources i.e. the Representative of your district in the next congress and to the President— You can at all times command my cooperation, it is in my power to bear strong testimony in your favor and it will give me much pleasure if I can contribute any thing to the promotion of your wish.

Again I will commend the wisdom of you[r] reflections; a superior mind may learn the profession of arms by the experience of service, but the process is slow and toilsome, and the knowledge never sits upon the possessor like a garmen[t] made for the wearer. An officer of Infantry has little opportunity to learn those things which pertain to artillery, still less those great lessons of Engineering the ignorance of which must always cause the useless expenditure of blood, if it does not bring defeat. The commander who is familiar with principles of fortification reconnoitres an enemy's position, sees a part, and knows the whole; without this knowledge he would probably attempt to avoid the salient which he saw, and fall upon the curtain where both salients would throw a converging fire upon his troops. Still more in defence than in attack are the resources of the Science of War put in requisition.

Present my sincere thanks to your Father[4] for his kind feeling and unmerited compliment to me – and with the renewed offer of my readiness to serve you to the extent of my power, in the mode most agreeable to you I am yr. friend

JEFFN. DAVIS

ALS (Myrtie C. Byrne). Addressed: "Geo. E. Metcalf Esqr. Kingston Adams Co. Missi."

[1] George Edward Metcalf (1829–1900), born at Chardon, Ohio, was reared in Mississippi. He left Oakland College to fight in the Florida wars and in 1846 enlisted in Co. C, 1st Miss. Rgt. Not admitted to the U.S. Military Academy, he traveled with his father to California in 1849. Two years later he joined the López filibustering expedition to Cuba, was captured and sent in irons to Spain. Soon released, he returned to Mississippi, living for a time on Davis Bend before settling on a farm in Wilkinson County. During the Civil War he served in the 10th Miss. Inf. (family recs. of Myrtie C. Byrne; Confed. Vet., 8:547; Natchez Dem., 1974 Pilgrimage Ed., B:14–15; Metcalf to Alexander K. Farrar, Mar. 9, 1854, Farrar Papers, LU-Ar; DNA, RG109, Comp. Service Recs.; 1860 Census, Miss., Wilkinson, family 145; ibid., 1880, enumeration dist. 154, 23).

[2] Brackets indicate letters supplied where the right margin is frayed.

[3] Francis Gildart, Jr., born about 1828 in Mississippi, entered West Point in 1846 but was dismissed in 1848 despite Davis' efforts in his behalf. Sometime after 1850 he moved to Texas, was an attorney in Austin, and actively supported the local Union Club (1860). In 1863, however, after working as a clerk for the New Orleans quartermaster, Gildart defected from a federal expedition to Texas and reported their plans to a Confederate general. Suspected as a spy, he was held prisoner for a time (1864) in Grimes County (Reg. Graduates, 1965, 238; Davis to William L. Marcy, Aug. 14, 1848; 1850 Census, Miss., Wilkinson, family 380; 1860 Census, Texas, Travis, family 605; Smyrl, "Unionism in Texas," SWHQ, 68:178; OR, Ser. 1, 26, Pt. 2:414–15, Ser. 2, 7:45, 371).

[4] Asa Baldwin Metcalf (1800–51), a Vermont-born physician, had lived in Ohio before settling in Adams County in 1829. Early in 1849 he migrated to California, where he died of cholera (family recs. of Myrtie C. Byrne).

To William L. Marcy

Warrenton, Mississippi. 29th June 1847

SIR:

Several companies have been raised in this state composed partly of the men of the Regt. I commanded in Mexico. applications have been made to me for information as to the mode by which they can be received into genl. Taylor's army and obtain transportation thither.[1] The greater part of them prefer to serve as mounted men, they are willing to engage for the War and if authority were given I have no doubt would soon fill up the incomplete Regt. called from Texas.[2] I believe it would require but a short time to raise another rifle Regt. to take the place of that lately disbanded, if this be desirable. Those who have spoken to me attach great importance to the difference between Volunteers as originally called out, and the organization provided for those who after the expiration of their twelve months' term shou[ld][3] reengage; because the first class have the right of electing their own officers whenever vacancies occur.[4]

Please inform me whether companies, or a battalion or a Regiment of Riflemen will be received; if so will they be allowed to go out as mounted men, <–if not can–> /or will/ they be received as foot, under the act of May <–14–> 13th. 1846. Vy. Respectfly yr. mo. o[5]

AL (DNA, RG107, Letters Recd., Book 65, D-114). LbC (RG27, Vol. 41, Ex. Jour., 125–26, Ms-Ar). Endorsed: "Rec July 19. '47. To be submitted to the President— War Dept Ansd July 16/47."

[1] Several days earlier a group of Mississippians had addressed Marcy offering to form a company of mounted riflemen but wanting assurance that they would be accepted before incurring additional expenses (Vicksburg *Weekly Sentinel*, July 14, 1847; Vicksburg *Tri-Weekly Whig*, July 27, 1847). Undoubtedly some of the would-be volunteers contacted Davis personally; no written "applications" dated June 1847 have been located. When the Miss. Btn. was organized, fourteen men from Davis' 1st Miss. Rgt. were among the members (DNA, M-863, rolls 1–3, 8–9).

[2] The 1st Texas Mtd. Vols. was not completed until July 1847 even though the secretary of war had called for cavalry regiments from Texas in November 1846. Under the command of John C. Hays, the new unit served with Scott, not Taylor (Houston *Dem. Telegraph and Texas Reg.*, Mar. 1, July 19, 1847; Barton, *Texas Vols.*, 83–84).

[3] The right margin is frayed.

[4] The act of May 13, 1846, provided that field officers be appointed according to the laws of the state in which the unit was raised. As Davis indicates, Mississippi militia officers were elected. By contrast, the act of

March 3, 1847, stipulated that reenlisting volunteers would serve under officers appointed by the president (*U.S. Statutes at Large*, 9:9–10, 184).

[5] The remainder of the complimentary closing and the signature have been clipped.

To Robert J. Walker

Brierfield, Mi. 29th June 1847

My Dear Sir,

I have just received your kind letter of the 17th Ult.[1] it having traveled to Mexico and back in pursuit of me. I thank you sincerely for the pleasure it gave you to see me promoted. Before this you will have received a letter which will inform you that my principles would not allow me to receive the commission tendered and that instead of seeing the end of the war, as I desired, I am again a "clod hopper."

After a careful examination of the published letter you sent me I would say it is in the main correct; but I cannot endorse the opinion that "Genl Taylor has been a Democrat all his life."[2] The statement in relation to his father as a supporter /of/ Jefferson is correct,[3] and it might have been added that the General has always referred to the strict Jeffersonian school as the one in which he had been taught, and the elements there acquired as the basis of his political opinions.[4] In another portion of the letter the sentence above quoted is answered, by this correct statement, "He entered the army in early life and has never been a politician." With his ideas of strict construction, with /his/ respect for state sovereignty, with his stern integrity and utter contempt for intrigue and those who seek their ends by indirect mea[ns][5] he must have been a Democrat had he ever been a Congressman: but is neither Whig nor Democrat. His assailants have been Democrats his defenders have been mainly Whigs, but his army connexions and habits have preserved him from the effect which such circumstances would have produced upon a man in civil life and as he stands free from any prejudice of party <–and–> his estimation of a politician would be no proof of party adherence. <–Thus–> His admiration of Jackson and of Clay[6] was not destroyed by their antagonism, and if as stated he approved the course of Simon Snyder[7] I should only infer from the fact that he thought him honest and capable.

Briefly I would say he is no party man, would not consent to be the candidate of a party, and probably would disagree with the ultra men of both parties.

I rejoice to hear of your improved health[8] and hope you may so moderate your labors as here after to preserve it and leave you long to serve your country and yet longer to witness the good fruit of your past labors.

Your good feeling for Genl. Taylor gives m[e] much satisfaction, felt the more sensibly because a long and very skillful article which appeared in the "Union" of the 6th Feby. arraigning the Genl. for the capitulation of Monterey and kindred subjects was ascribed to you.[9] I now regret that I did not write to you at the time concerning it.

Please present me most respectfully to Mrs. Walker, Miss Bache,[10] and the young folks to all of whom Mrs Davis sends her love, and joins me in sincerest regard for yourself. your friend

JEFFN. DAVIS

ALS (Emily Driscoll). Endorsed: "Private."

[1] Walker's letter has not been found.

[2] From this and subsequent references made by Davis it is clear that Walker had sent him a copy of Simon Cameron's letter of April 25 to Samuel D. Patterson, editor of the Norristown (Pa.) Register. First printed in the Register, Cameron's letter soon appeared in a number of newspapers (Philadelphia Pennsylvanian, June 1, 1847; Crippen, Cameron, 83, 98, 101).

[3] Cameron had stated that, as a presidential elector in Virginia, Taylor's father had voted for Thomas Jefferson. Actually Richard Taylor (1744–1829) had moved from Virginia in the mid-1780s and did not serve as an elector until 1812, when a resident of Kentucky (Hamilton, Zachary Taylor, 1:xvi, 25; Padgett, "Letters of Richard Taylor," Ky. Hist. Reg., 36:332).

[4] Taylor wrote in June that he regretted the publication of Cameron's letter, "notwithstanding I am & always have been a democrat of the Jeffersonian school, which embodies very many of the principles of the whigs of present day" (Letters, 109).

[5] Square brackets indicate material supplied where the right margin is cropped.

[6] Fellow Kentuckians Henry Clay and Taylor enjoyed cordial relations; contrary to Cameron's allusion, Taylor and Andrew Jackson were not always good friends (Hamilton, Zachary Taylor, 1:82, 112–13, 118).

[7] Cameron stated that while Taylor was stationed in Pennsylvania in 1808 he was reportedly "a supporter of Simon Snyder." An admirer of Jefferson, Snyder (1759–1819) was then governor of the state (DAB).

[8] In early May 1847 Walker was so dangerously ill with bronchitis that his recovery was in question, but by May 25 he was able to attend a cabinet meeting (N.Y. Herald, May 10, 1847; Polk, Diary, 3:35).

[9] An unsigned article entitled "The Capitulation of Monterey—Its History and Consequences" appeared in the Washington Union on February

3. Disclaiming any intention to impugn Taylor's patriotism, the writer nevertheless defended the House of Representatives' disapproval of the capitulation agreement and refuted Taylor's justifications for sanctioning it. After James Buchanan wrote him to say that no one in the cabinet bore him malice, Taylor replied that a friend had thought Walker the author of the article, "as it was his style," and further noted that "I might have remarked in presence of Col. Davis, who I knew was the friend of the Secretary as well as my own, that if it was the production of his pen, it was to be regretted he had not made himself in the first instance acquainted with the exact state of the case before attempting to assail me in that way" (*Letters*, 185; Taylor to John J. Crittenden, Nov. 1, 1847, Crittenden Papers, DLC).

[10] Perhaps Riny Bache, a friend of the Davises' in Washington (*Davis Papers*, 2:420, 535).

To Stephen Cocke

Brierfield, Mi. 15th July 1847

DEAR SIR, When we parted I hoped by this date to have been able to leave home free from the inconvenience and disagreeable exposure of hopping on crutches. My foot has not improved much and though just now its appearance is flattering I have been so often disappointed that I wait further evidence.

I thank you for the interest you take in the appointment of U. S. Senator and am really obliged to Govr. Brown for feelings which by others I had been led to believe he did not entertain towards to me.[1]

With the hope that I will soon have the pleasure of seeing you I am as ever very sincerely your friend

JEFFN: DAVIS

ALS (Z735, Davis Papers, Ms-Ar).

[1] After the death of Jesse Speight on May 1 Davis was mentioned as a candidate for senator. The appointment was to be made by Governor Albert G. Brown pending election by the state legislature in January. Not a close friend of Davis' before the Mexican War, Brown undoubtedly viewed the wounded hero as a serious political rival. Moreover, Brown and one of Davis' relations, Thomas E. Robins, were openly antagonistic.

From William L. Marcy

War Department July 16'. 1847

SIR,

I am directed by the President to inform you, in reply to your letter of the 29. ultimo, that he will accept of such a battalion of riflemen as you suggest, to serve during the war, to be raised in the State of Mississippi. You indicate the employment of these under Major General Taylor, but it is probable that the more active operations will be with the column under the command of Major General Scott, and their services may be required in connection with that column. Presuming that they will prefer the most active service, and that a different destination from that mentioned by you will not impede the raising of it, I shall send forthwith a request to the Governor to aid in the organization thereof.[1]

In regard to your suggestion that the battalion should be mounted, I would remark that the mounted force already called out is deemed to be sufficient for the service which may be required of that description of troops, and it is not now proposed to add to their number.[2] Very respectfully, Your Obt Serv

W L. MARCY
Secretary of War

LbC (DNA, RG107, Letters Sent, Mil. Books, 1823–53, 27:457). L, draft (ibid., Letters Recd., f/w Book 65, D-114). LbC (RG27, Vol. 41, Ex. Jour., 126, Ms-Ar).

[1] On July 17 Marcy authorized Governor Albert G. Brown to call for a battalion of riflemen. On July 29 Brown requested the organization of five rifle companies and simultaneously released the correspondence between Davis and Marcy to "show the circumstances under which the President granted the authority." Only two days before he wrote to Davis, Marcy had informed a group of Mississippians that there was no immediate need for more volunteers from their state (Jackson *Mississippian*, July 30, 1847; Vicksburg *Tri-Weekly Whig*, July 27, 1847).

[2] The call for an infantry unit rather than mounted riflemen contributed significantly to the delay in raising the Miss. Btn. As the Vicksburg *Tri-Weekly Whig* (Sept. 30, 1847) commented, "the boys in this State wish to go as *mounted men* to *Gen. Taylor*, while the perverse and obstinate administration swears they *must* go as *footmen* to *Gen. Scott*." By the governor's announced deadline of August 23 only one company was complete; finally in December the battalion was on its way to Mexico (Jackson *Mississippian*, Aug. 25, Dec. 24, 1847).

From Officers of the Second Mississippi Regiment

BUENA VISTA, MEXICO July 16th, 1847.

SIR:— As you will doubtless have learned before this reaches you,[1] the office of Colonel of the 2nd Mississippi Rifles will be vacated on the 1st of September next, by the resignation of Col. Reuben Davis.[2]

Feeling a deep interest in the selection of his successor, the officers held a meeting on last evening to ascertain, if possible, who was the choice of the regiment.

Knowing and appreciating the high reputation you have acquired as commander of the 1st Mississippi Regiment, there was on the part of the meeting a unanimous expression of opinion in your favor, and the undersigned were appointed a committee to ascertain the preference of the whole regiment, to communicate with you upon the subject, and to know if you would accept the command if tendered to you. We have made such enquiry among the men, and we are happy to be able to state, that you are the *unanimous* choice of the whole regiment. We therefore request that you will communicate to us at the earliest practicable period, what your views are upon the subject, so that we may communicate the same to the regiment.

Permit us to indulge the hope personally that it may not be incompatible with your wishes and interests to assume the command, and that we may soon have the pleasure of greeting you as our leader. We have the honor to be, Very respectfully, Your ob't serv'ts,

A. McWILLIE,[3]

Capt. 2nd Miss. Rifles.

E. DOWSING,[4]

1st. Lieut. 2nd Miss. Rifles.

F. AMYX,[5]

1st. Lieut. 2nd Miss. Refles.

A. J. TRUSSELL,

2nd Lieut. 2nd Miss. Rifles.

Vicksburg *Weekly Sentinel*, Sept. 29, 1847. Enclosed: Davis to John Jenkins, Sept. 21, 1847. Sent to both Davis and the *Sentinel* on July 19, the letter was first published on August 18.

[1] The announcement of Reuben Davis' resignation appeared in the Vicksburg *Sentinel* on July 28. Davis may have heard the news even earlier since Reuben Davis reached New Orleans on July 20 and presumably

traveled upriver several days later (New Orleans *Picayune*, July 21, 1847; Jackson *Mississippian*, July 30, 1847).

[2] Reuben Davis (1813–90), born in Tennessee, was a lawyer from Aberdeen. Having reluctantly accepted the colonelcy of the 2d Miss. Rgt. in January 1847, he resigned because of ill health in July. Resuming his career and Democratic political activities, he became an attorney for the New Orleans, Jackson & Great Northern

Railroad, a state legislator (1855–57), and a congressman (1857–61). A maj. gen. of state troops in 1861, he served in the Confederate Congress (1862–64) and after the war won recognition as a successful criminal lawyer. Despite some political differences with Davis during the Civil War, Reuben Davis remained his unstinting admirer (*DAB*; R. Davis, *Recollections*, passim; R. Davis to Davis, Jan. 10, 1854, Davis Papers, KyLxT, Aug. 2, 1863, MWA, Nov. 24, 1888, ViRC).

[3] Adam McWillie (1821–61), eldest son of Mississippi politician William McWillie, was born in South Carolina. Unsuccessful in attempts to join the 1st Miss. Rgt. as capt. of the Attala Guards, he served in the 2d Miss. from January 1847 until February 1848. A planter in Madison County during the 1850s, McWillie was elected capt. of a rifle company attached to the 18th Miss. Inf. in

1861. He was killed while rallying his men at Bull Run (*Miss. Official Reg., 1908*, 406–407, 415; DNA, M-863, roll 6; *Biog. and Hist. Memoirs of Miss.*, 1:1243–45; *OR*, Ser. 4, 2: 932).

[4] Everard Dowsing, born in Georgia about 1820, returned home to Columbus, Mississippi, in 1848 and was living there as late as 1860. He was a clerk by occupation (DNA, RG15, Mexican War Bounty Land Applics.; 1860 Census, Miss., Lowndes, family 320).

[5] Fleming Amyx, a native Virginian born about 1813, was a resident of Lexington, Mississippi, before the Mexican War. Afterward he migrated to California and was elected to the legislature (1855, 1861) from Tuolumne County (DNA, RG15, Mexican War Bounty Land Applics.; Jackson *S. Reformer*, June 21, 1845; Allen, *Legis. Sourcebook*, 297).

To John S. Clendenin

BRIERFIELD, Miss., 20th July, 1847.

DEAR SIR: Lieutenant Moore failed to make a report of the events particularly connected with Company H., on the 22d and 23d of September last, at Monterey. Captain Taylor has written to me[1] that the company officers, when we were in New Orleans, had contemplated calling on me to ask that their reports both of Monterey and Buena Vista should be published. I had always designed to send a copy of them to our Government, and thus hoped they would be given to the public.[2]

You will oblige me if you will make a full report of the occurrences of the last two days of the battle of Monterey,[3] which I the more desire, because yours was the only company which went out with me on the morning of the 23d, and remained constantly on duty throughout the day.

With my best wishes and kindest recollections, I am, as ever, your friend,

JEFFERSON DAVIS.

New Orleans *Delta*, Oct. 20, 1849. Clendenin included the text of this letter in a statement written to refute implications in two other New Orleans newspapers that his services in Mexico "were not held in high estimation" by Davis.

[1] James H. R. Taylor's letter has not been found.

[2] See Davis to Albert G. Brown, October 3, 1847. The company reports were not released for publication.

[3] If Clendenin reported as Davis asked, his account has not been found.

To [Simon Cameron] [1]

Brierfield, Mi 26th. July 1847

DEAR SIR,

With much pleasure I receivd your kind letter of the 9th Inst. and yesterday wrote to genl. Taylor[2] giving him the important and complimentary intelligence communicated by you. I agree with you as to the propriety of his declining to answer letters written either to draw out his opinions or to connect him with little cliques or political hacks in newspaper publication. Indeed if it were proper, he could not without being exposed to misconstruction answer to the various points which politicians raise. In every field of knowledge there are many conventional terms, recognized by the laborers, in a sense not generally apprehended, and one who has never engaged in politics would not probably understand the <−full−> /true/ import of a politicians letter, still less would his answer convey with precision his own opinion.[3] For instance no student of political economy would understand that "free trade" meant duties levied to raise revenue, and varied in direct proportion to the money required; yet those who use the term commonly mean no more than this.

Every thing is suspended here as to the next Presidency and there will probably be no more until further developments.[4] From an early period I have been convinced that the Whigs would not present the name of genl. Taylor as their candidate. Your meeting at Harrisburg[5] and my expectations of the effect which a more general knowledge of the opinions of genl. Taylor will have, induce the belief that he will be without a nomination supported by the Democracy generally and by the South without regard to Party.

We have drawn near to that which has been for many years my

196

dread, a division marked not by opinions, but by geographical lines. It is for the patriotic to show their devotion to the principles of our federation and save the Republic from the evil consequences so likely to follow from a geographical issue.

at present I forbear to suggest correspondents to you but in due time will avail myself of your invitation to do so.

Please let me hear from you occasionally and believe me with great regard yrs, truly

JEFFN. DAVIS

ALS (Washington County, Md., Hist. Soc.).

[1] Internal evidence, as well as information derived from Davis' letter of June 29 to Robert J. Walker and Zachary Taylor's letter to Davis of August 16, suggests that Simon Cameron was the addressee. At this time Cameron (1799–1889) was a Democratic senator from Pennsylvania (*DAB*).

[2] The letter of July 9 and Davis' letter of July 25 to Taylor have not been found.

[3] Davis and his correspondent undoubtedly had in mind the political shockwaves generated by Zachary Taylor's "Signal letter." Dated May 18, 1847, and addressed to the editor of the Cincinnati *Morning Signal*, the letter appeared in the Washington *Union* on July 1. In it Taylor disavowed basic Whig principles and indirectly sanctioned the Wilmot Proviso, opinions that discomfited Whigs everywhere and astounded his southern supporters. On the resulting controversy Taylor commented that he had not written for publication, hence his lack of "critical attention to the terms employed which politicians appear so much to require" (Vicksburg *Tri-Weekly Whig*, July 13, 1848; *Niles' Reg.*, July 24, 1847, 335; Washington *Union*, July 6–8, 1847; New Orleans *Delta*, July 11, 1847).

[4] Although there had been meetings and pronouncements in many states regarding the 1848 campaign, the Mississippi Democratic convention "did not even allude to the subject." Mississippi Whigs eschewed a state meeting altogether in 1847 (Jackson *Mississippian*, June 11, 1847; Young, "Miss. Whigs," 103–105).

[5] On June 26 a Democratic meeting in Harrisburg, Pennsylvania, adopted a set of resolutions praising Taylor and proposing him for president. Cameron, a leading participant in the meeting, was named to a committee of correspondence charged with promoting the general's candidacy (Harrisburg *Dem. Union*, July 7, 1847).

From Albert G. Brown

Executive Chamber   Jackson Mi 27th July 1847.

SIR

I am informed by the Secretary of War, that your (1s. Mi) Regt had issued to them one thousand stand of arms, and that our State stands charged with that number subject to a deduction of so many as were not actually on hand at the time the Regement was mustered out of the Service. You will recollect that it was at my instance the arms were left in the hands of the Volunteers,[1] it is therefore desireable to me that the account should be adjusted before I go out of office. Will you inform me therefore how many rank and file you had mustered out at New Orleans, how many stand of arms were retained *if you know* & whether any more guns were retained than there were privates mustered out of the Service. I have addressed a note to each one of the captains asking them to state their accounts, but a letter from you will greatly aid me in the settlement.[2] Very Respfl Your obt serv't

A.G. BROWN

LbC (RG27, Vol. 42, Ex. Jour., 177, Ms-Ar).

[1] See Brown's letter of May 17.
[2] Brown's letter to the ten captains of the 1st Miss. Rgt. was dated July 30 (RG27, Vol. 42, Ex. Jour., 177, Ms-Ar). For Davis' response to Brown's request, see his letter of October 3 and his letter to George Talcott dated November 7.

From Zachary Taylor

Camp near Monterey Mexico July 27th 1847

MY DEAR GENERAL,

Your very acceptable & interesting letter of the 24th, ulto,[1] from Brierfield has just reached me, for which you have my sincere thanks, & I hardly need say the pleasure it afforded me which is not a little, to hear & particularly to know after so long an absence, undergoing so many hardships & privations, encountering so many dangers, as well as suffering so much, you had reached home if not entire well, at least in good spirits, which I am not surprised at, as you found your excellent Lady, brother, his family & friends all well, & your affairs as prosperous <–as prosperous–> as you could have expected; that your wound had very much improved, & that it will I truly hope continue to do so rapidly, until it is not only entirely healed, as well as that you will have the use of your limb, fully as well as you had previous to the injury. Notwithstanding all the medical officers who have examined it have assured me there was no permanent injury to be apprehended from it, I must say /I have felt/ & still do much uneasiness about it, & fear it will be some time before you entirely recover from its effects, & before doing so, you will /be/ subjected to some pain, & great inconvenience, but in this I sincerely hope I may be mistaken—

The course pursued towards me by the head of the war dept, I can but consider rather a rough one to say the least of it, & it seems to me had I been properly supported by those whose duty it was to have done so, much more would or might have been acomplished than has been by this comd, at any rate had my force been what it should have been at Buena Vista, the Mexican foot or the greater portion of them, with their baggage & mu/ni/tions of war would have fallen into our hands of every description & perhaps Santa Ann; if all our disposable force had been concentrated on this line after we took posession of Saltillio, we might have reached the City of Mexico some time since, & succeeded in bringing about a peace; be this as it may it would not do for me to get into /an/ angry correspondence with the Secretary of War, as it might lead to <–lead to–> unkind feelings between the president & myself, which I do not wish, & will not knowingly do anything to produce it[2]–

I have been for some time saisfied as regards Genl. Scotts want of sincerety, while he was professing the kindest feelings for me, he was unscrupuously stripping me of my command, & leaving me to the tender mercies of the enemy; nor would he have had or felt the slightest compunction let the consequences been what they might, so he was not implicated in the same– I do not believe he would hesitate a moment to sacrifice <–to sacrifice–> me or anyone else who stood in his way, or interfered with /his/ interest, ambition or vanity in any way, or in the slightest degree; his sugared letter to me from N. York of Nover last (a copy of which was sent to his friend Mr, Marcy to be pulished if any misfortune over took me, to let the people see how kindly they felt towards us after our throats had been cut) which letter was published in the Union when it was supposed we had been annihilated by the Mexicans,[3] was sufficient evidence of his want of proper principles, & his participation in a dirty intrigue to get me out of the way, independed of his letter to Cadwallader,[4] which is conclusive evidence it was not intended that I should do anything on this line;[5] but it may be all for the best, &

at any rate such double dealing & duplicity generally results in due season disadvantageously to those who trafic in it, & I trust it will not fail in this instance, to do so–

Most truly & sincerely do I unite with you my dear genl, in wishing for a speedy peace, of which there are some little prospects, if for no other reason than the effect it would have of saving the lives of so many of our young gallant respectable /volunteer/ soldiers, who have volunteered in the cause of their country, who are daily falling victims to the hardships, privations &c common to a soldiers life, & to the diseases that accompany the march & attend the camp of young volunteers everywhere, & particularly under a tropical /sun/ vastly more distructive to human life than all the material invented for its destruction; many of whom if this war continues /say hundreds & thousands/ will find graves in a foreign land, who in the event of a speedy peace, might return to their home, to alleviate the sorrows & sufferings of helpless wives[6] & chidren, & gladden the hearts of aged parents & friends– We have recd. here news from Mexico up /to/ the 28th, ulto, though papers printed in that City, which stated that Genl, Scott with his army was in Puebla; & that Mr, Trist had joined him; & there had been a communication opened with the Mexican authorities on the subject of peace, the result of which had not transpired; it was however cheering to know that the first <–first–> steps had been taken in that important matter, <–matter–> & sincerely do I hope the result will be most fortunote– It appears Mr, T– is fully authorised to enter into all the preliminaris, as well as to conclude a peace[7]– It seems to me that we are now in posession of as much of the enemies territory as we want for any useful purpose, independent of what may be in posession of the Southern Column; the fact is I much fear if the war continues, we will have to occupy, & finally to annex more Mexican Territory to the Union than will be to our advantege in the fin[a][8]l adjustment of matter[9] From your genl, acquaintance with the prominent <–mi–> politi/cal/ men of our Country, I much fear if not annoy[ed] you are very much plagued with inquiries as to my vie[ws] on many of the greant nation/al/ subjects which have divide[d] the two prominent political parties of the country;[10] let who [wi]ll be at the hd. of the Nation if this war continues much l[on]ger a much larger amt, of revenue must be raised to mee[t] its expenses, & Congress must decide whether it will be best to fa[ll] back on the

tarif of 42, or resort to direct taxation; I am oppo[sed] to the bor-
rowing system by individual or by the govt, at any r[ate] a stop
must be put to it as soon as a peace can be brought a[bo]ut; when
we must have a revenue <–which–> to carry on th[e] govt, the
expences of which must be greatly increased with [the] acquisitions
of immense baren regions, to pay the interest of [the] National
debt,[11] & establish a respectable sinking fund— [Re?]establishing a
National Bank will hardly be again agitate[d] during /my/ time, nor
will there be during the same any surplu[s] revenue to dispose of
from the sales of the public lands; & [the] Wilmot provis/o/ is a
mere bugbare, & amounts to nothing; it wa[s] gotten up to produce
some important effect for the mome[nt] by creating excitement in
certain quarters, & will soon [die away?] & be looked on a seven
days wonder[12]– No man of ord[i]nary capacity can believe for a
moment that /if we/ annex the [wh]ole or any part of <–the
Union–> Mexico to the U. States that co[n]gress will ever permit
a state made from it /to/ enter our U[ni]on with the features of
Slavery connected with /it/; it has been ab[ol]ished by the people
of Mexico or their rulers,[13] & will never be revi/ved/d by ours; In-
ternan /improvements/ will carried on in spite of vetoe[s] or anything which the president can interpose to preve[nt] it— So far as
Slavery is concerned, we of the south must thr[ow] ourselves on
the constitution & defend our rights under /it/ to t[he] last, &
when arguments will no longer suffice, we will appeal to the sword,
if necessary to do so, I will be the last t[o] yield one inch– It will
be a source of much pleasure to m[e] to be so fortunate to
<–me–> be able to meet my Southern fri[en]ds, as well as all
others of the democratic party on the sa[me] ground, or at any rate
to meet half way; but enoug[h] on this subject as I am writing /to/
one who knows m[y] every thought in regard to political matters;
& I must again say I am no politician, nor have I a wish to be president of the U. States, much less of a party; & can truly say that I
feel much more interest in the recovery from your wound, & in the
termination of this war, so that the Volunteers who are suffering
so much fron disease, could git to their homes, than I do of being
president of the U States– I know I have many warm & devoted
friends in the gallant State of Mississippi who are warmly /devoted
to me/ & whose kind feelings are duly appreciated; But greatly fear
they have overrated not /my/ wishes but my ability to do good–

From the meeting of Congress to the election for the chief magistrate of the country, which is in Novr. 1848 the most outrageous assaults no doubt will be made on my character public & private, which however I must not suffer to disturb me, & let it pass without notice, & should a national convention think proper to nominate some one else for that high office, & shoul he be elected, it will not give me one moments concern in the way of unpleasant feelings– But should the major[ity][14] of the people think proper to elevate me to the office in que[s]tion I will serve them as a matter of duty honestly & faithfully to the best of my ability, strictly in conformity to /the/ principles of the constitution, as narly as it can be, in the way it was construed & acted on by our first presidents, two of whom at least participated so largely in completing & putting in operation that glorious instrument; which has made us what we are, the first people on the globe, & which will continue our growth & prosperity as long as its principles are adhear to, & our greatness will leave us in my humble opinion, whenever its provisions are lost sight of, as you corrcelly say–

I think it best to take things as they are & not attempt to speculate to deeply into futurity, events must thake their course; I was opposed to the annexation of Texas believing as I did the manner it was done, was at varience with /the/ Constitution,[15] & which no one now living will see the effects, & bad effects which is to result from this war, which has grown out of it on the institution[s?] of our great & hitherto prosperous country; but I will not make my self unhappy at what I cannot prevent; nor give up the constitution or abandon it because a rent /has/ been made in it, but will stick by & repair it, & nurse it, as long as it will hang togather–

The kind [re]membrances of your family is to me a source of the deepest gratification, they owe me nothin[g] in fact I feel under the deepest obligations to them for sparing you to me, who has redered me, as well as his cou[n]try such important services on so many trying occasions, which can never be forgotten by me; & I hope to be able <–to–> yet to thank them all in person as soon as I am relieved from my duties here, or the war is brought to a close; for <–it–> /it/ would be much more congenial to my feelings to be sitting with you under your own /vine/ & figtree with a few of your friends & neighbour including of corse your worthy brother, discussing the best mode of raising cotton corn &c, than the "cir-

cumstances /<-& pomp of->/ of glorious war," or all the parade
of splendor of the White House.– Altho, I miss you very much, &
should be more than gratified to have you with me, yet I could not
wish nor would desire you to make so great a sacrifice; you have
already gone far enough in that way, & at any rate for the present
require some repose, at any rate until you get the entire use of your
foot, ancle & leg as well as to set your affairs in order– On the subject of the appt, of <-the the appointment-> /Briger Genl,/ I
would consutl my own fe[e]lings & interest[s] in regard to it, I
[ho]pe there will be no more figting in Mexico, & even if there
shoul unfortunately be, it will I apprehend be somewhat <-guer->
of the guerilla character where little of reputation can be gained—
without imbarking in electioneering operations /should/ the Legislature of your State offer you the vacant position of Senetor in the
U Senate & it did not interfere too much with your private affairs,
it <-it-> seems to me you ought not to dectine; it is one of the
hig/h/est most dignified & conspicuous positions in the Country;
but your own feeling, & the opinions of your friends around you,
must govern you in this matter[16]–

Simce you left we have been doing but little, securing our communications, getting up supplies & watching the movements of gen-
erat Urrea,[17] who we hear is occasionally at Tula & Victo/ria./
my force has been too small to accomplish anything of importance;
the object of the dept heretofore seems to have been to throw all
the /<-disposable on [the?]->/ other line, leaving <-them->
/us/ to act purety /much/ on the defensive; of this I have not complained, believing it to be right & proper that that /command/
should be placed in point of force, beyond the possibility of disaster.
We but seldom hear from it, except through the letter writers by
way of N. Orlans; occasionally a stray newspaper reaches us across
the country from the City of Mexico– But a part at least or I may
say most of the reenforcements which have been so long promised
me,[18] have or /are/ about reaching the Rio Grande, if so I hope to
be able to make a forward movement on San Luis Potosi, or on
Zacatecas by the first of Septr, if peace is not made, which I again
repeat I sincerely hope will be the case. I am heartily tired of inaction, & will feel in much better health & spirits when again in the
Saddle; my greatest fears are occasioned by the sickness among the
new troops which have reached here duri/n/g the last three or four

months, both on the Ri[o Gr]ande, & at Saltillio; the Mississippi Regt, which I sent to Salt[illo w]ith the hope of i[mproving?] its health, ha[s] still a large sick rep[ort. I]ts Col, has again left on [furlough?] & suppose will hardly agai[n] return.[19] Several other of the N. Regts /are/ as badly off; it seems to me [wh]enever new troops are [b]rought togather fresh from the countr[y] they are liable to be atta[c]ked by all & every disease known to the human family–

I hope still to be able to /leave/ early in Novr, for the U. States if not before,[20] but in this I may be [d]isappointed; at any ra[t]e I shall do so the first moment I ca[n] leave with propriety–

I was highly gratified to learn your plantation or crop had not been injured b[y h]igh water, & that both cotton & corn was quite promising, & tr[ul]y do I hope that the yield [wi]ll be a most abundent o[ne]– My overseer[21] writes /me/ his /[p]rospects/ for a crop /of/ both corn & cotton are v[e]ry gloomy, owing to the severe droug[ht] which had follow[e]d the overflow, on part of the plantation there had not been a particle of rain for two months, & that the [cu]t worms & other insects had made great ravages in /what/ had [b]een replanted–

I will afford /me/ always much pleasure to hear from you no matter how often you may write, & y[o]ur views on political as well as other subjects will be read <–them with–> with much intere[st] & no doubt with profit– I <–fear–> I have inflicted you with [a] long & I fear a very uni[n]teresting epistle, but you are not [bou]nd to wade throu[gh] it, but can throw it aside wh[en]ever it is not of sufficien[t] /[interest?]/ pay for the trouble & time for reading it–

Present me most kindly to your good lady & worthy brother & family, including Dr, M[22]—& wishing you & them continued heath & prosperity I remain truly & sincerely Your Friend

Z– TAYLOR

ALS (Taylor Papers, DLC). Endorsed by Davis: "Ansd. 23d Sept. 47." Manuscript damaged; right margin of two pages clipped; last page torn.

1 Davis' letter has not been located. Allusions to some of its contents may be found in this letter and in Taylor's letter of July 20 to his son-in-law (Taylor, *Letters*, 119).

2 Taylor's relations with Secretary of War William L. Marcy were far from cordial and had recently been exacerbated by the publication of Taylor's letter to Edmund P. Gaines as well as by Marcy's failure to in-

form Taylor beforehand of the Veracruz expedition. For his part, President Polk was unhappy with what he viewed as Taylor's indiscretions, bad temper, and general incompetence (*House Ex. Doc. 60*, 30:1, 1100–1102; Polk, *Diary*, 2:248–50, 355–57).

3 Scott's letter of November 25 was published in the Washington *Union* on March 20, 1847, at a time when "painful apprehensions" were felt for the safety of Taylor's army (Polk, *Diary*, 2:433).

4 George Cadwalader (1806–79), a Philadelphia attorney, businessman, and militia officer, was appointed brig. gen. of vols. in March 1847; he served until mid-1848, participating in the capture of Mexico City. A Union maj. gen. of vols. during the Civil War, he was also military adviser to the president (*NCAB*, 12:269; Warner, *Gens. in Blue*).

5 Scott ordered on April 25 that Cadwalader rush all the newly organized regiments to Veracruz, explaining that Taylor would not need additional troops (Taylor Papers, DLC).

6 Taylor first wrote the word *widows*.

7 Nicholas P. Trist (1800–74), chief clerk of the State Department, was appointed by President Polk to negotiate with the Mexican government. Given "full power" to conclude a treaty, Trist left in April for Mexico, arriving at Scott's headquarters on May 14 (*DAB*; Polk, *Diary*, 2:466–67, 477–78; Smith, *War with Mexico*, 2:127–29).

8 Unless otherwise noted, square brackets indicate manuscript damage.

9 There were ardent expansionists in the Polk administration, notably Robert J. Walker, but Trist's instructions were to insist upon only the Rio Grande boundary and the cession of upper California and New Mexico. If possible, he was to negotiate for lower California and the right of passage across the Tehuantepec Isthmus (Buchanan, *Works*, 7:

271–79; Polk, *Diary*, 2:472–75, 3:229–30).

10 Evidence that such inquiries were being made is found in a letter from Robert B. Rhett to John C. Calhoun dated May 20, 1847: "I write today to Jefferson Davis to know what we are to expect from Genl. Taylor on the subject of the Tariff" (Boucher and Brooks, eds., "Corres. to Calhoun," *AHA Ann. Rep., 1929*, 377).

11 There being no direct taxation, government revenues were derived principally from customs duties and the sale of public lands. To meet the cost of waging war the Polk administration had resorted to the sale of treasury notes and bonds in the amount of $33 million. In spite of the additional income, the national debt nearly quadrupled during Polk's presidency, from about $17 million to over $65 million (Smith, *War with Mexico*, 2:255–67).

12 An even stronger version of the original Wilmot Proviso was introduced in the House in February 1847. Although not enacted, it led to considerable debate in Congress and nationwide. Only after his return from Mexico did Taylor seem to understand the deep sectional antagonism the proviso had unleashed (Taylor to Davis, Apr. 20, 1848).

13 The decree of Guerrero (1829) abolished slavery in Mexico but, in response to the protests of American colonists, Texas was exempted (*Handbook of Texas*).

14 Ink blot.

15 Whigs generally agreed with Taylor and his friend John J. Crittenden that annexation of a foreign state was illegal and that using a joint resolution of Congress to accomplish it was both unconstitutional and a usurpation of the Senate's treaty-making powers (Coleman, ed., *Life of Crittenden*, 1.227–31).

16 On July 20 Taylor wrote his son-in-law that he had received a letter from Davis: "he appears undeter-

mined what course to pursue as regards accepting the appr of Brig Genl or not; if the war continues I think he is inclined to accept. . . . The Col speaks of Genl Scott in harsh terms" (Taylor, *Letters*, 119).

[17] José de Urrea (1795–1849), a career soldier who was one of Santa Anna's ablest lieutenants during the Texas revolution. Leading a cavalry unit posted at Tula, Urrea harassed Taylor's army throughout 1847 by disrupting lines of communication and supply (Rives, *U.S. and Mexico*, 2:365; *Handbook of Texas*; Smith, *War with Mexico*, 1:400, 2:165–66).

[18] Most of the regular units promised Taylor had arrived by July 27; of the volunteer regiments he hoped to receive, the great majority were diverted to Scott's command (Smith, *War with Mexico*, 2:417–18).

[19] Col. Reuben Davis of the 2d Miss. Rgt., himself in poor health, was furloughed for sixty days on April 12. He returned to Mexico in June but on July 10 resigned his commission effective August 31 (DNA, M-29, roll 3, Special Orders No. 33, Apr. 12, No. 86, July 10, 1847; DNA, M-863, roll 4).

[20] In early December Taylor returned home on leave, before peace was concluded but after the capture of Mexico City (Hamilton, *Zachary Taylor*, 1:248–50).

[21] Thomas W. Ringgold was Taylor's overseer at his Cypress Grove plantation near Rodney, Mississippi (ibid., 2:31).

[22] Joseph E. Davis and his family, including his son-in-law Dr. Charles J. Mitchell, who had recently been in Mexico.

To John Jenkins

BRIERFIELD, Mississippi, 4th August, 1847.

DEAR SIR: I send you herewith the correspondence between the Secretary of War and our Governer, in relation to the arms of the first Mississippi Rifles.[1]

One of the letters passed out of my possession at New Orleans, to satisfy the United States Mustering officer[2] of our right to retain the Rifles, and has been recently recovered, or I should have presented this correspondence to you earlier, and asked its insertion in your paper. The prompt and early attention of Gov. Brown to a feeling so deep in our Regiment, has received as it deserved, our especial thanks; and it has seemed to me worthy of being made public. Very respectfully, Your friend, &c.,

JEFFERSON DAVIS.

Vicksburg *Weekly Sentinel*, Aug. 25, 1847.

[1] The enclosures were: Governor Albert G. Brown to Secretary of War William L. Marcy, April 20; Marcy to Brown, May 11; Ordnance Department officer George Talcott to Marcy, May 5; Brown to Davis, May 17; and Mississippi Secretary of State Wilson Hemingway to Davis, May 21.

[2] Sylvester Churchill (1783–1862), col. and inspector gen. (*Appletons'*; Heitman, *Hist. Reg.*, 1:301).

To Albert G. Brown

WARREN COUNTY, MISS., 15th Aug., 1847.

SIR—I have the honor to acknowledge the receipt of your very kind letter of the 10th inst., accompanying the commission (which you have conferred upon me) of U. States Senator, to fill the vacancy occasioned by the death of the late Senator Speight.

In the deep and sincere regret experienced at the loss of our tried and faithful representative, none can sympathize more truly than myself; none more fully realize the calamity we have sustained, in the death of this pure politician, this fearless exponent and vigilant guardian of the interests of our state.

It is with a grateful sense of the distinction bestowed, and a high estimate of the responsibilities which I am about to assume, that I accept the commission you have tendered, with so much of delicate and gratifying encouragement.

The approbation which you convey of my services in the twenty-ninth congress is especially pleasing, because therein was manifested my fixed opinion on the taxing and expending powers of the federal government, my uniformly entertained and often avowed creed of strict construction for the constitution of our Union.

I cannot express adequately my thanks for the high commendation you bestow on the services rendered in Mexico by the first Mississippi Riflemen. As the representative of the people you give us that meed of praise, which is the great incentive, the only reward of the citizen soldier for all which he may suffer or do in the cause of his country. As state troops, under your organization, we entered the service of the United States. Proud of the name of Mississippi; proud of her former achievements in war; anxious to burnish on the battle field her shield, rusted in the repose of peace; it was my wish, it was my effort to preserve our distinct organization, our state individuality; that thus we might bring back whatever of honorable distinction we should have the good fortune to acquire, and lay it at the feet of Mississippi, as our contribution to the joint property of her citizens, the reputation of the State.

You have justly anticipated my views in relation to a peace with Mexico; an event to be desired not merely from its influence on our domestic policy, but also to save from monarchical alliance, or entire prostration, a republican confederacy, which, despite our caution and magnanimous forbearance has forced us into war. The common desire of our countrymen to see the principle of self-government extended over this continent, and recognized as the policy of America, has justified past administrations in tolerating serious offences by Mexico, and still seeking to cultivate friendly relations. This desire has, I doubt not, led to a general approval of the course pursued by the present administration, in its steady efforts to open negotiations for a treaty of peace. Should these efforts continue to be unsuccessful, we will have the satisfaction to know, that our government has acted as became the United States, in avoiding unnecessary injury to a weak, though perverse and offending neighbor. Sincerely thanking you for your kind expressions and generous confidence, I promise all which zeal and industry can effect in the duties of the high station to which I am assigned. Very respectfully, Your ob't serv't,

JEFF. DAVIS.

Jackson *Mississippian*, Aug. 27, 1847.

From Zachary Taylor

Head Quarters Army of Occupation
Camp Near Monterey, Mexico
Augt, 16th, 1847

MY DEAR GENERAL,

Your two acceptable & interesting letters of the 16th, & 23d, ulto,[1] were duly received the latter by the last mail which reached here, the other six days previously for both of which you have my sincere thanks, & I can truly say the receipt of a letter from you is to /me/ at all times a source of much gratification, particularly if I can lear/n/ from it that your own health (with the exception of your wound which I flatter myself if not entirely well, has greatly improved, which I hope is the case in the present instance) as well as that of your excellent Lady & near relatives <-[illegible]-> are all good, & your affairs prosperous. The next subject /of/ interest if this unfortun war was brought to an end, would be, to discuss with you & other agricultural friends residing on the margin of the Mississippi as to the best mode of cultivating corn & cotton, as well as to pursue to protect our plantations from inundation—

However little inclination I may have for embarking in political life, yet I duly appreciate the interest Senator Cameron has taken in my reaching the first office in the gift of a great & free people, as well as for the conspicuous manner he has aided in bringing my humble name before the people of Pensylvania, for that elevated position; for to his influence & agency I am in a great measure indebted for my recent nomination at Harrisburg by a large & respectable number of the citizens of his State <-for pr-> as a candide for the <-for the-> office in question, at the coming election[2] —

I belive if the election was to take place immediately or even next November, I would in all probability be elected to that important office; but there is nothing more uncertain or fluctuating than popularity with the masses, & by the /time the/ election comes on, which is in November 39,[3] more than a year distant, some one else may be taken up & elected; I can assure you should this be the case, it will not give me one moments concern, on the contrary it would be more agreeable than mortifying; & I can but indulge the hope that this may be broughtabout— I observe by a few papers that a national Convention is contemplated by some, will be assembled by each of the great parties,[4] to select their respective candidates for the presidency &c; should this be done I hope both will pass me by if not unknown at least unnoticed—

Owing to the intimate relations known to exist between you & myself I fear you are greatly troubled if not harrassed with letters from your numerous political acquaintan/ces/ <-acquaintances as-> & others, in relation to my views on various matters which have divided the two great parties Whigs & Democrats (which subjects, many of them may for the most part be considered as settled at any /rate/ for many years to come, if not by the act of limitation at least by common consent; yet many rabid politicians on both sides, hold on to the whole of them with greatest tenacity, & enter on their discussion when generally acknowledged to be dead, with the same warmth & zeal as if the existance of the union depended on thire doing so; to reply to all or a considerable portion of them, must be too heavy a tax on your valuable time & I hope you will cut them as short as possible—

As regards my letter published in the signal,[5] which is making it seems some stir among politicians & newspaper editors, altho it may

not have been worded as carefully as it might have been, (as I intend it should have been very genl, in its terms; & by no means to
indorse the opinions of the editor or his editorial nor /do/ I think
on a fair construction it would bear such /an interp[retation]⁶/
<–[illegible]–>; nor how the people of the South can draw infer-
rences from any thing in said letter that I was unfindly to /the/
South or Southern interests /is hard to say/. My position, feelings &
associations independt of pecuniary considerations, should allay any
apprehensions on that head– While I would on the question of
Slavery respect the opinions & feeling of the non Slave holding States
on that subject & be careful not to do any act which would interfere with legal rights as regards the same, I would be equally /care-
ful/ that no encroachments will made on the rights of the citizens
of the slave holding, as /regards/ that description of property, or in
fact any thing els; let justice be don[e] to & in every part of the
Country North, East, South & West in accordance to the provisions
of the Constitution, which seems to me to be the proper & only
course to pursue by the Ch/i/ef magistrate, Congress & Judiciary
as the best & only one to preserve the Union. I look on the question
of Slavery as the most important /one/ now or that has ever been
before the country, since the organization of the government, as regards the perpetuity of the union, for such appears to be the feelings
of the people in the two portions of our country whose institutions
differ alone in that respect, brought about by the intemperate zeal
of the faintics of the north, & the intemperate zeal of a few politicians of the South, that the subject will no longer admit <–admit–>
of a proper & calm discussion, neither in the pulpit, in Congress, in
the newspapers, or in primary assemblies <–assemblies–> of the
people, the moment anny thing of the kind is attempted, men appear
not only to lose their temper as well as as their reason, the result of
which is instead of allaying it appears to have a contrary effect on
the temper & passion of the masses; only adding fuel to the flames,
& to widen insted of healing the breach between the parties concerned; I will not say interested, for those of the non Slave holding
States, have no interes in the matter; let them go on to discuss the
institutions of the South without notice as regards the matter in
question, with/out/ its being noticed, but the moment they go beyond that point where resistance becomes right & proper, let the
South act promptly, boldly & decisively with <–with–> arms in
their hands if necessary, as the union in that case will be blown to

atoms, or will be <–be–> /no longer/ worth preserving,– But I pray to god this state of things will not occur in my day or in your, or that of our children or children children, if ever <–if ever–> it is therefore best neither to think /about/ or discuss /<–[illegible]–>/ <–[illegible] I very much–> ourselves about that which may never occur—

I receive by every mail which reach here a large number of letters from different portions of the States on various subjects, most of them in some way connected with the coming election for the presidency; all of which I make out to read, & notwithstanding the good advice of genl Cameron & many other friends, altho, some may be written & no doubt are with sinister views & intententions, yet courtesy seems to /require/ that I should reply to them, which <–which–> I have done as far as my public duties would permit,[7] which are only a fe[w?] out of the many that reach me; & in doing so I have been brief; & in very general terms or intended to do so, yet in the hurry of the moment, & frequent interruptions I may not in some instan[c]es (as in the letter in the Signal, have been <–in some ins–> sufficiently guarded, if so it will be doubtless laid hold of with great avidity by the organ of the White House,[8] & other kindred editors, & used to my injury as far as it can be, by per-/ver/ting my meaning if not my language, at the expensene of truth, decency & everything else which they imagine will accomplish their ends— On one subject I have been explicit which was, when called on to know (which is frequently the case) whether I was a Whig or democrat, I have sta/ted/ in reply, that I had never meddled in or been mixed /up/ with political matters, not so much as having ever voted for one of /our/ Chief Magistrate before or since I entered the army, which was near forty years, having most of which time, been serving or stationed beyond the limits of the states; but if I had voted at the last presidential election, it would have been for Mr, Clay, & altho, Mr, Richie <–Richie–> & his Co laborers in vituperation & detraction, may & will I apprehend attempt to /use this to/ my disadvantage, yet I would not disguise or withhold my opinion /on/ that head did I know it would jeopard my election for the office in question, was I ever so anxious to reach it, which is by no means the case; I consider it would be dishonorabl to have any concealments on this or any other sub<–ject [illegible]–>, as I do not intend to look one way, & talk an other—

I will now <–will–> say to you what I have for the most part

stated to those with whom I have communicated with, on the subject of the presidency, some of which will will find their way into
some of the newspapers, to <–which–> should that be the case,
I shall refer those who may wis/h/ to know my views, or political
creed, which is, that I have no wish for said /office/ or to be exclusively the candidate of any party; that I was no politician, & if a
Candidate or to be made one at the coming election, I would be
made so by others, & by no act of mine in the matter; & besides the
want of inclination for civil office I very much doubted my qualifi-
catons to discharge properly the important duties connected with
that office, an office which had been filled & adorned by a Washington, a Jefferson & several others of the purest, wisest & most accomplished statesmen & patriots of this or any other age or country I
almost tremble at the thoughts of the undertaking; yet should the
good people think proper to elevate me to that <–elevated–> position I will serve them from a sense of duty, if not of inclination &
will do so honestly & faithfully to the best of my abilities, strictly
in conformity to the provisions of the Constitution, as near as I
can do so, as it was construed & acted on by our first presidents, two
of whom at least acted so conspicuous a part not only in framing
that instrument, completing it, as well as putting it in operation. But
many important changes may tak plac between now & holding the
election for a new chief magistrate, at home & abroad so much so as
to make it desirable for the general good that some other individual
should be selected better versed in state affairs than I am <–should
be selected–> for the same, & could he be elected I will not say
I would yield my pretentions to that office (for I have not the
vanity to believe I have any, but would not only acquiesce with
pleasure in such an arrangement, but would rejoice that the Republic had one citizen more [w]orthy & better qualified than I am,
(& no doubt there are thousands, to discharge the duties appertain-
ing to that high station. Be this as it may, if I ever occupy the White
House it must be by the spontaneous movement of the people without any act of mine, unpledged & untrammeled otherwise than what
I have already stated as regards the constitution, so that I could
enter on the arduous duties connected with that elevated position
in such a way as to be the president of the nation, & not of a party—

   Some two months since I received a communication from the
Secretary of War, asking my opinion as to the best manner to carry

on our operations against the enemy to bring about a peace; I recommended that we should <-should-> hold on to what we had
here, sending after keeping a sufficient force to hold this line as far
as we had gone, any surplus force to reenforce the other column,
that it would not do to risk a failure in that quarter; I have just received an answer to the same, in which the Secretary says, the president highly approves my views, & that I could send all the troops I
could spare to vera Cruz to report to Genl Scott,[9] which I shall immediately do, sending there 2,500, men, or more,[10] which will greatly aid in keeping open his communications with his base, if he is in
pos[ses]sion of the capitol, which I presume is the case;[11] unless
negotiations are going on for peace, which may prevent his advancing farther than Puebla, where he was when last heard from. We
have not heard directly from that column by the way of Vera Cruz
for some time, or in any other way; reports across the country
which <-can-> cannot be relied on, are contradictory; a short
time since a report reached here that the Mexican /congress/ had
convened & authorised Santa Anna to negotiate, & that three Commissioners had been appointed to meet Mr, Trist on the part of
Mexico; this was soon followed, by another, that /<-a->/ <-pro-
posed by Trist-> the terms proposed by Mr, T- had been rejected, & the <-de-> Congress dissolved; this has been followed by a
third that negotiations were still going on,[12]—

Going back to political matters it appears to me that no president
should hesitate a moment to veto any law passed by Congress which
conflicted with the provisions of the constitution; but on matters of
expediency great forbearance should be used, & only aft[er] the
most mature consideration. It appears to me & has for some time
that we are considering the office of Chief /Magistrate/ & will soon
make it so, of too much importance, & instead of its being what it
was intended to be, a Co-ordinate branch of the government, it is
rapidly swallowing up the other two, & should be closely looked
/to/ by the people; let each of the three great departments revolve
within their proper circle, & all will go right; it is this party spirit
which has the effect of strenghing the hands of the president in such
a way if he is not looked up to, to legislate for the country, he will
be <-as-> /considerd/ the source from which all /[illegible]/
honors are to flow, & the hand which is to confer them As we are
to act only on the defensive on this line I hope to be able to leave

the /country/ for the U. States in a few months,[13] but may be disappointed– It seems to me you acted wisely in declining the appt,
tendered you of Br, Genl, it was offered at the eleventh hour, &
altho, this war may continue for some time it will in that case be
all/t/ogater of the guerilla character in which no reputation can be
gained—

I deeply regret to hear you were still on crutches & truly hope
this will not long be the case, & that you will soon be able to throw
them aside if you have not already done so; at any rate I hope your
little niece has become reconciled to seeing you hobbling about on
them, & that you are not /such a [cripple?]/ in that situation as she
had imagined[14]—

I very much regret you could not make your contemplated visit
to B- Rouge, before Mrs. Taylor left for Pascagoula on the Lakes
back of New Orleans, having abandoned her contemplated trip to
Kentucky, which was declined on on acct, of hearing the Ohio
River was very low & falling, so much so, to make it doubtful
whether Steam Boats could get to Louisville— She will return to
B- Rouge early in November, where she & the family will be delighted to see you, & I hope you will not disappoint them in making
the promised visit

Be so good as to present my kindest regards to your good Lady &
worthy Brother & family including my friend Dr, Mitchell, & accept my Sincere wishes for the continued health & prosperity of
you all Truly [& si]ncerly Your Friend

Z Taylor

P. S. I much doubt your being able to make out to read this
<-long-> long & fear uninteresting epistle, as much of it will
hardly pay you for the trouble of wading through it, if at all, but
there is no necessit[y] for your doing so; & when ever you find it
about to [put you] to sleep, you; <-you-> c[an thr]ow it aside
or into the fire as you may think best—

Z- T

ALS (Taylor Papers, DLC). Endorsed by Davis: "ansd. 23d Sept.
47." Manuscript worn and damaged
by tape.

[1] Davis' letters have not been located.

[2] See Davis' letter dated July 26.

[3] Taylor must have intended to
write "48."

[4] Although national party conventions had occurred regularly since
1832, the Washington *Union* (June
15, July 9, 1847) felt it necessary to

urge Democrats to hold a national meeting in 1848. Taylor did not consider such gatherings useful or desirable; Davis favored them (Taylor, *Letters*, 153–54; Davis to Charles J. Searles, Sept. 19, 1847).

[5] Taylor's letter of May 18 to James W. Taylor (no relation) was published in the Cincinnati *Morning Signal* on June 26 and widely reprinted and discussed. See Davis to [Simon Cameron], July 26.

[6] Unless otherwise noted, square brackets enclose material supplied where the manuscript is damaged.

[7] Despite advice to the contrary, Taylor continued to answer his mail, described by a fellow officer as "scores of letters . . . from the National Whig at Washington down to the smallest small potato affair in the country" (New Orleans *Delta*, July 23, 1847).

[8] The Washington *Union*, edited by Thomas Ritchie.

[9] Secretary of War William L. Marcy addressed Taylor on May 6, was answered on June 16, and wrote again on July 15 (*House Ex. Doc. 56*, 30:1, 311–13, 367–68, 383–84).

[10] The same day he wrote Davis, Taylor ordered the 13th Inf., Ohio, Indiana, and Massachusetts regiments, and a light artillery battery to embark for Winfield Scott's command via Veracruz (DNA, M-29, roll 3, Gen. Orders No. 96).

[11] Scott did not capture Mexico City until mid-September.

[12] By late June, Trist learned that Santa Anna had asked for the opening of negotiations; in mid-July the American initiative was rejected and the Mexican congress adjourned (Smith, *War with Mexico*, 2:129–32).

[13] Taylor left Mexico on furlough in November.

[14] Davis apparently had reported the comments of his grandniece, Lise Mitchell, upon hearing of his wound at Buena Vista. See Joseph E. Davis' letter dated April 23.

To Officers of the Second Mississippi Regiment

BRIARFIELD, Warren co., Miss.,
August 19th, 1847.

GENTLEMEN:—I have the honor to acknowledge the receipt of your most gratifying letter of the 16th ult., conveying to me the information that my esteemed friends of the 2nd Mississippi Riflemen unanimously offer to elect me their regimental leader.

The honorable post you offer has every thing to commend it to me; it is the free gift of Mississippians; it invites me to field service in a region where the energy and health of the troops will not be impaired by the climate, and it assures me of being in the column of the general in whom I have unmeasured confidence.[1]

Your proposition under all the circumstances which attend it, is an honor of which the highest reputation might well be proud, and for which I feel more grateful than I have power to express. In declining a station so honorable, so acceptable to my tastes, feelings

215

and associations, and offered in a manner so highly complimentary, I have three reasons to submit to you in justification of my decision:

1st. I have not so far recovered from my wound as to be able to travel immediately; the probable date of your advance admits of no delay in one who would join you in your present position, and the anticipated character of your movement, in the event of an advance, renders it doubtful whether an individual could join you on the march.

II. Before the receipt of your letter I had accepted a commission to fill a vacancy in our Representation in the U. S. Senate.

III. I have held that vacancies occurring in the field afford opportunities to reward merit among yourselves, and that policy dictates, and esprit du corps demands, that promotions should thus be made. I feel that your kindness has made me an exception to a rule, and that I best show myself worthy of your generosity by declining to take advantage of it.

Though I shall not be with you to share the glory, it is permitted me to hope that at no distant day the fortune of war will give you an opportunity to fulfill the expectations of you, so early and confidently announced by myself, in common with your many friends and admirers.[2]

To you alone now is Mississippi's standard confided. Rent and blood-stained it may be; but in your hands, can never be dishonored. It may droop with the cypress, but will be crowned with the laurel.

For yourselves, gentlemen, please receive my sincere thanks, for the gratful terms in which you have conveyed the flattering wishes of my friends and fellow citizens of the 2nd Mississippi Rifles, to whom I pray you make my acknowledgements acceptable.

With assurances of the deep interest I will always feel in your prosperity and fame, and with the hope that under the blessing of peace we may be early reunited at home. I am very cordially, Your friend and ob't serv't.

JEFFERSON DAVIS.

Vicksburg *Weekly Sentinel*, Sept. 29, 1847. Enclosed: Davis to John Jenkins, Sept. 21, 1847.

[1] Although the 2d Miss. Rgt. sailed early in 1847 under orders to join Winfield Scott's army, it was soon reassigned to Zachary Taylor's command (R. Davis, *Recollections*, 230–32, 235–36).

[2] The 2d Miss. Rgt. saw no active service in Mexico, being on garrison duty most of their year's enlistment (ibid., 235–36; *Miss. Official Reg., 1908*, 417).

From Zachary Taylor

Head Quarters army of Occupation
Camp near Monterey Mexico
September 18th, 1847

MY DEAR GENERAL,

Your very acceptable & interesting letters of the 1st & & 8th ulto, with the several accompaniments have been received, the first a few days after I had written you a very long epistle,[1] the latter by the last mail which reached us a day or two since, whiich owing to the yellow fever, or some othe cause there had been an interval of near a month without our getting a Mail, or hearing from New Orleans, for all of which you have my best thanks— As regards the sketches referred to, the first I consider overdone; or rather I have been too much flattered, the artist having permitted his kind feelings to get the better of his judgment; while he of the wood has, hardly done me justice; for I cannot believe I look as bad as I am there represented[2]–

Finding an apparent reluctance from want of inclination, or ability, as well as great vacilation on the part of the War department to plac a proper force on this line for me to make a forward movement with, & believing the /best/ plan to bring about a peac was to take & hold posession of the city of Mexico, or to let the enemy see we could do so, & at the same time keep our communications open with Very Cruz, which if it did not effict that object, no other military operation would be so likely to do so; I addressed a letter to the Secetary stating I considerd one strong, better than two weak columns, & from the then state of things I thought it would be advisable to make the command under genl, S- astrong as posible; in reply he the Secretary informed me that my views had been submitted to the president who highly approved them[3] (which I apprehend was the first time he had done so for a considerable time, at any radte since I crossed the Rio Grande) & that I would after retaining such a force as I deemed sufficient to hold this line as far as we had gone, & send the balance to Vera Cruz to report to genl, Scott, which was immediatly done, sending there some 3000 men; this I considerd it to be my duty to do, as we had "to few to make war properly with, & too many for negotiation" or rather we had too small a force to carry the war with a fair prospect of success into the heart of the enemies Country in the direction of their Capitol, & more than was necessary to hold what we had taken posession of—

A short time after returning here from Saltillio I stated to <–Mr,–> Mr, Marcy that in the event of my moving forward towards the City of Mexico, I wished to have two or three of the old Regts, of Infy, placed under my orders, in answer to the same he stated that my wishes would be submitted to genl, Scott, who he did not expect could spare them, <–them,–> at the same time placing me under the command of that officer, or subject to his orders.[4] When I made the sugges/tion/ to reenforce the the other <–other–> line, I thought it not unlikely but I would be ordered there with the troops sent from this quarter; yet I am now convinced & ought to have been so for sometime past, that it never was intended since the taking of Monterey, that I should have an oportunty to accomplish anything more than I had done; with the exception of a few courteous letters <–letters–> which amo/u/nt to little or nothing the same course has been pursued towards /me/ since that time, <–which–> which no doubt they expected would lay me on the shelf, or drive me from the Country or perhaps from the Army; had I left in disgust while the war was going on, it would have been used as far as it could have been done, to my injury; it was never intended that I should have fought the batle of Buena Vista, /which had it/ been lost, or the army which won it, been withdrawn to Monterey as recommended by genl, Scott, it would have destroyed him & all concerned in the disgraceful intriegue carried on against me; as falling back would <–be–> /have been/ scarcely less disasterous than a defeat, for in either case besides <–besides–> many infortunate results which would have grown out of the same /amons other/ instead <–instead–> of Col, Doniphans March (which is a very extraordinary one, being lauded as it is in many of the newspapers throughout the land, they would now been lamenting Col. D– unfortunate retreat if nothing worse[5]— I have no hesitation in saying the battle of the 23d, of Febry, altho, I was not permitted to travel it, opened the road to the City of Mexico & the doors of the Halls of the Montezumas that others might revel in them.

Under all the circumstances of the case I think you acted wisely in not accepting the appt, of Brigr, /genl/ in the volunterrs, & altho, there is not an individual in the whole land I would have preferred having with me /as yourself/ if as much /so/ had I advanced into the heart of Mexico, knowing I could rely to the utmost on both your head & heart in consel, or in battle, yet I did not wish to see you undergo the trouble labor & anxiety of organizing traing & fitting an other volunteer Corps for battle– Had they given you the appt, conferred on Hopping[6] (who poor old man died at Mier a short time since) having been broken down before he left home) I could have truly wished you to have accepted it; as to any delicacy about commanding old officers of the Regular Army, you ought not to have considerd that for one moment, for I am sure such as have proper ideas & feelings in regard to such matters, would greatly prefer being under your command, a soldier by education & practice, to that of such men as genl, H— or any other without military mind & experience but I apprehend it was determined even had /I/ moved forward that you were not to accompany me; however I hope the war is at an end; genl, Scott having entirely defeated <–defeated–> the Mexican Army near the City which had resulted in an armistice for negotiations for peace, all of which you must have seen in the Newspapers ere this reaches you, as well as many particulars we are not apprised of, not having seen any thing like an official or detailed account of the affair; We must as regards the course which others have pursued towards /us/ however improper <–we must–> bear & forbear, as well as to forgive as we <–[illegible]–> /expect/ to be forgiven—

The internal improvement committee /or convention/ which met at Chicago[7] have gone pretty deeply into that subject or in favor of it, & as I stated to you in a former letter I think, no matter as to the views of the <–views as to the–> Chief magistrate of the Country, internal improvement will go on, & even beyond what it ought to, in the way of making harbors on on the lakes, as well as on the ocean, & removing obstructions in rivers &c, in spite of vetoes or any thing else, the /west/ will be too strong in a few years to check it by any act of the executive, & as I fear it may be somewhat a log roling business, we of the south must try & come in for a share of the spoils in some way or other if we do not acquire the outlay—

I think it unfortunate that any of our good Citizens of the <–good Citizens–> of the South, Should give themselves any trouble about what may not happen in thier time, in regard to the Wilmot proviso, which I think at best a trifling affair, for depend on it no Country will be attached to the /Union/ South of the Missouri Compromise; the free states will not agree to /it/ without the said proviso or an equivolent) nor can two thirds of the Senate /be brough/ to vote for the acquisition of territory with any such restriction; so that there is no probability of the same producing any great evill in our time, & as to those that come after us they mustake care of themselves; let us look to the Constitution & preserve & enforce if necessar all our rights under it, as long as we are charged with those sacred duties at every hazard, leaving it to posterity to do the same, which they will do if intelligent, bold & determined; & if not so the constitution will prove a mere rope of sand in their hands, & as easily broken to pieces, & all the guards which we can throw around it, would be of no aveail—

As regards the election for the next Chief Magistrate it<–s–> is so very far off, that I frequently indulge the hope that something may occur between now & Novr, 1848 which may have the effect of laying me aside as a candidate alltogather; I have already advised some of the leading politicians that in the event of its being /deemed/ necessary by either, or both of the great political parties which divide the country to hold national conventions for the purpose of nominating candidates for the two highest of<–o–>fices in the gift of the people, I hoped they would pass me by unnoted, & let their favors fall on some one else; beside I have uniformly stated that if I ever entered the White House to occupy it, it must /be/ untrammeled & unpledged, which it seems to me I would be departing from in some measure, were I to intimate even indirectly as to how I would form my Cabinent, should the people think proper to elect me /of/ which /I am/ very doubtful; & have thought for some time it was very <–doubtful–> /problemalicat/ if we would have a Chief magistrate of the nation, from any the Slaveholding states, particularly a slaveholder /for many years/ & I still entertain that opinion; under these circumstances, <–[illegible]–> as it might prevent a great many ilnatured remarks hereafter, it <–[illegible]–> appears to me it would be most prudent for this subject to be entirely laid over, until after the election— The three gentlemen referred to are among the brighest ornaments of our Country, posessing the most gigantic intilects, but I do not believe that either of them would occupy a seat in the Cabinet if offered to them; & notwithstanding their talents & experience, I think the people would prefer new men; Mr C—[8] went into Mr, Tylers as it was understood at the time, solely for the purpose of carrying through the annexation of Texas, & for no other object, nor would he have done /so/ under any other circumstances; as there is no telling what a day, much less a year may bring forth, I believe I have gone as far as I should do in stating if elected, I would <-seve-> /serve/ the people honstly & faithfully to the best of my abilities, strictly in accordance with the provisions of the Constitution, as the same was construed & acted on by our first presidents as nearly as I can do so; two of whom at least, acted so conspicuous a part not only in framing & completing that instrument, but in putting it in operation; at any rate I hope to appoint none to those or any other offic[e][9] who are not hones, capable & true to the constitution, if I am ever placed in a situation to assume those responsible duties.

I am very much gratified the way you have expressed yourself /on/ the statements you have made when writing to you[r] democratic friends;[10] without ever being mixed up with po[l]itics or political men, I have considerd my self /a/ Whig believing on the whole the opinions they advocated were more nea[r]ly allied to those advocated by Mr, Jefferson, in whose politi[cal] cred I was raised that those of their opponents; & which [I] have always intended to conform to; I recd, from him my first appt. in the army, & have ever since disapprove[d] either violence or proscription, come from what party it might — I have recd, through a friend from Kentucky by the last mail, similar information in regard to /a/ contemplated meeting in or near Lexington for the purpose of nominating me as a candidate for the presidency at the coming election, without regard to party, but the whigs could not be brought to the scratch;[11] the /writer/ suppose they were affraid of offending Mr, Clay— Among the numerous letters I recive on the Subject of the presidency, a few have reached me urging me not to suffer my /name/ to be placed before the /country/ as a candidate for the chief magistracy, but to urge the election of MrClay; thise letters as a matter of course I have not nor do I intend to notice them—I think it not unlikely <-it is not unlikely-> that many of the rabid Whigs in Ky, & elsewhere, still indulge the hope that Mr, C— will yet be brought /forward/ as the whig candidate; & how far he wishes, or encourages the same I am unable to say; an old friend who now resides in Paris Burlour County Ky, for many years the representative in congress from the Lexington district[12] & a fast friend of MrClay for the offices in question until now, writes me that the State is for me, under any circumstances, but many of the Whigs are waiting to see whether Mr, Clay is to be a candidate

bef/ore/ they declare themselves; Such men as him & MrCretten-
den[13] who has avowed himself in my favor have no concealments,
& are sincere in what they say & do in this matter; the/re/ is
nothing but plain dealing so far as they are concerned– I for one
cannot look on the republic in danger we are perhaps about to have
a terable storm <–but–> I much fear growing out of the abolition
question, the most important one in my humble opinion whi has
ever <–a–> agitated the country <–country–> since the adoption
of the constitution; as to internal improvements it is a small matter,
for it will extend to a certain /extent/ to every portion of the country & what <–was–> /is/ drawn from the treasury for that object
will be circulated among the whole people; but /I have/ entire faith
in the good old ship the Constitution if properly managed by those
who will stick by her, in good & evil report, she will <–she–> will
never touch /bottom/ or go down in our day–

No one can possible regret the violince of party or the unhappy
effects of /the same/ more than I do; it has besides other evils interrupted /in/ neighbourhood intercous, among people who had
been raised togather, & allways friends until party was carried to
such great lengths– Our constitution was made up by compromises,
by the sages & heroes of the revolution, men who had at every
hazard, & at all odds against <–had acted–> /them/ just achieved
our indeindependence, men too who acted for their Country & not
for themselves, & we should not on/ly/ forbear /but bear/ a great
deal bebefore defacing much less destroying that pure fabric made
by their clean hands; nothing so perfect in the way of government
has ever been created by the wit of man to compare to it; & surely
there is yet leven enough left among the descendants of those pure
patriottes to preserve theat ark of /our/ liverty made by them, or
to repair any breach that may be made in it, so as <–to–> to transmit /it/ whole & unimpaired from generation to generation, to the
end of time; I for one will not, nor never have despaired of the
common weath—

As soon as I hear negotiations between Mr, Trist & the Mexican
authorities have been brought to a close, or have been broken off
(which I do not expect will be the case, & genl, Scott has taken the
City of Mexico, which /he/ must be abundantly able to do, I shall
ask permission to return to the U. States, & if not granted I must do
so even if under the necessity of quitting the service—

You say nothing about your /wound/ which I am in hope is, if not entirely well is nearly so— Our friend Dr, Mitchell writes me under date of the 16th, of August, in reegard to the crops generally; the corn crop he says will be an abundant one, the Cotton he thins owing to the great rains will be a moderate one, as the picking will commence very late, much more than usual; & altho, the weed is unusually large he thinks there will be only a limited quantity of bolls; alltogather, he doubts whether the crop of the present, will be much larger than that of last year.[14] I flatter myself yours will be an abundant one— Mine of course [mu][15]st be very limite[d] The Dr says "two days [ago] Col, Davis [w]as doing well, his foot is healing but slowly but ne[ar]ly well, yet sometime must elapse before he will be able to use it;" this I very much regretted to learn, as <-now-> /I know/ your active disposition, as well as the anxiety you will have of superintending at this particular season of the /year/ all the details & operations of your plantation [&] how incovenient it is to do so with a lame foot; but trust it will not greatly interfere with your doing so on horse back, as well as attending to to all your concerns in that way— It appears that the govr of your State has tendered you the appt, of U. S. Senator in the place of genl, Spate[16] deceased; you understad those [ma]tters so much better than I do, that I hardly dare venture an opinion [as] to the course you ought or it was best to pursue; had you been elected [by] the legislature to full his term, the case would be somewhat different, altho, /there is n[o]/ doubt their confirming the same whenever that body comes togather; you must however consult /your/ interest, feelings & inclinations & act accordingly—

I feel under the deepest obligations to your excellent lady, & worthy brother /for the deep interest they/ take in all that concers my wellfare, for which I am truly gratful, & beg leave though you to tender to them my most cordial thanks, as well as to Dr, M- for his very acceptable letter— And wishing you all continued [health &?][17] prosperity I remain truly & sincerely Your Fiend

Z- TAYLOR-

P. S.

I inclose you a scrap sent me under <-cover-> a blank cover post marked Boston cut from the Tribune in relation to the Wilmot provis[18]

Z. T-

ALS (MS Coll., NjP). Edges of several pages clipped or indistinct; last page torn in places.

[1] Davis' letters have not been found; Taylor's last known letter to Davis is dated August 16.

[2] Undoubtedly a reference to two portraitists, William Garl Brown, Jr. (1823–94), of Richmond and Jesse Atwood (c1802–54) of Philadelphia, who had visited Taylor's Walnut Springs headquarters (Philadelphia *Public Ledger*, July 28, 1847; Washington *Union*, Sept. 27, 1847; N.-Y. Hist. Soc., *Dictionary of Artists*).

[3] Taylor's letter to the adjutant gen. concerning Scott's strategy was dated June 16; Secretary of War Marcy answered on July 15 (*House Ex. Doc. 60*, 30:1, 1177–78, 1193–94).

[4] Taylor arrived at Saltillo on March 9 and wrote the War Department on March 14, stating that he needed 2,000–3,000 seasoned regulars. On April 30 Marcy sent Taylor's letter on to Scott (ibid., 922, 1118–19).

[5] Alexander William Doniphan (1808–87), a Kentucky-born attorney from Liberty, Missouri, was col., 1st Mo. Mtd. Vols. Leading a band of less than 1,000 men from Santa Fe to Chihuahua, Doniphan twice defeated superior Mexican forces, occupied El Paso and Chihuahua, and by late May had reached Monterrey (*DAB*; Smith, *War with Mexico*, 1:298–314).

[6] Enos D. Hopping (c1805–47), born in New York City, had been appointed brig. gen. in March 1847 to please a faction of New York Democrats. Assigned to command the 10th, 13th, and 16th Inf. rgts., he died on September 1 (*Appletons*'; Polk, *Diary*, 2:399–405; *House Ex. Doc. 60*, 30:1, 924).

[7] Eighteen states were represented at the Northwestern Harbor and River Convention in Chicago on July 5–7, 1847. In a series of resolutions the delegates endorsed government expenditures for the improvement of rivers and lakes (Washington *Nat. Intell.*, July 14, 15, 1847).

[8] John C. Calhoun was secretary of state in Tyler's cabinet.

[9] Until noted otherwise, square brackets enclose letters supplied where edge of page is clipped.

[10] See, for example, Davis' letter of July 26.

[11] "Without distinction of party," the citizens of Fayette County met on June 15 to consider presidential possibilities but did not nominate anyone (Richmond *Enquirer*, Aug. 14, 1847; Washington *Union*, June 21, 1847).

[12] Garret Davis (1801–72), a Whig from Bourbon County, represented Henry Clay's Ashland district in Congress, 1839–47 (*DAB*).

[13] John Jordan Crittenden (1787–1863), for twenty years senator from Kentucky, also served as attorney general and as governor. An intimate of Taylor's, he also enjoyed a long, warm friendship with Davis, despite partisan differences (*DAB*; Davis to Ann C. Coleman, Sept. 17, 1871, Crittenden Papers, Perkins Lib., NcD).

[14] Damaged by heavy rains and boll weevils, the 1847 Mississippi cotton crop was nonetheless larger than that of the previous year (Jackson *Southron*, Sept. 3, 1847; Watkins, *King Cotton*, 171, 173).

[15] Unless otherwise noted, material enclosed in square brackets hereafter indicates places on page 9 of Taylor's letter where the paper is torn.

[16] Jesse Speight.

[17] Manuscript indistinct.

[18] Although the enclosure is missing, Taylor likely refers to some article from the New York *Tribune*, whose editor, Horace Greeley, strongly advocated passage of the proviso. See, for example, articles in the *Tribune* of July 21, 29, and August 12, 1847.

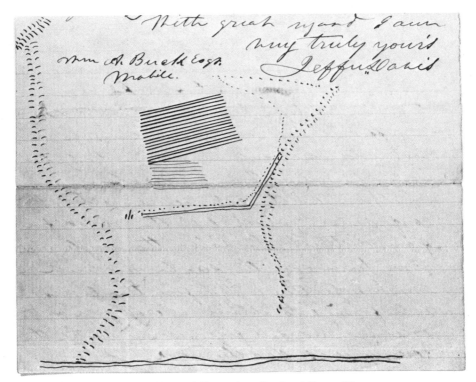

Sketch of the V Formation, Battle of Buena Vista

PLAN OF THE SENATE CHAMBER

1ST SESSION 30TH CONGRESS

A. Dickins, Secretary

G. M. Dallas, Pa.
President

D. McClelland Sc. Wash.

INDEX TO DIAGRAM OF THE SENATE CHAMBER.

Seating Chart, United States Senate, 1847–48

To Charles J. Searles

BRIERFIELD, *19th Sept.* 1847.

MY DEAR SIR: Your highly valued letter of the 3d Inst.,[1] came duly to hand, but found me quite sick,[2] and I have not been able at an earlier date to reply to it. Accept my thanks for your kind solicitude for my welfare.

Your past conduct enabled me to anticipate this from you and I am therefore doubly grateful.

The political information you communicate was entirely new to me, and it is only under the belief that the crisis renders important the views of every southern man, that I can account for any speculations having arisen about my opinions as to the next Presidency. I have never anticipated a separation upon this question from the Democracy of Mississippi, and if such intention or expectation has been attributed to me, it is not only unauthorised but erroneous.[3]

That it might become necessary to unite as southern men, and to dissolve the ties which have connected us to the northern Democracy: the position recently assumed in a majority of the non-slave holding states has led me to fear.[4] Yet, I am not of those who decry a national convention,[5] but believe that present circumstances with more than usual force indicate the propriety of such meeting. On the question of Southern institutions and southern rights, it is true that extensive defections have occurred among Northern democrats, but enough of good feeling is still exhibited to sustain the hope, that as a party they will show themselves worthy of their ancient appellation, the natural allies of the South,[6] and will meet us upon just constitutional ground. At least I consider it due to former association that we should give them the fairest opportunity to do so, and furnish no cause for failure by seeming distrust or aversion.[7]

I would say then, let our delegates meet those from the north, not as a paramount object to nominate candidates for the Presidency and Vice-Presidency, but before entering upon such selection, to demand of their political brethren of the north, a disavowal of the principles of the Wilmot Proviso; an admission of the equal right of the south with the north, to the territory held as the common property of the United States; and a declaration in favor of extending the Missouri compromise to all States to be hereafter admitted into our confederacy.

If these principles are recognized, we will happily avoid the worst of all political divisions, one made by geographical lines merely. The convention, representing every section of the Union, and elevated above local jealousy and factious strife, may proceed to select candidates, whose principles, patriotism, judgement, and decision, indicate men fit for the time and the occasion.

If on the other hand, that spirit of hostility to the south, that thirst for political dominion over us, which within two years past has displayed such increased power and systematic purpose, should prevail; it will only remain for our delegates to withdraw from the convention, and inform their fellow citizens of the failure of their mission. We shall then have reached a point at which all party measures sink into insignificance, under the necessity for self-preservation; and party divisions should be buried in union for defence.

But until then, let us do all which becomes us to avoid sectional division, that united we may go on to the perfection of Democratic measures, the practical exemplification of those great principles for which we have struggled, as promotive of the peace, the prosperity, and the perpetuity of our confederation.

Though the signs of the times are portentous of evil, and the cloud which now hangs on our northern horizon threatens a storm, it may yet blow over with only the tear drops of contrition and regret. In this connection it is consolatory to remember, that whenever the tempest has convulsively tossed our Republic and threatened it with wreck, brotherly love has always poured oil on the waters, and the waves have subsided to rest. Thus may it be now and forever. If we should be disappointed in such hopes, I forbear from any remark upon the contingency which will be presented. Enough for the day will be the evil thereof,[8] and enough for the evil, will be the union and energy and power of the south.

I hope it will soon be in my power to visit you and other friends at Vicksburg, from whom I have been so long separated.[9] I am, as ever, truly your friend,

JEFFERSON DAVIS.

Vicksburg *Weekly Sentinel*, Oct. 6, 1847.

[1] Not found.
[2] According to the *Sentinel* (Sept. 29, 1847), Davis was "suffering both from an attack of fever and from his wounded foot, which has never yet healed."

[3] Prefacing Davis' letter was a state-

ment by Searles explaining that on a trip "in the interior" of Mississippi he had discovered that Davis' opinions were being misunderstood "in relation to the principles of the Democratic party, and his feelings towards the Administration." Davis later recalled (1852) that Searles informed him "of certain misrepresentations . . . in circulation; among them was one which implied hostility to Mr. Polk." Davis had been criticized for comments about the administration's treatment of Zachary Taylor (see the June 14 Natchez speech), but Searles reported a "totally different reason" for the rumored breach. To show the president's "kind appreciation of me, and my thankfulness for it," Davis sent Searles copies of his most recent correspondence with Polk, letters dated May 19 and June 20 (Davis, *Papers*, ed. Rowland, 2:141–42). Meanwhile, an influential Democratic journal observed that, since Davis was both "a Calhoun democrat, and a very strong Taylor man," his position in Congress might very well "disappoint some of his constituents" (*Miss. Free Trader and Natchez Gazette*, Aug. 12, 1847; see also Jackson *Mississippian*, Aug. 20, 1847).

⁴ By late summer 1847 the legislatures of ten northern states had instructed their congressional delegations to vote for the Wilmot Proviso (Rayback, *Free Soil*, 26–27).

⁵ Among the principal voices condemning national conventions was John C. Calhoun's. Early in 1847 he denounced such meetings as "irresponsible bodies, not known to the constitution" (Washington *Union*, Mar. 27, 1847).

⁶ A maxim Davis attributed later to Thomas Jefferson. William H. Seward used a variant of the same saying in an 1848 campaign speech, also attributing it to Jefferson (Jackson *Mississippian*, Oct. 5, 1849; Seward, *Works*, ed. Baker, 3:289; see also Davis' speech at Jackson, Sept. 23, 1848).

⁷ Despite widespread opposition to the extension of slavery, there were no "extensive defections . . . among Northern democrats." Only in New Hampshire and New York were the party schisms cause for alarm. Davis' optimism that northern and southern Democrats could resolve their differences echoed a recently published article, which noted that seventeen northern Democrats had "stood boldly by the South" in preventing passage of the revived Wilmot Proviso (Rayback, *Free Soil*, 77–80; Jackson *Mississippian*, Sept. 10, 1847).

⁸ A paraphrase of Matt. 6:34: "sufficient unto the day is the evil thereof."

⁹ Davis apparently had not been in Vicksburg since June; available evidence suggests that he returned for the first time in early November.

To Albert G. Brown

Brierfield 20th Sept. 1847

SIR,

From the preceding report much was omitted which would have been supplied had it been originally written for one who was not himself an actor in the events described.¹ Some portion of the facts thus omitted I deem it proper here to append.

Having as stated in my report of the transactions of the 21st, been marched at the close of that day to our encampment at the "Walnut Springs," the Regiment was dismissed to its quarters for the night. In the morning of the 22d I was warned that our Regiment was required for field service. The Companies were formed and marched to the regimental parade. The severe service of the previous day had reduced the number, but had in no degree impaired the ardor or energy of our men. I announced the duty for which the Regiment was drawn out and marched it from the encampment. The report that we were off for another fight brought out all who were able to march, and I have often recurred with pride to the recollection, that when I subsequently counted the files for the issue of ammunition, we had forty seven men more, than when we formed on our Regimental parade.

By directing our march through some fields which concealed us from the view of "the Citadel," we reached the plain above "fort Teneria", the work which we had taken on the previous day, before we came under the enemy's fire. Here his artillery in the fort "el Diablo" opened upon us, and before we reached fort "Teneria", one shot took effect, killing Private Dubois and wounding Private Grigg of Company "H."

In conjunction with the Tennessee Regiment, under the command of Lt. Col. Anderson, we relieved the guard found in "Fort Teneria", and under the assignment of Brigadier Genl. Quitman took post for further orders. This work, "La Teneria", was composed of two field entrenchments and a stone house;[2] the salient, was a <–round fort–> /circular redoubt/ mounting four guns, one at an open embrasure, and three in barbet; the next, was /an/ irregular redan resting on the stone building; on the top of the stone building was a breast work of sand bags, from behind which the defenders had an upper tier of fire against their assailants, and at the last moment a plunging fire into the interior of the works below.

The Tennessee Regt. was was placed in the round work, the Mississippi Riflemen with Major Ridgely's battery[3] in the redan and Stone building. From the top of this house I made frequent observations during the day upon the positions and movements of the enemy at the east end of the town, without acquiring any other valuable information, than that he had a large force at the north east angle of his defences.

Working parties were detailed throughout the day, and under

the direction of Maj. Mansfield and Lieut. Scarrett of the Engineers, threw up a traverse to connect the round work with the redan, and made some additions to the more defective part of the breast work. From the fort "el Diablo" and "the Citadel", the enemy continued throughout the day to throw shot and shells at us; by constant vigilance we avoided injury from them, though the walls of the intrenchment were much too low to defile the interior of the work. At the approach of night Capt. Taylor's company was posted in the north-west <–[illegible]–> part of the stone building, the same in which we had taken the prisoners on the preceding day, with instructions to defend the gates in the event of a night attack, and by sentinels on the roof and at other suitable places to keep vigilant watch upon the enemy. The other companies were distributed along the breast work of the redan.

We had left camp without preperation, were in light clothing and entirely without food. Our Quarter Master had been directed to bring out the blankets and the day's rations for the companies, he informed me subsequently that he made several ineffectual attempts to do so, and failed from being unable to get an escort for his waggon, across the plain, where it would have been exposed to attack. Thus unprovided, rain and a norther came together upon us. The work which we occupied was rudely constructed and unfinished, earth had been taken from the inside of the parapet, the rain collected in holes and men already shivering with cold had to stand in the water when called to the breastwork. We were so near the enemy as to hear his guard calls, and the turning out of his cavalry patrols. His signals indicated that some concerted movement was to be made during the night; as he ought to have attacked us it was therefore to be expected, and we remained at the breast work, though the exposure was extremely severe.

Thus passed the night of the 22d. At dawn of the 23d, our sentinels on the house top reported that very few persons were visible in the fort "el Diablo", my own observations connected with the events of the night induced me to believe that the greater part of the garrison had been withdrawn. I communicated these things to Genl. Quitman, commanding the post, who authorized me to make a sortie with four companies, two of Missi: Riflemen and two of Tenn: Infantry.[4] We entered the suburbs of the city, and saw the enemy retreating rapidly before us. Having passed on sufficiently far to secure an approach on the gorge of the fort, and thus to avoid the fire of artillery if that arm had not been removed, the <–line–> /column/ was <–hfiled–> /headed/ to the left and marched rapidly upon the fort.

We found it's garrison and armament had been withdrawn, the traverse at its gorge had been dug down so as to render it more untenable by us, and the man who had been seen /in/ it claimed to be non-combattants. With a small party of Riflemen commanded by Lieut Hampton, I then proceeded with the assistance of Lieut: Scarrett of the Engineers to examine /the ground and/ a redoubt upon our right.[5] It had been also evacuated, and the houses in it's vicinity, which had been pierced with loop holes, were generally abandoned. In this reconnoissance we took some fifteen prisoners who informed us that the enemy had retired to the main Plaza. Lieut: Scarret proposed to report these events to genl. Taylor and to apply for sapping tools to advance into the city. For this purpose he soon after left us, and circumstances prevented his returning, as was desired. With the prisoners taken we returned to the fort "el Diablo."

I next proceeded with a few riflemen commanded by Lieut. Moore to reconnoitre the position to our left. The first was a <–n–> tenail connected by a line of abattis with a stone wall in it's rear, thence the defences were continued <–by the–> along the bluff of the city, by houses, the stone walls of yards, and the barricades constructed at the ends of the streets, to the South-eastern angle of the Town, where an old Hospital,[6] standing out in a salient position to the rest of the line, had been fortified and garnished with guns, to command one of the principal entrances to the Town, that by the Cadareita road. All the works along this line had been abandoned except the last mentioned, and from the obstinacy with which it was maintained, it is probable that the enemy then had in contemplation a retreat by that route, the only /one/ then open to him on which he could /have/ carried *artillery*.

When returning from this reconnoissance to the fort "el Diablo" I saw Lieut: Greaves with his Company, on the plain below the city, the facts connected with the duty he was performing will be found stated in Lieut. Greaves' Report.[7]

After our return to the fort "el Diablo" one of the Missi Companies "G"[8] was relieved by Company "B." and returned to the

"Teneria." Company "D" was then ordered up, and my original command was changed, as noticed in my report to genl. Quitman of the operations of the 23d. With Companies "B", Capt. Cooper & "D," Lieut. Russell & "H," Lieut Moore, and one company of the 1st Tenn. Volunteers, I advanced under Genl. Quitmans orders. As the <–works–> line, upon this side of the enemys defences, was a system of detached field works they were each of course untenable by us as long as the enemy /could/ hold those in their rear, we therefore proceeded, over the ground I had reconnoitred, to the block of the city, where the enemy first contested our progress,[9] and the action commenced, as described in my report of the 23d.

The cheif preperations of the enemy had been made against an attack upon the northern and eastern side of the Town. We were expected to approach by the Marin or Cadareita road, and from the enceinte of out<–er–> works, to the main plaza, nothing had been omitted to increase the resistance upon these approaches. Barricade, succeeded barricade, along the streets; the dwellings were supplied with ammunition, and prepared for its use, Infantry posted on the tops of the houses were securely sheltered by the stone parapet which surrounds their flat roofs, and /though forced from these positions/ it must be conceded that they firmly resisted. The Mississippi and Texas Riflemen[10] were vastly their superiors at sharp shooting and drove them back; but they slowly retired from house to house and from square to square, obstinately defending the crossing of every street. We continued to advance until abreast of the Cathedral of the main plaza, here we seized a two story house,[11] and maintained a contest, under the converging fire of the enemy, which lasted several hours, he was finally /driven/ from every exposed position within the range of our Rifles. The command at this position consisted of the advance of Col. Woods Texan Rangers, under genl. Henderson; and the advance of the Missi. Riflemen.

The prisoners taken in our reconnoissance of the morning, and a Mexican found in our second reconnoissance, to the left, concurred in stating that the main plaza was a square to the right of the Cathredral, but we now found that the Cathedral was upon one side of the plaza, and that our direction had been too far to the right. On the next square, immediately before us, was an unusually high house, from which it seemed a plunging fire could be thrown into the plaza.

To this house, after consultation with genl. Henderson, it was decided to advance, and secure it as a position to be held through the night. The task was more difficult than any we yet had performed, Throughout the day we had /been/ under the fire of the Enemy's artillery, generally throwing shells, but now we were close upon his field guns, which covered by a permanently constructed barricade swept the narrow pebble<–d–> paved street /over/ which we had to pass. The deadly efficiency of artillery in such a situation rendered it necessary to construct a shelter for our men whilst crossing the street. For this purpose we had to rely on such material as the neighboring yards and houses contained, of which /we/ were fortunate in getting enough <–for purpose–> and in form as convenient as would probably be found among articles not designed for such use.

Whilst engaged in this construction, I despatched Sergeant Major Harlan to the rear, to inquire of Genl. Quitman what had become of the field piece which he had said would cooperate with us;[12] and to direct Major Bradford, with the portion of the Regiment under him,[13] to join me. Sergt. Maj. Harlan returned and informed me that all the troops in our rear had retired, and that he was told the order to withdraw had been three times sent to me. He also informed Genl. Henderson that a like order had been sent by the commanding Genl. to him.

This intelligence was received with regret by all. As the resistance of the enemy became more obstinate, as the danger and difficulty of advancing increased, the energy and resources of our men rose with the demand, and all their views were onward. To none is this remark more applicable than to those who had encountered the greatest hardship, the men of Company "H." This Company after the exposure and fasting of the previous day and night had marched out with me early in the morning, before the supplies had been received from our encampment, and had been actively engaged ever since. I regret that, their gallant leader, Lieut. Moore had not made a report, of this day (23d Sept. 1846) when he fell in the Battle of Buena Vista.

As we retired the enemy who had passed to our rear, Kept up a constant fire upon us, especially at the crossings of the streets. We found no support in our rear until we reached the suburbs of the city, the first was Capt. Bainbridge[14] /with a company/ of the 3d U. S. Infantry and a piece of light artillery

About five O.Clock, <–we rejoined the balance of the Regiment at "La Teneria"–> having been actively engaged the whole day, we <–[illegible]–> rejoined the other part of our Regiment, at the Fort we had left in the morning,[15] and the whole were soon afterwards ordered to the encampment at the "Walnut Springs."

Early in the morning of the next day, a flag was sent out by the enemy, asking for a truce, and a conference; from which followed without further hostile operations the "Capitulation of Monterey." Very Respectfully yr. obt. Svt.

JEFFN. DAVIS

ALS (RG27, Vol. 26, Corres., Mexican War Docs., Ms-Ar). Endorsed by Davis: "No. 3. Statement of occurrences of the 22d & 23d Sept. 1846." Enclosed: Davis to Albert G. Brown, Oct. 3, 1847.

[1] Davis refers to his official battle reports (Sept. 26, 1846), copies of which he forwarded to Brown on October 3 along with this letter and a number of other documents.

[2] The fortified stone building.

[3] Randolph Ridgely commanded Co. C, 3d Art., at Monterrey. An 1837 West Point graduate, he died following a riding accident in October 1846 (Cullum, *Biog. Reg.*, 1:693; Ridgely's rep., Sept. 26, 1846, DNA, RG393, W. Dept. and Div., Reps. of Div. Comdrs. Engaged with the Enemy in Mexico).

[4] Cos. G and H of the 1st Miss., A and B of the 1st Tenn.

[5] See no. 9 on the map of Monterrey.

[6] See no. 12 on the map of Monterrey.

[7] Greaves's report is dated October 18, 1846.

[8] The letter G is written over *was*.

[9] See no. 11 on the map of Monterrey.

[10] 2d Texas Mtd. Vols.

[11] No. 13 on the Monterrey map.

[12] Two guns of the 3d Art. were withdrawn about three o'clock.

[13] Cos. C, E, G, and K had come up with Bradford; some had advanced with Davis while the rest remained under Bradford's command.

[14] Henry Bainbridge (1803–57), an 1821 West Point graduate, was wounded at Monterrey but as maj., 7th Inf., participated in the Mexico City campaign (Cullum, *Biog. Reg.*, 1:273–74; *Appletons'*).

[15] Co. I had remained at El Diablo.

To John Jenkins

BRIERFIELD, *Sept. 21st*, 1847.

DEAR SIR:— In your paper of the 1st inst., I observed a notice of a long article in the "Mississippi Advertiser," being an attack upon my "friends" in general, and myself in connection with the fact, that the 2d Mississippi Regiment, had offered to elect me their Colonel, and that I declined to accept.[1] Much stress is laid upon a paragraph in a number of your paper issued whilst I was in Mexico, referring to a rumor that I would probably become the commander of the 2d Mississippi Regiment.[2] I saw the paragraph, and at the same time a notice of it in a New Orleans paper, which treated the rumor as ridiculous. Either or both views seemed to me very unimportant, as no vacancy existed, and there was no prospect that one would happen. Col. R. Davis left his Regiment on leave of absence, not to resign, but to make such arrangements as would enable him to return to his command, and remain during the war. This information communicated to me, by himself, I frequently gave to others, to correct an impression that he would not return.

He rejoined his Regiment very soon after I left Monterey. Ill health has subsequently compelled him to resign, and a vacancy thus unexpectedly occured. In the mean time your paragraph, which the Advertiser considers as so effective, had become old,—if you can bear the supposition, perhaps Sir, it was forgotton in the 2d Regiment; the more supposible, as the report you noticed came from them,[3] and could acquire no additional importance by travelling back. The "Advertiser" says: "The announcement of the rumor of some circumstances, had time to reach the camp of the 2d Regiment in Mexico, and also the refusal of the tender of the Brigadier Generalship." Now, Sir, I have just said I thought the announcement had too much time, and I have some reason to believe the refusal had not enough.[4] A Physician formerly a member of the 1st Mississippi Regiment, now on duty in the medical staff of the division which includes the 2d Mississippi Regiment, wrote to me from camp Buena Vista, on the 10th July;[5] five days before the letter of the committee, from whose letter I make the following extract: "The 2d Mississippi, leave for Augua Nueva, in a few days, and more troops are expected up. We were all delighted to hear that you have been promoted to Brigadier, and would take command of this Division."

The idea of electing me Colonel of the 2d Mississippi Regiment, I have been informed by some of the officers, was as old as its organization, and repeatedly when we were at Monterey, members of the 2d Mississippi Regiment, expressed a wish, in the event of their Colonelcy becoming vacant to have my services in that capacity. These will [re][6]member, whilst I acknwledged the complim[e]nt, the extent to which I allways discouraged the proposition, and will recognize in the third reason of my letter to their committee a principle they have heard me more fully present. By them my reply might have been anticipated; yet if they supposed I could not resist an invitation so generously and unexpectedly given, they were not far wrong. Had I been physically able, and free to accept, they would probably have been right.

Now Sir, to return to the article of the "Advertiser," having gratuitously made the supposition, that the invitation of the 2d Regiment, was procured to subserve some purpose, and be refused, the editor[7] with all the solemnity of an endictment proceeds: "If Col. Jefferson Davis, has at any time, or in any form,"[8] &c &c, to instruct me what it is requisite for me to do in the case. To the low suspicion, I have nothing to reply. It must find its rebuke in every ingenerous mind, and its refutation must come from my friends of the 2d Mississippi Regiment, who best know the degree of its falsehood. How an unprejudicated mind could originate such things, it is difficult to conceive. Nor is it more easy for me to imagine whose vanity has been wounded, whose envy excited, whose jealousy has prompted him to this misrepresentation of a free offering, an honorable distinction, which my fellow citizens of the 2d Regiment, have been pleased to confer upon me.[9]

At the close of the Advertiser's article, is a call for infor[mati]on as to the ground on which I declin[ed] the proffered command.— Those who [v]olunteer advice, ought to have a great deal of information, and I am happy to have it in my power to contribute any.— I therefore send you for publication the correspondence in relation to this transaction. It is comprised entire, in two letters herewith enclosnd. No. 1 the letter of the committe, No. 2, a copy of my reply.[10] Very truly your friend,

JEFFERSON DAVIS.

Vicksburg *Weekly Sentinel*, Sept. 29, 1847.

[1] The Aberdeen *Mississippi Advertiser* published an article critical of Davis on August 25. First noted by the Vicksburg *Sentinel* on September 1, the article was printed in its entirety on October 20.

[2] On June 2, 1847, the *Sentinel* reported: "There is a rumor of some circumstances which may induce Col. Jefferson Davis to decline the appointment of Brigadier General tendered him by the President, and take the command of the 2d Mississippi Regiment in case of Col. Reuben Davis' resignation."

[3] According to the *Sentinel* (Sept. 1, 1847), word of the 2d Miss. Rgt.'s interest in Davis came from "a gentleman, formerly a member of the 1st Regiment . . . who heard it at Monterey, and repeated it here . . . as a well known fact."

[4] The so-called announcement, carried in the *Picayune* on June 4, could have been seen by officers of the 2d Miss. Rgt. before they wrote to Davis on July 16. Davis' refusal of the briga-

dier generalship was dated June 20 and not widely publicized for some days; most likely it was not known in Mexico by mid-July. See, for example, Zachary Taylor to Davis, July 27.

[5] James D. Caulfield had joined Davis' command as a pvt. Discharged on September 14 to serve as a contract assistant surgeon to the Mississippians, he subsequently was assigned to the Virginia regiment at Buena Vista (DNA, M-863, roll 1; DNA, M-29, roll 3, Special Orders No. 76, June 6, 1847). His letter of July 10 to Davis has not been located.

[6] Brackets enclose letters supplied where the newspaper is damaged.

[7] William D. Chapman, born in New York about 1816, was a newspaper publisher and editor associated in the 1840s with the Aberdeen *Monroe Democrat* and *Mississippi Advertiser*; he became coproprietor of the Columbus *Southern Standard* in 1851 (*Mississippiana*, 2:2, 16; 1850 Census, Miss., W. Monroe, family 445).

[8] The sentence reads: "If Col. Jefferson Davis has, at any time, or in any form, given the 2d Miss. Regiment to understand that he would accept the command, if tendered him, there is no excuse for his declining, unless from absolute inability to comply" (Vicksburg *Weekly Sentinel*, Oct. 20, 1847).

[9] Contending that Davis never intended to accept the colonelcy, the *Advertiser* asserted that the rumor was started by Davis' sycophantic friends "anxious to draw around his name much artificial applause" and "extraneous public puffing." Further, the *Advertiser* complained, the vaunting of Davis' achievements was "cruel to another whom it was depriving of distinguished soldiership by warping public opinion from an act of noble daring, in which life was perilled"— almost certainly a reference to the wounded Alexander K. McClung, who had raised a company for the 1st Miss. Rgt. in the Aberdeen area (ibid.).

[10] Officers of the Second Mississippi Regiment to Davis, July 16, and Davis' reply dated August 19.

To Concordia Parish Citizens

BRIERFIELD, Miss., *Sept.* 24, 1847.

DEAR SIR—When I recived the letter of your committee,[1] inviting me on behalf of the citizens of Concordia, to a barbecue to be given on the 30th inst., as a compliment to the character and gallant services of Gen. Z. Taylor; I hoped it would have been in my power to meet you on an occasion to me so interesting and grateful to the warm personal attachment I feel for the patriot hero whom you propose to honor. Valuable and brilliant as have been the public services of Gen. Taylor, attracting the admiration and gratitude of his countrymen throughout our broad Union, those who have known him best will equally remember and honor him for the purity, the generosity, and unostentatious magnanimity of his private character. His colossal greatness is presented in the garb of the strictest republican simplicity; and to this, no doubt, in a great degree, may be referred the feeling you describe when you say, "we are learning to regard him with a filial affection."

To speak of Gen. Taylor as one who had known him long and well, I will say, that his life has been devoted to the service of his country for no other reward than the consciousness of serving it well—and that for many years past, the goal of his desire has been a private station, as soon as his official obligations would permit, to retire to the enjoyment of the sovereignty of a citizen of the United States.

Before closing I will recur to a recent and characteristic exhibition of his disinterested patriotism. He was called on by the Administration for his opinion as to the best mode of prosecuting the war with Mexico. In view of the embarrassments which surrounded Gen. Scott, and the importance of the operations in which he was engaged, Gen. Taylor recommended that a portion of his own command be sent to reinforce the southern column.[2] For the good of his country, he sacrificed his long deferred hope of an advance at the moment of its fulfilment, and doomed himself to the worst punishment of a soldier—inactivity on a line of defence. For the good of his country all personal ambition, all rivalry were forgotten—he gave his vest also to the man who had taken his coat, and left him exposed to the storms of Buena Vista.

Permit me to offer you for the occasion:

Gen. Taylor.—The soldier who "never surrenders," the citizen whose love is "for the country, the whole country;"[3] the man whose sacrifices are all of himself.

Accept for yourselves, gentlemen of the committee, and please tender to those whom you represent, assurances of my high esteem and the regret which I feel at not being able to meet you as invited.[4] Very respectfully, yours,

JEFFERSON DAVIS.

New Orleans *Picayune*, Oct. 5, 1847.

[1] Davis' letter was addressed to Caleb G. Forshey, a member of the committee of invitation. Other members were Thomas P. Farrar, Thomas Edwards, George C. McWhorter, Joseph E. Miller, and J. Welch (Vidalia, La., *Concordia Intell.*, Oct. 2, 1847). Their letter has not been found.

[2] See Zachary Taylor to Davis, August 16, 1847.

[3] Davis quotes Lt. Thomas L. Crittenden's words to Santa Anna at Buena Vista during the exchange of white flags and paraphrases a sentence from Daniel Webster's Boston speech of June 17, 1825: "Let our object be our country, our whole country, and nothing but our country" (New Or-

leans *Delta*, Mar. 27, 1847; *Bartlett's*, 443).

[4] According to the Natchez *Courier* (Oct. 6, 1847), the reading of Davis'

letter was "received with token of enthusiastic approbation" and his toast "elicited universal and heartfelt applause."

To Varina Howell Davis

Brierfield 30th Sept. 1847

MY DEAR WIFE,

I have just received your letter by "magnolia" also your Ma's[1] and am cheered by the intelligence of your improved health.

I am getting on as well as surrounding circumstances and my own condition would lead you to expect. Yesterday was at the Hurricane, May-Jane is improving but very weak, Eliza was sick; in bed. Lize is greatly better the rest well.[2] Our family has changed since your departure, by the leaving of Mr. Payne,[3] the introduction into the house of two kittens, and under of a slut with a litter of whelps. Eliza is a little slow, somewhat dull and but a little neat or orderly.[4] Tis strange that the great first law of God, *order*, a law written in all his works and by which animated creation on land and /in/ water enjoys existence should so little impress itself upon the portion of his works made in his own image. This sermon to be concluded by yourself.

We have had three deaths here, Louisa's Melissa's and Amanda's children.[5] Others are quite sick. And the little which I can suggest is rendered to a great extent unavailing by the want of faithful executives.

Luther went down to Feliciana[6] on hearing of the death of Mr. Boyle.[7] The same cause will render proper a postponement of our visit.

I have not seen the resolutions of which you speak,[8] but it is well that somebody works for me when there are so many engaged in barring the gates to exclude <–them–> me. At all of which labor I am in no wise surprised; the public could not gain much if any thing from my labors, and I have not contracted to work for individuals.

My eyes have not permitted me to do much writing, of my general health [I][9] wrote to you last week[10] and regret you should have come to the conclusion that I designed to give you any thing else than correct information. We are all of us poor judges of our own case, whether morally or physically considered, and if the information you received from Brother Joe. was more correct than that which I gave you, the defect was of my judgement.

Having no body to direct the cooking of the apples and not presuming to eat them raw, they are of no use to *me*, of Bread there yet remains a large part of that you sent me, or rather of the half thereof which reached the *Brierfield*. Take thanks my dear and no more <–trouble–> /care/ of what we shall eat.

I heard the boat this morning and thought it sounded like you were on it, then nobody came down for a long time, what explanation could be given for this fact except that delay had occurred in getting the buggy and that you had forbidden an avant courier to effect a a su[r]prise. Your letter came not by Mercury nor a "carrier dove" though white was the steed and dark in the face the bearer of the precious freight. I did not ask the messenger whether over effort had sent the blood in such excess to his cheeks as to discolor the same.

Mr. Phillips[11] (miserabile dictu) has co[me] and interrupte[d] the progress of this valuable letter.

Present me most kindly to Judge Winchester and give him my congratulations on his improved health. Give my love to your Pa & Ma and all the children— as ever, your husband in the bonds of affection.

JEFF'N. DAVIS

P. S. your presents have arrived, and I am now bountifully supplied with Soda, Bread, and Apples – the last came in good time Eliza had just sent down for an apple if I had one. Somebody must have seen the note to Miss Gains[12] before you, I did not impress the wax with my finger but with the end of my pencil. yrs.

D.

The amiable man has given me a visitation, talked me down quite prostrate, prevented me from doing any thing and thus rendered me as cross as a Bear. [B]rother Joe has come and God bless him will I hope[13] Friday morning—[14]

ALS (ViRC). Addressed: "Mrs. Varina Davis Briars (near) Natches." Manuscript torn, parts obscured by tape. Found on Davis' plantation near Jackson, undoubtedly in July 1863, by Lt. Charles R. Ford, 76th Ill. Inf., the letter was given to the Confederate Museum in 1935 by his daughter.

[1] Delivered on the regular packet steamer *Magnolia,* neither the letter from Davis' wife nor the one from Margaret K. Howell has been located. Varina Davis may have taken refuge in Natchez for a few weeks because that city, unlike Vicksburg and other river towns, reported no outbreak of fever during September (Natchez *Courier and Jour.*, Sept. 15, 1847).

[2] Mary Jane Bradford, Davis' niece; Eliza Van Benthuysen Davis, his sister-in-law; and Mary Elizabeth Mitchell, his grandniece, all residents of Joseph E. Davis' neighboring Hurricane plantation, probably were suffering from the same kind of illness that swept Vicksburg. Although denying it was yellow fever and reporting only two deaths, both local newspapers admitted that the unnamed fever was epidemic (*Tri-Weekly Whig*, Sept. 14, 1847; *Weekly Sentinel*, Sept. 29, 1847).

[3] Perhaps Philanzo Payne, who on September 25 had received $350 from Davis for "an unsettled account."

[4] Undoubtedly a house servant, Eliza was described in an earlier letter from Varina Davis to her parents as "dirty, dirtier, dirtiest, and useless more useless, most useless" ([Jan. 5, 1847], Davis Coll., AU).

[5] Referring to servants.

[6] Luther L. Smith, Jr., Davis' nephew, was born and reared in West Feliciana Parish, Louisiana; recently he had been living on Davis Bend (Joseph E. Davis to Davis, Dec. 16, 1846).

[7] William D. Boyle, a Virginian, had married Davis' niece Lucinda Jane Smith, in 1836 and settled near St. Francisville, Louisiana. In 1844 Boyle was one of the attorneys who prosecuted John T. Mason for the murder of Davis' brother-in-law David Bradford. Soon thereafter Boyle was appointed a district judge. Charged with several improprieties in the discharge of his duties, he narrowly won the right to retain his judgeship in May 1847. On his way to hold court sev-

eral months later, he was stricken with yellow fever and died near Plaquemine on September 20, at the age of forty-one (DAR, *La. Tombstone Inscriptions*, 7:41; 1840 Census, La., W. Feliciana; Watts and De Grummond, *Solitude*, 14–16; *Be It Known and Remembered: Bible Recs.*, 4:18; Richmond, La., *Compiler*, May 24, 1844; New Orleans *Jeffersonian*, May 30, 1846; New Orleans *Delta*, July 1, 1846, Apr. 30, May 2, Sept. 25, 1847).

[8] Varina Davis must have told her husband of the proclamation first printed on September 3, 1847, in the Jackson *Southron*, the state Whig organ. Signed by "THE PEOPLE," the proclamation castigated Mississippi representatives Jacob Thompson and Robert W. Roberts for supporting a resolution censuring Zachary Taylor and the Monterrey capitulation commissioners. According to the proclamation, Thompson and Roberts, "regarding Col. Davis as a RIVAL at home, and fearing his great popularity . . . wished to throw a cloud over his prospects for the Senate . . . or for Governor." For "this act of ingratitude and misrepresentation of the will of their constituents," Thompson and Roberts were severely criticized. The other members of Mississippi's congressional delegation were praised for "their patriotic course" in voting against the resolution.

[9] Except as otherwise noted, material in square brackets is supplied because the manuscript is damaged.

[10] Not found.

[11] Probably Laughlin Phillips, an overseer aged about thirty-two, who in 1850 resided nearby with the carpenter who worked on Davis' plantation house (1850 Census, Miss., Warren, family 740; Z774, *Davis v. Bowmar* [1874], 480–82, Ms-Ar).

[12] Perhaps Matilda Gaines, born in Mississippi about 1820 and apparently a neighbor of Varina Davis' family (1850 Census, Miss., Adams, S. Natchez, family 258).

¹³ Gap in the text caused by repair of fold with tape; approximately half a line missing.

¹⁴ The second postscript appears on the back of the last page.

To Albert G. Brown

Brierfield 3d Oct. 1847

SIR,

Herewith I have the honor to transmit to you the reports of the Regimental officers of the Battles of Monterey and Buena Vista, as far as the same were in my possession.[1] I had hoped before this to have received full information in relation to the number of Rifles for which our state will be justly responsible and to have sent you a consolidated return; but regret to say that no company return has been made to me, since that of which I advised you.[2]

It was my purpose to have made a report to you, which should have been a history of our Campaign in Mexico, but ill health at last compels me to abandon the design. A wish on the part of the company officers to have their reports published, has been communicated to me by one of their number, and I have replied that they would be furnished to the Executive.[3] Very Respectfully yr. mo. obt. svt

JEFFN. DAVIS

ALS (Z735, Davis Papers, Ms-Ar).

[1] Davis enclosed twenty-nine documents, seventeen pertaining to Monterrey and twelve to Buena Vista: his three official reports (two dated Sept. 26, 1846, and one of Mar. 2, 1847); a supplemental report to Brown (Sept. 20, 1847); the returns of killed, wounded, and missing for the two battles; and twenty-three reports by his officers (Sept. 26–Nov. 1, 1846, Feb. 28–Mar. 6, 1847, and undated). Of the transmitted documents, the ten Buena Vista officers' reports are originals; several others—the casualty returns and Maj. Bradford's Monterrey report (Sept. 26, 1846)—are in the hand of Adj. Richard Griffith; Davis' reports to Bliss (Mar. 2, 1847) and Brown (Sept. 20, 1847) are in his own hand; and

the remainder, all of which concerned Monterrey, are copies made by Davis and/or his wife. Most of the latter reports, which Davis retained for his personal use, apparently were scattered when Union troops seized his library in July 1863 (see the descriptive note to Russell's report, Sept. 26, 1846). On October 24, 1847, Davis forwarded Brown a final Monterrey report.

[2] See Brown to Davis, July 27, 1847, to which no immediate reply has been located. See also Davis' letter to George Talcott dated November 7, 1847.

[3] In 1848 the Mississippi legislature voted to deposit the reports and accompanying documents in the secretary of state's office but made no provision for their publication. Sup-

posedly filed in the state library, the documents were missing for a number of years but are now included among the gubernatorial papers of Albert G. Brown (*Miss. Laws, 1848*, 535–36); Jackson *Semi-Weekly Mississippian*, Sept. 9, 1859; Davis to John F. H. Claiborne, Oct. 13, 1877, Davis Papers, DLC; endorsement dated Apr. 6, 1885, to memorandum on Monterrey, [Dec. 31], 1846, Z777f, Davis Papers, Ms-Ar). Davis' correspondence concerning publication of the reports has not been located.

From Charles T. Harlan

Vicksburg Oct 17. 1847.

DEAR COL.

[In reply to Your favor of the 29th Ult.[1]][2] I beg leave /have the honor/[3] to state that the 1st Miss Regt. on the 22nd. Sept were in Garrison at the fort attacked by them on the preceding day[4]—that at day break on the morning of the 23rd. you discovered that the enemy had evacuated or partially so the second[5] of line of forts which protected the entrance to the lower part of the City of Monterey. Selecting two Companies[6] you <–had–>[7] /led/ them <–follow–>[7] to its occupation—from thence You entered the town— about 8 Oclock Major Bradford with the remaining 8 Companies[8] was ordered to your support as also Col. Woods Regt. of Texans– In the desultory strife thro the City I became seperated from him[9] and found myself Close to a position occupied by Genl Quitman and Yourself having with You a few Tennessee troops and Your two Companies of Rifles[10]—with Your Command alone You struggled thro several squares of the City– In a short time You were joined by Genl Henderson <–and–>[7] /with/ a portion Col Wood's regt and together forced Your way to within a few squares of the plaza. The Miss Regt. remained disunited throughout the day. Therre were no bayonets with us[11] and two pieces of artillery attempting an advance had fallen back from want of efficient support, after firing a few discharges along the streets.[12] The sun was fast declining–   Genl H. now consulted you as to the most desirable course to be purssud– a further advance would have been impracticable with the forces[13] under Your Commands and nothing but the enemies ignorance of your Numbers and /unsupported/ position could have prevented Your destruction—The result of the Conference was an <–d–> order to Me /to bear a message/ from Genl. H–

to Genl. Taylor and from Yourself to Genl Quitman <–requesting their wishes with regard to Your relative Commands.–>[7] I could not find those Commanders or the /portion of/ Miss Regt.– /under Maj. Bradford/ in the pursuit of this Object I arrived at the extreme edge of the town where I found a detachment from I think Capt Bragg's Battery—from its Officer[14] I learned that our forces had fallen back—at this moment Mr. Ezra Price (serving with but not attached to the Miss. Regt.) Met Me– He came from the commanders to whom I had been sent, bearring orders for all our troops to return from the town, and although these Chiefs were not distant More than 1/2 mils, yet as the Night was fast closing, I thought it <–not im–>[7]proper /for me immediately/ to convey the commands as delivered by Mr. Price. On returning, I found You alone, <–Genl Henderson having already withdrawn his force–>[15]– the amunition had been reduced to a few rounds–the Men had not partaken of food for 36 hours, had been under arms all night without the protection of a blanket from a chilling rain which had fallen during the time and had been subjected to a most ardous days duty— It was under these circumstances the Order was delivered to You and gathering Your Men You retired from the town <–without loss–>[7] tho Not without opposition.[16]

I have above endeavored to Give you My remembrances of the 23rd. Sept. If you do not find it sufficiently perspicuous please write and say in What respect I Can refresh my Memory, for it is upon that I have to rely—

I cry Your Mercy for so long and So Seeming neglect of your request– a some what prolonged absence from V.Burg has prevented an earlier Compliance—I trust it May Not Now be too late and that it May answer any purpose intended–

You will have read of the Victories which are not Victories and the depressing Situation of Genl. Scotts Command[17]– Eight regiments now have been Called for by the Government but the apportionment among the States not Yet divulged[18]—Will it be pardonable to ask if my request has been preferred by you to the department[19]– I am so much opposed to the *election of Company* Officers that I would Not accept a position so obtained—the inefficiency of Volunteers is I think mainly attributable to this Course– there is too Much Subserviency to Company feeling[20]–

My desire is so strong to leave this Country, that I may have intruded My wishes at too great a length upon You– Pray Excuse me– I offer Very Many wishes for Your happiness– Very Truly Yours

C. T. Harlan

ALS (Davis Papers, KyLxT). ALS (RG27, Vol. 26, Corres., Mexican War Docs., Ms-Ar). Harlan apparently made a second copy of that portion of his letter dealing with the Battle of Monterrey and incorporated into it changes indicated by Davis on the original. The latter version, which is undated, bears the heading "Statement of C. T. Harlan Sergeant Major of the 1st Miss Riflemen in the battle of Monterey. Sept 23. 1846." Significant textual differences between the two versions are pointed out in footnotes, as are Davis' emendations to the original.

[1] Not found. In late September Davis was preparing his Mexican War reports for transmittal to Governor Brown (see Davis to Brown, Oct. 3, 1847). When Davis sent Harlan's report to Brown on October 24, he observed that it contained information on the third day's action at Monterrey not available elsewhere.

[2] The brackets were probably added by Davis.

[3] All interlineations were made by Davis and incorporated in Harlan's second copy.

[4] The 1st Miss. was posted in the fortified stone building and a redan connecting it with the Tenería.

[5] El Diablo.

[6] Besides Cos. G and H of the 1st Miss., Cos. A and B of the 1st Tenn. Rgt. moved with Davis to El Diablo.

[7] Marked for deletion, probably by Davis, and omitted on Harlan's second copy.

[8] Harlan's second copy reads, "with the remaining Companies." Before Davis entered the city his command was changed, Co. G being replaced by Cos. B and D; Co. H and a single Tennessee company remained with him. Since Co. I had been left as a rear guard, Bradford brought only four companies—C, E, G, and K—to Davis' support.

[9] Harlan's second copy reads, "from this reinforcement."

[10] Three Mississippi companies—B, D, and H—were with Davis.

[11] Harlan refers to members of the 1st Tenn.; the Mississippians did not carry bayonets.

[12] The two guns sent in by Braxton Bragg were withdrawn about three o'clock (Bragg's rep., Sept. 26, 1846, DNA, RG393, W. Dept. and Div., Reps. of Div. Comdrs. Engaged with the Enemy in Mexico).

[13] Harlan's second copy reads, "a further advance required a increase in the forces."

[14] Probably Lt. John F. Reynolds, who had been posted "to cover the troops as they retired" (Bragg's rep., Sept. 26, 1846, DNA, RG393, W. Dept. and Div., Reps. of Div. Comdrs. Engaged with the Enemy in Mexico).

[15] Marked for deletion, probably by Davis, and omitted on Harlan's second copy. Davis states elsewhere that Henderson had not yet withdrawn (Davis to Brown, Sept. 20, 1847).

[16] Harlan's second copy closes at this point with a sentence that reads, "The foregoing remembrances are respectfully submitted and I am Yours Very respectfully."

[17] Even though it had won "victory after victory" on the march from Veracruz to Mexico City, Scott's army seemed unable to "conquer a peace." Recent reports from Mexico confirmed that the enemy was resolved to continue fighting and that American

troops, numbering only about 10,000 and reduced by sickness, could not anticipate any substantial reinforcement (Vicksburg *Tri-Weekly Whig*, Oct. 12, 1847; New Orleans *Picayune*, Sept. 16–Oct. 15, 1847, passim; Scott, *Memoirs*, 2:431, 460, 498, 529–30).

[18] On October 5 the Washington correspondent of the Baltimore *Sun* reported that the president was going to call up eight additional volunteer regiments; in fact, the August 1847 call for volunteers was the last (New Orleans *Picayune*, Oct. 14, 1847; Polk, *Diary*, 3:147).

[19] On November 30 Davis addressed the president, recommending Harlan for a regular army appointment.

[20] The election of volunteer officers most frequently was opposed on the grounds that "strong talk and strong whiskey" during electioneering were key factors in the men's decision. Although many of the officers so chosen were ignorant of military training and were poor disciplinarians as well, some observers thought the elected officers excellent (Bloom, "With the American Army into Mexico," 12, 15–16; Meade, *Life and Letters*, 1:110, 162–63).

To George Talcott

(near) Warrenton, Mi. 7th Nov. 1847

SIR, Herewith I have the honor to enclose to you a return of the ordnance stores for which I was responible, with vouchers in relation thereto. Also please find the receipt of Capt. Howard which could not be obtained to send on with my last return to which it belongs.[1]

The fine rifles which you issued to the Regt. I had the honor to command in Mexico are worthy of the highest commendation, I doubt whether as many pieces were ever issued from any other ordnance Dept. so perfect in their construction and condition, In accuracy of fire they are equal to the finest sporting rifles, their range I think exceeds that of the (old pattern) Musket, and they less often miss fire, or want repair than any small arms I have seen used in service.[2] Very Respectfully yr. obt. svt.

JEFFN. DAVIS
(ex) Col. 1st Missi. Rifln.

ALS (DNA, RG156, Letters Recd., D 191-1847).

[1] The enclosures, now missing, were transmitted to the second auditor's office on November 24, the day after Davis' letter was received. Davis' "last return" has not been found, and according to Talcott there was "no record of any former return" except a receipt "for a pair of pistols" (Nov. 24, 1847).

[2] The second paragraph of Davis' letter was printed in circulars issued

by Eli Whitney to advertise his "new model Percussion Rifle" (1850) and his "New Model Mississippi and Minnie Rifle" in January 1860 (RG27, Vol. 27, Corres., Ms-Ar; DNA, RG 156, Special Files—Inventions, 6-447). See also Davis' letter to William L. Marcy, November 30, 1847.

To ———

Brierfield 8th Nov. 1847

My Dear Sir,

I have this morning received your kind letter of the 26th Ult. in which you inform me that the "Marshall guards" and their numerous friends would be gratified by the publication of a letter which I wrote some time since to your gallant Son[1] in relation to the brave and efficient company your County gave to the service of the country. I have no copy of that letter, and cannot closely remember it's contents, but can have no objection to it's publication unless on account of it's style which, as it was a friendly letter to a brother soldier, might well be unsuited to the purpose of publication. This point I refer to your discretion and friendly regard not doubting but that I shall be content with your decision—

In a few days I leave for Washington City[2] and will be happy to hear from you at that place. Very sincerely yrs.

JEFFN: DAVIS.

ALS (NNPM).

[1] Neither Davis' letter to the addressee's son, who apparently was a member of Co. I, 1st Miss. Rgt., nor the letter dated October 26 has been found.

[2] Davis left for Washington on November 11, stopping briefly in Vicksburg and traveling to Jackson before boarding the steamer *Ben Franklin* in Vicksburg for the trip upriver. On November 17 he was in Louisville and the next day reached Cincinnati, where he met with former President John Tyler. As Davis recalled, Tyler heard Davis "was at the landing and . . . kindly came on the boat" to greet him. Davis and his fellow senator, Henry S. Foote, arrived in Washington on November 25, after being delayed for a day in Baltimore by bad weather (V. Davis to Margaret K. Howell, Nov. 12, 1847, Davis Coll., AU; Jackson *Mississippian*, Nov. 12, Dec. 3, 1847; Louisville *Courier*, Nov. 18, 1847; Cincinnati *Enquirer*, Nov. 19, 1847; Davis to Lyon G. Tyler, Aug. 5, 1886, Tyler Papers, DLC).

From Daniel R. Russell

Carrollton 24re Novr 1847

DEAR SIR

Allow me to trouble you in the midst of cares, to aid. the pretensions of a freind both of yours[1] & mine

A Goran. Rowe[2] a young gentleman of this village desires to obtain a place at West Point Academy as a Cadet—

I am fully prepared to bestow on Mr. Rowe the highest compliment, He is a gentleman high toned & chivalric, of fine attainments for one of his age, being now 19 years old. He was a member of my company in Mexico & in the battle of Monterey though but a boy his bearing was most gallant. He was in the field during the 3 days & my attention was frequently attracted to him during the fight, cool & energetic, always prompt, & though then enfeebled by sickness phisically he kept up bravely <–during–> while the contest lasted— My estimation of him as a *gentleman* will be seen when I say that I kept him in my tent & mess while he remained in the service — He has been educated principally at the centennary college,[3] & has acquired an ordinary knowledge of the dead languages, some proficiency in the French language & mathematics, His brother in law & Guardian Genl J. Whitmore, is one of the members elect from this County to the next Legislature, whom you probably know, Perhaps he has addressed you on this subject[4]—

I will take this occasion to thank you most sincerely for the manner in which you were pleased to speak of me in your reply in July last to Mr Somerville's letter,[5] It has not only saved my reputation as a soldier, but I am constrained to attribute my success in the last election mainly to it,[6] My only regret upon the occasion is, that my pecuniary <–affae–> condition would not allow me to present myself as a candidate before this County for a seat in the Legislature, my vote in the County under circumstances which you do not know, warrants me in supposing that I would have been elected, then I might have given practical & perhaps serviceable demonstration of my gratitude towards you — I should have voted for you with pleasure — I remain your Obdt Servt

DANL R. RUSSELL

P. S. Perhaps it may serve Mr Rowe in this application to let it be known that he is a democrat in politics, this you are aware I do not regard as a recommendation, however.

R.

ALS (DNA, RG94, USMA Recs., Applics. of Cadets, 1848/240). Enclosed: Davis to Joseph G. Totten, Mar. 12, 1848.

¹ The word *mine* is overwritten.

² Andrew Goran Rowe, a native of South Carolina, became 3d cpl., Co. D, on September 14, 1846. Discharged on a certificate of disability in December, he returned to Carrollton, but by 1850 was working as an attorney in Holly Springs (DNA, M-863, roll 3; 1850 Census, Miss., N. Marshall, family 941).

³ Centenary College, a Methodist school founded in 1839, was first located at Brandon but in 1845 was re-established in Jackson, Louisiana (Skipwith, *East Feliciana*, 21).

⁴ Joshua Whitmore, born in South Carolina about 1810, was a Carrollton attorney. A Democrat, he served one term in the legislature before moving to Holly Springs. After a trip to California in 1850, Whitmore returned to Mississippi and in late 1851 became proprietor of the *Marshall Jeffersonian*. From 1853 until 1858 he was a state district attorney (1850 Census, Miss., N. Marshall, family 941; *Miss. Official Reg., 1908*, 122; Jackson *Mississippian*, July 21, 1848; Vicksburg *Weekly Sentinel*, July 31, 1850; Vicksburg *Tri-Weekly Sentinel*, Nov. 18, 1851; Ms-Ar to Davis Assn., Aug. 6, 1979). No letter from him to Davis has been found.

⁵ James Somerville (1822–77), a native of Virginia, served as pvt., Co. D. During the Civil War he reportedly was a militia officer and afterward practiced law in Carrollton (Rowland, ed., *Mississippi*, 3:782; Rowland, *Heart of the South*, 3:35; DNA, M-863, roll 3). Any correspondence between him and Davis has not been found but must have concerned criticism of Russell's performance in Mexico. Following another officer's *"insinuation"* of some misconduct, twenty-seven former members of Russell's company, including Somerville, signed a public letter attesting his "gallantry and character" (Vicksburg *Tri-Weekly Whig*, Oct. 4, 1847).

⁶ Russell, a Whig, had just been elected clerk of the district chancery court.

To Stephen Cocke

Washington, 30th Nov. 1847

MY DEAR FRIEND, your very kind letter of the 7th has just reached me having been forwarded by my Brother,¹

I truly thank you for the interest you manifest in my election, which is of course a subject upon which I now feel greater interest than I should have done had I remained at home, because to be beaten under present circumstances is to be recalled.²

Genl. Foote mentioned to me this morning that he had received a letter informing him that Thompson's friends were endeavoring to incite a feeling in the North[3] by stating that I had opposed his election. My opinion of Mr. Thompson is known to you and if I had been in his district I should certainly have opposed his nomination, but my notions of propriety caused me to refuse when requested to write to some of my friends and urge them to put him aside by a renomination at a new convention[4]— Briefly, I never interfered in the contest. The report may be of no importance, if however it should appear to you advisable you can say thus much to any of our friends in the Legislature whose opinion may be affected by the underground attack.

The President is in good health & fine spirits,[5] feels confident of being able to dis comfit the enemy as signally at home as abroad. The Southern and Western Whigs are understood to be with us on the War question, which will be in the beginning at least the chief ground of contest. I think the Wilmot Proviso<-n-> will will soon be of the things which were— Cass is heartily with us, and says he always was but saw the necessity last spring of caution, lest the fire which would go out if let alone should be kindled by attempting to extinguish it too suddenly.[6]

I have not been able to find the books and papers which I left here and have no list of Correspondents. I wish at your leisure you would from time to time send me names especially of those we met in our joint canvass[7]—

With great regard I am Yr. friend

JEFFN. DAVIS

Give my respects to Messrs Price and Fall — I will try to write to them this evening — if not ask them to send me the Mississippian,[8] which request I did not make be cause I took as granted they would know my wish upon that point.

JEFFN. DAVIS

ALS (Z735, Davis Papers, Ms-Ar).

[1] Cocke's letter has not been found.

[2] The election of senator was to be a major item of business before the Mississippi legislature in January. In contrast to the concern expressed here, Davis earlier had impressed Zachary Taylor as "indifferent" about the election (Taylor, *Letters*, 145).

[3] Since Henry S. Foote was from the southern part of the state, there was some sentiment that the second senator should come from northern Mississippi (Jackson *Southron*, July 23, 1847; Vicksburg *Weekly Sentinel*, July 28, 1847).

[4] Any correspondence on this topic has not been located; Davis' antagonism toward Jacob Thompson stemmed from Thompson's introduction of a motion to censure Zachary

Taylor after the Monterrey capitulation. Thompson was reelected to the House of Representatives from Mississippi's First Congressional District in November 1847.

[5] Davis had called on President Polk at the White House on November 26 (Polk, *Diary*, 3:232).

[6] Although Cass favored the Wilmot Proviso when first introduced in 1846, he argued on March 1, 1847, that it was "merely sectional" and that the United States ought to win the war before disposing of conquered territory (Woodford, *Lewis Cass*, 245–47).

[7] As candidates for Congress and the state chancellorship, respectively, Davis and Cocke had traveled together during the 1845 campaign (*Davis Papers*, 2:338–39, 351–52).

[8] Charles M. Price and George R. Fall published the state Democratic organ, the Jackson *Mississippian*. Rather than championing Davis as senator in the weeks prior to the election, the paper adopted a neutral stance between him and his chief rival, Roger Barton of Marshall County (see, for instance, articles published on Sept. 24 and Dec. 31, 1847).

To William L. Marcy

Gadsby's Hotel[1] 30th Nov. 1847

SIR, at the request of Mr. Eli Whitney[2] constructor of the rifles issued to the 1st Rgt. of Missi. Vols. I have the honor to address you and to bear testimony to their high value, whether viewed in relation to their neatness, their accuracy of aim, or their durability in field service. Having served with troops bearing the musket and subsequently with those who used the patent carbine, I have had opportunity to test both in the field, and have no hesitation in giving the preference to the rifle recently used by my command in Mexico as having greater certainty of fire and simplicity of[3] construction, and recommend the constructor to the most favorable consideration of your Department. very respectfully yr. obt. svt.

JEFFN. DAVIS

ALS (Z43, Rosenstock-Davis Papers, Ms-Ar).

[1] Located on the northwestern corner of Pennsylvania Avenue and Third Street, Gadsby's New Hotel was a Washington landmark for nearly a century. Davis soon moved to Mrs. Owner's boarding house on Capitol Hill (Brown, *Washington*, 427–28; Federal Writers' Project, *Washington*, 632; Davis to Robert J.

Walker, Dec. 9, 1848; *U.S. Cong. Dir., 1848*, 22).

[2] Eli Whitney (1820–95), only son of the cotton gin inventor, became president of the Whitney Arms Company and founder of the New Haven Water Company (*NCAB*, 10:155; Mirsky, *Eli Whitney*, 290–91; Colt, *Own Record*, 3).

[3] Davis apparently first began the word *and*.

To Isaac S. K. Reeves[1]

Washington D. C. 16th Dec. 1847

DEAR SIR,

Excuse my delay in replying to your favors of Nov. 14 & Dec. 6[2] and pray attribute it to my many engagements and imperfect health, not to any disposition to neglect a subject to me of such peculiar interest.

Col. Hardin was not a graduate of the Military academy.

The Register of 1844[3] which you had the kindness to send contains a correct account of my military positions when in the U. S. Army, except in an unimportant particular i. e. that I served first in the 6th Infantry under a rule which at the time of my entrance into the line of the army assigned all cadets to the schools of practice at Jefferson Bks. and Fortress Monroe, for temporary service.

after leaving the service the only appointments I have held were under the state government of Missi — viz— In

1844 — State Presidential Elector — in
1845 — Representative in the U.S. Congress
1846 — Colonel of a /volunteer/ Rifle Regiment, which served twelve months in the Mexican War.
1847 — Senator in the U.S. Congress.

Born in the State of Kentucky
Appointed from the state Mississippi.

It will give me great pleasure to add any thing which may have been accidentally omitted or forgotten and in any way to promote your design of presenting proofs of the general usefulness of our Alma Mater[4] — very truly your's,

JEFFN. DAVIS

ALS (Cullum File, NWM).

[1] Isaac Stockton Keith Reeves (c1819–51), born in South Carolina, was an 1838 West Point graduate. After serving in the 1st Art. in New York and Maine (1838–40), he returned to the academy, undertaking duties as asst. professor, quartermaster, and adj. (Cullum, *Biog. Reg.*, 1:700; Heitman, *Hist. Reg.*, 1:822).

[2] Reeves's letters have not been found.

[3] U.S. Military Academy, *Register of Officers and Graduates of the United States Military Academy, from 1801 to 1844* (New York: W. L. Burroughs, 1844).

[4] Since the academy records were maintained by the adjutant, Reeves was "the logical compiler and publisher" of the school's official register.

In addition to the information Davis provides here, the following facts were included in a subsequent register (1850): he was a commissioner for the capitulation of Monterrey; he was wounded at Buena Vista; he declined the brigadier generalship tendered in 1847; and he served as chairman of the Military Affairs Committee, 1849–50 (Cullum, comp., *Officers and Graduates*, 149; NWM to Davis Assn., June 12, 1979).

From Patrick W. Tompkins

Copy

Washington, Dec. 25, 1847

DEAR SIR

I perceive from the tone of the last Missi. papers received here, that it is assumed by a portion of the press of our party, that you would reject a seat in the U. S. Senate, if conferred on you by the assistance of the Whigs in the legislature, and by the other that the Whigs under such circumstances ought not to cast their votes for you.[1] I have reason to know that some of the Whigs members of the legislature, under the conviction that no whig could be elected to the senate, preferred you to any other democrat for that station and were pledged to your support. From my knowledge of your character and my belief that in the U. S. Senate you could not narrow yourself down to the mere representation of a party, but that you would be in the sense of the constitution, the representative of the great interests and rights of the whole state, I could not notice those newspaper passages without some concern, nor without believing that no one was authorized to commit you to grounds so narrow and as I think so dangerous.

In view of all the circumstances and in view of your patriotic devotion, your brilliant military services, your abilities and attainments and known conservative principles, I have desired and do desire to see the legislature of Missi. retain you in your present station. With high esteem yr. obt. svt.

(signed) P. W. TOMPKINS

L, copy by Davis (William L. Richter).

[1] Patrick W. Tompkins, the only Whig in the Mississippi congressional delegation, obviously refers to recent statements in such party papers as the Jackson *Southron* and Vicksburg *Whig*. When the *Southron* (Nov. 19) announced itself in favor of Davis'

election as senator, the *Mississippian*, state Democratic organ, responded (Nov. 26) that Davis would not welcome Whig support. Summarizing the dilemma facing his party, the editor of the Vicksburg *Daily Whig* (Dec. 1) stated that, although he would rejoice to see Davis in the Senate, he believed that "Col. Davis wishes to be elected by his *own party*; he does not wish to be elected by *Whig votes*; and we think that a manly independence would dictate to the Whigs to cast their votes for some good and true Whig."

To Patrick W. Tompkins

Copy

Washington D.C. 25th Dec. 1847

DEAR SIR, I thank you for your friendly letter of this date and especially for the kind and generous interest you evince for my political success. I have not seen the newspaper statements to which you allude and can only answer in general terms, which your confidence leads me to hope may be satisfactory. I have not authorized any one to act or speak for me in the matter of the approaching senatorial election, nor would my opinions or my feelings as a Mississippian have permitted me to say that I would reject the support of the Whigs in our legislature, and refuse a seat in the Senate if they contributed to confer it upon me. I hold that an U. S. Senator in part represents the state sovereignty, that his services belong to the whole people, and that he would be unworthy of such elevation if he could consider himself in that station the representative of a party. My principles and adherence to democratic measures are so well known that I should attribute any support the Whigs might be pleased to give me as the result of a personal confidence, the manifestation of which I would gratefully receive and highly appreciate. By accepting the executive appointment I became in some degree a Candidate before the legislature for the Senate, but determined to take no action in relation to it, deeming it improper in the first place to interfere in County canvasses between the people and their future Representatives, or in the second place to canvass with those Representatives in relation to the manner in which they would carry out their delegated trust. To this rule of conduct I intend to adhere, though I am aware that not having held correspondence or recent intercourse with the members of the legislature, unscrupulous and designing men have a more than ordinarily good opportunity to misrepresent me.[1] With great regard I am yrs.

JEFF'N. DAVIS

ALS, retained copy (William L. Richter).

[1] On January 10 Democratic legislators caucused at Jackson, selecting Davis over Roger Barton as the senatorial candidate by a vote of 54 to 34, whereupon the nomination was declared unanimous. The following day the Mississippi house and senate elected Davis by acclamation, an occurrence that the *Mississippian* (Jan. 14, 1848) claimed to be unprecedented in any state. Despite Davis' ostensibly easy victory in the election, the thirty-five Whig votes in the 1848 Mississippi legislature might have proved decisive if Barton's supporters had been intractable (Vicksburg *Daily Whig*, Feb. 25, 1848).

Remarks on the Ten-Regiment Bill

Editorial Note: On December 22, 1847, Lewis Cass, chairman of the Committee on Military Affairs, reported "a bill to raise, for a limited time, an additional military force." A week later he urged its passage, noting that details of the legislation had been arranged during the last session and that its sole aim was to secure an early peace. The vote to consider the bill on January 3 was 19–19, Davis voting yea; Vice-President George M. Dallas cast the deciding affirmative vote (*Cong. Globe*, 30:1, 63, 78–79, 81).

January 3, 1848

Mr. DAVIS, of Mississippi. I deem it proper, as one of the Military Committee, to say, that this bill for ten additional regiments was prepared and submitted early to the Senate, under the impression that an exigency existed, that troops should be promptly raised. The chairman, under instructions of the committee, announced his intention to bring up the bill at the first possible moment, and press it to a speedy passage. It is now one week—[Mr. CASS: Two weeks][1]—two weeks, then, Mr. President, since this announcement was made. One week, I had hoped, would have been sufficient to have passed the bill; surely it was long enough to relieve us from any charge of a design to interpose it between the resolutions of the senator from South Carolina and the consideration of the Senate.[2]

It appeared to us, that unless active operations are renewed in Mexico, thus exciting the military ardor of the people of the United States, it would require all the intervening time between the present and the period of yellow fever to organize and forward the necessary troops into the interior of Mexico. The senator from Florida is right; there may justly be entertained apprehensions for our troops in Mexico, and that further efforts may yet be required on the battle-field.[3] What induced Santa Anna to attack Gen. Taylor at Buena Vista, but the knowledge that his forces had been reduced so low, that an easy and certain victory might be expected? Had his force upon that line been undiminished, the battle of Buena Vista would never have been fought. Let the past instruct us of the future. Tardiness in furnishing supplies of men and munitions has been the great cause of the expenditure of life which has occurred in the progress of this war.[4] Had General Scott possessed enough of men, of transportation, and other supplies, to have advanced into the interior immediately, and after the battle of Cerro Gordo to have pressed close upon the retreating enemy, it is most probable that Santa Anna would have remained in his refuge at Orizaba,[5] Scott's march have been unopposed, no fortifications erected around the capital, and the city of Mexico have surrendered without firing a gun. Sir, to secure a peace, we must show our power to compel submission. Our weak columns have induced attacks. Our gallant soldiers, outflanked, encircled—as it were engulphed in sea of enemies—have been equal to the emergency. American valor has triumphed over every disparity; but they have done so at immense sacrifice of blood. Shall such sacrifice be demanded for the future? Shall treasure be weighed against the blood of our countrymen? Let us not, by delay, expose the lives of our patriot soldiers; defer the public necessity to discuss general positions of no applicability to the question before us. Those occasions on which our men have performed such prodigies were not anticipated until it was too late to give relief. We shall show ourselves more wise only by avoiding in future similar contingency.

The Secretary of War, with all the information before him—the Executive of the United States, with all the knowledge his position gives him—asks for these additional regiments. On what rule shall we determine the propriety of the demand?

Sir, all history concurrently establishes the fact, that when civil governments at home attempt to direct military operations in a foreign country, failure is the result. Upon the generals must fall the responsibility of failure—upon their reports must decisions here, as to means, mainly rely. These come to us through the Executive and War Department.

As to the special order for to-morrow,[6] I will say that the Military Committee have certainly not sought any parliamentary advantage; nor have the senators, with whom I have conversed, any wish or intention to prevent the senator from South Carolina from discussing his resolutions.

I shall be pleased to hear that distinguished senator upon any great question; and certainly do not object to his offering his remarks upon his resolution rather than upon the bill. Nor do I perceive any antagonism between the resolution and the bill. I do not wish to annex the whole of Mexico, or govern it as a province. The President does not look to such end; nor, sir, does the sending of these troops, in my opinion, tend to it. To secure indemnity for the past, is more easy than to attain security for the future. This last object, and to leave behind us a republican government sufficiently stable to maintain treaty obligations, and give us some guaranty for the observance of neutral rights, are objects which I hope to see promoted by this addition to our army.

To me it is easy to concur in the main proposition of the resolutions, and yet insist on the augmentation of our army, and refuse to withdraw our forces.

I shall be pleased, as on other occasions, to hear the senator from South Carolina; but, after his remarks, shall insist on resuming the consideration of the bill now before the Senate;[7] leaving those who may wish to reply, to do so after the public service has been attended to; and when, for one, I shall be more willing to listen attentively to a general discussion.

Washington *Union*, Jan. 5, 1848. When Davis' remarks first appeared in the *Globe* (30:1, 92–93) and *Union* (Jan. 4), "some inaccuracies" were discovered, leading the *Union* to republish his speech "in a corrected form."

¹ Brackets in the original.
² On December 15, 1847, John C. Calhoun introduced two resolutions: first, "that to conquer Mexico, and to hold it either as a province or to incorporate it in the Union, would be inconsistent with the avowed object for which the war has been prosecuted"; second, he proposed that no policy should be adopted which might lead to the conquest of Mexico. He requested an early discussion of his resolutions, duly slated for consideration on January 4. When Cass pressed for debate of the ten-regiment bill on December 30, Calhoun asked more time to study the measure and stated his belief that the committee's "object in calling up his bill at present is . . .

to get a parliamentary advantage—to compel the Senate to discuss this bill before an opportunity is afforded for discussing the resolutions which I have offered" (*Cong. Globe*, 30:1, 26, 54, 78–80, 89).

³ Speaking for early consideration of the ten-regiment bill, James D. Westcott pointed out that American forces in Mexico were scattered in relatively vulnerable detachments among "embittered foes," that they were susceptible to tropical diseases, and that indecision and delay would encourage the enemy to prolong the struggle (ibid., 89–90).

⁴ At the conclusion of Davis' remarks, John J. Crittenden objected to the Mississippian's supposition that "any of the disasters of this war are attributable to the tardy legislation of Congress." Davis reminded Crittenden that an item for camp and garrison equipage had been struck by the House from the quartermaster's estimate when the original volunteer bill was passed in 1846 (ibid., 93).

⁵ Following the Battle of Cerro Gordo (Apr. 17–18, 1847), Santa Anna fled some fifty miles to the southwest, to the town of Orizaba, where he reorganized his army (Bauer, *Mexican War*, 271).

⁶ Calhoun's speech in defense of his resolutions was the special order of the day for January 4; the resolutions were tabled in order that the army bill could be discussed (*Cong. Globe*, 30:1, 96–100).

⁷ On the motion of Ambrose H. Sevier, the ten-regiment bill was made the special order of the day for one o'clock on January 5 (ibid., 93).

Remarks on the Ten-Regiment Bill

Editorial Note: Arguing that Mexico no longer posed a serious threat, John J. Crittenden offered a substitute amendment authorizing the president to call up as many as 30,000 volunteers for three years if needed rather than increasing the regular army by ten new regiments (*Cong. Globe*, 30:1, 111–13).

January 5, 1848

Mr. DAVIS, of Mississippi, then said: It is not my purpose at this time to go into a discussion of the ten-regiment bill, but to address myself especially to the amendment of the Senator from Kentucky. I have been surprised at the introduction of that amendment; I certainly did not expect it.

The gentleman has not anticipated the ground upon which I would oppose the substitution of that amendment for the bill. He seems to rest it on the supposition that we are to oppose the substitution of volunteers for regulars because regulars are better than volunteers. I take no such ground, and fortunately stand in an attitude in which I can have no prejudices for one or the other, having served with both. But, sir, the question lies deeper and far beyond the mere availability of the one over the other. And I would say to the honorable Senator from Kentucky, who has seen service,[1] that if he will revert to the period when he returned from his campaign, and met the aged patriot, who wrung his hand and enquired for his son who had died on the field of battle—when he met the mother who, with tears streaming down her cheeks, put to him the same question, he will at once say, however necessary it may be to call forth the chivalry of the country to fight its battles, let us not send such men, to be wasted in the mere duties of the sentinel, by the attacks of disease and an unfriendly climate, whilst engaged in a service where neither patriotism is elicited, nor glory is to be won. If this country were invaded, I would turn to the great body of the militia—for I use the terms "volunteers" and "militia" as synonymous—for its defence. But when we carry on a foreign war, and especially when defensive operations, merely, are carried on, we have reached a point where regulars are the force which should be employed in the nice routine of the service, in which the duties are not sufficiently important to justify that disruption of society, that injury to the commercial interests of the country, which would result from bringing out men of that high class, which the honorable Senator from Kentucky has correctly said constitutes the great body of the volunteers.[2] There is a great difference in the material of the volunteers and the regular force. There is an enthusiasm that spreads over every neighborhood when the call for volunteers goes forth. When Kentucky is called on to send her regiment, and every county its company, an enthusiasm bursts out everywhere, and the State pours forth its best material—material too good for common use.

The gentleman inquires why it is that we prefer regulars?[3] I will answer: we prefer regulars, first, because they are cheaper; secondly, because they can be maintained in better discipline. They will maintain a better state of police. They will be healthier, and therefore more effective, in proportion to their numbers, for mere garrison duties. As long as you keep the high-bred gentlemen for the battle, they will bear any privation, submit to every restraint, and discharge to the utmost every duty. But do you expect that those men, who have broken all the endearing ties of home in order to fight their country's battles, will sacrifice themselves to the mere duties of the sentinel—will be content with the performance of the police of a garrison? Will they be suited better for the one, or as well for the other, as men of a lower grade in society, and more accustomed to such duties?

But the gentleman has made an argument which I regard as more congenial to his feelings. He has alluded to the gallantry of the army, and the battles won by small forces, affording evidence against the necessity of this increase of our force.[4] But it is one thing to beat the enemy and another to hold him in subjection, and the argument of the honorable Senator, which rests upon the supposition that Mexico is conquered, I hold to be by no means indisputable. Is Mexico conquered? Is any part of it conquered? Conquest, as laid down by some writers, is of three kinds.[5] Ruin is one of these kinds of conquest; but we have not ruined Mexico, and God forbid we ever should. The moral feeling of this country would never justify such a course. Another mode of conquest is, to hold a country by controlling its government. That is not suited to the genius of our country. We send no proconsul abroad—no provincial army to direct the government of the country. We recognize as the great basis of all institutions self-government. The other mode of conquest is by colonizing a country. We cannot do that. In neither of these modes, then, have we conquered Mexico. We have not even suppressed the hostility of the Mexican people. I hazard the assertion, that there is more hostility against us in Mexico now than there was at the beginning of the war. Mexico is not conquered.

But the honorable Senator asks, how will you employ this large force? Not to take cities; not to fight battles. And I agree with him that our army could now march through all South America and defeat every enemy. But we want this force to hold towns and posts in Mexico—to convince the Mexicans that resistance is idle, and beyond all this, to afford protection to all the citizens of Mexico who are ready to recognize our authority and give us supplies. These are some of the great objects to be obtained. To effect them, large bodies of men will be needed. We must garrison our posts with forces adequate to make a sortie, if necessary, and not be shut up when any partisan chief chooses to come and sit down before their gates.

Again, the army of General Scott, which achieved such victories before the city of Mexico, did it at a heavy sacrifice of blood, and that resulted from the want of force. The length of their lines was far inferior to that of the enemy's. Our gallant men fell under the converging fire of the foe, and therefore their blood was spilled like water. American courage, the skill of the officers, and the science of our incomparable staff, achieved those victories, and God forbid that they should ever be tested again at such a fearful sacrifice. But that army in its present state is not combined, whilst there are many posts without a garrison, which we ought to hold.

Then again, the resources of Mexico, must contribute to the support of that army. We cannot afford to keep down anarchy in Mexico at the expense of our treasury. We must not depend on the petty amount of property that might be wrung from the poor rancheros. Such a thing has never been contemplated by our Government, nor practised by our officers. In Zacatecas you can have possession of the mint. In Potosi are the richest mines in Mexico; and if, as has been stated, the annual produce of these mines amounts to nearly twenty-five millions, and we claim the revenue which the Mexican Government extracted from mining operations,[6] and by protecting the entrance of goods into the country, furnish a new source of revenue from the duties on imposts, then we have something to support our armies, without touching private property, and the expenses of the war are borne by Mexico herself.

The object now is, not to prepare to fight a battle, but to prevent a battle. The great object now is, to allow the ability which yet remains in Mexico to establish federal government on republican principles, to exert itself. We have taught Mexico salutary lessons. We have convinced them that they are not what they supposed they were; and I hope it will not excite a laugh when I mention that supposition to have been, that they were the greatest military power on the continent; for it was not until after the battle of Buena Vista that they began to doubt it. Let us now give them an opportunity to create a government somewhat stable, and capable of adhering to its obligations. I reject the idea of taking her Federal Government under our protection as altogether impracticable, and because it would certainly tend to render it odious to the people. Our policy should be directed by the purest reason and most patriotic motives to that end which will hasten a peace and leave Mexico the power to erect again her nationality.

If I believed that this additional force were unnecessary, I should vote against the bill. If I believed that regulars were not better calculated to occupy garrisons, and that the gallantry of our volunteers in the field should decide this question, I would vote against it. But I believe the force to be necessary, and that these regulars are the proper force. The Senator from Kentucky spoke of giving a discretionary power to the President to call out thirty thousand volunteers. Well, I doubt not the wisdom of the Executive—I doubt not his nerve to encounter that responsibility. I would be quite willing to make him responsible, and to rely upon the good feeling, patriotism, and intelligence of the country, to sustain him in calling out these men for the present purpose, and still further for the ultimate object, when the forces may be reduced, of recalling the volunteers, now making sacrifices beyond the duty which they undertook to perform. And at this moment, sir, the honorable Senator from South Carolina, before me, recalls to my mind, appropriately, in this connection, the fact that the regiment which has covered the Palmetto State with laurels and cypress, now numbers only about one hundred and fifty fit for active service.[7] I would recall that regiment at once. I would return its members to their social and commercial duties, and substitute for them a regular regiment, equally able to perform, at all events, the duties they have now to discharge.

I did not rise for the purpose of making any extended remarks, and have been led to say more than I intended. I hope the amendment will not be adopted.[8]

Cong. Globe, 30:1, 114–15.

[1] Crittenden had served as an aide-de-camp in the Kentucky militia in 1813, participating in the Battle of the Thames (Coleman, ed., *Crittenden*, 1: 15).

[2] Crittenden had noted that regulars and volunteers "to some extent consisted, perhaps, of the same materials." It was Lewis Cass, replying to Crittenden, who said that the volunteers "were formed of the very best material our country afforded" (*Cong. Globe*, 30:1, 113, 114).

[3] Crittenden said that volunteers were subject to the same laws as regulars, were equally effective, and felt their obligations as strongly (ibid., 113).

[4] The battles of Buena Vista and those preceding the conquest of Mexico City were cited by Crittenden as evidence that Americans needed a relatively small force to win decisive victories (ibid., 112).

[5] Machiavelli, *The Prince*, ch. 3.

[6] Davis' figure seems inflated. Waddy Thompson, former minister to Mexico, estimated the total production of gold and silver at about \$22–24 million in 1846, and a correspondent of the New Orleans *Commercial Times* reported on December 1, 1847, that the annual yield of the mines in Zacatecas, Guanajuato, and San Luis Potosí together totaled only \$20 million. Mined gold and silver had been taxed by Mexican authorities at the rate of 3 percent; the same rate was

fixed in Winfield Scott's order of December 31, which assessed the various Mexican states to help defray the cost of American military occupation (Thompson, *Recollections*, 204; Washington *Union*, Jan. 11, 26, 1848).

[7] Suffering severe losses at Churubusco in August, the Palmetto Rgt. reportedly had less than one hundred men able to enter Mexico City. So reduced was the unit that several officers returned home in December to recruit replacements, and it was rumored the Carolinians might be recalled upon passage of the ten-regiment bill. Davis' information on regimental strength may have come from Gens. James Shields and John A. Quit-

man, former commanders of the South Carolinians, who had recently arrived in Washington (*Niles' Reg.*, Oct. 2, 1847, 76; Natchez *Courier and Jour.*, Dec. 8, 1847; Washington *Nat. Intell.*, Dec. 28, 1847; *Miss. Free Trader and Natchez Gazette*, Feb. 12, 1848; Moore, "Pvt. Johnson," *S.C. Hist. Mag.*, 67:222, 224).

[8] Crittenden's proposal was defeated 19–26. Davis' speech in opposition was called "one of the most forcible speeches ever delivered in the Senate." Even John C. Calhoun, a staunch critic of the bill, admitted that Davis had presented a "strong view" (*Cong. Globe*, 30:1, 115; New Orleans *Picayune*, Jan. 15, 1848).

To John J. Crittenden

23d Jany. 1848

DR. SIR,

I have just received the enclosed letter from *our* noble boy[1] and would have handed it to you in person if my foot had been only usually troublesome to day, but being unable to put on a shoe without pain I send a servant with it and not even his Father can derive more pleasure than I did from its perusal—Truly yr. friend

JEFFN. DAVIS

ALS (KyLx).

[1] Thomas L. Crittenden's letter has not been found.

From Joseph Henry

Washington Feby 2nd 1848

MY DEAR SIR

I beg that you will pardon me for not having paid my respects to you since your appointment as one of the Regents of the Smithsonian Institution.[1] I was called out of the city soon after your appointment and since my return I have been so much occupied with the duties of my office that I have been unable to command the time for making a number of visits

Please inform me by the Bearer on which evening I may find you disengaged I would be pleased to give you a full account of the plan of organization and of all the proceedings of the Institutions. I have made an engagement for this evening and also one for Saturday evening— Perhaps some evening next week would suit you and would be more convenient for me.[2]— I remain very Respectfully your obt– serv.

JOSEPH HENRY[3]

ALS (Henry Papers, DSI).

[1] Having served on the select committee to establish the Smithsonian in 1845–46, Davis was named regent (trustee) on December 30, 1847, replacing Lewis Cass, who had resigned. Word of Davis' appointment reached Mississippi shortly before the legislature voted on whether to retain him as senator, prompting a family friend to write that the news could only prove beneficial since it "gave the *lie* to another *slander* that he was inimical to the administration." Davis was reappointed regent in 1851 (*Davis Papers*, 2:397; *Cong. Globe*, 30:1, 78; William Laughlin to V. Davis, Jan. 11, 1848, Davis Papers, KyLxT; *Smithsonian*, 1:482).

[2] Davis proposed on February 4 that they meet Monday the seventh "or at any time more convenient to you."

[3] Joseph Henry (1797–1878) was a native New Yorker who joined the Princeton faculty in 1832. His research and publications in physics led to his appointment as first director of the Smithsonian, a post he held from 1846 until his death (*DAB*). Enjoying a warm personal relationship with Davis in the prewar years, Henry wrote in 1861, "I am pleased that Jefferson Davis has been appointed President ... for I put confidence in his talents and integrity" (Henry to Frederick A. P. Barnard, Feb. 23, 1861, Univ. MSS, NNC; Coulson, *Joseph Henry*, 235–36).

Exchange with John Bell on the Ten-Regiment Bill

Editorial Note: In the four weeks preceding this exchange, eleven senators had delivered major speeches on the ten-regiment bill. The twelfth was John Bell of Tennessee. Beginning on February 2, he questioned the goals of the administration in prosecuting the war, the need for the additional regiments, and the possibility of negotiation with the present Mexican government. Continuing his remarks on February 3, Bell mentioned Davis' "argument in favor of regulars" as garrison troops, an argument that supported Bell's contention that the administration planned not to treat with Mexico but "to continue the military occupation of the country" (*Cong. Globe*, 30:1, App., 189–95).

February 3, 1848

Mr. DAVIS, of Mississippi. It is true, as stated by the Senator,[1] that, in the course of this debate, the remarks which I have offered have been to isolated points, such as were supposed to be directly connected with the bill under discussion, and presented as briefly as the nature of the case would allow—so briefly that it appears my meaning has been misconstrued. My observations upon the subject of military posts and the character of troops suited to the service of permanent garrisons were made with no such purpose, under no such idea, as the Senator seems to suppose.

I contended that "regulars" were to be preferred for the reasons then offered, in positions which were to be held by a stationary force, retained in possession for military purposes; not to fix the limit of territorial acquisition, still less to interfere with the political institutions of Mexico. I distinctly declared my opinion that our Government, by the fundamental principles upon which it rests, is forbidden from dictating the policy or interfering in the internal affairs of any other Government. Posts and garrisons are necessary to preserve lines of communication. Extended military lines were spoken of as required to destroy cooperation between the different sections of the enemy, and to prevent the General Government of Mexico, against which this war has been directed, from reëstablishing its power and again concentrating the scattered fragments of its army to renew active hostilities against us. The occupation of these lines recommended itself to me, not as a mode of permanent possession, but as a means to hasten the often-declared object, the much-desired consummation of this war, an honorable peace.

Convinced that regulars were better suited than volunteers to garrison posts, that our volunteers should not be required to remain in service for mere garrison duties longer than necessity demands, and that we require new posts in remote regions, this bill is commended by every consideration which has been conclusively presented to my mind. As a reason for supporting the bill under consideration, I spoke on the occasion referred to by the Senator of a military line[2] which should extend from the Atlantic to the Pacific. I did not then define the line, but will now do so if the Senator wishes. That line, as contemplated by me, would begin at Tampico, ascend the valley of the Panuco to the mountains, then turn northward and follow the range of the Sierra Madre, keeping always the ridge which overlooks the waterless desert to the west and south, pass around the lakes of Parras, cross the valley of Chihuahua, follow the range of mountains which bound it on the west, at about the parallel of thirty degrees north latitude, bear west and pursue the highlands which limit the valley of the Gila cross the Colorado river, and terminate on the Pacific so as to include the harbor of San Diego. This was proposed as a military line. I believed that a vast country north and east of it would be rendered quiet by the occupation of the four practicable passes through the natural barrier along which it runs; that great results would be effected at the least expenditure of means and of men; and that regular troops were most appropriate to the service. My policy, I repeat, was not the permanent occupation of Mexico, but to force from her a peace by every proper means of pressure, and hasten the termination of our general occupation of that country.[3] Again, I will state as my reason for wishing to increase our army so largely, the belief that its visible strength must be such as to destroy in the enemy all hope of resistance before he will seriously incline to peace. Though very unwilling to occupy the time of the distinguished Senator, his pointed reference required me to reply. I desire an early peace, and believe that a Government exists in Mexico which has the ability to treat; that President Herrera,[4] sustained by the new Congress and the new army of Mexico,[5] is competent to suppress factious opposition to negotiation, and under an honorable peace to maintain his Government against revolutionary assault. With such a Government we ought to treat, and I devoutly pray we may treat, even before the honorable Senator shall have concluded his remarks.[6]

Mr. BELL. I unite heartily in the prayer of the Senator that we may have peace. In regard to his remarks, I have only to say that there may have been, as I stated yesterday, a modified policy adopted, and one which would be consistent with the line of the Sierra Madre as the "security" which they want. But I think this is at last a new construction, assumed by the distinguished Senator from Mississippi as one satisfactory to him.

Mr. DAVIS. Assumed last November a year ago.[7]

Cong. Globe, 30:1, App., 195.

[1] John Bell (1797–1869), a Nashville attorney, was elected to the state senate and the House (1827–41) before serving two terms as senator (1847–59). A conservative and slaveholder, Bell was affiliated with the Whig and American parties; in 1860 he was the presidential nominee of the Constitutional Unionists (*DAB*).

[2] Probably referring to Davis' remarks on January 17 (*Cong. Globe*, 30:1, 188).

[3] In March Davis attempted to amend the Treaty of Guadalupe Hidalgo, to include substantial portions of the states of Tamaulipas, Nuevo León, and Chihuahua and all of Coahuila in the territory ceded to the United States (Miller, ed., *Treaties*, 5:251). For a map showing the line he proposed, see Paullin, *Atlas*, Plate 94.

[4] José Joaquín Herrera (1792–1854) served as president of Mexico from December 1844 to December 1845 and again from June 1848 until January 1851. In August 1847 he was appointed a commissioner to negotiate with the United States, although it was assumed by many, including Davis, that he was chief executive at the time (Cotner, *Herrera*, 106–71, 315; New Orleans *Picayune*, Feb. 6, 1848).

[5] By October 1847 Santa Anna had relinquished both military and political control, leaving the Mexican government and army in the hands of leaders disposed to conclude a peace settlement (Cotner, *Herrera*, 163, 166; Smith, *War with Mexico*, 2:235–40).

[6] On February 2 Mexican officials signed the peace treaty at Guadalupe Hidalgo.

[7] See Davis to Robert J. Walker, November 30, 1846.

To Alexander Hamilton, Jr.[1]

Washington 9th Feb. 1848

MY DEAR SIR,

Many thanks for your kind attention, and let me assure you though by constant engagement I have been slow to acknowledge the favor of your correspondence, it is most highly valued.[2] My situation does not permit me to avail myself of the favorable opportunity presented to visit Annapolis, the reason suggested though powerful cannot remove the obstacles official and physical, and the attractions were sufficient without it to create an earnest desire to see under existing circumstances that place of so many and memorable historic associations. We are employed in the senate with long talking about minute points of history, which in a small degree only bear on the question of the Texas boundary, and surely in no practical manner upon the existing war, and the supplies necessary to its prosecution. The present course of Congress is directed to no end, unless to the next presidency, which though the people's business, has too often been the occupation of their Representatives. Nothing has transpired so far as I am informed to change the attitude in which you left us, many leading whigs openly declare that Mr. Clay will not be a candidate but the visible signs portend otherwise.[3] Unconnected with any party of President makers I have very little information on the subject, none beyond that which is generally possessed. Genl. Taylor does not intend to come northward, as you have probably seen by his answer to the Committee of the Missi. Legislature, who invited him to visit our state Capitol.[4]

I have not been able to find the letters of <–y–>our distinguished countryman, your Father, written to Genl. Washington and Maj. McHenry on the extension of territory.[5] An extract of the McHenry letter was published in a speech of Mr. Woodbury and I used it in the senate[6] to answer a position taken by Mr. Miller[7] of N. J. If you could send me these letters it would be esteemed as a great obligation— Your letter to Genl. Taylor was promptly forwarded— Hoping soon to see you and wishing you great happiness and prosperity, I am vy. truly yrs.

JEFFN: DAVIS

ALS (Hamilton Papers, DLC).

[1] Alexander Hamilton, Jr. (1786–1875), born in New York City, was educated at Columbia (1804), served in the War of 1812, and afterwards resided for several years in France. Returning in 1820, he practiced law, was appointed a federal district attorney and land commissioner, and became a New York real estate developer (N.Y. *Times*, Aug. 3, 1875, 4; Hamilton, *Intimate Life*, 217).

[2] Other correspondence between Hamilton and Davis in 1847–48 has not been found.

[3] The Washington *Union* (Feb. 5, 7, 1848) noted that Henry Clay's "stock [was] rising," the result of recent endorsements in Pennsylvania and New York. Although Clay was not declaring his availability, the *Union* believed that no one could mistake "his own wishes or the determination of his friends."

[4] Zachary Taylor had declined the Mississippi legislators' invitation on January 24, 1848, explaining that he considered such a trip improper while on leave of absence from the army (Jackson *Mississippian*, Feb. 4, 1848). The general was also suffering from rheumatism; see his letter of February 16.

[5] Hamilton's letter of June 27, 1799, to his friend, Secretary of War James McHenry (1753–1816), includes the following sentence: "Besides eventual security against invasion, we ought certainly to look to the possession of the Floridas & Louisiana—and we ought to squint at South America" (Hamilton, *Papers*, 23:227; *DAB*, s.v. "McHenry, James"). The letter to Washington has not been located.

[6] Davis refers to Levi Woodbury's remarks on the annexation of Texas, delivered in the Senate on February 17, 1845. In a response to Jacob Miller's speech of February 8, 1848, Davis denied that he would assign soldiers to degrading duty in Mexico and, ac-

cording to the *Globe* reporter, "made some further observations concerning the moderation which marked what had been called progressive Democracy, to show that the fathers of our country had more grasping views than the present Administration" (*Cong.*

Globe, 28:2, App., 237; ibid., 30:1, 321).

[7] Jacob Welsh Miller (1800–62), a Whig attorney from Morristown, New Jersey, served in the state legislature (1832, 1838–40) and in the Senate, 1841–53 (*BDAC*).

From Zachary Taylor

BATON ROUGE, LA., Feb. 16, 1848.

MY DEAR GENERAL: Your very acceptable and interesting letter of the 29th ult.,[1] with its several inclosures, has just reached me, for which, as usual, you have my sincere thanks.

The letter inclosed was from a Dr. Masi, a Mexican of some note, formerly a resident of Victoria, where his family was when we were there last winter, but now living in Matamoras, in relation to detaching Tamaulipas, New Leon and Coahuila from the central government of Mexico, and to set up for themselves under the auspices or protection of the United States;[2] which should have been sent by him to the State Department, for the consideration and action of the government; I will, however, transmit them to the Secretary of War, who can give them such direction or take such action on them as he may think best. I regret to hear there is so much time devoted by members of Congress to President making. I would greatly prefer seeing them attending to their appropriate duties in making such appropriations as were calculated to bring this miserable war with Mexico to an end, as well as passing such laws as were necessary for the good of the country; after which if there was nothing to do, let them adjourn and return to their homes, leaving it to the people to say at the ballot-box who should be their Chief Magistrate after the fourth of March, 1849.

So far as I am personally concerned there are but few individuals in the Union, who take less interest as to who will be the successful candidate for the Presidency at the coming election than myself; and should another receive a majority of the votes of the good people of the country for said office in November next, I should be neither disappointed or mortified at the result, particularly if he is honest, truthful, and patriotic. I observe both the great parties, Democrats and Whigs, intend holding a National Convention at no distant day, to nominate candidates for the two highest offices known to our laws; I trust I shall not be the nominee of either, if it is expected I am exclusively the candidate of their party, and to carry out if elected, their particular views; as I could not accept it under such considerations, but should both, or either, think proper to nominate me without pledges or trammels, other than the Constitution imposes, leaving me free to occupy the ground I have taken, which I cannot recede from, which is to be the President of the nation, and not of a party, I shall not decline the honor; I do not, however, expect anything of the kind, as I am satisfied from present appearances that, so far as the ultra whigs and democrats are concerned, this matter will settle down to a strict party vote and candidates; and the contest will be between the trading politicians, office holders and seekers on both sides, and the people. So far as I am concerned, I shall remain quiet, leaving to the people, in whose hands I consider myself, to drop me, or those who brought me forward for said office, for I am no candidate further than they have made me so, which will give me no concern, for if I go into the White House it would be more from a sense of duty than inclination.

I have read the letters addressed by me in reply to the resolution nominating me for the presidency by two meetings in Pennsylvania, whigs and democrats, which you was so good as to forward in the slip enclosed, nor can I perceive anything in either worthy of notice, or at any rate of animadversion; the individual who took so much pains to bring them so conspicuously before the public by placing them side by side on the same sheet, no doubt thought he had discovered a "mare's nest" and richly deserves having his name placed on record in the Patent Office, for his wonderful inventive powers.[3] I shall be singularly fortunate if nothing more objectionable can be urged against me between this and the first Monday in November next; such attacks give no concern, and they can pass for what they are worth: I regret the course of Mr. Clay and some others,[4] although I do not doubt the purity of their motives as regard the Mexican war; it seems to be now unnecessary to discuss its legality or necessity, or whether or not it could have been avoided; we are now engaged in it, and let us all lay our shoulders to, and pull together until it is brought to a close; for us the sooner the better, in my humble opinion; for unless it is done before a great while, pestilence if not famine may drive us from the country. The ship fever, I learn, is making sad ravages among our people along the line from Vera Cruz to the City of Mexico,[5] particularly at the two ends, and the sooner we can get out of the country the better. I have no fears after what has passed ever to retire or withdraw our troops in a way which would dishonor our country or its flag.

I see nothing to induce me to change my views as to the course we ought to have pursued after the battle of Monterey, for had the same been adopted, we should have saved some thousands of lives and millions of money, which I conceive have been most unnecessarily sacrificed and expended; and I think it a good rule when we are in error, the sooner we get right the better. In all changes and operations which may take place and be carried on for the presidency, I must beg you, my dear General, that you will, without regard to what concerns me, look to your interest; you are young and I hope have many years of prosperity before you, while my days are numbered, or nearly so, by the age allotted to man by his Creator; at any rate my days of ambition have passed away.

I was truly gratified to learn by letter from Major Bliss soon after getting to Washington[6] that he had seen you and that you had greatly improved in health, particularly your wounded foot, which had so much improved; he thought you would soon be able to dispense with your crutch, which was most gratifying intelligence to me, which I hope will soon be realized. I have been for near four weeks and still am confined to the house with something like rheumatism, attended with slight fever, the penalty we sometimes pay for many years exposure in various latitudes, but hope to get about very soon, as I am improving. I have in consequence of said attack done no business since my return, having been only once to my plantation, but hope to do so again very soon, when, if my health will permit, I intend making a short visit to the hurricane.[7]

Information has just reached here from New Orleans that the preliminaries of a treaty, informal of course, had just reached there direct from the city of Mexico on its way to Washington,[8] which had been entered into by Mr. Trist and Gen. Scott, with some of the Mexican authorities, which I flatter myself is the case, and that the terms will prove satisfactory to all concerned.

Mrs. Taylor, who has been quite unwell ever since my return, but is now on the mend, and Betty[9] desires to be most kindly remem-

270

bered to you and wishing you and yours every property and happiness through a long life, I remain truly your friend,

Z. TAYLOR.

Boston *Advertiser*, Oct. 1, 1863. Taken in July 1863 from Davis' library in Hinds County, this letter was sent by a Union soldier to friends in Boston.

[1] Davis' letter and its enclosures have not been found.

[2] In November 1846 "Aelaria de Masa, M.D.," a resident of the Mexican state of Tamaulipas, wrote President Polk "that inhabitants of the Northern Provinces of Mexico were ready to revolt & establish an independant Republic" if the United States would guarantee its existence. Secretary of State James Buchanan urged that such assurances be given, but Polk was unwilling to commit himself and declined to answer Masa's communication (Polk, *Diary*, 2:254–56; John Slidell to Polk, Nov. 4, 1846, Polk Papers, DLC).

[3] The two letters referred to were dated August 2 and 3, 1847, wherein Taylor commented on the proceedings of a Democratic meeting in Harrisburg and a Whig rally in Philadelphia. Although the clipping Davis sent has not been found, the device Taylor describes—placing his political statements "side by side on the same sheet" to show contradictions—was used later in the 1848 campaign (see, for example, Washington *Union*, Oct.

6, 1848). *Niles' Register* had placed notice of the two letters in tandem on October 23, 1847.

[4] Undoubtedly a reference to Henry Clay's resolutions on the Mexican War (Nov. 13, 1847) and the recent speeches in Congress on the ten-regiment bill and the possibility of annexing all of Mexico.

[5] Ship fever (typhus) was rampant in New Orleans, but the greater threat to Winfield Scott's army in Mexico seemed to be typhoid (New Orleans *Picayune*, Feb. 11, 13, 15, 1848; Smith and Judah, eds., *Chron. of the Gringos*, 328, 330, 364–65, 497).

[6] Taylor's aide William W. S. Bliss was in Washington from January 18 until January 23, 1848 (Washington *Nat. Intell.*, Jan. 21, 1848; N.Y. *Tribune*, Jan. 25, 1848).

[7] Taylor had checked on conditions at his Mississippi plantation in mid-December. Returning there in March, he also traveled upriver for a brief visit to Hurricane, home of Davis' brother Joseph (Taylor to Joseph P. Taylor, Mar. 10, 1848, Taylor Papers, DLC; Taylor to Davis, Apr. 20, 1848).

[8] Confirmation that the treaty had been signed first appeared in the New Orleans *Delta* on February 15, 1848.

[9] Taylor's daughter Mary Elizabeth.

To Francis A. Wolff

Washington. 23d Feb, 1848

MY DEAR FRIEND,

I have verry often thought of you since we parted; and regretted that I did not see you again after our brief interview in New Orleans. It gave me great pleasure to hear from you, and to learn of your improved health;[1] and /the/ well merited support your neighbors have given to your claims in public estimation.[2] The incident you mention is wholly forgotten by me, I wish it were so by you, and yet I should then have lost the gratification it gives me to feel /that/ my comrade in privation and danger remembers my infirmities only to forgive them.[3]

Accept my thanks for the compliment you paid me in giving my name to your nephew. I hope some day to see him and to fulfil the obligation of the time honored custom.[4] By this mail I will send to your address a copy of the new edition of the Constitution[5] for the young gentleman. it[6] will be his first book I suppose, and one which I hope he will study early and well; that in after life, should the sacred compact of our Union be even less respected than now, he will stand its able and devoted champion, perhaps in high places to administer it & thro life to feel for it the reverence which impressed on childhood, age seldom obliterates

X X X X X X[7]

As ever, your friend

JEFF'N DAVIS

L, copy by Wolff (La. Hist. Assn.–Davis Coll., LNT). Enclosed: Wolff to William T. Walthall, May 15, 1879 (ibid.).

[1] Wolff, a sgt. in the 1st Miss. Rgt., was wounded in the chest at Monterrey and discharged in November 1846 (Holly Springs *Gazette*, Dec. 12, 1846; DNA, M-863, roll 3). His letter to Davis has not been found.

[2] Wolff may have been elected to a county office in November 1847; complete returns for Tippah are unavailable.

[3] Wolff recalled in 1879 that when Davis first went to the Senate Wolff had written him, reminding his former commander of a wartime incident: "The day before we reached Walnut Springs near Monterey . . . I had the honor of leading a pioneering party. Our principal work was to set large stones across the brooks for the infantry to cross over dry shod. The head of the column was pressing us closely. Col. Davis galloped up & reproved me harshly" (Wolff to William T. Walthall, May 15, 1879, La. Hist. Assn.–Davis Coll., LNT).

[4] According to Wolff, Davis owed his namesake a coat (ibid.).

[5] Several thousand copies of a new edition of the Constitution, "with an alphabetical analysis, prepared and published by W. Hickey," were ordered purchased for the use of the Senate in February 1847 (*Cong. Globe*, 30:1, 623).

[6] Marked for capitalization, undoubtedly added later.

[7] Apparently an indication of omitted material.

From Ferdinand L. Claiborne

Natchez Feb 27th. 1848

DEAR SIR:

I beleive the appointment of *Collector* of the Port of Natchez will expire in a few months— *John*. D. Elliot Esqr. is the present, incumbent— I have heard that charges of some character will be preferd agaist him, & that an effort is to be made, to induce the President to send in another name to the Senate for the office of Collector[1]—

Now Sir, if this turns out to be true & if the Mississippi Delegation in Congress determi[ne][2] to refuse their support to Mr Elliot may I ask you to get me the appointment.

Understand me distinctly, I make *no* charges against Mr Elliot. I would scorn to get station by injuring any man— If he is a faithful & honest officer & posseses your confidence, let me beg you to *retain* him over all others, but only in event of a change being determined on, I ask your aid — — If Congress passes an appropriation to erect a Custom House at Natchez[3] Govenor Brown has promised to use his exertions to get for me any appointment that might grow out of it— The appointment I ask for, if the contingency arrives, is very small— Local in its nature & yeilding a sallay of only $500 Yet this sum would assist in the Education of a large family[4]—

As far as I know Mr Elliot is worthy of the office— I know he is a good Democrat— This is my opinin— Others may be able to show otherwise— I for one would regret his removal & more so, if there was cause for it— In relation to the Hospital at Natchez, I trust you will succeed in getting the appropriation, as the memorials that are before [Con][5]gress will fully justify the measure[6]—

I am known to all our Delegation— on terms of friendship with all save Mr Featherston,[7] to whom I am a stranger— Do me the kindness to show this Letter to our members & if you feel warranted from your knowledge of me, you will speak favourable to Mr Featherston in my behalf—

I ask not for these small appointments on account of services to the Democratic Party— If I have rendered services, it was no more than my duty as a good citizen, who beleved our Principles best adapted to secure the hapiness & glory of the county— — I not only ask you to show this Letter to our Delegation, but to the Secraty of the Treasury— — When Gov Poindexter[8] assailed Mr Walker many years ago, my Brother, now deceased, was the first man in the state to defend his reputation & in a series of Resolutions at a Meeting, in Madison County, was the first to propose his name for United States Sennator[9]—

On a Recent occasion, when his official & private character was violently attacked, I was the first of his old friends to come to the rescue— I got up a large meeting in Natch[ez]— Challenged all his enemyes & he has many here, to join issue with me— In this Hot bed of Whiggery I offered the resolution annexed— carried it by acclamation & it was published in evey City and Village in the united States as the vindication of his character by *those who knew him best*[10]— I want Mr Walker to Know plainly that I ask his aid, if he can conciencuosly give it & I have requested his perusal of this letter, that he may know, I am no sycophant, but simply ask a reciprocity of favours— I would not have the smallest favour as a boon— But am always grateful for the assistance of friends—

I speak frankly when I say that all your Democratic constituents sustain the course of our Congre[ssio]nal Delegation, except that of Hon Patrick Thompkins[11]—

Our State is thoroughly Democratic— So is Louissiana— If Gen Taylor could or would <-[illegible]-> /advocate/ & proclaim Democratic Principles, we would all rally around the old chieftain to

The same enthiusiam that characterized our support of Gen Jackson, would mark our devotion to Gen Taylor— But as his Principles are not known he will fail to receive the support *even* of a fragment of the Party in this State— of one thing you may rest convinced— that the nominee [of][12] the Democratic Convention, will get a larger vote in this State than President Polk received[13]— I Know of no Man, who has been seduced into the Whig or Taylor rank[s?]

I may be deceved, but venture to declare that the future will prove true, as I have sai[d]

Apologzing for the liberty I have take[n] & offering my services in any way & any time to seve you, I am with high regard yours Truly

F. L. CLAIBORNE[14]

Extract from the Washington. Union.[15]

ALS, photocopy (DNA, RG200, Walker Papers).

1 John D. Elliott had held the collectorship since 1844. The charges leveled against him in 1848 had to do with a case of trespassing on public lands, which occurred while Elliott was acting as assistant timber agent under the supervision of Claiborne's brother John. No disciplinary action was taken, and in May 1848 Elliott was reappointed, serving until August 1849. On February 22, 1848, Davis and two other Mississippians recommended Natchez attorney James B. Haggin for Elliott's position, should a vacancy occur. Learning that Haggin had been suggested, Ferdinand Claiborne later withdrew his own application (*Davis Papers*, 2:94–95; Claiborne to Davis, Mar. 11, Davis to Walker, June 17, Walker to Davis, June 21, 1848; John F. H. Claiborne to Joseph Smith, July 29, 1847, DNA, RG45, Letters from Timber Agents; see also Davis to John Y. Mason, July [25], 1848).

2 Ink blot.

3 Despite its location and the amount of commercial business transacted there, Natchez was not selected as the site for a federal customhouse.

4 By September 1850 Claiborne and his wife had eight children (1850 Census, Miss., Adams, family 15).

5 Until otherwise noted, square brackets indicate manuscript damage.

6 Beginning in 1806 Congress had received several memorials on the subject of the Natchez hospital; in 1837 a ten-acre site was purchased. When the Thirtieth Congress convened, the *Mississippi Free Trader* (Dec. 11, 1847) editorialized on the need ·for such a facility, noting that Davis and Albert G. Brown "have both warmly entered into the wishes and wants of Natchez in respect to the hospital." Appropriations were provided, 1848–51, and the building was virtually complete by June 1852, when custody was transferred to the local customs

collector (U.S. Cong., *American State Papers, Class IV, Commerce,* 1:667; *Senate Doc. 90,* 17:1; ibid., *33,* 17:2; ibid., *137,* 24:2; *House Rep. 745,* 27:2, 4–6; *House Ex. Doc. 1,* 32:2, Pt. 2:228; *Cong. Globe,* 30:1, xlvii; for Davis' actions in the Twenty-ninth Congress, see *Davis Papers,* 2:612–14).

7 Winfield Scott Featherston (1820–91), born in Tennessee, served as a Democratic congressman from Houston, Mississippi (1847–51). Col., 17th Miss. Inf., and subsequently promoted brig. gen. (1862), he practiced law in Holly Springs after the war, served in the state legislature, and was a leader in the overthrow of Republican governor Adelbert Ames (*DAB*; Warner, *Gens. in Gray*).

8 George Poindexter (1770–1853), a native of Virginia, settled in Natchez in 1802. A member of the territorial assembly, congressman, and district judge, he played an important role in drafting the first state constitution (1817). After serving another term in Congress, he was elected governor (1820–21) and was appointed to the Senate in 1830 (*DAB*).

9 In the summer of 1834 Senator George Poindexter charged Samuel Gwin and, by implication, Walker with misconduct in the Chocchuma land sales. As a result of the bitter public controversy that followed, Poindexter lost his Senate seat to Walker in 1835. At a public dinner in Walker's honor, held at Madisonville on September 11, 1834, Osmun Claiborne offered several "spirited resolutions" favoring the course of the Andrew Jackson administration and disapproving Poindexter's actions. Despite Ferdinand Claiborne's assertion, Walker credited John H. Mallory with being the "first man who publicly proposed me for the Senate" (Miles, *Jacksonian Democracy,* 94–111; Jackson *Mississippian,* Sept. 12, 19, 1834, Oct. 2, 1835; Stanard, "Abstracts," *Va. Mag. Hist. and Biog.,* 1:324).

10 Criticized by the Whigs since the

adoption of the independent treasury bill and passage of the tariff of 1846, Robert J. Walker was vilified in April and May 1847 for his part in the regulations concerning collection of duties in Mexican ports and for what some viewed as misconduct in the handling of an $18 million federal loan. Claiborne's resolution in defense of Walker was offered on May 6, 1847, at a routine Democratic meeting in Natchez. It was reprinted in the Washington *Union* on May 27 (Washington *Nat. Intell.*, Apr. 3, 5, 10, 14, 22, 1847; *Miss. Free Trader and Natchez Gazette*, May 1, 4, 8, 1847; Jackson *Southron*, May 14, 1847).

11 Mississippi Whig congressman Patrick W. Tompkins was severely criticized for his abstention during the vote for Speaker, which Democrats felt had contributed to the election of Robert C. Winthrop, an "ultra Wilmot Proviso man." After Tompkins subsequently denounced the president for his refusal to release some confidential instructions to John Slidell, the Vicksburg *Sentinel* scoffed that, while Tompkins' chief opponent in the debate had been serving in the war, Tompkins had remained at home "studying the honeyfuggling speeches with which he wormed himself into his seat" (Vicksburg *Weekly Sentinel*,

Dec. 22, 29, 1847, Jan. 5, Feb. 9, 16, 1848; *Cong. Globe*, 30:1, 202–205).

12 Hereafter square brackets indicate that the right margin is cropped.

13 Polk received 25,126 votes in 1844, nearly 6,000 more than Henry Clay. In 1848 Lewis Cass narrowly won Mississippi, receiving 26,537 votes to Taylor's 25,992 (*Miss. Official Reg., 1908*, 246).

14 Ferdinand Leigh Claiborne, younger brother of John F. H. Claiborne, was born about 1811 in Natchez, where he was active in Democratic politics and local affairs. In 1855 he settled on a plantation in Pointe Coupee Parish, Louisiana. Elected several times to the state legislature, he was also a member of the 1879 constitutional convention (Menn, *Large Slaveholders*, 316; *Biog. and Hist. Memoirs of La.*, 1:349; Natchez *Courier and Jour.*, May 12, 1847; Washington *Union*, July 8, 1848; Claiborne to Davis, June 8, 1853, Misc. MSS—Davis, NHi; Rawson, "Party Politics," 165–66, 242–43).

15 In the margin. Clipping headed "Hon. Robert J. Walker," from the *Union* of May 27, 1847, is attached to the bottom of the page. The words "Washington Union," in Claiborne's hand, are repeated at the lower edge of the clipping.

To Linn Boyd

WASHINGTON CITY, March 16, 1848.

DEAR SIR: We are just informed of your unanimous nomination by the democratic convention of Kentucky, as their gubernatorial candidate at the approaching election.

We bear cheerful evidence of the well-founded confidence which this act of your friends in Kentucky manifests, but at the same time would express our deep regret that any circumstances should impose upon you the necessity of vacating your seat in the House of Representatives at this critical and important crisis.

The fact (with which you are familiar) of the nearly equally balanced state of parties in the House[1]—the important questions of national interest which must be passed upon by the present Congress, in connexion with the existing war; upon the proper and judicious decision of which so much depends, apart from the no less imposing consideration of your long experience and intimate acquaintance with these subjects—demand, in our estimation, that you should not adopt, in relation to this matter, any course which will require you to vacate your seat during the present session of Congress.[2]

Our apology for thus obtruding these opinions upon your consideration, is to be found in our anxious desire to promote, as far as our present position in Congress will enable us to do it, the great principles of democratic faith, so immediately identified with the permanent prosperity of our country; and the success of which might be greatly endangered by your withdrawal from Congress at this time, when a single vote might determine the most important issue. We are, very respectfully, your obedient servants, [. . .][3]

JEFFERSON DAVIS,

Washington *Union*, Mar. 17, 1848.

[1] Whigs outnumbered Democrats in the House 115 to 108; 4 representatives were affiliated with neither major party (*U.S. Hist. Statistics*, 1083).

[2] Boyd had been informed of his nomination by telegraph on March 16; almost immediately he declined the nomination. Replacing him on the ticket was Lazarus W. Powell, who lost the August election to John J. Crittenden (Washington *Union*, Mar. 17, 1848; Collins, *Hist. of Ky.*, 1:57).

[3] Signing with Davis were nine other senators and fifty-three congressmen.

Exchange with John C. Calhoun on the Ten-Regiment Bill

Editorial Note: Since Davis' last speech on the ten-regiment bill, he had exchanged remarks with Jacob W. Miller (Feb. 8) and had heard sixteen other senators address the question. His exchange with Calhoun, prompted by the latter's March 16 speech as well as by comments on March 17 by Henry Johnson, Daniel Webster, and Lewis Cass, was lauded by the Jackson *Mississippian* (Apr. 7, 1848) for its "lofty independence" from Calhoun's position.

March 17, 1848

Mr. DAVIS, of Mississippi. The Senator from Louisiana [Mr.

JOHNSON[1]][2] has expressed his conviction of the certainty of an immediate peace, and on that he based his argument in presenting his motion to recommit the bill, with instructions.[3] I have just received a letter from Mexico, which certainly does not encourage me in the prospect of peace. This letter states that the road from Vera Cruz to Mexico is infested by guerilleros, and that a party for Orizaba had been attacked by them, and been compelled to return to Vera Cruz. Though reported that the Mexicans had been dispersed, yet the American party left their dead on the field, and all their property fell into the hands of the guerilleros. Those reports which we have had of Santa Anna asking his passports, and leaving the country, are all pretext. Instead of leaving the country, it is said that he is now recruiting his forces, and looks to future operations. Perhaps he is raising nothing more than an escort—but peace is not his object.[4] I beg to say to the honorable Senator from South Carolina, that that party in Mexico to which he alludes, as being neither unfriendly nor inimical to us, is the party on which Santa Anna is falling back for support in his hostile movements—the party of Puros, which invited him to return to Mexico, as the enemy of monarchical government,[5] in order to overthrow Paredes.[6]

I cannot, for myself, approve of any such policy as that spoken of by the Senator from South Carolina, nor can I at all conceive why he should regard the raising this additional force in the light of mere braggadocio.[7] We propose to raise it for the moral effect which it may produce on Mexico. We may with great propriety pass this bill in order to give Mexico to understand that if she do not give us peace willingly, we will coerce a peace. But that gallant army which has performed so many glorious deeds is rapidly wasting away. The yellow fever has appeared in Vera Cruz, and our troops are dying in the interior of other diseases. The volunteers are becoming daily more and more dissatisfied with the service; and, in my opinion, the spirit of the contract under which they entered the service justifies their discharge as soon as active hostilities cease. They entered for the war, but they believed that on the cessation of active hostilities they would be discharged. Already the question is mooted whether, if there can be war without a declaration of war, there may not be peace without a treaty.

But the honorable Senator from South Carolina not only directs his attention to the present measure, which he reprobates as mere braggadocio, but this goes back to an old subject—the removal of the army to the banks of the Rio Grande. He says:

> "The whole affair is in our own hands. Whether the treaty fails or not, we still have the complete control, if we act with wisdom and firmness, and avoid, what I detest above all things, a system of menace or bravado, in the management of our negotiation. I had hoped that that system had been abandoned forever. It nearly involved us in a war with England about Oregon. It was only prevented by the wisdom and firmness of this body. It was resorted to in our negotiations with Mexico, and the march of the army under General Taylor to the Rio Grande, was but intended to sustain it. Unfortunately, the circumstances prevented the Senate from interposing as in the case of Oregon, and this war was the consequence."[8]

Now the President has clearly the right to move the army of the United States into any portion of its territory.

Mr. CALHOUN (in his seat.) Certainly not into disputed territory.

Mr. DAVIS. The Senator says that the President has not the right to move the army into any disputed territory. When we annexed Texas, we left this boundary question open for negotiation. The Administration sought assiduously to settle the question by negotiation. What, then, is the argument of the Senator? When the opposite party refuse to settle the question by negotiation, are we to be estopped? Are we to allow the enemy to wrest from us the dominion which we claim as ours of right? If so, what is this but a broad invitation to every land to dispute the boundary with us? But I would ask the honorable Senator, how comes it, that even before the annexation of Texas, the navy of the United States was ordered to the Gulf of Mexico for the protection of Texas?

Mr. CALHOUN. The answer is obvious. The Gulf of Mexico is the common property of all nations. It is not disputed. But though we had a right to lay off Vera Cruz, we had not the right to enter the harbor of Vera Cruz.

Mr. DAVIS. Was it not the gentleman's own order to make a naval demonstration against Vera Cruz.[9]

Mr. CALHOUN. I have no knowledge of such an order. Will the Senator permit me to notice another point? He indicated that the President had a right to march the army into any disputed territory. Am I right?

Mr. DAVIS. I do not consider it disputed territory.

[Calhoun, though admitting that there was disputed territory, asserts that the president had acted without authority in ordering Zachary Taylor from Corpus Christi to the Rio Grande. He adds references to boundary disputes during the administrations of Washington and Tyler in which neither president "dreamt of attacking . . . without authority of Congress."]

Mr. WESTCOTT. I beg to remind the Senator that Mr. Jefferson and Mr. Madison seized upon the country west of the Mississippi.

Mr. CALHOUN. Oh! that was a trifling case. You could cover the whole country with a blanket!

Mr. DAVIS. I repeat, that I cannot perceive on what grounds the Senator will justify the order sending the navy to the Gulf of Mexico, whilst we were negotiating the annexation of Texas, and yet deny that after annexation was completed——

Mr. CALHOUN. They were issued when Congress was in session. If any attack had been necessary, application would have been made to Congress for authority.

Mr. DAVIS. The whole case is matter of record; and we know as well as the actors in it, that our navy did stand off and on the coast, looking into Mexican harbors, to keep our Government advised of any hostile movements, and be prepared to act, if necessary, for the protection of Texas. For the like purpose, a large portion of our army was concentrated upon the border, and put in correspondence with the President of Texas. The Senator from South Carolina, then Secretary of State, communicated to the Texan Government this disposition of our land and naval forces, and announced it to be the purpose of the President, as a duty under the then existing circumstances, to use all his constitutional power to protect Texas from foreign invasion.[10] If the whole power to grant the protection thus offered, consisted in asking for authority by an act of Congress, it was a promise likely to be filled with hope deferred. In view of the delays which would probably have attended the passage of such an act, what justification can there be for so early a movement of the army and navy to the immediate proximity of anticipated operations. Does the Senator deny the power of the President to order the army into any part of the United States?

Mr. CALHOUN. He has no right to order it into disputed territory.

Mr. DAVIS. What! shall a foreign Power dispute our territorial limits—refuse to settle the boundary by negotiation—seize, by force, territory rightfully ours, and our Executive stand powerless by and see the enemy gain the advantage of occupying all the commanding positions of the country. This would be an alluring invitation to every coterminous Power to select their opportunity and dispute our boundary. At another time, during the recess of Congress, according to the Senator's general position, the territory thus disputed could be seized with entire safety. Upon the question of the northeastern boundary, to which the Senator alluded, my recollections are different from his. I think by both the Committee on Military Affairs and by the Committee on Foreign Relations reports were made at the time, recognizing the power of the Executive to use the military force of the country—to call out the militia—to protect the territory claimed by Maine from hostile invasion, or an attempt by military force to exercise exclusive jurisdiction within the disputed territory.[11] But I was about to say, when I yielded to the honorable Senator, that after Texas became a part of the American Union, and we failed by negotiation to adjust the boundary with Mexico, the question became closed against us, and the United States had no other mode by which to determine the territory of Texas, than by reference to her limits, as defined before annexation to the United States; all which having been asserted and maintained, we were bound to insist on and defend from forcible seizure. By annexation, Texas lost the power to negotiate or to carry on the war; and co-extensive with this surrender were the obligations imposed upon the United States. The President did what every man of patriotic impulses will say he should have done—afford to Texas that protection which a State had the right to demand; and in ordering the army to the Rio Grande, he did no more than might have been done in the case of the northeastern boundary, when that was an open question. But the Senator has laid down the position that this was done to intimidate Mexico. Not so. Our army was encamped at Corpus Christi, which had been made a port of entry. Was that, then, in the disputed territory? Where was the disputed territory? Mexico claimed up to the Sabine. She has continued to assert that claim; and any intermediate line between the Sabine and the Rio Grande, is of our suggestion, and not of Mexican origin. When, at a recent period, Santa Anna returned to Mexico, he promised to restore the severed territory of Texas, and to gather laurels on the banks of the Sabine, and lay them at the feet of the Supreme Government.[12] A right to the whole of Texas, a determination to restore it to Mexico, has, by her soldiers and her statesmen, been uniformly asserted—adhered to with the pertinacity characteristic of the Spanish race. The whole of Texas, then, was included in this disputed territory, and if the President had no right to march the army to the Rio Grande, he had no right to order it across the Sabine. Mexico claimed the whole of Texas. In the controversy on the part of Mexico the question was not whether the Nueces or the Rio Grande was the boundary, but whether Texas was a part of the United States or not. Upon the part of the United States that question was closed, forever closed. Before her army was ordered into the territory of Texas, nothing was open but the adjustment of boundary. This was sought by negotiation with Mexico, and our advances were insultingly repelled. That the boundary of revolutionary Texas was the Rio Grande—at least the lower part of that river—has been too often and too conclusively demonstrated to require more than a passing notice. Without adverting to the mass of evidence which has been presented here on other occasions, I will refer only to that on which I mainly rely. After the battle of San Jacinto, and when Santa Anna was a prisoner in the hands of the Texans, General Filisola, commanding the Mexican army, wrote to his Government, communicating the fact of President Santa Anna's capture, and giving the saddest account of the condition of the troops under his command. The President *ad interim* replied, and gave the General authority to do whatever should be necessary to procure the release of the captive President, and to save his troops and munitions of war.[13] These results were obtained by treaty. General Filisola was one of the parties to that treaty, and the consideration given to Texas for the vast benefits thus secured was the recognition of the Rio Grande as a boundary, and the immediate withdrawal of all Mexican troops beyond it. It is true this treaty was never formally ratified by Mexico,[14] but having obtained the full benefit of all its stipulations, I submit whether the moral obligation was not complete henceforth and forever to recognize the Rio Grande as the true boundary. That is the only argument on which I have ever found it necessary to rest this point.

Not being a lawyer, I will not attempt to discuss a legal question with the eminent jurist on the other side of the Chamber, [Mr.

WEBSTER,]² but cannot forbear from expressing my surprise at the view which he, in connection with the distinguished Senator on this side of the Chamber, [Mr. CALHOUN,]² takes of the legitimate rights of our army when invading a foreign country.¹⁵ They would restrain our army from the moment it enters a hostile country, so as to prevent it from availing itself of any of the public funds—they would restrict it to such contributions as they might wring from the citizens. Now, one of the evidences of the advancement of civilization in the conduct of war has been seen in that very procedure on the part of an army which these distinguished Senators condemn. Instead of wringing from poverty, from the agricultural citizen, the means of maintenance, our army have seized only upon the public resources of the country, and have thus illustrated the intelligence, the chivalry, and humanity of the American people.

The Senators contend that legislation is necessary to appropriate the public revenues of Mexico to the maintenance of our army, whilst they admit the right to seize private property for its use. Sir, I had thought our war was waged against the general government of Mexico, and that our policy was as far as possible to relieve the peaceful population from the ordinary sufferings of war. Sir, I am at a loss to conceive how we could properly legislate upon a country which had not been conquered—for a people in open war against us—or how the laws, if enacted, could be properly executed under such circumstances. The foreign government must have been displaced by our arms, before there was space for our legislative and judicial departments to flow in; and the roar of those arms must have been hushed, before the voice of the lawgiver could be heard. The Constitution of the United States makes provision for the organization and maintenance of our army and navy, and for calling out the militia by legislative enactments. It makes the President the commander-in-chief of the army and navy, and the militia, when called into service. Congress declared that war existed. It passed laws for raising men and money. The President, as commander-in-chief, assumed the command of the army; and, as has been stated by the Senator from Michigan, from that moment all the rights which appertain to a state of war, attached to the army. The exercise of legislative rights only follows when Congress takes possession of a conquered country. Up to that point nothing but the power of the Executive department flows in. The power belongs not to the President merely, but to the Executive department; and, without orders from the President, every officer in the army could exercise it. The right is conferred by war, and the only difference between the action of our army and that of any other, has consisted in this, that ours has demanded less, and taken nothing by force. It has not committed pillage. The government opposed to us has been deprived of power, and the resources by which it was sustained naturally flowed to the army which took the country and people in charge. In laying duties—in collecting taxes, they have collected but a portion of the revenue which would have flowed to the Mexican Government if it had not been displaced by our arms. Both could not exist together. Such is the plain, common sense view of the matter. The legal view I must leave to others. The honorable Senator from South Carolina fears that if the President exercise this power, immense abuses may follow—that armies may be raised, and treaties may be made with other countries; and that, he says, would be in violation of the Constitution of the United States.[16] The Constitution of the United States is a temple, gradually extending itself, and covering acre after acre, State after State, spanning rivers and mountains, but not yet gone to foreign lands. It is still limited to the United States. It cannot be violated in Mexico. It does not extend to Mexico, and God forbid it ever should! It is the Constitution of our own Union and our own people, and none but territory annexed to our Union can claim to be under that Constitution. If the President has violated the Constitution, in the progress of this war, you must prove that he has failed to comply with the law which declared the war and authorized him to prosecute it, giving him men and money for that purpose. Until that be shown, the President cannot have violated any provision of the Constitution in Mexico.

But the main purpose for which I rose, sir, was to speak of the effect of the passage of this bill in Mexico. We had information from a special agent sent to Mexico in 1844 that he had commenced preliminaries, and had the prospect of a settlement by negotiation, of all the difficulties then pending. On the fourth day after the negotiation had been opened, two celebrated letters published in that year reached Mexico. One dated at Raleigh, and the other at Lindenwold.[17] On the arrival of these letters, forwarded, it is said by the Mexican minister at Washington City, the negotiation was immediately suspended. Again, Mexico probably intended to enter into a negotiation for the settlement of the questions then in dispute, when Mr. Black received intimation, in the terms so often referred to here, of a willingness on the part of Mexico to receive a commissioner;[18] though I think that there has been altogether a misunderstanding of the language in which the note was written. *Commissionado* was the term employed, meaning one commissioned, empowered to settle the question in dispute. Now, they may have meant no other questions than those growing out of the annexation of Texas; but, as the Senator from Michigan remarked, they sought refuge in the subterfuge of the distinction between the terms "minister" and "commissioner," and thus evaded the obligation of the contract into which they had voluntarily entered.[19] And why? Because, at that time a controversy had arisen with regard to the boundary in Oregon. The Mexicans then cherished the hope that there would be war between this country and England, and that, with the latter as an ally, they would be able to regain Texas. The old hope was thus revived. They refused to enter into negotiations. And now, if they have their hopes revived again with the prospect of a refusal here to supply men and money to prosecute the war, they will again reject negotiations in the expectation that a new administration may come into power in the United States more favorable to them. If we change the policy which we have heretofore pursued, there can be no doubt they will refuse to ratify the treaty.

In our intercourse with Mexico, if we have erred, it has been in undue consideration and misplaced leniency. For a long term of years we have borne national insult, and left unredressed the personal outrages and pecuniary injuries done to our citizens by Mexico. We have passed unnoticed the offences repeatedly offered in their official correspondence; it was the strong rendered patient, with the captiousness of the weak, by the consciousness of his ability to punish. This course, so long observed by our Government, has surely not been departed from by the present Administration.

I cannot conceive, sir, how the President could have exhibited greater forbearance towards Mexico. He sent out a minister[20] to treat with her on the first intimation of any desire on her part to enter into a negotiation for the purpose of restoring amicable relations. Acting in the forbearing and friendly spirit of the power, who had taken that infant republic by the hand when it first essayed to walk, we studiously avoided collision. Collision, however, from the causes to which I have alluded, became at last inevitable. Yet it is gravely asserted, that the President had determined to extend the territory of the United States to the Rio Grande, "peaceably if he could, forcibly if he must;"[21] most certainly not to extend the territory of the United States, but to settle the question of boundary; and had we been the aggressive party, as it has been alleged—had we been reckless of the feelings, rights, and interests of Mexico, we certainly never should have incorporated a provision in the terms of annexation, securing to us the right of settling the limits of Texas—that was done to guard against the possibility of a collision with Mexico; we did not adopt the extreme claims of Texas, but reserved to ourselves the right to settle the question of boundary. Nothing could have been done more indicative of the friendly spirit which we entertained towards Mexico.

At this late hour, I certainly shall not attempt to enlarge; but I must take occasion to say, that I do not think that Mexico is about to cede any territory to the United States; I think that we are about to retrocede territory to Mexico. I hold that in a just war we conquered a larger portion of Mexico, and that to it we have a title which has been regarded as valid ever since man existed in a social condition—the title of conquest. It seems to me that the question now is, how much we shall keep, how much we shall give up, and that Mexico cedes nothing.

Mr. WEBSTER was understood to inquire if that view was in accordance with the terms of the paper?

Mr. DAVIS. I have seen papers in English and Spanish, and I think in none was the term cede employed. As a moralist I would not undertake to defend the seizure of country from the inhabitants, but the question was settled long before the oldest member of the Senate entered it. These very Mexican people settled it when they conquered the ancient Aztecs. If they had the right to take the territory from that people, who did not cultivate it, the argument is equally good against them now. They produce little to that which the country is capable of yielding; and year by year the amount is steadily decreasing. The country is going to waste, villages are depopulated, fields once highly productive in all that nature in her bounty yielded to the industry of man, now lie uncultivated, and marked only by the remains of the irrigatory ditches by which they were formerly watered. The exuberant wealth of Mexico once flowed out to sustain the American colonies of Spain—the governments of Louisiana and Florida received contributions from her. Turn, now, and contemplate the change which the difference of government has wrought, and tell me whether all the arguments of utilitarianism and of humanity may not now be more successfully applied to the Mexican than by them against the Aztec population.

The Senator says this war is "odious."[22] Odious! Odious for what? On account of the skill and gallantry with which it has been conducted? Or is it because of the humanity, the morality, the magnanimous clemency which has marked its execution? Odious! Why, in any newspaper which I take up, I find notices of large assemblages of the people gathered together to do honor to the remains of some dead soldier brought back from Mexico; or around the festive board to greet the return of some gallant member of the army. The conductors of the press, without distinction of party, express the highest approbation of the conduct of the army. Where is the odium? What portion of our population is infected with it? From what cause does it arise? It cannot be on account of the origin of the war, the extraordinary unanimity with which it was declared by both Houses of Congress, the eagerness with which our citizens pressed to the service, forbid that conclusion. A long and unbroken succession of victories has satiated the public appetite for military triumph. There may be a surfeit, for more has been offered than needed for a feast. An over anxiety for immediate peace is the natural result; with this I sympathize; beyond this I am not prepared to believe the popular feeling of the country extends.

We have cause to be proud of the record this war will leave behind it—a monument more lasting than brass. We, the actors of today, must soon crumble to dust; the institutions we now maintain, and hope will be perpetual, may pass away; the Republic may sink in the ocean of time, and the tide of human events roll unbroken over its grave; but the events of this war will live in the history of our country and our race, affording, in all ages to come, proof of the high state of civilization amongst the people who conducted it— proof of the intelligence which pervaded the rank and file who fought its battles—proof of the resources of such a Government as ours, wholly unembarrassed in the midst of war, conquering one nation and feeding another! Where, sir, are the evidences of evil brought upon us by this "odious" war? Where can you point to any inroad upon our prosperity, public or private, industrial, commercial, or financial, which can be, in any degree attributed to the prosecution of this war? All that is yet to be shown, and I confidently await the issue.

Cong. Globe, 30:1, 497–99.

[1] Henry Johnson (1783–1864), an attorney born in Virginia, was elected senator from Louisiana in 1818. Governor from 1824 until 1828, he served as a Whig congressman before returning to the Senate in 1844. After his defeat for reelection, he resided on his plantation in Pointe Coupee Parish (*BDAC*; *NCAB*, 10:75).

[2] Brackets in the original.

[3] Evidently the *Globe* printed out of sequence Johnson's motion to recommit the ten-regiment bill, since both the Washington *Union* (Mar. 17) and the *National Intelligencer* (Mar. 18) reported its having been offered prior to Davis' remarks. Johnson stated that he would have voted for the bill, "but the change of circumstances that had taken place . . . render[ed] it unnecessary." He then suggested a proviso that no new officer be appointed under the bill unless it was deemed "indispensable" (*Cong. Globe*, 30:1, 501).

[4] Part of the letter, "from a distinguished officer at Vera Cruz, dated March 4," appeared in the *Union* on March 17. The party attacked on its way to Orizaba was "a detachment of ninety cavalry"; beset by 500–600 Mexicans, the volunteers lost a lieutenant and five men in addition to their wagons. Santa Anna was said to have "some 800 men, and is rapidly recruiting" near Oaxaca, a region where the people reportedly had declared they would not recognize the recent treaty.

[5] In his March 16 speech Calhoun remarked that the Puros were unwilling to see peace concluded, not because they were "our friends or enemies," but because they wanted to overthrow the Mexican government (*Cong. Globe*, 30:1, 478). As Davis notes, the Puros (liberals) had been hostile not only to the United States but to any group that worked for centralism or the monarchy. "Desperate for leadership" in 1846, the Puros saw Santa Anna as their best "hedge against monarchism and the best hope of organizing resistance against the United States" (Pletcher, *Diplomacy of Annexation*, 175, 360, 443–44).

[6] Mariano Paredes y Arrillaga (1797–1849), soldier and politician, overthrew the Herrera government in January 1846 but was himself forced to resign six months later. President at the outbreak of war, Paredes reportedly was too fearful of losing his office to act decisively against the Americans (*Enciclopedia de México*; Cotner, *Herrera*, 152–53).

[7] Calhoun had declared that "passage of this bill, if it be intended either for the purpose of intimidation or of coercion, [would] be entirely useless—an unmeaning bravado." The "policy" Davis mentions may be Calhoun's suggestion that the Americans "fall back and take the line of the treaty," indicating to the Mexican people "that we are satisfied if they are" (*Cong. Globe*, 30:1, 478).

[8] Ibid.

[9] Secretary of the Navy John Y. Mason, not Calhoun, instructed Commodore David Conner on April 15, 1844, to "occasionally show yourself at or before Vera Cruz" (*Senate Doc. 341*, 28:1, 78–79).

[10] Calhoun's letter of April 11, 1844, to Isaac Van Zandt, the Texas chargé in Washington, and J. Pinckney Henderson, then Texas envoy to England and France (ibid., *349*, 28:1, 11; see also ibid., *1*, 28:2, 28–29, 38).

[11] On the previous day Calhoun discussed limitations upon the president as commander-in-chief, pointing out that he was specifically authorized to use the militia and army for "suppressing insurrections" and "repelling invasion" (*Cong. Globe*, 30:1, 479). Davis apparently believed the South Carolinian alluded to the "Aroostook War," a conflict that erupted in 1839 over the boundary between Maine and New Brunswick. After the militia was called out, Congress authorized a force of 50,000 and $10 million for defense, if needed (Rich, *State O' Maine*, 152–54).

[12] Santa Anna's "favorite vaunt," from a letter to James Hamilton of February 18, 1842, in which he rejected an offer to pay Mexico $5 million in return for a treaty recognizing Texas independence: "the Mexican army has again taken a position of offence, and she will not vary her attitude till she plants her eagle standard on the banks of the Sabine" (*Niles' Reg.*, Mar. 26, 1842, 49–51; Carleton, *Buena Vista*, 154–55).

[13] Vicente Filisola (1785–1850), a native of Italy, took part in Mexico's struggle for independence and served as Santa Anna's second-in-command in the war with Texas (*Diccionario Porrúa*). Filisola's letters of April 25 and May 14, 1836, were addressed to the naval secretary, José M. Tornel; Tornel replied in the name of the acting president, José J. Corro, on May 15, 1836 (Jenkins, ed., *Papers of the Texas Revolution*, 6:63, 258–66, 303–304).

[14] The Treaty of Velasco (May 14, 1836). The secret version promised Santa Anna's liberation if he would work for recognition of Texas independence (*Handbook of Texas*).

[15] Referring to Webster's comments, delivered earlier in the day (*Cong. Globe*, 30:1, 484–85).

[16] Calhoun's March 16 speech (ibid., 478–79).

[17] The antiannexation letters written by Henry Clay and Martin Van Buren in April 1844. Gilbert L. Thompson was the "special agent sent to Mexico" (Pletcher, *Diplomacy of Annexation*, 154).

[18] John Black (1792–1873) was the American consul in Mexico City during 1843–47 and 1848–61. On October 15, 1845, he received confirmation that Mexico was willing to receive "the commissioner of the United States, who may come . . . with full powers . . . to settle the present dispute" (Manning, ed., *Diplomatic Corres.: Inter-American Affairs*, 8:167n, 762–63, 900; *Appletons'*).

[19] Lewis Cass, speaking on March 17 (*Cong. Globe*, 30:1, 493).

[20] John Slidell.

[21] Recalling Henry Clay's remarks in Congress on January 8, 1813, which paraphrased Josiah Quincy's comments of January 14, 1811, regarding the admission of West Florida (Stevenson, ed., *Home Book of Quotations*, 58).

[22] Daniel Webster: "The war is odious. Generally speaking, taking the whole country together, the war is odious in a high degree" (*Cong. Globe*, 30:1, 485).

To James K. Polk

Senate Chamber 28th March 1848

SIR,

I have been asked to give for your inspection my opinion on the value of Colts revolving pistol for mounted troops.[1]

Horses are in my opinion no more than transportation to Riflemen, giving celerity of movement but necessarily to be left in rear of any field on which Riflemen are to be brought into action. For cavalry the revolving pistol is far preferable I think to the carbine, and for the attack of Mexico guerilleros they have been and no /doubt/ will be found most efficient. The only doubt entertained by me is whether they can under the exposures incident to active service be kept "in order" on this point Col. Harney and Majr. McCullough[2] can speak positively, both these officers having used them in the field vy. truly yrs &c

JEFFN: DAVIS

ALS (DNA, RG46, 30 Cong., Colt Arms File No. 7).

[1] The day this letter was written Senator Thomas J. Rusk of Texas offered a resolution asking the president for information on Samuel Colt's "repeating firearms," especially in regard to adopting them for army use. Polk replied on April 13, noting that the War Department had contracted for 2,000, had requested more, and had investigated the possibility of buying Colt's patent. A subsequent report recommending purchase of 5,000 Colt pistols included abstracts of several testimonial letters, among them Davis', on the weapons' usefulness and dependability (*Cong. Globe*, 30:1, 549, 632–33, 676; *Senate Rep. 136*, 30:1; see also Colt, *Own Record*, passim).

[2] Col. William S. Harney, 2d Dragoons, had served in the army with Davis in the 1830s. Ben McCulloch (1811–62) was capt., Texas Mtd. Vols., in Mexico. Both recorded favorable opinions on the Colt pistols (*DAB*; Barton, *Texas Vols.*, 81; *Senate Rep. 136*, 30:1, 6).

To ————

Washington 29th March 1848

DEAR SIR,

Your kind letter of the 22d Inst has just come to hand,[1] many thanks for your kind feelings towards myself, such as you have shown on other occasions and which have been well and gratefully remembered. The enclosure you sent me in a former letter was so complimentary that however acceptable as the over kind commendation of a friend I could not get permission of my modesty to put it in the line of publication. It was not I assure you the less valued for being seen in the manuscript of a friend rather than in a public print. I am sorry that you are agrieved by the conduct of Mr. Walker[2] to one less conversant with public affairs I would suggest that public agents frequently do things disagreeable to the private man are forbidden by official obligations from making explanations which would give a new phase to the transaction.

It will give me much pleasure to hear from you often and to see you at this place when you come to the East.[3] accept my congratulations on your good fortune, and doubly do I congratulate you that your prosperity rests on the broad, enduring basis of popular confidence, not on the shifting quick-sand foundation of executive patronage. Very truly your's

JEFFN: DAVIS

ALS (Joseph Rubinfine).

[1] No letter dated March 22 has been found.

[2] Robert J. Walker had been attacked in the House on February 15 concerning the loan bill. A month later Congressman Willard P. Hall pointed out some discrepancies in several treasury reports, leading "A Mississippian" to reply publicly in Walker's behalf to the "innuendo" that the secretary had pocketed public funds.

On the other hand, Davis' correspondent may have been disturbed by Walker's recent handling of federal loans, one of which had just been taken by a London firm (*Cong. Globe*, 30:1, 355–59; Washington *Nat. Intell.*, Mar. 17, 1848; Washington *Union*, Mar. 8, 22, 1848; see also Ferdinand L. Claiborne to Davis, Feb. 27, 1848). Davis defended Walker in the Senate on May 25, 1848.

[3] Davis first began to write the word *north*.

To Robert J. Walker

Washington 30th March 1848

DEAR FRIEND,

You will recollect that the President asked /you/ some time since to recommend Marshall Smith to the collector of New orleans for an Inspectors appointment, the appointment has not been given.

The President asked me to communicate this fact to you and said the appointment must and should be given to young Smith.[1]

as the coons said and sung in "40, it may be said of southern Europe in relation to republican principles "It is the ball a rolling on, a rolling, rolling, rolling on".[2]

I was happy to heer yesterday of your unusually good health— as ever truly your's

JEFFN. DAVIS

ALS (George H. Edwards).

[1] Although Davis assured Smith prior to June 1848 that his appointment as a New Orleans customs inspector "should be made forthwith," Smith did not receive the position (Smith to James K. Polk, June 1, 1848, Polk Papers, DLC).

[2] Referring to Whig electioneering techniques in the 1840 presidential election.

To Beverley Tucker[1]

Washington 12th April 1848

MY DEAR SIR,

I have the pleasure to acknowledge the receipt of yours of the 6th Inst. It is with sincere regret that I find my unjustifiable delay in answering your former communication[2] has created a doubt as to the estimation placed upon it. I pray you to accept assurances of the real gratification it gave me and my apology for the delay which has occurred in answering it.

Col. J. P. Taylor,[3] the brother of the genl. was here when your first letter reached, he like myself was grateful for your good services and kind wishes towards Genl. Taylor. It was difficult for me to decide on a channel of communication worthy of yourself and bearing the proper relation to the genl. and myself.[4] The prominent papers here and elsewhere at that time were either hostile to genl. T. or stood aloof from him, neither could be trusted.

I believed that genl. Taylor's true position was on the Democratic side but every thing seemed to drive him from us, my connection with him rendered my efforts especially valueless, and I have now no hope that the Democratic party will avail itself of his strength in the coming contest. The Whigs may, and if so as a necessary consequence his affiliations must be with our opponents. In such case my confidence, admiration, and affection for the man, will be opposed by my convictions, and aherence to measures— Believing it[5] necessary that a candidate should have the organized support of one party or the <−r−> other and that it is impossible for genl. T. to be adopted now by the Democrats, the preliminary contest becomes one for Whig nomination, if in this the better caste of that party should alone be found, and the ultras be driven off a new party might arise from which better things could be expected.

For myself I will confess that I have been disappointed in the course of events, and look despondent upon a progress which I have no power to control or conform to. Your early advocacy of genl. T. cannot fail in any event to be to him a source of gratification and will be remembered by me.

accept my real regrets for the <–momentary–> delay which has caused a misapprehension of my feelings, and be assured of my highest esteem and regard, to which I will add my obligation for having been selected for a correspondent by you. It will give /me/ <–with–> much pleasure to hear from you, and I hope with improved health to be found a more prompt correspondent—Very truly yrs.

JEFFN. DAVIS

ALS (Tucker-Coleman Papers, ViW).

[1] Nathaniel Beverley Tucker (1784–1851), a native Virginian, was professor of law at the College of William and Mary. An exponent of states' rights, he published several works on political economy and three novels (*DAB*).

[2] Neither letter has been found.

[3] Joseph Pannill Taylor (1796–1864), born in Kentucky, was a career soldier, serving in the Commissary Department for thirty-three years and as commissary gen., 1861–64 (Warner, *Gens. in Blue*; Heitman, *Hist. Reg.*, 1:947–48).

[4] Tucker planned to write a series of open letters to Taylor, offering advice on contemporary issues (Brugger, *Beverley Tucker*, 175).

[5] The word *it* is in the margin.

To James K. Polk

Washington 13th april 1848

SIR,

In conformity with the understanding of this day I have the honor submit the following statement and opinion in relation to the claim of Brig. Genl. Twiggs for a brevet on account of services in the battle of Monterey.[1]

On the 21st of Sept. being the first day of active operations against the Town of Monterey, I was with the party who carried the first fort taken, and on passing through the fort in pursuit of the retreating enemy, I saw Genl. D. E. Twiggs in a position of great personal exposure and heard him cheering our men to active pursuit,[2] My orders and duties soon removed me to another part of the field and I did not again see Genl. Twiggs during the day— For the estimate placed upon his services by the comdg. genl. I refer to the commen-

293

dation bestowed on /Genl. Twiggs in/ the official report of the investment and reduction of Monterey.[3]

On the morning of the 21st Sept 1846, when the Troops were marched against the east end of Monterey, the purpose was not understood to be an attack, but only to make such demonstration as would enable Genl. Worth's command to pass round to the position selected for it at the West end of the Town, upon such assurance Genl. Twiggs who was quite ill turned over his command to the second officer (Col. Garland)[4] and as I was informed at the time retired by advice of Genl. Taylor to his tent; but fearing that an attack might be made or contest otherwise occur he returned to the field and went direct to the point on which his division had marched, he found the volunteers storming the Fort, and I found him close behind the retreating enemy. It has been stated that Genl. Twiggs was not with his division and therefore not entitled to a brevet, to which I answer, he went to the place against which his division had been marched but before he arrived that division had been withdrawn from the attack and was in fractions, in and on houses, behind fences, and in the corn;[5] the Volunteers who had been /brought/ forward to sustain the attack on the first fort, renewed the assault and carried it by storm.[6] Immediately after passing through the fort thus taken I saw genl. Twiggs and he was the only Genl. officer I did see with the advance of the assailants.

In conclusion I will say that according to the principle upon which the brevets were granted I consider it just and due to genl. Twiggs that he should be breveted, for services at Monterey on the first day of the attack, and that Genl. Taylor's report is sufficient warrant for such brevet. Very truly yr. friend,

JEFFN: DAVIS

ALS (Polk Papers, DLC).

[1] Promoted brig. gen. after Palo Alto, Twiggs was recommended for promotion after Monterrey but was not brevetted. On March 2, 1847, he was voted a sword by Congress for his services at Monterrey and on April 12, 1848, was nominated brevet maj. gen. for gallantry at Cerro Gordo. Withdrawn five days later, the nomination was resubmitted, this time for his good conduct at Monterrey, the brevet to date from September 23, 1846. In the midst of the Senate's consideration of the matter, Twiggs arrived in Washington and was received at the White House on April 21. His brevet was confirmed May 10 (*DAB*; Heitman, *Hist. Reg.*, 1:976; *Senate Ex. Jour.*, 7:381, 396, 410; Polk, *Diary*, 3: 430).

[2] Davis refers to the capture of the buildings in the Tenería complex. Not

mentioned in Davis' battle reports, Twiggs's presence was noted in Daniel R. Russell's account (Oct. 18, 1846), in Davis' memorandum ([Dec. 31], 1846), and by implication in Davis' letter to Joseph E. Davis (Jan. 26, 1847).

[3] See Zachary Taylor's report (*Senate Doc. 1*, 29:2, 85, 88).

[4] Lt. Col. John Garland, 4th Inf., had served with Davis in the Michigan Territory in the early 1830s.

[5] After the futile attempt to storm the Tenería, Garland's command dispersed, some moving toward the *tête-de-pont*, some taking a position in a building behind the tannery, and others going "into a cornfield"; see the map of Monterrey (Garland's report, Sept. 29, 1846, DNA, RG94, Letters Recd., f/w 38-T-1847; Backus, "Brief Sketch," *Hist. Mag.*, 10:208–10; Johnston, *A. S. Johnston*, 138; Smith, *War with Mexico*, 1:250–51).

[6] The attack by the 1st Miss. and 1st Tenn. rgts.

Remarks on the Cumberland Island Dam Bill

Editorial Note: Navigation of the Ohio River was rendered both difficult and dangerous in early 1848 because recent freshets had damaged the wing dams erected in 1833–34 from the head of Cumberland Island across the northwestern river channel. After receiving memorials on the subject from Tennessee citizens, the Committee on Roads and Canals reported on April 7 a bill recommending an appropriation of $50,000 for repairs. Senator Arthur P. Bagby of Alabama spoke against the measure, saying the central government had no authority "to improve any river." John C. Calhoun responded that the federal power to regulate commerce was ample authority because the Ohio was a multi-state watercourse; he used as an analogy the government's construction of buoys and lighthouses. Bagby viewed the latter as falling within the constitutional provision for maintaining a navy (*Cong. Globe*, 30:1, 558, 593, 633–34; see also Stephen H. Long to John J. Abert, Apr. 6, 1848, DNA, RG77, Topog. Bureau, Letters Recd., L-189-1848).

April 14, 1848

Mr. DAVIS, of Mississippi. Entertaining views similar to those which have been expressed by the Senator from Alabama,[1] viewing the whole system of internal improvement by the Federal Government as an assumption of power not conferred by the Constitution, and believing that if the power were possessed, the experience we have had shows that its exercise would be inexpedient and demoralizing, I think it necessary to explain why I shall vote for this bill, and to show what peculiarity there is in the case, which constitutes it an exception to the general rule. The appropriation is not, as the Senator from Alabama seems to think, to remove a bar in the Cumberland river, but it is to repair a dam which the Federal Government constructed in the Ohio river. For the purpose of improving the navigation of the Ohio, and the passage from the Cumberland into the Ohio river, a dam was built from the "Cumberland Island" to the Illinois shore, which forced the water of the Ohio river into the channel on the Kentucky side, which was by nature the inferior channel of the two, but which was no doubt selected because an incidental improvement would thus be made at the mouth of the Cumberland river. This dam has given way, the artificial advantage to the smaller channel is lost, and the larger one is obstructed by the remains of the work which the Federal Government erected. The natural navigation being thus impaired, those who are interested in it have a right to expect of this Government that it will remove the impediment; at least, restore them to their natural advantages. The broken dam is a nuisance, an injury to vast interests, private and public; and having been introduced by this Government, I hold we are bound to abate it. The practical question is, how can it be most efficiently and economically done? According to the best information in my possession, it will cost less of time and of money to repair the dam than to remove the *debris*. Large masses of stone, which have imbedded themselves in the sand, could only be removed by immense labor, to be performed only at the lowest stage of water. To remove the dam would, therefore, require that we should wait until after the present favorable season for navigation had passed by, and the injury done by the obstacle during this period would greatly exceed the expense of repair. As a measure of justice and of economy, I shall vote for an appropriation to repair the dam; and thus, at as early a day as possible, to restore the navigation to a condition which I hope will equal, if it does not exceed, its natural advantages.

In arriving at this conclusion, my reflections have not brought me to the position of the Senator from South Carolina, [Mr. CALHOUN.][2] If I were compelled to rely on the power "to regulate commerce" as a justification for this appropriation, my adherence to the doctrine of literal interpretation of the terms of the Constitution would compel me to vote against this bill, intimately connected as it is with the interests of the great valley of which I represent a part. To regulate is to make rules, not to provide means. The power was given by the States to the Federal Government, as part of the great purpose, the establishment of a more perfect union, and the promotion of domestic tranquillity. The common agent was intrusted with this power, because it could only be used by the States as sovereigns making treaties with each other, and because its exercise was probably to be a detriment to the commercial interests of our political family, and a cause of dissension among us. The same clause which conveyed this power in regard to the commerce of the States, gave it also in relation to foreign nations and Indian tribes. If the construction were admitted that the power to regulate commerce carries with it the right to improve the channels through which it is transmitted, there would be no limit to our appropriations within the most remote port which our merchantmen visit, or the least known Indian tribe with whom our fur traders hold intercourse.

Any rule which could be laid down as a limit to the extent which the Federal Government may constitutionally go in works of improvement, must be found in practice defective, and liable, in the progress of legislation, to be lost sight of, unless that rule has within it its own limitation. It might, with great fairness, be urged that the Federal Government is bound, as one who uses the public highways, to contribute its proportion of the labor necessary to keep them in repair; and if this were an occasion proper to the discussion of the general subject, it might easily be shown that both historically and practically the Ohio river is emphatically a national highway, and entitled as such to all which the Federal Government has a right to bestow. If appropriations to rivers and harbors were limited to the amount collected by charges imposed upon their commerce, we should have a guide and a check to expenditures on their improvement. On our great western rivers, so often selected as the foundation of an argument, a very light tonnage duty would suffice to make all the improvements which have been, or ever will be, required for their successful navigation. The general application of such a rule would impose the burden upon those who receive the benefit of improvements; our legislation would be freed from alliances which corrupt it at the fountain, and overburden the national treasury by appropriations for local objects.

Whilst I agree with the Senator from Alabama in the general principles which he has stated, I disagree with the view which he has taken of the particular case. To tap a stream, or to remove a natural dam, is among the most difficult problems of civil engineering, and admitted to be attended by all the dangers which the Senator has indicated; but to improve the bed of a stream, to increase without radically changing the natural advantages of a national highway, are cases widely differing from those put by the Senator, whether they be viewed as questions of engineering or of constitutional construction. The cases put by the Senator endanger the natural navigation, by drawing off the original pools, or, by leaving the highway common to the States, and entering with a canal the territory of a particular State, invade its sovereignty over the soil. These are objections which do not apply to the question before us, if it were presented for original decision, instead of being, as it is, a proposition to remedy an evil which the former action of the General Government has inflicted.

The Senator from South Carolina [Mr. CALHOUN][2] offers the practice of erecting light-houses and buoys in the harbors on our seacoast, as an argument for the existence of the power to improve the channels of interior commerce. With great deference to the acknowledged ability of that Senator, I differ entirely from his conclusion, and deny the analogy upon which he insists. The erection of light-houses upon our maritime coast, and the placing of buoys to mark the entrance into our harbors, are mainly referable to the power to maintain a navy, and provide for the common defence; though I will admit that the construction of light-houses and buoys may also be drawn from the power to regulate commerce, and for like reasons as apply to the construction of docks, ways, and warehouses. For convenience and security in the collection of imposts, we require goods imported into the country to be laid down at particular places; thence arises an obligation to facilitate the entrance of vessels to the places so designated, and, facility and security being the common benefit of the parties, tonnage duties and port charges are imposed, and serve to create the means for harbor improvements. Surely this cannot be considered parallel to the improvement of the route over which the commerce is to pass.

Mr. DAVIS,[3] of Massachusetts. How does that agree with the provision of the Constitution which gives power to the General Government to regulate commerce among the States?

Mr. DAVIS, of Mississippi. The power to prescribe the rules for commerce among the States was surrendered to the General Government; the States were thenceforward deprived of the power to impose restrictions or levy duties upon the commerce of each other;

and the Federal Government received that power under limitations which mark the purpose of those who gave it. Our Constitution was to bring the States nearer to each other; and this power, transferred to the General Government, it was foreseen, would be the fruitful cause of jealousy and strife; the barriers then opposed by some States to the commerce of others were swept away by the compact of union, and no foundation was left upon which they could be rebuilt. All had been done which constitutions can achieve to give to the people of the United States one commerce and interest. The Constitution of these United States is a monument to free trade; and the various clauses in it bearing upon this power to "regulate commerce among the States" show that it was not to give activity to the exercise of it, but to restrain the States, that it was conferred upon the Federal Government. It was not my purpose to enter into the discussion of the great principles which have been alluded to, but only to point out some of the peculiarities of the case under consideration, which, in my opinion, make it an exception to the general rule, and, therefore, free it from objections which might generally obtain.

[Noting that congressional power to establish ports of entry and to provide for the collection of duties was not confined to the seaboard, Calhoun reiterates his opposition to internal improvements in general but restates his contention that "the great highways, common to all the States" should be a federal concern.]

Mr. DAVIS, of Mississippi. The Senator from South Carolina has misconstrued the admission made by me as to the right to erect light-houses and buoys. In addition to that which was referable to the navy power, I said there also existed a power incident to the regulation of commerce, to construct light-houses and buoys where necessary to the safety of those on whom our regulations were imposed. By making it a consequence of the laws which require imported goods to be landed at particular places, it was sufficiently indicated that the works should be connected with the places thus prescribed. The reference to the tonnage duties and port charges, as laid in consideration of the harbor facilities furnished, certainly exhibited with sufficient clearness the extent of my admission. I believe it was originally the practice to limit appropriation for a harbor to the amount of port and tonnage duties collected at it.[4] I wish the rule was now in force. No admission has been made by me which can be fairly construed as recognizing the right to expend means drawn from the national treasury upon harbors which have no taxable commerce, and which therefore supply no funds to the Government. Least of all, can anything advanced by me be tortured into an admission of the right to go abroad, from the place for which the regulation is made, to create a commerce upon which the regulation shall operate.

The Senator selects landing on the upper Mississippi and Ohio, and asks if these are not ports of entry,[5] and if vessels cannot go up to them from the sea. For the later question I will refer him to his recollections of the trip he made from Memphis, after the celebrated convention held at that place,[6] and then inform him that he was in a very deep river when compared to those he would have passed over if he had ascended to the ports of entry he has named.

The Senator is certainly aware that the places named by him as ports of entry have no foreign commerce brought to them in sea vessels; and if they had, he could only apply my admission to the landing place, which would not in the least aid his purpose, or their commerce. It will be long before I admit as an incident to laws prescribing the rules for commerce that the Federal Government can create channels through which commerce may flow, or that an act of Congress can make the entrance to a harbor equal the distance from the sea to the landing for river boats on the head branches of our longest rivers.

If to declare by law a landing on some interior river to be a port of entry can confer the power to remove all obstructions between that landing and the sea, what limit have we to the burdens which may be imposed upon the industry of the country to support the visionary or corrupt schemes which theory or selfishness may devise? If, under the power to make rules, to enact laws for the government of commerce, we have the right to appropriate money to provide for it channels of transportation, who shall discriminate between rivers, and creeks, and canals, and railroads, or who can say that from channels it may not be extended to vehicles for conveyance? So far as we may constitutionally improve our national highways, it must be for other purpose than the promotion of commerce; and the power must be drawn elsewhere than from the right to regulate it. The transportation of troops, of supplies, and munitions of war, the transfer of public moneys, the proper discharge of the civil functions and military duties of the Federal Government, may require the improvement of public highways, and under the war power and the duty to provide for the common defence, it may as far as necessary be done. This is a necessity which the settlement of our territory removes. It has limitations both of time and of purpose. Not so with the improvements for commerce, which will increase with increasing population, and has its application to every town and village of the Union. The interests of those whom I represent, and my own conviction and feelings, unite in resistance to a construction than which none was ever adopted more latitudinous in its nature, or tending to more flagrant abuse. I have admitted that at a place where imposts are collected, where tonnage duties are paid, where imports are required to be landed, an obligation is imposed to point out the safe approach to the place so designated. The mere declaration that a certain place shall be a port of entry does not fulfill any of the conditions; and if they were all fulfilled, no application could be made of my admission to the route over which the vessel had passed in its voyage.[7]

Cong. Globe, 30:1, 634–36.

[1] Arthur Pendleton Bagby (1794–1858), native Virginian, settled in Alabama in 1818, serving his adopted state as legislator, governor, and senator, 1841–48 (*DAB*).

[2] Brackets in the original.

[3] John Davis (1787–1854), a Yale graduate, was elected to the House in 1824, serving eight years. Subsequently governor, he was Whig senator from Massachusetts, 1835–40, 1845–53 (*DAB*).

[4] Although Congress continued several state laws permitting the collection of tonnage duties to maintain specific port facilities, by the 1820s it was more common to finance harbor improvements with federal appropriations (*U.S. Laws Relating to Rivers and Harbors*, 1:15–24; U.S. Cong., *American State Papers*, Class IV, Commerce, 2:626–27).

[5] Calhoun had mentioned St. Louis and Cincinnati as ports of entry (*Cong. Globe*, 30:1, 635).

[6] A reference to Calhoun's November 1845 trip from Memphis to New Orleans (*Davis Papers*, 2:365, 370–71).

[7] After a brief rejoinder by Calhoun, the bill was passed 31–8; Davis and Calhoun both voted in the affirmative. Subsequent efforts to include funds for the work in the general appropriations bill failed (*Cong. Globe*, 30:1, 636, 943, 1029).

To Varina Howell Davis

Washington 18th. April 1848

DEAR WIFE,

I have the pleasure to acknowledge the receipt of your's of the 30th ulto. informing me of your arrival at the Hurricane, and the reasons which had hastened your return. I fear you have exposed yourself to hazard, for which the cause does not afford justification, but as it has been done it only remains to me to hope that God will bless your good motives and save you from harm in their pursuit. You will have received letters before this reaches you,[1] giving my fears of a very protracted session, nothing is certain which depends on a vote of Congress, but all the indications are that the presidential canvass is to be conducted here. Mrs Tuley[2] left this place yesterday. She and Miss Garner[3] and Parson Brown[4] send their kind remembrances to you. Mrs Tuley invites you to spend the recess of Congress with her. Keyworth[5] has finished the braid and it is the handsomest I ever saw. He showed me a neat little clasp set with jet and pearls, which he said you had noticed and admired. I therefore told him to put it on. As it may not be soon in my power to send it to you by safe conveyance, there will remain to me in the mean time the pleasure of possessing it. A small lock of hair was returned to me as all which remained.

My health is almost restored, very little lameness, and seldom any pain, or other inconvenience except an inability to write for long periods continuously. There was no cause for anxiety about me, and it grieves me that you should have been thus injured either in health or spirits.

I had hoped that with cheerful friends and left in our separation to the full force of your affection for me, you would have enjoyed more equanimity than when we were together. Of disagreeable subjects I hope I have never shown a disposition to speak unnecessarily, and if sometimes unprofitably, it has not been deliberately done except for good ends, thus is it now that I refer to memories to which I recur with pain and for objects which will be apparent. I cannot bear to be suspected or complained of, or misconstrued after explanation, *by you.* Circumstances, habits, education, combativeness, render you prone to apply the tests which I have just said I cannot bear. You do not wish to destroy my sensibility, or to drive me for relief to temporary stupefaction, and vicious associations; through these channels alone could I reach the condition suited to such treatment as I have received. We are apt by viewing our own heart, to construe our acts differently from others, and conscious of your love for me, you may not have understood how far your treatment of me was injurious. I will only say, that I hoped when you saw that your course if continued would render it impossible for us ever to live together, that my ill health rendering me less able to bear abuse, produced a necessity for separation at a time when a wifes kindness was most needed, and that the dread of constant strife was so great, as not to be overcome by a threat of exposure to the public, of the real cause of my going alone from home; with body crippled, nerves shattered, and mind depressed.— I had hoped your memory instead as you say dwelling on "the weary past and blighted future" would have grappled with substantial facts, and led you to conclusions, which would have formed for your future a line of conduct suited to the character of your husband, and demanded by your duties as a wife. Your two previous letters were very discouraging, this is better, and I have spoken more fully than in the answers to the two last.

I hope soon to hear from concerning affairs at home and the people, very little detail information has been given to me.

You should as a moral duty as a social obligation exercise such prudence and self-control in all things as will conduce to your health physical and mental. If it would be agreeable to you to spend this summer in the North Mrs Walker[6] has kindly proposed to me to let you remain with her at the springs and elsewhere during the recess of Congress — I need not say that (because I love you) it would always make me happier to be with you, if kind and peaceful.

With love to all our family, I am Affectionately Your husband — Truth & Love ever attend upon you — Good night

(signed) JEFFN. DAVIS.

L, copy (Dearborn Coll., MH-H). In 1939 the letter printed above was owned by Mrs. Irene N. Harmon of Wells, Maine. Her daughter gave the document to a physician, who in turn gave it to a niece; the letter has since been misplaced. Harvard acquired a handwritten copy in 1957 (*Maine Ref. List of MSS*, 2:244; corres., Davis Assn., June 9, 1977–June 4, 1979).

[1] Varina Davis' letter has not been found. Having visited Davis relations in Louisiana in January–March, she wrote her mother from home in mid-April describing how busy she was with preparations for a niece's wedding (Zachary Taylor to Davis, Apr. 20, 1848; V. Davis to Margaret K. Howell, Jan. 31, [Apr.], 1848, Davis Coll., AU). No other Davis letters to Varina have been found for early 1848.

[2] Mary W. Tuley, born in Virginia about 1809, was first married to Dr. Thomas Jackson, was widowed, and then was married to Joseph Tuley (1796–1860), a wealthy farmer in Clarke County, Virginia. She was residing in Philadelphia as late as 1882 (Tuley, *Tuley Family Memoirs*, 10, 58; 1850 Census, Va., Clarke, family

47; New Orleans *Picayune*, Sept. 20, 1882).

[3] Ediland Garner, born in Virginia about 1833, was a member of Joseph and Mary Tuley's household (1850 Census, Va., Clarke, family 47).

[4] Obadiah B. Brown (1779–1852), a native of Newark, New Jersey, was for forty-three years (1807–50) pastor of the First Baptist Church in Washington (Cathcart, ed., *Baptist Ency.*).

[5] Robert Keyworth was a longtime Washington jeweler whose shop was on Pennsylvania Avenue. Born in England about 1797, he died prior to May 1861 (1822–55 Washington dirs.; 1850 Census, D.C., 3d ward, family 54; J. T. Pickett to Davis, May 17, 1861, DNA, RG109, Gen. and Staff Officers' Papers).

[6] Mary Bache Walker, wife of the treasury secretary.

From Zachary Taylor

Baton Rouge Louisiana April 20th 1848

MY DEAR GENERAL,

It is sometime since I wrote you or since I had the pleasure of receiving a line from you, altho, I hear from you occasionally through those who have met you in Washington, & occasionally by letters written by friends from that place; they for the most part say, your health with the exception of your wound which was giving you some trouble was pretty good, which we were very much pleased to hear; I sincerely hope if you have not entirely recoverd ere this from the effects of your wound, you are in a fair way to become so, & that you will very soon be able if it is not already the case, to dispense with your crutch, & to use your disabled limb without pain or inconvenien[ce][1] of any kind. I am aware your engagements are & have been such as to occupy both your time <–time–> & thoughts in more important matters than in writing private letters even of a friendly character; & such has been my situation for the last three months, what with sculptors, portrait painters & letter writers I have barely had time to attend to the most trivial matters, much less important ones. I am now sitting to three artists eight hours daily, & at one time been in the hands of six, which in addition to the receipt & replying to a small portion of some thirty letters every week, most of them relating to political matters connectted with the coming presidential election, some of them very long ones, has given me as much or even more than I could get through with; such however as was written with the view of drawing from me /my opininions/ as to the justice & necessity of the Mexican War, the Wilmot proviso, the authority of Congress under the Constitution to establish Banks &c, I dispose of in a most sumary way; I also receive many letters urging me to decline in favor of Mr Clay or to run as Vice President on the same ticket with him; one writer stating as a reason for my agreeing to such an arrangement was that many of the leading politicians among the Whigs particularly in N. York & Pensylvania, who were most prominent in advocating my claims to the Presidency, were doing so to bring about a schism on the meeting of the Whig N. Convention in June, between Mr, Clays friends & mine, by which they hoped to have both of us withdrawn, & Genl, Scott substituted as a compromise; this may be all true, yet I have not replied to any such letter nor do I intend doing so, but to let such schems tak their course if they exist. I consider this getting /up/ a N. <-Convention-> Whig Convention will have the effect if it was not intended to do so, to defeat my election, as I cannot see how my friends can go [illegible], for if I am not the nominee of said convention, they will have no authority to give any pledges that I will withdraw in favor of anyone; I consider myself now in the hands of the people a portion of whom have brought me before the Country as a candidate for the presidency without any agency of mine in the matter, & if they think proper to drop me & take up an other & cast their votes for him at the proper time, which they ought to do if he is more available & better qualified to discharge the duties of that high station, & succeed in electing him, I will be neither disappointed or mortified at the results; on the contrary if he is honest, truthful & patriotic qualities we have not recently met with in those filling high places, I will be more than gratified at the result, be he whom he may. But I cannot withdraw from the contest whether nominated by said convention o[r] not which I do not expect to be, if I do not get the vote of a single State, or the whole; I must be /consistent/ even should my being so defeats my election—

I presume Mr, Clay who is very anxious to do so, or genl, Scott will get the nomination of the Whig N. Convention which is to meet in Philadelphia on the 7th, of June, as the devoted friends of both those individuals will from what I lear/n/ do all in their power in the first place to get me out of the way considering I am somewhat of an interloper in this matter; but be this as it may if the first receives the nomination, & is elected I will not complain; & if defeated after being nominated, & his being a candidate should have the effect of defeating my election, it will not produce a partile of unkindness on my part towards him; for there are many circumstances which will allay so far as I am concerned, & smooth down many causes of irritation which may spring up out of this Presidential contest; his son[2] having fallen by my side while gallantly sustaining his country's honor & her flag at Buena Vista, is of itself was there no other cause to make /me/ under all circumstances to feel kindly towards his father; while on the other hand there is not a single redeeming quality or circumstance so far as I am concerned to soften the hard feelings which I am free to say I entertain for the latter; he intrigued & flattered Mr. P–[3] until /he got authority to [illegible]/ me & my command was placed subject /to his orders/ which he stripped me of /the greater portion of my force/ in the most uncourteous & I may say indecent manner that could have been devised leaving me in a situation that nothing hardly short of a miracle could have saved me & those under my command from annihilation; I will not say he wished me & those with me destroyed or that he would have rej/o/iced at such an event; but had it turned out so, I do not believe it would have given him one moments concern so his own selfish orguls & view ha/d/ been answerd— Mr, Webster is no doubt preparing to take ground in favor of Genl. Scott for the presidency if he cannot get the Whig nomination himself at the meeting of the Whig N. Convention, he will use the Genl, if he can again do so, as he did at the Harrisburg Convention in forty,[4] to defeat Mr, Clays nominati[on] as well as mine— Great efforts will be made by mr, Webster as well as many other prominent politicians of the North Whigs & Democrats, to make the Wilmot proviso one of the grea[t]est if not the principal element in the coming presidential election; & every effort will be made by them to array the people /of the/ free States & those of the Slave holding against each other; Mr, Websters great speech in the Senate on I believe the appropriation bill recently deliverd cannot be misunderstood in regard to that matter;[5] which if they succeed in doing, which I should not be surprised at, & a ca[n]didate for the presidency should be taken up from one of the former & they should coalesce on him the matter will be settled, as they have the numbers— It seems to me that Mr. Clay in his Lexington speech bid for the votes of the Wilmot proviso men, & Cass, Buchanan & Dallas in <–their–> defining their position in their letters addressed to the public in relation to that subject,[6] bid for the votes of the people of the Slave holding portions of the Union; which I apprehend will have the effect to prevent the election of either, particularly the three latter; this Wilmot question should never have been agitated, nature has so arranged matters as regards the ceded Territory, which will prevent the existence of Slavery in any portion of it; for no one will while in his senses carry his slaves there unless <–unless–> he wishes to get them out of the rea[ch] of some civil process; this proviso was gotten up with no other object but to array the North against the South, & I much fear its injurious effects before it [is] finally disposed of; but I hope for the best—

We have not as yet heard of the fate of the Trist treaty, which seems after undergoing certain alterations was ratified by the U. S. Senate,[7] & I sincerely wish since it has gone so far that it may be favorably recd. & acted on by the Mexican authorities; at the same time I am free to say I do not like it, & would have greatly preferred the plan I suggested or recommended which was, to have taken as much territory for indemnity as would have compensated our Citizens for all their los/s/es on acct. of spoliations, & paid them what was justly due; but would not have given Mexico one cent for any territory beyond or for that object, as I think we have "paid too dear /already/ for the Whistle";[8] I would have taken at any rate to the Rio Grande, & all upper California, & more if necessary for the object stated; but not an other acre, & /if/ she would /not/ treat on such terms I would at once have withdrawn our army, occupied the Country necessary to pay our Citizens & let her /have/ driven us from it if she was able, but which she would never / <–[illegible]–> have/ attempted to have done, as she would have found an abundance for many years to come in settling her own internal quarrels; but I am not disposed to cavil at the terms of said treaty, & shall say amen with a hearty response if it is carried into operation in good faith—

When I last wrote you I was just recovering from an attack of neuralgy in one of my legs, which confined me to the House for about five weeks, as soon as I was able to get about I made a visit to my unfortunate plantation, & while there made a short visit to your excellent brother /&/ his kind lady, & was so fortunate as to meet there his daughter Mrs, Robins your Sister Mrs, Bradford, her interesting family & several other family relatives including Dr,

Mitchel who got there the evening I left; but regret to say I was truly disappointed in not meeting your good lady which I had expected to have done; she being then on a visit to your Sister in Feliciana.[9] I spent a most delightful day with them, & had my time permitted, I could have gladly remained several; but such was my previous arrangements or engagements I felt under the necessity of leaving the next day, on the return of the same boat from Vicksburg, which carried me up; while I remained I felt not if among strangers or even acquaintances but as if I was among near & dear relatives; your accomplished sister in law, while your brother was engaged took me over the plantation which is a most desireable one, & handsomely arranged; as well as over Brierfield where all appeared to be going on very well, & pointed out the spot where the workmen were preparing the materials on which your new dwelling was to be erected; the only objection to which seemed to me, was a small pond of standing water nearby, which may possibly have the effect of producing intermittent fevers, but it may not have that effect— I deeply regret to say I found your worthy brother not in as robust health as I expected & could have wished to have done, I fear he is & has been for some time past overworking himself; he ought now to think more about the preservation of his health than making cotton & corn; for altho, he has <–elf–> a little paradise & surrounded it with every comfort & I may say luxury, which he may be reluctant to leave, yet he ought not to hesitate to do so for a moment, at least for a time to try the benefit of a change of climate, & /I/ was highly gratified to learn from him, that he though[t] he would leave home in May in time to meet the N. Democratic convention,[10] which was to meet in Baltimore in that month, to nominate candidates for the two highest offices known to our laws; after attending which I trust he will visit Washington, where he can spend a few weeks very pleasantly, & then go East & while away his time during the summer at some of the large Cities & pleasant watering places of the North, returning home in autum by way of the Virginia Springs, which he should do annally, should he be benefited by such a course; the first /object/ with him should be the restoration of his health, & its preservation, he has enough, & more to make all his family independent & his life is of more importance to <–his family–> /them his/ relatives & friends as rgards his advice & example, than all the wealth ten times told he can amass for them or rather the former—

I found the plantation we were speaking about belonging to Mr, Turner,[11] which you considerd one of the best in Mississippi, joined your brothers above on the river; in conversing with him about it, he stated it could have been purchase he thought about the time I made the investment near Rodney; had I been aware of it, & could have succeeded in making the arrangement for it, I would have been much better satisfied at this time to have located myself on it, & to have passed my spare time with you your brother & your families, much more to my satisfac/tion/ than I could in the White H[ou]se where I never expect to get. I must again say to you as regrds political matters do not let your friendship for me interfere with your political prospect[s] for I take greater interest in your political advancement than in my own— Since I commenced this & just as I was bringing it to a close, which you will doubtless say I ought to have done long since I received your highly esteemed letter of the 4th, inst, & a Uunion the govt, paper of the 6th, /referred to/ in your letter, you mention the call made on you by the honbe, Revardy Johnson <–Johnson–> one /of/ the Senator from Maryland, & the substance of a conversation he had with you, as regards my position in relation to the Presidency, & the N. Whig Convention, & the view you took & reply you made to him was entirely correct; I have just recd, a letter from him on the subject in question, which was recd, in the kindest terms, the same spirit in which it was written, & immediately replied to /it/ & I hope in a way that will be satisfactory[12]—

I apprehend before the presidential contest is over, or at any rate by the time it is gotten through with, that the Wilmot proviso is a matter of more importance than you at one time immagined;[13] & that I was not far wrong in believing it would be best for our whole country in settling the terms of a treaty with Mexico, not /to/ have taken any territory South of the Missouri compromise line; the Wilmost proviso or the <–extion–> extention of Salvery will in all probability be the test question at both conventions Whigs & Democrats, as well as throughout the country at the coming election, in which case as I have before stated, someone from the free States Whig or Democrat mu/st/ be elected, in which event the South

<-South-> will hardly have an other Chief Magistrate day, if ever, for it will become disreputable even to reside in a slave holding state—

I consider I would have acted highly improper had I not avowed that I was a Whig (altho, I have no doubt I am a much better & a consistant republican than thousands who profess themselves to be Democrats of the purest water, yet I had previous to the last presidential election avowed myself /as/ belonging to the Whig party to all with whom I conversed; & therefore had I changed my position at this time or since I have been spoken of as a candidate for the presidency, I might have been charged with great appearance of truth that I had done so in order to reach that high position believing the Democrats were the strongest— I have no concealments on that head, & if I was ever so anxious to reach the White Hous, which is by no means the case, I would not do so by making a false issue or under false preten[ces] In an artic[l]e in the Union which you enclosed me, headed "Greek against Greek, Clay Whigs vs. Taylor Whigs" Mr, Richie goes on to say, now we have a letter from the chairman of the Joint Committee of the Legislature of Mississippi who went to invite Genl, Taylor to the seat of Govt, to pay due honors to him– "He states expressly /that/ in a conversation with him, the old soldier to/ld/ him the South should never agree to the /provisions of/ Wilmot proviso," /"But to the letter,"/ I certainly never intended to have made any such statement; I might have said the South would never agree to any treaty with Mexico containing such an article in it, even if I said that much— <-"But to the letter"-> I/n/ regard to the conversation had with Genl, Taylor I have to say he did not talk on the Tariff— We did on the war. He expressed himself in favor of the War &c &c"[14] the greater portion /of said conversation/ I must believe was manufactoried perhaps by Mr. R— himself for I do not believe any chairman selected by so reputable a body, & that body selected by so highly respectable & dignified body as the Legislature of Mississippi for the object in question, would have made such a representation, there must be something wrong in this matter; at any rate /I/ <-[illegible]-> must have been greatly mistaken; for such opinions ha<-ve-> to say the least of <-it-> /them they/ were never entertained by me, & I hardly think could have been advanced by me— As to the statements of Dr, Baden brought on the floor of Congres by Mr, McClernand of Illinois & Henley[15] from Indiana the greater portion of which is a tissue of falsehood Dr, B– may have called on [u]s & been introduced with [h]undred[s] of others, & no doubt if he did so I treated /him/ with every courtesy in <–in–> my power; but I do not recollect any such individual & have no hesitation in saying no such conversation ever passed between us; but I will not say it was not manufactoried <–by the venerable editor–> by the venerable Editor of the Govt. paper, or some other equally abandoned politician for the worst /of/ purposes— Mr, Brown too appears to figure as a willing witness <–witness–> as to the unblemished caracter /of/ one Dr, Timmothy Tugmutton or Kemball, of Hines Country Mississippi who if he made the statements refferred to by Mr, Brown of <–Miss–>/ss/<–ippi–> Mississippi is no doubt a most infamous Character & must have left his native /st/ for <–the–> /no/ good, <–of his state–> Maine[16]—Mr, Henley figures largely in w/h/at he must have known to be false as regards Dr Baden's statements which was that I advised the withdrawal of the troops of my command, previous to <–being to–> thier being taken from me by genl, Scott; or ralther he states this on his own knoledge after an interview with the Secretary of War;[17] Dr, Badens was on an other point equally false; & the member from Baltimore <–[and?]–> Mr, McClain[18] in /his/ over zeal to exculpate the administration for its course towards Genl, Scott & myself lugs in Lt, Col Duncan[19] & attempts at the expense of truth to make him figure in a way unknown to all who were present unless it was such as posessed a like fertile imagination[20]— Those who repeat or inclose <–the–> the falsehoods of others are as ville contemplable & as much to be detested as those who originate them.

Majr, Bliss who has this moment got here, informs us that you had nearly recoverd from the effects of your wound, which we all delighted to hear Mrs, Taylor joins me in <–in–> kindest wishes for your <–for your–> continued health happiness & fame— Your Frien Truly & Sincerely

ZAYLOR

P. S.

We are to have an other flood & overflow in the Miss[21]

ALS (Soc. Coll., PHi). An incomplete draft dated April 18 is in the Zachary Taylor Papers, Library of Congress.

[1] Square brackets enclose material supplied where the manuscript is damaged.

[2] Henry Clay, Jr.

[3] President Polk.

[4] Daniel Webster did not attend the

1840 Whig convention but, according to one insider, his friends contrived to secure delegates for Winfield Scott, "who was to be made the cat's-paw to defeat Mr. Clay" (Wise, *Seven Decades*, 166).

[5] Speaking on March 23 about the loan bill, Webster forcibly declared his opposition to the admission of any new states, particularly on the country's southern boundary (*Cong. Globe*, 30:1, 532–35).

[6] Henry Clay spoke in Lexington on November 13; Lewis Cass's "Nicholson letter" was dated December 24; James Buchanan addressed a Pennsylvania committee on August 25; and Vice-President Dallas had expressed his views on the proviso in a Pittsburgh speech on September 18 (*Niles' Reg.*, Sept. 4, Nov. 27, 1847, Jan. 8, 1848, 4, 197–200, 293–94; Washington *Union*, Sept. 24, 1847; see also Rayback, *Free Soil*, 114–30, and Davis to Hugh R. Davis, June 4, 1848).

[7] The Treaty of Guadalupe Hidalgo was ratified by the Senate on March 10, Davis voting yea. A motion to add the Wilmot Proviso was defeated, as were amendments by Davis and Sam Houston to annex more territory. Finally, few substantive changes were made in the version submitted by Polk on February 23 (*Senate Ex. Doc. 52*, 30:1, 3–37; Miller, ed., *Treaties*, 5:207–60). For Davis' proposals, see his motions offered on March 4, 6, and 9.

[8] A paraphrase from Benjamin Franklin's *The Whistle*, written in 1779 (Stevenson, ed., *Home Book of Proverbs*, 2486).

[9] After checking on conditions at Cypress Grove, near Rodney, Mississippi, Taylor visited Joseph and Eliza Davis and other members of the family at Hurricane plantation on March 17 (Vicksburg *Weekly Sentinel*, Mar. 22, 1848). Varina Davis was with Anna Davis Smith at Locust Grove plantation in West Feliciana Parish, Louisiana.

[10] Named in January as a delegate to the national convention, Joseph E.

Davis received his credentials in April but was not listed among the official delegates when the convention opened on May 22 (Jackson *Mississippian*, Jan. 14, Apr. 28, June 9, 1848).

[11] Henry Turner, born about 1810 in Mississippi, owned 2,000 acres valued at $50,000 (1850). Brother-in-law of John A. Quitman, Turner was active in state Democratic politics (1860 Census, Miss., Warren, family 1374; ibid., 1850, agric., 813; Vicksburg *Weekly Sentinel*, Jan. 5, 1848; Z913, Quitman Papers, folder 16, Ms-Ar).

[12] Reverdy Johnson (1796–1876), Whig senator from Maryland, became Taylor's attorney general (*DAB*). Davis' letter of April 4 has not been found, nor has any record of the Johnson-Davis conversation and Johnson's correspondence with Taylor.

[13] Davis' privately expressed views to Taylor have not been located; see Davis to Stephen Cocke of November 30, 1847, for one statement on the Wilmot Proviso. Taylor himself believed in 1847 (July 27, Sept. 18) that the proviso was "a mere bugbare" and "a trifling affair."

[14] Taylor quotes from an article in Thomas Ritchie's Washington *Union* of April 6. Reuben H. Boone, Democratic senator from Tishomingo County, led the joint legislative committee that invited Taylor to Jackson in January 1848 (Jackson *Mississippian*, Jan. 14, Feb. 4, 1848; *Davis Papers*, 2:93).

[15] Thomas Jefferson Henley (1810–65), Democrat from Richmond, Indiana, was a state legislator (1832–42) and congressman (1843–49). Moving to California, he served in the legislature, 1851–53, and was state superintendent of Indian affairs, 1855–58 (*BDAC*).

[16] Albert G. Brown, serving his first term as representative from Mississippi, identified the doctor as "a most reputable and clever gentleman" believed to be "formerly from Maine" and now a resident of Hinds County (*Cong. Globe*, 30:1, 587).

[17] During House debate on April 6,

Democrat John A. McClernand read from that day's *Union* a letter written by Dr. Timothy Kemmell to Albert G. Brown and purporting to give the substance of an interview between a Dr. Baden and Taylor. In the letter Taylor is reported to have admitted that he, not Polk, ordered American forces to the Rio Grande in 1846. A different troop movement, the transfer of a large part of Taylor's army to Scott's command in 1847, was discussed by Thomas J. Henley. Stating he had studied the letters exchanged by Scott and Taylor and had also called on Secretary of War Marcy for additional official correspondence, Henley concluded that Taylor himself had initiated the transfer (ibid., 584–86; Washington *Union*, Apr. 7, 1848).

[18] Robert Milligan McLane (1815–98), an 1837 West Point graduate, resigned from the army in 1843 and began the practice of law. Elected four times to the House as a Democrat (1847–51, 1879–83), he also served as commissioner to China and minister to Mexico and France (*BDAC*).

[19] James Duncan (1811–49), born in New York, graduated from West Point in 1834 and was capt., 2d Art., during the Mexican War. Brevetted three times while in the commands of Taylor and Scott, Duncan was later col. and inspector gen. (Cullum, *Biog. Reg.*, 1:569–70; *NCAB*, 11:519).

[20] By early 1848 Winfield Scott, like Taylor, found himself embroiled in political intrigue. A well-publicized letter by Duncan that extolled William J. Worth at the expense of Scott as well as anonymous correspondence lauding Gideon Pillow—and actually penned by Pillow—culminated in Scott's arrest of Worth, Pillow, and Duncan and the subsequent recall of Scott. On December 31, before making his decision to supersede Scott, Polk consulted with Davis, who advised that Taylor be sent to replace Scott in Mexico. Defending the administration during House debate on March 21, Robert McLane praised Duncan, recounting an incident said to have occurred after the Battle of Palo Alto, in which the artillery officer asked that the regulars alone be allowed "to rout and destroy" the Mexicans the next day. According to McLane, "Taylor had given them no answer . . . but had laid his hand upon Duncan, and ordered him to say to Major Bliss that they should fight the enemy to-morrow" (*Cong. Globe*, 30:1, 518; Elliott, *Winfield Scott*, 568–72; Polk, *Diary*, 3:269–70).

[21] In mid-April the Mississippi River at Natchez, about thirty miles from Taylor's Jefferson County plantation, was rising but still below the 1847 high-water mark. The widening and deepening of the Raccourci cutoff downriver helped prevent an overflow in 1848 (Vidalia, La., *Concordia Intell.*, Apr. 15, 22, 29, 1848; *Miss. Free Trader and Natchez Gazette*, Apr. 25, 1848).

Remarks on the Protection of Property

Editorial Note: On April 15 the sloop *Pearl* left Washington for a northern port with seventy-seven fugitive slaves. Captured early April 17 by a group of private citizens, the *Pearl* was returned to Washington and all on board were jailed. The following evening angry crowds filled the streets; one group moved on the office of an antislavery newspaper, breaking windows and threatening the editor. On April 20 in both the House and Senate northern legislators offered resolutions concerning the incident. Senator John P. Hale of New Hampshire proposed a bill to indemnify property owners for damages caused by "any riotous or tumultuous assemblage." He was instantly challenged by Arthur P. Bagby and John C. Calhoun, who advised rejection of the bill and threatened retaliation if abolitionists continued to encourage slaves' escape. The debate, described as being "of a most exciting and personal character," ended inconclusively as Hale's bill received no further consideration (Washington *Union*, Apr. 19, 20, 1848; Poore, *Perley's Reminiscences*, 1:398–99; *Cong. Globe*, 30:1, 649, 656, App., 501–10; Wiltse, *Calhoun*, 3:341–42).

April 20, 1848

Mr. DAVIS, of Mississippi. The Senator from South Carolina has remarked that he expected that younger members of this body would notice the motion of the Senator from New Hampshire to introduce a bill, the purpose of which is the protection of incendiaries and kidnappers.[1] I have only to say that it is from no want of accordance in feeling with that honorable Senator, but from deference to him who has so long and so nobly stood foremost in defence of the institutions of the South, that I remained silent. It was rather that I wish to follow him than that I did not feel the indignation which he has so well expressed. The time has come when Congress should interpose the legislation necessary for the punishment of those men who come within our jurisdiction, acting, in fact and in morals, as incendiaries—coming here within the legislative limits of Congress, to steal a portion of that property which is recognized, as such by the Constitution of the United States, and, therefore, entitled to our protection. Is this District to be made the field of abolition struggles? Is this Chamber to be the hot-bed in which plants of sedition are to be nursed? Why is it that in this body, once looked to as the conservative branch of the Government—once looked to as so dignified that it stood above the power of faction—that we find the subject of this contest so insulting to the South—so irritating always when it is agitated—introduced on such an occasion? Is this debatable ground? No! It is ground upon which the people of this Union may shed blood, and that is the final result. If it be pressed any further, and if this Senate is to be made the theatre of that contest, let it come—the sooner the better. We who represent the southern States are not here to be insulted on account of institutions which we inherit. And if civil discord is to be thrown from this Chamber upon the land—if the fire is to be kindled here with which to burn the temple of our Union—if this is to be made the centre from which civil war is to radiate, here let the conflict begin. I am ready, for one, to meet it with any incendiary, who, dead to every feeling of patriotism, attempts to introduce it.

[In a bitter exchange between Hale and Davis' colleague Henry S. Foote, the latter declares that Hale would be hanged—with Foote's help, if need be—should he venture to Mississippi. Counseling calm, Willie P. Mangum suggests that the citizens of the District be consulted. Calhoun disagrees, stating that the Senate must act since the object of Hale's bill is to disarm the citizens and "arm the robbers." Stephen A. Douglas states that the bill is harmless but ill timed, the harsh words of southern senators serving only to enhance Hale's position. Foote then notes that Douglas would feel differently if he lived where "insurrection exhibit(s) its fiery front" and repeats that anyone expressing himself as Hale had would "meet death upon the scaffold." Douglas sympathizes with Foote's fears of "a negro insurrection."]

Mr. DAVIS, of Mississippi. I do not wish to be considered as participating in the feeling to which the Senator alludes. I have no fear of insurrection; no more dread of our slaves than I have of our cattle. Our slaves are happy and contented. They bear the kindest relation that labor can sustain to capital. It is a paternal institution. They are rendered miserable only by the unwarrantable interference of those who know nothing about that with which they meddle. I rest this case on no fear of insurrection; and I wish it to be distinctly understood, that we are able to take care of ourselves, and to punish all incendiaries. It was the insult offered to the institutions which we have inherited, that provoked my indignation.

Mr. FOOTE. Will the honorable Senator allow me to make a remark?

Mr. DOUGLAS.[2] With a great deal of pleasure.

Mr. FOOTE. If it be understood that I expressed any fear of insurrection which might grow out of this movement, it is a mistake. I said that such an audacious movement as this could not be tamely submitted to without encouraging its authors to proceed; and in that, I think, all who have spoken on this side of the Chamber concur.

Mr. DAVIS, of Mississippi. I did not intend to imply that my colleague had taken any such course as that which I disclaimed. His ground was that which the peace and security of the South has justified, and which will, of necessity, be their position in future. When Dr. Johnson heard that a man, whose life had been a course of villany, had committed suicide by hanging himself, he replied, "it was right that a life which had been uniformly oblique should be terminated by a perpendicular."[3]

Cong. Globe, 30:1, App., 501–506.

[1] Calhoun, recalling his long years as the defender of slavery, said he "had hoped that younger members... might have taken the lead, and relieved me from the necessity of ever again speaking upon this subject" (*Cong. Globe*, 30:1, App., 501).
[2] Stephen Arnold Douglas (1813– 61) was serving his first term as senator from Illinois (*DAB*).
[3] From a parody published shortly after the appearance of Boswell's *Life*, on the subject of scoundrels: "It is proper, Sir, that a man whose actions tend towards flagitious obliquity, should appear perpendicular at last" ([Newman], *Lounger's Common-Place Book*, 1:73, 77).

To William L. Marcy

Washington 5th May 1848

Sir,

Some time since I called your attention to the case of Lieut L. B. Northrop 1st Regt. Dragoons who was ordered to be dropped from the service.[1] I stated to you that I felt convinced the case had not been understood, further inquiry convinces me that the decision is less justified than even was supposed by /me/ at the date of our conversation. Lieut. Northrop was selected for a difficult and dangerous service, in the discharge of which he was accidentally wounded by a ball which lodged in his knee. When under apprehension that he would not again be able to render service, he applied for three years leave of absence that he might apply himself to the study of Medicine, and mentioned his intention if permanently crippled, to retire from the army, if he should recover, the knowledge gained was spoken of as adding to his future usefulness. This the adjt. genl. has most strangely construed into a contract by which Lieut. Northrop was to surrender his commission at a fixed time. You sir will not fail to perceive that the position of the adjt. genl. could only be correct where an officers commission could be bargained away for an indulgence; but in the case of Liut. Northrop there was no indulgence he was on sick leave, and required to report monthly like other officers thus circumstanced, and no one will say that his case is less deserving of kind consideration than others who have been longer invalids; who are disabled for life; yet remain upon the army Register. Lieut Northrop from the most honorable considerations determined to leave the army as soon as he could support himself, if his injury left him permanently a cripple; from feelings of the nicest delicacy, he consented to waive all claim to promotion whilst absent from his Regt. For these declarations which do honor to him as a man and a soldier a distinction has been made between him and others similarily situated towards the service. Lieut Northrop continued from time to time to seek duty on the staff, only representing himself unable to do Regimental duty, by an examination of the correspondence, especially the last letter of Lieut. Northrop (of October) it will be seen that he never was knowingly aparty to any contract for the surrender of his commission.[2]

He was entitled under surgeon's certificate to be "absent sick", this was his condition, and if there had been a contract it would seem there should have been some advantage to him, but none appears, he acquired no new right, or privi[leg][3]e. I ask of you to examine this case assured th[a]t you will find a gallant officer and an honorable man has been unju[stly d]eprived of his commission, and if you agree with me as to the merits of the c[a]se I trust you will show the error of the Adjt. genls construction to the President, that he may rescind the order dropping Lieut Northrop from the rolls of the army[4]— Truly yours

JEFFN. DAVIS

ALS (DNA, RG94, Letters Recd., 48-N-1848, f/w 56-N-1860).

[1] Lucius B. Northrop was notified on January 8 that he had been dropped from the army. Davis soon contacted Adj. Gen. Roger Jones about the case (Jan. 19, 25) and apparently talked with Marcy on the evening of January 19 (Jones to Davis, Jan. 20, 1848).

[2] Wounded in October 1839, Northrop was on active duty for only five months (in the winter of 1842–43) during the next eight and a half years. When he applied for a three years' leave in December 1843, it was granted, according to Roger Jones, with the "express understanding" that he would resign in 1846 if he were still disabled. In September 1847, having received only the required monthly reports, Jones asked whether he intended to resign or return to the Dragoons. Northrop replied on October 11, denying that he had ever agreed to resign, reviewing his various attempts to undertake some regimental assignments, and reiterating that he was physically unfit for active service (Northrop to Jones, Oct. 11, 1847, Jones to William L. Marcy, Nov. 24,

1847, DNA, RG94, Letters Recd., 91-N-1847 and 126-N-1847, f/w 56-N-1860).

³ Brackets indicate portions of the original obscured by ink smears.

⁴ Marcy's reply to Davis, dated May 24, concurred with Jones. In a letter to the president about Northrop (June 23), Davis complained that "the answer of the secty. does not go beyond the report and correspondence of the Adjt. Genl. [and] consequently does not reach the matter at issue." An endorsement by Marcy on Davis' June letter ordered that at the first opportunity Northrop be restored to the position he would have accepted if he had not been dropped. On July 26 Davis assured Northrop that he would be returned to the army lists. On August 12 he was not only reinstated but also—thanks to Davis' intercession—promoted capt., 1st Dragoons, to rank from July 21, 1848 (Davis to Northrop, [Aug. 9], 1848; *Senate Ex. Jour.*, 7:468–69, 476, 481). See also Andrew P. Butler and John C. Calhoun to President Polk, July 6, 1848.

Remarks on the Occupation of Yucatan

Editorial Note: Long an unstable region alienated from the rest of Mexico, Yucatan was plunged in 1846 into a civil war that gradually escalated into a deadly conflict between white and Indian. So desperate did the situation of the white population become by 1848 that on March 25 an appeal was sent to the United States, Spain, and Great Britain, offering sovereignty to whichever nation responded first. Polk's message to Congress (Apr. 29) emphasized the possible extermination of Yucatan's white population by the Indians, the peninsula's strategic location, and the dangers of European interference. On May 4 Senator Edward A. Hannegan reported a bill authorizing a "temporary military occupation," the use of volunteers, and the distribution of arms to the white citizens. In the "protracted discussion" that followed, Davis responded to John M. Clayton, who opposed the bill. Noting the Yucatan's unhealthy climate, Clayton warned against "precipitate action" and further annexation of territory, particularly while the treaty with Mexico was pending (Merk, *Monroe Doctrine*, 202–11; *Cong. Globe*, 30:1, App. 590–99).

May 5, 1848

Mr. DAVIS, of Mississippi. I have no disposition to follow the Senator from Delaware[1] into any discussion of the treaty, or the probabilities of future annexation. On the treaty I consider my lips yet sealed. The subject of future annexation I leave to the future. The President's message distinctly announces that he seeks no annexation of Yucatan. It is not the acquisition of territory to which he directs his attention. He merely points out the sole motive which has prompted him on this occasion to invoke the action of the legislative branch of the Government. Nor do I conceive it necessary at present to assert that principle, which, when the time arrives, I, like others, shall be ready to maintain: the non-intervention of European Powers in the affairs of the North American continent. I do not think that that principle is involved in this question. We are at war with Mexico. Yucatan is recognized as a part of Mexico, standing neutral, it is true, through the greater part of the war, but, on one occasion, throwing off her neutrality, and identifying herself with Mexico, in her war against the United States. Being thus a part of Mexico, the Mexican war covers Yucatan. The President requires no more than a sufficient force to enable him to prosecute his military operations in Yucatan or elsewhere, to save him from the necessity of applying to Congress for any action at all. It is well known that a response to his application for an increase of the army has been long delayed. The measure has been long discussed in this body, and it remains to be seen how long action upon it may be deferred in the other branch of Congress.[2] In these circumstances, an urgent demand for the presence of American troops in Yucatan arises, and the President calls upon Congress to give him the means to carry out what was his plain duty, as the chief officer of the Executive Government. A portion of that country, against which we made war, and rendered especially helpless by our act of invasion, calls to us in a voice of deep suffering for aid. That is the ground upon which I put this question. This measure is an incident of the Mexican war, which past legislation has declared and recognized.

The President only asks for troops to enable him to carry out an object entirely consistent with the prosecution of the war against Mexico. It is true that he alludes to the present condition of Yucatan in connection with Great Britain. This is no new announcement. We have seen Great Britain year after year extending her naval stations, until, by a line of circumvallation, she almost surrounds the Gulf of Mexico. We see her posts at telegraphic distances from the banks of the Bahamas to the mouth of the Oronoco. And certainly we may be jealous of any attempt on her part to seize a cape which actually commands the entrance into the Gulf from the Caribbean Sea. The chairman of the Committee on Foreign Relations has appropriately connected with this the question of the possession of Cuba.[3] Yucatan and Cuba are the salient points commanding the Gulf of Mexico, which I hold to be a basin of water belonging to the United States. Whenever the question arises whether the United States shall seize these gates of entrance from the south and east, or allow them to pass into the possession of any maritime Power, I am ready, for one, to declare that my step will be forward, and that the cape of Yucatan and the island of Cuba must be ours.[4]

Mr. CLAYTON. Will the honorable gentleman allow me to ask him a question?

Mr. DAVIS. Certainly.

Mr. CLAYTON. Suppose there should be a negro insurrection in Cuba, and that, from motives of humanity, Great Britain should interfere and take military possession of that island, for which course we are about to make a precedent, would the honorable Senator hesitate to go to war?

Mr. DAVIS. Not a moment!

Mr. CLAYTON. It is the answer that I expected.

Mr. DAVIS. I have no confidence in the humanity of Great Britain, the great slave-trader of the world. If she should interfere, on any pretext, in the affairs of Cuba, in order to obtain a footing there, I would regard it as a proper occasion to interfere. Great Britain has already attempted, under a pretext of establishing a hospital on the island of Cuba, in connection with her slave-ships, to build up a Gibraltar to overlook the Spanish Moro Castle; and if the government of Cuba has yielded to that demand, the weak court of Spain not denying it, I would have considered it as demanding the immediate interference of the United States. The very necessity of defending the United States requires that we should take whatever steps should be necessary always to secure the freedom of the great point of exit and entrance to a large portion of the American coast. But I understand the question of the Senator as making the interference of Great Britain in the affairs of Cuba a parallel case with the present.

Mr. CLAYTON. I put that case to show the Senator the effect of his own declaration.

Mr. DAVIS. I saw the conclusion, and was prepared for it.

Mr. CLAYTON. It is a foregone conclusion.

Mr. DAVIS. If we were not at war with Mexico, and a war of castes had sprung up in Yucatan, in which we had no right as a belligerent Power to interfere, however I might have been pained in beholding the spectacle, I should have viewed it as I did the case of Guatemala, in which the Indian race triumphed,[5] and established, as I will concede to the Senator, a better government than Guatemala ever had before. If such were the case at present, I would stand quietly by, and let the people decide which race should rule them. But I place this case of Yucatan solely on the ground of the Mexican war. I have not yet seen any convincing proof that Great Britain has interfered. She has been asked to send some troops, and I believe has sent three companies of artillery.[6]

Mr. CLAYTON. Is there not an armistice now existing?

Mr. DAVIS. That originally constituted a difficulty with me, which, by one best calculated to construe it, has been removed, and does not now interpose any obstacle to my action. I am not apprized at what date that armistice expires,[7] but I think it will come to an end before we can possibly get troops to Yucatan. Again, that armistice points directly to the fact that no new posts are to be taken in Mexico, except on account of hostile movements on her part. Here is a movement, the result of which we cannot determine. It is like the war of factions all over Mexico. It may be for the purpose of interfering with the progress of the American army in the conclusion of the treaty. Is the Senator from Delaware prepared to say it is not?

I do not rely upon the argument of the honorable Senator, the chairman of the Committee on Foreign Relations, based upon the fact that these Indians have been furnished with arms, bearing the Tower mark.[8] It does not follow from that fact, that these arms were furnished by Great Britain. Caesar, Frederick, and Napoleon, the three greatest generals, have demonstrated that celerity of movement is the great groundwork of military success. Great Britain, aware of the value of the maxim, has been constantly reducing the weight of her arms. The Tower muskets have been condemned and sold as unfit for service. Hence, they are found all over the South American States.

Mr. HANNEGAN. Has not Great Britain established a great depôt of arms at the Balize?[9]

Mr. DAVIS. Certainly, I am aware of that fact. If she was sending muskets there, however, she would send them from her own armories, and of the present standard. These Tower muskets were also found in the hands of the Mexicans, having been purchased by those who could obtain only cheap arms, or had less skill in the use of them. Great Britain may be interfering in the affairs of Yucatan, but I am not prepared to jump to that conclusion. Like ourselves, she may only be answering the call of humanity; or she may be insidiously arming the Indians. But whether it be the one or the other, it is immaterial to my argument. I take the ground, that as we are at war with Mexico, we have a right to establish posts in any part of Mexico, if it be necessary to the prosecution of that war; and if Great Britain steps in when we have prostrated the Mexican Government, to take advantage of the condition of affairs and seize Yucatan, we have the right to interpose. We are the belligerent Power; we may take up positions within that territory, and, with the highest motives of humanity and policy, assert our right to exclude any other Power from seizing Mexico, or any portion of her territory in the present prostrate condition to which she has been reduced by us. In my judgment, therefore, the President has placed the question on the true ground.

I rise to offer an amendment to the bill, upon the ground simply of the urgent demand which exists for the immediate increase of the army, and to give power to the President to call out troops to supply the place of those withdrawn from the army, for the purpose of holding posts in Yucatan. With these introductory remarks, I beg to offer my amendment.

The amendment, which is as follows, and is a substitute for the whole bill, was then read:

> *Be it enacted, &c.*, That the President be, and he is hereby, authorized and empowered to accept the services of an equal number of volunteer troops to supply the place of such as may be withdrawn from their present duty, to answer to the exigent demand for the immediate presence of a portion of our army in Yucatan: *Provided*, Their services shall be required. The same to be raised for service during the war with Mexico, agreeably to the provisions of the act of May thirteenth, eighteen hundred and forty-seven.

Mr. UPHAM.[10] I would ask if the President has not the right now to increase the army to the extent of twelve thousand volunteers?

Mr. DAVIS. The President is authorized to call out a certain number of volunteers by regiments. These regiments were called out. They have wasted away in the service, and it would take perhaps the number named to fill up the ranks of regiments already existing in the volunteer service; but the only way in which that can be done, is by recruiting, and recruiting for volunteer regiments has been found to be so difficult, that no one looks to it as a means of increasing the army with the rapidity required by this exigency.

The Senator from Delaware, I may remark, before I resume my seat, represents Yucatan as a sickly country, and speaks of the sufferings of our troops in Mexico. Now, I do not believe that the interior either of Yucatan or of Mexico, is sickly; but when new troops are sent to a tropical climate in the summer season, exposed to the inclemencies of camp life, and put upon soldier's fare, they are liable to contract disease, partly in consequence of their want of knowledge of the proper mode of encampment, and of the best means of protecting themselves. Hence the necessity for sending into a new country troops that have had some experience; and in sending out fresh volunteers, they should be mingled for a time with troops that have been in service, from whom they can learn all the necessary means of taking care of themselves in a climate the peculiarities of which are to be learned.

[Crittenden argues that Davis' amendment "entirely changes the character of this bill" by simply proposing to increase the military force in Mexico, thus changing the president's aim—"to rescue an unhappy people overwhelmed by a savage foe." He also refers to the likelihood that adoption of Davis' proposal would violate the existing armistice.]

Mr. DAVIS, of Mississippi. I beg to call the attention of the Senator to the fact that there was an express provision in the armistice, that in the case of any military movements being made, we had the right to send our troops to counteract them.[11]

Mr. CRITTENDEN. I suppose it may be fairly inferred that that provision had reference only to such military operations as were supposed to be hostile to us.

Mr. DAVIS, of Mississippi, (in his seat.) Yes; I have no doubt such was the understanding of the provision.

[Crittenden recalls that, since "civil war raged in the Yucatan" when the armistice was signed, it would have been mentioned if the terms were not intended to include it. Urging caution, he requests more information on the extent of the occupation and its probable cost.]

Mr. DAVIS, of Mississippi. If I understood the Senator from Kentucky, his objection to the bill, as I have proposed to amend it, arises out of the existing armistice between the United States and Mexico. In addition to the stipulation before mentioned by me, the Senator will find two general exceptions to the condition of the armistice. One to restrain the Indians from predatory incursions upon the Mexican settlements; the other, where armed men may be found banded together acting without the authority of either of the contracting parties. The first case gives the right to pass limits of present occupation; the second makes it the duty of both contracting parties to suppress such lawless or insurrectionary movements. Within one or other of these exceptions the contemplated campaign in Yucatan must be included.[12]

Cong. Globe, 30:1, App., 599–601.

[1] John Middleton Clayton (1796–1856), Whig senator from Delaware, was a Yale graduate who served Zachary Taylor as secretary of state, negotiating the Clayton-Bulwer Treaty in 1850 (*BDAC*).

[2] Referring to the ten-regiment bill, passed by the House on May 8.

[3] Edward Allen Hannegan (1807–59), a Democrat from Covington, Indiana, had served in the state legislature and the House (1833–37) before becoming senator (1843–49). His speech on May 5 forcefully proclaimed Great Britain's designs in South America. Belize, the Bay Islands, the Mosquito coast of Nicaragua, and the mouth of the San Juan River were already under British control, and, according to Hannegan, "the entire Isthmus" was threatened. British possession of the Yucatan, he said, "would soon be followed by the possession of Cuba" and total domination of the Gulf (*DAB*; *Cong. Globe*, 30:1, App., 596–97; see also Perkins, *Monroe Doctrine*, 18–20, 165–67).

[4] Some weeks after this speech, on June 23, Davis visited the president, taking with him three Cubans who "had information" about an imminent revolution on the island. If the revolt were successful, they reported, their countrymen "would desire to be annexed to the U. S." After listening to

their comments and to Davis' reading of a letter from Cuba, Polk gave only "a general evasive reply" (Polk, *Diary*, 3:499–500).

[5] In 1838–40 Rafael Carrera led a rural uprising in Guatemala, enabling Indians and mestizos to become a viable political force for several decades (*Ency. of Latin America*, s.v. "Carrera").

[6] In his remarks James D. Westcott quoted a Campeche newspaper of March 31, 1848, to show that the British governor of Belize had sent three companies of soldiers to the Yucatan village of Bacalar (*Cong. Globe*, 30:1, App., 607).

[7] Signed on February 29, the armistice was "to remain in force during the period fixed by the treaty [four months], unless notice of terminating it [was] given" (Smith, *War with Mexico*, 2:468, 470).

[8] Hannegan suggested that the Indians were armed with muskets, "bearing the mark of the Tower of London" and supplied by a British agent in Belize (*Cong. Globe*, 30:1, App., 597).

[9] Approximately 100 soldiers were sent to Belize to defend against the Yucatecan Indians (Merk, *Monroe Doctrine*, 214n).

[10] William Upham (1792–1853) was Whig senator from Vermont, 1843–53 (*BDAC*).

[11] For the terms of the armistice, see

the Washington *Union* of March 28, 1818.

[12] Debate continued until May 17, when Hannegan, having learned of a treaty between the whites and Indians, withdrew his bill (*Cong. Globe*, 30:1, App., 603–40).

To Hugh R. Davis

Washington 4th June 1848

MY DEAR NEPHEW,

I am not able to account for my silence which you notice in your kind letter.[1] There is no one of whom I think with more affectionate solicitude than yourself, no one to whom I could write with more pleasure or from it would give me more gratification to receive frequent letters. It has been my misfortune to witness in my political course but little of that elevated statesmanship of which it would give me pleasure to speak to a younger relation, and therefore politics have not presented to me a theme for correspondence between us.[2] Before this you will have received the nominations of the Baltimore convention,[3] both men are in private life worthy of the highest estimation neither of them are great, and the first on the ticket would be more respectable in any other position than an *executive* office.

His opinions upon the question of slavery in the territories are very unpalatable to me, and whether viewed as an original question or referred to the past practice of our government wholly untenable in argument. His creed and practice on "internal improvement" are not such as has heretofore been considered democratic.[4] This narrows the ground of controversy to the issues declared to be obsolete or suspended, and reduces the contest to little more than a choice of agents. To have democratic officers is certainly in my opinion an advantage, for the time being, but ultimately it were better for our party that its measures should be abandoned under a Whig than a Democratic Administration. Believing that the policy of internal improvement is to be the distinguishing mark of the next four years, and that all the attendant evils of extravagance and public debt are to be visited upon us, I feel little interest in the Presidential canvass— The anti slavery feeling in the North and the Internal improvement policy of the West, were strong enough in the convention to defeat any sound man. The Whigs are busyly engaged in combinations for their convention, the Clay, McLane,[5] and Scott men are combining, they will unite if possible to defeat Genl. Taylor's friends in the convention, I have rather avoided than sought information, and cannot pretend to judge of events connected with Whig schemes. It is probable however if the northern men succeed that the Taylor men, the southern whigs, will withdraw and present his name to the south as a southern independent candidate. Then a *geographical* division will occur, the event which I have always deprecated, and which must be the precursor of *disunion*. The northern Democrats could relieve us from this danger if they would brave the abolitionists.

Please present me affectionately to my niece Ann and the young Hugo,[6] I hope to enjoy the pleasure you promise me of seeing them on my return, in the latter part of the summer.

You mention the matter of Jenny's troubles with "Jim",[7] if it is wished to sell him I would be glad to own him and <−will−> authorize you to have his price paid by Messrs. Laughlin & co. of New Orleans,[8] or to make any other arrangement which may be more agreeable.

Let me hear from you as often as convenient and believe me ever affectionately your Uncle

JEFFN: DAVIS

ALS (ViRC).

[1] Not found.

[2] Hugh Davis was active in Wilkinson County Democratic party affairs (Woodville *Repub.*, June 13, Aug. 29, 1848; Davis to Wilkinson County Citizens, Oct. 6, 1848).

[3] Lewis Cass and William O. Butler were selected the Democratic standard-bearers on May 25.

[4] A reference to Cass's firm stand on the doctrine of popular sovereignty as expressed in the Nicholson letter and to his voting record for federally financed internal improvements (Woodford, *Lewis Cass*, 251–53, 266–67; see also Davis' speech of Sept. 22 and his public letter of Oct. 23, 1848).

[5] John McLean (1785–1861) of Ohio, former congressman and postmaster general and longtime Supreme Court justice (1830–61), was "a perennial candidate" for president. His name was presented to the Whig convention but withdrawn before the first ballot (Hamilton, *Zachary Taylor*, 2:59–60; Weisenburger, *Life of McLean*, esp. ch. 9).

[6] Hugh Davis' wife was the former Ann Jane Boyle (1823–June 17, 1882). Their son Hugh Landon Davis (July 2, 1846–July 5, 1898) attended the University of Virginia, 1865–68, and became an attorney (H. Davis, *Davis Family*, 173; Davis genealogy files, Ernesto Caldeira; family recs. of Douglas M. Moore; ViU to Davis Assn., Nov. 2, 1979).

[7] Jane Davis Farish, Davis' niece, lived in Woodville, not far from her cousin Hugh's plantation. In 1846 she

had inherited from her grandmother a young slave named Jim (*Davis Papers*, 1:458; H. Davis, *Davis Family*, 94).

[8] William Laughlin was Davis' commission merchant, 1845–51 (*Davis Papers*, 2:16).

Speech at Washington

Editorial Note: On June 12 John J. Crittenden resigned his Senate seat to run for governor of Kentucky. The same day he accepted the invitation of a large group of friends, including Davis, to be honored at a public dinner. "Without distinction of party," members of Congress and local citizens gathered at the National Hotel on the eve of Crittenden's departure. Davis was asked to respond "to a toast given in honor of the army." Nearly three months later a Whig campaign paper gave the substance of his extemporaneous remarks "in regard to the character, military and civil," of Zachary Taylor (*BDAC*; Washington *Nat. Intell.*, June 13, 15, 16, 1848; Washington *Battery*, Sept. 7, 1848).

June 13, 1848

Colonel Davis commenced his remarks by observing that he would, in order to illustrate the value and importance to the nation of that arm of the public service, honored in the sentiment which had just been announced and most generously applauded, glance at the services and character of a distinguished officer of the army, who, he regretted to see, had been placed before the nation, without his own seeking, as the candidate of a party for the high office of Chief Magistrate of this Union.

He then alluded to the cool, intrepid, noble, and judicious conduct of Captain Zachary Taylor in defending Fort Harrison, in the war of 1812, against a vastly superior force of infuriated savages and gave, in vivid terms, an account of the exploit. He then followed the young Hero through his frontier hardships and exploits in the arduous service of his country, exhibiting ever those high and noble traits of character, honesty, firmness, forecast, and humanity, which still characterize the man, down to the Florida war and the memorable battle and victory of Ocheechobee, where he displayed in so eminent a degree his thorough knowledge of the Indian character and mode of warfare, his great skill and courage, and his never-failing humanity.

Next he presented him as the well-selected instrument of the Gov-

ernment to lead our army, first to the protection of the Texas frontier, and next to repel the attack of the Mexican army under Arista
and Bustamente.[1] He pictured the dangers which surrounded him—
the smallness of his force, in comparison with that of the enemy—
the disadvantages of his position—his lack of ponton trains and supplies—his march to Point Isabel—his cool judgment and determined
purpose while at that Point; on which occasion he wrote that he
should return to the rescue of the portion of his force he had left at
Fort Brown, and that if the enemy opposed his march, whatever his
numbers, he should fight him—his return march, when he did meet
the enemy and whipped him splendidly at Palo Alto and Resaca de
la Palma, and afterwards drove him from Matamoros on the southern side of the Rio Grande—and the judgment and humanity he
exhibited on these occasions, as well as the confidence his bearing,
manner, and character infused into the breasts of all, volunteers as
well as regulars, who participated in those thrilling scenes!

He then traced the same noble Hero to the storming and capture
of Monterey, with such portion only of his command as his limited
means of transportation and subsistence would allow of his taking
along with him from the banks of the Rio Grande. After depicting
the brave General during the sanguinary engagement—the coolest
of the cool, inspiring full confidence wherever he moved—he
touched upon the kind-hearted benevolence and humanity of the
brave old Chief, as exhibited after the battle was over, first, in taking
the very best care of his own wounded, and then going about among
the wounded and suffering of the enemy, and ordering his soldiers
to pour cold water down their parched throats.[2] The picture which
he here drew evidently took a deep hold upon his auditory, for all
was as hushed as death.

Next he led the company on, in imagination, to the critical and
hazardous time for General Taylor, when, at or near Saltillo, with
the flower of his command, all his own favorite regulars, except
about 500 men, taken from him, leaving him with this handful of
regulars and some five thousand volunteers, and Santa Anna, who
had been passed from exile into Mexico, coming down upon him
with the veteran troops of the Mexican army, composed of more
than 20,000 men, far better clothed and disciplined than our own
men!

Upon this ungrateful and outrageous conduct towards General

Taylor—without aiming to decide where and with whom the responsibility of the black act laid—the eloquent orator was severely indignant. Passing on from the rebuke, which he could not help uttering, though he did not exactly locate it upon any particular shoulders,[3] he vividly described the battle at Buena Vista, and the great part performed in it and throughout it by General Taylor, as well as the beneficial effects which that mighty victory produced, in contrast with what would inevitably have been the disastrous consequences, had the Mexican hosts led by Santa Anna been the victors!

Having traced General Taylor through all his brilliant military achievements, the truth-loving and eloquent Senator spoke of the old hero as a man, a civilian, a member of society, a pillar of the State, and declared that in all these stations he had no superior. He was proverbial for his modesty, firmness, intelligence, uprightness, and humanity. He had known him long and known him well, and he had never known a man with a purer or better character. In whatever station he might be placed of honor and trust, he would adorn it. He was a man of great wisdom and firmness of character, and *he had never undertaken any step and failed to carry it out!*

Washington *Battery*, Sept. 7, 1848.

[1] Mariano Arista (1802–55), later president of Mexico, and Anastasio Bustamente (1780–1853), a former president; the latter did not participate in any Mexican War battles (*Diccionario Porrúa*).

[2] Taylor's special care of the Mexican wounded was reported after the Battle of Buena Vista, not Monterrey (see, for example, Vicksburg *Daily*

Whig, Apr. 2, 1847).

[3] Accused later (1852) of having criticized the administration in the course of his speech, while "leaving it doubtful . . . whether [he] intended to cast censure on Mr. Polk or Gen. Scott," Davis explained that he "felt deeply" about the withdrawal of Taylor's men but had "never censured Mr. Polk for it" (Davis, *Papers*, ed. Rowland, 2:141).

Exchange with Henry S. Foote

July 1, 1848

Mr *Davis of Missii.* Some time since I presented to the Senate a /national/[1] flag, being the particular flag raised upon the <–Capital–>[1] /Citadel/ of Mexico, after <–it was captured.–> /the Capitol was taken/[2] The Officer who <–gave–> /entrusted/ it to me for presentation gave me no special history of the Circumstances Connected with it, beyond the fact, that it was the first National flag that had been raised over the Citadel[3] of Mexico after the Capture of that City. <-In fact-> I believed,[4] that in was in Consequence of the accounts being somewhat contradictory as to the individual by whose immediate agency the flag was raised, that he declined saying any thing at all in regard to the matter. I have recd. <-however-> this morn /from a distinguished citizen of Iowa/ from the officer who raised the flag <-a-> letters[5] in which <-he-> /it is/ stated,[6] that he considers <-that-> some injustice has been done him, in Consequence of the report made by him to Genl. Twiggs, giving an account of the transaction <-had-> not having[7] been Communicated to the Senate. He has forwarded to me /a duplicate of/ that report,[8] and as an act of justice to him, I now present it to the Senate, and ask that it may be read, & printed[9]

The report was read by the Secy:

Mr. Foote.[10] complained that he had not been consulted by his colleague before he presented the flag. There was an impression among the friends of Major General Quitman, that injustice had been done to him, by the total suppression of his name in the remarks which his colleague had made on introducing the flag. He had intended, however, to let the matter rest, and he would have done so but for the revival of the subject this morning. Without intending the slightest disrespect to General Twiggs, he thought he should not be doing his duty, if he permitted the name of General Quitman, who had ordered the flag to be raised, and who was a distinguished son of Mississippi, to be silently passed over. He had in his possession documentary evidence on this point, which he hoped to be able at an early period to submit to the Senate, in order that justice should be done to all on the official records of this body.

Mr. DAVIS, of Mississippi, expressed himself a little surprised at the course of his colleague. The officer who had placed the flag in his hands, had said nothing on the subject, and if there was any wrangling for the honor among subordinates, he would not stoop to mingle in it. He did not expect that there existed any misunderstanding between the commanding officers. He should be found as ready to defend the reputation of General Quitman, whenever a proper occasion offered itself, as any man; and he should feel great grief if anything took place to ruffle a single plume in his wreath of renown. The fame of this distinguished man, and of others who had performed a conspicuous part in the late war, he was willing to hand over to the historian; and he would not wish to be numbered among those who desired to make political capital out of it.[11]

MS, emended by Davis (Davis Papers, KyLxT); *Cong. Globe*, 30:1, 890–91.

[1] All interlineations and deletions by Davis.

[2] On June 2, "in the name of Brigadier General Twiggs," Davis presented what was described as "a Mexican flag, taken in Mexico" and pronounced "an eulogium on the exploits of our army." After he disagreed with a suggestion that the flag be deposited in the State Department, the subject was laid over (*Cong. Globe*, 30:1, 811).

[3] Davis corrected the word *City*.

[4] Davis added the letter *d* and the comma.

[5] Davis added the letter *s*.

[6] Davis changed the final *s* to *d*.

[7] Davis added the word *having*.

[8] Benjamin S. Roberts' report to Twiggs was dated September 17, 1847. In it he detailed the history of the "stand of national colors" that Twiggs had given him and that Roberts claimed was the first flag to fly over both the *garita* of Belén and the Mexican capitol. A Senate investigation later determined that, though the second claim was true, John A. Quitman deserved credit for having ordered the first American flag flown at Belén (*Senate Rep. 32*, 34:1, Washington *Union*, July 25, 1847; see also Claiborne, *Quitman*, 1:360–65).

[9] Davis added "& printed."

[10] The manuscript portion of the item ends here.

[11] After Andrew P. Butler stated his support of Quitman's claim, "some further discussion took place between Mr. FOOTE and Mr. DAVIS, which became at first warm and then personal in its character." Solon Borland spoke, also crediting Quitman with raising the flag, before William L. Dayton moved successfully to table the subject. According to one observer, the possibility of a duel between Foote and Davis was "very broadly mentioned"; the clash was averted by the intervention of their colleagues (*Cong. Globe*, 30:1, 891; Jackson *Southron*, July 14, 1848). Not on amicable terms for some time, Davis and Foote had actually come to blows and narrowly avoided a duel the previous December (see *Davis Papers*, 2: 86).

Andrew P. Butler and John C. Calhoun to James K. Polk

Senate Chamber 6th July 1848

Sir,

Having learned that the case of Lieut. L. B. Northrop late of the 1st Regt of Dragoons, is before you, for restoration to his command we beg leave to ask for him your fevorable consideration

Mr. Northrop bore a high reputation in the army and was wounded when in the discharge of a difficult and hazardous duty — from this wound his present disability resulted — other officers we are informed have been permitted to remain in the army when permanently disabled, and we hope no invidious distinction will be made against this gallant, honorable, and unfortunate officer. Very Respectfully yrs.—

A. P. BUTLER[1]—
J. C. CALHOUN

AL by Davis/S by Butler and Calhoun (DNA, RG94, Letters Recd., 88-N-1848, f/w 56-N-1860).

[1] Andrew Pickens Butler (1796–

1857), native South Carolinian, was elected to the state house and senate before joining his mentor Calhoun in the Senate in 1846 (*BDAC*).

Speech on the Oregon Bill

Editorial Note: Despite the passage of almost two years since the treaty with Britain, Oregon did not yet have a territorial government when the Treaty of Guadalupe Hidalgo introduced the problem of organizing California and New Mexico. Tabled since February 1848, the Oregon bill was brought up on May 31. Desultory discussion over the next three weeks ended on June 23, when John P. Hale offered an amendment extending the provisions of the Northwest Ordinance to Oregon and Davis countered with an amendment opposing any prohibition of slavery in the territory. During the ensuing debate Davis rose to defend his amendment and to give his views on slavery, his first congressional speech focusing directly on the subject (*Cong. Globe*, 30:1, 309, 656, 804–805, 818, 862, 870–71, debate in App., passim; V. Davis, *Memoir*, 1:400; for a general discussion, see Potter, *Impending Crisis*, 65–73).

July 12, 1848

Mr. PRESIDENT: Shall jealousy, discord, and dissension—shall political strife, for sectional supremacy—be permitted to undermine the foundation of our republican fabric? Shall an interference with the domestic affairs of the people in one portion of our Union, wounding to their pride and sensibility, and unwarranted by the compact of confederation, be pressed, to the destruction of that fraternal feeling and mutual confidence on which alone can our institutions securely repose? Shall a discrimination against one section of the Confederacy, the palpable object of which is totally to destroy political equality, be sanctioned by the common agent of the States, and receive here an impulse to hasten its progress to the inevitable goal of such a principle—the disunion of the States?

These, and such as these, are the grave, the melancholy questions which arise from the consideration of this bill and the character of the discussion we have heard upon it. Happy, thrice happy,[1] will it be if the answers to these questions shall be given by a lofty patriotism and enlightened statesmanship, which, disregarding the passions of the hour, look to the general welfare and the permanent good. But, if personal considerations govern our actions—if each Senator reflects the prejudice and extreme opinion which may exist in the section he represents—then it may be our lot to witness the fulfillment of the foreboding fear of Mr. Jefferson, when such agitation as that which surrounds us caused him to express the apprehension, that the sacrifices of the generation of 1776 had been made in vain.[2]

Deeply impressed with the gravity and importance of the subject, I shall offer my opinions dispassionately and candidly, briefly and decidedly, as the occasion requires, and my deep-rooted love of the Union demands.

I consider the 12th section of this bill to establish a Territorial Government in Oregon, to be practically the abolition of slavery in said Territory by the Government of the United States; and seeing no adequate disposition to strike that section out of the bill, I introduced the amendment now under consideration. To this I was prompted by a sense of duty to myself, of duty to those whom I have the honor to represent, of obligation to the principles avowed as the basis of my political creed, and which are the cardinal points by which my political course must be directed. This amendment has received an interpretation which its language in no degree justifies. To this misconstruction I will first call attention, as upon it rests a position, assumed in several quarters, which it is important to combat. Senators have treated this amendment as a proposition to force slavery into the Territory of Oregon.[3] Sir, I had no such purpose, no such desire; and surely the most ingenious must fail to extract any such intent from its letter. It is but a distinct avowal of the ground uniformly maintained by all statesmen of the strict construction school, and adhered to by southern men generally throughout the entire period of our confederate existence. Its direct aim is to restrain the Federal Government from the exercise of a power not delegated—its ultimate effect to protect those rights which have been guarantied by the Federal Constitution. The amendment is in these words: "That nothing contained in this act shall be so construed as to authorize the prohibition of domestic slavery in said Territory whilst it remains in the condition of a Territory of the United States."

There is nothing directory, or enactive, or proposed for enactment. It is restrictive, and directed against a prohibition which is covertly contained in the bill. Though it is not expressly declared that slavery shall be prohibited in Oregon, this would be virtually enacted by the twelfth section of the bill, which gives validity and operation to the laws enacted by the "Provisional Government established by the people" who inhabit that Territory. It is known that one of the laws passed by the people of Oregon prohibits slavery.[4] To give validity to those laws is therefore equivalent to the passage of a law by Congress to prohibit slavery in that Territory. Does Congress possess such power?

If the right to migrate with their property to territory belonging to the United States attaches equally to all their citizens, and if, as I have been credibly informed, citizens have migrated with their slaves into Oregon, to pass the bill before us without amendment would be abolition of slavery by the Federal Government. Entertaining this opinion, I submitted an amendment to meet the case distinctly and singly. Now, for the first time in our history, has Congress, without the color of compact or compromise, claimed to discriminate in the settlement of territories against the citizens of one portion of the Union and in favor of another. This, taken in connection with all which is passing around us, must excite the attention of Senators to the fact, and forces on my mind the conclusion, that herein is sought to be established a precedent for future use. Here upon the threshold we must resist, or forever abandon the claim to equality of right, and consent to be a marked caste, doomed, in the progress of national growth, to be dwarfed into helplessness and political dependence. As equals, the States came into the Union, and, by the Articles of Confederation, equal rights, privileges, and immunities were secured to the citizens of each; yet, for asserting in this case that the Federal Government shall not authorize the destruction of each equality, we have been accused of wishing to claim for the citizens of the southern States unusual rights under the Constitution.[5] This accusation comes badly from those who insist on provisions for exclusion; and cannot find its application to a demand that nothing shall be done to affect the constitutional relations of citizens or the constitutional rights of property. We do not ask of the Federal Government to grant new privileges, but to forbear from interfering with existing rights—rights which existed anterior to the formation of the Constitution, which were recognized in that instrument, and which it is made the duty of the Federal Government, as the agent of our Union, to protect and defend.

Such obligations as belong to other species of property, nor more nor less, we claim as due to our property in slaves. Nor can this claim be denied without denying the property right to which it attaches. This, it has been contended, is the creation of local law, and does not extend beyond the limits for which such laws were made; and, with an air of concession, we are told that it is not proposed to interfere with slavery as it exists in the States, because the Constitution secures it there.[6] Sir, slavery is sustained but was not created by the local law of the States in which it exists; nor did those States ask of the Federal Government to secure or maintain it within their borders; beyond their own jurisdiction, and there only, could the protection of Federal laws be required. Before the formation of our Confederacy, slavery existed in the Colonies, now the States of the Union; and, but for the union of the States, would have no legal recognition beyond the limits of the territory of each. But when the fathers of the Republic had achieved its independence, they sought to draw closer the bonds of union, and to remove all cause for discord and contention. For this holy purpose, they met in council and formed the Constitution under which we live. This compact of union changed the relation of the States to each other in many important particulars, and gave to property and intercourse a national character. Property in persons held to service was recognized; in various and distinct forms it became property under the Constitution of the United States, was made coextensive with the supremacy of the Federal laws, its existence subject only to the legislation of sovereign States possessing powers not drawn from, but above, the Constitution. Thus, provision was made for the recovery of fugitive slaves, and the question of right to such property as absolutely precluded, as the guilt or innocence of one charged with "treason, felony, or other crime." In both cases, it is made the duty of the State authorities to deliver up the fugitive, on demand of the State from which the felon fled in the one case, and of the person to whom the service is due in the other.[7]

By the second section of the fourth article of the Constitution, it is provided that—

"A person charged in any State with treason, felony, or other crime, who shall flee from justice, and be found in another State, shall, on demand of the executive authority of the State from which he fled, be delivered up, to be removed to the State having jurisdiction of the crime."

"No person held to service or labor in one State, under the laws thereof, escaping into another, shall, in consequence of any law or regulation therein, be discharged from such service or labor, but shall be delivered up on claim of the party to whom such service or labor may be due."

Thus was the property recognized, and the duty to surrender it to the claimant made as imperative as in the case of fugitives from the State authority and law.

This property was further recognized by including it in provisions which are only to be drawn from the power to regulate commerce. By the ninth section of the first article of the Constitution, it is provided that—

"The migration or importation of such persons as any of the States now existing shall think proper to admit, shall not be prohibited by the Congress prior to the year one thousand eight hundred and eight, but a tax or duty may be imposed on such importation, not exceeding ten dollars for each person."

Could there be a more distinct recognition of the property-right in slaves? Here is not only a permission to import, but a duty to be laid upon them as a subject of commerce. The fact that an exception was made against the entire control of such importation by Congress, is conclusive that, but for such exceptions, it would have been embraced in the general grant of power to the Federal Government to regulate commerce. If the framers of the Constitution had intended to recognize no other than the right to recapture fugitives—if they had denied the existence of property in persons, they surely would not have used the word importation, as found in the clause of the Constitution just cited. In further support of this opinion, I would refer to the fact that exception was so strictly construed, that laws prohibiting such importation into territories not included in the exception were enacted. I was, therefore, surprised that the Senator from New York should have cited as a proof of power of the Federal Government to legislate on the subject of slavery in the territories, the law to prohibit the importation of Africans into the Mississippi Territory before the year 1808.[8] That territory was not included in the exception which restrained the Federal Government from prohibiting the importation of slaves before 1808; therefore it was exercised under the general power over the subject, as a matter of commerce. Upon this power over commerce, and of the property-nature of the persons so considered, must rest all our laws for the abolition of the foreign slave trade. To deny this general basis, would draw after it the sequence that all our laws upon that subject were enacted without any grant of authority, and were therefore unconstitutional. Nor is it thus alone that this property in persons has been recognized. During the Revolution, and by the men who framed our Declaration of Independence, throughout all the States of the Confederacy, the propriety of refusing liberty to a certain caste of persons was admitted, and in the earliest legislation under the Constitution, those to whom the services of such persons were due were denominated their "owners."[9]

In the treaty of peace which closed the war of our Revolution, the phrase "negroes or other property" shows the position assumed upon our side, as well as the admission made by Great Britain, that the persons so referred to were recognized in their character as property. Again, in 1815, after the adoption of the Constitution, the same construction was explicitly admitted in the treaty of Ghent, in the first article of which we find the expression "any slaves or other private property." With what propriety, with what fairness can it now be assumed that that which we have called property, and negotiated upon as such in our diplomatic relations and international acts, from the birth of the Republic down to 1815, has no existence among the States of the Union, no claim to recognition or protection beyond the limits of the States where it is ordained and sustained by local law? The Constitution recognized slavery; by it the Federal Government was constituted the agent of the States, intrusted with the power of regulating commerce with the States, and with the conduct of all foreign relations. In the discharge of its appropriate functions, the Federal Government, as shown above, has maintained this property right against a foreign Power, and it is equally bound to defend it, within the limits of Federal jurisdiction, against the encroachment upon its security and use, as guarantied by the Constitution.

To those who argue this extension of the property in slaves beyond the limits of the States which they inhabit as an unequal obligation or unusual right, I will render the admission, that but for the Constitution the right to property in slaves could not have extended beyond the State which possessed them. But gentlemen should recollect that all the territory northwest of the river Ohio, from which five non-slaveholding States have been carved, was originally the property of Virginia,[10] and but for the compact of our Union the institutions of that State would have been extended over it. This territory, thus interposed between the northern Atlantic States and the vast region which has been acquired west of the Mississippi, must have prevented those States from all such acquisition. How, under this contingency, would have been the relative size of the slave and non-slaveholding territory? The answer to this inquiry should silence complaint of advantages accruing to the South from the guarantees of the Constitution.

To avoid the possibility of misconstruction, I repeat that we do not seek to establish slavery upon a new basis; we claim no such power for the Federal Government. We equally deny the right to establish as to abolish slavery. We only ask that those rights of property which existed before the Constitution, and which were guarantied by it, shall be protected. If it can be shown that the southern States would, as independent sovereignties, have possessed no right of extension, or that the right of territorial acquisition was transferred to the Federal Government, subject to the condition that it should be used for the benefit of the northern States exclusively, then we will have, what has not yet been presented, a foundation for the assumption that from all territory thus acquired slavery or involuntary servitude should be forever excluded. Sectional rivalry, stimulated by the desire for political aggrandizement, party zeal, local jealousies, and fanaticism, maddened by recent success, have each brought their contribution to the mass of assertion which has been heaped upon the claim of the South to an equal participation with the North in the enjoyment of the territory belonging in common to the States. But assertion is not proof, abuse is not demonstration; and that claim, sustained by justice and supported by the staff of truth, stands yet unbent beneath the mountain of error which has been accumulated upon it.

The various modes which have been proposed to exclude slaveholders from entering territory of the United States with their property may be referred to three sources of power: the Federal Government, the territorial inhabitants, and the law of the land anterior to its acquisition by the United States.

The Federal Government can have no other powers than those derived from the Constitution. It is the agent of the States; has no other authority than that which has been delegated; cannot, by the character of its creation and the nature of its being, have any inherent, independent power. To the Constitution, as the letter of authority for this Federal agent, we must look for every grant of power. All which is not given is withheld; all which is prohibited is doubly barred. It is not to be supposed that the sovereign States, when forming a compact of union, would confer upon the agent of such compact a power to control the destiny of the States; nor is it in keeping with the avowed objects, "to insure domestic tranquillity, provide for the common defence, and promote the general welfare," that it should be used to disturb the balance of power among the States. Were one portion of the Union to increase whilst the other remained stationary, the result would be reached in the course of years which led to the war of our Revolution, and the separation of the Colonies from the mother country. What would it profit a minority to have Representatives in Congress, if opposed to a majority of mastering strength, and of will as well as power to sweep away all the protecting barriers of the Constitution? It was not for representation in Parliament that the fathers of our Republic dissolved the political bands which connected them with the parent Government; but to maintain the freedom and equality which could not be secured by a hopeless minority in common legislation—to defend their inalienable rights from aggression by those who were irresponsible to them—that they pledged their lives, their fortunes, and their sacred honor. To such men it was of paramount importance, in forming a General Government, to guard against interference with domestic institutions, and to preserve such equality among the different sections and interests as would secure each from aggression by the others. This purpose is deeply graven on the Constitution, pervades it as a general spirit, and appears both in its grants and prohibitions. Thence arose the different basis of representation in the two Houses of Congress; thence the Executive veto; the limitations on the power to regulate commerce among the States; the prohibition against interference with private property; against discrimination in favor of one port over another; the partial representation of persons held to service; and the many other provisions which will occur to Senators, illustrative of the design to preserve such equality as is necessary to prosperity, to harmony, to union among sovereigns.

The right of the Federal Government to legislate for the Territories has been claimed from two sources of power—the grant to Congress "to dispose of, and make all needful rules and regulations respecting, the territory or other property belonging to the United States,"[11] and as a power necessarily incident to the right to acquire territory. The power drawn from the first-mentioned source is plainly a power over the territory as public land; the expression "territory or other property" shows the idea too distinctly to require elucidation. The territory belonging to the United States at the formation of the Constitution was such as had been ceded by particular States as a common fund of the Union. The Federal Government, as agent of the States, was charged with the disposal of public domain, under the needful rules and regulations which Congress were authorized to make. The source from which this addition to the common stock was derived, the object for which it was given, the conditions of the cession, all unite with the general provisions of the Constitution to forbid the idea of a transfer of absolute powers of legislation, as the existence of a power in the Federal Government to make laws for the Territory which would affect the political rights or interests of the States. The laws of Congress in relation to territory belonging to the United States must be "needful" to execute the trust conveyed by the States; and none of the grants of the Constitution are to be so "construed as to prejudice the rights of the United States or of any particular State."[12] To promote the sale of the public land where no settled government exists, it may be claimed as an incident to the power to dispose of such property, that Congress should provide for courts and such government generally as will give security to settlers and certainty to titles in the region to which we invite emigration.

Thus far the powers of a trustee may properly extend—thus far the agent may go in good faith to those to whom he acts—the sovereignty still remaining, where alone it can reside, in the States to whom the Territory belongs. It will probably not be contended, that to exclude a portion of our citizens, or to prohibit a certain kind of property, is a "needful regulation" for the disposal of public lands. Certainly, such a position could not be maintained; and those who contend for the power of Congress to prohibit slavery in the Territories, have usually relied upon the second source of power, the right of acquisition.

Before considering how much may be derived from that right, it might have been well to examine into its existence, and inquire to whom its benefits attach. The power to admit new States into the Union was conferred by the Constitution, but not to acquire territory as such. The former was a power properly conferred upon a Confederation which looked to the addition of new members; the latter belongs to sovereignty, and can be possessed by nothing less. The right to acquire belonged to the States as an inherent right of independent existence—one which attaches to all bodies, animate and inanimate. Stones gather accretions, vegetables collect increments, animals assimilate food, and incorporate it with their bodies: by like operation of this general law, the States, as independent sovereigns, had a right to acquire; but the means of acquisition—the war and treaty-making powers—were intrusted to the Federal Government. The right to acquire was not delegated, save as the means were to be used by the Federal Government, and therefore the acquisition must inure to the benefit of the States, in whose right alone it could be made. The power to govern, as an absolute, ultimate authority, remains in the States, and their agent can only exercise so much of that power as has been granted. Our legislation for the territory must, if this view be correct, be drawn from the specific grants, and be subject to all the limitations and prohibitions imposed on them by the Constitution. The rule that the right to acquire carries with it the right to govern, receives a modification in its application to the Federal Government, in this, that it acquires as agent for the States, by the blood or common treasure of the States, or as, in past cases, by a cession for the common benefit of the States, and can, therefore, only govern as authorized by the sovereign owners of the territory.

The question, then, is reduced to this: has the Federal Government, under the grants of the Constitution, power to prohibit "slavery" in the Territories of the United States? The right to property in slaves being recognized by the Constitution, this question is convertible into another: has the General Government the right to exclude particular species of property from the territory of the United States, and thus confine the enjoyment of its advantages to a portion of their citizens? A proposition so repugnant to justice, so violative of the equal rights which every citizen of the United States has in the common property, so destructive of the equality in privileges and immunities secured by the Constitution, would seem to be answered by its statement. Yet, palpable as the outrage appears, it has been perpetrated in legislative resolutions by eleven States of the Union,[13] bound by the Federal compact to recognize the coequality of the States; and repeatedly asserted by Senators in this Chamber, pledged to maintain the Constitution. This Federal Government, designed to render more perfect the union of the States, and to promote their common defence, is thus to become the most formidable enemy of some, the great seedsman of discord among all.

The union of the States into one Confederacy gave no power to destroy local rights of property, or to change the condition of persons; but much to protect and preserve the existing rights of property and relative condition of persons, by extending the limits of their recognition, and enlarging the provisions for their security. Thus the Federal Government cannot take "private property," except for "public use," and by making "just compensation" therefor; the States cannot pass laws to impair the obligation of contracts; duties cannot be imposed on articles of commerce passing from the limits of one State to another; nor apprentices, indented servants, or slaves, by escaping into another State, be discharged from their obligations under the laws of that from which they fled.[14] In these and similar instances the Federal Government can do and has done much, which is beyond the power of a State, to protect and enlarge the value of property. To determine what shall be property, what the condition of persons, are functions of sovereignty beyond its delegated authority, which can only be exercised by a sovereign State within its limits, and beyond that, by the majority of States required to amend the Constitution. I deny, then, that the Federal Government may say to any class of citizens, you shall not emigrate to territory which belongs in common to the people of the United States; equally deny that it can say what property shall be taken into such territory, or legislate so as to impair after his arrival in the territory, any of the preëxisting rights of the emigrant to the property he may carry with him. Many of the reasons and principles presented to establish the absence of power in the Federal Government to exclude slavery from territory belonging to the United States, bear with like force against the second class of opinion—that the power rests in the territorial inhabitants. In the unwearied search of those who, from the foundation of our Government, have sought in every quarter for the fountains of power by which the sovereignty of the States might be submerged, this, until recently, remained undiscovered. When territorial governments were first established in the territories, now the States of the Northwest, a very different doctrine obtained, and quite opposite was the practice under it. There, though the foreign inhabitants were mainly those who had taken part with us in the wars against Great Britain, they were not considered so capable of self-government as to be intrusted with the powers of local legislation, and the restricted governments established in Indiana and Michigan were required to adopt the laws of some State of the Union for their rule and government. Thus, in relation to French settlers at Vincennes, and Canadian refugees in Michigan, it was decided.[15] Now, sir, for whom is it proposed to reverse the decision, not only so far as to recognize local legislation, but to admit the power to pass fundamental laws controlling the action of Congress, and determining the future policy and institutions of Oregon? For a small settlement, composed, to a large extent, of the late dependents of the Hudson's Bay Company; subjects of the British Crown; the very men who were arrayed against us to dispute our right to the soil; the same who, by fraud and violence, wrested from our citizens their property and possessions on the Columbia river; the same who, in violation of the faith of our treaty with Great Britain for the joint occupancy of Oregon, made regulations the effect of which was to destroy the valuable furs in that portion of the country which they expected to become exclusively the property of the United States, whilst they were preserved in that which was expected to pass at a subsequent day to the sovereignty of Great Britain. So much for those who formed a large, if not controlling, part of this population of Oregon when this policy of excluding slavery was adopted there. Shall they be permitted to sit in judgment on the constitutional rights of American citizens? Shall they decide the future institutions of our territory? Looking further to the south, in the valley of the Willamette, we find, it is true, settlements of American citizens, on whose patriotism and love for the States from which they are distant wanderers, we can safely rely. They are American citizens—a name which all who are born beneath the flag of our Union must cherish with such affection and pride that their bond of allegiance needs no endorser. Giving them full confidence, so far as their conduct might be involved in any contest for the interest or honor of our common country, there arises from the question before us an inquiry of a very different nature. I have said that the power to prohibit the introduction into Oregon of slavery, as recognized under the Constitution, is such control over property and persons as can only be exercised by sovereignty. If this be correct, the proposition to leave the whole subject to the territorial inhabitants is equivalent to acknowledging them to be sovereign over the territory. If they are so, by their own right, then it is not "territory belonging to the United States." If it be territory of the United States, Congress has no right to surrender the sovereignty of the States over it; no right to intrust to other hands the formation of the institutions which are in future to characterize it. In connection, however, with this proposition, I have spoken of one portion of the territorial inhabitants as men having no claim upon our confidence, and suggested that there were other inquiries than those connected with their patriotism which required consideration in relation to the other portion of the settlers in Oregon. Are they statesmen? Have they such political experience and wisdom that the settled practice of the country should be changed in order that they may fix the fundamental principles on which their future institutions shall rest; that they may lay the corner-stone of that republican edifice which is in after time to overlook the Pacific? Or are they, as we have heretofore believed them, missionaries of religion, whose studies have been devoted to subjects which, however high and holy, have not been those which would qualify them for the labor of forming temporal governments? And, beyond this, traders, trappers, adventurers in the forest and in the mountain, whose pursuits and character have least led them to contemplate, or to value, the forms and blessings of civil government.

Such is the character of the inhabitants of Oregon; and, if there be little to justify the surrender of the highest powers of legislation to them, there is still less to warrant it in the character of the inhabitants of those Territories we have recently acquired, and which must soon be the subject of governmental organization. There we find a people educated to opinions and habits hostile to our own, mongrels of the Spanish and Indian races, inheriting from both the characteristics, pertinacity, treachery, and revenge, and fresh from conflicts the history and consequences of which are well calculated to excite the bitterest animosity towards our citizens and our Government; a people whose religious prejudices are so strong that they have recently sought to transfer a large part of their country to a foreign colony,[16] for the purpose of excluding the immigration of American citizens, to whom they gave the name of "Methodist wolves;" morally, socially, and intellectually degraded to such a degree, that with the forms of free government, they have never enjoyed any of its essential rights. With the writ of habeas corpus as the established law of the land, citizens were nevertheless transported by order of the Central Government across several States of the Republic, and incarcerated, without question, or power to obtain legal redress.[17] Are these the men who shall prescribe the fundamental law of the land? Shall they determine the rights, privileges, and immunities of the American citizens who may migrate into that country? Shall they decide with what property one of your citizens, to whom you have granted land for services in the war with Mexico, shall be permitted to take possession of his grant? If so, the territory we have acquired belongs not to the United States, but to the people so recently conquered, now become sovereign over the rights of our citizens, our laws, and our Constitution. This opinion in favor of the sovereignty of territorial inhabitants, of such recent origin and rapid growth, seems to have found an equally rapid decline, and has not, I think, sufficient importance now to justify me in detaining the Senate by further remarks upon it. To the citizen who presses beyond the limits of civilization to open up to cultivation and settlement the forest domain of the United States, I have always been willing to extend protection and such peculiar advantages over other joint owners of the common stock as are due to the services he has thus rendered to the common interest. But the civil rights, the political principles of our Government, are not to be transferred to those who shall be first in the race to reach newly-acquired possessions, or who shall by accident be found upon them. To point this opinion by a single application, I will refer to a large body of American citizens, who, under the control of religious enthusiasm, have gone beyond the limits of State jurisdiction to found a sectarian colony in the unexplored wilderness of the Tlamath lake.[18] My remarks will, of course, be understood to apply to the Mormons, and I introduce the case to ask if any one is prepared to welcome the consequences to civil and religious liberty which would flow from the exercise of sovereignty by them over the country of which they may take possession?

I now pass to the third source of power from which it is claimed the right may be derived to exclude slavery from a Territory of the United States: The inviolability of the law as it exists at the period of acquisition.

Did I seek protection under a principle which I believe to be wrong, I would concede this point to those who make it, because I hold it to be conclusive against them in the case of Oregon. That Territory, whether derived from France as a part of Louisiana, by the treaty of 1803, or from Spain as a part of the vice-royalty of Mexico, in 1819, would, by the application of this rule, be slave territory, that institution having existed under the laws of both France and Spain, in the provinces, and at the dates referred to. If, then, the law existing at the date of acquisition be inviolable, the case is closed. Those who have set this mine, have sprung it to their own destruction. But, believing this to be wrong in fact, I claim no advantage from it. The progress of humanity softening the rigors of war, has constantly modified and restricted the rights of the conqueror; it has gone so far as to leave the municipal regulations, the private rights of property, and existing relations of persons, undisturbed. The laws are permitted to remain, so far as they do not conflict with the rights of the conqueror, not so much to satisfy a supposed claim of the conquered, as to prevent anarchy, to promote order, and to preserve the necessary relations in society until the new sovereign shall give other laws to the country. The object for which such continuance of existing laws is permitted, clearly marks the limitation of their effect to the existing condition of those who inhabit the territory. To extend it beyond this, so as to affect the property or personal rights of those by whom the territory has been acquired, either by conquest or purchase, would be to render the acquisition nugatory, and present the absurdity of sovereignty without jurisdiction, of a conqueror made subject by his conquest. The laws of Spain, or of Mexico, if they should remain paramount in the territory acquired from either, would exclude a large portion of our citizens, and many kinds of property which are articles of free commerce among the States. The mass of our citizens would never submit to restraint on their religious worship. The monopolies of Mexico, and the free trade throughout the United States, guarantied by the Constitution, could not exist together. The power to exclude one species of property can be no better founded than that to exclude any other; the Constitution protects all which it recognizes, or none. Those who contend that the laws of Mexico will prevent the introduction of slaves, as held among us, into California and New Mexico, have not shown why the same laws, by their course of reasoning, will not exclude the introduction of tobacco.[19] Believing that the principles and guarantees of the Constitution extend over all territory belonging to the United States, and that all laws violative of either are abrogated by the act of acquisition, it imports to me nothing by what authority such laws were passed. To those who hold that municipal laws are to be held sacred, I commend inquiry as to the character of the laws prohibiting slavery in Mexico. They are not municipal, but general laws: were not passed by the State Legislatures, but by the Central Government, and, I have been informed, in opposition to the wishes of the northern and eastern States of that Republic. The Central Government, against which we have waged war, from which as indemnity for long-continued flagrant wrongs we have taken territory, will surely not be permitted to leave its legislation over the country we have acquired, as a form on which its institutions are to be moulded. Shall the citizen, who, rejoicing in the extended domain of his country, migrates to its newly acquired territory, find himself shorn of the property he held under the Constitution by the laws of Mexico? Shall the soldier who locates his grant in California find himself under the authority he had contributed to conquer? Shall the widow and the orphan of him who died in his country's quarrel, be excluded from the acquisition obtained in part by his blood, unless they will submit to the laws of the power he bled and died to subdue? Never, never! Reason and justice, constitutional right and national pride, combine to forbid the supposition.

I have thus presented my view of the three sources from which it is claimed to draw the power to prohibit slavery in territory of the United States. From the considerations presented, my conclusion is, that it cannot properly be done in either of the modes proposed; that, not being among the delegated powers of the Federal Government, or necessary to the exercise of any of its grants, Congress cannot pass a law for that purpose; that the Territorial Government is subordinate to the Federal Government, from which it derives its authority and support, and that neither separately nor united can they invade the undelegated sovereignty of the States over their territory; that the laws of a former proprietor, so far as they conflict with the principles of the Constitution, are abrogated by the fact of acquisition; that territory of the United States is the property of all the people of the United States; that sovereignty of the territory remains with them until it is admitted as an independent State into the Union; and that each citizen of the United States has an equal right to migrate into such territory, carrying with him any species of property recognized by the Constitution, until sovereignty attaches to the Territory by its becoming a State, or until the sovereign States, by agreement or by compact, shall regulate specifically the character of property which shall be admitted into any particular Territory. Against such conclusions, those who take an opposite view of this question have cited precedents to sustain their positions. In the long course of years, and under the widely-differing circumstances of the various cases which have arisen, the practice of our Government has not been so uniform as in my judgment to furnish any settled rule of construction. Nor am I prepared to admit, either on this or other occasions, the binding force of precedent over the legislation of Congress. I yield to it such authority as is due to the wisdom and purity of those by whom it was established; more than this it cannot claim. In referring to the early legislation of Congress in relation to Territories, I have not been able to perceive the general application of more than one principle, which is, that a Territory, politically considered, should be treated as an embryo State; therefore, the guards thrown around it have been mainly those which would prepare it for a republican form of government, this being the only restriction which Congress is authorized to impose on the constitution of a new State at the period of its admission into the Union. In the organization of territorial governments in the earlier days of our Republic, we find no attempts by Congress to legislate for them. Where powers of legislation were not conferred upon the territorial inhabitants, their laws were to be adopted from the statutes of some State in the Union; and, to show that no claim was set up by the Federal Government to regulate property or change the condition of persons, I would refer to the States formed out of the Northwest Territory, over which the often-cited ordinance of 1787 was extended. There we find, notwithstanding the provisions of that ordinance, that slavery continued to exist, as to some extent it still exists, in the State of Illinois.[20] In the act of 1793, passed to carry out the ordinance of 1787, the following language occurs: "Where a person held to labor in any of the United States, or in either of the Territories on the northwest or south of the Ohio, under the law thereof,"[21] &c., which is a distinct recognition by Congress of the existence of slavery in the territory covered by the ordinance of 1787, and is conclusive against the pretension here set up, that by the ordinance of 1787 the power to prohibit slavery in the Territories was claimed, exercised, and admitted. The whole extent and force of precedents upon this subject have been so fully and ably investigated by others who have spoken on the same side of the subject with myself,[22] that I will not pursue this branch of the investigation further. I therefore dismiss it with the remark, that whatever of validity they possess is to be drawn from the idea that each was a compact ratified by the acquiescence of the States, and can have no other application than to the particular case for which each was formed. There is, however, a marked difference between territory acquired by joint efforts or common treasure of the States and that which was derived by the cession of a particular State. In the former case the sovereignty attaches to the States of the Union by the fact of acquisition, and no other functions could be vested in the Congress than those derived from the Constitution. In the latter, sovereignty and jurisdiction could be transferred in any form which it might please the giver and the receiver to adopt. If, then, Virginia or Georgia has conferred upon the Federal Government higher powers than would necessarily belong to its character of trustee for the public domain, it could not thence be inferred that equal powers would be possessed over territory acquired in common by the States. Thus, the legislation in one case would form no precedent for the other, because of the different sources of authority. In this connection, I will notice a position taken by the Senator from Massachusetts in relation to the cession made by Virginia of the territory northwest of the Ohio river. He assumes that it was made to preserve the existing ratio between the slave and non-slaveholding States.[23] If, sir, I have the history of that transaction aright, it was founded on far more noble considerations—upon motives alike honorable and patriotic in the State which ceded and in those which demanded the cession: it was to preserve that just relation between the confederates which was deemed essential to preserve the equality of the States, the prosperity, the perpetuity, and the harmony of the Union.

The States of Maryland and Delaware objected to the Articles of Confederation because of the immense territory held by Virginia, maintaining that it gave her a controlling power which might be destructive of the prosperity of the smaller States, as it would be subversive of the equality essential to the confederacy of sovereigns. In the act of New Jersey for ratifying the Articles of Confederation this objection was noticed, and their delegates instructed to sign the articles, "in the firm reliance that the candor and justice of the several States will, in due time, remove, as far as possible, the inequality which now subsists." The Legislature of Delaware passed resolutions, one of which contained the following:

"That this State thinks it necessary, for the peace and safety of the States to be included in the Union, that a moderate extent of limits should be assigned for such of those States as claim to the Mississippi or South Sea," &c.

In 1779, the delegates from Maryland laid before Congress the instructions of their General Assembly. That paper was an able argument against the propriety and justice of the extensive claims of some of the States to the western territory—strongly exhibited the political and financial evil which would probably result from the admission of them, and, after asserting the right of all the thirteen States to the unpeopled territory as a common property, declared:

"We have coolly and dispassionately considered the subject; we have weighed probable inconveniences and hardships, against the sacrifice of just essential rights, and do instruct you not to agree to the Confederation unless an article or articles be added thereto in conformity with our declaration."[24]

It does not appear that any question of domestic institutions influenced the action of the States upon this subject; indeed, an opposite conclusion is forced upon us by the character of the parties by whom the cession of this territory was insisted on. Slave States cannot be supposed to have insisted on a cession of territory, that the power of the non-slave States should be increased. Who then looked to the ignoble war of sections, which it has been our shame and misfortune to witness? Who then would have consented to any measure which looked to the reproduction of that inequality, the revival of that interference with the domestic affairs of the States, which had caused the revolution?

The reason most strongly urged was, the injury likely to result to some from the disproportionate power of others; the object most sought was, the security which would result from equality. In keeping with these, the Congress of the Confederation, in 1780, took into consideration the addresses of the different States on the subject of the western territory, and recommended to—

"Those States which can remove the embarrassments respecting the western country, a liberal surrender of a portion of their territorial claims, since they cannot be preserved entire without endangering the stability of the General Confederacy."

And,

Resolved, "That it be earnestly recommended to those States who have claims to the western country to pass such laws, and give their delegates in Congress such powers, as may effectually remove the only obstacles to a final ratification of the Articles of Confederation."[25]

By force of such appeals, urged by the conviction that it was necessary to place the Federal Union on a permanent basis, and to make it acceptable to all its members, Virginia, with that devotion to the common good which became the land of Washington and Jefferson, ceded her rich birthright, the vast territory from which has arisen the five northwestern States of our Union. This surrender of individual interest to the general welfare—this concession to secure the tranquillity of the States, marked by a dignity and patriotism in the contemplation of which paltry struggles for political advantage should be forgotten, is now cited as a measure for the apportionment of strength to the slave and free States, as contending parties. With what probability can it be argued that Maryland would demand or Virginia give for such a purpose?[26]

No, sir, it was fraternity, not strife—it was the general good, not sectional advantage—it was the sovereignty, the equality, and the prosperity of all the States, for which the men of the Revolution made their sacrifices, both of war and of peace. It was to perfect the Confederation, to remove the distrust and dissatisfaction of slaveholding States, that Virginia ceded the Northwestern Territory to the common stock of the Union. And this act of magnanimity, of generous confidence, is now cited as authority against those who were weakened by it. Nor is it in this case alone that the South may complain of such injuries and unfair construction. In every instance concession has been made the basis of aggression, and the language of conciliation has been answered by objurgation and abuse. The right to representation in proportion to population was waived so far in relation to slaves as to exclude two-fifths of their number, yet those who have the advantage of this concession, those who deny that there can be property in persons, are those who attack this compromise of the Constitution, and denounce it as an unequal privilege bestowed on the property of the South. The partial representation of slaves is in accordance with their mixed character, being both persons and property; but with much more reason might it be contended that they were entitled to full representation in the Federal Government than to no representation at all. Indeed, if the South had yielded no claim to full representation in proportion to the number of slaves, how could those who deny that there can be property in persons resist such claim? Population is the basis and the measure of Federal representation. Representatives are assigned to numbers, not to white men, nor to citizens, nor to voters. Each State fixes its own standard of citizenship, and no State has a right to inquire what amount of political privileges are enjoyed, or what may be the condition of the inhabitants of another.

The partial representation of slaves is a compromise of the Constitution, a concession made to northern delegates who opposed their representation on the ground that they were chattels. The argument is changed, but the opposition continues. There is another concession which has been often referred to in this debate, the Missouri compromise.

With the right to extend slavery into any portion of the territory of Louisiana, secured by the treaty of acquisition,[27] there was, nevertheless, a fierce resistance against the admission of Missouri into the Union as a slaveholding State. During its territorial condition the right had been unquestioned—the controversy only arising in view of the political power which would attach to a sovereign State. I will not dwell upon the nugatory character of any law which should attempt to control the domestic institutions of a State, but pass to the result of this controversy about the admission of Missouri. Again, the South, in the spirit of concession which had marked the conduct of her sons at a former period, surrendered their unquestioned and unquestionable right to extend slavery over the whole of that territory which had been acquired under the name of Louisiana, and agreed, except within the limits of Missouri, to confine it to the south side of the parallel of latitude 36°30′ north. Again was sectional interest abandoned to the hope of permanently establishing tranquillity in the Union. If that hope is now to be destroyed, it will be by those who derived all the benefit from the compromise—not by those who waived by it a portion of their rights, and who are now willing to extend its provisions, if fairly applied, to all other territory, though the division which would thence follow would give to the South less than a fourth of the territory which would fall to the North. In the compromises of the Constitution, and the concessions which have followed its adoption, the advantages have mainly accrued to the North; yet the South has steadily and faithfully observed them. Can as much be said of the North? The Constitution recognizes the institution of slavery, which thence acquired a general, instead of its previous merely local character. It was made the duty of the State authorities to deliver up fugitive slaves to their owners, and the free commerce among the States secured to each citizen, was a prohibition against State legislation to disturb the right of the master to pass from one State to another with his slave property. The duty has been neglected; the right has been obstructed; slaves have been torn from their masters, when exercising the right of every American citizen to pass from one part of the Union to another; the magistracy have stood silent when these outrages were perpetrated, and the legislation of three States, instead of looking to prevention and punishment of said cases in future, have enacted laws best calculated to magnify the evil. Even here, in the course of debate, it has been asserted that, to carry a slave out of the limits of the jurisdiction of a State in which slavery is recognized, emancipates him.[28] If that were true, the recognition of slavery by the Constitution would be a nullity. The master who, in discharge of a duty to the Government, should enter an arsenal or dock-yard under the exclusive jurisdiction of the United States, would thereby lose the right to property in his slave. Or, if he should sail from Norfolk to New Orleans, by going to sea he would pass beyond the jurisdiction of a State, and thus incur the forfeiture. Beyond the limits of a State, whether in territory or on the deck of an American vessel, the Constitution and laws of the United States follow our citizens and protect their property. The recognition of slavery by the Constitution, therefore, presents a case arising here, in a very different view from one in Great Britain. The difference destroys the value of the argument based on British practice and analogy.[29]

Eleven States of the Union have spoken through their Legislatures against the further extension of slavery, with the clearly-indicated, sometimes even expressed, intention thus to prepare the way for a more direct and fatal attack upon the institutions of the South. When we are told that slavery is an "immense moral and political evil, which ought to be abolished as soon as the end can be properly and constitutionally attained;" when we are admonished of the design "to resist the admission of any new State into the Union while tolerating slavery,"[30] he must be blind indeed who does not see the purpose, by thus forbidding the growth of the slaveholding States, and devoting all our vast territorial domain to the formation of those in which slavery is forbidden, to obtain in the future such preponderance of free States as will enable them constitutionally to amend the compact of our Union, and strip the South of the guarantees it gives.

If factious opposition and sectional disregard of the common good have been able thus to obliterate the great landmarks—equality among the States and non-interference with domestic affairs—in so brief and such partial enjoyment of power, how can we expect moderation and forbearance when swelled to a three-fourths majority? Those who seek to appropriate our Territories to the exclusive formation of non-slaveholding States, must not hope by catch-words and abusive epithets against slavery to conceal their real purpose, the political aggrandizement of the North.

Was their object the benefit of the slaves; did they seek, as a paramount object, their emancipation, the policy would certainly be the reverse—instead of confining, to disperse them. Nothing can be more plain than that, if confined to a small space, they must accumulate in the hands of a few, and, if dispersed, that they must have many masters.[31] Whatever there is of harshness arises from their accumulation, so that the master and slave are necessarily separated, and the latter placed under the authority of a hired agent. Whilst the number owned by one person is small, he has immediate charge of them; from their daily intercourse, permanent connection, and real identity of interest, arise those kindly relations usual in such condition. The power to oppress dependents exists in all countries, and bad men everywhere abuse the power. In no relation which labor bears to capital is such oppression better guarded against than in that of master and slave. There is in it all which naturally excites the forbearance and kindness of the generous and the good; and, this failing, there are considerations of interest, of pecuniary advantage, to restrain the sordid and the vicious, which do not exist in cases of hired laborers. To confine slavery to a small district would go further than any other means to strip it of its kind paternal character; when the master would no longer know his slave, when the overseer would have the proprietor's power, then would disappear many of the features which commend it to those who have been reared amidst it; then would cease the moral and intellectual progress of the slave; then would steadily diminish the feelings promotive of emancipation, and the power to effect it. It has been from the association with a more elevated race that the African has advanced; it has been from their mutually kind offices that the master has in many instances liberated his slave as a mark of affection. For this association and for this feeling, it is required that there should not be a great disproportion in the number of the races where they reside together. The power to emancipate must depend upon property considerations and upon public policy conjointly. A large community of free men would have the pecuniary ability to emancipate a small number of slaves; the reverse would be beyond their power. Upon a large territory, a few blacks might be turned loose without injury to the progress of society; but on a small territory, a large number of blacks could only be released by surrendering the country to them. If, then, as proposed, slavery, as it exists among us, should be confined to the States in which it now exists, the consequence will be, not its extinguishment, but its perpetuation. Each State, when it finds within its borders as many Africans as safety and policy will permit, will enact laws to prevent their further introduction; the tide which has flowed regularly on from New England to Texas will be checked, and they will thenceforward continue to accumulate, and when they reach the density which renders involuntary labor no longer profitable, they must still be held, from the impolicy of liberating them in the country and the inability to send them away—the latter increasing in a compound ratio, because the augmentation of number will bring with it a diminution of profit from their labor.

Gentlemen have spoken of the spirit of the age as opposed to slavery.[32] Sir, I think there is no foundation for the presumption of moral change, but that all the changed action which has occurred is referable to density of population. It may be taken as a general rule, that involuntary service is less profitable than voluntary labor; and there is a singular uniformity in the degree of density at which, in different countries, it has been abandoned—the villeinage of England and the serfdom of Russia both becoming a burden to proprietors at the same point; that is, when the population reached the point of forty persons to the square mile. But our slaves are a distinct race, physically differing so much from ourselves that no one can look to their emancipation without connecting with it the idea of removal, separation of the races. When they cease to be profitable, we cannot, like the ancient Britons in the case of their villeins, say, Be free, and see, with the announcement, all cause for distinction cease.[33] Therefore, it is to be observed, that those States of our Union which have passed acts of emancipation have first found themselves nearly rid of the caste, or made their laws prospective and so remote that this result would be reached before the act went into operation.

With what justice or propriety do those who have availed themselves of the demand for their slaves in the more southern and sparsely settled States, now insist upon closing the door against their egress to newer countries, as the white population, gathering behind them, would press them still further on? They have sold their slaves when they ceased to be profitable, and slavery became to them a sin of horrid enormity when the property was transferred from themselves to their brother. Therefore they will confine it to the country in which it now exists, and deprive others of the means used by themselves, and which forms the only practicable mode of getting rid of it. To those who are sincere in their professions of a wish to banish slavery from the United States, and feel it is only to be effected by the voluntary action of those among whom it exists, I say, leave your territories open, and let the white race, as it flows in from the North, gradually, by its greater energy and intelligence, bear the African race before it to regions unsuited to the labor of the white man, as the tide bears the foam to the shore, and gives back to the beach the things which are its own.

The Senator from Vermont objects to the introduction of slave property into Territories, and says it should not be forced upon an infant community, but left to be adopted, if they desire it, when they have power to organize an independent government.[34] I have expressed my opinion of the constitutional rights of the holders of that property, and distinctly stated that I desire no Congressional legislation beyond that which is necessary to secure those rights. Non-interference with the subject of slavery is our main position, and is equally opposed to force for or against it.

So far from perceiving the propriety of excluding slaves from infant communities, as urged in this debate, the experience of our pioneers, the condition of those who first grapple with the difficulty of taming the wilderness, furnishes a forcible illustration of the truth of the relation I have attempted to show exists between involuntary servitude and density of population. The hard necessity which maintains the power of capital over labor in old settled countries, is not known among the forest adventurers. The bond between the employer and the servant is therefore so weak, that in the first settlement of a country, more than at any subsequent period, would involuntary servitude be advantageous and desirable. I can readily conceive that slaves would be taken into countries where they would cease to be profitable as soon as other labor flowed in. Such instances have occurred in our northern Territories, and early emancipation was the result. Why is it assumed that slavery degrades labor, and its presence excludes the white laborer? It may be true as regards the whites and free blacks of the North, that they will not toil together: there is rivalry between them. But if thence a conclusion is drawn that the same condition exists in the slave States, it is false in reasoning and in fact. Slaves are capital; and, in the mind of the master, there can be no contest between capital and labor—the contest from which so much of human suffering and oppression has arisen. In slave States there is an equality among white men which cannot exist where the same race fill the places of master and menial. The white laborer is elevated by having a caste below him. That he would not be excluded from territory by the presence of slaves, the constant emigration to the South from the non-slave States conclusively establishes. No, sir; it is for no such reason that the present position is taken.

This opposition to slavery is political, and rapid are the strides it is making in aggression. The mighty State of New York is now convulsed to its centre.[35] Men who were justly entitled to the appellation of statesmen, in its most dignified sense, who have filled the highest stations of honor and trust, are now identified with a movement at war with justice, at war with the Constitution, and which, disturbing the tranquillity of to-day, will, if not checked in its onward progress, reach disunion to-morrow. The time is not remote when an abolition meeting could not have been held in New York; but it has become political, and therefore this new form of the monster. Duty, fraternity, faith, give way, and masses worship the idol without the fanaticism which alone could excuse the apostacy. With political abolitionists, what argument can avail? The security, the prosperity, the growth of a section only is considered; and all which would benefit those to whom they believe their interest opposed, must find therefrom resistance. Theirs is the policy so deeply and sadly deprecated by Mr. Jefferson, when he spoke of a geographical line coinciding with a marked principle, moral and political, which every new irritation would mark deeper and deeper. Theirs is the policy which Mr. Monroe described in his letter to Mr. Jefferson as "an effort to give such a shape to our Union as would secure the dominion over it to its eastern section." That patriot statesman, in the same letter, as a justification for the treaty by which Texas was surrendered, describes the sectional struggle which existed at the time as so fierce and uncompromising that it was necessary for the internal peace to make the sacrifices of the treaty, and draws from the contest the conclusion, "that the further acquisition of territory to the west and south involves difficulties of an internal nature which menace the Union itself." This letter of

Mr. Monroe, taken in connection with that of Mr. Jefferson, to which it was a reply,[36] shows how deep-seated and extreme was the opposition at that day to the growth and prosperity of the southern and western sections of the Union. From the hazard which then impended over us we were saved by the patriotic devotion of those northern men who sacrificed themselves for the peace and general welfare of the Confederacy. Now, when like hazard and difficulty surround us, it is my pride and comfort to believe that like sacrifices, if necessary, will be made. To those who consider the Union worth preserving, it must be a primary object to give peace and security to its members. The pure and wise men who formed our Republic foresaw, what events have so clearly demonstrated, that these objects were only to be certainly attained by approximating equality among the sections, and leaving all domestic affairs entirely to the control of the States. This policy has been generally adhered to, by admitting alternately slave and non-slaveholding States into the Union, and by affirming in solemn manner, at different periods in our history, the restricted character and general purposes of our Federal Government. Thus, on the 6th of January, 1838, the Senate of the United States, by a vote of thirty-one to eleven—

"*Resolved*, That it is the solemn duty of the Government to resist, to the extent of its constitutional power, all attempts by one portion of the Union to use it as an instrument of attack upon the domestic institutions of another, or to weaken or destroy such institutions."[37]

But ten years have passed since this declaration was made, yet mark how great has been the advance of aggression on the constitutional guarantees and principles of our compact as at that day admitted. It is openly asserted, as a principle of action, that slaves shall be confined to the territory upon which they are now located, not for their benefit, but for the political advantage of the non-slave-holding States;[38] or, in other words, to weaken (who can doubt finally to destroy?) slave institutions. No longer is the claim to humanity set up, but the thirst for power goes step by step in this aggression with hostility to the African race. The Senator from New York, [Mr. Dix,][39] my friend who sits near me—and I do not use the phrase in a merely complimentary sense—in opposing the extension of slavery to wider limits, uses the following language:

"The tendency of the human race is to increase in a compound ratio of the extent and productiveness of the surface on which it is sustained. * * * The multiplication of the human species is governed by laws as inflexible and certain as those which govern the repro-duction of vegetable life. * * * I believe it may be satisfactorily shown that the free black population in the northern States does not increase by its own inherent force. * * * Under the most favorable circumstances it is and must continue to be an inferior caste in the North. * * * A class thus degraded will not multiply. This is the first stage of retrogradation. The second almost certainly follows. It will not be reproduced; and in a few generations the process of extinction is performed."[40]

And this is the moral teaching of those who assume to be our pastors, and offer their vicarious repentance for the sins of slavery. With surprise and horror I heard this announcement of a policy which seeks, through poverty and degradation, the extinction of a race of human beings domesticated among us. We, sir, stand in such a relation to that people as creates a feeling of kindness and protection. We have attachments which have grown with us from childhood—to the old servant who nursed us in infancy, to the man who was the companion of our childhood, and the not less tender regard for those who have been reared under our protection. To hear their extinction treated as a matter of public policy or of speculative philosophy arouses our sympathy and our indignation. If I believed slavery to be the moral, social, and political evil which it is described; if I believed the advantage of rendering our popula-tion homogeneous to be as great as it is asserted, not then—no, nor if both were ten times greater—would I be reconciled to such a policy for such a purpose.

It has been usual for southern men to decline any discussion about the institution of domestic slavery, in the midst of which they have grown up, and of which they may be supposed to know something, however vituperative and unfounded the accusations made against it. Agreeing in the general propriety of this course, I nevertheless propose on this occasion to depart from the ordinary practice. The question is forced upon us by our northern brethren to such extent that silence, if persevered in, might be construed into admission of the truth of their accusations. In debates of Congress, by the press, by Legislatures of the States, in the pulpit, and in primary assem-blies, it has become customary to denounce slavery as a political evil; as a burden on the Government; as the sin and opprobrium of the nation; as destructive of good order and human advancement; as a blighting curse on the section where it exists, and a gangrene, extending its baleful influence to every portion of the Union. Now, sir, upon what do these assumptions rest? Have we been less faithful as citizens? Have riots, conflagrations, or destruction of private property, been more frequent in the slave than in the non-slave States? Have their churches been less harmonious, their divines less pious, their statesmen less eminent, their soldiers less efficient than yours? If not, then why this unwarrantable denunciation—why this unfounded assumption? If it be a sin, you are not otherwise involved than by your connection with its introduction; with its existence you have nothing to do. As owners of the commercial marine, you were the importers of Africans; you sold them in the South; you are parties to a compact which recognizes them as a property throughout the United States, and secures to their owners rights which, but for the Confederation, would have been local. Show, then, your repentance, if you feel any, for having contributed to the increase of this property, by observing the obligations imposed by the circumstances of the case upon you, and the rights recognized in the fundamental, paramount law of our Union. The Constitution did not create the institution of domestic slavery; it was not part of the object for which it was formed to determine what should be property, but an important portion of its duty to generalize and protect the rights of citizens beyond the limits of State jurisdiction. From this duty has arisen all the intermediate acts in relation to slave property; yet, at this late period of the practice under our Constitution, Senators assert that slavery is so purely local, that if a master pass with his slave into the limits of a State or Territory where such property is not recognized by local law, the slave by that act becomes free. This is in keeping with the legislation of those States in which the legal and constitutional obligations to surrender fugitive slaves have been nullified. It is in keeping with the repeated declaration here, made with the condescending air of a sovereign granting a favor, that there is no intention to interfere with slavery as it exists in the States, but that its further extension cannot be permitted.

Do Senators forget that this Government is but the agent, the creature of the States; that it derives its powers from them; not they their rights and institutions from it? Slavery existed in the States before the formation of the Constitution; it needed no guarantee within their limits; its recognition beyond this was part of the more perfect Union, as its protection against all enemies whomsoever is part of the common defence for which that Constitution was adopted. There is not a more prominent feature in the federal compact than the prohibition to the States to interfere with commerce. But if a citizen of Maryland cannot pass through Pennsylvania or Ohio, on his way to Kentucky or Missouri, without submitting his property to the tests of those States through which he is merely travelling, the right to free commerce among the States has no practical value. The right to uninterrupted transit is not varied by the character of the property—the power is the same, whether the question arise upon a slave or a bale of goods. There is no discretionary power; and a total prohibition would be less offensive than an invidious distinction, claiming to spring from a moral superiority. Each State is responsible for its own institutions— the sovereignty and coequality of all the States forbid the idea of moral responsibility on the part of one for the acts of another. If slavery be a sin, it is not yours. It does not rest upon your action for its origin, or your consent for its existence. It is a common-law right to property in the service of man; it traces back to the earliest Government of which we have any knowledge, either among Jews or Gentiles. Its origin was Divine decree—the curse upon the graceless son of Noah. Slavery was regulated by the laws given through Moses to the Jews. Slaves were to be of the heathen, and with their offspring to descend by inheritance: thus, in the main particulars, being identical with the institution as it exists among us. It was foretold of the sons of Noah that Japhet should be greatly extended, that he should dwell in the tents of Shem, and Canaan should be his servant.[41] Wonderfully has the prophecy been fulfilled; and here, in our own country, is the most striking example. When the Spaniards discovered America they found it in the possession of the "Indians;" many tribes were enslaved, but the sons of Shem were not doomed to bondage; they were restless, discontented, and liberated, because they were unprofitable. Their places were supplied by the sons of Ham, brought across the broad Atlantic for this purpose; they came to their destiny, and were useful and contented. Over the greater part of the continent Japhet now sits in the tents of Shem, and in extensive regions Canaan is his servant. Let those who possess the best opportunity to judge, the men who have grown up in the presence of slave institutions, as they exist in the United States, say, if their happiness and usefulness do not prove their present condition to be the accomplishment of an all-wise decree. It may have for its end the preparation of that race for civil liberty and social enjoyment.

Compare the slaves in the southern States with recently-imported Africans, as seen in the West Indies, and who can fail to be struck with the immense improvement of the race, whether physically, morally, or intellectually considered? Compare our slaves with the free blacks of the northern States, and you find the one contented, well provided for in all their physical wants, and steadily improving in their moral condition; the other miserable, impoverished, loathsome from the deformity and disease which follows after penury and vice; covering the records of the criminal courts, and filling the penitentiaries. Mark the hostility to caste, the social degradation, which excludes the able from employment of profit or trust, and leaves the helpless to want and neglect. Then turn to the condition of this race in the States of the South, and view them in the relation of slaves. There no hostility exists against them—the master is the natural protector of his slave, and public opinion, common feeling, mere interest would not allow him to neglect his wants. Those who urge that exclusion of slavery from the Territories does not exclude the slaveholder, because he may dispose of his property before emigration, show such inability to comprehend the attachment which generally subsists between a master and his slaves, that I will only offer to them interest as a motive for the care which is extended to those persons—securing comfort to the aged and to the infant, attention to the sick, and adequate provision to all. Such is the difference between the condition of the free and slave blacks under circumstances most favorable to emancipation. Does it warrant the desire on the part of any friend of that dependent race to hasten upon them responsibilities for which they have shown themselves so unequal? If any shall believe that the sorrow, the suffering, the crime which they witness among the free blacks of the North have resulted from their degradation by comparison with the white race around them, to such I answer, does the condition of St. Domingo, of Jamaica, give higher evidence? Or do the recent atrocities in Martinique encourage better hopes?[42] Sir, this problem is one which must bring its own solution, leave natural causes to their full effect, and when the time shall arrive at which emancipation is proper, those most interested will be most anxious to effect it. But as the obligation is mutual, so must the action be joint; and it is quite within the range of possibility that the masters may desire it when their slaves will object, as was the case when the serfs of Russia refused to be liberated by their landlords. Leave the country to the South and West open, and speculation may see in the distant future slavery pressed by a cheaper labor to tropical regions, where less exertion being required to secure a support, their previous preparation will enable them to live in independent communities. They must first be separated from the white man, be relieved from the condition of degradation which will always attach to them whilst in contact with a superior race, and they must be elevated by association and instruction; or, instead of a blessing, liberty would be their greatest curse. Under these considerations, I cannot view the policy proposed to confine them to the present limits of the slave States, as having one point either of humanity or sound policy to recommend it, or that it can do other wise than perpetuate slavery even beyond its natural term in the States where it now exists.

When the colonies made common cause against the parent country and conquered their independence, no one State claimed the right to interfere with the domestic affairs of another. Each was recognized sovereign within its limits, and all were disposed to respect the rights and feelings of each. Had it been otherwise, our Confederation would never have been formed. This is changed, and, strange as it may appear, the change follows the action of the very Government whose interference with the domestic affairs of the colonies led to the Revolution; stranger still, the first State to follow is the same which was most oppressed in the colonial condition, and, to her honor be it remembered, first raised the standard of revolutionary resistance.

When it was discovered that colored foreigners (from St. Domingo) had instigated the blacks of Charleston to murder the whites and burn the city, as a measure of policy warranted by humanity and necessary precaution, a law was passed to exclude foreign colored persons from the city. For fourteen years this law was enforced without objection. Then came British emancipation in the West Indies, British agitation, British publications against slavery, and then for the first time Massachusetts discovered that a duty was imposed on her to resist a law necessary to protect the lives and property of those for whom it was passed—a police regulation, not directed against her inhabitants, but general in its effect and unmistakable in its purpose. In the day of her colonial tribulation, Massachusetts sent an ambassador to South Carolina: she now sent another, but how different the missions. Then, domestic interference was the grievance; now, it was the purpose and the end of the mission to maintain a right of colored inhabitants to violate a police regulation, which those best informed believed to be necessary to guard against the highest crimes and greatest misfortunes. A like mission was deputed to New Orleans, where security to property had rendered similar regulations necessary.[43] All this for the maintenance of a speculative philosophy which sees no guilt in crimes flowing from it, and asks for no practical result. Of all who engage in this agitation on the question of slavery—this indecent intrusion on the domestic affairs of others—I ask, what remedy do you propose?

We have heard you denounce it in coarsest abuse. We have felt your interference by legislative enactment to render our property less secure, by individual organization to seduce our slaves from comfort and contentment, to turn them penniless upon a community where they are despised and oppressed, and in a climate to which, by constitution, they are unsuited. We have seen you unite with our foreign enemies to defame us, and join those who, for commercial purposes, have warred against slavery as the cause of our supremacy in the cotton market of the world. But we have not seen the good you have done, or any other effect you have wrought than to generate distrust among the whites, and to produce a necessity for increased rigor over the slaves. What, then, do you propose? You speak of emancipation, but you know that immediate emancipation is impracticable; that, if the States would consent, the treasury of the Federal Government would not approximate the purpose. More than this, you know that without slaves cotton could not be produced to supply your factories, and that ruin and want would stalk over your own villages, where now wealth and plenty reign. What prompts to your agitations? Not an instinctive opposition to involuntary servitude, as is shown by your readiness to give validity to the Mexican laws over California and New Mexico, and thus continue the peon system, far more harsh and repulsive to my mind than our domestic slavery: liable to the same abuses, but without the controlling restraint which interest and the relation of permanent dependence creates in the case of the slave.[44] Is it love for the

African? No! His civil disability, his social exclusion, the laws passed by some of the non-slave States to prevent him, if free, from settling within their limits, show, beyond the possibility of doubt, that it springs from no affection for the slave. Is it the moral conviction that there cannot be property in persons? No, you imported Africans and sold them as chattels in the slave-markets, and you are constantly objecting to their representation as persons in the councils of the Federal Government. Is it because, as has been said in this debate, slavery is a burden on the Government, diminishing its power in peace and war?[45] If so, let the exports of the country answer what section of the Union contributes most to supply our treasury; let the history of our wars reply, as to the number and conduct of the troops which the slaveholding States have given to the service of the country. Those answers must show that this position is wholly untenable. The only conclusion is, that you are prompted by the lust of power, and an irrational hostility to your brethren of the South. I say irrational, because an injury inflicted upon us would surely recoil upon you, and because the sons of the South may proudly challenge the citation of an instance when they have opposed the interest of the North, because it was such, or been recusant to any of the compromises of or under our Constitution.

Whilst northern men contend that the slave States shall not be extended, by participation in any acquired territories, they should remember, and blush to remember, that Oregon was acquired by a treaty which ceded a large southern territory, and that southern men have been, throughout, those who have led in the efforts to secure exclusive possession of Oregon. Floyd, Benton, and Linn[46] stopped not to balance political power, nor paused from their labors to secure Oregon to the settlement and use of our own people, because its climate and productions indicated the future erection of non-slave States. I have claimed for southern men that they have faithfully adhered to all compromises. Is there one which has been fully kept by the opposite party? The ordinance of 1787, which may be considered a compact by subsequent acquiescence of the States, contained a provision for the restoration of fugitive slaves, that being the only consideration given to the South. It has been flagrantly violated. In establishing the ratio of representation, the

South compromised by deducting two-fifths of the persons held to service, and the North has been from that time to this endeavoring to get rid of the compromise. Without a shadow of propriety, the admission of Missouri as a State of the Union was opposed because of her domestic institutions; the slave States, to secure harmony, conceded that slavery should be excluded from all the remaining part of the territory which was north of 36° 30'; but now, when other territory is acquired, the North assert it all to be free, and refuse to declare the territory south of 36° 30' to be open to the introduction of slaves, as good faith would require, if their assertion were tenable, and the territory in fact not equally open to the property of all the people of the United States. But, inflamed by success in former contests, you march boldly to the conflict, and demand the whole. The mask is off, the purpose is avowed that there shall be no further extension of "the slave power."[47] The question is before us; it is a struggle for political power, and we must meet it at the threshold. Concession has been but the precursor of further aggression, and the spirit of compromise has diminished as your relative power increased. The sacrifices which the South has in other times made to the fraternity and tranquillity of the Union are now cited as precedents against her rights. To compromise is to waive the application, not to surrender the principles on which a right rests, and surely gives no claim to further concession. It has been said that we are contending for an abstraction, a thing of no practical importance. If so, then why is it so obstinately resisted? Do you wish to gain another and a broader precedent for future use? The course of this debate justifies the supposition, and demands caution on our part. If to contend for principle the practical effect of which may be remote is an abstraction, then, sir, the war of the Revolution and the war of 1812, so far as the South was concerned, were both fought for abstractions. In the colonial condition, the southern States were especially fostered by Great Britain, and their prosperity was rapidly increasing at the commencement of hostilities against the mother country. The acts of unjust and oppressive legislation were applied to the northern colonies. Sympathy, fraternal feeling, and devotion to principle, brought the South to your side in your first step to resistance. Again, in the war of 1812, it was your seamen, not ours, who were impressed, and again, from devotion to principle and the obligations of our alliance, the South stood fore-most in that conflict. The blood of her sons stained the battle-fields from Niagara to New Orleans; her exports, main dependence for her support, were cut off, and distress came to every hamlet and cottage; yet she murmured not, railed not, raised not the standard of opposition against the Government whilst engaged in a foreign war.

I have said that the South has, on all occasions, been prompted by a sincere desire for domestic tranquillity, and an ardent love for the Union. The conduct of her sons on this occasion has, I think, sustained her past character. To prevent further agitation, to secure peace, to perpetuate our Union, I am willing to go as far as my principles will allow. To compromise, it is necessary that both parties should, to some extent, yield. To prevent continuance of the agitation, it is necessary that the conditions of the compro-mise should be express; that nothing should be left to doubtful con-struction. Finally, the value of any compromise we may make must depend on the feelings of those for whom it is made, and to whom it is intrusted. If the spirit of compromise has departed from our people, it is idle to propose its forms. If the principles of the Con-stitution are to be disregarded by a self-sustaining majority, the days of the Confederation are numbered. The men who have en-countered past wars for the maintenance of principle, will never consent to be branded with inferiority—pronounced, because of the domestic institutions, unworthy of further political growth. If such be your determination, it were better that we should part peaceably, and avoid staining the battle-fields of the Revolution with the blood of civil war. Abraham said to his nephew Lot, when strife arose among their people, "Go thou to the right hand, and I will go to the left, and let there be peace between us."[48]

If the folly, and fanaticism, and pride, and hate, and corruption of the day are to destroy the peace and prosperity of the Union, let the sections part like the patriarchs of old, and let peace and good will subsist among their descendants. Let no wounds be inflicted which time may not heal. Let the flag of our Union be folded up entire, the thirteen stripes recording the original size of our family, untorn by the unholy struggles of civil war; its constellation to re-main undimmed, and speaking to those who come after us of the growth and prosperity of the family whilst it remained united. Unmutilated, let it lie among the archives of the Republic, on some future day, when wiser counsels shall prevail, when men have been sobered in the school of adversity, again to be unfurled over the continent-wide Republic.

Sir, can it be possible that we have those among us who are willing to hazard such fearful results for the paltry consideration of political supremacy over those who do not possess the power, and have never shown their desire, to intrude on the domestic affairs, to impede the growth, or to mar the prosperity of their northern brethren? Can such considerations palliate this crusade against the South? Shall the fabric of human liberty and republican government, which was founded and built by the wisest and purest of our land, and left as a heritage for their children forever, to be torn down by the first generation which succeeded to it, and left in ruin, an object for the republican's pity, the monarchist's scorn?

I hear and see the agitation of politicians, but from those I turn to the people. In their patriotism and good sense is my hope and confidence. They have no interest beyond the public good. To them, in this critical emergency, this imminent hazard, I look for safety, trusting that they will reject every interpolation on our compact which may endanger the perpetuity of our Union, and consign to the obscurity they merit every demagogue who caters to popular excitement, and seeks to elevate himself by an agitation which draws in its train the destruction of the compromises, the subversion of the principles on which the durability of our Confederacy depends.

Mr. President, I have intentionally extended my remarks to many points not involved in the amendment I proposed to the Senate. That amendment was confined to the case presented by the bill under consideration, which, though not in terms, does in fact, as I have shown, authorize the prohibition of slavery in Oregon. It asks no additional guarantee, no privilege, no concession, but is to prevent a construction which would recognize in the Federal Government, as in those who derive their authority from it, power to control the subject of slavery without the concurrence of the States. If this amendment be rejected, I shall view it as ominous of the future, and stand prepared for whatever consequences may follow.[49]

Cong. Globe, 30:1, App., 907–14. Also issued in pamphlet form: Davis, Speech . . . on the Oregon Bill.

[1] Horace, Odes, Book I, xiii, line 20: "Thrice happy they, and more, whom an unbroken bond unites" (Bartlett's, 38).

[2] Jefferson's letter to John Holmes (Apr. 22, 1820) on the Missouri Compromise was quoted in full by Calhoun on June 27 (Cong. Globe, 30:1, App., 870).

[3] Davis' amendment was opposed by John A. Dix because it asserted the principle of slavery extension (ibid., 865).

[4] In a prohibition similar to that in the Northwest Ordinance, the provisional Oregon government banned slavery in 1845 (Palmer, Journal, 300–301).

[5] Davis refers to the "privileges and immunities" clause—Article IV, section 2, of the Constitution. John Davis of Massachusetts had argued that southerners were claiming "extraordinary privileges" with regard to slaves, "a right of property rising above the rights of other citizens" (Cong. Globe, 30:1, App., 895).

[6] A reference to the opinion of John Davis (ibid.).

[7] Davis again refers to the Constitution, Article IV, section 2. Like other southern politicians, he did not accept the 1842 decision of the Supreme Court in Prigg v. Pennsylvania, wherein the court held that the return of fugitive slaves was exclusively a federal obligation (U.S. Constitution, 787; Kelly and Harbison, American Constitution, 338–39).

[8] To support his argument that Congress possessed power to legislate on slavery in the territories, John A. Dix cited the act of April 7, 1798, prohibiting the importation of slaves into the Mississippi Territory from outside the United States (Cong. Globe, 30:1, App., 864; U.S. Statutes at Large, 1:549–50).

[9] One early statute (1807) referring to owners was "An Act to prohibit the importation of Slaves" (U.S. Statutes at Large, 2:429).

[10] Not only Virginia, but New York, Massachusetts, and Connecticut also ceded claims northwest of the Ohio River (Carter, ed., Terr. Papers, 2:3–12, 22–24).

[11] Article IV, section 3 of the Constitution.

[12] Article IV, section 3 reads in part: "construed as to prejudice any claims of the United States, or of any particular state."

[13] From January 1847 through June 1848, the state legislatures of Vermont, New York, Pennsylvania, Ohio, New Jersey, New Hampshire, Michigan, Massachusetts, Maine, Connecticut, and Wisconsin passed resolutions against the admission of new slave states or in favor of excluding slavery in any new territory (Washington Nat. Intell., Aug. 23, 1848).

[14] Davis alludes to the Fifth Amendment, Article I, sections 10 and 9, and Article IV, section 2, of the Constitution, respectively.

[15] The Northwest Ordinance required the territorial governor and judges to adopt civil and criminal laws from the original states during the first phase of territorial government. Indiana and Michigan, formed from the original Northwest Territory, were so organized (Carter, ed., Terr. Papers, 2:42–43, 7:7–10, 10:5–7). Davis also refers to laws regarding slaves held by French and Canadian residents of the Northwest Territory. In 1788 a congressional committee decided that the prohibition of slavery applied only to the introduction of new slaves and not to those already present. However, in 1831 the Supreme Court let stand a state court ruling excluding slavery in territories north of the Ohio River (ibid., 2:49n, 149–50; Menard v. Aspasia, 30 U.S. 505 [1831]).

[16] Immediately prior to the outbreak

of the Mexican War, Great Britain dismissed several overtures aimed at placing California under its protection (Pletcher, *Diplomacy of Annexation*, 212, 422–25).

[17] The specific incident to which Davis refers is not known. As to the protection of Mexican citizens under law, he may be speaking of amparo, a legal procedure roughly analogous to the writ of habeas corpus. Part of the Yucatan constitution of 1841, amparo was not incorporated into Mexican law until 1847 (Baker, *Judicial Rev.*, 12–34).

[18] Lake Klamath, located in southwestern Oregon. The name originally was Tlámét, in the Alikwa Indian language (Gatschet, *Klamath Indians*, 2, Pt. 1:xxxiii).

[19] John Dix contended that if slavery did not exist in a territory when it was acquired, "its introduction ought to be prohibited." Along with Davis, Calhoun and Herschel V. Johnson denied such a viewpoint, Calhoun terming it "an absurdity" (*Cong. Globe*, 30:1, App., 867, 871, 892). Davis' mention of tobacco refers to the fact that in Mexico production of that staple was a state-owned monopoly (Thompson, *Recollections*, 192).

[20] While part of the Indiana Territory, Illinois was governed by territorial laws allowing indentured servitude. Separated from Indiana in 1809, Illinois retained the indenture system as late as 1843 (Berwanger, *Frontier against Slavery*, 8–14, 17n).

[21] Although the Northwest Ordinance was reenacted under the Constitution, the Fugitive Slave Act of 1793 established procedures and penalties regarding the return of fugitives from labor. Davis quotes section 3 (*U.S. Statutes at Large*, 1:302–305).

[22] See the remarks of John M. Berrien, June 28 (*Cong. Globe*, 30:1, App., 873–80, esp. 874–76).

[23] John Davis had argued that, although a ratio of free and slave states was included in the planned division of territory north and south of the Ohio River, the acquisition of new territories that might alter the ratio had not been contemplated by the founding fathers (ibid., 895–96).

[24] New Jersey's ratification resolution was received in Congress on November 25, 1778; Delaware's resolutions were entered on February 23, 1779; Maryland's demand for additional articles was submitted on May 21, 1779 (*Jour. Cont. Cong.*, 12:1161–63, 13:236, 14:619–22).

[25] Congress' resolution was sent to the states on September 6, 1780 (ibid., 17:806–807).

[26] Virginia reluctantly ceded the western territory in 1780 after Maryland insisted that ratification of the Articles of Confederation depended on such an action (Billington, *Westward Expansion*, 201).

[27] Article III of the treaty of cession guaranteed the inhabitants of Louisiana "the free enjoyment" of their liberty and property (Miller, ed., *Treaties*, 2:501).

[28] Prior to the 1830s state courts north and south of the Mason-Dixon line agreed that transit through a free state or territory freed slaves from their masters. By the 1840s, however, southern courts had changed their opinion, holding that free states could not void what in essence was a contract between master and slave. Senator Samuel S. Phelps of Vermont exemplified the northern view when he argued that the master, having placed himself and his slave in a different jurisdiction, was subject to its laws—presence in free territory brought freedom. Davis also alludes to the personal liberty laws of several northern states, which severely limited the aid those states would grant in returning fugitive slaves (*Cong. Globe*, 30:1, App., 881; Morris, *Free Men All*, 109–25; Kettner, *American Citizenship*, 302–308).

[29] Phelps declared that "the fugitive slave arriving upon the soil where

slavery is not recognized, becomes free. This is the doctrine of the English common law." To buttress his argument, he cited the emancipation of slaves in the *Amistad* and *Creole* incidents (1839, 1842). The doctrine that a positive law sanctioning slavery was necessary for the institution's existence followed from an English court decision in the *Somersett* case (1772), an opinion that had "a deep impact" in America (*Cong. Globe*, 30:1, App., 881; Morris, *Free Men All*, 13–14).

30 From the resolutions of the Massachusetts and Vermont legislatures, respectively (Washington *Nat. Intell.*, Aug. 23, 1848).

31 Davis paraphrases a theme proposed by Jefferson that the diffusion of slaves "over a greater surface would make them individually happier, and proportionally facilitate the accomplishment of their emancipation, by dividing the burden on a greater number of coadjutors" (Jefferson to John Holmes, Apr. 22, 1820, *Writings*, ed. Bergh, 15:249–50).

32 On June 29 Samuel Phelps remarked: "Sir, I am opposed to this extension of an institution which I hold to be utterly at war with the opinions and moral sentiments of the age" (*Cong. Globe*, 30:1, App., 882–83).

33 Villeinage in England had gradually evolved into freeholding by the fifteenth century. Although Nicholas I initiated reforms, serfdom was not abolished in Russia until 1861 (Page, *End of Villainage*, 77; Blum, *Lord and Peasant*, 545–51, 611). In 1850 there were 309,878 slaves in Mississippi; the total population was 606,526 (Dodd and Dodd, comps., *Hist. Statistics*, 34).

34 A reference to the argument of Samuel Phelps (*Cong. Globe*, 30:1, App., 882).

35 The Barnburners, a free-soil faction of New York Democrats, recently had nominated Martin Van Buren for president (Rayback, *Free Soil*, 206–12).

36 The letter from James Monroe is a reply to Jefferson, but the Jefferson letter that Davis quotes was addressed to John Holmes (May 1820, Monroe, *Writings*, ed. Hamilton, 6:123; Apr. 22, 1820, Jefferson, *Writings*, ed. Bergh, 15:520).

37 Responding to a Vermont resolution in opposition to Texas annexation, John C. Calhoun in December 1837 introduced a series of resolutions, one of which Davis quotes. The others dealt with Calhoun's compact theory of union, reserved powers of the states, and the danger to the Union of attacks on slavery (Wiltse, *Calhoun*, 2:370–71; *Cong. Globe*, 25:2, 55, 81, 98).

38 A reference to remarks made by John Davis four days earlier (*Cong. Globe*, 30:1, App., 896).

39 Brackets in the original.

40 Excerpts from a speech by John Adams Dix (1798–1879), Democratic senator, 1845–49, and 1848 gubernatorial candidate of the free-soil Democrats in New York (*Cong. Globe*, 30:1, App., 865–66, 896; *BDAC*).

41 Davis refers to texts that formed part of the classic biblical defense of slavery, Gen. 9:25–27 and Lev. 25:44–47. For a fully developed example of the argument, see McKitrick, ed., *Slavery Defended*, 86–98.

42 A frequent defense of slavery stressed the system's beneficial aspects compared with the treatment received by free blacks in the North and the Caribbean. In May 1848 a slave revolt in Martinique had resulted in some bloodshed and was followed immediately by a proclamation of emancipation (Jenkins, *Pro-Slavery Thought*, 245–46, 296–98; *Niles' Reg.*, July 5, 1848, 15).

43 After the Denmark Vesey conspiracy in 1822, South Carolina passed the Negro Seamen's Act, requiring free black sailors to be imprisoned in

Charleston while their ships were in port. Although the British were not to abolish slavery completely in the West Indies until 1838, they quickly protested the action of South Carolina and similar measures enacted in other southern states. Secretary of State John Quincy Adams unsuccessfully sought a solution in the courts and in 1843 raised the issue in Congress. When the House failed to act, Massachusetts sent state commissioners to Charleston and New Orleans to lobby for repeal of the laws (Wiecek, *Antislavery Constitutionalism*, 132–40; Rice, *Rise and Fall of Slavery*, 257–58).

[44] The Spanish and Mexican system of debt peonage, often harsher than slavery, was prohibited by act of Congress in 1867 (W. Davis, *El Gringo*, 231–34; *U.S. Statutes at Large*, 14: 546).

[45] Possibly a reference to remarks by Thomas Hart Benton on May 31: "this Federal Government was made for something else than to have this pestiferous question constantly thrust upon us to the interruption of the most important business." At the time Benton was concerned with securing relief for Oregon settlers from the peril of an Indian uprising (*Cong. Globe*, 30:1, App., 686).

[46] Dr. John Floyd (1783–1837), a Democratic congressman from Virginia, 1817–29, had spearheaded the drive to acquire all the Oregon country. After his retirement from Congress, Missouri senators Lewis F. Linn and Benton continued the agitation for annexation (Pletcher, *Diplomacy of Annexation*, 104–107; *BDAC*).

[47] If slaves remained under their masters' control when they went into free jurisdictions, Phelps argued, "that doctrine would place the slave power above all the institutions of this Government" (*Cong. Globe*, 30:1, App., 881).

[48] Gen. 13:9 reads: "if thou wilt take the left hand, then I will go to the right; or if thou depart to the right hand, then I will go to the left."

[49] Immediately after Davis' speech, John M. Clayton of Delaware proposed a compromise solution. As head of an eight-member select committee, evenly divided between North and South, Whigs and Democrats, Clayton foresaw a settlement permitting Oregon, California, and New Mexico to be organized without a prohibition against slavery. In the two latter cases, however, a slave transported there might bring suit for his freedom, thus forcing federal courts to decide the issue of congressional power over slavery in the territories. The Senate accepted the proposal on July 26, sending it to the House, where it was tabled. Subsequently the House passed its own bill for Oregon, leaving aside the Mexican cession lands and incorporating the Northwest Ordinance provision against slavery. The Senate refused to accept the House measure, instead amending the bill to prohibit slavery because Oregon lay above the extended Missouri Compromise line. Davis favored adoption of 36°30′, but just before final passage he attempted to substitute the Clayton compromise. Upon the urgent request of several senators, he withdrew his motion and the Oregon bill again passed. When the House still refused to concur, the Senate receded from its insistence on the Missouri Compromise line; Davis and most other southerners voted nay. The first session of the Thirtieth Congress ended on August 14, 1848, with the Oregon Territory organized under the provisions of the Northwest Ordinance and the status of California and New Mexico undecided (*Cong. Globe*, 30:1, 927–28, 1002–1005, 1027, 1043, 1061–63, 1078–80, 1083–85; Wiltse, *Calhoun*, 3:349–57).

To William L. Marcy

Senate Chamber 12th Aug. 1848

SIR,

Govr. J. W. Matthews of Mississippi wrote to me on the 24th Ult.[1] requesting that the 2d Missi. Regt. and the Missi. Battalion should be allowed to keep their arms, and if not otherwise, then by charging them to the state for arms to which it may be now or here after entitled. When the letter was received a resolution was before the Mil. committee to give to all volunteers their arms, that resolution was adversely treated, and has been returned to the senate. I now apply to you on the part of the Governor of Mississippi that the arms of the Missi. Vols. be turned over to the state as provided, in such cases.[2] Very Respectfully yrs.

JEFF'N: DAVIS

ALS (Richard W. Davis).

[1] Not found.
[2] An endorsement by ordnance officer George Talcott indicates that there was "no objection" to Davis' request. In September Talcott ad-

dressed the governor, stating that a balance of 365 rifles would be charged against Mississippi's quota of arms and stores (Sept. 22, 1848, RG27, Vol. 27, Corres., Ms-Ar). See also Albert G. Brown to Davis, May 17, 1847.

Speech at Raymond

Editorial Note: Davis' participation in the presidential campaign was restricted, as the Jackson *Mississippian* (Sept. 1, 1848) explained, by "considerations of a private character." By early September he was on his way home after the adjournment of Congress (Davis to William L. Marcy, Sept. 3, 1848). Later in the month he spoke at Raymond, Jackson, and Vicksburg and on October 19 at Port Gibson. He also released two public letters (Oct. 6, 23) on current political issues.

September 22, 1848

He ran over some of the prominent measures of public policy in which he took an interest during the late session of Congress—spoke in terms of severe condemnation concerning the "defection" of Benton and Houston on the Oregon Bill[1]—said nothing about Polk—gave out that the Northern Democrats were no longer worthy of being called "allies of the South" and that he should never again speak of them as such, and came at last, with evident reluctance, to the Presidential contest.—He said that if any persons expected him to speak evil of Gen. Taylor, they would be disappointed. He knew no evil of the old hero, and spoke of him as one of the purest and noblest men the world had ever seen. The Colonel seemed greatly moved in speaking of Gen. Taylor, and his eulogy on the old man was beyond all question the finest we ever heard. It was received with thunders of involuntary applause.—He referred to the kindness and almost paternal regard shown by Gen. Taylor to the Mississippians under his command, and was again interrupted by a storm of cheers. He said the old General stood god-father to the sons of Mississippi when, amid the war and smoke of the fight, they were baptized in blood on the heights of Buena Vista—and was again compelled to pause by a hurricane of applause. He said that, during the progress of the battle, after he (Col. Davis) was wounded, Gen. Taylor came and sat down by him—the firm determination on his brow seemed struggling with an expression of deep sorrow for the brave fellows who had fallen and those who were yet to bite the dust—when, on being interrogated as to his purpose, he replied, while the fire of an unconquered will gleamed in his eye—"MY WOUNDED ARE BEHIND ME, AND I SHALL NEVER PASS THEM ALIVE!" About this time, the crowd became so excited that they were almost ready to carry the Colonel from the stand. But he was not done yet. He said that, after all, Gen. Taylor in a political point of view, must be regarded as identified with the party which had nominated him, and that, therefore, he (the Colonel) would be obliged to vote for Cass and Butler. This announcement was received with loud shouts by the Democrats; and the Colonel, after scolding them a little for seeming to suppose that he ever intended to do anything else,[2] proceeded to remark that Martin Van Buren was a very corrupt man—very!—that he had always been so, but that he had stuck up to his pledges so long as he remained in office, and that *Cass* would, in all probability, do the same! He told us that the doctrine (advocated by some) of leaving the question of slavery to the mongrel population of our Mexican territories, was palpably wrong and exceedingly contemptible, and, being pressed for time, he omitted mentioning that it was the most-prominent doctrine advocated by Cass in the Nicholson letter.[3] He also took occasion to inform us that (though he was going to support a

Northern man himself) the South must rely upon herself in the great struggle which must soon come upon the slavery question, and that the Presidential canvass should be conducted with such forbearance as to prepare the way for that amalgamation of parties which the coming crisis would render necessary.

Vicksburg *Tri-Weekly Whig*, Sept. 26, 1848.

[1] Thomas Hart Benton and Sam Houston, along with Presley Spruance of Delaware, were the only slave state senators to cast affirmative votes on the question of receding from the Missouri Compromise amendment to the Oregon bill; the final vote was 29–25 (*Cong. Globe*, 30:1, 1078).

[2] According to the Vicksburg *Weekly Sentinel*'s account of the speech (Sept. 27, 1848), Davis was "indignant" that anyone doubted his position, denouncing as "*false* and a *slander*" the idea that he would desert the Democratic party. Since the summer of 1847 it was rumored that Davis' connection with Taylor had alienated the Mississippian from the Polk administration. Indeed, as early as October 1847 there was a suggestion that Davis might be Taylor's secretary of war, a notion that persisted during late 1848. Whig support of Davis' election as senator in January did nothing to dispel the idea that he was "a Taylor man" and the *Mississippian* (Sept. 1, 1848) felt compelled to state that Davis' limited ac-

tivity in the fall canvass was not a sign of disaffection with the Democratic cause. Although Davis continued publicly to eulogize Taylor and urge Mississippians to vote for Cass and Butler, privately he mourned that Taylor would not be on the Democratic ticket and expressed some misgivings about the nominees (Benjamin F. Dill to John A. Quitman, Sept. 7, 1847, Z239, Claiborne Coll., Ms-Ar; Jackson *Mississippian*, Oct. 1, 29, 1847; Vicksburg *Weekly Sentinel*, Jan. 5, 12, Dec. 6, 1848; James M. Howry to James K. Polk, Jan. 17, 1848, Polk Papers, DLC; Davis to Beverley Tucker, Apr. 12, and to Hugh R. Davis, June 4, 1848).

[3] Davis later explained that he had supported Cass's election despite the Michigan senator's identification with popular sovereignty because he believed the doctrine was "unconnected with the functions of the President." Furthermore, he considered that Cass would be "reliable for defence against . . . Congressional legislation for the interdiction of slavery in the Territories" (Davis, *Papers*, ed. Rowland, 2:111–14; see also Davis' public letter of Oct. 23, 1848).

Speech at Jackson

September 23, 1848

COL. DAVIS, in his introductory remarks, spoke of the gratification he felt at returning to the land where he was reared—to the midst of his friends and neighbors—to the home of his affections, his interests and his hopes.

He referred to his unanimous election to the Senate, and feelingly acknowledged his indebtedness for an honor so far exceeding his deserts, and so little to have been expected by one whose party alliances had been so close and so constant. He said he had, by devotion to the interests of the State, endeavored to make such return, as was within his power, for the personal confidence, which those who differed from him politically had manifested.

He then gave some account of his stewardship, especially in relation to the light-houses on the Gulf coast, and the establishment of a navy yard, at Ship Island. He believed the report of the coast survey would show a harbor at Ship Island, the best between the Tortugas and Vera Cruz.—That a navy yard was necessary as connected with the defence of the coast and the commerce of the Gulf, and that it would open a rich source of wealth to the people of East Mississippi, by creating a demand for the ship timber which abounds there.[1]

He spoke of the Mexican war, which he viewed as forced upon the United States, and which had demonstrated a problem heretofore denied—the fitness of militia for all the purposes of war. They had been tried in invasive marches, in holding positions in the attack of fortified places, in battle on the open field, and had not been found wanting. To maintain the honor, or protect the rights and interests of the country, we could safely rely on the arms and breasts of the patriotic citizens of the land. This lesson, thus taught to the States of Europe, will probably secure to the United States a long exemption from foreign aggression, and give, in protracted peace, an increased consideration, indemnity for much that the war has cost us. But whilst a continuous succession of victories brought laurels in such profusion, there was another and more enduring species of fame—the triumph of civilization and humanity, softening all the rigors of war to such degree, that the helpless, the non-combatant and the conquered saw, in your victorious troops, their best protectors. He said there had been much in the treaty of peace, which did not meet his approval; he explained his efforts to amend the treaty, especially on the subject of boundary, in which he had been unsuccessful; and in the mode of payment, in which he had obtained a modification, which requires the sum to be paid in instalments,[2] and thus constitutes a bond on the Mexicans for good behaviour, the best that could be had, where there is such total want of national faith and disregard of treaty obligations.

He said, the question which, in the late session of Congress, excited the greatest interest, and which would probably produce the most important results, was the organization of territorial governments. Upon that, all the opposition to the South, both political and fanatic, was displayed in its concentrated force. He spoke of the different forms in which the question was presented, first covertly, seeking, through the acts of the provisional government of Oregon, to enact the prohibition of slavery within that territory, for all time to come. He advocated the Senate bill as strictly constitutional and more likely to secure our rights, according to the terms of the confederate compact, than an appeal to any other mode provided under the government, to secure all guarantied by the constitution, was the extreme which could be hoped for from any of the departments of government; to be encroached on was the ordinary fate of the minority, and no one who considered the course of Congress, at its late session, could expect the guaranties of the constitution to be enlarged, for the benefit of the South, by federal legislation.

He showed the determination on the part of the House of Representatives, to resist the claims of the South, by the summary manner in which the bill to adjudicate the rights of southern slaveholders, emigrating to the United States territories, was disposed of, and from this he drew two conclusions—that southern men were sincere and confident of their right, and therefore willing to risk the decision of the courts—that their northern opponents, confident of a congressional majority, and regardless of our rights, refused such mode of settlement. He denied that the necessity for a territorial government in Oregon was greater or more pressing than in California and New Mexico; he viewed the case of Oregon as pressed for a precedent, and expected it to be so quoted; he said that the President, when the Oregon bill was presented to him, was reduced to the consideration of the bill before him, and though as a member of Congress he probably would have voted against it, to withhold his approval as President, he had no other ground than the want of power in Congress to legislate upon the subject; this position, if taken, would have required him to veto the Missouri Compromise, if presented to him. The message sent with his signature to the Oregon bill presents the President's opinion upon the moral force of that compromise,[3] which has long presented the most practicable ground, if not the only mode, in which the question of slavery in the territories can be settled.

He treated the assurance, that it was not designed to interfere with slavery in the States, as utterly valueless; there being no power, there was no forbearance; but in the resolve of the non-slaveholding States to claim the whole territory for their own extension, the ultimate design was visible; steadily increasing in numbers, they could first control all legislation and bend the laws to their own purposes, and finally reaching the limits of a three-fourths' majority, they could, by a change of the constitution, abolish slavery in the South, if previous interference by the law-making, President-electing, judge-appointing, governing majority, should not previously, by indirect means, have effected that object. He maintained equality of sections and great interests was essential to the preservation of the Union; and compared the condition of the South, if a decided minority in the Union, to that of the colonies when connected with Great Britain. Our fathers rejected the offer of a representation in Parliament, because their representatives would have been powerless. All who loved the Union more than sectional advantage must see, that to preserve the confederacy, the slaveholding States must be multiplied, increasing *pari passu* with the other States, unless they indulge the vain expectation that the South will surrender her claim to equality and sovereignty, and permit her institutions to be dictated by her pride-swolen neighbors.

Upon the question of slavery extension, the issue was made; one or the other side must yield; the opponents of the South refused to permit slavery to enter any of the territories, which, though our common property, they resolve to appropriate exclusively to themselves; we claim no more than the right of joint proprietors, to the joint use of the common property, and it was a claim which we could not and ought not to yield.

He animadverted upon southern representatives who had abandoned the South, and thus driven from our side those northern men who had, at their own hazard, and as a measure of unquestionable right, claimed that a compromise of conflicting pretensions should be made. When representatives of slaveholding States postponed or abandoned the claims of those States, we could not expect support from those whose constituency were arrayed against our pretensions. There was a time when the northern democracy were properly called the allies of the South;[4] that term could not appropriately be applied now; both the great parties at the North are opposed to us, but as the votes upon test questions, at the last session of Congress would show, the friends of the South are to be found in the ranks of the democracy. There had been a rapid progress to sectional division—that evil so long deprecated and justly feared; the Union could not long survive the perfect organization of geographical parties, and he hoped the democracy of the South would adhere to their fraternity of principles, would stick to the ship, composed of materials from every condition of society and every quarter of our broad Union, as long as there was a stick to bear our colors, or a plank to stand on. He felt, however, that there should be co-intelligence and union among southern men, as the best mode of checking the progress of opinions which, through geographical divisions, must in their onward course reach disunion. He said, the warning "Put not your trust in Princes,"[5] might well be applied to our present condition. The South had little to hope from Congress, the opposition to the further extension of the slave-holding States was active, and not limited to one form; if one form should prove to be impracticable, others would be sought; the majority in Congress being opposed to the introduction of slaves into territories, will withhold appropriations for a government, and thus drive the people of the territory into slavery prohibition, or pass laws prohibiting slavery in the territory, as one mode or the other may be the more effectual. The form will vary with the case, the resistance being constant. He believed nothing could succeed which did not reach the source, and operate on public opinion at the North. If assured of the determination of southern men to sustain their ultimatum, even by force of arms, reflection and patriotism might change the current of popular feeling at the North, and the politicians who now ride the hobby of slavery, would as readily answer to the change, as the mercury in a thermometer responds to the increase or diminution of heat. Thus only can we expect any radical and permanent benefit. Your representatives cannot hope to effect a change of opinion in the representatives of those who are antagonist to you, nor expect that their voices will be heard in the storm of anti-slavery agitation, which is sweeping over the northern portion of our land. You must rely upon yourselves to arrest this politico-geographical war upon your rights; as in the last resort, you must stand shoulder to shoulder; your voice, to be heard and heeded, must be united.

He said he was aware that he addressed those who were preoccupied with the Presidential canvass, and that the present was not, therefore, the time to discuss questions at length which were unconnected with that engrossing subject. At some future time he might seek to be heard more fully, and more generally by the people, on the questions to which he had alluded. He had now come among them to make to his fellow-citizens the limited visit which his private affairs would allow, in order that he might confer with them, and as their representative, give an account of his stewardship. For these purposes, and to extend his acquaintance with the people and the interests he represented, he had made his present hurried visit, and he regretted that circumstances restricted it to so narrow a limit.

In relation to the Presidency he said, that he had been unconnected with any movement or combination to effect the nomination, and that it was not his purpose to enter, as a partisan, into the canvass. Before he became a member of Congress, he had avowed his objection to Congressional interference with the Presidential nomination, and a change in his position had wrought no change in his opinion. As a member of Congress, he had acted out his creed, and waited, an observant spectator, for an expression of the popular will, through primary assemblies, and their delegates in convention. Subsequent reflection had only confirmed him in his position; and he would go further, and say, that he would prefer to see all intervening machinery dispensed with; that instead of Congressional interposition, the electoral system should be abandoned, and the people of each State be permitted to vote directly for whomsoever each might choose, as President and Vice President of the United States.

He said, as a Mississippian, his highest allegiance was to the State; as a Senator, he considered himself a representative of her sovereignty, and speaking to the people he would use the language of soberness and truth, not partisan zeal. Always a democrat, his political conduct had been guided by the principles of the democratic creed; having never doubted their correctness, he had never swerved from them, and might claim to be excused from offering extraordinary proofs of his sincerity. The result of the approaching Presidential election in Mississippi could not be considered a debateable question. The democracy had slowly acquired an overwhelming majority, and those who feared their defeat must have much less confidence in their adherence to principle than he believed to be due.

Strong in numbers, efficiently organized, ably and industriously represented in the canvass, he doubted not that their overpowering majority would be still further augmented, at the approaching election. He felt that whatever he might be able to effect was not required for the success of our ticket, or the maintainance of our party majority.

He said he had been informed that some speculation had arisen, as to the course he would pursue in the Presidential election. If this arose from his having abstained, in his position as Senator, from all connection with President-making, he would add to what he had already said, that his ideas of propriety dictated that course. By theory and organization, the Senate was the conservative branch of our government; in no contingency could the election of the President be referred to it; between the Senate and the Executive exist close and confidential relations, involving all important appointments, and the foreign negotiations, on which American, not party feelings should decide. In the case of impeachment, the Senate would sit in judgment; these and kindred considerations, led him to the conclusion, that above all other officials, Senators should keep aloof from the strife and excitement of partisan controversy, in a Presidential canvass.

If any had inferred from the high opinion he had publicly expressed of General Taylor, soon after returning from Mexico, that he would abandon his political faith, and unite with a party which he held to be wrong in principle, and against which he had struggled during the whole of his political life, they had fallen into the error of confounding personal estimation with political alliance. No part of the esteem or confidence he had heretofore expressed in relation to General Taylor was abated. His opinion was the growth of many years, and of observation under varied and trying emergencies; it had not sprang up in a night—it would not wither in a day. But a President, coming into power by the support of a party, must be viewed as identical with that party from which his advisers must be drawn, and by which his measures must be passed. He honored him as a patriot and a gallant soldier; but on this, as on past occasions, he must oppose the whig candidate for political office. He believed the principles and measures of the democracy to be essential to the preservation of the Union, and to the prosperity and security of the southern planting States; to this conviction, all personal considerations were subordinate. To his political principles he was ready to sacrifice his affections; but if any expected him, in supporting the democratic ticket, to assail or depreciate Gen. Taylor, they expected that which he was neither able nor willing to perform. He knew no evil to tell; he had ever found him just, generous, wise, good and great; equal to every emergency and to any fortune. He had not forgotten the kindness and paternal care extended to the sons of Mississippi, when in Mexico; he remembered, on the eventful evening of the second day of the battle of Buena Vista, General Taylor, when speaking of his wounded who had been carried to rear, referred to their gallant services with the pride and feeling of a father, and nobly declared that he would never pass them alive. Remembering these things, he would be less than a man, could he fail gratefully to feel and willingly acknowledge the services and merits of that distinguished citizen and soldier.

He said the principles which divided the two great parties of the Union were well known and of remote origin. He knew of no concession that had been made by our political opponents, involving any principle. What though they say, it is not proposed to establish a national bank, or a tariff "of protection for protection's sake," the power is still claimed to legislate upon the currency and the exchanges of the country, and to impose duties for other purposes than revenue. He denied any other power to have been granted than to coin money and to regulate the value thereof; the constitution no where contemplates any other federal currency than specie; and the wisdom of its hard money framers had recently been manifested in a most convincing form. England, the country with which our principal commercial relations exist, had been covered with the pall of bankruptcy, and distress knocked at the door of the palace and the hovel,[6] yet the shock was scarcely felt in the United States; he referred to the past to show how different would have been the result, if the commerce of the two countries had been bound together by the intangible links of banking. He spoke of the tariff of 1846; of the increased revenue produced by it, and of its still higher claim to estimation as approximating the principle in taxation which requires the citizen to contribute to the support of the government, in proportion to the benefits received. This could not be absolutely done by any mode of direct taxation, but as consumption would generally be in direct proportion to property, if duties were laid on all articles consumed, according to their value, the only just mode is approximated as nearly as possible, by indirect taxation. He said under existing circumstances, it was unnecessary to speak of direct taxation.

On the policy of internal improvement, the whig party occupied their old position; and candor required of him, when speaking to his constituency, to say, that the doctrine of internal improvement, by the general government, found so much favor with the Northern and Northwestern democracy, that he expected it to prevail, for years to come, to run its course to the creation of a large public debt, the result of fruitless appropriations, then to become odious, the impolicy to be demonstrated, and in the soberness of repentance, the true principles of the constitution to be redeemed.

He expressed his surprise that the whig dogma in relation to the veto power of the President, should still find favor in the South. It is one of the checks interposed for the benefit of the minority. You of the South are the minority, and such you must remain; your safety is in the terms of the compact; your policy is conservative. Among the safeguards erected against the will of the majority, he viewed the veto as the wisest and most effectual. The diversity of mind and interest would usually maintain contending parties, such as have heretofore existed in our country; upon a question of vital importance to a minority, it may always make terms with one party or the other, and elect a President who would shelter the threatened interest by the interposition of the Executive veto. As its whole effect was to restrain, he could not see why it should be dreaded by a minority, but could readily understand why it should be denounced by an aggressive majority.—He referred to the charge that the veto was a monarchical power; he said that it was popular in its origin, and so truely popular in its use, that it was only found in countries of free institutions. It was first given to the Tribunes of Rome, to restrain the patricians from legislative oppression of the people. In the limited monarchy of Great Britain, it had only a nominal existence, not having been applied for more than a century. In our own country, it had never been overruled by the constitutional majority, and with not more than one exception, the position of the President's veto had been sustained by the people.[7] He said no power was less likely to be abused—none could afford less temptation to the corrupt and ambitious, because its only effect was to restrain, and it must necessarily be exercised against the dominant party in Congress.

Viewing the old principles of the whig and democratic parties as at issue in this contest—convinced as he had long been of the vital importance of the measures and policy of the democratic party, it could hardly be necessary for him to say that he should, at the November election, vote for the democratic electoral tickit.

Of the democratic candidate for the Presidency, he said that he knew General Cass well, and esteemed him as a scholar, a patriot and a statesman of the greatest ability and experience, and an honorable man upon whose pledges they might safely rely. A long life of public service, in the camp, the wilderness, the councils of the nation, the executive cabinet and at foreign court, had so often and in such eminent degree exhibited his capacity and devotion to his country, as to render his character and history familiar with his fellow-citizens.

It is urged however, that he is a northern man, and cannot be trusted by the South. So long as we have friends at the North, it is not only a moral duty to cherish and sustain them, but it is dictated by policy also. If those northern men who encounter opposition fierce as civil war, because of their adherence to you, are to be distrusted because of their locality, how long can you expect to have such friends? In proportion as the number of those northern men who maintain the rights and interests of the South, is small, so is their sincerity proven, and their claim to our kindest consideration established.

But our opponents charge that we have heretofore advocated a northern man—that he betrayed us; and they urge this against confiding in another from the same section. This is a position neither sound in reasoning nor in fact; we admit that Mr. Van Buren has proved faithless to the southern men who confided in him, but he kept his pledges as long as he held station, and it may be that his recent defection is the result of disappointment; he did not betray his official trust. But grant all that is said of him—admit that the democracy were mistaken in him—that he was as corrupt as the whigs charged, by what mode of reasoning would it be established, that all northern men are, therefore, unworthy of confidence? Those who take this position have reached the point of disunion; nothing could justify the continuance of the connexion beyond the demonstration of such a truth. He urged upon the South the propriety of resisting the formation of geographical divisions; he described the valley of the Mississippi as one country by laws which it was not in the power of man to subvert. He deprecated the disunion of the States as an evil only to be contemplated as a remedy, when every thing else had failed. He spoke of our government as the centre from which free principles were extending over the wide surface of christendom, and of the shock which would be given to confidence in representative government, if this great experiment should be, in any respect, unsuccessful.

He contended that the constitution, literally construed, so as to leave all domestic interests to local legislation, might embrace within its operation a confederacy as extended as our race could occupy. He saw no limit until we reached a people incompetent for self-government; he, therefore, had favored the annexation of Texas, because possessed by Americans, with language and institutions and capabilities like our own; he was willing to take uninhabited territory coterminous to our own, and suitable for emigration from the United States. He would add new members to our family, not to form new republics, but to extend the glorious government we had inherited from the thirteen States of the revolution. Let the stripes, which on our federal flag are recordant of the original size of our family, never be dimmed, unless by the lustre of the stars, which multiplying, may finally extend over and conceal them.

He appealed to his friends of all political parties to cultivate harmony and good understanding; pointed to the effect which he hoped would be produced on popular feeling at the North, by entire unanimity among ourselves upon questions involving, however remotely, the rights of the South; he said these were questions paramount to all others, and not proper to be connected with our political divisions—that their decision lay beyond the pending election, and far transcended it in importance—that above the contest there should be seen the spirit of fraternity and harmony, upon all such questions as involved Southern rights, so that others might understand what was to be expected when the forbearance of the South should be exhausted, and know that her concessions had sprung from affection to the whole Union, not from local division or conscious weakness. He said he hoped no extenuation would be attempted on either side, of any position taken by the partisans of either, which opposed or hazarded the rights of the South, as connected with their slave property. We had reached a point, in this controversy, where one or the other must yield; the question at issue was whether the territory of the United States should be open to the settlement of all citizens with their property, or whether we of the South should be excluded from taking our slaves into such territory. This admitted of no compromise, and could only be yielded by southern men, when they are willing to be marked as unfit for the equality in the Union which they inherited from their sires of the revolution—to be curbed from further growth, as carrying the seeds of moral and political evil in their institutions. This surrender, your pride, your knowledge of the truth, your respect for yourselves, for those from whom you inherited these institutions, your convictions of duty and public interest, will never allow you to make. And the sooner and more fully this is known among your enemies, the greater the hope of peaceful and honorable adjustment of this question, dangerous to the Union, and vital to the honor, to the prosperity, to the existence of the slaveholding States.

Col. Davis, in conclusion, expressed his obligations to the people of Mississippi, of both political parties, for the unmerited honors conferred upon him, and as their representative, he had striven zealously, however feebly, to requite their many acts of kindness. For the future, he pledged all that affection for the land, with which his memories were associated and his hopes identified, could give; all that entire devotion to their interests would prompt and enable him to accomplish.

Jackson *Mississippian* (Dem.), Oct. 20, 1848.

1 Davis had favored establishment of a Gulf Coast navy yard since 1844 and in 1846 had requested a report on the capacity of Ship Island for such a facility (*Davis Papers*, 2:74–75, 310, 410). On March 8, 1848, he introduced resolutions for a lighthouse on Ship Island and a navy yard in the harbor of Cat and Ship islands.

2 Davis made several vain attempts to amend Article 5, which defined the boundary between the United States and Mexico. He succeeded, however, in removing from Article 12 an option by which two years after ratification the Mexicans might elect to receive the balance due them ($12 million) in one payment rather than in annual installments (Miller, ed., *Treaties*, 5:243–44, 251).

3 Stressing his fears of sectional strife, Polk had advised settlement of the slavery question by adoption of the Missouri or "some other equitable compromise" (U.S. President, *Messages and Papers*, 4:606–10).

4 Attributed by Davis to Thomas Jefferson (see Davis to Charles J. Searles, Sept. 19, 1847).

[5] Ps. 146:3.

[6] Referring to the recent financial crisis in England, during which hundreds of mercantile and banking establishments failed. The crisis had its roots in the Bank Act of 1844, which required that Bank of England notes be covered by bullion and prohibited issuance of notes by new banks. Coinciding with widespread railroad speculation and the Irish famine, the act only contributed to what was described as "universal panic," unmitigated until October 1847, when the prime minister recommended suspension of the law (Evans, *Commercial Crisis,* esp. ch. 2).

[7] Davis is restating Calhoun's famous argument (1842) that the veto power was a constitutional safeguard of minority rights. The one instance in which a veto had been overridden occurred at the end of Tyler's administration with enactment of the revenue cutter bill (Jackson, *Presidential Vetoes,* 83–84; for Calhoun's speech of February 28, 1842, on the veto, see *Cong. Globe,* 27:2, App., 164–68).

Speech at Port Gibson

October 19, 1848

Col. Davis was cheered by both parties, and divided his speech pretty equally between them, the whigs being quite as well pleased with it as were the Democrats. Col. Davis *possesses* the candor which was *professed* by others, and frankly admitted that the great bulk, of the Democratic party of the North were equally as hostile to the institution of slavery as the whigs of those states. That he could no longer claim them as he once did, as the allies of the south, but that *he* was *wrong* and the *whigs* of Mississippi were *right* when they told him, some years ago, that Martin Van Buren professed principles which he did not entertain, and that his party at the North were abolitionists at heart. Col. D. advised those present who thought that the interests of the South required them to vote for Gen. Taylor, to do so, an injunction which will be observed by fully two thirds of those present.[1]

Col. D. then replied to various questions which were propounded him, many of which told *against* his party.

Port Gibson *Herald and Corres.* (Whig), Oct. 20, 1848.

[1] A week after the speech, Richard T. Archer, a well-known Claiborne County citizen, wrote Davis a public letter, telling why he planned to vote the Whig ticket. Archer recalled: "In your address you *politically* passed over the unassailable PATRIOTISM, fitness, and unquestioned fidelity of Gen. Taylor . . . and you compared the *head* of your ticket with the *tail* of that ticket for which, though a *no-party man,* I shall freely give my suffrage. But I give this suffrage without

confidence in Millard Fillmore. . . . When you appealed to me whether I would vote for Fillmore, why bore you not in mind that *you* were about to vote for *Cass*, and that you were preaching proselytism to those who distrusted him?" (Port Gibson *Herald and Corres.*, Oct. 27, 1848). Taylor carried Claiborne County 464–358 (ibid., Nov. 10, 1848).

To Woodville Citizens

WARREN County. 23d Oct. 1848.

GENTLEMEN:[1]—I have the honor to acknowledge the receipt of your polite invitation to attend a mass meeting at Woodville, on the 4th of Nov. next. A previous invitation to meet my fellow citizens of Yazoo county on the 31st inst. had been accepted before the receipt of your letter, subject only to the condition of my being able to leave home.[2] Thus I am deprived of the pleasure it would have given me, to have met my early friends, and the sons of my early friends, in primary assembly.

The great principle which has divided the people of the U. States into two political parties from the formation of the confederacy, is strict, or latitudinous construction of the terms of compact. To the majority, strict construction is an obstacle, to the minority, it brings confidence, and security. As the representative strength of the Southern States has relatively diminished in the growth of our Union; so, to us, has the importance of this principle increased, until it has reached a value which should make it the political Shibboleth of the South.

No longer is the doctrine of implied powers confined in its application to means expedient or convenient to the federal government; but drawing authority from numerical power, and disregarding the restraints of written fundamental contract, its advocates assume to decide by majorities the rights, and privileges of sovereign states of the Union. Denouncing your institution of domestic slavery, they call upon the federal government to exclude the citizens of the South from migrating with their slaves into the territories belonging to the United States. In this they demand the exercise of a power not granted in the constitution; and thus the advocates of strict construction answer, whatever their private views or sectional interests may be, and this answer satisfies the position of the South; which is to be left to the uninterrupted enjoyment of the guarantees of the constitution, securing to them in all things equality with other states of the confederacy.

He must be a careless observer who supposes any right of the southern States touching the subject of slavery can be submitted to the congress and preserved. Shall Southern men then affiliate with a party which would extend federal legislation to any, even the most remote branch of this democratic institution of the South?

There is another opinion among northern politicians to which I refer, lest silence should be construed into acquiescence; it is that the territorial inhabitants have the power to decide upon the right of slaveholders to migrate with their property to the territories. This like the position that Congress may prohibit such migration, I hold to be absolutely wrong; and being neither the apologist or defender of either creed, will not here enter into an inquiry as to which is more or less tenable. The rights of the states not delegated to the federal government, are as absolutely their own as if no union existed; and surely it requires no argument to prove that their dependencies, the territories, do not form a third estate with power to modify the relation of the contracting parties to whom they belong. There is this difference between the two opinions as involved in the selection of a president; the former is connected with him officially, the latter not at all. A law of Congress must be approved by the executive, or receive his veto. An act of the territorial legislature does not reach him. His opinions therefore upon the powers of congress are important, upon the powers of territorial legislatures unimportant, so far as his official acts are concerned.

Whilst the opponents of Southern institutions are steadily and zealously engaged in demolishing the constitutional barriers which the fathers of the republic raised for our peace, protection, and fraternity; we should show the unbelieving, that we are united and resolved to resist their encroachment. The questions involved in this canvass surpass in importance, and enduring influence, a hundred, yea, a thousand fold, the mere consideration of personal preference between the candidates.

If the South hesitates in the assertion of her rights, or gives rise to a doubt as to the unanimity with which she will maintain them, the days of "northern men with southern principles" will soon be numbered; and we shall have united to meet the evil which an earlier exhibition of unanimity might have prevented.

Accept, gentlemen, individually, my thanks for the terms in which you have been pleased to address me, and pray make for me a suitable apology to the friends who have desired my presence. Hoping to see the state rights county of Wilkinson numbered as in olden time, among the supporters of the democratic ticket,[3] those who deny to the federal government the exercise of doubtful powers, I am very truly, Your friend,

JEFFERSON DAVIS.

Woodville *Repub.*, Nov. 7, 1848.

[1] Claiborne Farish, Isaac D. Gildart, *Republican* editor John H. Leatherman, H. E. Sale, and A. Morningstar were the committee of invitation appointed by Woodville Democrats.

[2] The letter inviting Davis to speak has not been found. Davis later confirmed that he did speak in Yazoo County (Davis, *Papers*, ed. Rowland, 2:137).

[3] Wilkinson County supported Andrew Jackson, but from 1836 through 1848 returned Whig majorities in every statewide and presidential election (Burnham, *Presidential Ballots*, 568; Hodge, "Attitude of the Repub.," 12–26).

From William H. Sparke

Vicksburg Nov 17th 1848

DEAR DAVIS

I am disposed to be as good as my promise and if /it/ proves agreeable I will keep you advised of what occurs that you are interested in,[1]

A good democrat called on me a few days since and remarked that Robbins[2] had left and that I would have to defend my personal friend Col Davis, I informed him that I would willingly do so on all occasions, he informed me that a report was in circulation that you stated on the evening of the election that The nomination of *Gen* Cass was a prostitution of the Democratic party, this <–has–> report has ben started by a Whig of varasity, and, I assert if you did make the remark you certainly gave some qualifycation to it The democrats of *VB* feel quite tender on there defeat[3] especially those that bet, I am not one of those as I never risk anything but a party contest, I feel assured that *Gen* Taylor will make a popular President, I do not consider him pledged to the Whigs so fare as to change or recommend any change of the leading measures of the

Democratic party, As a matter of corse he will make some changes in the principal offices of *Government*, this will be all right,

I have asserted that the first who begin to complain of his administration will be the Whigs,

Please advise me of the matter which I inform you of as early as convenient and I will write you again[4]

We are all well Respectfully your friend

W. H. SPARKE

N. B. I remember we conversed on the subject of Gen Cass & his soundness as a statesman, you remarked that you had served with him in committee,[5] and found him an excellent agreeable and gentelmanly old fellow and decidedly with the South on the Question that divides the two parties, *ie* the Wilmot proviso[6]

ALS (Davis Papers, KyLxT).

[1] Davis evidently visited Vicksburg just before leaving home for Washington. On November 20 he arrived in New Orleans and on December 1 reached the capital. Three days later he attended the opening session of Congress and on December 12 was reappointed to the Military Affairs and Library committees. During the session Davis resided at Mrs. Duvall's boarding house on Missouri Avenue near 4½ Street, along with fellow southern Democrats William R. King, Solomon W. Downs, and Emile La Sere (New Orleans *Picayune*, Nov. 21, 1848; Washington *Union*, Dec. 2, 1848; *Cong. Globe*, 30:2, 1, 27–28; *U.S. Cong. Dir., 1849*, 30).

[2] Thomas E. Robins, a prominent local Democrat married to Davis' niece, was registered as a Vicksburg voter in October 1848 (*Weekly Sentinel*, Oct. 25, 1848). His whereabouts in November are unknown.

[3] Vicksburg Democrats lost heavily in the 1848 election. In the two city precincts, Taylor received 534 votes to Cass's 346. Taylor carried Warren County 890–478 (*Tri-Weekly Whig*, Nov. 9, 1848).

[4] No subsequent correspondence of this period has been located.

[5] Cass was chairman of the Senate Military Affairs Committee during the first session of the Thirtieth Congress.

[6] Sparke's postscript appears in the left and top margins of the first page.

From Francis G. Baldwin

Columbus Mi Novr 19th 1848

DEAR SIR

Tho personally a stranger to you yet I have so far presumed upon my admiration of your character & the near affinity of political feeling as far as I have learnd your's as to address you on a subject involving my intents. I may farther mention that I have voted

for you with pleasure on two occasion's first as a democratic elector & subsequently for congress. I hope these considerations will
constitute in your estimation a sufficient apology for your being
troubled by so humble & unknown individual as myself. Before
proceeding farther I may mention that, I am the Brother in law of
the Honl Geo R Clayton[1] & J B Cobb[2] of this place who are probably known to you. As my object in addressing you is to solicit
your influence & intercession in obtaining a political appointment
I will briefly sum up my claim, I am a democrat a whole democrat
& nothing but a democrat. In this respect I am v.s my whole connexion I have voted in three Presidential contests viz in '40 in '44
& in the one just over. In the two first I supported the democratic
nominees. In the last struggle upon a review of the whole-ground
I felt bound to vote for Genl Taylor. Even upon a strict party
issue I would have voted against such a model of human nature
with reluctance & as between Taylor & Cass the former occupying
an independent & American position The latter a very exception-
able specimen of democracy to say the least why I could not hesitate to give my vote as my *feelings* dictated. I am thus candid in
order that you may have all necessary light in adjudicating my
claim. The office to which I aspire is that of Marshal of the Northern district of this state just vacated by the death of Col Kincannon
the late incumbent, Should Mr Polk appoint me the place would be
filled by a democrat who would be retained by the incoming administration whereas should he on the eve of his exit appoint an
opponent of Taylor would he not be soon remov'd & be replace'd
by a whig? There are a number of the latter stripe fixing up their
papers to be ready by the 4th of March.[3] Be this as it may I shall
be grateful if you will cooperate with the following gentleman to
whom I refer you for any farther information in soliciting for me
the appointment. Honl H V Johnson[4] of Geo. Hon John H Lumpkin[5] do—Honl Howell Cobb[6] do.– Yours &c

FRANCIS. G. BALDWIN.[7]

ALS (DNA, M-873, roll 4).

[1] George R. Clayton (1808–67), an
attorney, served in the legislature of
his native Georgia before moving to
Columbus, Mississippi, in 1836. In 1843
he was the Whig gubernatorial nomi-

nee (Rowland, ed., *Ency. Miss. Hist.*,
1:454). His sister Julia S. was married
to Baldwin (Miller, *Bench and Bar*,
1:183).

[2] Joseph Beckham Cobb (1819–58)
was the son of former Georgia senator Thomas W. Cobb. A Whig attor-

ney, Joseph Cobb served in the state house from Noxubee County (1842) and in the senate from Lowndes (1854–57). He was also the author of a novel, some political essays, and *Mississippi Scenes* (1851), a collection of descriptions and anecdotes (Alderman et al., eds., *Lib. of S. Literature*, 15:88–89; *Miss. Official Reg., 1908*, 49, 74). Like Baldwin, Cobb had married a sister of George Clayton's (Miller, *Bench and Bar*, 1:183).

[3] See the letters of Lock E. Houston (Dec. 3, 8), Stephen Cocke (Dec. 8), and Thomas H. Williams (Dec. 10) for the names of Whigs recommended to Davis. As Baldwin predicts, Polk's appointee was replaced in 1849 (*Senate Ex. Jour.*, 8:6, 132).

[4] Herschel Vespasian Johnson (1812–80), Democratic senator (1848–49) and governor (1853–57) of Georgia, subsequently served in the Confederate Senate, 1863–65 (*DAB*).

[5] John Henry Lumpkin (1812–60), Democratic congressman from Georgia, 1843–49, 1855–57 (*BDAC*).

[6] Howell Cobb (1815–68) had served with Davis in the Twenty-ninth Congress. A Democratic representative from Georgia almost continuously from 1843 until 1857, Cobb was secretary of the treasury under Buchanan. During the Civil War he was Confederate brig. and maj. gen. (*DAB*). Davis described Cobb years later as a "pure patriot . . . whose brain and heart and means and energies were all at the service of his country" (*Rise and Fall*, 2:566).

[7] Francis G. Baldwin, born about 1817 in Georgia, was editor and proprietor of the Columbus *Primitive Republican* in 1851 and copublisher of the *Democrat* in 1853 (1850 Census, Miss., Lowndes, family 917; *Mississippiana*, 2:15, 16).

Remarks on the Report of Robert J. Walker

Editorial Note: In his final report as secretary of the treasury, Walker stressed the importance of the revenue tariff, recommended the establishment of a branch mint in New York City, espoused a plan for payment of the debt, noted the progress of the coast survey, suggested that sections of land be set aside in Oregon for education, and proposed reorganization of the Treasury Department. According to President Polk, the most praiseworthy features of Walker's financial system were the tariff of 1846 and the "constitutional treasury," which Polk believed had saved the nation from "the almost universal paralysis of commerce and industry" experienced in Europe during 1847–48 (*Cong. Globe*, 30:2, App., 5–9, 11–20). Walker's report (*House Ex. Doc.* 7, 30:2), read to the Senate on December 11, was called by the Washington *Union* (Dec. 12, 1848) "the capital of the column of the Secretary's fame."

December 11, 1848

Mr. DAVIS, of Mississippi, moved that twenty thousand extra copies thereof be printed. He said he disliked very much to make a motion to print so large a number of any document; but he looked upon this report as embodying a new system of finance—which, however, had been in operation long enough to be tested by the people.

[Simon Cameron opposed such a motion, saying the country "had decided against" Walker's system; William R. King, however, favored Davis' suggestion as it would give the public an opportunity to decide the merits of the secretary's policies.]

Mr. DAVIS, of Mississippi, was sorry that the honorable Senator from Pennsylvania [Mr. CAMERON][1] had introduced the subject of the tariff in this irregular manner. But, since it had been introduced, he would ask, has that Senator, or has any other member of this honorable body, ever presented the issue of the tariff of 1846, or known it to have been fairly and distinctly presented, to the people of the United States during the late Presidential contest?[2] If so, I should like to know where. It is not the financial system of the Secretary of the Treasury alone. The Democratic party in the two Houses of Congress enacted the tariff of 1846. The Secretary has carried it out as an Executive officer, and the people should understand the manner in which he has discharged that duty. And I add, is it fair, if it has been decided against him, as the Senator from Pennsylvania [Mr. CAMERON][1] says, that the Secretary should not be heard in relation to the manner in which he has executed the high and imperative law of the United States? Why does he wish to conceal the facts and arguments embodied in the Secretary's report? Has the decision of the people—the honorable gentleman's constituents—been given upon a false showing? Why not allow the testimony in favor of the system to go before the country as broadly and freely as the accusation against it?

[William Allen agreed with Davis that the citizenry should be allowed to examine Walker's report, "that all might see for themselves whether the pledges of the Democratic party have been violated or not." Cameron retorted that he did not see any reason to give the report "peculiar attention" unless "for some other reasons than its mere connection with the financial policy of the present Administration." John M. Niles[3] remarked that he was unwilling to treat Walker's report with more consideration than the president's; also, he wished to learn more of the report's contents. Davis, Niles, chided, "ought not to be uneasy not particularly anxious" about the subject, since it would be fully discussed in due time.]

Mr. DAVIS, of Mississippi, replied, that if the honorable Senator from Connecticut [Mr. NILES][1] imputed to him that he was one who had been anxious to go into the merits of this system of finance, he had done him injustice. He had only asked that it should go to the country, not that he wished to treat it with more respect than the President's message, but because the subject was one of peculiar interest, of peculiar historical interest, and formed, he thought, the most striking example ever presented to the world of a Government carrying on its financial operations, while engaged in a foreign war, without the aid of any other machinery than the ordinary revenue of the country, derived from its imports, and without suffering any loss by its greatly increased and multifarious disbursements. That the revenue of the country has increased under such circumstances, notwithstanding all adverse influences, is true. These are facts, not arguments; and it is these facts that we wish to lay before the people, that the public mind may be prepared for that powerful argument which the Senator from Connecticut [Mr. NILES][1] will make when the subject shall be brought before the Senate. That is why he went for the printing of so large a number of copies of the report.[4]

Cong. Globe, 30:2, 18–19.

[1] Brackets in the original.

[2] Cameron had not specifically cited the tariff of 1846 in his comments but stated that the Democrats lost the 1848 election "chiefly on account of the opposition of the people . . . to this financial system of the present Secretary of the Treasury." He later indicated that the tariff was the issue most frequently discussed in Pennsylvania during the campaign (*Cong. Globe*, 30:2, 18, 19).

[3] John Milton Niles (1787–1856), a Jacksonian Democrat, served in the Senate, 1835–39 and 1843–49 (*DAB*).

[4] Debate continued among Henry S. Foote, John P. Hale, Cameron, James D. Westcott, and Thomas Metcalfe, before Davis' motion was adopted by a vote of 29–21 (*Cong. Globe*, 30:2, 19–20).

Remarks on the Petition of Robert Wallace[1]

Editorial Note: First submitted in 1837 and again in 1846, a bill for Wallace's relief came before the Senate on December 21, 1848. Subsequently misidentified in the *Congressional Globe* as Cadwalader Wallace, Robert Wallace requested payment for his services as an aide-de-camp and compensation for loss of a horse in 1812. His claim was supported by testimonials from Lewis Cass and Thomas S. Jesup. When debate on the bill resumed, Kentucky Senator Joseph R. Underwood pleaded Wallace's case while Davis, the recently appointed (Dec. 22) chairman of the Committee on Military Affairs, raised some objections (*Cong. Globe*, 30:1, 298, 530, 535, 558, 887; ibid., 30:2, 80, 86; Quaife, ed., *War on the Detroit*, 195n).

December 26, 1848

Mr. DAVIS, of Mississippi. The case to which the honorable Senator from Florida refers rests upon very peculiar ground. The claim was not for his services as aid, but as inspector general and mustering officer for the troops.[2] And I would observe to the honorable Senator from Kentucky,[3] that in such cases as these we should always make a discrimination. There can be no claim for services on the part of any volunteer aid, because, as has been stated by the Senator from Alabama, a commanding officer has no right to select his aids from those who are not commissioned officers of the army.[4] If an individual serves as a volunteer, he must do it for the honor of the position; he cannot expect to be paid. If paid, it is out of gratitude for services rendered, without an obligation to render them, and cannot be demanded as a right. And if Congress decide that any particular person shall be paid for such services, it must be after a full examination of what such services were, and upon a just discrimination in regard to them. The pay department of the army cannot exercise any discretion in the matter. It is altogether outside of the regular business of that department.

I will state simply—as I do not intend to detain the Senate, and as the matter has been examined by the Military Committee—that, as an individual member of this body, I was not in favor of the claim in either case—that of Florida, or the present one. In regard to the claim for the horse, although the law does, as the Senator from Kentucky supposes, authorize the payment for horses killed in battle, I have never heard of horses, or any other property, being paid for, which had been surrendered to the enemy by the volition of the individual himself to whom such property belonged.

If General Hull[5] had been fighting against a semi-barbarous foe, we might easily believe that the troops would be plundered of their property; but we all know the usages of war too well to believe that in this case the private property of individuals was taken away from them. If the Senator from Kentucky will make it apparent that his property was rendered amenable to seizure by the British troops by the action of his commander solely, then I will admit that a case is made out, and that, if you recognize the man as having been in service, he should be paid for the horse so lost. But I put the Senator on his guard that he must first fully establish these facts.

[Underwood states that an Indian was seen on Wallace's horse, noting that when frontier armies surrendered to combined British and Indian forces "the rules of civilized warfare . . . were not respected."]

Mr. DAVIS, of Mississippi. Seeing an Indian on the horse, or in possession of the horse, is not the proof I called for.

[Underwood repeats his explanation, adding that the horse was forcibly taken.]

Mr. DAVIS, of Mississippi. If the honorable Senator from Kentucky will allow me, I will put him on his guard in relation to these matters.

There is a very great distinction between an officer losing his horse in the moment of battle—whether surrender follow or not—and that of his horse being taken from him in violation of the rules of war. If the officer abandons his horse, if the horse runs away and is taken by an Indian, the loss is chargeable to the loser's own neglect. If, however, the honorable Senator shows that this officer was entitled to serve on horseback, and was dismounted at the surrender of Hull's army, and his horse taken from him, regardless of the rights of private property, his claim should be granted; otherwise, it should not.

[Underwood concludes from the evidence at hand that Wallace and his horse were surrendered "and that the enemy tolerated this Indian in taking the horse," thus violating the rules that Davis described. The Kentuckian adds that Hull was a general, not just a territorial governor.]

Mr. DAVIS, of Mississippi. He was a military governor merely.[6]

Cong. Globe, 30:2, 100.

[1] Robert Wallace, born in the District of Columbia about 1790, was a prosperous Kenton County, Kentucky, farmer. He had volunteered for the Ohio militia early in 1812, serving as a pvt. and later as an aide to Governor Return J. Meigs and Gen. William Hull (1850 Census, Ky., Kenton, family 511; DNA, RG15, War of 1812 Bounty Land Applics.).

[2] James D. Westcott noted that Charles L. Hill had been remunerated for services rendered to the governor of Florida (*Cong. Globe*, 30:2, 100).

[3] Joseph Rogers Underwood (1791–1876), member of a prominent Kentucky family, was educated at Transylvania and served in the War of

1812. He was elected as a Whig to the House, 1835–43, and later to the Senate, 1847–53 (*DAB*).

4 William Rufus Devane King (1786–1853), senator from Alabama for nearly three decades, was elected vice-president in 1852 (ibid.). His comments followed Underwood's detailed description of Wallace's service record and a listing of precedents in which compensation had been granted for loss of a horse (*Cong. Globe*, 30: 2, 98–99).

5 William Hull (1753–1825), a Revolutionary War officer, was appointed governor of Michigan Territory in 1805 and brig. gen. in April 1812. After surrendering his army to the British in August 1812, he was court-martialed for treason; his death sentence was remanded (*DAB*; Heitman, *Hist. Reg.*, 1:553–54).

6 Before the vote, Underwood rejoined that Hull was a general and added notice of another precedent of payment for a horse. With passage of the bill, Wallace was granted the sum of $914 (*Cong. Globe*, 30:2, xxxix, 100).

UNDATED ITEMS
[1846–48]

Statement on the Capture of the Tenería

the Brigade com[p]¹osed of the Tenn. and Missi. Regts. I felt that it was great injustice or little discrimination

The Tenesseeans were with us in the attack, but no man can go upon the ground and see the position of the Regts. without admitting that the Missi Regt. must have faltered or entered the Fort before the Tenesseeans could get up; but when it is Known that the Mexcans made no stand, but were found flying out of the Fort as we entered it and still more when it is known that the Mississippi Regt. advanced by the front at <–s–> full speed, and that the Tenessee Regt. was marched up by a flank, the claim to have shared <–the–> equally in the storming of the Fort becomes ridiculous to the mind least informed in military movements.

What then shall I say of a claim presented through the press. to the first place on the part of the Tenessee Regt. and the assertion that they carried the Fort at the point of the bayonet?²

Can I who found the Fort evacuated (save the few who could be seen crowding out of the sally porte³) when I entered it, at the head of those who started first and run over the shortest line of approach, who pursued the enemy firing on him in retreat, believe that any man without the intent to lie can say he led a Regt. in advance of mine — I have forborne to collect⁴ statements, perhaps too confidently relying on the conclusiveness of our claim <–to the first place in a fast–> to the storming of the Fort. We were supported by the Tenesseeans, who alone were with us in the attack and as it would have given me pleasure to bear testimony to their services so I regret that I must notice things which it would never have <–[illegible]–> been my choice to preserve or remember⁵—

401

But this question must be decided in a manner that will leave no ground for future contest.

AD (ViRC), paginated by Davis: "14"; AD (Davis Papers, DLC), paginated by Davis: "15." The first portion, donated to the Museum of the Confederacy by Jefferson Hayes-Davis, was endorsed by Varina Davis: "Fragment of a paper in Mr Davis' own hand upon the mooted point of who was first in the Black Fort [the Teneria] at Monterey when it [was] captured." For provenance of the Library of Congress fragment, see Daniel R. Russell's report, September 26, 1846.

[1] Manuscript torn.
[2] A reference to the published letters of Balie Peyton and William B. Campbell.
[3] The gorge of the Tenería.
[4] End of the first fragment.
[5] Perhaps a reference to the criticism that Campbell leveled at his regiment; see Davis to Joseph E. Davis, January 26, 1847.

Statement on the Withdrawal from Monterrey

After capturing the redoubt and Fort Taneria on which it rested,[1] and receiving the sword of the condg, Officer I moved my Regt across the stream to attack the salient of the system of detached works in our front,[2] but after proceeded some distance far enough to be so close to the work as to be in comparative safety, an order was sent by genl, Quitman through his A. D. C. Lieut Nichols of the U. S. Infantry requiring us[3] to retire, and we were directed to a position occupied by the Ohio & Tenn. Regts. under the command of Genl. Butler. That position was in front of the curtain and under the artillery /and long range musketry/ fire of the two salients.[4] After conference with the Ins. Genl. A. Sidney Johnston with his advice I moved my Regt, towards the salient to the westward[5]— leaving Genls. Butler, Hamer & Quitman where I found them, Soon thereafter Genl, Butler was wounded & Genl. Hamer succeeded to the command of the Division. On reaching the front of the salient I met the chief Engineer Maj. Mansfield who informed that some U. S. Infy, was there and under his direction commenced with the Infy, a movement to attack the works at the Purissima bridge. Genl. Hamer soon arrived and ordered us to move to the rear. In making the movement Capt Field comdg the U. S. Infy, who obeyed the order was Killed.[6] The Missi Regt. followed Genl. Hamer's column and entered a corn field, where the Lancers

AD (Z37, Walthall Papers, folder 8, Ms-Ar). Part of the collection of William T. Walthall, an attorney and journalist who aided Davis in preparing *The Rise and Fall of the Confederate Government.*

[1] The redoubt before the fortified stone building, not the building itself, was usually called the Tenería. Compare Davis' statement in his letter to Albert G. Brown, September 20, 1847.
[2] El Diablo.
[3] The word *me* is overwritten.
[4] Both El Diablo and the *tête-de-pont* could direct fire onto the American troops collected in the lane. See Davis' description of the position in his memorandum dated [December 31], 1846.
[5] The *tête-de-pont* (no. 6 on the Monterrey map).
[6] In other accounts—his report to Quitman, September 26, 1846, and his memorandum dated [December 31], 1846—Davis states that he and Field pursued an enemy party before being joined by Mansfield and taking a position before the *tête-de-pont.*

From Douglas H. Cooper

Statement of Capt. D. H. Cooper Co. B Miss Vols. in regard to the battle of the 21st.

The Brigade under Gen Quitman approached the round fort near the distillery at the South[1] Eastern Corner of Monterey[2] by <–the–> a file movement by the left flank— the column formed by the Mississippi Regiment filed to the right[3] <–left,–> /<–then to the right–>/ and then formed by Company into line— the left file of each arriving first upon the line.[4] The fire upon the fort commenced on the left of the regiment and was taken up successively by each Company as it arrived on the line. Being in Command of the extreme right of the regiment I arrived on the line after the firing had commenced and My Company formed- fired & by some mistake of the men fell back perhaps ten paces- loaded and were again brought up to the former position & fired— obliquely to the left at the fort. The noise & confusion at this time <–became–> was great & I could not hear any command from the field officers,[5] but observing a forward movement I gave the command to advance— Which was executed rapidly. <–[illegible–]> When I arrived close enough to the breastwork to see any thing distinctly. the first thing I observed was Col. McClung waiving his sword upon the fort, I called out to my men to hurry in pointing to Col. McClung. When I reached the ditch the mississippi riflemen were running into the fort. Many of my men were in the fort before I could get over the ditch

& up the embankment when I jumped into the fort men from different companies of our Regiment were pouring in on all sides & around on the embankment I passed on immediately, out at the rear of the round fort and on to the right across the branch which runs between the distillery & the 3rd. fort[6] with some of my own company & some of other companies of the Regiment inclining to the right up the creek or ditch under the hill upon which stands the 3rd. fort. I have no recollection of seeing any soldiers but the riflemen in the fort when I passed through it and do not believe any others got in before the enemy were driven out by the Missippi riflemen. Those immediately with me were close upon the heels of the Mexicans fireing upon them as they ran over to the 3rd. fort. & into the bushes along the creek After recrossing the creek above where I previously crossed it. Some few perhaps 20 riflemen were conducted by Col. Davis to the right still further until we reached the corner where the first street to the right of the fort,[6] intersects the road[7] leading from the distillery to the right. I posted the riflemen behind a house & wall within the garden on the corner. A considerable number of regular troops & a portion of Gen Hamers command[8] had by this time collected in the lane. near the corner. The Mexican guns raked the Street on our right. Col Davis endeavoured to prevail upon the officers in command of the troops with which we were thrown to charge the battery on right under cover of the fire of our rifles. But we were ordered out[9] & retired across the street and into the fields without again returning to the fort. We were exposed to the fire of the cannon in crossing the fields & were threatened with a charge from the Mexican cavalry. After remaining for a considerable time exposed to fire from the forts, toward evening the remainder of the Miss Regiment under Maj Bradford joined Col. Davis. We were then ordered to go to the relief of Gen Taylor at the fort & distillery. After advancing a part of the way under a raking fire from the Enemy's Forts we /were/ ordered to retire to Camp. Having crossed the range of the cannon I think four times in Marching & countermarching across the fields.

D. H. Cooper
Commdg Co. B.
1st. Regt Miss. Vols.

ALS (Davis Papers, DLC). L, copy by V. Davis (RG27, Vol. 26, Corres., Mexican War Docs., Ms-Ar). For provenance of the Library of Congress manuscript, see Daniel R. Russell's report (Sept. 26, 1846).

1 The letter *S* is written over an *N*.
2 The Tenería and the fortified stone building were located on the northeastern edge of the city.
3 The word *right* is in the margin.
4 After Quitman's brigade had marched to the Tenería by the left flank, the 1st Miss. fronted 300 yards before the fort. Davis then ordered his men into the maneuver Cooper describes, which gained ground to the front and left, bringing the Mississippians into line at a distance of about 180 yards from the fort (Davis'

memorandum dated [Dec. 31], 1846).
5 A reference to the dispute between Davis and Lt. Col. McClung, both of whom claimed to have ordered the charge.
6 El Diablo.
7 The lane (no. 4 on the map of Monterrey).
8 The 1st Ohio Rgt.
9 Despite his unsuccessful conference with Gens. Butler, Hamer, and Quitman, Davis moved Cooper and a small party of Mississippians into position to attack the *tête-de-pont* (see nos. 5 and 6 on the Monterrey map); it was there that Davis received Hamer's order to withdraw (Davis' report to Quitman, Sept. 26, 1846, and his memorandum dated [Dec. 31], 1846).

From Carnot Posey

Statement of Lieut Carnot Posey (of Company "B") of the charge of the Missi Riflemen on the South Eastern fort[1] of Monterey. 21st. September. 1846.

On the morning of the 21st. Brig. Gen Quitman's Brigade approached the south eastearn corner of the town, after two or three volleys were fired, the order was given to the Missi Riflemen to charge the fort, which was forthwith, and unhesitatingly obeyed, when I arrived within twenty or thirty paces of the fort, I observed Lieut. Col McClung waving his sword on the top of the breast work, and calling on the men to rush on. As I reached the brink of the ditch, I turned and called on Co. "B" to rush<-e-> on, calling their attention at the same time to their Lieut, Col on the top of the fort. In turning to call on our company I was particular to look round me, and did not see any men near the fort except the Missi. Riflemen, Of this I am certain. I threw myself, and crossed the same, passing round the "Round fort"[1] to the second fort, by the distillery.[2] When I approached the second fort, I observed two officers of the mexican army, holding /up/ the hilts of their swords, and surrendering to our men. I immediately turned to our men calling on them not to shoot, as the fort had surrendered, and observed none except the Riflemen near me. Not entering either fort, I passed, and <–cross–> crossed the creek beyond the fort pursuing the flying ennemy. Col Davis, and Capt. Cooper, being with me, with men from each company. After crossing the creek we turned to the right, being about two hundred yards from the third fort,[3] and approaching the same we crossed a ditch to the right, and then turned to the <–left up a lane–> left up a lane or street, being continually exposed to a shower of <–bullet–> bullets, the men returning the fire of the enemy from every hut and wall.,

When in the act of charging the third fort, we were called on to retire from the town which was done under a continued, and heavy fire from the enemy. After reaching the field, we were charged by the cavalry of the enemy, which were repulsed by a few volleys. Col Davis was then joined by Maj. Bradford with the rest of the Regt. when the Regt. was ordered to the assistance of Gen Taylor. Before reaching the town, the Regt. was ordered to return<–ed–> to the camp, which was done, being under the cross fire of the enemy's cannon for some time.

(signed) CARNOT POSEY 1st Lieut. Co. "B."

L, copy by V. Davis (RG 27, Vol. 26, Corres., Mexican War Docs., Ms-Ar). Endorsed by Davis: "No. 5 Compy. 'B.' Statement of Capt. Cooper and of Lieut. Posey." Enclosed: Davis to Albert G. Brown, Oct. 3, 1847.

[1] The Tenería, located on the north-eastern edge of the city.
[2] The fortified stone building.
[3] Probably El Diablo, although Posey's later reference to the "lane or street," which was on the opposite side of the creek from El Diablo, suggests that he may be describing the attack on the *tête-de-pont*. Presumably Posey accompanied Davis and Cooper to their position north of the *tête-de-pont* (no. 5 on the map of Monterrey), where Davis received the order to withdraw. Compare the reports of Daniel R. Russell, October 12, 1846, and Douglas H. Cooper, n.d.; see also Davis' report to Quitman, September 26, 1846, and his memorandum dated [December 31], 1846.

William Delay to Richard Griffith[1]

Report
Of the operations of Company F. of the first Regiment of Miss Riflemen on the days of the 22d & 23d of Feb 1847. in the Battle of *Buona Vista*

UNDATED ITEMS

On the morning of the 22d Feb '47. this company encamped with its Regiment at Saltillo, received orders to prepare each member with one days provision and march immediately with the Regiment to the Pass Buona Vista about 6 miles from our then encampment. This order was immediately executed, and at the signel to form the Regiment each member of the company appeared in his place excepting 3 one left sick in hospital at Monterey <–and–> one sick in camp & one on extra duty as Wagoner, the two latter both manifested much anxiety to join there Company and march The Regiment took up the line of march and after arriving within one mile of the above named pass. no guns had been heard fire as yet, but an immence column of the Enemy was seen a few miles beyond the Pass advancing,[2] As the Regiment was advancing near the pass by the right flank, by order of the Col it filed to the left and marched 2 or 3 hundred yards and formed on the left of an Indiana Regiment which position it held until dark.[3] At 27 minuts a past 3. P.M. a cannon was heard to fire from the Mexican Army. and soon after several others in succession but none from our army that i kew of. At about an hour & ahalf by sun P.M.[4] a large party of Mexicans had ascended a ridge of the mountain on our left flank and opened a brisk fire upon a portion of our troops (I learned was the Kentucky Cavalry) <–which–> who had ascended another Ridge in the Mountain) which fire was briskly returned by them; the firing was kept up by both parties until after dark when our Regiment returned to Camp. Early next morning (23d) we heard a report of a cannon from the Enemy, and so soon as it was sufficiently light we could see that the firing was resumed upon the mountain; the Regiment took up the line of march as the morning previous,— when we arrived in about a mile and a quarter of the scene of action we heard a number of cannons in quick succession with a multitude of Small arms, we then marched hurriedly until we arrived at the scene of action,—we filed to the left as the day previous, to take our position on the left flank. As we advanced near, we discovered a considerable portion of the troops on the left flank of our Army retreating[5] and a large column of the Enemy of both Cavalry & Infantry passing through A number of the troops retreating passed our Regiment <–r–> rapidly while we were hurriedly advancing, and I was told they were the 3d Indiana Regiment. I heard many voices in our Regimet soliciting them to return which some of them did, though but few.[6] We had now arrived in plain view of the

407

whole Mexican force which had passed through whch looked to be between 6000 & 8000 in numbers. I saw no other Regiment or piece Artilery to support ours. in a Charge So soon as the Regiment arrived in shooting distance /with Rifles/ of the Emey we opened a fire[7] upon <–tha–> a Column immediately in our front which column I discovered <–re–>turn to retreat,—We were then ordered to charge and after crossing a deep Ravine,[8] we continued our fire for a short time, when it was discovered that the Enemy were firing upon us from three different directions—on our right in front & on our left flank. we were then ordered to retire a short distance to Rally again[9] whilest retiring I learned that Sergant Hagomy, Corporels Blakely & Butler & privats Donovent, Jones and Garrott /of my Company/ were all killed, & that Bigbie,[10] Simpson Morris[11] and Caatney[12] /of the same/ were severely wounded & Malone & Lieut. Stockard slightly wounded 3 members of the company were dispatched to take the wounded to hospital, all the wounded went except Liut. Stockard & J. F. Malone who kept their[13] Places in the company during the whole day—2 of the 3 who went back with wounded returned to their places in time for the next charge the other one did not return during the day.[14] Each of my Lieutenants had Rifles, and I noticed them firing frequently during the day at the Enemy Every member of the company then present kept his place until the company with the Regiment returned to camp at night.

The many interesting scenes which transpired during the latter part of the day, I leave for others more competemt to depict Your Obt Servt

WM. DELAY Capt
Comp F 1st Reg Miss Riflen

ADS (RG27, Vol. 26, Corres., Mexican War Docs., Ms-Ar). Endorsed by Davis: "No. 7 Com. 'F.'" Enclosed: Davis to Albert G. Brown, Oct. 3, 1847.

[1] Griffith received this and three other battle reports while Davis was recuperating from his wound in Saltillo.

[2] Before noon on February 22 "a vast cloud of dust" heralded the arrival of Santa Anna's cavalry on the road leading to Buena Vista. By about one o'clock the rest of the Mexican army had arrived (Carleton, *Buena Vista*, 32, 38).

[3] Very likely the Mississippians were stationed near the 3d Ind. Rgt., whose position at about 1 P.M.—approximately the time Davis' command arrived—was "upon a height immediately in rear of Washington's battery, and overlooking the battery and the road"

(*Senate Ex. Doc 1*, 30:1, 186). See no. 1 on the map of Buena Vista.

4 An hour and a half before sunset, or between three and four o'clock (ibid., 146; Vicksburg *Daily Whig*, Apr. 7, 1847).

5 The 2d Ind. Rgt., Ind. Rifle Btn., Ky. and Ark. Cav. rgts.

6 Some members of the 2d Ind. Rgt. were rallied by the Mississippians; the 3d Ind. had not yet arrived on the field.

7 For the site of the Mississippi regiment's first volley, see no. 2 on the map of Buena Vista. The effective range of the volunteers' rifles was about one hundred yards (Sawyer, *Our Rifles*, 144).

8 The northern ravine, particularly its eastern branch. See no. 3 on the Buena Vista map for the Mississippians' advance.

9 The regiment recrossed the ravine to the site marked no. 5 on the Buena Vista map.

10 James N. Bigbie (c1826–1905), a native of South Carolina, lost his left arm at Buena Vista. After the war he was a farmer in Harris and Clay counties, Georgia (DNA, RG15, Mexican War Pension Applics., OWW 14538).

11 Joseph W. Morris, born in Tennessee about 1827, was a farmer in Lafayette County (1850 Census, Miss., Lafayette, family 503).

12 Thomas Courtney, born in England or Ireland about 1815, worked as a ditcher before his enlistment in the 1st Miss. Rgt. Described as "wholly disabled" by his wound, he was a farmer in Lafayette County as late as 1860 (ibid., family 39; ibid., 1860, family 897; DNA, RG15, Mexican War Pension Applics., OWIF 9211).

13 Delay first wrote the word *them*.

14 Undoubtedly a reference to the hospital facilities at the Buena Vista hacienda, where it was reported there were 700–800 able-bodied men, many of whom "had deserted the field . . . by carrying off the wounded" (French, *Two Wars*, 82).

CALENDAR
July 13, 1846–December 31, 1848

Items in italics are printed in this volume.

1846

July 13	*To the People of Mississippi*
July 18	*To Varina Howell Davis and Joseph E. Davis*
July 22	*To Robert J. Walker*
July 22	Discharge certificate. DS (DNA, RG15, Mexican War Bounty Land Applics.). Jesse Read.
July 23	To Roger Jones. L, copy (DNA, M-863, roll 1). Transmits resignation of Philip J. Burrus and recommends acceptance.
July 29	*To Varina Howell Davis*
[Aug. 1]	Pay and mileage account. DS (DNA, RG217, 1st Aud., House of Reps., 29:1, folio 197). Acknowledges receipt of $3,488 for Jan. 21–Aug. 1, 1846.
[Aug. 1]	Regimental return for July. DS (DNA, RG94, Vol. Muster Rolls, Mexican War).
Aug. 3	*From Zachary Taylor*
Aug. 4	From James H. Piper. LbC (DNA, RG49, Div. C, Misc. Letters Sent, New Ser., 21:237a). In reply to inquiry (*Davis Papers*, 2:565), Davis Bend will be resurveyed when Congress appropriates funds.
Aug. 7	Discharge certificate. ADS (DNA, RG15, Mexican War Bounty Land Applics.). William R. Hemby.

Aug. 8   Discharge certificates. DS (ibid.). James M. Childress, John W. Cummings, David R. Jameson (Jimerson), John W. Kirk, Charles A. Lewers, James P. Moore, Adkinson Stewart.

Aug. 9   Discharge certificate. D, copy (ibid.). Joseph S. Fuqua.

Aug. 9   Discharge certificate. DS (ibid.). William H. Gee.

Aug. 10   Discharge certificate. DS (ibid.). James C. Hays.

Aug. 11   Discharge certificate. DS (ibid.). George W. Shaifer, James J. V. Steele.

Aug. 11   Discharge certificate. D, copy (ibid.). James O. Ragsdale.

Aug. 16   *To Varina Howell Davis*

Aug. 19   Discharge certificates. DS (DNA, RG15, Mexican War Bounty Land Applics.). Littleton J. Mapp, James Richards.

Aug. 20   *To John McNutt*

Aug. 20   From Benjamin L. Hodge. ALS (DNA, M-863, roll 2). Resigns as 2d lt., Co. D. Enclosed: Davis to William W. S. Bliss, Sept. 3, 1846.

Aug. 20   Discharge certificates. DS (DNA, RG15, Mexican War Bounty Land Applics.). Alfred G. Browning, Ransom C. Higginbotham, James L. Powell, William W. Wadsworth.

Aug. 21   Discharge certificates. DS (ibid). Albert L. Abston, William Creight, James C. Davis, A. T. Powell.

Aug. 22   Discharge certificates. DS (ibid.). George and Robert F. Williams.

Aug. 24   *To Robert J. Walker*

Aug. 24   Invoice. DS (Mrs. Joseph H. Howie). Eighty rifles and accouterments were furnished John M. Sharp.

Aug. 24   Discharge certificates. DS (DNA, RG15, Mexican War Bounty Land Applics.). Warler Davis, Noland S. Dixon, James D. Stewart.

Aug. 29   *From Albert G. Brown*

Sept. 1   Regimental return for August. DS (DNA, RG94, Vol. Muster Rolls, Mexican War).

Sept. 3   To William W. S. Bliss. LS (ibid.). Transmits resignations of Benjamin L. Hodge and Philip J. Burrus; seeks authority to fill vacancies.

Sept. 3   *To George H. Crosman*

Sept. 24   *Terms of Capitulation*

Sept. 25   *To Joseph E. Davis*

Sept. 26   *To John A. Quitman*

[Sept. 26]   *To John A. Quitman*

Sept. 26   *From Alexander B. Bradford*

Sept. 26   *From Reuben N. Downing*

Sept. 26   From Bainbridge D. Howard. ALS (DNA, M-863, roll 2). Requests leave of absence because of illness.

Sept. 26   *From William P. Rogers*

Sept. 26   *From Daniel R. Russell*

Sept. 27   *From James H. R. Taylor*

[Sept.]   *From Varina Howell Davis*

Oct. 1   Regimental return for September. DS (DNA, RG 94, Vol. Muster Rolls, Mexican War).

Oct. 1   Field and staff muster roll. DS (ibid.).

Oct. 5   *To ———*

Oct. 5   *To Varina Howell Davis*

Oct. 7   *From Joseph E. Davis*

Oct. 7   *Memorandum on the Capitulation of Monterrey*

Oct. 12	*To Robert J. Walker*
Oct. 12	*From William P. Rogers*
Oct. 14	Certificate of service. DS (DNA, RG15, Mexican War Bounty Land Applics.). D, copy (DNA, RG 94, Personal Papers, Med. Officers and Physicians). Testifies to James D. Caulfield's services as surgeon.
Oct. 16	From John Willis. ALS, AES by Davis (DNA, M-863, roll 3). Requests furlough; approved by Davis.
[Oct. 18]	To John S. Clendenin (New Orleans *Delta*, Oct. 20, 1849). Requests a note on the surrender of the stone building at Monterrey.
Oct. 18	*From Stephen A. D. Greaves*
Oct. 18	*From John L. McManus*
Oct. 18	*From William H. H. Patterson*
Oct. 18	*From Daniel R. Russell*
[Oct. 19]	To Zachary Taylor. ALS (DNA, M-863, roll 3). Recommends that attached resignation of Carnot Posey be accepted.
Oct. 20	Certificate of disability. ADS (DNA, RG15, Old War Pension Applics., OWIF 5748). States that Alexander K. McClung was wounded at Monterrey.
Nov. 1	*From John Willis*
Nov. 1	*To Balie Peyton*
Nov. 3	*From Balie Peyton*
Nov. 10	*Speech at Vicksburg*
Nov. 11	To Robert J. Walker. ALS (DNA, M-873, roll 73). Recommends Philip A. Roach for Cádiz consulship.
Nov. 14	*To Balie Peyton*
Nov. 16	*To John Jenkins*
Nov. 25	*From J. Pinckney Henderson*

413

Nov. 30	*To Robert J. Walker*
Dec. 3	Real estate tax roll (RG29, Vol. 570, Ms-Ar). Davis' 1,290 acres in Warren County are assessed at $16,770.
Dec. 6	To William L. Marcy. ALS (DNA, RG107, Applics. for Appt., 1846–48). Recommends Clinton W. Lear for army commission.
Dec. 8	*To Elizabeth Maury Holland*
Dec. 10	*To Varina Howell Davis*
Dec. 16	*From Joseph E. Davis*
Dec. 22	From Franklin E. Smith. ALS, retained copy (Z 618, Smith Diary, Ms-Ar). Asks help in obtaining furlough.
Dec. 30	*From Joseph E. Davis*
[Dec. 31]	*Memorandum on the Battle of Monterrey*

1847

Jan. 4	From Albert G. Brown. LbC (RG27, Vol. 42, Ex. Jour., 129, Ms-Ar). Transmits blank commissions for use in filling vacancies among officers.
Jan. 6	*To Thomas Ritchie*
Jan. 13	*To John A. Quitman*
Jan. 26	*To Joseph E. Davis*
Feb. 1	Regimental return for January. DS (DNA, RG94, Vol. Muster Rolls, Mexican War).
Feb. 8	*To Varina Howell Davis*
Feb. 8	To James K. Polk. Autograph dealer's cat. entry (Madigan, "Autograph Letters, MSS, and Hist. Docs." [1940], item 40). Recommends William H. H. Patterson for army commission.
Feb. 13	*From Joseph E. Davis*

Feb. 20	To James K. Polk. ALS (DNA, RG107, Applics. for Appt., 1846–48). Recommends Samuel R. Harrison for army commission.
Feb. 25	*To Varina Howell Davis*
Feb. 28	*From Crawford Fletcher*
Mar. 1	*To Waddy Thompson*
Mar. 1	*Douglas H. Cooper to Richard Griffith*
Mar. 1	*From Amos B. Corwine*
Mar. 1	*Reuben N. Downing to Richard Griffith*
Mar. 2	*To William W. S. Bliss*
Mar. 2	*From Alexander B. Bradford*
Mar. 3	*John S. Clendenin to Richard Griffith*
Mar. 3	*From Henry F. Cook*
Mar. 6	*From William P. Rogers*
Mar. 8	To [Watson Van Benthuysen?]. (New Orleans *Jeffersonian*, Mar. 26, 1847). Reports that the enemy was routed at Buena Vista.
[Mar.]	*From James H. R. Taylor*
Mar. 25	*To John E. Wool*
Apr. 16	*From Joseph E. Davis*
Apr. 20	To Robert J. Walker. ALS, photocopy (DNA, RG 200, Walker Papers). Recommends William H. H. Patterson to command voltigeur company from Mississippi.
Apr. 20	*Court of Inquiry Deposition*
Apr. 23	*From Joseph E. Davis*
Apr. 30	*To Joseph E. Davis*
May 7	*To Jackson Citizens*
May 13	*From Joseph E. Davis*

May 17	*From Albert G. Brown*
May 17	Commission as brigadier general. DS by James K. Polk and William L. Marcy, copy (DNA, RG94, Reg. of Army Comns., 12:83).
May 19	*From James K. Polk*
May 21	*From Joseph E. Davis*
May 21	From Wilson Hemingway (Vicksburg *Weekly Sentinel*, Aug. 25, 1847; Davis, *Papers*, ed. Rowland, 1:92). Transmits correspondence mentioned in Albert G. Brown to Davis, May 17, 1847. Enclosed: Davis to John Jenkins, Aug. 4, 1847.
May 24	*To George H. Crosman*
May 27	*To Varina Howell Davis*
May 27	*To Thomas B. Eastland*
May 27	*To Thomas B. Eastland*
May 28	*To John C. Calhoun*
June 10	Discharge certificate. DS (DNA, RG15, Mexican War Pension Applics., OWIF 9211). Thomas Courtney.
June 10	*Speech at New Orleans*
June 11	To Natchez citizens (Natchez *Weekly Courier and Jour.*, June 16, 1847; Davis, *Papers*, ed. Rowland, 1:85). Accepts invitation to June 14 reception for 1st Miss. Rgt.
June 11	To Vicksburg citizens (Vicksburg *Tri-Weekly Whig*, June 15, 1847; Davis, *Papers*, ed. Rowland, 1:73–74). Accepts invitation to June 15 reception for 1st Miss. Rgt.
June 12	Pay voucher and affidavit. DS (DNA, RG217, 2d Aud., Settled Accts. of Army Paymasters, no. 7008A, Voucher 7). Acknowledges receipt of $1,685.22 pay and allowances for himself and two servants, July 18, 1846–June 12, 1847.

June 12	Discharge certificate. DS (DNA, RG15, Mexican War Bounty Land Applics.). John J. Poindexter.
June 12	Field and staff muster roll. DS (DNA, RG94, Vol. Muster Rolls, Mexican War).
June 14	*Speech at Natchez*
June 15	Speech at Vicksburg (Vicksburg *Tri-Weekly Whig*, June 17, 1847; New Orleans *Delta* [nonpartisan], June 24, 1847). States that he would not accept commission as brig. gen.; lauds Taylor's leadership at Buena Vista.
June 20	*To James K. Polk*
June 20	To Roger Jones. ALS (DNA, RG94, Letters Recd., 212-D-1847, f/w 38051 AGO 1896). Declines commission as brig. gen.
June 20	*To Robert J. Walker*
June 22	To Daniel O. Williams (Jackson *Mississippian*, July 9, 1847). Hopes to attend July 3 barbecue at Clinton for 1st Miss. Rgt.
June 23	*To George E. Metcalf*
June 24	To William L. Marcy. ALS (DNA, RG107, Applics. for Appt., 1846–48). Recommends Junius R. Hutchinson, formerly 1st Miss. Rgt., for appointment in Quartermaster's Department.
June 29	To Lowndes County citizens (Jackson *Southron*, July 16, 1847; Davis, *Papers*, ed. Rowland, 1:85–86). Regrets inability to attend dinner honoring Co. K.
June 29	*To William L. Marcy*
June 29	*To Robert J. Walker*
July 15	*To Stephen Cocke*
July 16	*From William L. Marcy*
July 16	*From Officers of the Second Mississippi Regiment*

July 20	*To John S. Clendenin*
July 26	*To [Simon Cameron]*
July 26	To William L. Marcy. ALS (DNA, RG107, Applics. for Appt., 1846–48). Recommends James C. Wilson for a.q.m., 2d Miss. Rgt.
July 27	*From Albert G. Brown*
July 27	*From Zachary Taylor*
Aug. 4	*To John Jenkins*
Aug. 10	From Albert G. Brown. LS (Davis Papers, DLC). LbC (RG27, Vol. 42, Ex. Jour., 185, Ms-Ar); printed in Davis, *Papers*, ed. Rowland, 1:92–93. Transmits senatorial commission. DS by Brown and Wilson Hemingway (DNA, RG46, 30:1, Miss., Credentials).
Aug. 15	*To Albert G. Brown*
Aug. 15	To James K. Polk. ALS (DNA, RG107, Applics. for Appt., 1846–48). Recommends James D. Caulfield as army surgeon.
Aug. 16	*From Zachary Taylor*
Aug. 19	*To Officers of the Second Mississippi Regiment*
Aug. 24	To John M. McCalla. ALS (DNA, RG217, 2d Aud., Old, Old Ser., no. 5795). Transmits records of Mitchell M. Robins, formerly 1st Miss. Rgt.
Sept. 18	*From Zachary Taylor*
Sept. 19	*To Charles J. Searles*
Sept. 20	*To Albert G. Brown*
Sept. 21	*To John Jenkins*
Sept. 24	*To Concordia Parish Citizens*
Sept. 25	Receipt. AD, AE by V. Davis (Davis Papers, KyLxT). Philanzo Payne acknowledges payment of $350.

Sept. 30	*To Varina Howell Davis*
Oct. 3	*To Albert G. Brown*
Oct. 17	*From Charles T. Harlan*
Oct. 24	To Albert G. Brown. ALS (RG27, Vol. 26, Corres., Mexican War Docs., Ms-Ar); printed in Davis, *Papers*, ed. Rowland, 1:178. Transmits Charles T. Harlan's report on third day of Battle of Monterrey.
Oct. 24	Receipt. AD (Davis Papers, DLC). Carpenters William Zeigler and Albert N. Marcy acknowledge receipt of $1,000 draft on William Laughlin & Company, New Orleans.
Nov. 2	From Vicksburg citizens (Vicksburg *Weekly Sentinel*, Nov. 17, 1847; Davis, *Papers*, ed. Rowland, 1:178–79). Davis invited to public dinner in his honor.
Nov. 2	To Vicksburg citizens (ibid.). Declines invitation to public dinner because of poor health and imminent departure for Washington.
Nov. 7	*To George Talcott*
Nov. 7	Receipt from Dr. George A. Yearly. ADS (Davis Papers, KyLxT). Acknowledges payment of $151 for medical services, Feb. 1845–Aug. 1847, including two visits to Jane Davis Nicholson and six to Ferdinand Carroll, formerly 1st Miss. Rgt.
Nov. 8	*To* ——
Nov. 24	*From Daniel R. Russell*
Nov. 24	From George Talcott. LbC (DNA, RG156, Misc. Letters Sent, 38:430–31). Acknowledges Davis' letter of Nov. 7 and requests previous ordnance returns.
Nov. 30	*To Stephen Cocke*
Nov. 30	*To William L. Marcy*

Nov. 30   To James K. Polk. ALS (Ruder Coll., Beauvoir). Recommends Charles T. Harlan, Samuel R. Harrison, and Samuel W. Marsh, all formerly 1st Miss. Rgt., for army commissions.

Dec. 3   From Richard M. Young. LbC (DNA, RG49, Div. C, Misc. Letters Sent, 23:94). Replies to Davis' query of Nov. 30, concerning use of land certificate in a second state.

Dec. 6   To ———. ALS (W. Americana MSS, S-1083, D 294, CtY). States that during Zachary Taylor's absence in Mexico mail may be sent to his plantation at Rodney, Jefferson County, Mississippi.

Dec. 6   To James K. Polk. Autograph dealer's cat. entry (Kingston Galleries, cat. 15, item 43). Recommends William B. Spinks, formerly 1st Miss. Rgt., for army commission.

Dec. [9]   To Francis P. Blair and John C. Rives. ADS (Beauvoir). In response to inquiry of December 9 as to the disposition of Davis' twelve copies of the *Congressional Globe*, directs that one copy be retained for himself and the others sent to Wilson Hemingway, Stephen Adams, Lloyd Selby, John J. McCaughan of Mississippi City, W. W. Worthington of Columbus, Robert Josselyn, Stephen A. D. Greaves, John Jenkins, Andrew A. Kincannon, Joseph E. Davis, and Dr. McCauly of New Orleans.

Dec. 9   To Robert J. Walker. ALS (Davis Assn., TxHR). Recommends E. B. Grayson for Land Office clerkship.

Dec. 11   From John M. McCalla. LbC (DNA, RG217, 2d Aud., Letters Sent, Property Div., L:92). Requests ordnance returns of 1st Miss. Rgt. prior to fourth quarter 1846.

Dec. 12   To James K. Polk. ALS (DNA, RG107, Letters Recd., Book 66, P-516). Transmits letter of revenue service capt. John A. Webster and recommends him for further service in Mexico.

Dec. 13	To James K. Polk. ALS (DNA, RG107, Applics. for Appt., 1846–48). Recommends William H. Scott, formerly 1st Miss. Rgt., for army commission.
Dec. 15	Moves that Military Affairs Committee inquire into establishing a hospital in New Orleans; remarks on need for such a facility (Washington *Nat. Intell.*, Dec. 16, 1847).
Dec. 16	*To Isaac S. K. Reeves*
Dec. 18	From Joseph G. Totten. LbC (DNA, RG94, USMA, Letters Sent, 15:26). Answers Davis' query about a cadetship for Zachary Taylor's grandson, Robert C. Wood, Jr.
Dec. 20	Moves that memorial of Clements, Bryan, & Co. be referred to Claims Committee (*Senate Jour.*, 30:1, 62).
Dec. 20	Moves that Henry Child's petition be withdrawn (ibid., 64).
Dec. 21	To Rufus L. Baker. ALS (Baker Coll., NWM). Introduces Mr. Powell, who is concerned with small arms improvements.
Dec. 22	From Isaac S. K. Reeves. ALS (DNA, RG46, 30A H9.1). Transmits memorial requesting equal compensation for Military Academy and regimental adjutants. Davis presents memorial, Dec. 23 (ibid.; *Senate Jour.*, 30:1, 71).
Dec. 23	To James K. Polk. ALS (DNA, RG107, Applics. for Appt., 1846–48). With Henry S. Foote recommends John G. Arnold for army commission.
Dec. 25	*From Patrick W. Tompkins*
Dec. 25	*To Patrick W. Tompkins*
Dec. 25	From A. H. Davidson. ALS (DNA, RG15, Mexican War Bounty Land Applics.). Transmits document for warrant of Robert L. Shook, formerly 1st Miss. Rgt. Enclosed: Davis to James L. Edwards, n.d. ALS (ibid.).

Dec. 29　To [Thomas Ritchie]. ALS (deCoppet Coll., NjP). Requests that the Washington *Union* be sent to Reuben H. Grant, Macon, Mississippi.

Dec. 29　Moves that two petitions of James Edwards, one on behalf of Edward M. Wanton, be referred from the Military Affairs Committee to the Claims Committee (*Senate Jour.*, 30:1, 79).

Dec. 30　From John M. McCalla. LbC (DNA, RG217, 2d Aud., Letters Sent, Property Div., L:113). Acknowledges receipt of 1st Miss. Rgt. camp and garrison equipage return for July 14, 1846–June 12, 1847.

Dec.　From Hugh W. Dobbin. ALS (DNA, RG46, 30A H13). Encloses documents for War of 1812 pension claim. Davis presents documents, Jan. 5 (*Cong. Globe*, 30:1, 110).

[Dec.]　From Zachary Taylor. ALS (Taylor Papers, DLC). Favors American withdrawal from all of Mexico except San Francisco Bay, Tampico, and San Juan de Ulloa, thus eliminating the Wilmot Proviso as an issue; discusses views on internal improvements, national bank, tariff, war debts, and extension of slavery; expects the Whigs to nominate Clay, the Democrats, Cass or Buchanan; comments on his reply to forged Joseph R. Ingersoll letter; advises Davis to follow his own political interests in presidential election; thanks Davis for compliments in his letter to Concordia Parish citizens (Sept. 24, 1847) and for offer to defend Taylor's actions; mentions intrigues of Scott and Worth; hopes for Davis' election to Senate.

1848
Jan. 3　To James L. Edwards. ALS (DNA, RG15, Mexican War Bounty Land Applics., Adams Brownlee). Transmits evidence sent by Rufus K. Arthur in undated statement to Davis (ALS, ibid.) concerning Adams Brownlee, J. Wesley Maples, and J. O. Woodruff, formerly 1st Miss. Rgt.; inquires about Albert M. Newman's papers.

Jan. 3   Receipt. DS (DNA, RG217, 3d Aud., Manning File). Acknowledges compensation as senator of $300.

Jan. 3   *Remarks on the Ten-Regiment Bill*

Jan. 5   From William H. Emory. ALS (Davis Papers, KyLxT). Discusses Dr. Adolphus Wislizenus' map of the Southwest.

Jan. 5   *Remarks on the Ten-Regiment Bill*

Jan. 6   From William L. Marcy. LbC (DNA, RG107, Reps. to Cong., 6:52). Reports to the Senate on accommodations for troops in New Orleans.

Jan. 6   Moves to amend the bill providing bounties for volunteers to include regiments of dragoons and mounted riflemen (*Cong. Globe*, 30:1, 121–22).

Jan. 6   Moves that Joseph De La Francia's petition be referred to the Judiciary Committee (*Senate Jour.*, 30:1, 96).

Jan. 11   To James L. Edwards. ALS (DNA, RG15, Mexican War Bounty Land Applics.). Transmits claim by heirs of William E. Harris, 1st Miss. Rgt.

Jan. 11   To McClintock Young. ALS (DNA, RG90, Letters Recd. by Marine Hosp. Service, M1848, 16). Inquires whether New Orleans Marine Hospital can soon be made available for disabled soldiers.

Jan. 12   From Stephen H. Long, L, copy (DNA, RG109, Citizens File). Requests Davis' help for his son Henry C. Long, formerly 1st Ky. Rgt. and aide to Gen. Hamer at Monterrey.

Jan. 12   From McClintock Young. LbC (DNA, RG90, Letters Sent by Sec. of Treas. re Marine Hosp. Service, 1:599–600). States that construction at the New Orleans Marine Hospital will not be completed for several months and cannot accommodate soldiers.

Jan. 13 Presents petition of Henry V. Keep, formerly 1st Miss. Rgt., requesting compensation for Mexican War service (*Senate Jour.*, 30:1, 108; DNA, RG46, 30A H9.1).

Jan. 17 Remarks on ten-regiment bill; declares in response to Andrew P. Butler that more regular units are needed in Mexico to protect American posts and force Mexico to treat for peace (*Cong. Globe*, 30:1, 188).

Jan. 17 Presents petition of Robert M. Martin, formerly 1st Miss. Rgt., requesting bounty land for Mexican War service (*Senate Jour.*, 30:1, 113; DNA, RG46, 30A H13).

Jan. 19 To Roger Jones. ALS (DNA, RG94, Letters Recd., 4-N-1848, f/w 56-N-1860). Inquires about 1st Lt. Lucius B. Northrop's removal from army rolls.

Jan. 19 Moves that Gad Humphries' petition be transferred from Military Affairs Committee to Claims Committee (*Senate Jour.*, 30:1, 121).

Jan. 20 From Roger Jones. ALS (DNA, RG94, Letters Sent, 23:411). Transmits papers on Lucius B. Northrop.

Jan. 20 Reports Military Affairs Committee bill for retirement of disabled army officers (*Senate Jour.*, 30:1, 125; DNA, RG46, 30A B1). Moves that bill be considered, May 4 (*Cong. Globe*, 30:1, 727). Moves to postpone consideration of bill, May 5 (*Senate Jour.*, 30:1, 317). Remarks on bill, June 12 (*Cong. Globe*, 30:1, 827).

Jan. 20 Moves that the petition of Eugene Van Ness and John M. Brush, executors of Nehemiah Brush, be transferred from the Military Affairs Committee to Claims Committee (*Senate Jour.*, 30:1, 125).

Jan. 22 — From Rufus R. Williamson. ALS (DNA, RG15, Mexican War Bounty Land Applics.). Former member of 1st Miss. Rgt. sends documents for land claim. Enclosed: Davis to James L. Edwards, Feb. 6, 1848. ALS (ibid.).

Jan. 23 — To "My dear Judge." ALS (Richey Coll., OOxM). Transmits several letters, one from A. L. Morgan concerning Samuel Ragsdale's land claim.

Jan. 23 — *To John J. Crittenden*

Jan. 23 — To Richard M. Young. ALS (DNA, RG49, Misc. Letters Recd., D22850). Transmits letter of N. L. Morgan on Samuel Ragsdale's claim.

Jan. 24 — To Roger Jones. ALS (deCoppet Coll., NjP). Requests views on promoting army officers to new corps.

Jan. 24 — From Roger Jones. LbC (DNA, RG94, Letters Sent, 24:421–22). Opposes promotion of army officers to new corps.

Jan. 24 — From Thomas J. Usrey. ALS (DNA, RG15, Mexican War Bounty Land Applics.). Former member of 1st Miss. Rgt. requests assistance with his land claim. Enclosed: Davis to James L. Edwards, Feb. 3, 1848. ALS (ibid.).

Jan. 24 — Remarks on first battles of Mexican War (*Cong. Globe*, 30:1, 233).

Jan. 25 — To Roger Jones. ALS (DNA, RG94, Letters Recd., 26-D-1848, f/w 56-N-1860). Requests reinstatement of Lucius B. Northrop.

Jan. 25 — To John Y. Mason. ALS (DNA, RG45, Misc. Letters Recd., 144). Requests brevet for marine capt. John G. Reynolds.

Jan. 25 — To John A. Quitman. Autograph dealer's cat. entry (Carnegie, "Autograph Letters," cat. 305 [1968], item 88). Requests favor for John G. Reynolds.

Jan. 25   Reports Military Affairs Committee bill to provide additional quarters near New Orleans for troops (*Senate Jour.*, 30:1, 133; DNA, RG46, 30A B2). Remarks (*Cong. Globe*, 30:1, 241).

Jan. 25   Moves that Oscar F. Pitman's petition claiming compensation for carrying mails in 1834 be referred to Post Office Committee (*Senate Jour.*, 30:1, 132; DNA, RG46, 30A H14.2).

Jan. 26   To Nathan Towson. ALS (DNA, RG99, Letters Recd.). Requests refund for John P. Stockard, formerly 1st Miss. Rgt.

Jan. 27   To John M. McCalla. L, copy (Walker Papers, DLC). With Henry S. Foote recommends E. B. Grayson for clerkship.

Jan. 27   From John Y. Mason. LbC (DNA, RG45, Gen. Rec. Book, 39:275). Favors brevet for John G. Reynolds.

Jan. 28   To Richard M. Young. ALS (DNA, RG49, Misc. Letters Recd., D22987). Transmits letter of Jacob A. Van Hoesen concerning a land patent.

Jan. 29   From John M. McCalla. LbC (DNA, RG217, 2d Aud., Letters Sent, 39:27). John P. Stockard's claim has been received from paymaster gen.

Jan. 29   From Eugene Van Ness. LbC (DNA, RG99, Letters Sent, 28:340). Has recommended refund for John P. Stockard.

Jan. 31   To Joseph W. Matthews. LS (RG27, Vol. 27, Corres., Ms-Ar). With others recommends William C. Enos' appointment as commissioner for Mississippi in Pennsylvania.

Jan. 31   From William Medill. LbC (DNA, RG75, Letters Sent, 40:288). Returns letter of Thomas C. Hindman concerning William Compton's claim.

Jan. 31   From Richard M. Young. LbC (DNA, RG49, Div. D, Letters Sent re Private Land Claims, 13:474). Information requested will be forwarded.

Jan. 31　　Commission as senator. DS by Joseph W. Matthews and Samuel Stamps (DNA, RG46, 30.1, Miss., Credentials).

Feb. 2　　To James L. Edwards. ALS (DNA, RG15, Mexican War Bounty Land Applics.). Transmits documentation for claims of Tolbert Dockery and John Standin, formerly 1st Miss. Rgt.

Feb. 2　　*From Joseph Henry*

Feb. 2　　Reports Military Affairs Committee bill to provide pensions for enlisted men of Ordnance Department (*Senate Jour.*, 30:1, 149–50; DNA, RG46, 30A B2). Remarks (*Cong. Globe*, 30:1, 292).

Feb. 2　　Public notice (Washington *Union*, Feb. 2, 1848). Davis to be among managers of "National Birth-Night Ball," Feb. 22.

Feb. 3　　To Thomas Lawson. ALS (Haskell Coll., MiU-C). Recommends appointment of James D. Caulfield to Miss. Btn.

Feb. 3　　To William L. Marcy. ALS (Hay Scrapbook, DLC). Introduces Thomas Worthington of Ohio.

Feb. 3　　To James K. Polk. DS (DNA, RG94, USMA Applics. for Appt., 1848/171). With others recommends Claudius F. LeGrand for cadetship.

Feb. 3　　*Exchange with John Bell on the Ten-Regiment Bill*

Feb. 4　　To Joseph Henry. ALS (Henry Papers, DSI). Suggests they meet on Feb. 7.

Feb. 4　　Moves that the Wyandot Indians' petition be withdrawn (*Senate Jour.*, 30:1, 153).

Feb. 7　　Remarks on plan for holding a military, not defensive, line in Mexico (*Cong. Globe*, 30:1, 311).

Feb. 8　　From Thomas Lawson. LbC (DNA, RG112, Letters Sent, 18:419). Has recommended James D. Caulfield's appointment to Miss. Btn.

Feb. 8	Exchange with Jacob W. Miller on the ten-regiment bill; Davis denies he called regular soldiers inferior to volunteers; opposes annexation of all Mexico (*Cong. Globe*, 30:1, 321, App., 296–97).
Feb. 9	To James Buchanan. ALS (DNA, M-873, roll 52). Recommends William R. Lewis, former Vicksburg merchant, for Belfast consulship.
Feb. 9	*To Alexander Hamilton, Jr.*
Feb. 10	To William L. Marcy. ALS (DNA, RG107, Letters Recd., Book 66, D-34). Inquires about need for surgeon's certificate to obtain land warrant.
[Feb. 10]	To James K. Polk. ALS (DNA, RG107, Applics. for Appt., 1846–48). Recommends Cornelius D. Hendren for army commission.
Feb. 10	From John J. Abert. DS (DNA, RG46, 30A E4). Comments on inadequate pay of military storekeepers.
Feb. 10	From Richard M. Young. LbC (DNA, RG49, Div. D, Letters Sent re Private Land Claims, 13:487–88). Transmits documents concerning Mississippi lands.
Feb. 13	From Woodson Wren. ALS (DNA, RG46, 30A E7). Natchez postmaster discusses pay and allowances of postmasters, abuses in postal system; Davis presents communication, Feb. 29 (*Senate Jour.*, 30:1, 194).
Feb. 14	From Joseph W. Matthews. LbC (RG27, Vol. 42, Ex. Jour., 233, Ms-Ar); printed in Davis, *Papers*, ed. Rowland, 1:183. Transmits Mississippi legislature's resolution (Feb. 10) on condition of 2d Miss. Rgt. and Miss. Btn. in New Orleans.
Feb. 14	Presents Samuel F. Butterworth's petition for balance due him on mail contract (*Senate Jour.*, 30:1, 172).
Feb. 15	Presents military storekeepers' petition concerning pay (ibid., 173).

Feb. 16   From Horatio J. Harris. L, copy (DNA, RG49, Cong. Letters Recd., D24445). On behalf of Joseph E. Davis, requests official documents for Diamond Place litigation. Enclosed: Davis to Joseph S. Wilson, Mar. [16], 1848. AES (ibid.).

Feb. 16   *From Zachary Taylor*

Feb. 16   Remarks supporting resolution of thanks to Zachary Taylor; regrets that discussion has included talk of war policy and "President-making" (*Cong. Globe*, 30:1, 368).

Feb. 17   To William Medill. ALS (DNA, RG75, Claims, Reserve File A, Case 444). Transmits letter of Richard T. Archer.

Feb. 17   From "Brutus" (Washington *Union*, Feb. 17, 1848; Davis, *Papers*, ed. Rowland, 1:183–89). Defends Mexican War declaration against criticism leveled by Supreme Court justice John McLean.

Feb. 17   From Joseph G. Totten. LbC (DNA, RG94, USMA Letters Sent, 15:142). Acknowledges receipt of letter recommending Claudius F. LeGrand.

Feb. 18   To James K. Polk. ALS (DNA, RG94, USMA Applics. for Appt., 1848/208). Recommends George E. Metcalf for cadetship.

Feb. 19   From Rufus K. Arthur. ALS (DNA, RG15, Mexican War Bounty Land Applics.). Writes concerning claim of David Sims, formerly 1st Miss. Rgt. Enclosed: Davis to [James L. Edwards], Mar. 7, 1848. ALS (ibid.).

Feb. 19   From William Medill. L, copy (DNA, RG75, Claims, Reserve File A, Case 461). Returns Richard T. Archer's letter; says claim will be considered. Enclosed: Davis to Archer, Feb. 19, 1848. ALS (Lester Coll., LU-Ar).

Feb. 22   To James K. Polk. LS (DNA, RG56, Letters Recd. re Appts., Customs Collectors Applics.). With others recommends James B. Haggin as collector at Natchez.

Feb. 22   Receipt. DS (DNA, RG217, 3d Aud., Manning File). Acknowledges compensation as senator of $200.

Feb. 23   *To Francis A. Wolff*

Feb. 26   From Enoch Steen. ALS (DNA, RG107, Applics. for Appt., 1846–48). Dragoon officer requests help in securing the transfer of his son Alexander from 12th Inf. to 1st Dragoons. Enclosed: Davis to William L. Marcy, Mar. 23, 1848. ALS (ibid.).

Feb. 27   To William L. Marcy. ALS (DNA, RG107, Letters Recd., Book 66, D-57). Recommends William H. Emory for a brevet and transfer to topographical duty in Mexico.

Feb. 27   *From Ferdinand L. Claiborne*

Feb. 28   To James L. Edwards. ALS (DNA, RG15, Mexican War Bounty Land Applics.). Transmits papers for claim of James M. Shelton, formerly 1st Miss. Rgt.

Feb.   To James K. Polk. DS (DNA, M-873, roll 46). With others recommends Thomas J. Johnston, Jr., for judgeship in Minnesota Territory. Enclosed: Davis to Polk, Mar. 2, 1848. ALS (ibid.).

Mar. 1   From Joseph W. Matthews. LbC (RG27, Vol. 42, Ex. Jour., 234, Ms-Ar). Transmits Mississippi legislature's resolution (Feb. 25) concerning appropriation for the railroad from Jackson to Alabama border.

Mar. 3   From Charles McDougall. ALS (DNA, RG94, USMA Applics. for Appt., 1848/106). Requests support for appointment of Alexander S. Hooe to West Point. Enclosed with recommendation: Davis to James K. Polk, Mar. 8, 1848. ALS (ibid.).

Mar. 4   From ——— (Washington *Union*, Mar. 17, 1848). Officer stationed at Veracruz reports on condition and movements of army.

Mar. 4   Moves that the following sections be stricken from Arts. 5 and 22 of the peace treaty with Mexico: mutual consent to any change in the boundary; definition of the border; protection of and compensation for noncombatants' property (*Senate Jour.*, 30:1, App., 623–25; *Senate Ex. Doc. 52*, 30:1, 15–17).

Mar. 4   Presents resolution on appointment of Smithsonian regents (*Senate Jour.*, 30:1, 201).

Mar. 6   From William L. Marcy. ALS (DNA, RG107, Draft Letters Sent by Sec. of War). Explains failure to act on resignation of army capt. George B. Crittenden.

Mar. 6   Withdraws motion on boundary definition, Art. 5 of peace treaty; moves to annex parts of Tamaulipas, Nuevo León, Chihuahua, and all of Coahuila and to provide for a border survey (*Senate Jour.*, 30:1, App., 626–27).

Mar. 6   Presents petition of enlisted men of Ordnance Department concerning bounty land (*Senate Jour.*, 30:1, 203).

Mar. 6   Resolution instructing Library Committee to consider subscribing for maps of American operations in Mexico. AD (DNA, RG46, 30A B6); submitted (*Senate Jour.*, 30:1, 203). Resolution instructing purchase, Apr. 10. AD (DNA, RG46, 30A B6); reported (*Senate Jour.*, 30:1, 268–69).

Mar. 7   Presents petition of Ark. Cav. Rgt. requesting pay for period they were imprisoned by Mexicans (*Senate Jour.*, 30:1, 204).

Mar. 8   To Robert J. Walker. ALS (DNA, RG56, Letters Recd. from Cong., 1847–48, 46). Transmits treasury note of Joseph Koger for indemnity.

Mar. 8   Resolutions recommending establishment of customhouse at Biloxi, Mississippi, establishment of navy yard at Ship and Cat islands, and erection of lighthouse at Ship Island. AD (DNA, RG46, 30A B6); submitted (*Senate Jour.*, 30:1, 205–206).

Mar. 9   Moves that payment option be stricken from Art. 12 of the treaty (*Senate Jour.*, 30:1, App., 639–40).

Mar. 9   Presents petition of John Johnston, Sr., et al. for compensation as Choctaw Indians' counsel (*Senate Jour.*, 30:1, 206; DNA, RG46, 30A H7); submits additional documents, Mar. 16 (*Senate Jour.*, 30:1, 216).

Mar. 10   From John Jenkins. ALS (DNA, RG217, 2d Aud., 1817–53, 3d Ser., Acct. 6352). Requests help in securing payment for advertisements placed by the army in Vicksburg *Sentinel*. Enclosed: Davis to Thomas S. Jesup, Mar. 23, 1848. ALS (ibid.).

Mar. 10   From McClintock Young. LbC (DNA, RG56, Letters Sent to Cong., 4:392–93). Requests additional evidence in Joseph Koger's claim.

Mar. 11   From Ferdinand L. Claiborne. ALS (DNA, RG56, Letters Recd. re Appts., Customs Collectors Applics.). Withdraws application for Natchez customs collectorship.

Mar. 12   To James K. Polk. ALS (DNA, M-873, roll 52). Recommends William R. Lewis for Belfast consulship.

Mar. 12   To Joseph G. Totten. ALS (DNA, RG94, USMA Applics for Appt., 1847/133, 1848/240). Recommends Patrick H. Hargon, a Madison County student, and Andrew G. Rowe for cadetships.

Mar. 13   From John Y. Mason. LbC (DNA, RG45, Gen. Rec. Book, 39:405). Reports registration of midshipman applications of Samuel Dabney and Robert W. Mitchell.

Mar. 13   From William Medill. LbC (DNA, RG75, Letters Sent, 40:384). Provides copy of his letter to the Land Office concerning Thomas C. Hindman's inquiry.

Mar. 14   From Henry L. Heiskell. LbC (DNA, RG112, Letters Sent, 18:486). Transmits permission for W. P. S. Compher to take exam for appointment as army surgeon.

Mar. 15   From Daniel Graham. LbC (DNA, RG53, A:194). Transmits bounty land warrant for John Standin.

Mar. 16   *To Linn Boyd*

Mar. 17   From Samuel Stamps (DNA, RG46, 30A J4; *Senate Misc. Doc. 126*, 30:1, 2). Transmits Mississippi legislature resolution (Mar. 4) in support of the administration's prosecution of the Mexican War; presented Apr. 20 (*Senate Jour.*, 30:1, 292).

Mar. 17   *Exchange with John C. Calhoun on the Ten-Regiment Bill*

Mar. 18   To Robert J. Walker. ALS (Personal Misc. Papers–Davis, NN); printed in Davis, *Papers*, ed. Rowland, 1:191. Transmits recommendations and asks Walker's support for William B. Howell as Natchez postmaster.

Mar. 18   Receipt. DS (DNA, RG217, 3d Aud., Manning File). Acknowledges compensation as senator of $54.85.

Mar. 19   To James L. Edwards. ALS (DNA, RG15, Mexican War Bounty Land Applics.). Transmits claim by heir of Daniel F. Kenner, 1st Miss. Rgt.

Mar. 19   To William L. Marcy. DS (Ruder Coll., Beauvoir). With others recommends J. Camp Perkins, formerly 1st Miss. Rgt., for army commission.

Mar. 22   Presents memorials of Mississippi legislature requesting improved transportation of mail and improvement of navigation on the Big Black River (*Senate Jour.*, 30:1, 227; DNA, RG46, 30A H14.2 and 30A H17.2).

Mar. 24   From Edward J. C. Kewen. ALS (DNA, RG94, Letters Recd., 103-K-1848). St. Louis attorney and former editor of Columbus *Whig* requests help in procuring discharge of brother Thomas, formerly 1st Miss. Rgt., from 2d Miss. Rgt.

Mar. 24   Remarks on need for military asylum in preference to acting on individual cases (Washington *Nat. Intell.*, Mar. 25, 1848). Reports Military Affairs Committee bill for establishment of asylum, Mar. 28 (*Senate Jour.*, 30:1, 241; DNA, RG46, 30A B2).

Mar. 27   Submits resolution authorizing Aaron H. Palmer to revise his memoir on Siberian and Manchurian resources (*Senate Jour.*, 30:1, 236). Report of joint committee, Mar. 31. ADS (DNA, RG46, 30A B6).

Mar. 28   *To James K. Polk*

Mar. 28   To Robert J. Walker. ALS (Walker Papers, DLC). Transmits request (ALS, Mar. 29) of William G. Grandin, lawyer from New York, for different employment.

Mar. 29   *To ———*

Mar. 29   To James L. Edwards. ALS (DNA, RG15, Mexican War Bounty Land Applics.). Transmits document for application of Ferdinand Carroll.

Mar. 30   To Joseph G. Totten. ALS (DNA, RG77, Letters Recd., D-3611). Requests copy of Military Academy's course of study and admission requirements.

Mar. 30   *To Robert J. Walker*

Mar. 31   To William L. Marcy. ALS (DNA, RG107, Letters Recd., Book 67, D-71). Transmits two letters commending William H. Emory; recommends his promotion in Topographical Engineers.

Mar. 31   From Richard M. Young. LbC (DNA, RG49, Div. D, Letters Sent re Private Land Claims, 14:89–91). Provides information requested by Horatio J. Harris on Diamond Place.

Apr. 1   To Lewis Cass. ALS (DNA, RG107, Letters Recd., Book 66, D-57). Transmits information concerning William H. Emory.

Apr. 1   To James L. Edwards. ALS (DNA, RG15, Mexican War Bounty Land Applics.). Transmits claim by heir of William Mallett, 1st Miss. Rgt.

[Apr. 1] From James H. R. Taylor. ALS (ibid.: Robert L. Shook). Requests help in securing land warrants for John Long and Leonard H. Murphree, both formerly 1st Miss. Rgt.; comments on peace treaty, ten-regiment bill, and Planters' Bank bonds. Enclosed: Davis to James L. Edwards, Apr. 11, 1848.

Apr. 2   To ———. ALS (Wirt Coll., Mahoning Valley Hist. Soc.). Reports that new senators have not been supplied with copies of the Constitution for distribution.

Apr. 3   To Robert J. Walker. ALS (NIC). Requests Virginian John W. Smith's retention as watchman at Treasury Department.

Apr. 3   From Richard M. Young. ALS (DNA, RG49, Div. B, Letters Sent re Bounty Land Warrants, 9:387). Transmits Samuel Frisby's warrant.

Apr. 4   To John F. H. Claiborne. ALS, photocopy (DNA, RG200, Walker Papers). Explains that he attributed Ferdinand L. Claiborne's letter of Feb. 27 to addressee; reports negative results on John Claiborne's earlier request despite help of Robert J. Walker and George Bancroft.

Apr. 5   To William L. Marcy. ALS (DNA, RG94, Letters Recd., 103-K-1848). Requests disability discharge for Thomas Kewen.

Apr. 6   Remarks on resolution to the French people; praises action of provisional government (*Cong. Globe*, 30:1, App., 467).

Apr. 7   Presents Christopher Cunningham's petition for pension (*Senate Jour.*, 30:1, 260). Bill for Cunningham's relief, Apr. 12. AD (DNA, RG46, 30A B2). Reported (*Senate Jour.*, 30:1, 272). Remarks on bill (*Cong. Globe*, 30:1, 622–23).

Apr. 10	From Daniel Graham. LbC (DNA, RG53, A:208). Transmits bounty land stock certificate for heir of John C. Peyton, 1st Miss. Rgt.
Apr. 10	Presents citizens' petition proposing government purchase of Mount Vernon (*Senate Jour.*, 30:1, 265).
Apr. 11	To James L. Edwards. ALS (DNA, RG15, Mexican War Bounty Land Applics.). Transmits evidence for Robert L. Shook's warrant and inquires about the papers of John Long and Leonard H. Murphree.
Apr. 12	To James K. Polk. ALS (DNA, RG107, Letters Recd., Book 67, D-80). Recommends Robert H. Chilton for brevet.
Apr. 12	*To Beverley Tucker*
Apr. 12	From McClintock Young. LbC (DNA, RG56, Letters Sent to Cong., 4:417). Responds concerning Joseph Koger's treasury note.
Apr. 13	*To James K. Polk*
Apr. 13	Reports Military Affairs Committee bill explanatory of the act to raise additional troops (*Senate Jour.*, 30:1, 276; DNA, RG46, 30A B1). Moves consideration of bill, May 12 (*Cong. Globe*, 30:1, 763).
Apr. 14	To William L. Marcy. ALS (DNA, RG107, Letters Recd., Book 67, D-80). Recommends Robert H. Chilton, William H. Emory, ordnance officer Charles P. Kingsbury, and Bennet Riley for brevets.
Apr. 14	*Remarks on the Cumberland Island Dam Bill*
Apr. 17	To James L. Edwards. ALS (DNA, RG15, Mexican War Bounty Land Applics.). Transmits claim of James Richards, formerly 1st Miss. Rgt. Transmits additional evidence, June 22. ALS (ibid.).
Apr. 18	*To Varina Howell Davis*

Apr. 18   To James L. Edwards. ALS (DNA, RG15, Mexican War Bounty Land Applics.). Testifies that Noland S. Dixon was honorably discharged from service.

Apr. 18   From Zachary Taylor. AL (Taylor Papers, DLC). Recommends James M. [Waller?] as agent for an insurance company at Baton Rouge.

Apr. 18   From Zachary Taylor. AL (ibid.). Draft of Apr. 20 letter.

Apr. 19   From Cave Johnson. LS, AE by Davis, AES by V. Davis (Davis Papers, KyLxT). Informs Mississippi congressional delegation that a special agent to investigate mails is not necessary.

Apr. 20   *From Zachary Taylor*

Apr. 20   *Remarks on the Protection of Property*

Apr. 25   To David E. Twiggs (Washington *Union*, Apr. 29, 1848). With others invites Twiggs to a testimonial dinner.

Apr. 26   To George E. Badger. ALS (DNA, RG107, Letters Recd., Book 67, C-152). Concurs in recommendation of Richard C. Gatlin for brevet.

Apr. 26   From David E. Twiggs (Washington *Union*, Apr. 29, 1848). Declines invitation of Davis et al. to testimonial dinner.

Apr. 26   Remarks on the payment of California claims (*Cong. Globe*, 30:1, App., 566–67); further remarks, Apr. 28 (ibid., 30:1, 707–708); calls for division on amendment requiring that agents not allow any claim in which they have a part or permit an assignee to receive more than he paid for claim (ibid.; Davis, *Papers*, ed. Rowland, 1:201–204).

Apr. 27   From Richard M. Young. LbC (DNA, RG49, Div. C, Misc. Letters Sent, 24.32). Transmits a statement on public lands in Mississippi.

Apr. 27	Presents David Baker's petition for a renewal of his patent on a sawmill for ship timber (Washington *Union*, Apr. 28, 1848).
Apr. 29	From Daniel Graham. LbC (DNA, RG53, A:266). Returns letter and scrip of Thomas R. Griffin, formerly 1st Miss. Rgt.
Apr. 29	Receipt. DS (DNA, RG217, 3d Aud., Manning File). Acknowledges compensation as senator of $200.
May 1	From John S. Clendenin. ALS (DNA, M-873, roll 16). Asks support for consular appointment.
May 1	From Daniel Graham. LbC (DNA, RG53, A:227). Transmits certificate for William Mallett's heir.
May 3	Receipt. DS (DNA, RG217, 3d Aud., Manning File). Acknowledges compensation as senator of $241.63.
May 5	*To William L. Marcy*
May 5	*Remarks on the Occupation of Yucatan*
May 6	From Roger Jones. LbC (DNA, RG94, Recruiting Div., Letters Sent, 5:377). 2d auditor to pay John Jenkins and Franklin C. Jones for advertisements in Vicksburg *Sentinel*.
May 6	Receipt. DS (DNA, RG217, 3d Aud., Manning File). Acknowledges compensation as senator of $200.
May 8	Remarks on occupation of Yucatan; fears "collision" with Great Britain (*Cong. Globe*, 30:1, App., 607).
May 9	To James Buchanan. ALS (DNA, M-873, roll 5). Recommends John S. Clendenin for consular post.
May 10	Pension Committee report recommending a bill for the relief of Nehemiah Brush. AD (DNA, RG46, 30A D1); *Senate Rep. 150*, 30:1. Submitted (*Senate Jour.*, 30:1, 329).

May 12   Presents David Hunt's petition for confirmation of land title (*Senate Jour.*, 30:1, 333).

May 13   From [James L. Edwards]. LbC (DNA, RG15, Letters Sent, 165:183). Provides information on Ferdinand Carroll's military service.

May 13   Presents memorial of J. Anthony King and Cuyler W. Young proposing organization of force to serve in Yucatan; moves they have leave to withdraw memorial, May 18 (*Senate Jour.*, 30:1, 334, 346; DNA, RG46, 30A H6.1).

May 14   From William H. Emory. ALS (Emory Folder, ICHi). Remarks on Davis' support of and Thomas Hart Benton's opposition to his brevet; asks Davis' aid in speeding the printing of Emory's report.

May 21   To James L. Edwards. ALS (DNA, RG15, Mexican War Bounty Land Applics.). Transmits claim by heir of James Langston, 1st Miss. Rgt.; requests copies of revised instructions for claims. Requests return of document, May 25. ALS (ibid.). Transmits evidence for claim, Dec. 26. ALS (ibid.).

May 24   From William L. Marcy. LbC (DNA, RG107, Letters Sent, Mil. Books, 28:299). Transmits copies of correspondence and report concerning Lucius B. Northrop.

May 25   From Roger Jones. LbC (DNA, RG94, Letters Sent, 25:126). Rejects request for Thomas Kewen's discharge.

May 25   Remarks on inquiry concerning Robert J. Walker and payment of public debt interest (*Cong. Globe*, 30:1, 787).

May 27   To Francis A. Wolff. ALS (Ben S. Nelms). Forwards bounty land certificate; advises on documents for pension.

May 27   To Richard M. Young. ALS (DNA, RG49, Misc. Letters Recd., D26576). Transmits B. M. Hines's land receipt for patent.

May 27   From James L. Edwards. LS, AES by Davis (DNA, RG15, Mexican War Bounty Land Applics.). Provides information about documents needed for claim of Isham C. Laird, formerly 1st Miss. Rgt.; Davis forwards instructions to Laird.

[May 28]   To J. R. Hunter. Autograph dealer's cat. entry (Benjamin, "Collector," cat. 69 [July–Aug. 1956], item j611). States that he received Hunter's letter of May 18.

May 31   Remarks on recommitment of the bill to establish a government in Oregon (*Cong. Globe*, 30:1, App., 688–689).

June 1   Resolution that additional copies of Smithsonian Institution regents' report be printed for Senate use. ADS (DNA, RG46, 30A B6); submitted (*Senate Jour.*, 30:1, 366).

June 2   Presents first U.S. flag raised over Mexican capitol (*Senate Jour.*, 30:1, 367).

[June 2]   Undated resolution that Baron de Kalb's portrait be placed in Library of Congress. AD (DNA, RG 46, 30A B6); submitted, June 2 (*Senate Jour.*, 30:1, 367).

June 4   *To Hugh R. Davis*

June 4   To James L. Edwards. ALS (DNA, RG15, Mexican War Bounty Land Applics.). Transmits claim of Robert B. Swisher; inquires about the cases of Plummer M. Martin and Milton F. and Hugh Gourley, all formerly 1st Miss. Rgt.

June 9   To James L. Edwards. ALS (ibid.). Provides information on Abner W. Teague and Reuben Russell; inquires into cases of Louis A. and William G. Cooper, all formerly 1st Miss. Rgt.

June 10   To Dr. John Torrey. Autograph dealer's cat. entry (Bloomfield, "Autographs of Distinction," list DI-2 [1949], item 42). Manuscript being sent to printing office for revision.

June 10   Receipt. DS (DNA, RG217, 3d Aud., Manning
           File). Acknowledges compensation as senator of
           $50.

June 11   To Richard M. Young. ALS (DNA, RG49, Misc.
           Letters Recd., D27149). Transmits James W.
           Wyly's letter concerning land patent.

June 11   From Persifor F. Smith. ALS (DNA, RG107,
           Letters Recd., Book 67, T-152). Reports on troops
           in Mexico; recommends 1st Lt. Earl Van Dorn, 7th
           Inf., for brevet. Enclosed with recommendation:
           Davis to William L. Marcy, June 30, 1848. ALS
           (ibid., D-139).

June 12   To John J. Crittenden (Washington *Nat. Intell.*,
           June 15, 1848; Coleman, ed., *Life of Crittenden*,
           1:303–304). With others invites Crittenden to a
           testimonial dinner.

June 12   From John J. Crittenden (ibid.). Accepts invitation
           of Davis et al. to testimonial dinner.

June 12   Moves to consider House bill to amend 1841 act on
           sales of public lands and preemption rights (*Cong.
           Globe*, 30:1, 828).

June 12   Presents petition of James Farrell for pension
           (*Senate Jour.*, 30:1, 376; DNA, RG46, 30A H13).

June 13   Remarks on adjournment date; desires to lay over
           "important measures" to next session (*Cong. Globe*,
           30:1, 834).

June 13   *Speech at Washington*

June 14   To James L. Edwards. ALS (DNA, RG15, Mexi-
           can War Bounty Land Applics.). Provides informa-
           tion on service of Abner W. Teague and Reuben
           Russell.

June 15   From James W. McCulloh. LbC (DNA, RG217,
           1st Compt. Office, Letters Sent to Land Officers,
           4:229). Provides information concerning Solomon
           Clark's accounts as receiver of public moneys at
           Pontotoc.

June 15	Order form. DS (Personal Misc. Papers—Davis, NN). Agrees to purchase 500 copies of Albert G. Brown's speech.
June 17	To Robert J. Walker. ALS (DNA, RG56, Letters Recd. re Appts., Customs Collectors Applics.). Transmits documents in case of John D. Elliott.
June 18	To Stephen Cocke. ALS (Z735, Davis Papers, Ms-Ar). Approves bill drafted in case of Gordon Boyd et al., to be presented by Winfield S. Featherston.
June 19	Receipt. DS (DNA, RG217, 3d Aud., Manning File). Acknowledges compensation as senator of $200.
[June 19]	Undated joint resolution authorizing adjudication of certain Choctaw claims. AD (DNA, RG46, 30A B3); submitted (*Senate Jour.*, 30:1, 396).
June 20	Remarks supporting bill to prohibit adulterated drugs (*Cong. Globe*, 30:1, 858).
June 21	To William L. Marcy. Autograph dealers' cat. entries (Carnegie, "Recent Acquisitions," cat. 39, item 605, and Black, "American Panorama," cat. 96 [1964], item 46). Recommends discharge of John R. Bilton since peace with Mexico seems imminent.
June 21	From Robert J. Walker. LbC (DNA, RG56, Letters Sent to Cong., 4:455). Has requested copy of charges against John D. Elliott.
June 22	To William L. Marcy. ALS (DNA, RG107, Letters Recd., Book 67, D-135). Military Affairs Committee opposes placing Capt. Manuel L. Domínguez' Mexican force on equal footing with American troops.
June 22	From Henry L. Heiskell. LbC (DNA, RG112, Letters Sent, 19:104). Acknowledges receipt of John V. Wren's application as army surgeon.
June 23	To James K. Polk. ALS (DNA, RG94, Letters Recd., 74-N-1848, f/w 56-N-1860). ALS, draft

(Z735, Davis Papers, Ms-Ar); printed in Davis, *Papers*, ed. Rowland, 1:205–206. Reviews case of Lucius B. Northrop and requests his reinstatement.

June 23   Remarks leading to an amendment disallowing prohibition of slavery in Oregon (*Cong. Globe*, 30:1, 871, App., 860).

June 24   To William L. Marcy. Autograph dealer's cat. entry (Benjamin, "Collector," cat. 64 [1951], item W1497). Commends services of George D. Ramsay during the Battle of Monterrey.

June 26   From Henry L. Heiskell. LbC (DNA, RG112, Letters Sent, 19:109–10). Responds to request for information on increased medical staff; notes need for doctors at posts in newly acquired territory.

June 26   From Roger Jones. LbC (DNA, RG94, Letters Sent, 25:199–201). Responds to inquiry concerning relative rank and precedence of land and sea officers.

June 29   To James K. Polk. LS (DNA, M-873, roll 59). With others recommends William D. Merrick for Mexican claims commissioner.

June 29   To William C. H. Waddell (Vicksburg *Weekly Sentinel*, July 26, 1848; Davis, *Papers*, ed. Rowland, 1:206–207). Explains provisions of bill for volunteers' clothing allowance and defends Lewis Cass against censure in matter.

June 29   Remarks concerning appropriations for a seawall at Great Brewster's Island and the dam at Cumberland Island (*Cong. Globe*, 30:1, 883–84); moves to strike appropriation for Great Brewster's Island (*Senate Jour.*, 30:1, 431).

June 30   Moves that 10,000 copies of reports of secretary of war and William H. Emory be printed (*Senate Jour.*, 30:1, 432).

June   Public notice (Washington *Union*, July 16, 1848). With others recommends former St. Louis attorney

Ferdinand W. Risque as agent in claims against the government.

July 1   *Exchange with Henry S. Foote*

July 5   To Andrew J. Donelson. ALS (Donelson Papers, DLC). Introduces John Perkins, Jr., of New Orleans, a friend of long standing.

[July]   To James A. Pearce. ALS (NBuHi). Requests letters of introduction in Europe for his friend and neighbor John Perkins, Jr.

July 6   *Andrew P. Butler and John C. Calhoun to James K. Polk*

July 7   To Richard M. Young. ALS (DNA, RG49, Cong. Letters Recd., 27925). Requests estimate of acreage north and south of 36°30′ in the western territory.

July 10   From Zachary Taylor. ALS (Emmet Coll., no. 1441, NN). LS (Taylor Papers, DLC). Asks Davis to forward his letter to John M. Morehead requesting notification of Taylor's nomination by Whig convention; met returning troops, some from 2d Miss., in New Orleans; hears Joseph E. Davis and family will visit Washington while in the North; thanks Davis for his statement on Taylor to William L. Dayton.

July 11   From Joseph G. Totten. LbC (DNA, RG94, USMA Abstract Letterbooks, Engr. Dept., 2:35–36). Writes Davis and Armistead Burt requesting equal allowances for Military Academy professors.

July 11   Moves that Military Affairs Committee be discharged from consideration of appointment of additional cadets to West Point (*Senate Jour.*, 30:1, 461). Report of Military Affairs Committee, July 12. AD (DNA, RG46, 30A D2).

July 11   Moves to postpone further consideration of the Oregon bill (*Senate Jour.*, 30:1, 462).

July 12   *Speech on the Oregon Bill*

July 18   From Richard M. Young. LbC (DNA, RG49, Div.
             C, Misc. Letters Sent, 24:111). Provides requested
             information on acreage north and south of 36°30′
             in the western territory, based on maps by Henry S.
             Tanner and John Disturnell.

July 18   Reports conference committee's amendments on the
             supplemental Mexican War bill (*Cong. Globe*, 30:
             1, 949).

July 18   Presents resolution that John C. Frémont be com-
             pensated for preparing maps and memoir of Oregon
             and California (*Senate Jour.*, 30:1, 475; DNA, RG
             46, 30A B6).

July 18 or 19 Moves that consideration of the naval appropria-
             tions bill be postponed and that the Senate proceed
             to executive business (*Cong. Globe*, 30:1, 954;
             Senate Jour., 30:1, 477).

July 22   From Gideon J. Pillow. ALS (DNA, RG107,
             Letters Recd., Book 68, T-51, 1849). Transmits
             communication at request of Col. George W.
             Hughes, Md. and D.C. Vols.

July 22   Questions Hannibal Hamlin concerning extension
             of the Missouri Compromise line (*Cong. Globe*,
             30:1, App., 1146).

July 24   To Winfield Scott (Washington *Nat. Intell.*, Aug.
             14, 1848). With 107 other senators and representa-
             tives invites Scott to public dinner in his honor.

July 25   To James L. Edwards. ALS (DNA, RG15, Mexican
             War Bounty Land Applics.). Transmits documents
             for heirs of Cornelius O'Sullivan, 1st Miss. Rgt.

July [25]   To John Y. Mason. ALS (DNA, RG45, Misc.
             Letters Recd.). Transmits bill of Vicksburg attor-
             neys William C. Smedes and Thomas A. Marshall
             for services rendered to John D. Elliott.

July 25   From Joseph G. Totten. LbC (DNA, RG77, Offi-
             cial Papers—Totten, 6:527). Introduces Prof. Jacob

W. Bailey, who wants to confer on allowances for West Point instructors.

July 26 — To Lucius B. Northrop. Autograph dealer's cat. entry (Driscoll, "Autographs," cat. 21 [1961], item 39). Assures Northrop that he will be reinstated.

July 28 — From [James L. Edwards]. LbC (DNA, RG15, Letters Sent, 167:417). Reports that William H. Miller, formerly 1st Miss. Rgt., has not filed a bounty land application.

July 28 — Remarks that he had pledged not to vote for a fixed adjournment date (*Cong. Globe*, 30:1, 1009).

July 29 — To James K. Polk. LS (DNA, M-873, roll 17). With others recommends Mississippi adj. gen. Robert Cook for judgeship in California or Oregon.

July 30 — To James L. Edwards. ALS (DNA, RG15, Mexican War Bounty Land Applics.). Verifies Frederick W. Fauntleroy's service in 1st Miss. Rgt.

July 30 — To John Y. Mason. ALS (DNA, RG45, Misc. Letters Recd.). Requests John G. Reynolds' release from arrest and his return to duty.

July 30 — To Robert J. Walker. ALS (DNA, RG56, Letters Recd. from Cong., 1847–48, 53). Inquires about Joseph Koger's claim.

July 31 — To James K. Polk. ALS (DNA, M-873, roll 85). With Mississippi delegation recommends James H. R. Taylor for Mexican claims commissioner.

July 31 — From Francis Gildart. ALS (DNA, RG94, USMA Letters from Sec. of War to Chief Engr., S4932). Requests help in having son Francis, Jr., readmitted to West Point; comments on current political issues. Enclosed with recommendation: Davis to William L. Marcy, Aug. 14, 1848. ALS (ibid.).

July 31 — Presents John Crawford's petition concerning a land claim; requests withdrawal, Dec. 6 (*Senate Jour.*, 30:1, 513, 30:2, 49).

Aug. 1   From Robert J. Walker. LbC (DNA, RG56, Letters Sent to Cong., 5:3). First comptroller will act promptly on Joseph Koger's claim.

Aug. 4   To William L. Marcy. ALS (DNA, RG107, Letters Recd., Book 67, D-161). Recommends George W. Hughes for brevet; encloses William J. Worth's letter of recommendation.

Aug. 4   From Henry L. Heiskell. LbC (DNA, RG112, Letters Sent, 19:153). Responds to inquiry concerning appointment of James D. Caulfield to the army medical staff.

Aug. 4   Submits amendment adding Mississippi to bill giving Alabama right-of-way and public lands for a railroad (*Cong. Globe*, 30:1, 1038).

Aug. 5   From James L. Edwards. LbC (DNA, RG15, Letters Sent, 168:86). Transmits requested forms.

Aug. 7   Remarks supporting bill to grant certain unsold lands to Arkansas (*Cong. Globe*, 30:1, 1048).

Aug. 7   Offers amendment to an amendment concerning approval of Oregon territorial statutes (ibid.).

Aug. 8   To William L. Marcy. ALS, photocopy (Campbell Coll., ViU). Requests Lucius B. Northrop's promotion to capt.

Aug. 8   Presents and speaks on resolution instructing secretary of war to furnish a map showing American operations in Texas and Mexico (*Cong. Globe*, 30:1, 1051).

[Aug. 9]   To Lucius B. Northrop. Autograph dealer's cat. entry (Goodspeed's, "Autographs," cat. 517 [1964], item 126). Informs Northrop he has been nominated to lieutenancy; Davis, with concurrence of Military Affairs Committee, is recommending captaincy; illness will prevent Davis from leaving Washington as soon as session ends.

447

Aug. 9	To James K. Polk. ADS (Polk Papers, DLC). Introduces Robert D. Howe, a teacher from Vicksburg.
Aug. 9	To James K. Polk. LS (DNA, RG107, Letters Recd., Book 72, B-162, 1850). With other senators recommends Bennet Riley for brevet.
Aug. 9	Remarks opposing amendment granting discharges to the mounted rifle regiment intended for California (*Cong. Globe*, 30:1, 1056).
Aug. 9	Presents Military Affairs Committee's amendments to military appropriations bill (ibid.).
Aug. 10	From William Medill. LbC (DNA, RG75, Letters Sent, 41:158). Acknowledges receipt of John W. Vick's deed and promises to forward it to the General Land Office.
Aug. 10	Moves to substitute original Senate bill for House bill on Oregon territorial government (*Cong. Globe*, 30:1, 1061).
Aug. 11	Remark on post routes bill (ibid., 1066).
Aug. 12	*To William L. Marcy*
Aug. 12	To William L. Marcy. ALS (DNA, RG107, Letters Recd., Book 67, M-305). Recommends artillery lt. James G. Martin for brevet.
Aug. 12	To William L. Marcy. ALS (ibid., Book 72, B-162, 1850). Recommends Bennet Riley for brevet.
Aug. 12	Moves that the Military Affairs Committee be discharged from subjects not reported (*Senate Jour.*, 30:1, 581).
Aug. 14	To Joseph W. Matthews. ALS (RG27, Vol. 27, Corres., Ms-Ar). Presents John J. Plume of New Jersey for consideration as commissioner of deeds.
Aug. 14	Receipt. DS (DNA, RG217, 3d Aud., Manning File). Acknowledges compensation as senator of $1,662.32.

Aug. 14   Moves that J. P. Parker and R. Knott be allowed to withdraw their petitions (*Senate Jour.*, 30:1, 598).

Aug. 16   From Thomas J. Johnston, Jr., and James W. Gibbons. ALS (Davis Papers, KyLxT). Thank Davis for his willingness to support their rights as Treasury Departments clerks.

Aug. 24   From James Thompson. LbC (DNA, RG217, 3d Aud., Cong. Letters Sent, 10:251). Transmits forms needed for reimbursement of funds paid James H. R. Taylor by Mississippi.

Sept. 1   Personal property tax rolls (RG29, Vol. 571, Ms-Ar). Davis is taxed $51.40 for 79 slaves, 2 horses, 50 head of cattle, and a watch.

Sept. 3   To William L. Marcy. ALS (Misc. MSS–Davis, KyLoF). Asks that Zachary Taylor's letter of recommendation be returned to Henry H. Hall of New York City.

Sept. 7   From John Y. Mason. LbC (DNA, RG45, Misc. Letters Sent, 40:338). Transmits copy of John F. H. Claiborne's letter concerning claim of Smedes and Marshall; states that John D. Elliott was not authorized to hire attorneys.

Sept. 8   From Richard M. Young. LbC (DNA, RG49, Div. K, Letters Sent re Indian Lands, 13:337–38). Transmits land patent for John W. Vick.

Sept. 22   *Speech at Raymond*

Sept. 23   *Speech at Jackson*

Sept. 26   Speech at Vicksburg (Vicksburg *Weekly Sentinel* [Dem.], Oct. 4, 1848). Discusses current issues; declares he will vote for Cass and Butler; eulogizes Taylor.

Oct. 6   To Wilkinson County citizens (Woodville *Repub.*, Oct. 24, 1848; Davis, *Papers*, ed. Rowland, 1:213–

17). Declines invitation to October 14 meeting at Cold Springs because of "domestic affliction"; believes Democratic principles coincide with southern interests, especially on rights of slaveholders.

Oct. 11 — To Richard M. Young. ALS (DNA, RG49, Cong. Letters Recd., D31047). Acknowledges receipt of John W. Vick's land patent.

Oct. 19 — *Speech at Port Gibson*

Oct. 23 — *To Woodville Citizens*

Oct. 24 — From Daniel O. Williams. ALS (Davis Papers, DLC). Requests establishment of a post office at Deer Creek, Hinds County.

[Oct. 27] — From Richard T. Archer (Port Gibson *Herald and Corres.*, Oct. 27, 1848). In undated response to Davis' speech of Oct. 19, Archer explains his support of the Taylor-Fillmore ticket.

Nov. 16 — To Joseph W. Matthews. ALS (Misc. MSS–Davis, NHi). Recommends Gleason F. Lewis, a Detroit exchange broker, for commissioner of deeds.

Nov. 17 — *From William H. Sparke*

Nov. 19 — *From Francis G. Baldwin*

Nov. 20 — From Joseph W. Speight. ALS (DNA, M-873, roll 82). Son of former U.S. senator requests aid in procuring the appointment as marshal for northern district of Mississippi.

Nov. 21 — From Isaac N. Davis. ALS (ibid., roll 55). Requests aid in procuring for William McCarthy, a Columbus planter, the appointment as marshal for northern district of Mississippi.

Nov. 22 — From John M. Grant. ALS (ibid., roll 34). Macon resident requests aid in procuring the appointment as marshal for northern district of Mississippi.

Dec. 3 — From Lock E. Houston. ALS, AE by Davis (ibid., roll 57). States that Whig William McQuiston of

Monroe County would be acceptable to Democrats as marshal of northern district of Mississippi.

[Dec. 4–18]   To James K. Polk. LS (DNA, M-873, roll 34). With other senators recommends Andrew B. Gray to survey Mexican boundary.

Dec. 6   To Robert J. Walker. ALS (Davis Coll., ICHi). Recommends William H. Bell to be marshal of northern district of Mississippi.

Dec. 8   From Stephen Cocke. ALS, AE by Davis (DNA, M-873, roll 45). Recommends appointment of his nephew, Columbus attorney William P. Jack, as marshal of the northern district of Mississippi; says Jack, a Whig, supported Davis' election, is highly regarded by Joseph E. Davis, and would be acceptable to Democrats.

Dec. 8   From Lock E. Houston. ALS (DNA, RG45, Letters Recd. re Appts., Customs Collectors Applics.). Recommends Dr. John M. Anderson of Aberdeen to be collector of San Francisco if the post is created.

Dec. 10   From Thomas H. Williams. ALS, AE by Davis (DNA, M-873, roll 57). Former U.S. senator recommends William McQuiston to be marshal of northern district of Mississippi.

Dec. 11   From Joseph W. Speight. ALS (DNA, RG56, Letters Recd. re Appts., Customs Collectors Applics.). Recommends Dr. John M. Anderson to be customs collector at San Francisco if the post is created.

Dec. 11   *Remarks on the Report of Robert J. Walker*

Dec. 11   Joint resolution recommending that Rufus Choate and Gideon Hawley be reappointed to the Smithsonian Institution's board of regents. D, AE by Davis (DNA, RG46, 30A B3). Introduced (*Senate Jour.*, 30:2, 52).

Dec. 12   Presents petition of Thomas M. Taylor, navy purser, requesting release from liability for funds lost in bank failure (*Cong. Globe*, 30:2, 27).

Dec. 13   To John Y. Mason. ALS (DNA, RG45, Misc. Letters Recd.). Transmits request for extension of midshipman Reuben Harris' leave.

Dec. 13   From Roger Barton. ALS (DNA, M-873, roll 21). Introduces Thomas J. Davidson of Ripley, Mississippi.

Dec. 14   Recommends prompt action on bill concerning construction of a railroad across the Isthmus of Panama (*Cong. Globe*, 30:2, 40).

[Dec. 14–22] Resolution. DS (Hunter Papers, 25064, Vi). With thirteen other southern senators proposes that a committee of five be appointed to determine those southern members willing to unite in an address opposing the Wilmot Proviso if applied to territory acquired from Mexico below 36°30′.

Dec. 15   To James Buchanan. ALS (DNA, RG59, Recs. of Bureau of Accts., Misc. Letters Recd., 1848:1776). Introduces Philip A. Roach, consul to Cádiz, who wishes to settle his accounts.

Dec. 15   From Edward B. Stubbs. ALS (ibid., Misc. Letters Sent, 19:591). Informs Davis that case of Philip A. Roach will receive immediate attention.

Dec. 15   From Nathan Towson. LbC (DNA, Letters Sent, 29:552–53). States that he will recommend that additional paymaster Albert G. Bennett of Mississippi be retained.

Dec. 18   Presents William H. H. Shover's petition for arrears of pay (*Senate Jour.*, 30:2, 66).

Dec. 18   Submits memorial of ordnance officers asking amendment of Aug. 23, 1842, act to allow equal allowances for officers stationed at armories and arsenals (ibid.; DNA, RG46, 30A H9.1).

Dec. 20   From Samuel D. King. ALS (DNA, RG46, 30A H16). Requests resubmission of Joseph Vidal's representative's petition concerning land claims.

Dec. 21   To James L. Edwards. ALS (DNA, RG15, Mexican War Bounty Land Applics.). Transmits papers for claim by heir of Garland Anderson, 1st Miss. Rgt.

Dec. 22   From John M. McCalla. LbC (DNA, RG217, 2d Aud., Letters Sent, Claims, 3:120). Responds to inquiry concerning Tolbert Dockery's claim.

Dec. 26   *Remarks on the Petition of Robert Wallace*

Dec. 26   Submits bill to grant Mississippi public lands for construction of a railroad from Brandon to the Alabama border (*Senate Jour.*, 30:2, 84; DNA, RG46, 30A B1).

Dec. 26   Presents credentials of Augustus C. Dodge of Iowa (*Senate Jour.*, 30:2, 81).

Dec. 27   From Richard M. Young. LbC (DNA, RG49, Div. B, Letters Sent re Mil. Warrants under Act of Feb. 11, 1847, 1:287). States that warrant for Robert H. Lowry, formerly 1st Miss. Rgt., was sent to Liberty, Missouri.

Dec. 27   Resolution requesting information on the expenditures and results of the coast survey since 1807. D, AE by Davis (DNA, RG46, 30A B6); submitted (*Senate Jour.*, 30:2, 85).

Dec. 27   Remarks opposing charter for Washington & Alexandria Steamboat Co. as a monopoly and "invasion of State rights" (*Cong. Globe*, 30:2, 101).

Dec. 28   Presents petition of N. B. Hill on behalf of Gilbert Stalker asking payment for transportation provided army in Seminole Wars (*Senate Jour.*, 30:2, 88).

Dec. 29   From William H. Aspinwall et al. (*Senate Misc. Doc. 6*, 30:2, 27–28). Acknowledge communication from Military Affairs Committee concerning contract with New Granada to build a railroad across the Isthmus of Panama.

Dec. 29   From John Chamberlain. ALS (RH 991, CSmH). Professor of natural philosophy requests set of standard weights and measures for Oakland College, Mississippi.

Dec. 29   Presents petition of teamster George Martin for Mexican War disability pension (*Senate Jour.*, 30: 2, 91; DNA, RG46, 30A H13).

Dec. 29   Gives notice he will introduce bill concerning illegal entries at the Columbus, Mississippi, land office (New Orleans *Picayune*, Jan. 5, 1849).

Dec. 30   To William L. Marcy. LS (DNA, RG94, USMA Recs., Applics. for Appt., 1848/270). With others recommends Charles E. Sims of Hinds County for cadetship.

Undated

[*1846*]   *Statement on the Capture of the Tenería*

[*1846*]   *Statement on the Withdrawal from Monterrey*

[*1846*]   *From Douglas H. Cooper*

[*1846*]   *From Carnot Posey*

[*1847*]   *William Delay to Richard Griffith*

[1847]   Return of killed and wounded. DS (RG27, Vol. 26, Corres., Mexican War Docs., Ms-Ar). Records that the 1st Miss. Rgt. suffered 96 casualties at Buena Vista, including 39 killed.

[1846–48]   Notes for speech on the Mexican War. AD (Davis Papers, KyLxT). Gives names of Mexican leaders, mentions Texas annexation, early battles, and topics such as "justice of the War . . . necessity of its prosecution . . . end to be attained."

ADDENDA, 1824–46

1824, Aug. 2   To Amanda Davis Bradford. ALS (William L. Richter). Expresses grief at the news of his father's death. Will leave Lexington soon for West Point: "It was no desire of mine to go on, but as Brother Joseph evinced some anxiety for me to do so, I was not disposed to object."

1833, Nov. 13   List of stores. DS (Davis Papers, NWM). As adj. of 1st Dragoons, certifies he has delivered two horses and some riding equipage to Lt. Thomas Swords.

1833, Nov. 20   Requisition. DS (ibid.). As adj. of 1st Dragoons, receives "one paper and book case."

1833, Nov. 30   Requisition. DS (ibid.). As adj. of 1st Dragoons, receives forage for his horse.

1833, Dec. 31   Requisitions. DS (ibid.). As adj. of 1st Dragoons, receives forage for three horses.

1841, Jan. 5   Tax roll (RG29, Vol. 570, Ms-Ar). Listed as owner of 25 slaves, Davis is taxed $16.00.

1842, Apr. 17   To Hugh R. Davis. ALS (ViRC). Advises his nephew to draw on Jacob U. Payne for needed supplies; discusses family news.

1844, [after May 1]   Speech. AD (Davis Papers, KyLxT). Twenty-two-page fragment of an address in which he deplores the corrupting influence of personal campaigning by presidential candidates, "a demoralizing tendency" started in 1840 and continuing in 1844, as reflected by Henry Clay's recent southern tour. Notes that "two great parties" have existed since the foundation of the Republic, one upholding strict construction of the Constitution, the other "seeking by latitudinarian construction to enlarge the powers of the federal government." As a minority, the South must rely on the Constitution and support the candidate who is true to its doctrines:

"to ask an unbridled majority, irresponsible to us, to modify their policy out of regard to our interests or respect to our rights [is as] idle as asking mercy of the winds and waves." Sees five major national issues in the 1844 campaign: the tariff; disposition of funds received from the sale of public lands; constitutional revision to abolish the executive veto power; the exercise of undelegated authority by the central government; and the question of permitting slavery in any newly acquired territory. Reviews the history of the U.S. Bank, concluding that its establishment was not provided for in either the "general welfare" or "commerce" clauses of the Constitution, nor was the bank needed as a treasury agent or supplier of uniform currency; denounces the institution as "a great political machine." Considers the protective tariff—an "affiliated measure" of the bank—part of the reason for the prevalence of "redundant currency upon the country at large and especially the planting states."

1845, Jan. 31 To Varina Banks Howell. ALS (Davis Assn., TxHR). Sympathizing with his fiancée who suffers from an inflamed thumb, Davis puns on the word *felon* and two other words. Comments that "few things were in my younger days more sad to me than the mirth of a professed clown . . . it was a fellow feeling which just now made me think of it, in a genuine moody fit I sat down to write you a cheerful letter, but . . . I cannot write what it could give pleasure to Varina to read, better then not to write."

1845, Feb. 25 To Varina Banks Howell. Autograph dealer's cat. entry (Richards, "Autographs," cat. 84 [1978], item 9). On the eve of their wedding, sends Varina Howell a ring and informs her that the minister will call at her home at 10 A.M. Advises her to "be calm and meet the contingency of this important change as becomes you . . . and be assured, I will try to do better than I have ever promised to fulfil brighter hopes than I have ever inculcated." Signs the letter "Uncle Jeff:"

1845, Dec. 22 To Robert J. Walker. Autograph dealer's cat. entry (Benjamin, "Collector," cat. 651 [July–Aug. 1946], item J1376). With three other members of the Mississippi congressional delegation, writes concerning "funds approved by Congress for Mississippi and 'the district ceded by the Chickasaws.' "

1845, Dec. 28 From Henry S. Foote. ALS (DNA, RG45, Applics.

for Appt.). Asks help of Davis and other members of the Mississippi congressional delegation in securing appointment of Dr. George W. Williams as assistant surgeon in navy.

1846, Jan. 7 To James K. and Sarah Childress Polk. AL by V. Davis (Polk Memorial Auxiliary, on deposit in T). "Mr. & Mrs. Jeffn. Davis and their neice Miss [Mary Jane] Bradford have the honor to accept the invitation of the President & Lady, to dinner on Tuesday next."

1846, Jan. 21 From Albert S. Johnston. Autograph dealer's cat. entry (Sweet, "Autograph Letters," list 116, item 45). Asks Davis' "support in obtaining command of a U. S. regiment."

[1846], Jan. 29 To George Bancroft. Autograph dealer's cat. entry (Richards, "Autographs," cat. 11 [1964], item 89). With "three others," Davis endorses "the application of a midshipman."

1846, Jan. 29 To James K. Polk. Autograph dealer's cat. entry (Madigan, "Autograph Letters," 1936 cat., item 40). Recommends West Point classmate Thomas B. W. Stockton for an army commission.

1846, Feb. 20 To James K. Polk. Autograph dealer's cat. entry (Argosy, "Autographs Historical & Literary," cat. 453, item 48). With 23 other congressmen from Mississippi, Louisiana, and New York, Davis requests a lieutenancy for Samuel C. Reid, a hero of the War of 1812.

1846, May 17 To James K. Polk. Autograph dealer's cat. entry (Madigan, "Autograph Album," cat. 1 [Apr. 1934], item 55). Requests a commission for Lancaster P. Lupton, a comrade from West Point and early army days.

1846, May To William L. Marcy. Autograph dealer's cat. entry (Goodspeed's, "Autograph Letters," cat. 369 [1943], item 783). Recommends a constituent for an army appointment.

[1846, June 22] To Varina Howell Davis. ALS (Robert E. Canon and Newton Wilds). Regrets to learn from her letter of the 20th that she is ill; he would bring her back to town immediately were not the mountain air more beneficial than the "disagreeable" weather in Washington; his plans to visit depend on congressional action on the tariff bill, but "if my presence is necessary to you all other

things must yield"; reports that Mrs. Henrietta has undertaken Varina Davis' commission; the "ladies of the White house" inquired for his wife at the president's levee, which he attended with the Perkins family Friday evening; since few ladies have called on John A. Quitman's family during their visit in Washington, "I took occasion to say you would regret not having been here to introduce them to your acquaintances"; Mrs. Potter sends her love to Varina and Mary Jane Bradford; Davis asks to be remembered to Mary Jane, to Col. Joseph Tuley and family, and to Mrs. Stephen Adams; relies on Betsy to care for his wife; signed "your 'Hubbin.'"

1846, [before July 3] To James K. Polk. Autograph dealer's cat. entry (Barker, "Autographs for Sale," list 791-1). With Linn Boyd and four other congressmen, Davis signs a letter of recommendation.

SOURCES

MANUSCRIPT COLLECTIONS

American Antiquarian Society, Worcester, Mass. (MWA)
Archivo Histórico Militar, Secretaría de la Defensa Nacional, Mexico City
  Operaciones Militares, 1846
Beauvoir, Biloxi, Miss.
  Lucius Scott Ruder Collection
Boston Public Library and Eastern Massachusetts Regional Public Library System (MB)
  Manuscript Collection
Buffalo and Erie County Historical Society (NBuHi)
Chicago Historical Society (ICHi)
  Jefferson Davis Collection
  William H. Emory Folder
  John E. Wool Collection
Clemson University, Clemson, S.C. (ScCleU)
  John C. Calhoun Papers
College of William and Mary, Williamsburg, Va. (ViW)
  Swem Library
  Tucker-Coleman Papers
Columbia University, New York, N.Y. (NNC)
  Columbia University Manuscripts
  John A. Dix Papers
Cornell University, Ithaca, N.Y. (NIC)
Duke University, Durham, N.C. (NcD)
  Perkins Library
  Campbell Family Papers
  John J. Crittenden Papers
Emory University, Atlanta, Ga. (GEU)
  Jefferson Davis Papers
The Filson Club, Louisville, Ky. (KyLoF)
  Miscellaneous Manuscripts—Jefferson Davis

SOURCES

Harvard University, Houghton Library, Cambridge, Mass. (MH-H)
    Dearborn Collection
    John Anthony Quitman Papers
Historical Society of Pennsylvania, Philadelphia (PHi)
    Society Collection
Henry E. Huntington Library, San Marino, Calif. (CSmH)
Illinois State Historical Library, Springfield (IHi)
    Jesse J. Ricks Collection
Indiana Historical Society, Indianapolis (InHi)
    William H. English Collection
Indiana State Library, Indianapolis (In)
    William R. Haddon Collection
Lexington Public Library, Lexington, Ky. (KyLx)
Library of Congress (DLC)
    Papers of John J. Crittenden
    Papers of Jefferson Davis and Family
    Papers of Andrew Jackson Donelson
    Papers of Alexander Hamilton
    John Hay Scrapbook
    Papers of the Benjamin Montgomery Family
    Papers of James K. Polk
    Papers of William T. Sherman
    Papers of Zachary Taylor
    Papers of John Tyler
    Papers of Robert J. Walker
Lincoln Memorial Shrine, Redlands, Calif.
Louisiana State University, Department of Archives and Manuscripts (LU-Ar)
    Alexander K. Farrar Papers
    George M. Lester Collection—Jefferson Davis Letter
Mahoning Valley Historical Society, Youngstown, Ohio
    Benjamin F. Wirt Collection
Miami University, Oxford, Ohio (OOxM)
    Samuel Richey Confederate Collection
Minnesota Historical Society, St. Paul (MnHi)
    Allyn K. Ford Collection
Mississippi Department of Archives and History, Jackson (Ms-Ar)
    Official Records

Record Group 8	Superior Court of Chancery
Record Group 27	Governor
Record Group 28	Secretary of State
Record Group 29	Auditor
Record Group 33	Adjutant General
Record Group 60	Work Projects Administration

SOURCES

Private Manuscripts
Z37	William T. Walthall Papers
Z43	Fred A. Rosenstock Collection of Jefferson Davis Papers
Z133	Philip Crutcher Notes on the History of Vicksburg
Z156f	John A. Quitman Papers
Z239	John F. H. Claiborne Collection
Z355f	James C. Browning Diary
Z618	Franklin E. Smith Diary
Z659f	Robert J. Walker Papers
Z735	Jefferson Davis Papers
Z774	*Jefferson Davis v. J. H. D. Bowmar et al.* (1874)
Z777f	Jefferson Davis Papers
Z790f	William Burr Howell and Family Papers
Z913	John A. Quitman Papers
Z1028	Joseph E. Davis and Family Papers
Z1401m	James L. Power Papers

Subject Files
  Richard Griffith
  Alexander K. McClung
  Mexican War
Pierpont Morgan Library, New York, N.Y. (NNPM)
Museum of the Confederacy, Richmond, Va. (ViRC)
National Archives (DNA)
  Microfilm Series

M 29	Records of the Adjutant General's Office, Orders of Zachary Taylor
M-183	Records of the Department of State, Diplomatic and Consular Instructions
M-863	Records of the Adjutant General's Office, Compiled Service Records, Mexican War
M-873	Records of the Department of State, Letters of Application and Recommendation, 1845–53

  Manuscripts

Record Group 15	Records of the Veterans Administration
Record Group 26	Records of the United States Coast Guard
Record Group 45	Naval Records Collection of the Office of Naval Records and Library
Record Group 46	Records of the United States Senate
Record Group 48	Records of the Office of the Secretary of the Interior
Record Group 49	Records of the Bureau of Land Management
Record Group 53	Records of the Bureau of the Public Debt
Record Group 56	General Records of the Department of the Treasury

SOURCES

Record Group 59	General Records of the Department of State
Record Group 60	General Records of the Department of Justice
Record Group 75	Records of the Bureau of Indian Affairs
Record Group 77	Records of the Office of the Chief of Engineers
Record Group 90	Records of the Public Health Service
Record Group 92	Records of the Office of the Quartermaster General
Record Group 94	Records of the Adjutant General's Office, 1780s–1917
Record Group 99	Records of the Office of the Paymaster General
Record Group 105	Records of the Bureau of Refugees, Freedmen, and Abandoned Lands
Record Group 107	Records of the Office of the Secretary of War
Record Group 109	War Department Collection of Confederate Records
Record Group 112	Records of the Office of the Surgeon General (Army)
Record Group 153	Records of the Judge Advocate General (Army)
Record Group 156	Records of the Office of the Chief of Ordnance
Record Group 200	National Archives Gift Collection
Record Group 217	Records of the United States General Accounting Office
Record Group 393	Records of United States Army Continental Commands, 1821–1920

New-York Historical Society, New York, N.Y. (NHi)
    Miscellaneous Manuscripts—Jefferson Davis
    Miscellaneous Manuscripts—Robert J. Walker
New York Public Library, New York, N.Y. (NN)
    Emmet Collection
    Personal Miscellaneous Papers—Jefferson Davis
New York State Library, Albany (N)
    John E. Wool Papers, JT12777, Box 5, Folder 5
Old Court House Museum Library, Vicksburg, Miss. (MsVO)
    Fisher Funeral Home Records
James K. Polk Memorial Auxiliary, Columbia, Tenn.
Princeton University, Princeton, N.J. (NjP)
    Andre de Coppet Collection
    Manuscript Collection
Rice University, Houston, Texas (TxHR)
    Jefferson Davis Association
    Jefferson Davis Papers, Woodson Research Center
Smithsonian Institution, Washington, D.C. (DSI)
    Joseph Henry Papers

SOURCES

Tennessee State Library and Archives, Nashville (T)
    Mexican War Collection
Texas State Library and Historical Commission, Austin (Tx)
    Confederate Muster Roll Index
    Governor's Papers
Transylvania University, Lexington, Ky. (KyLxT)
    Jefferson Davis Papers
Tulane University, New Orleans, La. (LNT)
    Mrs. Mason Barret Collection of Albert Sidney and William Preston Johnston Papers
    Lise Mitchell Journal
    Lise Mitchell Papers
    Louisiana Historical Association: Jefferson Davis Papers
United States Military Academy, West Point, N.Y. (NWM)
    Rufus Lathrop Baker Collection
    Cullum File of Graduates
    Jefferson Davis Papers
    Mexican War Papers
University of Alabama, Tuscaloosa (AU)
    Jefferson Davis Collection
University of Michigan, William L. Clements Library, Ann Arbor (MiU-C)
    Clinton H. Haskell Collection
University of Mississippi, Oxford (MsU)
    Mississippi Collection
University of North Carolina, Chapel Hill (NcU)
  Southern Historical Collection
    Quitman Family Papers
    Trist Wood Papers
University of Texas, Austin (TxU)
    Charles T. Harlan Papers
University of Virginia, Charlottesville (ViU)
    Mrs. Thomas Campbell Collection
Washington County Historical Society, Hagerstown, Md.
Yale University, New Haven, Conn. (CtY)
    Western Americana Manuscripts

PRIVATE RECORDS

Florence N. Bruce, Vicksburg, Miss.
Myrtie C. Byrne, Natchez, Miss.
Ernesto Caldeira, Woodville, Miss.
Robert E. Canon and Newton Wilds, Houston, Texas
Barbara Clarke, Hinsdale, Ill.
Richard W. Davis, Acton, Mass.

SOURCES

Lucinda G. Dietz, New York, N.Y.
Emily Driscoll, New York, N.Y.
George H. Edwards, Hollywood, Fla.
Harold C. Fisher, Yazoo City, Miss.
Albert F. Ganier (deceased), Nashville, Tenn.
Mrs. Joe H. Howie, Jackson, Miss.
Kathryn C. Kimble, Vicksburg, Miss.
Elizabeth K. Kuebel, New Orleans, La.
Douglas M. More, New York, N.Y.
Ben S. Nelms, Houston, Texas
Thomas V. Noland, Biloxi, Miss.
William L. Richter, Manhattan, Kan.
Joseph Rubinfine, Pleasantville, N.J.
Adele D. Sinton, Colorado Springs, Colo.
Clarence L. Yancey, Shreveport, La.

TYPESCRIPTS

Bloom, John Porter. "With the American Army into Mexico, 1846–1848." Ph.D. dissertation, Emory University, Atlanta, 1956.

Dorman, John F. "Genealogy of the Preston Family." Typescript, The Filson Club, Louisville.

Everett, Frank E., Jr. "Vicksburg Lawyers Prior to the Civil War." Typescript, Vicksburg, Miss., 1968.

Hinton, Harwood P. "The Military Career of John Ellis Wool, 1812–1863." Ph.D. dissertation, University of Wisconsin, Madison, 1960.

Hodge, Sara W. "Attitude of the Woodville Republican Toward National Questions, 1823–1848." M.A. thesis, University of Mississippi, Oxford, 1929.

Jackson, Maurice Elizabeth. "Mound Bayou—A Study in Social Benevolence." M.A. thesis, University of Alabama, Tuscaloosa, 1937.

Rawson, Donald M. "Party Politics in Mississippi, 1850–1860." Ph.D. dissertation, Vanderbilt University, Nashville, 1964.

Shepperd, Gladys Byram. "The Montgomery Saga: From Slavery to Black Power." Typescript, 1971. Benjamin Montgomery Family Papers, Library of Congress.

Young, David Nathaniel. "The Mississippi Whigs, 1834–1860." Ph.D. dissertation, University of Alabama, Tuscaloosa, 1968.

NEWSPAPERS AND PERIODICALS

Mississippi
    Aberdeen *Mississippi Advertiser*
    Benton *Yazoo Banner*
    Carrollton *Mississippi Democrat*

SOURCES

Columbus *Southern Standard*
Holly Springs *Gazette*
Holly Springs *Mississippi Palladium*
Jackson *Mississippian* (title varies)
Jackson *Southern Reformer*
Jackson *Southron*
Natchez *Democrat*, Pilgrimage editions
Natchez *Mississippi Free Trader and Natchez Gazette*
Natchez *Weekly Courier and Journal*
Natchez *Weekly Democrat*
Oxford *Falcon*
Port Gibson *Herald and Correspondent*
Vicksburg *Post*
Vicksburg *Sentinel* (title varies)
Vicksburg *Sentinel and Expositor*
Vicksburg *Whig* (title varies)
Woodville *Republican*
Yazoo City *Whig*

Others

Austin *Texas Democrat*
Boston *Advertiser*
Brookville *Indiana American*
Cincinnati *Enquirer* (title varies)
Dubuque *Daily Herald*
Eaton, Ohio, *Weekly Register*
Galveston *Civilian and Galveston Gazette*
Galveston *Daily News*
Greenville, S.C., *Mountaineer*
Harrisburg, Pa., *Democratic Union*
Houston *Democratic Telegraph and Texas Register*
Huntsville, Ala., *Democrat*
Indianapolis *Indiana State Sentinel*
Little Rock *Arkansas State Gazette*
Louisville *Courier*
Matamoros *American Flag*
Nashville *Tri-Weekly Nashville Union*
Nashville *Whig*
New Orleans *Bee*
New Orleans *Daily Crescent*
New Orleans *Daily Delta*
New Orleans *Daily Picayune*
New Orleans *Jeffersonian*
New Orleans *Southerner*
New Orleans *Times-Democrat*
New York *Herald*

SOURCES

New York *Morning Express*
New York *Spirit of the Times*
New York *Times*
New York *Tribune*
New York *World*
Niles' National Register (Baltimore)
Omaha *World-Herald*
Philadelphia *Pennsylvanian*
Philadelphia *Public Ledger*
Richmond, La., *Compiler*
Richmond, Va., *Dispatch*
Richmond, Va., *Enquirer*
St. Louis *Globe-Democrat*
Saltillo *Picket Guard*
San Francisco *Alta California*
Vedette (Washington, D.C.)
Vidalia, La., *Concordia Intelligencer*
Washington, D.C., *Battery*
Washington, D.C., *Daily National Intelligencer*
Washington, D.C., *Daily Union*

DEALERS' CATALOGS

Argosy Book Stores, New York
Conway Barker, Dallas
Walter P. Benjamin, New York
Robert K. Black, Upper Montclair, N.J.
Ben Bloomfield, New York
Carnegie Book Shop, New York
Dodd, Mead & Company, New York
Emily Driscoll, New York
Edward Eberstadt & Sons, New York
Goodspeed's, Boston
Kingston Galleries, Somerville, Mass.
Thomas F. Madigan, New York
Paul C. Richards, Brookline, Mass.
Forest H. Sweet, Battle Creek, Mich.

LEGAL CASES

R. C. Ballard v. *Joseph E. Davis*, 31 Miss. 525 (1856).
Davis v. *Bowmar*, 55 Miss. 671 (1879).
Menard v. *Aspasia*, 30 U.S. 505 (1831).
State v. *Samuel W. Fullerton*, 7 Robinson 210 (Louisiana 1844).

SOURCES

ARTICLES

Backus, Electus. "A Brief Sketch of the Battle of Monterey; With Details of That Portion of It, Which Took Place at the Eastern Extremity of the City." *Historical Magazine*, 10 (1866), 207–13.

———. "Details of the Controversy Between the Regulars and Volunteers, in Relation to the Part Taken by Each in the Capture of Battery No. 1. and Other Works at the East End of the City of Monterey, on the 21st of September, 1846." *Historical Magazine*, 10 (1866), 255–57.

Barringer, Graham A., [ed.]. "The Mexican War Journal of Henry S. Lane." *Indiana Magazine of History*, 53 (1957), 383–434.

Boucher, Chauncey S., and Robert P. Brooks, eds. "Correspondence Addressed to John C. Calhoun, 1837–1849." *Annual Report of the American Historical Association for the Year 1929*. Washington: Government Printing Office, 1930.

Brand, Carl F. "The History of the Know Nothing Party in Indiana." *Indiana Magazine of History*, 18 (1922), 47–81, 177–206, 266–306.

Buley, R. C. "Indiana in the Mexican War." *Indiana Magazine of History*, 15 (1919), 260–326, 16 (1920), 46–68.

Burr, Frank A. "Jefferson Davis, the Ex-Confederate President at Home." *Tyler's Quarterly Historical and Genealogical Magazine*, 32 (1951), 163–80.

Coleman, J. Winston, Jr. "Kentucky River Steamboats." *Kentucky Historical Society Register*, 63 (1965), 299–322.

Day, Mrs. John W. "Brig. General Carnot Posey." Woodville, Miss., *Republican*, 1975 Pilgrimage edition, 11, 15.

Estes, William E. "Battle of Monterey." Fort Worth, Texas, *Gazette*, Jan. 5, 1885, 3–4.

Fesler, Mayo. "Secret Political Societies in the North During the Civil War." *Indiana Magazine of History*, 14 (1918), 183–286.

German, S. H. "Governor George Thomas Wood." *Southwestern Historical Quarterly*, 20 (1916–17), 260–68.

Kendel, Julia. "Reconstruction in Lafayette County." *Mississippi Historical Society Publications*, 13 (1913), 223–71.

McFarland, Baxter. "A Forgotten Expedition to Pensacola in January, 1861." *Mississippi Historical Society Publications*, 9 (1906), 15–23.

Monette, John W. "The Mississippi Floods." *Mississippi Historical Society Publications*, 7 (1903), 427–78.

Moore, John Hammond, ed. "Private Johnson Fights the Mexicans, 1847–1848." *South Carolina Historical Magazine*, 67 (1966), 203–28.

Morris, Cheryl Haun. "Choctaw and Chickasaw Indian Agents, 1831–1874." *Chronicles of Oklahoma*, 50 (1972), 415–57.

SOURCES

"Notes and Documents: Oklahoma Historical Markers and Monuments, 1960–1966." *Chronicles of Oklahoma*, 44 (1966), 216–29.

Pace, Eleanor Damon, ed. "The Diary and Letters of William P. Rogers, 1846–1862." *Southwestern Historical Quarterly*, 32 (1928–29), 259–99.

Padgett, James A. "The Letters of Colonel Richard Taylor and of Commodore Richard Taylor to James Madison, Together with a Sketch of Their Lives." *Kentucky Historical Society Register*, 36 (1938), 330–44.

Patridge, Isaac M. "The Press of Mississippi." *De Bow's Review*, 29 (1860), 500–509.

Rainwater, Percy L., ed. "Letters to and from Jacob Thompson." *Journal of Southern History*, 6 (1940), 95–111.

Sexton, F. B. "J. Pinckney Henderson." *Texas State Historical Association Quarterly*, 1 (1897–98), 187–203.

Sioussat, St. George L., [ed.]. "Mexican War Letters of Col. William Bowen Campbell, of Tennessee, Written to Governor David Campbell, of Virginia, 1846–1847." *Tennessee Historical Magazine*, 1 (1915), 129–67.

Smyrl, Frank H. "Unionism in Texas, 1850–1861." *Southwestern Historical Quarterly*, 68 (1964–65), 172–95.

Stanard, W. G. "Abstracts of Virginia Land Patents." *Virginia Magazine of History and Biography*, 1 (1894), 310–24.

"Story of Brierfield." St. Louis *Globe-Democrat*, Oct. 24, 1886, 8.

Viola, Herman J. "Zachary Taylor and the Indiana Volunteers." *Southwestern Historical Quarterly*, 72 (1968–69), 335–46.

Washburn, Wilcomb E. "The Influence of the Smithsonian Institution on Intellectual Life in Mid-Nineteenth-Century Washington." *Columbia Historical Society Records*, 63 (1963–65), 96–121.

Watson, Douglas S., and Dorothy H. Huggins, [eds.]. "To California Through Texas and Mexico: The Diary and Letters of Thomas B. Eastland and Joseph G. Eastland, His Son." *California Historical Society Quarterly*, 18 (1939), 99–135, 229–50.

Webber, Mabel L., ann. "Records from the Blake and White Bibles." *South Carolina Historical and Genealogical Magazine*, 36 (1935), 14–19, 42–55, 89–93, 113–21, 37 (1936), 38–44, 65–70.

Wright, Muriel H. "General Douglas H. Cooper, C. S. A." *Chronicles of Oklahoma*, 32 (1954–55), 142–84.

BOOKS

Alcarez, Ramón, et al. *The Other Side; or, Notes for the History of the War Between Mexico and the United States.* Translated and edited by Albert C. Ramsey. New York: John Wiley, 1850.

SOURCES

Alderman, Edwin A., Joel C. Harris, and Charles W. Kent, eds. *Library of Southern Literature*. 16 vols. New Orleans, Atlanta, and Dallas: Martin & Hoyt, 1907–13.

Allen, Don A. *Legislative Sourcebook: The California Legislature and Reapportionment, 1849–1965*. [Sacramento]: Assembly of the State of California, [1965].

American Almanac and Repository of Useful Knowledge, for the Year [1830–61]. Boston: Gray & Bowen, 1829–61.

Anderson, John Q., ed. *Louisiana Swamp Doctor*. Baton Rouge: Louisiana State University Press, 1962.

Appletons' Cyclopaedia of American Biography. Edited by James Grant Wilson and John Fiske. 6 vols. New York: D. Appleton, 1887–89.

Ashe, Samuel A'Court, ed. *Biographical History of North Carolina from Colonial Times to the Present*. 7 vols. Greensboro: C. L. Van Noppen, 1905–1907.

Baker, Richard D. *Judicial Review in Mexico: A Study of the "Amparo" Suit*. Austin: Institute of Latin American Studies, University of Texas Press, 1971.

Bakewell, Peter J. *Silver Mining and Society in Colonial Mexico: Zacatecas, 1546–1700*. Cambridge, England: University Press, 1971.

Balbontín, Manuel. *La Invasión Americana, 1846 a 1848*. Mexico: Gonzalo A. Esteva, 1883.

Bancroft, Hubert Howe. *The Works of Hubert Howe Bancroft*. 39 vols. San Francisco: A. L. Bancroft, 1882–90.

Bartlett, John, comp. *Familiar Quotations: A Collection of Passages, Phrases and Proverbs Traced to Their Sources in Ancient and Modern Literature*. 13th ed., rev. Boston: Little, Brown, 1955.

Barton, Henry W. *Texas Volunteers in the Mexican War*. Waco: Texian Press, 1970.

Bauer, Karl Jack. *The Mexican War, 1846–1848*. New York: Macmillan, 1974.

Baylies, Francis. *A Narrative of Major General Wool's Campaign in Mexico in the Years 1846, 1847 & 1848*. Albany: Little, 1851.

Be It Known and Remembered: Bible Records. 4 vols. Baton Rouge: Louisiana Genealogical and Historical Society, 1960–67.

Berwanger, Eugene H. *The Frontier Against Slavery: Western Anti-Negro Prejudice and the Slavery Extension Controversy*. Urbana: University of Illinois Press, 1967.

Billington, Ray Allen. *Westward Expansion: A History of the American Frontier*. 2d ed. New York: Macmillan, 1960.

Biographical and Historical Memoirs of Louisiana. 2 vols. Chicago: Goodspeed, 1892.

Biographical and Historical Memoirs of Mississippi. 2 vols. Chicago: Goodspeed, 1891.

SOURCES

Biographical Encyclopedia of Kentucky of the Dead and Living Men of the Nineteenth Century. Cincinnati: J. M. Armstrong, 1878.

Birkhimer, William E. *Historical Sketch of the Organization, Administration, Matériel and Tactics of the Artillery, United States Army*. 1884. Reprint. New York: Greenwood Press, 1968.

Blum, Jerome. *Lord and Peasant in Russia, from the Ninth to the Nineteenth Century*. Princeton: Princeton University Press, 1961.

Booth, Andrew B., comp. *Records of Louisiana Confederate Soldiers and Louisiana Confederate Commands*. 3 vols. New Orleans: n.p., 1920.

[Boynton, Charles B., comp.]. *History of the Great Western Sanitary Fair*. Cincinnati: C. F. Vent, [1864].

Brooks, Nathan C. *A Complete History of the Mexican War: Its Causes, Conduct, and Consequences*. Philadelphia: Grigg, Elliot, 1849.

Brown, George R. *Washington: A Not Too Serious History*. Baltimore: Norman, 1930.

Bruchey, Stuart W., comp. *Cotton and the Growth of the American Economy: 1790–1860*. New York: Harcourt, Brace & World, 1967.

Brugger, Robert J. *Beverley Tucker: Heart over Head in the Old South*. Baltimore: Johns Hopkins University Press, 1978.

Buchanan, James. *The Works of James Buchanan, Comprising His Speeches, State Papers, and Private Correspondence*. Edited by John Bassett Moore. 12 vols. Philadelphia: J. B. Lippincott, 1908–11.

Burke's Presidential Families of the United States of America. Edited by Hugh Montgomery-Massingberd. London: Burke's Peerage, 1975.

Burnham, Walter Dean. *Presidential Ballots, 1836–1892*. Baltimore: Johns Hopkins Press, 1955.

Caldwell, Joshua W. *Sketches of the Bench and Bar of Tennessee*. Knoxville: Ogden Brothers, 1898.

Capers, Gerald M. *Occupied City: New Orleans under the Federals, 1862–1865*. [Lexington]: University of Kentucky Press, 1965.

Carleton, James Henry. *The Battle of Buena Vista, with the Operations of the "Army of Occupation" for One Month*. New York: Harper & Brothers, 1848.

Carter, Clarence E., ed. *The Territorial Papers of the United States*. 26 vols. Washington: Government Printing Office, 1934–62.

Carter, Samuel. *Blaze of Glory: The Fight for New Orleans, 1814–1815*. New York: St. Martin's Press, 1971.

Cathcart, William, ed. *Baptist Encyclopaedia*. Philadelphia: Louis H. Everts, 1881.

Chamberlain, Samuel E. *My Confession*. New York: Harper & Brothers, 1956.

SOURCES

Claiborne, John Francis Hamtramck. *Life and Correspondence of John A. Quitman.* 2 vols. New York: Harper & Brothers, 1860.

Clark, Thomas D. *A History of Kentucky.* Lexington: John Bradford Press, 1950.

Coleman, Ann Mary Butler. *The Life of John J. Crittenden.* 2 vols. 1871. Reprint. New York: Da Capo Press, 1970.

Collins, Lewis and Richard H. *History of Kentucky.* 2 vols. Reprint. Frankfort: Kentucky Historical Society, 1966.

Colt, Samuel. *Saml. Colt's Own Record.* Hartford: Connecticut Historical Society, 1949.

Corbin, Diana F. M. *A Life of Matthew Fontaine Maury.* London: Sampson Low, Marston, Searle, & Rivington, 1888.

Cotner, Thomas Ewing. *The Military and Political Career of José Joaquín de Herrera, 1792–1854.* Austin: University of Texas Press, 1949.

Coulson, Thomas. *Joseph Henry: His Life and Work.* Princeton: Princeton University Press, 1950.

Crippen, Lee F. *Simon Cameron: Ante-Bellum Years.* Oxford, Ohio: Mississippi Valley Press, 1942.

Cullum, George W. *Biographical Register of the Officers and Graduates of the U.S. Military Academy at West Point, N.Y., from Its Establishment, in 1802, to 1890 with the Early History of the United States Military Academy.* 8 vols. Boston: Houghton, Mifflin, 1891–1930.

—————. *Register of the Officers and Graduates of the U.S. Military Academy at West Point, N.Y., from March 16, 1802, to January 1, 1850.* New York: J. F. Trow, 1850.

Daughters of the American Revolution. Louisiana. *Louisiana Tombstone Inscriptions.* 11 vols. [Shreveport?]: Louisiana Society NSDAR, 1954–57.

Davis, Harry Alexander. *The Davis Family (Davies and David) in Wales and America.* Washington: Harry Alexander Davis, 1927.

Davis, Jefferson. *The Address on the Mexican War and Its Results as Delivered by the Hon. Jefferson Davis before the Louisiana Associated Veterans of the Mexican War, at Exposition Hall, New Orleans, Tuesday, March 7th, 1876.* New Orleans: L. McGrane, 1876.

—————. *Jefferson Davis, Constitutionalist: His Letters, Papers and Speeches.* Edited by Dunbar Rowland. 10 vols. Jackson: Mississippi Department of Archives and History, 1923.

—————. *Private Letters, 1823–1889.* Edited by Hudson Strode. New York: Harcourt, Brace & World, 1966.

—————. *The Rise and Fall of the Confederate Government.* 2 vols. New York: D. Appleton, 1881.

SOURCES

————. *Speeches of the Hon. Jefferson Davis, of Mississippi, Delivered during the Summer of 1858.* Baltimore: John Murphy, 1859.

————. *Speech of Jefferson Davis, of Mississippi, on the Oregon Bill, Delivered in the Senate of the United States, July 12, 1848.* Washington: Towers, [1848].

Davis, Reuben, *Recollections of Mississippi and Mississippians.* Boston: Houghton, Mifflin, 1891.

Davis, Varina Howell. *Jefferson Davis, Ex-President of the Confederate States of America: A Memoir by His Wife.* 2 vols. New York: Belford, 1890.

Davis, William W. H. *El Gringo; or, New Mexico and Her People.* New York: Harper & Brothers, 1857.

DeRosier, Arthur H. *The Removal of the Choctaw Indians.* Knoxville: University of Tennessee Press, 1970.

Diccionario Porrúa de Historia, Biografía y Geografía de México. 2d ed. Mexico City: Editorial Porrúa, 1965.

————. *Suplemento.* 1966.

Dictionary of American Biography. Edited by Allen Johnson et al. 11 vols. New York: Charles Scribner's Sons, 1964.

Dodd, Donald B., and Wynelle S. Dodd. *Historical Statistics of the South, 1790–1970.* Tuscaloosa: University of Alabama Press, 1973.

Dufour, Charles L. *The Mexican War: A Compact History, 1846–1848.* New York: Hawthorn, 1968.

Dyer, Brainerd. *Zachary Taylor.* Baton Rouge: Louisiana State University Press, 1946.

Ellet, Charles. *The Mississippi and Ohio Rivers: Containing Plans for the Protection of the Delta from Inundation.* Philadelphia: Lippincott, Grambo, 1853.

Elliott, Charles W. *Winfield Scott: The Soldier and the Man.* New York: Macmillan, 1937.

Enciclopedia de México. 12 vols. Mexico City: Instituto de la Enciclopedia de México, 1966–77.

Encyclopedia of Latin America. Edited by Helen Delpar. New York: McGraw-Hill, 1974.

Estienne, Henri. *Les Prémices, ou le I livre des proverbes épigramatizéz, ou des épigrammes proverbializéz.* 1593. Reprint. Geneva: Slatkine, 1968.

Evans, David Morier. *The Commercial Crisis, 1847–1848.* [1848–49.] Reprint. New York: Augustus M. Kelley, 1969.

Federal Writers' Project. *Washington, City and Capital.* Washington: Government Printing Office, 1937.

Ficklin, Slaughter W. *Genealogy of the Ficklin Family since 1720.* Charlottesville, Va.: James Alexander, 1870.

SOURCES

French, Samuel G. *Two Wars: An Autobiography of Gen. Samuel G. French.* Nashville: Confederate Veteran, 1901.

Gatschet, Albert S. *The Klamath Indians of Southwestern Oregon.* Washington: Government Printing Office, 1890.

Gibson, James M. *Memoirs of J. M. Gibson: Terrors of the Civil War and Reconstruction Days.* Edited by James G. Alverson and James G. Alverson, Jr. [San Gabriel?, Calif.: n.p., 1966.]

Gibson, [Thomas] W. *Letter Descriptive of the Battle of Buena Vista, Written upon the Ground.* Lawrenceburgh, Ind.: n.p., 1847.

[Giddings, Luther]. *Sketches of the Campaign in Northern Mexico in Eighteen Hundred Forty-Six and Seven.* New York: George P. Putnam, 1853.

Gregg, Josiah. *Diary and Letters of Josiah Gregg.* Edited by Maurice G. Fulton. 2 vols. Norman: University of Oklahoma Press, 1941–44.

Hamilton, Alexander. *The Papers of Alexander Hamilton.* Edited by Harold C. Syrett. 26 vols. New York: Columbia University Press, 1961–79.

Hamilton, Allan McLane. *The Intimate Life of Alexander Hamilton.* New York: Charles Scribner's Sons, 1910.

Hamilton, Holman. *Zachary Taylor.* 2 vols. Indianapolis: Bobbs-Merrill, 1941–51.

Hamilton, William Franklin. *A History of Carroll County.* [Carrollton, Miss.]: Carroll County Conservative, [1901].

Handbook of Texas. Edited by Walter Prescott Webb and Eldon S. Branda. 3 vols. Austin: Texas State Historical Association, 1952–76.

Hardee, William J. *Rifle and Light Infantry Tactics for the Exercise and Manoeuvres of Troops When Acting as Light Infantry or Riflemen.* 2 vols. Philadelphia: Lippincott, Grambo, 1855.

Harrison, Robert W. *Levee Districts and Levee Building on Mississippi: A Study of State and Local Efforts to Control Mississippi River Floods.* [Stoneville? Miss.]: Delta Council, 1951.

Heitman, Francis B. *Historical Register and Dictionary of the United States Army, from Its Organization, September 29, 1789, to March 2, 1903.* 2 vols. 1903. Reprint. Urbana: University of Illinois Press, 1965.

Henry, Jeanne Hand. *1819–1849 Abstradex of Annual Returns, Mississippi Free and Accepted Masons.* New Market, Ala.: Southern Genealogical Services, 1969.

Henry, William S. *Campaign Sketches of the War in Mexico.* New York: Harper & Brothers, 1847.

Hopkins, William P. *The Seventh Regiment Rhode Island Volunteers in the Civil War, 1862–1865.* Providence: Providence Press, 1903.

Humphreys, A[ndrew] A., and H[enry] L. Abbot. *Report upon the*

SOURCES

Physics and Hydraulics of the Mississippi River. Philadelphia: J. B. Lippincott, 1861.

Index to the Great Register of the City and County of San Francisco, 1872. San Francisco: n.p., 1872.

Indiana. Adjutant General's Office. *Indiana in the Mexican War*. Compiled by Oran Perry. Indianapolis: William R. Burford, 1908.

Jackson, Carlton. *Presidential Vetoes, 1792–1945*. Athens: University of Georgia Press, 1967.

Jefferson, Thomas. *The Writings of Thomas Jefferson*. Edited by Albert Ellery Bergh. 20 vols. Washington: Thomas Jefferson Memorial Association, 1907.

Jenkins, John H., ed. *The Papers of the Texas Revolution, 1835–1836*. 10 vols. Austin: Presidial Press, 1973.

Jenkins, William Sumner. *Pro-Slavery Thought in the Old South*. Chapel Hill: University of North Carolina Press, 1935.

Jewell, Edwin L. *Jewell's Crescent City, Illustrated*. New Orleans: n.p., 1874.

Johnston, William Preston. *The Life of Gen. Albert Sidney Johnston, Embracing His Services in the Armies of the United States, the Republic of Texas, and the Confederate States*. New York: D. Appleton, 1879.

Journal of the Congress of the Confederate States of America, 1861–1865. 7 vols. Washington: Government Printing Office, 1904–1905.

Journals of the Continental Congress, 1774–1789. 34 vols. Washington: Government Printing Office, 1904–37.

Kelly, Alfred H., and Winfred A. Harbison. *The American Constitution: Its Origins and Development*. 5th ed. New York: W. W. Norton, 1976.

Kettner, James H. *The Development of American Citizenship, 1608–1870*. Chapel Hill: University of North Carolina Press, 1978.

Lavender, David. *Climax at Buena Vista: The American Campaigns in Northeastern Mexico, 1846–47*. Philadelphia: J. B. Lippincott, 1966.

Lincoln, Waldo. *History of the Lincoln Family*. Worcester, Mass.: Commonwealth Press, 1923.

Lipscomb, William L. *A History of Columbus, Mississippi, during the 19th Century*. Birmingham, Ala.: Press of Dispatch Printing Co., 1909.

Lockett, Samuel H. *Louisiana as It Is: A Geographical and Topographical Description of the State*. Edited by Lauren C. Post. Baton Rouge: Louisiana State University Press, 1969.

Lubbock, Francis Richard. *Six Decades in Texas; or, Memoirs of Francis Richard Lubbock*. Edited by C. W. Raines. Austin: Ben C. Jones, 1900.

Lyman, Joseph B. *Cotton Culture*. New York: Orange Judd, 1868.

SOURCES

Lynch, James D. *The Bench and Bar of Mississippi*. New York: E. J. Hale, 1881.

McBride, Robert M., and Dan M. Robison, *Biographical Directory of the Tennessee General Assembly*. Vol. I, 1789–1861. Nashville: Tennessee State Library and Archives, 1975.

McCain, William D. *The Story of Jackson*. 2 vols. Jackson, Miss.: J. F. Hyer, 1853.

McCall, George A. *Letters from the Frontiers*. Philadelphia: J. B. Lippincott, 1868.

McElroy, Robert. *Jefferson Davis: The Unreal and the Real*. 2 vols. New York: Harper & Brothers, 1937.

McKitrick, Eric L., ed. *Slavery Defended: The Views of the Old South*. Englewood Cliffs, N.J.: Prentice-Hall, 1963.

McWhiney, Grady. *Braxton Bragg and Confederate Defeat*. New York: Columbia University Press, 1969.

Madray, Mrs. I. C. *A History of Bee County, with Some Brief Sketches about Men and Events in Adjoining Counties*. Beeville, Texas: Beeville Publishing Co., 1939.

Mahon, John K., and Romana Danysh. *Infantry*. Rev. ed. Washington: Office of the Chief of Military History, U.S. Army, 1972.

Maine. University. *A Reference List of Manuscripts Relating to the History of Maine*. Orono: University Press, 1938.

Manning, William R., ed. *Diplomatic Correspondence of the United States: Inter-American Affairs, 1831–1860*. 12 vols. Washington: Carnegie Endowment for International Peace, 1932–39.

Mayes, Edward. *Lucius Q. C. Lamar: His Life, Times, and Speeches, 1825–1893*. Nashville: Publishing House of the Methodist Episcopal Church, South, 1896.

Meade, George G. *The Life and Letters of George Gordon Meade, Major-General United States Army*. Edited by George Gordon Meade. 2 vols. New York: Charles Scribner's Sons, 1913.

Menn, Joseph Karl. *The Large Slaveholders of Louisiana, 1860*. New Orleans: Pelican, 1964.

Merk, Frederick. *The Monroe Doctrine and American Expansionism, 1843–1849*. New York: Alfred A. Knopf, 1966.

Miles, Edwin A. *Jacksonian Democracy in Mississippi*. Chapel Hill: University of North Carolina Press, 1960.

Miller, David Hunter, ed. *Treaties and Other International Acts of the United States of America*. 8 vols. Washington: Government Printing Office, 1931–48.

Miller, Stephen F. *The Bench and Bar of Georgia: Memoirs and Sketches*. 2 vols. Philadelphia: J. B. Lippincott, 1858.

Mirsky, Jeannette. *The World of Eli Whitney*. New York: Macmillan, 1952.

SOURCES

Mississippi. Department of Archives and History. *The Official and Statistical Register of the State of Mississippi, 1908*. Nashville: Brandon, 1908.

———. *Laws of Mississippi*. Jackson: publisher varies, 1842–57.

———. State Library Commission. *Mississippiana*. Vol II: *Union List of Newspapers*. [Jackson]: Mississippi Library Commission, 1970.

Monroe, James. *The Writings of James Monroe*. Edited by Stanislaus Murray Hamilton. 7 vols. New York: G. P. Putnam's Sons, 1898–1903.

Morris, Thomas D. *Free Men All: The Personal Liberty Laws of the North, 1780–1861*. Baltimore: Johns Hopkins University Press, 1974.

National Cyclopaedia of American Biography. 58 vols. and index. New York and Clifton, N.J.: James T. White, 1898–1979.

New English Dictionary on Historical Principles [OED]. Edited by James A. H. Murray. 10 vols. in 20. Oxford: Clarendon Press, 1888–1928.

[Newman, Jeremiah W.]. *The Lounger's Common-Place Book*. 4 vols. London: Kerby, 1796–99.

New-York Historical Society. *Dictionary of Artists in America, 1564–1860*. New Haven: Yale University Press, 1957.

Official Records. See *War of the Rebellion*.

Ohio Roster Commission. *Official Roster of the Soldiers of the State of Ohio in the War of the Rebellion, 1861–1866, and in the War with Mexico, 1846–1848*. 12 vols. Cincinnati, Akron, and Norwalk, Ohio: publisher varies, 1886–95.

O'Meara, Barry E. *Napoleon in Exile; or, A Voice from St. Helena*. 2 vols. 1853. Reprint. New York: AMS Press, 1969.

Overdyke, William Darrell. *The Know-Nothing Party in the South*. Baton Rouge: Louisiana State University Press, 1950.

Page, Thomas Walker. *The End of Villainage in England*. New York: Macmillan, 1900.

Palmer, Joel. *Palmer's Journal of Travels over the Rocky Mountains, 1845–46*. Cleveland: Arthur H. Clark, 1906.

Parker, Richard D. *Historical Recollections of Robertson County, Texas, with Biographical & Genealogical Notes on the Pioneers & Their Families*. Edited by Nona Clement Parker. Salado, Texas: Anson Jones Press, 1955.

Paullin, Charles O. *Atlas of the Historical Geography of the United States*. Edited by John K. Wright. Washington: Carnegie Institution and American Geographical Society, 1932.

Paxton, William McClung. *The Marshall Family; or, A Genealogical Chart of the Descendants of John Marshall and Elizabeth Markham, His Wife*. Cincinnati: R. Clarke, 1885.

SOURCES

Perkins, Dexter. *The Monroe Doctrine, 1826–1867*. 1933. Reprint. Gloucester, Mass.: Peter Smith, 1965.

Pletcher, David M. *The Diplomacy of Annexation: Texas, Oregon, and the Mexican War*. Columbia: University of Missouri Press, 1973.

Polk, James K. *The Diary of James K. Polk during His Presidency, 1845 to 1849*. Edited by Milo Milton Quaife. 4 vols. Chicago: A. C. McClurg, 1910.

Poore, Ben. Perley. *Perley's Reminiscences of Sixty Years in the National Metropolis*. 2 vols. Philadelphia: Hubbard Brothers, 1886.

Potter, David M. *Impending Crisis, 1848–1861*. Edited and completed by Don E. Fehrenbacher. New York: Harper & Row, 1976.

Rayback, Joseph G. *Free Soil: The Election of 1848*. Lexington: University Press of Kentucky, 1970.

Register of Graduates and Former Cadets of the United States Military Academy. West Point, N.Y.: West Point Alumni Foundation, 1965.

Rice, Charles Duncan. *The Rise and Fall of Black Slavery*. New York: Harper & Row, 1975.

Rich, Louise. *State O'Maine*. New York: Harper & Row, 1964.

Risch, Erna. *Quartermaster Support of the Army: A History of the Corps, 1775–1939*. Washington: Government Printing Office, 1962.

Rives, George L. *The United States and Mexico, 1821–1848: A History of the Relations between the Two Countries from the Independence of Mexico to the Close of the War with the United States*. 2 vols. New York: Charles Scribner's Sons, 1913.

Roa Bárcena, José María. *Recuerdos de la Invasión Norteamericana, 1846–1848*. 3 vols. Mexico City: Editorial Porrúa, 1947.

[Robertson, John Blount]. *Reminiscences of a Campaign in Mexico by a Member of "The Bloody-First."* Nashville: John York, 1849.

Rose, Victor M. *Victor Rose's History of Victoria*. Edited by J. W. Petty, Jr. Victoria, Texas: Book Mart, 1961.

Rowland, Dunbar. *Courts, Judges, and Lawyers of Mississippi, 1798–1935*. Jackson: Hederman Brothers, 1935.

———. *History of Mississippi: The Heart of the South*. 4 vols. Chicago and Jackson: S. J. Clarke, 1925.

———, ed. *Encyclopedia of Mississippi History*. 2 vols. Madison, Wisc.: Selwyn A. Brant, 1907.

———, ed. *Mississippi*. 3 vols. Atlanta: Southern Historical Publishing Association, 1907.

Sanders, John B., comp. *The 1850 Census, Panola County, Texas*. Center, Texas: J. B. Sanders, 1966.

Santa Anna, Antonio López de. *Apelación al Buen Criterio de los Nacionales y Estranjeros. Informe sobre las Acusaciones Presentadas por el Señor Diputado Don Ramón Gamboa*. Mexico: Imprenta de Cumplido, 1849.

SOURCES

Sawyer, Charles Winthrop. *Our Rifles*. Boston: Williams Book Store, 1941.

Scharf, John Thomas. *History of the Confederate States Navy from Its Organization to the Surrender of Its Last Vessel*. 2d ed. Albany, N.Y.: Joseph McDonough, 1894.

Scott, Winfield. *Memoirs of Lieut.-Gen. Scott, LL.D., Written by Himself*. 2 vols. New York: Sheldon, 1864.

[Scribner, Benjamin F.]. *Camp Life of a Volunteer: A Campaign in Mexico; or, A Glimpse at Life in Camp*. 1847. Reprint. Austin: Jenkins, 1975.

Sellers, Charles G. *James K. Polk: Continentalist, 1843–1846*. Princeton: Princeton University Press, 1966.

Seward, William H. *The Works of William H. Seward*. Edited by George E. Baker. 5 vols. New York: Redfield, 1853–84.

Shenton, James P. *Robert John Walker: A Politician from Jackson to Lincoln*. New York: Columbia University Press, 1961.

Sillers, Florence W., comp. *History of Bolivar County, Mississippi*. Edited by Wirt A. Williams. Jackson: Hederman Brothers, 1948.

Silver, James W. *Edmund Pendleton Gaines, Frontier General*. Baton Rouge: Louisiana State University Press, 1949.

Singletary, Otis A. *The Mexican War*. Chicago: University of Chicago Press, 1960.

Skipwith, Henry. *East Feliciana, Louisiana, Past and Present: Sketches of the Pioneers*. 1892. Reprint. Baton Rouge: Claitor's Book Store, 1957.

Smith, George Winston, and Charles Judah, eds. *Chronicles of the Gringos: The U.S. Army in the Mexican War, 1846–1848: Accounts of Eyewitnesses & Combatants*. Albuquerque: University of New Mexico Press, 1968.

Smith, Horatio D. *Early History of the United States Revenue Marine Service or (United States Revenue Cutter Service), 1789–1849*. [Baltimore: Press of R. L. Polk Printing Co., 1932].

Smith, Isaac. *Reminiscences of a Campaign in Mexico: An Account of the Operations of the Indiana Brigade on the Line of the Rio Grande and Sierra Madre, and a Vindication of the Volunteers against the Aspersions of Officials and Unofficials*. 2d ed., rev. Indianapolis: Chapmans & Spann, 1848.

Smith, Justin H. *The War with Mexico*. 2 vols. New York: Macmillan, 1919.

Smithsonian Institution. *The Smithsonian Institution: Documents Relative to Its Origin and History, 1835–99*. Edited by William Jones Rhees. 2 vols. Washington: Government Printing Office, 1901.

Stevenson, Burton E., ed. *The Home Book of Proverbs, Maxims and Familiar Phrases*. New York: Macmillan, 1959.

SOURCES

————, ed. *The Home Book of Quotations: Classical and Modern.* 6th ed., rev. New York: Dodd, Mead, 1952.

Stone, Sarah Katherine. *Brokenburn: The Journal of Kate Stone, 1861–1868.* Edited by John Q. Anderson. Baton Rouge: Louisiana State University Press, 1955.

Strode, Hudson. *Jefferson Davis.* 3 vols. New York: Harcourt, Brace, 1955.

Suetonius Tranquillus, C. *The Lives of the Twelve Caesars.* Translated by Alexander Thomson. Revised by T. Forester. London: George Bell & Sons, 1901.

[Tarpley, Collin S.]. *A Sketch of the Life of Jeff. Davis, the Democratic Candidate for Governor.* Jackson: Mississippian Power Press, 1851.

Taylor, Zachary. *Letters of Zachary Taylor, from the Battle-Fields of the Mexican War.* Edited by William H. Samson. Rochester, N.Y.: Genesee Press, 1908.

Tennessee. Civil War Centennial Commission. *Tennesseans in the Civil War: A Military History of Confederate and Union Units with Available Rosters of Personnel.* 2 vols. Nashville: Civil War Centennial Commission, 1964.

Tercentenary History of Maryland. Compiled by Matthew P. Andrews and Henry F. Powell. 4 vols. Chicago and Baltimore: S. J. Clarke, 1925.

Terrell, Josephine J. B., comp. *The Truitt Family (Truett, Trewit, Truit, Trewitt—Records for the Same Family) Genealogy and History, 1650–1964.* Littleton, Colo.: n.p., 1964.

Texas. Legislature. *Members of the Texas Legislature, 1846–1962.* Austin: n.p., 1962.

Thompson, Waddy. *Recollections of Mexico.* New York: Wiley & Putnam, 1846.

Tuley, William Floyd. *The Tuley Family Memoirs.* New Albany, Ind.: W. J. Hedden, 1906.

U.S. Census Bureau. *Historical Statistics of the United States: Colonial Times to 1970.* 2 vols. Washington: U.S. Commerce Department, Census Bureau, 1975.

U.S. Congress. *American State Papers.* Class II, Indian Affairs; Class IV, Commerce and Navigation; Class VI, Naval Affairs; Class VIII, Public Lands. Washington: Gales & Seaton, 1832–61.

————. *Biographical Directory of the American Congress, 1774–1961.* Rev. ed. Washington: Government Printing Office, 1961.

————. *Congressional Directory for the First Session of the Thirtieth Congress of the United States of America.* Washington: J. & G. S. Gideon, 1848.

————. *Congressional Directory for the Second Session of the Thirtieth*

SOURCES

Congress of the United States of America. Washington: J. & G. S. Gideon, 1849.

———. *Congressional Globe.* 27th–31st Congresses. Washington: publisher varies, 1841–51.

———. *House Executive Documents.* 29th–32d Congresses.

———. *House Reports.* 27th–30th Congresses.

———. *Journal of the Executive Proceedings of the Senate of the United States of America, 1789–1905.* 90 vols. Washington: publisher varies, 1828–1948.

———. *Senate Documents.* 28th–30th Congresses.

———. *Senate Journal.* 30th Congress.

———. *Senate Reports.* 30th, 34th Congresses.

U.S. Constitution. *The Constitution of the United States of America.* Edited by Norman J. Small. Washington: Government Printing Office, 1964.

U.S. Laws, Statutes, etc. *Laws of the United States Relating to the Improvement of Rivers and Harbors.* 3 vols. Washington: Government Printing Office, 1913.

———. *United States Statutes at Large.* Edited by Richard Peters. 10 vols. Boston: Charles C. Little & James Brown, 1845–55.

U.S. Library of Congress. *Report of the Librarian of Congress and Report of the Superintendent of the Library Building and Grounds for the Fiscal Year Ending June 30, 1906.* Washington: Government Printing Office, 1906.

U.S. Mississippi River Commission. *The Improvement of the Lower Mississippi River for Flood Control and Navigation.* 3 vols. in 1. St. Louis: M[ississippi] R[iver] C[ommission], 1932.

U.S. President. *A Compilation of the Messages and Papers of the Presidents, 1789–1897.* Compiled by James D. Richardson. 10 vols. Washington: Government Printing Office, 1896–99.

U.S. State Department. *Register of Officers and Agents Civil, Military, and Naval in the Service of the United States.* Washington: State Department, 1829–69.

U.S. War Department. *General Regulations for the Army of the United States, 1847.* Washington: J. & G. S. Gideon, 1847.

———. *General Regulations for the Army; or, Military Institutes.* Philadelphia: M. Carey & Sons, 1821.

Van Deusen, Glyndon G. *The Life of Henry Clay.* Boston: Little, Brown, 1937.

Vechères de Boucherville, René Thomas. *War on the Detroit.* Edited by Milo Milton Quaife. Chicago: R. R. Donnelley & Sons, 1940.

Walthall, William T. *Jefferson Davis: A Sketch of the Life and Character of the President of the Confederate States.* New Orleans: n.p., 1908.

SOURCES

Warner, Ezra J. *Generals in Blue: Lives of the Union Commanders.* Baton Rouge: Louisiana State University Press, 1964.

————. *Generals in Gray: Lives of the Confederate Commanders.* Baton Rouge: Louisiana State University Press, 1959.

War of the Rebellion: A Compilation of the Official Records of the Union and Confederate Armies [OR]. 70 vols. in 128. Washington: Government Printing Office, 1880–1901.

Watkins, James L. *King Cotton: A Historical and Statistical Review, 1790 to 1908.* 1908. Reprint. New York: Negro Universities Press, 1969.

Watts, Beulah de Verieré Smith, and Nancy Jane Lucas De Grummond. *Solitude: Life on a Louisiana Plantation.* Baton Rouge: Claitor's Publishing Division, 1970.

Weisenburger, Francis P. *The Life of John McLean: A Politician on the United States Supreme Court.* Columbus: Ohio State University Press, 1937.

Wiecek, William M. *The Sources of Antislavery Constitutionalism in America, 1760–1848.* Ithaca: Cornell University Press, 1977.

Wilcox, Cadmus M. *History of the Mexican War.* Edited by Mary Rachel Wilcox. Washington: Church News, 1892.

Williams, Frances Leigh. *Matthew Fontaine Maury, Scientist of the Sea.* New Brunswick, N.J.: Rutgers University Press, 1963.

Wiltse, Charles M. *John C. Calhoun.* 3 vols. Indianapolis: Bobbs-Merrill, 1944–51.

Winchester, Robert Glenn. *James Pinckney Henderson, Texas' First Governor.* San Antonio: Naylor, 1971.

Wise, Henry Alexander. *Seven Decades of the Union.* Philadelphia: J. B. Lippincott, 1872.

Woodford, Frank B. *Lewis Cass: The Last Jeffersonian.* New Brunswick, N.J.: Rutgers University Press, 1950.

Wright, E. W., ed. *Lewis & Dryden's Marine History of the Pacific Northwest.* 1895. Reprint. New York: Antiquarian Press, 1961.

INDEX

Abbreviations *edn* and *dsn* refer to editorial note and descriptive note, respectively.

INDEX

Camp Allen: Davis selects site, 64*n*

Campbell, William B. (sketch, 29): at Tenería, 25, 30*n*, 42*n*, 44–45, 47, 50, 75, 77*n*, 78, 87–88, 101, 103; relations with Davis, 83*n*, 114–15, 402*n*; criticizes 1st Tenn. Rgt., 115; mentioned, 35, 36, 38*n*, 42, 48, 84*n*, 85

Capitulation. *See* Davis—Mexican War; Monterrey capitulation

Carrasco, José M., 30*n*

Carrera, Rafael, 324*n*

Carroll, Ferdinand: land claim of, 434; mentioned, 419, 439

Carson, Stephen D.: Davis recom. for army comn., 180*n*

Cass, Lewis (sketch, 1:264): as candidate (1848), 12, 276*n*, 392*n*, 393, 422; and Wilmot Proviso, 249, 306–307, 392; and ten-rgt. bill, 254*edn*, 277*edn*; on vols., 261*n*; Davis supports candidacy, 325, 375–76, 385, 389*n*, 391, 449; and Nicholson letter, 326*n*, 375; letter to, 434; mentioned, 254, 263*n*, 283, 285, 396*edn*, 443

Cat Island: resolution on, 431

Caulfield, James D. (ident., 236): Davis recom. as surgeon, 413, 418, 427; letter from, quoted, 234; mentioned, 9*n*, 447

Centenary College (described, 248), 247

Cerro Gordo, Battle of, 255

Chamberlain, John: letter from, 453–54

Chance, Reuben N., 37

Chapman, William D. (sketch, 236): criticizes Davis, 233–35

Chevallie, Michael H., 170*n*

Chickasaw cession, 6, 456

Childress, James M., 411

Childs, Henry: petition of, 421

Chilton, John M. (sketch, 2:27), 169

Chilton, Robert H. (sketch, 2:687): and services to Davis in Mexico, 169–70, 172; Davis recom. for brevet, 436

Choate, Rufus: resolution on, 451

Choctaw cession, 275*n*

Choctaw Indians: resolution on, 442

Churchill, Sylvester (ident., 206), 206

Churubusco, Battle of, 262*n*

Cincinnati *Morning Signal*: Z. Taylor's letter to, 197*n*, 215*n*

Citadel (Monterrey) (described, 24), 22, 30*n*, 51, 58, 67, 73, 75, 108, 111, 228, 229

Claiborne, Ferdinand L. (sketch, 276): letters from, 273–74, 432; letter from, cited, 276*n*; mentioned, 435

Claiborne, John F. H. (sketch, 2:115): letter to, 435; mentioned, 18–19, 242*n*, 275*n*, 276*n*, 449

Claiborne, Osmun, 274

Claiborne County: support for Z. Taylor, 389*n*

Clariday (Clardy), Richard, 126*n*

Clark, Solomon, 441

Clay, Henry (sketch, 2:135): friendship with Davis, 183*n*; Z. Taylor and, 190, 211, 221–22, 305–306, 310, 422; Davis on candidacy, 267, 326, 455; on Mexican War, 269; and vote in Miss. (1844), 276*n*; opposes Texas annexation, 284; and West Fla., 289*n*; and Lexington speech, 306

Clay, Henry, Jr. (sketch, 183): killed at Buena Vista, 127*n*, 182, 306

Clayton, George R. (sketch, 393), 393, 394*n*

Clayton, John M. (sketch, 324): opposes Yucatan bill, 318*edn*, 320–21; and compromise proposal, 373*n*

Clements, Bryan & Co., 421

Clendenin, John S. (sketch, 150): Davis recom. for office, 438; letters to, 195, 413; letter from, 438; letter to R. Griffith, 154–56; mentioned, 10*n*, 145, 196*n*

Clifton, Caswell R.: letter to, 171

Clinton: barbecue for 1st Miss. Rgt., 417

Coast survey: Davis and, 6, 453

Cobb, Alpheus, 29

Cobb, Howell (sketch, 394), 393

Cobb, Joseph B. (sketch, 393), 393

Cobb, Thomas W., 393*n*

Cocke, Stephen (sketch, 2:339): letters to, 192, 248–49, 442; letter from, 451

Cohea, Edward M., 84*n*

Cold Springs: Davis invited to speak at, 450

486

INDEX

Coleman, Ann Crittenden: letter to, cited, 224n

Coleman, John W., 29

Colhoun, James (sketch, 32): praised by Davis, 28, 146; mentioned, 9n, 72, 129

Collingsworth, Addison S. (ident., 163), 163

Colt, Samuel, 290n

Colt revolver: Davis on, 289–90

Columbus *Democrat*, 394n

Columbus *Primitive Republican*, 394n

Columbus *Southern Standard*, 236n

Columbus *Whig*, 433

Compher, W. P. S., 433

Compton, William: claim of, 426

Concordia Parish: letter to citizens, 236–37; letter to citizens, mentioned, 422

Conger, Jonathan, 122n

Congressional Globe: Davis sends to friends, 420

Conner, David, 288n

Constitution, U.S.: Z. Taylor on, 201, 202, 210, 212, 213, 220–22; Davis on strict construction, 207, 295–301, 333, 338, 348, 389–91, 455–56; Davis sends copy to friend, 272; Davis on presidential powers, 279–81, 283–84; Davis on various provisions of, 339–40; and three-fifths compromise, 352, 366–67; and slavery, 352–54, 361–62, 378–80; and minority guarantees, 378–79

Contreras, Battle of, 127n

Cook, Henry F. (sketch, 2:227): praised by Davis, 37, 145; letter from, 157–58; mentioned, 9n, 28, 35

Cook, Robert: Davis recom. for office, 446

Cooper, Douglas H. (sketch, 31): at Monterrey, 26, 36, 72, 105, 231, 406; praised by Davis, 37, 146; statement of, 403–404; letter to R. Griffith, 128–30; letter from, cited, 131n; mentioned, 9n, 123

Cooper, Louis A.: killed at Buena Vista, 137; and claim for, 440

Cooper, William G.: claim of, 440

Corro, José J., 289n

Corwine, Amos B. (sketch, 134): praised by Davis, 146; letter from, 131–33; letters from, cited, 134n;

mentioned, 9n, 130

Coste, Napoleon L.: Davis commends, 18

Cotton, Charles F. (sketch, 34), 29

Courtney, Thomas (sketch, 409), 408, 416

Crawford, John: petition of, 446

Creight, William, 411

Creole, 372n

Crittenden, George B.: resignation, 431

Crittenden, John J. (sketch, 224): supports Z. Taylor, 222; and ten-rgt. bill, 257edn, 261; on Yucatan bill, 323; letters to, 262, 441; letter from, 441; letters to, cited, 123n; mentioned, 205n, 277n, 327edn

Crittenden, Thomas L. (sketch, 123): at Saltillo with Davis, 123; writes J. E. Davis re Davis, 123n, 164–65; at Buena Vista, 138n; Davis quotes, 237n; praised by Davis, 262

Crosman, George H. (sketch, 21): letters to, 20–21, 177–78

Crump, George P., 10n, 38n, 83n, 150n, 156n

Cuba: Davis and, 319–20, 324n

Cumberland Island dam: Davis on, 295–301, 443

Cummings, John W., 411

Cunningham, Christopher: petition and bill, 435

Cypress Grove (Z. Taylor plantation), 204, 271n, 307, 309, 420

Dabney, Samuel, 432

Dallas, Alexander J. (sketch, 98), 97

Dallas, George M. (sketch, 2:167), 254edn, 306

Dandridge, Mary Taylor (sketch, 1:476), 270

Davidson, A. H.: letter from, 421

Davidson, Thomas J.: introduced to Davis, 452

Davis, Amanda. *See* Bradford, Amanda Davis

Davis, Anna Eliza. *See* Smith, Anna Davis

Davis, Ann Boyle (niece-in-law) (sketch, 326), 326

Davis, Caroline. *See* Leonard, Caroline Davis

Davis, Eliza Van Benthuysen (sister-

487

INDEX

INDEX

INDEX

INDEX

INDEX

INDEX

503

INDEX

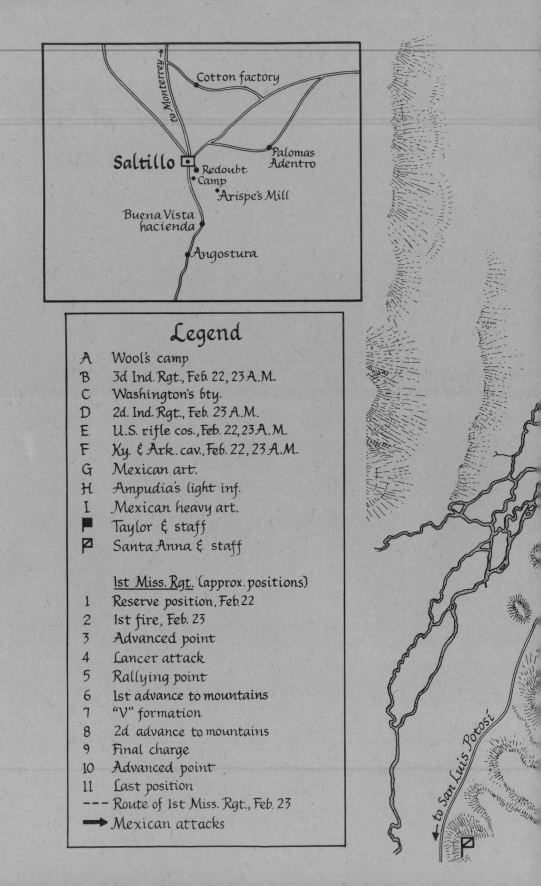

to Monterrey ↑

Cotton factory

Saltillo ◻

Redoubt •
• Camp

Palomas
Adentro •

• Arispe's Mill

Buena Vista
hacienda •

Angostura •

Legend

A Wool's camp
B 3d Ind. Rgt., Feb. 22, 23 A.M.
C Washington's bty.
D 2d Ind. Rgt., Feb. 23 A.M.
E U.S. rifle cos., Feb. 22, 23 A.M.
F Ky. & Ark. cav., Feb. 22, 23 A.M.
G Mexican art.
H Ampudia's light inf.
I Mexican heavy art.
⚑ Taylor & staff
⚑ Santa Anna & staff

1st Miss. Rgt. (approx. positions)
1   Reserve position, Feb. 22
2   1st fire, Feb. 23
3   Advanced point
4   Lancer attack
5   Rallying point
6   1st advance to mountains
7   "V" formation
8   2d advance to mountains
9   Final charge
10 Advanced point
11 Last position
--- Route of 1st Miss. Rgt., Feb. 23
➡ Mexican attacks

to San Luis Potosí ←